HUNGER

Basic Mechanisms and
Clinical Implications

HUNGER

Basic Mechanisms and
Clinical Implications

Edited by

Donald Novin, Ph.D.

Professor of Psychology
Department of Psychology
University of California
Los Angeles, California

Wanda Wyrwicka, Ph.D.

Research Anatomist
Department of Anatomy
University of California
Los Angeles, California

George A. Bray, M.D.

Professor of Medicine
Department of Medicine
UCLA School of Medicine
Harbor General Hospital
Torrance, California

Raven Press ▪ New York

QP
138
H86

Preface

All energy used by animals is ultimately derived from the food they eat. If for no other reason than that, knowledge of the regulation of food intake would be important for a complete understanding of the organism. When energy intake is below that required to provide for the various forms of energy expenditure, the organism must call on its stores of energy to make up the deficit or reduce, if possible, the expenditure.

When the energy contained in the food we eat exceeds the expenditure, the excess energy is stored—largely as fat. It is primarily this latter fact, or problem, so prevalent in developed (one is tempted to say overdeveloped) countries, that engages not only the curiosity of the basic researchers but that of the clinicians who are seeking solutions to a public health problem of almost epidemic proportions—obesity.

In the area of hunger research, and probably in most other areas as well, the distinction between basic and clinical research and interests is often blurred. Many fundamental findings, basic to our understanding of hunger, have evolved from clinical observation. The initial clues that the hypothalamus was central to energy metabolism were first observed in clinical medicine. On the other hand, basic research into behavioral processes, physiological and biochemical, is beginning to suggest, to the clinician, methods of approaching the problems associated with aberrations of hunger.

The tradition in this area of research—of advancements made by basic sciences, of clinical observations, and of studies on both man and animal, using a variety of methods—is continued in this volume. As is usual in a field in which rapid changes are occurring, more questions are raised than answers are given. However, many issues that are likely to remain of concern for some time to come are dealt with here.

Several chapters reveal that neurotransmitters involved in the regulation of food continue to be of interest and their role in hunger is becoming more clearly defined. Another theme that is reviewed is the necessity for a considerable revision in the classic view of hypothalamic "centers" controlling hunger and satiety. One new viewpoint, treated in several chapters, is that a principal role of these areas is not so much the direct control of hunger but rather the relation of energy storage to food intake. According to the theory, known as the "set-point" theory, the obvious relation that food intake determines body weight is turned around to state that energy stores (or, more properly, deviations from an appropriate level of internal energy) determine food intake. Also evident in this volume is the current importance being given, or recognized anew, to learning, taste, and visceral mechanisms. No longer can such mechanisms, peripheral in an anatomical sense, be considered peripheral in their role in hunger. The glucostatic hypothesis of the control of hunger is still an important idea and the evidence for specific glucose receptors in both central and peripheral areas is dealt with by a number of contributors. Finally, several chapters deal with the nature of hunger and particularly with approaches to the problem of obesity in humans. Here, especially, these works represent a dual interest in obtaining new information and the possibility of applying the data to issues of genuine human concern.

We believe that this volume offers a broad spectrum of approaches to the problem of hunger and weight control and should be of interest to scientists concerned with the implications and possible applications of research on hunger, and to those clinicians desiring greater depth to their understanding of the medical problems relating to the control of food intake.

Donald Novin

Acknowledgments

On January 15 to 17, 1975, a meeting was held in Los Angeles under the auspices of the Brain Research Institute of the University of California, Los Angeles. Much that was presented was either new data or new theoretical construction, or both. The chapters in this volume are based on the presentations at that conference.

We are very grateful to the following organizations who gave financial support necessary to hold the meetings and publish this volume: American Society of Bariatric Physicians, Hoffman–LaRoche, Lilly Research Laboratory, Merck, Sharp & Dohme Postgraduate Program, A. H. Robins, Smith, Kline & French, USV Pharmaceutical Corporation, and Weight Watchers Foundation.

We would like to thank Mr. Darrell Dearmore whose skillful handling of the audio-visual equipment was basic to a pleasant and fruitful conference. We also owe a great debt to Ms. Kay Collins, conference secretary, whose organizational abilities and tact were vital to the conference from its initial planning to the publication of this volume.

Donald Novin

Contents

Developmental and Motivational Properties of Hunger

Set-Point Theory and the Relationship of Weight Regulation and Food Intake

Short-Term Regulation of Feeding: Patterning, Peripheral, and Visceral Mechanisms

Hunger and Obesity in Man

Conclusion

Contributors

R. E. Barry
See George A. Bray

J. Benfield
See George A. Bray

Ilene L. Bernstein
Department of Psychology
University of Washington
Seattle, Washington 98105

Elliott M. Blass
Department of Psychology
The Johns Hopkins University
Baltimore, Maryland 21218

D. A. Booth
University of Birmingham
P. O. Box 363
Birmingham, 2TT B15 England

Katarina Tomljenović Borer
Neuroscience Laboratory
University of Michigan
Ann Arbor, Michigan 48104

Peter C. Boyle
See Richard E. Keesey

George A. Bray
Department of Medicine
UCLA School of Medicine
Harbor General Hospital
1000 West Carson Street
Torrance, California 90509

Pietro Castelnuovo-Tedesco
Department of Medicine
UCLA School of Medicine
Harbor General Hospital
1000 West Carson Street
Torrance, California 90509

Michael H. Chase
Department of Anatomy
University of California
Los Angeles, California 90024

Barbara J. Collins
See John D. Davis

J. Cytawa
See David L. Wolgin

John D. Davis
Department of Psychology
University of Illinois
Box 4348
Chicago, Illinois 60680

Alan N. Epstein
Department of Biology
Leidy Laboratories
University of Pennsylvania
Philadelphia, Pennsylvania 19174

Elzbieta Fonberg
Department of Neurophysiology
Nencki Institute
Pasteura 3
Warsaw, 22 Poland

J. Gibbs
See G. P. Smith

Roger A. Gorski
See Dwight M. Nance

M. R. C. Greenwood
See Joel A. Grinker

Joel A. Grinker
The Rockefeller University
66th and York Avenue
New York, New York 10021

Sebastian P. Grossman
Department of Behavioral Sciences
University of Chicago
Green Hall
5848 South University Avenue
Chicago, Illinois 60637

A. E. Harper
Department of Biochemistry
University of Wisconsin
420 Henry Mall
Madison, Wisconsin 53706

Bartley G. Hoebel
Department of Psychology
Princeton University
Princeton, New Jersey 08540

S. Ishibashi
See Taketoshi Ono

Richard E. Keesey
Department of Psychology
The University of Wisconsin
Madison, Wisconsin 53706

Joseph W. Kemnitz
See Richard E. Keesey

H. Kita
See Taketoshi Ono

F. Scott Kraly
See Elliott M. Blass

Sarah Fryer Leibowitz
The Rockefeller University
66th Street and York Avenue
New York, New York 10021

Jacques Le Magnen
College de France
11 Place Marcelin Berthelot
Paris 75231, France

Michael W. Levine
See John D. Davis

Mary Ann Marrazzi
Department of Pharmacology
Wayne State University
School of Medicine
Detroit, Michigan 48207

Joel S. Mitchel
See Richard E. Keesey

Gordon J. Mogenson
The University of Western Ontario
Department of Physiology
London 72, Ontario, Canada

T. Nakamura
See Taketoshi Ono

Dwight M. Nance
Department of Anatomy
University of California
Los Angeles, California 90024

Donald Novin
Department of Psychology
University of California
Los Angeles, California 90024

Taketoshi Ono
Department of Physiology
Kanazawa University
Kanazawa, Japan

Yutaka Oomura
See Taketoshi Ono

Charles A. Opsahl
See Terry L. Powley

Jaak Panksepp
Department of Psychology
Bowling Green State University
Bowling Green, Ohio 43403

Jeffrey W. Peck
Department of Psychology
University of Utah
Salt Lake City, Utah 84112

S. V. Platt
See D. A. Booth

Daniel Porte, Jr.
See Stephen C. Woods

Terry L. Powley
Department of Psychology
Yale University
333 Cedar Street
New Haven, Connecticut 06510

Judy M. Price
See Joel A. Grinker

Judith Rodin
Department of Psychology
Yale University
333 Cedar Street
New Haven, Connecticut 06510

Mauricio Russek
Department of Physiology
National School of Biological Sciences
Mexico City, 17, D.F., Mexico

John D. Sanderson
See Dennis A. VanderWeele

Douglas Schiebel
See Pietro Castelnuovo-Tedesco

Anthony Sclafani
Department of Psychology
Brooklyn College
Brooklyn, New York 11210

N. Shimizu
See Taketoshi Ono

G. P. Smith
The New York Hospital-Cornell Medical
  Center
21 Bloomingdale Road
White Plains, New York 10605

Edward M. Stricker
Department of Psychology
University of Pittsburgh
Pittsburgh, Pennsylvania 19122

M. Sugimori
See Taketoshi Ono

Ann C. Sullivan
Research Division
Hoffman-LaRoche, Inc.
Nutley, New Jersey 07110

P. Teitelbaum
See David L. Wolgin

F. M. Toates
See D. A. Booth

Joseph Triscari
See Ann C. Sullivan

Dennis A. VanderWeele
Psychology Department
Occidental College
1600 Campus Road
Los Angeles, California 90041

Barbara S. Williams
See Orland W. Wooley

David L. Wolgin
Department of Psychology
University of Illinois
Champaign, Illinois 61801

Stephen C. Woods
Department of Psychology
University of Washington
Seattle, Washington 98105

Orland W. Wooley
Department of Psychiatry
University of Cincinnati Medical School
Cincinnati, Ohio 45221

Susan C. Wooley
See Orland W. Wooley

Wanda Wyrwicka
Department of Anatomy
University of California
Los Angeles, California 90024

Michael J. Zigmond
See Edward M. Stricker

Hunger: Basic Mechanisms and Clinical Implications,
edited by D. Novin, W. Wyrwicka, and G. Bray.
Raven Press, New York © 1976.

Brain Catecholaminergic Mechanisms
for Control of Hunger

Sarah Fryer Leibowitz

The Rockefeller University, New York, New York 10021

Pharmacological studies of central mechanisms involved in the control of hunger have revealed strong evidence suggesting an important neurotransmitter function for catecholamines in the brain. The present report describes this evidence obtained in this and other laboratories.

CATECHOLAMINES AND HUNGER STIMULATION

Adrenergic Initiation of Feeding in Satiated Animals

In 1960, Grossman first demonstrated that *l*-norepinephrine (NE),[1] when injected through chronic cannulas directly into brains of satiated rats, could elicit a vigorous feeding response (1). This effect has since been confirmed by numerous investigators, in other species (2–4) as well as in the rat (5–10). In addition the catecholamine (CA) *l*-epinephrine (EPI) has also been found to produce the response, with perhaps even greater potency than NE (6, 7, 11, 12), whereas another CA, dopamine (DA), and the *d*-isomer of NE appear to be relatively ineffective (6, 7, 12). Dose-response studies with *l*-NE and *l*-EPI have revealed that the elicited eating response is dose-dependent (6, 10, 12, 13) and, furthermore, that it can be observed with doses as low as 4 ng (14, 15). The effectiveness of such low doses, as well as the demonstrated specificity of the biologically active *l*-isomer, provide a strong foundation for the idea that adrenergically elicited eating is a physiological phenomenon.

Feeding Initiation Mediated by Alpha-Adrenergic Receptors

Tests with selective stimulants of alpha- or beta-adrenergic receptors have generally demonstrated that a reliable eating response can be elicited by an alpha-receptor stimulant, such as metaraminol, but not by the beta-receptor stimulant isoproterenol (6, 7, 12; however, see refs. 3 and 16). This evidence, suggesting that alpha as opposed to beta receptors are mediating

---

[1] **NE,** *l*-norepinephrine; **CA,** catecholamine; **EPI,** *l*-epinephrine; **DA,** dopamine; **AMPH,** *d*-amphetamine; **CPZ,** chlorpromazine.

adrenergically elicited feeding, receives support from the studies of Booth (6) and Slangen and Miller (7), who found NE-induced eating to be abolished by the alpha-adrenergic blockers phentolamine and phenoxybenzamine but to be unaffected by the beta-adrenergic blocker propranolol. In a series of studies conducted in this laboratory (12, and *unpublished data*), additional blocking agents were tested in combination with EPI and with NE. The evidence obtained here supports the conclusion that alpha-adrenergic receptors are mediating the feeding response induced by either NE or EPI, and that beta-adrenergic, dopaminergic, cholinergic, and serotonergic receptors are not involved.

Localization of Alpha-Adrenergic Mechanisms for Feeding Initiation

The above evidence provides indirect support for the idea that there exists in the brain an alpha-adrenergic receptor mechanism involved in the initiation of feeding behavior. In order to determine the precise location of such a mechanism, a few investigators have examined in satiated rats the effectiveness of NE in eliciting feeding after injection into different sites throughout the brain. The convergence of evidence provided by earlier (5, 17) and more recent (8, 15, 18, 19) studies indicates that, with one or two exceptions, extra-hypothalamic structures are relatively or totally insensitive to the alpha-adrenergic feeding stimulation effect of NE. Within the boundaries of the hypothalamus, the medial portion appears to be very sensitive, in contrast to the lateral portion, which is almost totally insensitive (8, 15, 18, 20). Further analyses focused on the medial hypothalamic region have revealed the greatest sensitivity in the rostral portion, distinguishing the paraventricular nucleus at the anterior hypothalamic level as the single most sensitive site in the brain (15, 18, 19). Based on these results, it is our hypothesis that the paraventricular nucleus of the hypothalamus is a primary site in the mediation of alpha-adrenergic elicitation of eating. Regarding the involvement of the nearby perifornical hypothalamus originally shown by Booth (17) to be a particularly responsive site in the brain, it would appear that this region's sensitivity may actually reflect the diffusion of NE medially to the paraventricular nucleus itself (15).

Alpha-Adrenergic Potentiation of Feeding in Hungry Animals

In addition to initiating a new feeding response in food-satiated rats, NE [at a dose as low as 2.5 ng (21)] and EPI have both been found to potentiate the on-going feeding behavior of already hungry rats (15, 18, 22). Similar to the effect in satiated rats, this potentiation effect in hungry rats appears to be mediated by alpha-adrenergic receptors (Fig. 1). Moreover this effect seems to be localized to the medial region of the ventral diencephalon, with the most sensitive region apparently located at the rostral hypothalamic level (15, 18).

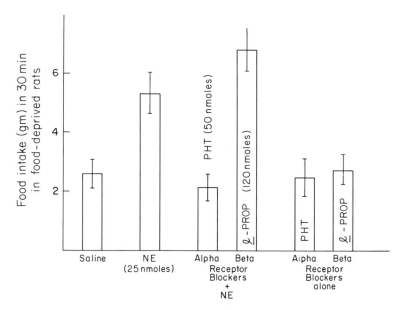

FIG. 1. Potentiation of feeding effect produced by unilateral norepinephrine (NE) injection into the paraventricular nucleus of 8-hr food-deprived rats. Local pretreatment with the alpha-adrenergic blocker phentolamine (PHT) abolished the NE-induced potentiation of feeding, while the beta-adrenergic blocker *l*-propranolol (*l*-PROP) caused a further increase in feeding. When injected alone, neither blocker had any effect on the rats' baseline food intake scores.

In light of these findings (and the above localization findings in satiated rats), it is important to note the recent work of Martin and Myers (23) demonstrating a reliable increase in the efflux of NE into the third ventricle of a feeding rat. This increase did not occur in the lateral ventricle or anterior hypothalamus, nor did it occur with DA in the substantia nigra, anterior hypothalamus, or third ventricle. These findings are remarkably consistent with our localization evidence in distinguishing the medial (perhaps periventricular) region of the hypothalamus as a primary site in mediating alpha-adrenergic stimulation of feeding behavior.

Possible Pathways Mediating Alpha-Adrenergic Stimulation of Feeding

Histofluorescence assays of CA nerve terminals in the hypothalamus have revealed a particularly rich innervation of the paraventricular and periventricular regions of the hypothalamus (24–28). The origin of the pathways giving rise to this dense innervation was first indicated by Olson and Fuxe (29) and Maeda and Shimizu (30) to be the midbrain "subcoeruleus" area. More recently, Lindvall et al. (26, 27), using the more sensitive glyoxylic acid fluorescence method, have identified two NE periventricular bundles, namely, the dorsal bundle which originates in the midbrain and caudal thalamus (cell group A11) and the ventral bundle, which is formed in the supramammillary region. In light of the above behavioral evidence obtained with exogenous NE, it seems possible that these prominent periventricular and paramedian NE fiber systems may act as substrates for alpha-adrenergic stimulation of natural feeding behavior. Another possible substrate, however, might also be the EPI projection system (31), which has been found to originate in the medulla and ascend to the hypothalamus, particularly the rostral medial and periventricular areas and the nearby perifornical region. As mentioned above, exogenous EPI has been found to be even more potent than NE in potentiating feeding behavior (7, 12).

Natural Versus Adrenergically Elicited Ingestive Behavior

Kissileff (32) and Fitzsimons and LeMagnen (33) have analyzed in detail the pattern of ingestive responses exhibited normally by rats under laboratory conditions. By comparing this normal pattern of ingestion with that exhibited after hypothalamic adrenergic stimulation, we have observed numerous similarities in the responses, with respect to both magnitude and temporal characteristics (10).

In the laboratory, rats normally take between six and 10 well-separated meals each day. As with the eating response induced by central adrenergic stimulation, the eating exhibited by rats at a normal meal occurs vigorously and continuously over a period of 5 to 15 min, and the size of the meal in both cases generally varies between 2 and 3 g. Drinking behavior is rarely observed during the meal. However, under normal conditions, rats frequently drink a small amount of water (0.5 to 3.0 ml) a few minutes before or after the meal. Interestingly, the same behavior, specifically drinking before a meal, has also been observed after central adrenergic stimulation (10). Within a minute or so after injection, NE or EPI frequently induces a drinking response of approximately 1 to 4 ml. This drinking response lasts 2 to 3 min, occurring vigorously and continuously throughout this interval and then, within a minute or so, is followed by the eating response. As with the drinking behavior observed under normal conditions, the amount of water ingested by individual rats after NE injection is found to be positively correlated with the size of his corresponding meal. Perhaps 70% or more of a rat's normal water intake is closely associated with feeding, and it appears from the above results that this same type of drinking behavior, called "food-associated" drinking (32), can also be observed after central adrenergic stimulation.

From the above analysis, it becomes clear that natural ingestive behavior and adrenergically elicited ingestive behavior bear striking similarities. These similarities provide strong support for the hypothesis that the responses observed with exogenous adrenergic stimulation reflect the normal function of an endogenous adrenergic system in controlling ingestive behavior. This hypothesis is further supported by the finding (see above) that quite low doses of NE or EPI, approaching probable physiological levels, are effective in producing these behaviors.

Tests with "Indirect-Acting" Drugs

If brain NE (or EPI) does indeed play a role in stimulating natural hunger, and if alpha-adrenergic receptors located in the medial hypothalamus are required for the mediation of this phenomenon, one would expect to observe specific changes in feeding behavior with central injection of drugs, which either selectively block alpha-adrenergic receptors or release or deplete endogenous stores of the adrenergic neurotransmitter. To test this prediction, we first examined the effects of the alpha-adrenergic receptor blocker phentolamine on food intake after injection into the medial or lateral parts of the hypothalamus (20). Consistent with the above hypothesis, we found phentolamine to suppress reliably the food intake of hungry rats after bilateral injection into the medial hypothalamus (Fig. 2) but not after injection into the lateral hypothalamus.

Additional tests with drugs that release endogenous NE from nerve endings

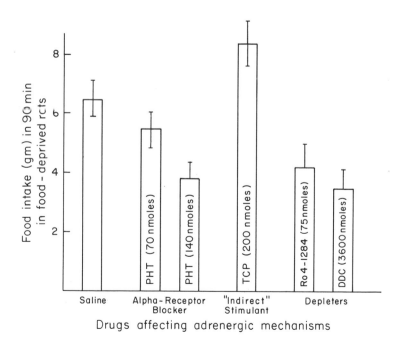

FIG. 2. Effects on food intake of various drugs injected into the medial hypothalamus of 18-hr food-deprived rats. The drugs injected were the alpha-adrenergic blocker phentolamine (PHT), the indirect catecholamine stimulant tranylcypromine (TCP), the short-acting monoamine releaser Ro4-1284, and the inhibitor of dopamine-β-hydroxylase diethyldithiocarbamate (DDC). All drugs were injected bilaterally, and the doses given refer to the amount of drug injected per side.

have similarly revealed supportive evidence for the existence of medial alpha-adrenergic receptors that stimulate natural hunger. In satiated rats, an increase in feeding has been observed after injection of a combination of drugs (a monoamine oxidase inhibitor plus monoamine releaser), which presumably causes an increase of NE in the synaptic cleft (7). A similar effect has been demonstrated after injection of the toxic agent 6-hydroxydopamine, which, through the destruction of NE-containing neurons, causes an initial release of this neurotransmitter (34). In hungry rats, a facilitation of feeding effect has been observed with desipramine, a drug that blocks the uptake inactivation of endogenous NE (35). A similar potentiation has been observed with medial hypothalamic injection of the drugs tranylcypromine (36; and Fig. 2) and d-amphetamine (AMPH) (20), both of which are known to be potent releasers of endogenous catecholamine (37–39). It is important to note that this feeding potentiation obtained with drug injection into the medial hypothalamus could not be observed after injection of the same drugs into the lateral hypothalamus (20, 36, 40).

To determine if local NE depletion affects food consumption, we tested the two drugs Ro4–1284 (a short-acting monoamine releaser) and diethyldithiocarbamate (a potent inhibitor of dopamine-β-hydroxylase) after injection into the medial or lateral hypothalamic regions (36). As predicted, medial hypothalamic injection of these drugs, which by different means cause a reduction in availability of endogenous NE, produced a reliable suppression of food intake (Fig. 2), an effect opposite to that observed with presumed release of endogenous NE (such as with tranylcypromine). Lateral hypothalamic injection of these drugs failed to produce this suppression.

Chlorpromazine

The phenothiazine chlorpromazine (CPZ) is a well-known tranquilizing agent, which has been found to affect CA mechanisms of the brain, producing a blockade of adrenergic receptors (41) as well as causing an increase in CA turnover (42–44). Although clinical reports have suggested that this drug may have a stimulatory effect on hunger, experimental evidence with systemically administered CPZ has failed to yield clear results along these lines (45–49). When administered directly into the brain (particularly the medial hypothalamic region), however, CPZ has been found to produce a marked increase in feeding behavior of satiated rats (50, 51; and Fig. 3), as well as of hungry rats (Leibowitz, *unpublished data*). Interestingly, additional tests with centrally injected NE in the same rats have revealed a strong positive correlation between the magnitudes of the effects produced by CPZ and NE (50). Furthermore CPZ-induced feeding, like NE-induced feeding, has been found to be abolished by a centrally administered alpha-adrenergic blocker, whereas it is somewhat potentiated by a beta-adrenergic blocker (Fig. 3).

To investigate the possibility that CPZ stimulates feeding by acting *in-*

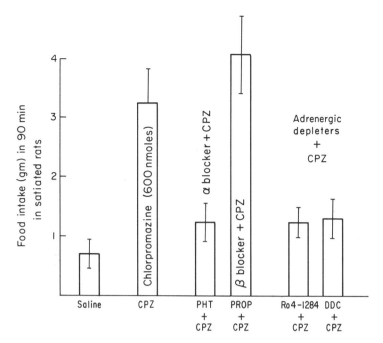

FIG. 3. Eating induced by chlorpromazine (CPZ) unilaterally injected into the medial hypothalamus of satiated rats. The response was abolished by the alpha-adrenergic blocker phentolamine (PHT, 50 nmoles) injected 10 min before (*bar 3*), the monoamine releaser Ro4—1284 injected 30 min before (*bar 5*), and the dopamine-β-hydroxylase inhibitor diethyldithiocarbamate (DDC, 6000 nmoles) injected 2 hr before (*bar 6*). In contrast, the beta-adrenergic blocker propranolol (PROP, 120 nmoles) injected 10 min before CPZ (*bar 4*) tended to potentiate the induced eating response.

directly through endogenous noradrenergic (or adrenergic) mechanisms, we tested this drug in combination with other drugs that either deplete or block the synthesis of endogenous NE (51). Local pretreatment with either type of drug was found to abolish the eating effect induced by central CPZ (Fig. 3). The same pretreatment, in contrast, was actually found to potentiate the eating effect of central NE. Although these results must be interpreted with caution, especially in light of the multiple and even toxic effects of CPZ on nerve tissue, they provide preliminary evidence that CPZ's effect on feeding may depend on intact stores of endogenous NE, which may in turn have a physiological function in the control of food consumption. These results become particularly interesting in light of the clinical reports of obesity in patients receiving CPZ treatment.

Circadian Rhythm Hypothesis

In contrast to the above reports of a NE stimulatory effect on food intake [lab chow (6, 7, 10, 22), Metrecal (13), or sweet milk (52)], Margules (53) reported that hypothalamically injected NE could have a suppressive effect on milk consumption. Based on the fact that Margules' experiments were conducted at night, in contrast to the daytime experiments of the other investigators, Margules suggested that the above conflicting results might reflect a dependency of exogenous NE's behavioral effect on a circadian rhythm of endogenous NE (54). To test this hypothesis, Margules examined his rats, which were maintained on lab chow pellets and then switched to sweet milk for the test, after NE injection in the daytime versus at night. As predicted, Margules found that when injected at the beginning of the dark cycle, NE indeed suppressed milk consumption, whereas when injected at the beginning of the light cycle, NE stimulated milk consumption.

In these studies on NE suppression of milk intake, Margules used as his site of injection the lateral hypothalamus at the level of the ventromedial nucleus. Since this site (as opposed to more medial sites) has generally been found to be relatively insensitive to NE's stimulatory effect on food intake (see above), we decided to test for Margules' day-night difference at a site where the stimulatory effect was more pronounced (Leibowitz, *unpublished data*). Accordingly, in rats with cannulas aimed at the hypothalamic paraventricular nucleus, we tested for NE's effect on food ingestion in rats maintained on lab chow and switched to milk for the test (procedure used by Margules), as well as in rats maintained and tested on the same food substance, either lab chow or milk. With the relatively high drug dose (25 μg) used by Margules, we found paraventricular nucleus injection of NE to stimulate food consumption reliably under all test conditions, regardless of time of injection (day versus night) or type of food used (milk versus lab chow). Thus a circadian rhythm of sensitivity to NE was not observed with paraventricular (medial) hypothalamic injection, in contrast to the day-night dependency demonstrated by Margules (54) with lateral hypothalamic injection. Based on the localization evidence showing maximal sensitivity of the paraventricular nucleus to NE's stimulatory effect on food intake (15, 19) and a complete loss, and perhaps reversal, of this effect at more lateral regions of the hypothalamus (15, 20, 36), it would appear that the site of injection was indeed a primary factor in yielding the different results described above.

Tests with Hypophysectomized Rats

As suggested above, the medial hypothalamus and, in particular, the paraventricular nucleus may have an important function in the mediation of alpha-adrenergic stimulation of hunger. Extensive work in the field of neuroendocrinology has indicated that these brain areas are involved in the control of hormone release by the pituitary. Furthermore, these areas are known to be richly innervated by CA nerve terminals (24–28), and it has been suggested that brain CA may play a role in mediating various hypothalamic neuroendocrine processes (55–58). To explore the possibility of a link between these hormonal and behavioral functions of the paraventricular and medial hypothalamic regions, we examined the effect that removal of the pituitary gland has on feeding and drinking behavior elicited by centrally injected NE (59). Tests conducted in hypophysectomized rats revealed that in the absence of the pituitary, NE (or EPI) was almost totally ineffective in eliciting a feeding response in satiated rats, whether the food substance used was lab chow, wet mash, milk, or cookies. A most interesting finding was that the NE-elicited drinking response, which is closely associated with the elicited feeding response (see above), appeared totally unaffected by hypophysectomy. Moreover drinking elicited by the cholinergic agent carbachol was reduced by only 30%. These results indicate a dependence of NE-elicited feeding on the pituitary and thus direct our attention to a possible involvement of hormones released by the pituitary. These hormones may either be directly involved, whereby their release by central NE actually induces the behavioral response, or, perhaps more likely, they may have an indirect, permissive function, possibly in maintaining normal adrenergic receptor activity in the brain.

CATECHOLAMINES AND HUNGER SUPPRESSION

The above results provide supportive evidence for the hypothesis that an alpha-adrenergic (NE or EPI) receptor mechanism, located in the medial hypothalamus, plays a role in the stimulation of natural hunger. In this section, I shall review results that suggest that catecholaminergic (beta-adrenergic and dopaminergic) receptor mechanisms, located in the lateral hypothalamus, play a role in the suppression of natural hunger.

Catecholaminergic Suppression of Feeding

When injected into the hypothalamus of hungry animals, each of the CA agonists [EPI (9, 60, 61; and Fig. 4), DA (62, 63; Leibowitz, *unpublished data*), isoproterenol (20, 60, 64–66; and Fig. 5), and NE (36, 53)] and the indirect CA stimulant amphetamine (20, 67, 68) have been found to have a suppressive effect on feeding behavior. As discussed below, this CA-induced suppression occurs most readily with injection into the lateral hypothalamus (as opposed to the medial hypothalamus for alpha-adrenergic potentiation of feeding) and also with injection in combination with blockers of alpha-adrenergic receptors.

The doses required to produce the CA suppression of feeding effect appear to be higher than the threshold doses for alpha-adrenergic-potentiated feeding. With d-AMPH (which is three times more potent than l-AMPH), a dose at least as low as 800 ng has been found to be effective (69), whereas 1- to 5-μg doses of the CA agonists appear to be necessary (59; Leibowitz, *unpublished data,* see also Fig. 5). Our efforts to determine if lower doses

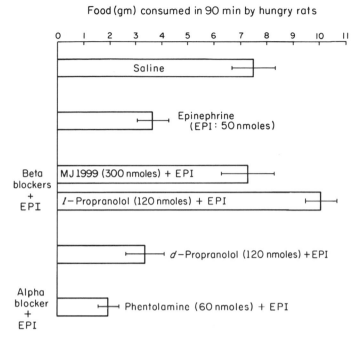

FIG. 4. Suppression of feeding effect produced by unilateral epinephrine (EPI) injection into the lateral (perifornical) hypothalamus of 18-hr food-deprived rats. This suppressive effect was abolished by the beta-adrenergic blockers MJ 1999 and *l*-propranolol, while potentiated by the alpha-adrenergic blocker phentolamine. A significant reversal, towards feeding potentiation, was obtained with *l*-propranolol, while no change was observed with the *d*-isomer of propranolol.

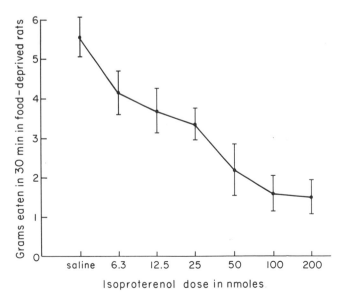

FIG. 5. Dose response for suppression of feeding effect produced by unilateral isoproterenol injection into the lateral (perifornical) hypothalamus of 18-hr food-deprived rats.

might be effective have shown that anorexia induced by EPI, DA, or AMPH can be reliably potentiated by the following: an alpha-receptor blocker (see Fig. 4), an inhibitor of the catabolic enzyme monoamine oxidase, and a blocker of the inactivating reuptake mechanism of the brain. Perhaps these various pharmacological manipulations will help one to reveal CA suppression of feeding at doses closer to physiological levels.

Feeding Suppression Mediated by Beta-Adrenergic and Dopaminergic Receptors

As with the alpha-adrenergic stimulation of feeding phenomenon (see above), the CA suppression of feeding effect appears to require the functional integrity of CA receptors in the hypothalamus. The receptors involved in this effect appear to be beta-adrenergic and dopaminergic in nature, as opposed to alpha-adrenergic, cholinergic, or serotonergic.

In tests with adrenergic receptor blockers injected in combination with EPI, isoproterenol, or d-AMPH, the suppressive effect of these CA stimulants has been found to be completely abolished by beta-receptor blockers, whereas it is somewhat potentiated by alpha-receptor blockers (60, 65, 68, 70); and Fig. 4). More recent tests with d-AMPH plus a wider variety of receptor blockers (40, 62, 69, 71) have revealed a total block of d-AMPH anorexia with DA as well as beta-adrenergic blockers, whereas no significant blockade with either alpha-adrenergic, serotonergic, or cholinergic blockers. In light of these AMPH results suggesting the involvement of DA as well as beta-adrenergic receptors in CA-induced feeding suppression, it will be important to determine whether this dual receptor involvement also applies to the anorexia induced by the agonists EPI or DA.

Localization of CA Mechanisms for Feeding Suppression

Localization studies conducted with EPI and d-AMPH strongly suggest that the CA (beta-adrenergic and DA) receptors involved in the inhibition of feeding phenomenon are located in the lateral, perhaps anterolateral, portion of the hypothalamus (15, 18, 40; and Fig. 6). As with the alpha-adrenergic stimulation of feeding phenomenon (see above), we have found that the suppression of feeding effect induced by CA stimulation could generally not be observed with drug injection into extra-hypothalamic structures. Within the hypothalamus, however, the region of greatest sensitivity was found to be the lateral hypothalamus [lateral hypothalamic lesions have been found to abolish amphetamine anorexia (72–74)], as opposed to the medial hypothalamus where alpha-adrenergic stimulation was most effective in producing a facilitation of feeding. Moreover it appears that the rostral portion of the lateral hypothalamus, just lateral to the fornix, may be considered the single most effective site for suppressing feeding with CA stimulation (15, 18, 40). This site lies perhaps 1 mm lateral to the paraventricular nucleus,

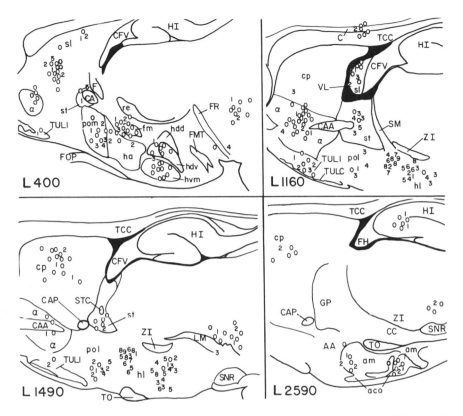

FIG. 6. Schematic diagrams of sagittal sections of the rat brain showing the sensitivity of different regions to the anorexic effect of amphetamine (AMPH). The diagrams and abbreviations are taken from the König and Klippel Stereotaxic Atlas of the Rat Brain. Each number indicates the site of AMPH injection for a particular rat and the magnitude of the effect produced at that site by AMPH. The number given is the first digit of the mean percent suppression of food intake observed with AMPH as compared to a saline vehicle baseline (for example, 5 = 50–59% suppression). (From Leibowitz, ref. 40.)

the single most effective site for stimulating feeding with alpha-adrenergic stimulation (19).

To test further the hypothesis that CA (specifically beta-adrenergic and DA) receptors for reducing eating are located in the anterolateral hypothalamus, we examined the effect of centrally administered receptor blockers on the anorexia induced by peripherally administered AMPH (69). When bilaterally injected into the lateral hypothalamus, the DA receptor blocker haloperidol and the beta-adrenergic blocker *l*-propranolol were each found to reliably antagonize the suppression of feeding observed with peripheral AMPH (haloperidol produced a 75% blockade and propranolol a 42% blockade). In support of the suggestion that the two CA blocking agents are indeed acting on receptors at or near to the lateral hypothalamic site of injection, we found that these blockers, when injected peripherally at the relatively low doses used centrally, were ineffective in altering the action of AMPH. By directly comparing the magnitudes of the reversals caused by central injection of the blockers, the effect produced by the DA blocker was shown to be significantly greater than that produced by the beta-adrenergic blocker. This difference in effectiveness of the two blockers may reflect a slightly different location or extent of the mediating DA and beta-adrenergic mechanisms, or it may possibly indicate a more predominant role for the DA mechanisms in mediating AMPH anorexia.

Possible Pathways Mediating CA Suppression of Feeding

Based on the above evidence for a lateral hypothalamic location of CA mechanisms for suppressing feeding behavior, we suggest three CA pathways as possible mediators of this phenomenon. With regard to the NE pathway which may be involved, it appears that the so-called ventral NE pathway (25) might act as a substrate for CA anorexia. This pathway, which originates primarily in the medulla oblongata (25–27, 29, 30), has been shown to innervate the basolateral hypothalamus (29, 30), in contrast to other known NE pathways that innervate either medial and periventricular areas of the hypothalamus or various thalamic and telencephalic regions (25–27, 29, 30). In support of this suggestion, Ahlskog and Hoebel (75, 76) have demonstrated that destruction of the ventral NE pathway leads to hyperphagia and obesity, in addition to attenuating the anorexic effect of peripherally administered AMPH.

Recently, Hökfelt et al. (31) provided evidence for an adrenergic pathway which with the ventral NE pathway ascends from the lower brainstem and terminates predominantly in the hypothalamus. Since EPI in the periphery is known to have more potent beta-adrenergic activity than NE (77), it is possible that this adrenergic pathway in the brain may be a mediator of CA anorexia. From Hökfelt's analysis of this projection system, it appears that it terminates particularly heavily in the anterolateral hypothalamus, precisely where we found exogenous CA agonists or AMPH to produce the strongest suppression of feeding effect. Based on this convergence of evidence, it seems possible, therefore, that this newly identified adrenergic innervation of the hypothalamus may act as an important substrate for beta-adrenergic control of eating.

With regard to a dopaminergic pathway mediating CA-induced anorexia, our evidence for a hypothalamic location of the nerve terminals (40) would tentatively lead us to reject the nigrostriatal and mesolimbic DA systems which innervate primarily telencephalic structures (25). [Destruction of the nigrostriatal system has actually been shown to produce aphagia (25, 78–81).] Rather, our localization evidence would appear to suggest a diencephalic projection system as the most likely candidate. Recently Lindvall and his associates (27) described an intradiencephalic DA pathway, which they called the incerto-hypothalamic DA system. This system has its origin in the caudal thalamus and hypothamus (cell group A11) and in the medial zona incerta and dorsal hypothalamus (cell group A13). (See ref. 82 for a detailed description of the diencephalic CA cell groups.) These cells give rise to short DA neurons that have intradiencephalic projections in the zona incerta and the dorsal anterior hypothalamus. This CA projection, which is distinct from the tuberal-hypophyseal DA system (25, 27, 83), may very possibly be an important neuroanatomical mediator of CA inhibition of feeding.

Tests with "Indirect-Acting" Drugs

There is abundant evidence to suggest that the effects of AMPH on behavior are mediated through this drug's indirect action on CA mechanisms of the brain. Biochemical studies have demonstrated that AMPH causes a release of CA (NE and DA) from nerve endings in the brain, as well as a blockade of CA reuptake inactivation (38, 39). Moreover pharmacological studies have shown the behavioral effects of peripherally administered AMPH to be antagonized by drugs that block the synthesis of brain CA (84–88). Results obtained in this laboratory with centrally injected AMPH (69) confirm the idea that AMPH anorexia is indeed mediated by endogenous CA, perhaps NE and EPI as well as DA. In these studies, we found that centrally injected α-methyltyrosine, an inhibitor of CA synthesis, abolished anorexia induced by lateral hypothalamic injection of AMPH. Similar results were obtained with hypothalamically injected Fla-63, a drug that leaves DA intact but inhibits the synthesis of NE and perhaps EPI. These findings indicate that AMPH-induced anorexia requires intact stores of brain CA, and this, in turn, provides support for the proposed physiological role of brain CA in the inhibition of natural hunger.

Further evidence for this hypothesis comes from additional tests (36) with the drug tranylcypromine, which is known to enhance the release, as well as inhibit the breakdown, of endogenous CA, and also with the drugs Ro4–1284 and diethyldithiocarbamate, which respectively deplete and inhibit the synthesis of endogenous CA. When injected into the anterolateral hypothalamus, tranylcypromine, like AMPH, produced a significant suppression of food intake. Ro4–1284 and diethyldithiocarbamate, in contrast, caused the opposite effect of facilitating food intake (see also ref. 89). These results in the lateral hypothalamus are consistent with the proposed presence in that region of a CA mechanism for feeding suppression. As described above, diametrically opposite results were obtained with the same drugs in the medial hypothalamus. This evidence supports the proposed presence in the medial region of an antagonistic alpha-adrenergic mechanism for feeding stimulation.

With regard to the actions of AMPH in the brain, a series of studies have suggested a role for central CA neurons in the control of glycogen metabolism in the brain. Hutchins and his colleagues (90, 91) have found that cerebral glycogenolysis induced by AMPH injection into the mouse can be antagonized by CA synthesis inhibitors, as well as by beta-adrenergic blocking agents. The AMPH-induced glycogenolysis can also be antagonized by CPZ, a drug that blocks DA receptors, as well as alpha-adrenergic receptors, but not by a drug that selectively blocks alpha-adrenergic receptors. In view of the evidence relating glucose utilization to feeding regulation (92–94), it seems possible that the suppressive effect of AMPH and CA stimulants on food consumption may reflect the control exerted by central CA mechanisms on glycogen breakdown in the brain.

SUMMARY AND CONCLUSIONS

The above studies provide evidence that, in the rat and perhaps in other mammals as well as man, there exist two central CA mechanisms for control of hunger. The first is a noradrenergic (and/or adrenergic) mechanism that *stimulates* feeding behavior. This stimulatory mechanism involves alpha-type receptors located in the medial (paraventricular) hypothalamic region and may be mediated by adrenergic pathways that originate in the midbrain and ascend through the periventricular region of the diencephalon. The second system involved in control of hunger appears to be a CA mechanism that *suppresses* feeding behavior. This mechanism involves beta-adrenergic and dopaminergic receptors located in the anterolateral hypothalamic region, and the mediating pathways may include recently identified adrenergic pathways and intradiencephalic DA pathways that originate in the midbrain and innervate lateral hypothalamic regions. Further work needs to be done to determine if these mechanisms have a physiological function in control of natural hunger. However, some supportive evidence for this hypothesis has been obtained with a variety of indirect-acting drugs that are believed to act through endogenous CA mechanisms. The effectiveness of such drugs in altering hunger in humans provides a basis for suggesting the existence in man as well as in animals of the CA mechanisms postulated in this chapter.

ACKNOWLEDGMENTS

I thank Kevin Chang and Steven Feiertag for their excellent technical assistance. This work was supported by U.S. Public Health Service research grant MH 13189 and by funds from the Grant Foundation, Hoffmann–La Roche, and Smith, Kline, and French.

REFERENCES

1. Grossman, S. P. (1960): *Science,* 132:301–302.
2. Yaksh, T. L., and Myers, R. D. (1972): *Physiol. Behav.,* 8:251–257.

3. Baile, C. A., Simpson, W. C., Krabill, L. F., and Martin, F. H. (1972): *Life Sci.,* 2:661–668.
4. Setler, P. E., and Smith, G. P. (1974): *Brain Res.,* 65:459–473.
5. Coury, J. N. (1967): *Science,* 156:1763–1765.
6. Booth, D. A. (1968): *J. Pharmacol. Exp. Ther.,* 160:336–348.
7. Slangen, J. L., and Miller, N. E. (1969): *Physiol. Behav.,* 4:543–552.
8. Davis, J. R., and Keesey, R. E. (1971): *J. Comp. Physiol. Psychol.,* 77:394–402.
9. Leibowitz, S. F. (1973): In: *The Neurosciences: Third Study Program,* edited by F. O. Schmitt and F. G. Worden, pp. 713–719. MIT Press, Cambridge, Mass.
10. Leibowitz, S. F. (1975): *Physiol. Behav.,* 14:731–742.
11. Grossman, S. P. (1964): *Int. J. Neuropharmacol.,* 3:45–58.
12. Leibowitz, S. F. (1975): *Physiol. Behav.,* 14:743–754.
13. Miller, N. E., Gottesman, K. S., and Emery, N. (1964): *Am. J. Physiol.,* 206:1384–1387.
14. Leibowitz, S. F. (1974): Paper presented at Vth International Conference on Physiology of Food and Fluid Intake, held in Jerusalem (p. 87 of Abstracts).
15. Leibowitz, S. F. (1975): Submitted manuscript
16. Antunes-Rodrígues, J., and McCann, S. M. (1970): *Proc. Soc. Exp. Biol. Med.,* 133:1464–1470.
17. Booth, D. A. (1967): *Science,* 158:515–517.
18. Leibowitz, S. F. (1973): In: *Frontiers in Catecholamine Research,* edited by E. Usdin and S. Snyder, pp. 711–713. Pergamon Press, Oxford.
19. Leibowitz, S. F. (1974): Paper presented at EPA Annual Meeting, held in Philadelphia.
20. Leibowitz, S. F. (1970): *Proc. Natl. Acad. Sci. USA,* 67:1063–1070.
21. Ritter, R. C., and Epstein, A. N. (1974): Paper presented at Vth International Conference on Physiology of Food and Fluid Intake, held at Jerusalem (p. 112 of Abstracts).
22. Grossman, S. P. (1962): *Am. J. Physiol.,* 202:872–882.
23. Martin, G. E., and Myers, R. D. (1974): Paper presented at 4th Annual Meeting, Society for Neuroscience, held in St. Louis (p. 325 of Abstracts).
24. Fuxe, K. (1965): *Acta Physiol. Scand.,* 64 (Suppl. 247): 37–102.
25. Ungerstedt, U. (1971): *Acta Physiol. Scand.,* Suppl. 367:1–48.
26. Lindvall, O., and Björklund, A. (1974): *Acta Physiol. Scand.,* Suppl. 412:1–48.
27. Lindvall, O., Björklund, A., Nobin, A., and Stenevi, U. (1974): *J. Comp. Neurol.,* 154:317–346.
28. Jacobowitz, D. M., and Palkovits, M. (1974): *J. Comp. Neurol.,* 157:13–28.
29. Olson, L., and Fuxe, K. (1972): *Brain Res.,* 43:289–295.
30. Maeda, T., and Shimizu, N. (1972): *Brain Res.,* 36:19–35.
31. Hökfelt, T., Fuxe, K., Goldstein, M., and Johansson, O. (1974): *Brain Res.,* 66:235–251.
32. Kissileff, H. R. (1969): *J. Comp. Physiol. Psychol.,* 67:284–300.
33. Fitzsimons, T. J., and Magnen, J. L. (1969): *J. Comp. Physiol. Psychol.,* 67:273–283.
34. Evetts, K. D., Fitzsimons, J. T., and Setler, P. E. (1972): *J. Physiol. (Lond.),* 233:35–47.
35. Montgomery, R. B., Singer, G., Purcell, A. T., Narbeth, J., and Bolt, A. G. (1969): *Nature,* 233:1278–1279.
36. Leibowitz, S. F. (1971): *Proc. 79th Annu. Convention APA,* 741–742.
37. von Euler, U. S. (1970): In: *New Aspects of Storage and Release Mechanisms of Catecholamines,* edited by H. J. Schümann and G. Kroneberg, pp. 144–158. Springer-Verlag, New York.
38. Carlsson, A. (1970): In: *International Symposium on Amphetamines and Related Compounds,* edited by E. Costa and S. Garattini, pp. 289–300. Raven Press, New York.
39. Glowinski, J. (1970): In: *International Symposium on Amphetamines and Related Compounds,* edited by E. Costa and S. Garattini, pp. 301–316. Raven Press, New York.
40. Leibowitz, S. F. (1975): *Brain Res.,* 84:160–167.

41. Thoenen, H., Hürlimann, A., and Haefely, W. (1965): *Int. J. Neuropharmacol.*, 4:79–89.
42. Da Prada, M., and Pletscher, A. (1966): *Experientia*, 22:465.
43. Corrodi, H., Fuxe, K., and Hökfelt, T. (1967): *Life Sci.*, 6:767–774.
44. Gey, K. F., and Pletscher, A. (1968): *Experientia*, 24:335–336.
45. Schmidt, H., Jr., and Van Meter, W. G. (1958): *J. Comp. Physiol. Psychol.*, 51:29–31.
46. Reynolds, R. W., and Carlisle, H. J. (1961): *J. Comp. Physiol. Psychol.* 54:354–356.
47. Stolerman, I. P. (1967): *Nature*, 215:1518–1519.
48. Stolerman, I. P. (1970): *Neuropharmacology*, 9:405–417.
49. Robinson, R. G., Hoffer, B. J., and Bloom, F. E. (1974): Paper presented at 4th Annual Meeting, Society for Neuroscience, held in St. Louis (p. 397 of Abstracts).
50. Leibowitz, S. F., and Miller, N. E. (1969): *Science*, 165:609–611.
51. Leibowitz, S. F. (1969): *Proc. 77th Annu. Convention APA*, 901–902.
52. Berger, B. D., Wise, C. D., and Stein, L. (1971): *Science*, 172:281–284.
53. Margules, D. L. (1970): *J. Comp. Physiol. Psychol.*, 73:1–12.
54. Margules, D. L., Lewis, M. J., Dragovich, J. A., and Margules, A. S. (1972): *Science*, 178:640–642.
55. Fuxe, K., Hökfelt, T., and Jonsson, G. (1970): In: *Neurochemical Aspects of Hypothalamic Function*, edited by L. Martini and J. Meites, pp. 61–83. Academic Press, New York.
56. Mueller, E. E. (1970): In: *Aspects of Neuroendocrinology. V. International Symposium on Neurosecretion, August 20–23, 1969, Kiel*, edited by W. Bargmann and B. Scharrer, pp. 206–214. Springer-Verlag, Berlin.
57. Wurtman, R. J. (1971): *Neurosci. Res. Program Bull.*, 9.
58. Ganong, W. F. (1972): *Prog. Brain Res.*, 38:41–57.
59. Leibowitz, S. F. (1974): Paper presented at 4th Annual Meeting, Society for Neuroscience, held in St. Louis (p. 301 of Abstracts).
60. Leibowitz, S. F. (1970): *Nature*, 226:963–964.
61. Leibowitz, S. F. (1972): *Neurotransmitters*. Res. Publ. ARNMD, 50:327–358.
62. Kruk, Z. L. (1973): *Nature*, 256:52–53.
63. Hansen, M. G., and Whishaw, I. Q. (1973): *Psychopharmacologia*, 29:33–44.
64. Margules, D. L. (1970): *J. Comp. Physiol. Psychol.*, 73:13–21.
65. Goldman, H. W., Lehr, D., and Friedman, E. (1971): *Nature*, 231:453–455.
66. Jackson, H. M., and Robinson, D. W. (1971): *Br. Vet. J.*, 127:51–53.
67. Booth, D. A. (1968): *Nature*, 217:869–870.
68. Leibowitz, S. F. (1970): *Proc. 78th Annu. Convention APA*, 813–814.
69. Leibowitz, S. F. (1975): *Brain Research, in press.*
70. Sanghvi, I., Singer, G., Friedman, E., and Gershon, S. (1972): *Proc. Vth International Congress on Pharmacology*, Abstr. 1196.
71. Barzaghi, F., Gropetti, A., Mantegazza, P., and Muller, E. E. (1973): *J. Pharm. Pharmacol.*, 25:909–911.
72. Epstein, A. (1959): *J. Comp. Physiol. Psychol.*, 52:37–45.
73. Carlisle, H. J. (1964): *J. Comp. Physiol. Psychol.*, 58:47–54.
74. Russek, M., Rodríguez-Zendejas, A. M., and Teitelbaum, P. (1973): *Physiol. Behav.*, 10:329–333.
75. Ahlskog, J. E., and Hoebel, B. G. (1973): *Science*, 182:166–169.
76. Ahlskog, J. E. (1974): *Brain Res.*, 82:211–240.
77. Innes, I. R., and Nickerson, M. (1970): In: *The Pharmacological Basis of Therapeutics*, edited by L. S. Goodman and A. Gilman, Chap. 24. Macmillan, New York.
78. Oltmans, G. A., and Harvey, J. A. (1972): *Physiol. Behav.*, 8:69–78.
79. Marshall, J. F., and Teitelbaum, P. (1973): *Brain Res.*, 55:229–233.
80. Fibiger, H. C., Zis, A. P., and McGeer, E. G. (1973): *Brain Res.*, 55:135–148.
81. Fibiger, H. C., Phillips, A. G., and Clouston, R. A. (1973): *Am. J. Physiol.*, 225:1282–1287.
82. Björklund, A., and Nobin, A. (1973): *Brain Res.*, 51:193–205.
83. Björklund, A., Moore, R. Y., Nobin, A., and Stenevi, U. (1973): *Brain Res.*, 51:171–191.

84. Weissman, A., Koe, B. K., and Tenen, S. S. (1966): *J. Pharmacol. Exp. Ther.,* 151:339–352.
85. Randrup, A., and Munkvad, I. (1966): *Nature,* 211:540.
86. Hanson, L. C. F. (1966): *Psychopharmacologia,* 9:78–80.
87. Dominic, J. A., and Moore, K. E. (1969): *Psychopharmacologia,* 15:96–101.
88. Holtzman, S. G., and Jewett, R. E. (1971): *Psychopharmacologia,* 22:151–161.
89. Friedman, E., Starr, N., and Gershon, S. (1973): *Life Sci.,* 12:317–326.
90. Hutchins, D. A., and Rogers, K. J. (1971): *Br. J. Pharmacol.,* 43:504–513.
91. Hutchins, D. A., and Rogers, K. J. (1973): *Br. J. Pharmacol.,* 48:19–29.
92. Smith, G. P., and Epstein, A. N. (1969): *Am. J. Physiol.,* 217:1083–1087.
93. Balagura, S. (1970): In: *The Hypothalamus,* edited by L. Martini, M. Motta, and F. Fraschini, pp. 181–193. Academic Press, New York.
94. Smith, C. T. V. (1972): *Physiol. Behav.,* 9:391–396.

Hunger: Basic Mechanisms and Clinical Implications,
edited by D. Novin, W. Wyrwicka, and G. Bray.
Raven Press, New York © 1976.

Brain Catecholamines and the Lateral Hypothalamic Syndrome

Edward M. Stricker and Michael J. Zigmond

Psychobiology Program, Departments of Psychology and Biology, University of Pittsburgh, Pittsburgh, Pennsylvania 15260

In 1951, Anand and Brobeck (1) reported that bilateral lesions of the ventrolateral hypothalamus of rats and cats resulted in the complete cessation of eating. Their lesioned animals usually starved to death within 10 days, despite the presence of familiar and nutritious foods. These results were interpreted as indicating that cell groups contained within the lateral hypothalamus functioned as a feeding center, which, together with a medial hypothalamic inhibitory mechanism, was critically involved in the central control of hunger.

Over the next 20 years, research provided three major developments in these concepts. (a) The same lesions that abolished feeding also eliminated other motivated activities, such as drinking, maternal, thermoregulatory, and punishment avoidance behaviors. These findings led to the postulation that the lateral hypothalamus contained overlapping centers for a variety of motivational states. (b) The initial aphagia that was observed after lateral hypothalamic lesions usually was not permanent, and, if the lesioned animals were kept alive by intragastric intubation of liquid nutrients, many of them began to ingest some food again and ultimately recovered voluntary feeding and drinking behaviors that were sufficient for body weight maintenance. This gradual recovery process could be separated into four easily distinguished stages, each representing a more complete return of function than the preceding one. (c) Despite the apparent recovery of function, detailed investigations revealed enduring deficits in the feeding and drinking responses of lesioned animals to specific nutritional needs, such as dehydration, decreased glucose utilization (glucoprivation), and sodium deficiency. These and other subtle deficits indicated that the animals had not recovered completely.

The initial aphagia and adipsia, progressive recovery, and persistent residual deficits in lesioned animals together constitute what has become known as the lateral hypothalamic syndrome (2, 3). In the past several years, four insights have provided a new perspective on this syndrome. The present report describes and discusses these recent ideas.

ASCENDING CATECHOLAMINE-CONTAINING NEURONS AND
THE LATERAL HYPOTHALAMIC SYNDROME

The lesions that are most effective in producing aphagia and adipsia have been localized in the far-lateral aspects of the tuberal hypothalamus, a region consisting largely of ascending and descending fibers of passage rather than compact cellular masses. This fact together with many reports that aphagia and adipsia can be obtained after electrolytic lesions or knife cuts that spared the lateral hypothalamus, has undermined the concept of hypothalamic feeding and drinking centers.

Ungerstedt (4) was the first to point out that lateral hypothalamic lesions, as well as most extrahypothalamic lesions that produced aphagia and adipsia, would interrupt dopamine-containing neurons of the nigrostriatal bundle as they coursed through the ventral diencephalon. In order to separate damage to these fibers from damage to other tissue, Ungerstedt (4) injected the neurotoxin 6-hydroxydopamine (6-HDA)[1] into various sites along the ascending dopaminergic pathways [this procedure is believed to cause a relatively specific degeneration of neurons containing the brain catecholamines (CA) norepinephrine (NE) and dopamine (DA); see Fig. 1] and observed aphagia and adipsia in rats. Although his intracerebral injections of 6-HDA also damaged adjacent catecholaminergic fibers, Ungerstedt emphasized the importance of striatal DA depletions, because selective damage of other fiber tracts did not significantly affect ingestive behaviors. These important results have been confirmed in other laboratories. Moreover the same progressive recovery of function that is seen after lateral hypothalamic lesions, as well as most of the residual deficits, have been observed in rats given intracerebral or intraventricular injections of 6-HDA that spared the lateral hypothalamus but depleted striatal DA by at least 80% (Fig. 2) (5–7). Collectively these findings are consistent with the important role of nigrostriatal DA fibers in the central control of food and water intakes that had been proposed.

However, there are several reasons for believing that lateral hypothalamic lesions may not be tantamount to the destruction of nigrostriatal DA neurons. (a) Intraventricular 6-HDA does not produce all of the residual deficits that have been observed in recovered laterals (e.g., reflex salivary secretions to food or thermal stimuli are not impaired) (6). (b) Complete disruption of ingestive behaviors following electrolytic lesions of the lateral hypothalamus has been associated with only 50 to 60% depletion of striatal DA (8, 9), whereas more than 90% depletion is required using intraventricular 6-HDA treatments (9). (c) Dopaminergic projections that terminate more rostrally than the striatum also ascend along portions of the nigrostriatal

---

[1] Abbreviations used in this chapter: **CA,** catecholamine; **NE,** norepinephrine; **DA,** dopamine; **6-HDA,** 6-hydroxydopamine; **AMT,** α-methyl-p-tyrosine.

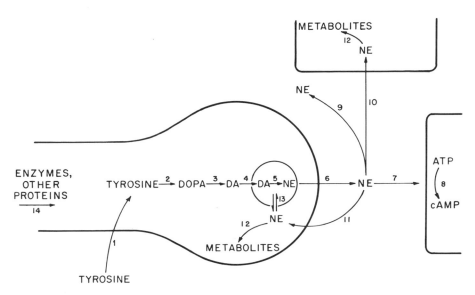

FIG. 1. The life cycle of NE. Tyrosine Is transported into the nerve terminal (1) where it is converted first to DOPA (catalyzed by tyrosine hydroxylase) (2), then to DA (by DOPA decarboxylase (3), and finally, following the transport of DA into vesicles (4), to NE (by dopamine-β-hydroxylase) (5). NE is released into the synaptic cleft by exocytosis (6). There it acts on the postsynaptic membrane (7), perhaps by influencing adenylate cyclase, an enzyme that catalyzes the conversion of adenosine triphosphate (ATP) to adenosine 3',5'-cyclic monophosphate (cAMP) (8). NE is removed from the synapse either by diffusion (9) or by uptake into surrounding cells (10), the most important of which are the noradrenergic terminals themselves (11). Once within the cytoplasm, NE can either be metabolized (by one of several routes, involving the enzymes monoamine oxidase and catechol-O-methyltransferase) (12) or taken up and stored in vesicles for reuse (13). The enzymes involved in the synthesis or catabolism of NE are formed in cell bodies and transported to their sites of action, as are various other proteins that may be important in the construction of vesicles, cell membranes, transport systems, and receptors (14). (Although this figure is drawn for noradrenergic neurons, the scheme is essentially the same for DA except that dopamine-β-hydroxylase is not present in the vesicles.

Using this diagram, the proposed actions of drugs that are mentioned in this paper may be visualized: 6-HDA is believed to gain preferential access into catecholaminergic neurons through amine-specific uptake mechanisms in their axon terminals, due to its structural similarity to the naturally occurring catecholamines, and to destroy the nerve terminals once within them; pargyline inhibits monoamine oxidase, and may promote the neurotoxic effects of 6-HDA by attenuating its catabolism within the brain; reserpine leads to CA depletions by destroying the presynaptic vesicles, thereby permitting the stored CA to be exposed to catabolic enzymes; AMT inhibits CA synthesis by competing with tyrosine for tyrosine hydroxylase; amphetamine increases CA release from vesicles and may also block its reuptake; apomorphine is believed to directly stimulate postsynaptic DA receptors; L-DOPA can be converted to DA outside of catecholaminergic neurons, due to the extraneuronal presence of DOPA decarboxylase, and will stimulate DA receptors until inactivated by uptake into terminals or enzymatic degradation; caffeine and theophylline inhibit the enzyme responsible for the catabolism of cAMP. (Reprinted from Stricker and Zigmond, ref. 10, with permission.)

bundle and are damaged by most lesions of this pathway. Although damage to these projections may not be involved in the initial deficits (4), they may be important to other aspects of the lateral hypothalamic syndrome. (d) Feeding and drinking deficits have been obtained with perifornical lateral hypothalamic lesions, which do not disrupt the nigrostriatal DA neurons

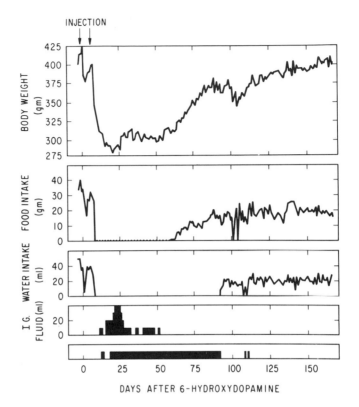

FIG. 2. Recovery of feeding and drinking behaviors in a rat given intraventricular 6-HDA (2 × 200 µg) after pretreatment with pargyline (50 mg/kg, i.p.). Intragastric (IG) feeding and the ingestion of special diets (*bottom line*) are shown. Although all rats progressed through the same stages of recovery, consideration of this animal, who recovered more slowly than most, permits a more detailed examination of the recovery sequence. At first this animal ate nothing and had to be maintained by daily intragastric intubations of liquid diet. After 4 days, the animal passed into a second stage in which it would ingest the palatable foods. Gradually, larger amounts of these special foods were consumed and eventually tube feeding was no longer required for maintenance of body weight. After 58 days, the animal entered a third stage in which it would eat dry chow, but only if hydrated. Although it still would not drink water, the rat would accept 5 to 10% sucrose solutions and thereby maintain body fluid hydration. Finally 92 days after the second 6-HDA treatment, the animal entered a fourth stage in which it maintained body weight on dry chow and tap water, although at a level that was considerably below that of control rats. (Reprinted from Zigmond and Stricker, ref. 9, with permission.)

(interestingly another catecholaminergic pathway, the dorsal bundle of NE fibers, was interrupted) (10). Therefore, the lateral hypothalamic syndrome is probably an amalgamation of many overlapping syndromes, resulting from damage to several different control systems, that together determine the outstanding disruptions in behavior that are observed.

BRAIN CATECHOLAMINE-CONTAINING NEURONS AND AROUSAL

Motivated behaviors have a broad, nonspecific component of arousal, which may be characterized by increased alertness, sensitivity to relevant sensory stimuli, and frequently locomotor activity. Reticular activation appears to be essential for the motivational responses, since stimuli cease to provoke electrocortical arousal and behavior when the reticulocortical input is depressed during ether or sodium pentobarbital anesthesia even though primary sensory pathways to the cortex are unimpaired (11). Catecholaminergic neurons appear to play a critical role in the reticular activating system. Like adrenergic neurons of the sympathetic nervous system, these central neurons are able to influence a large number of regions in response to input to a few, discrete cell groups. Their contribution to central arousal was first indicated by psychopharmacologic studies, which demonstrated that electrocortical activation and behavioral responsiveness are both decreased by drugs that depress activity in central catecholaminergic synapses, whereas the reverse effects are obtained with drugs that augment activity in those synapses (12). More recently specific groups of NE- and DA-containing cell bodies have been observed in the brainstem, which project throughout the telencephalon (13) and appear to be jointly responsible for these effects, although their individual contributions are not identical. Thus extensive damage to NE-containing cell bodies in the locus coeruleus increases the synchrony of EEG activity and allows only brief periods of behavioral orientation to sensory stimulation, whereas destruction of the DA-containing cells of the substantia nigra and ventral tegmentum eliminates behavioral responsiveness despite the presence of normal desynchronous EEG activity (14). These observations emphasize the independence of the systems mediating tonic cortical waking and those mediating more phasic behavioral arousal.

A preliminary formulation of our thoughts on the function of these pathways is diagrammed in Fig. 3. Each sensory stimulus is seen as having two effects: a specific one that activates the neurons involved in eliciting some appropriate motivational state and a nonspecific one that removes a gate and thereby permits such responses to actually occur. Note that a stimulus would

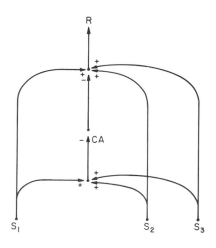

FIG. 3. Schematic representation of neural mechanisms by which sensory stimuli (S) might elicit an appropriate behavioral response (R). $\rightarrow$ Neuronal pathways (which are not necessarily monosynaptic), + excitatory influences, − inhibitory influences, CA indicates synapses of catecholaminergic terminals. Not shown are pathways containing serotonin, acetylcholine, or γ-amino-butyric acid, which are of known significance to cerebral arousal and motor function (12). (Reprinted from Stricker and Zigmond, ref. 10, with permission.)

not evoke a behavioral response if either the specific or the nonspecific (i.e., catecholaminergic) pathways were interrupted. Given the multiplicity of stimuli that impinge on an animal at any given time, we presume that the overt motivated response (for example, feeding, R) will be the one that is associated with the prepotent stimulus (in this case, decreased energy utilization, S_1). Additional stimuli (e.g., gustatory and olfactory cues associated with food, S_2 and S_3) would tend to augment the nonspecific arousal component, due to multisensory convergence onto single reticular neurons, and thereby facilitate responding. Thus a weak stimulus for hunger might still elicit feeding when combined with the incentive arousal from highly palatable food.

In this context it does not seem remarkable that animals sustaining extensive damage to both the dorsal NE bundle and the nigrostriatal DA bundle, as occurs following lateral hypothalamic lesions or intraventricular 6-HDA treatments, show increases in cortical EEG synchronization, are akinetic, and are unresponsive to interoceptive stimuli arising from homeostatic imbalances. Their initial aphagia and adipsia probably reflects the more fundamental problems they have of remaining alert and sustaining arousal in response to sensory stimulation. In fact, deficits in responding to olfactory and gustatory stimuli have been shown to parallel the ineffectiveness of regulatory stimuli in provoking feeding and drinking, and probably contribute to the initial absence of these behaviors (15).

If sensory signals increase neural firing in the residual catecholaminergic neurons of lesioned animals by the same amount as in the catecholaminergic neurons of intact animals, then the total amount of neurotransmitter released would be less than the amount released in intact animals. Thus a given sensory stimulus should not be as effective in activating postsynaptic CA receptors in lesioned animals, and, consequently, animals with fewer catecholaminergic neurons should be less sensitive to weak sensory stimuli than intact animals. For example, it should take a more intense stimulus for hunger to activate residual catecholaminergic neurons sufficiently for feeding behavior to occur. If the threshold for feeding is raised, then lesioned rats should eat less frequently than controls and should stop sooner when they do eat. This will inevitably lead to maintenance of body weight at levels below those of control rats. If the threshold is high enough, then lesioned animals might not be able to eat frequently enough to maintain their body weights, and intragastric feeding by the experimenter would be required for their survival. If the threshold was still higher, then lesioned animals might not eat at all. These considerations are obviously consistent with observations that aphagia is seen only after extensive damage to catecholaminergic neurons, and that long-term reductions in the rate of body weight gain after apparent recovery are generally proportional to the size of the lesions or the length of the initial periods of aphagia and anorexia (6, 16).

A second implication of this formulation is that nonspecific stimuli should be much more important to the activation of catecholaminergic neurons in lesioned animals than in intact rats, since the extra stimulation might be critical in providing sufficient arousal for motivation and behavior. The importance of incentives in providing arousal might therefore account for the extreme finickiness (i.e., the consumption of only highly palatable food and fluids) of rats soon after lateral hypothalamic lesions or intraventricular 6-HDA treatment. Similarly we have observed that simple handling often is sufficient to stimulate feeding briefly in anorexic rats that have been given intraventricular 6-HDA (6), and comparable results have been reported in anorexic rats with 6-HDA lesions of the substantia nigra (7).

Finally amplifying the weak signal that is generated by catecholamines at the postsynaptic membrane should restore feeding behavior in animals with damaged catecholaminergic neurons. This is exactly what seems to occur. For example, amphetamine, which is known to enhance CA release and reduce reticular arousal thresholds, has been shown to increase *ad libitum* food intake both soon after lateral hypothalamic lesions (10, 17) and following recovery of feeding and drinking behaviors (18). More recently, rats recovered from the initial effects of intraventricular 6-HDA or electrolytic lateral hypothalamic lesions have been found to increase food intake when acute glucoprivation is produced by systemic 2-deoxy-D-glucose (2-DG) if they had been pretreated with caffeine or theophylline (19) (see Fig. 1).

BRAIN CATECHOLAMINE-CONTAINING NEURONS AND RECOVERY OF FUNCTION

If destruction of central catecholaminergic neurons provides the basis for the aphagia and adipsia that is initially observed after electrolytic or 6-HDA lesions of the brain, then it is not immediately apparent how to account for recovery of ingestive behaviors since the NE and DA depletions are permanent. One possibility is that resumption of feeding and drinking results from functional recovery of the damaged pathway that is not revealed by measurements of amine concentration. In support of this hypothesis, we have observed that in animals who had recovered from the initial effects of intraventricular 6-HDA or electrolytic lateral hypothalamic lesions, further disruption of central catecholaminergic neurons by an additional intraventricular injection of 6-HDA or by administration of α-methyl-*p*-tyrosine (AMT, in doses that inhibit CA synthesis) reinstated aphagia and adipsia (9, 10). These results would not be expected if resumption of feeding had resulted from transfer of functions formerly served by the amines to another neurochemical pathway.

There is accumulating evidence that the activity of catecholamines is regulated at the synaptic level (10). For example, there are compensatory increases in release and synthesis of amine in the central nervous system following the administration of receptor antagonists and further increases in biosynthetic capacity through enzyme induction when elevations in turnover are prolonged. When receptor activity is reduced indirectly by chronic treatment with reserpine or AMT (see Fig. 1), increased sensitivity of the postsynaptic membranes appears to provide additional amplification. As in these pharmacological studies, there is an initial decrease in receptor activity following destruction of a portion of the catecholaminergic fibers since the number of neurons that are releasing the amine is reduced. Assuming that receptors are activated by catecholamines from many adjacent fibers, and that the communication within individual neurons is equivalent, it is possible that alterations of turnover, synthesis, and receptor activity at residual CA synapses also provide the basis for recovery of function following subtotal damage to CA projections (10, 20). The proposed sequence of events is summarized in Fig. 4.

Several lines of evidence support this concept of recovery. (a) Rats recovered from intraventricular 6-HDA or lateral hypothalamic lesions are considerably more sensitive to the anorexic effects of AMT than are control animals (9). Since CA depletion after the inhibition of tyrosine hydroxylase is dependent on the rate of turnover within the neurons, these data suggest that lesion-induced depletions of brain CAs are accompanied by an increase

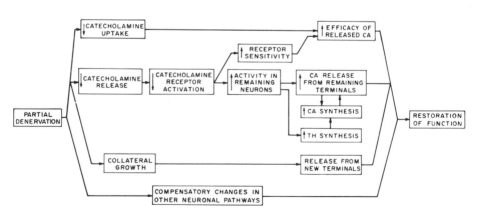

FIG. 4. A model for recovery of function within central catecholaminergic neurons following subtotal damage. Immediately following the lesion, net CA release will be reduced, reflecting the proportion of undamaged neurons that remain. Even though the loss of uptake sites will increase the efficacy of released amine, net decreases in receptor stimulation should occur and lead to increased CA release from residual neurons. This increased turnover should be accompanied by increases in CA synthesis. Prolonged stimulation should increase the neuron's capacity for CA biosynthesis (e.g., through an increase in the effective availability of tyrosine hydroxylase) and thus progressively raise their capacity for sustained increase in CA turnover, whereas enhanced sensitivity of the postsynaptic membrane should increase the effectiveness of the released CA and further promote the recovery of function. A decrease in the affinity of residual terminals for CA, collateral growth from intact axons, regeneration of the damaged fibers, and compensatory changes in other neuronal pathways might also contribute to recovery of function, as might the reversal of certain secondary effects of the lesions (not shown; e.g., vasomotor changes, hemorrhage, edema, proliferation of glial cells). (Reprinted from Stricker and Zigmond, ref. 10, with permission.)

in the turnover of the remaining neurons of the damaged pathway. This hypothesis is further supported by recent measurements of CA synthesis in rats following damage to the nigrostriatal DA fibers (21). (b) The uptake of exogenous NE into the telencephalon decreases following lateral hypothalamic lesions (22) or intraventricular 6-HDA (23). This decrease may result from a reduced affinity of the residual terminals for NE as well as a reduction in number of axon terminals (20). (c) There is an increase in the amount of motor activity that is elicited by apomorphine in 6-HDA-treated rats who are depleted of telencephalic DA by at least 85 to 90% (10, 24). This effect probably reflects a change in the postsynaptic membrane and may be distinguished from the presynaptic supersensitivity that is evident in the augmented response to L-DOPA of lesioned rats with more moderate depletions (10, 25) (see Fig. 1).

This model for recovery of function has two implications that should be made explicit. First, central CA pathways should be able to maintain function despite extensive and irreversible damage; in this regard, note the absence of conspicuous behavioral impairments in 6-HDA-treated rats or human Parkinsonian patients until 75 to 90% of striatal DA has been lost (9, 26). Second, the four stages of recovery following 6-HDA or lateral hypothalamic lesions may simply represent recognizable landmarks along a continuum of function, rather than discrete levels of cerebral control as has been proposed by others (27).

BRAIN CATECHOLAMINE-CONTAINING NEURONS AND RESIDUAL DEFICITS

Following damage to central catecholaminergic neurons, the synthesis of CA should be increased in residual neurons in order to support the elevated rate of turnover. However, in the absence of a proportionate increase in tyrosine hydroxylase, the neurons would then have less of this enzyme available to allow a further increase in CA synthesis when a stimulus provoked additional release. Consequently intense stimuli might increase neuronal activity so much that CA synthesis could not keep up with turnover, CA levels in the terminal would be depleted, and the resultant decrease in receptor stimulation would reestablish aphagia and adipsia.

These considerations may account for many of the impairments in feeding and drinking behaviors that have been observed in recovered laterals and other animals bearing extensive damage to central catecholaminergic projections. The experimental treatments that have revealed residual deficits typically involve the abrupt onset of large nutritional needs, often stimulating maximal behavioral responses in intact rats. Such treatments would be expected to produce stimuli that are well above the range that damaged CA systems can accommodate. Consequently, the failure of lesioned rats to eat or drink under such circumstances might reflect their general inability to behave appropriately after acute and profound stress, rather than the ineffectiveness of specific stimuli for hunger or thirst.

One illustrative example involves the feeding response of rats to acute glucoprivation. Treatment with 4 to 8 units of insulin produces such severe hypoglycemia that animals must eat in order to survive. Unlike controls, rats recovered from lateral hypothalamic lesions do not eat and therefore die (3, 28). These results have been interpreted as revealing a loss of glucoprivic

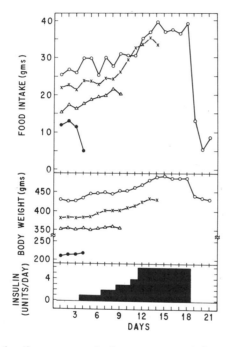

FIG. 5 The effects of daily injections of protamine zinc insulin on food intake and body weight of rats that had been given bilateral electrolytic lesions of the lateral hypothalamus. Each symbol depicts a representative animal. Of 13 lesioned rats that were tested, only four survived the entire 15 days of treatment; the others lasted for 1 to 13 days before the experiments were terminated. All four sham-lesioned control rats survived and showed increases in food intake and body weight that were comparable to those of the lesioned animals. (Reprinted from Stricker et al., ref. 29, with permission.)

feeding, a conclusion supported by subsequent reports that lesioned rats would not increase food intakes after the administration of 2-DG (3, 29). However, in collaboration with Dr. Mark Friedman, we have recently found that recovered laterals will become hyperphagic and gain body weight when they were made chronically hypoglycemic with smaller doses of long-acting protamine-zinc insulin (Fig. 5). Identical results were obtained with 6-HDA-treated rats which had not been aphagic (30), which also do not increase food intakes in response to acute and severe glucoprivation (29). Moreover lesioned rats were found to become hyperphagic when chronic decreases in glucose utilization occur in association with diabetes mellitus (30). Together with the above-mentioned potentiation of 2-DG-elicited feeding by caffeine and theophylline (19), these results indicate that damage to central catecholaminergic neurons does not abolish specific feeding responses to glucoregulatory needs.

Impairments in the feeding responses of lesioned rats following injections of insulin or 2-DG often are contrasted with the increased food consumption that is observed when the need for caloric intake is increased during exposure to a cold environment (7, 28, 29). In confirmation of these findings, we observed that rats with lateral hypothalamic lesions, which did not increase their food intakes in response to 2-DG, did increase their food intakes by

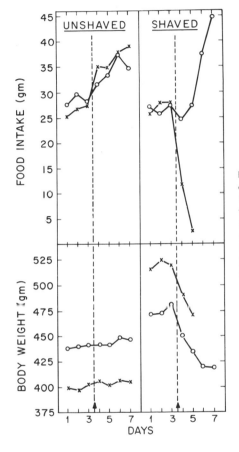

FIG. 6. The effects of continuous exposure to 5°C on food intakes and body weights of rats that had been given bilateral electrolytic lesions of the lateral hypothalamus. Values are for a representative control (O) and lesioned rat (X). Rats were either unshaved or shaved just before being placed in the cold environment (arrow). (Reprinted from Stricker et al., ref. 29, with permission.)

more than 20% during the first few days of exposure to 5°C (Fig. 6, left). Such results have been interpreted as indicating that the lesions had differential effects on glucoregulatory and thermoregulatory feeding mechanisms. However, 1 month later, when these animals were shaved before being placed into the cold again, 7 of 10 rats died within the first 2 days and the other three did not become hyperphagic for 4 to 7 days; in contrast, five shaved control rats increased their food intakes by the 2nd or 3rd day (Fig. 6, right) (30).

These results indicate that lateral hypothalamic lesions do not fractionate separate controls of feeding behavior. As with acute glucoprivation, lesioned rats will not increase their food intake soon after being exposed to a cold environment if the cold stress is made severe (in this case, by prior removal of the insulation provided by fur). Thus the permanent feeding deficits of lesioned rats after their apparent recovery may not reflect an inability to respond to certain qualitatively different stimuli, but rather to quantitatively different intensities of the same stimulus. Consequently, the failure of brain-damaged rats to eat during metabolic emergencies should not imply that they will be unable to respond appropriately to more moderate and gradually developing homeostatic imbalances such as arise when meals are taken *ad libitum* in the normal laboratory environment.

CONCLUSIONS AND SUMMARY

Like the peripheral adrenergic neurons in the sympathetic nervous system, central neurons containing the catecholamines NE and DA project diffusely to a large number of neural structures from only a few cell groups. This neuroanatomical organization is consistent with the apparent contribution of these neurons to the broad, nonspecific components of arousal that are associated with homeostatic imbalance and other conditions of excitement or alarm.

DA-containing neurons traverse the far lateral aspects of the hypothalamus, ascending to regions throughout the telencephalon from cell bodies in the mesencephalon. Specific destruction of 90% or more of these dopamine terminals, such as following intraventricular administration of the neurotoxin 6-hydroxydopamine, leads to aphagia, adipsia, akinesia, and sensory neglect in rats. It seems probable that these fibers are the critical tissue that is damaged by large lateral hypothalamic lesions, which are known to abolish motivated behavior.

Animals suffering damage to dopaminergic neurons may be characterized by an apparent insensitivity to relatively weak sensory stimuli and an intolerance of relatively intense ones. We believe that the former results from a reduction in the number of nerve terminals, with a greater increase in stimulus intensity now being needed to produce an equivalent increase in total dopamine turnover, whereas the latter may result from the decreased ability of the residual neurons to increase synthesis and thereby permit major increases in dopamine release. These changes contract the range of stimuli that the lesioned animals can respond to and underlie many of the specific behavioral deficits.

Gradual recovery of ingestive behaviors and sensory-motor functions occurs in most brain damaged animals within a few weeks after lesioning. Recovery of function appears to be due in part to compensatory processes that occur within residual neurons of the damaged pathway. For example, increased release of catecholamines from the remaining intact terminals, together with an increased efficacy of released neurotransmitter, helps to restore basal function despite permanent catecholamine depletions. As these and other neurochemical compensations proceed, the functional range widens. Nevertheless, even after the resumption of voluntary feeding and drinking behaviors, centrally sympathectomized animals maintain their body weight at much lower levels than controls and fail to respond appropriately during marked homeostatic imbalances. These residual deficits in behavior indicate that recovery is not complete.

Because of the great potential for compensation that is present in catecholaminergic neurons, and because of the nonspecific nature of the message that is probably conveyed by adjacent neurons within these fiber tracts, pathways of catecholaminergic neurons can sustain extensive damage before basal function is disrupted. However, even when brain damage is moderate, the neurochemical compensations that are required to maintain function result in a narrowing in the range of the animal's behavioral capabilities. These changes are much less prominent than when brain damage is severe and may go unnoticed unless specific examinations are conducted.

In summary we believe that models based on biochemical and neuropharmacological principles can be constructed that provide an appropriate perspective for analyzing motivated behavior in intact animals as well as recovery of function following brain damage.

ACKNOWLEDGMENTS

We are grateful for the contributions to this work of our students and associates: Dr. Mark Friedman, Mr. Thomas Heffner, Ms. Kathleen Moran, Ms. Debra Rubinstein, Ms. Suzanne Wuerthele, Ms. Jen-shew Yen, and Mr. Mark Zimmerman. Our research has been supported by U.S. Public Health Service Grants MH-20620 and MH-25140 from the National Institute of Mental Health, and grants from Eli Lilly Company and Smith, Kline and French Company.

REFERENCES

1. Anand, B. K., and Brobeck, J. R. (1951): *Yale J. Biol. Med.*, 24:123–140.
2. Teitelbaum, P., and Epstein, A. N. (1962): *Psychol. Rev.*, 69:74–90.
3. Epstein, A. N. (1971): In: *Progress in Physiological Psychology*, edited by E. Stellar and J. M. Sprague, pp. 263–317. Academic Press, New York.
4. Ungerstedt, U. (1971): *Acta Physiol. Scand.*, 367:69–93.
5. Fibiger, H. C., Zis, A. P., and McGeer, E. G. (1973): *Brain Res.*, 55:135–148.
6. Stricker, E. M., and Zigmond, M. J. (1974): *J. Comp. Physiol. Psychol.*, 86:973–994.
7. Marshall, J. F., Richardson, J. S., and Teitelbaum, P. (1974): *J. Comp. Physiol. Psychol.*, 87:808–830.
8. Oltmans, G. A., and Harvey, J. A. (1972): *Physiol. Behav.*, 8:69–78.
9. Zigmond, M. J., and Stricker, E. M. (1973): *Science*, 182:717–720.
10. Stricker, E. M., and Zigmond, M. J. (1976): In: *Progress in Psychobiology and Physiological Psychology, Vol. 6*, edited by J. M. Sprague and A. N. Epstein. Academic Press, New York.

11. French, J. D., Verzeano, M., and Magoun, H. W. (1953): *Arch. Neurol. Psych.,* 69:519–529.
12. Jouvet, M. (1972): *Ergebn. Physiol.,* 64:166–307.
13. Ungerstedt, U. (1971): *Acta Physiol. Scand.,* 367:1–48.
14. Jones, B. E., Bobillier, P., Pin, C., and Jouvet, M. (1973): *Brain Res.,* 58:157–177.
15. Marshall, J. F., Turner, B. H., and Teitelbaum, P. (1971): *Science,* 174:523–525.
16. Powley, T. L., and Keesey, R. E. (1970): *J. Comp. Physiol. Psychol.,* 70:25–36.
17. Teitelbaum, P., and Wolgin, D. L. (1975): *Prog. Brain Res., in press.*
18. Heffner, T. G., Zigmond, M. J., and Stricker, E. M. (1975): *Fed. Proc.,* 34:348.
19. Zimmerman, M. B., Friedman, M. I., and Stricker, E. M. (1975): Presented at the meeting of the Eastern Psychological Association, New York.
20. Zigmond, M. J., and Stricker, E. M. (1974): In: *Neuropsychopharmacology of Monoamines and Their Regulatory Enzymes (Adv. Biochem. Psychopharm.,* Vol. 12), edited by E. Usdin, pp. 385–402. Raven Press, New York.
21. Agid, Y., Javoy, F., and Glowinski, J. (1973): *Nature New Biol.,* 245:150–151.
22. Zigmond, M. J., Chalmers, J. P., Simpson, J. R., and Wurtman, R. J. (1971): *J. Pharmacol. Exp. Ther.,* 179:20–28.
23. Uretsky, N. J., and Iversen, L. L. (1970): *J. Neurochem.,* 17:269–278.
24. Schoenfeld, R. I., and Uretsky, N. J. (1972): *Eur. J. Pharmacol.,* 19:115–118.
25. Schoenfeld, R. I., and Uretsky, N. J. (1973): *J. Pharmacol. Exp. Ther.,* 186:616–624.
26. Hornykiewicz, O. (1973): *Fed. Proc.,* 32:183–190.
27. Teitelbaum, P. (1971): In: *Progress in Physiological Psychology,* edited by: E. Stellar and J. M. Sprague, pp. 319–350. Academic Press, New York.
28. Epstein, A. N., and Teitelbaum, P. (1967): *Amer. J. Physiol.,* 213:1159–1167.
29. Zigmond, M. J., and Stricker, E. M. (1972): *Science,* 177:1211–1214.
30. Stricker, E. M., Friedman, M. I., and Zigmond, M. J. (1975): *Science,* 189:895–897.

Hunger: Basic Mechanisms and Clinical Implications,
edited by D. Novin, W. Wyrwicka, and G. Bray.
Raven Press, New York © 1976.

Satiety: Hypothalamic Stimulation, Anorectic Drugs, and Neurochemical Substrates

Bartley G. Hoebel

Department of Psychology, Princeton University, Princeton, New Jersey 08540

The hypothalamus and its inputs and outputs are involved in the control of feeding. If we learn to control the hypothalamus electrically and chemically, we will understand a good deal about the basic mechanisms of hunger and their clinical implications.

The work described in this chapter addresses three questions. (1) Can we tap into the brain mechanisms for eliciting and reinforcing feeding by using implanted electrodes to stimulate the hypothalamus? (2) If so, what can the procedures for eliciting feeding, self-stimulation, and stimulation escape tell us about the action of appetite suppressant drugs? (3) Is it possible to identify the neurochemical bases of anorectic drug action? Following the above outline, this chapter progresses from brain stimulation to pharmacology to neurochemistry in an effort to analyze the mechanisms of satiety in the rat.

In discussing each of these three questions, the results are placed in a broader context by synthesizing and theorizing from them. With regard to brain stimulation, it seems likely that the reward and aversion measured as self-stimulation and stimulation escape reflect the animal's tendency to approach or withdraw from food. This conclusion is supported at the pharmacological level; an anorectic compound with relatively minor arousal or sedative properties emerges as a drug of choice for these studies. This drug has been sold to people who are trying to lose weight, but it was never proven effective; therefore tests of its clinical efficacy were undertaken and are summarized here. At the neurochemical level, techniques were developed for assessing the role of brain norepinephrine and serotonin in satiety. Depletion of norepinephrine caused hyperphagia during the waking hours; and treatment intended to deplete serotonin caused hyperphagia during the quiescent hours. These new means of producing hyperphagia are compared to classical hypothalamic hyperphagia. There are interesting differences. This leads to a discussion of the role of noradrenergic and serotonergic satiety functions in amphetamine and fenfluramine anorexia.

BRAIN STIMULATION AND SATIETY

Figure 1 (top) shows feeding elicited by half minute trains of lateral hypothalamic stimulation. The lower part of the figure is a record from a

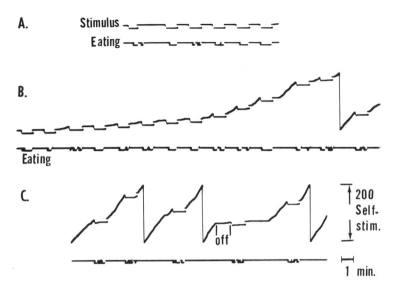

FIG. 1. A: Feeding induced by lateral hypothalamic stimulation. B: Development of self-stimulation inter-rupted by feeding during 1 min bouts of automatic stimulation at the same intensity. C: Well-practiced self-stimulation and elicited eating. (From Hoebel, ref. 47.)

rat as it learns to self-stimulate; it quickly learned to press the lever 3,000 times an hour for 0.5 sec trains of the same stimulation. Thus, when the current is on the rat eats, and when the current is off the rat turns it on for itself.

At this brain site, unlike some others, self-stimulation increases with food deprivation (1, 2); Blundell and Herberg (3) found this only occurred when the electrode was capable of eliciting feeding as well as self-stimulation. Conversely force-feeding decreased self-stimulation (4). The effect was selective as shown in Fig. 2, which contrasts a lateral hypothalamic electrode with a septal electrode in the same rat. Apparently lateral hypothalamic

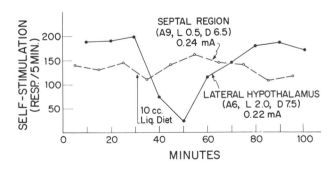

FIG. 2. Self-stimulation selectively inhibited at the lateral hypothalamic site but not at the septal site. (From Hoebel, ref. 9.)

stimulation can engender self-stimulation that is especially sensitive to food intake. Deprivation increases it, and postingestional satiety factors decrease it.

If the stimulation is turned on and left on, or turned on automatically for 0.5 sec every second, most of our rats eventually learn to turn it off by pressing a lever for 5 sec time-out. Figure 3 depicts the test cage with a lever at the left for self-stimulation, one at the back for food pellets and one at the right for stimulation escape.

We find that stimulation escape varies reciprocally with self-stimulation under most circumstances. When self-stimulation decreases after a meal, escape increases. The top line of Fig. 4 illustrates the decrease in self-stimulation after intragastric loading with a mixture of eggs, sugar, and milk. This decrease in responding is not just lethargy because during automatic stimulation, indicated on the bottom line, escape response increased as marked on the middle line.

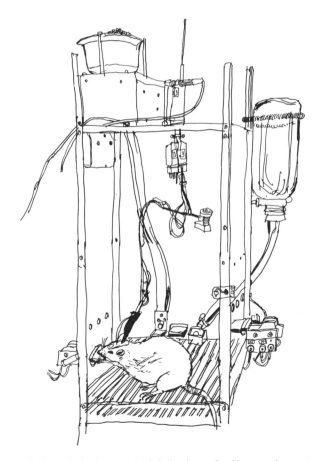

FIG. 3. Testing cage. Self-stimulation lever at the left, food tray, food lever and water trough at the rear, stimulation-escape lever at the right. (From Hoebel and Thompson, ref. 5.)

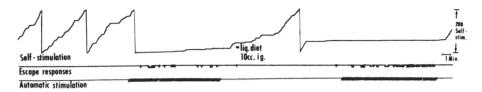

FIG. 4. Self-stimulation decreased by one-third (*top trace;* cumulative response record), but stimulation-escape tripled (*middle trace;* event marker) after this the rat was tube-fed. (From Hoebel, ref. 9.)

Decreased self-stimulation coupled with increased stimulation escape suggested a shift from hypothalamic reward to hypothalamic aversion resulting from postingestional factors. I have hypothesized that the brain controls the animals's willingness to eat by shifting this reward and aversion along a continuum such that the animal gets rewarded for eating when it needs energy and punished for eating when there is an energy surfit (5, 6).

If this is correct, then body weight should exert control over hypothalamic reward and aversion, just as it controls feeding. Figure 5 is an earlier demonstration that excess weight inhibits food intake. Daily insulin injections in nearly lethal amounts forced the rat to overeat to keep its blood sugar level up to a viable level. Obesity resulted from the overeating. When insulin treatment terminated, physiological factors correlated with obesity inhibited food intake until body weight returned to normal (7). This simply demonstrates weight regulation in a normal animal.

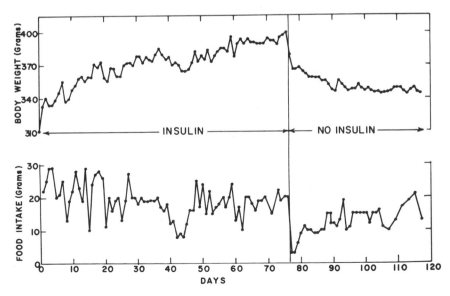

FIG 5. A normal rat forced to overeat and become obese by insulin injection, voluntarily restricts its food intake so that weight returns to normal after treatment is terminated. (From Hoebel and Teitelbaum, ref. 7.)

To determine if weight-related factors can inhibit self-stimulation, rats were force-fed (8) or chronically stimulated in the presence of food using the cage in Fig. 3. Figure 6 shows the result in our best rat (5). Self-stimulation decreased (top) and simultaneously escape increased (second line) when the rat became obese (third line) from overeating (bottom). Thus both fat-related and meal-related signals, control hypothalamic reinforcement.

This background information is necessary to understand the pharmacological studies to follow, but is really by way of review, having been

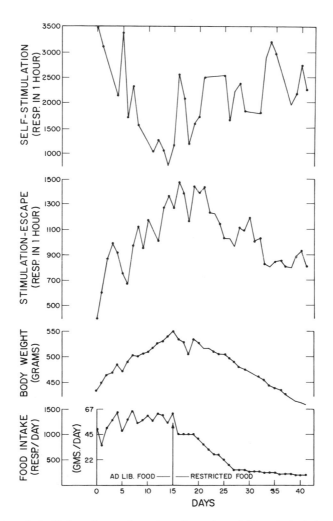

FIG. 6. This rat made itself obese by pressing a lever for prolonged (30 sec) stimulation, which caused overeating (*bottom* curve). In daily 1-hr tests, self-stimulation decreased, and escape from automatic stimulation increased, as the rat gained weight. Restricting food intake reversed the process. (From Hoebel and Thompson, ref. 5.)

summarized previously (9). The theory that hypothalamic approach and withdrawal represents approach and withdrawal in feeding behavior has been developed at length in this year's Nebraska Symposium on Motivation (6).

If this theory is to be of value, it must predict new experiments and, one would hope, contribute to human happiness. To test the theory and its relevance to human concerns, we have assessed the effects of appetite suppressant drugs on hypothalamic reinforcement and selected one of them for tests with humans who wanted to lose weight.

PHARMACOLOGY OF SATIETY

We were interested in three anorexigenic drugs: amphetamine, fenfluramine, and phenylpropanolamine. Figure 7 shows their structures and their structural likeness to putative neurotransmitters in the brain. Each of the anorectics has a methyl group on the alpha carbon to protect it from the destructive action of monoamine oxidase. They all lack the hydroxyl groups on the benzene ring so they can cross the blood-brain barrier. Thus they can pass into the brain and remain there. Once in the brain they may affect monoamine function. Structurally, as depicted in the figure, amphetamine parallels dopamine, phenylpropanolamine is similar to norepinephrine, and ephedrine corresponds to epinephrine. Phenylpropanolamine has the advantage that it is thought not to be a CNS stimulant and does not cause overt activity change (10). Fenfluramine has a radical departure from the others with the addition of a fluorine moiety to the ring. We chose to test this drug

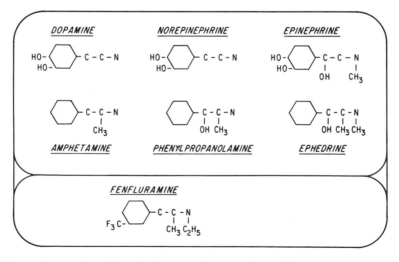

FIG. 7. Structural comparison of catecholamines and anorectic drugs used in the experiments described in the text.

because it is a good appetite suppressant, but definitely not a stimulant. If anything, it is a depressant.

Figure 8 summarizes our results with these three prototypic anorectic drugs. As shown by the first column of arrows all three drugs suppressed feeding at the doses we used. Self-stimulation was increased by amphetamine (11, 12). We attribute this to its arousal properties because it also caused escape to increase. Kornblith, when associated with my laboratory, found that fenfluramine had the opposite effect and caused both self-stimulation and stimulation escape to decrease (13). This is probably the result of general response suppression or sedation.

Phenylpropanolamine (Propadrine®) did what was expected according to the theory outlined above. Just as food intake was suppressed, so was self-stimulation (12). Escape on the other hand, was accelerated in tests lasting several hours (12). In short tests the effect was not seen (13), probably

FIG. 8. Of the three drugs used, only Propadrine (phenylpropanolamine) decreased self-stimulation and increased stimulation-escape; whereas amphetamine increased both, and fenfluramine decreased both, at the anorectic doses tested. (After Kornblith, ref. 13, and Hoebel and McClelland, ref. 12.)

because the drug at the doses used tended to debilitate the animal initially. After this effect abated, willingness to escape from stimulation increased above baseline levels. Therefore phenylpropanolamine decreased our measure of reward, while increasing aversion. This suggests that phenylpropanolamine is a drug of choice when an appetite suppressant that is neither a CNS stimulant nor a depressant is desired.

If the eating elicited by stimulating the hypothalamus is related to natural eating and self-stimulation, then this drug should have a suppressive effect on electrically elicited eating as well as self-stimulation. It did have this effect, but it was selective. Phenylpropanolamine inhibited feeding but did not depress drinking elicited with the same electrode. This occurred whether elicited feeding and drinking were tested simultaneously or separately (14).

This demonstrates that there is specific pharmacological control of hypothalamically induced eating. It also suggests that elicited feeding may be related somehow to feeding reward at certain self-stimulation sites. This may not be true of all self-stimulation sites, nor with all drugs, particularly those that affect cholinergic systems (15); in the present experiments, however, both elicited-feeding and self-stimulation were suppressed by the same drug. Both were also suppressed by food intake (16).

If this drug is capable of suppressing feeding without causing an overall change in activity or responsiveness and without suppressing other motivated behavior patterns, and if people have a similar mechanism, then it should be a good anorectic for patients who must lose weight. We tested phenylpropanolamine in humans. It is sold over-the-counter in large quantities, but has never adequately been proven effective (17). The U.S. Food and Drug Administration (FDA) accepted it as being safe because its effects on blood pressure are minimal; soon the FDA will want to know if it is effective in causing weight loss.

Our subjects were Princetonians interested in their weight. They took the drug or a placebo, before meals in a double-blind, subject crossover design. The subjects lost weight on phenylpropanolamine (Hungrex®). They also lost some weight on the placebo as shown in Fig. 9. When they were crossed-over to the opposite treatment those that had been taking the drug then got the placebo and lost no more weight. Those who had started on the placebo and then were given the drug continued to lose. This difference was statistically significant (18). There is not time to discuss whether this was also medically significant. That is a difficult problem (17). However, at least from the scientific point of view, the evidence showed that this drug, which worked so well in rats, can also be effective in humans.

The weight loss with phenylpropanolamine was probably the result of decreased food intake. In separate tests with subjects drawn from the same population, phenylpropanolamine taken before a lunch of chocolate liquid

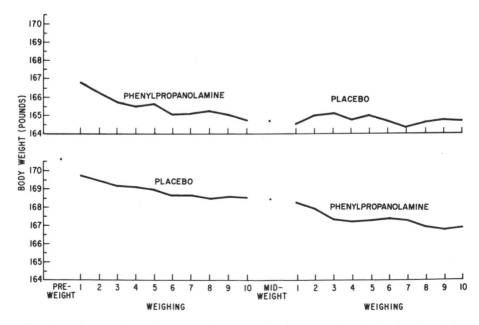

FIG. 9. Top: Patients taking phenylpropanolamine for 2 weeks followed by placebo for 2 weeks lost weight with the drug and gained slightly with the placebo. Bottom: Patients taking placebo first and then drug lost weight during both periods. N = 70. (From Hoebel et al., ref. 18.)

diet (Metrecal®) caused a significant decrease in intake. This was confirmed in a second test again using the lunch technique of Jordan et al. (19). Each subject served as his or her own control in a double-blind design. Based on Jordan's experience with amphetamine tests, we ran a third group of subjects but gave them no food-related expectations by informing them that the drug was a nasal decongestant. Incidentally, this is true—the same drug is an active ingredient in Contac®, Allerest®, Propadrine®, and many other popular cold-relief remedies. In this third group, the population was selected for their interest in being paid rather than an interest in their weight, so they were younger, mostly students, and thinner than our early groups of Princeton townspeople. This time the drug did not suppress lunch intake, perhaps because of the different expectations or the different population of subjects.

In summary, we conclude that phenylpropanolamine causes decreased food intake and weight loss relative to a placebo when it is taken by weight-conscious people. From the clinical point of view, this is acceptable because these are the people who need it. It appears, however, that unknown factors can override the anorectic effect of the drug. Actually, this may be beneficial clinically because the drug is used for purposes other than anorexia, such as nasal decongestion.

My overall assessment of this popular drug is that it is effective, statistically speaking, with the population who is likely to use it for weight control; this legitimizes its use for that purpose; however, more weight will actually be lost by the placebo effect than by the actual drug effect. People taking the drug should be made aware of several related facts. (a) If they take phenylpropanolamine for nasal decongestion they may also lose their appetite, and if they take it for weight control they may constrict mucous membranes (currently these facts are not on the labels). (b) Because the drug probably affects brain feeding mechanisms directly (as we shall see in a moment), it may affect other brain systems with similar neurochemical substrates; if this is so, it could also affect other behaviors (which behaviors is currently unknown). Therefore, a drug that acted exclusively by way of natural physiological satiety signals instead of directly on the brain might be preferable. (c) Most people who lose weight gain it back; and the advisability of temporary weight loss is currently a moot point. (d) There may be personality shifts associated with weight loss that should be correctly interpreted so as to reinforce the weight loss if the change is for the better and not be blamed on other circumstances if the change is for the worse.

NEUROCHEMISTRY OF SATIETY

The next question is how and where anorectic drugs act. Lesion studies have shown that amphetamine depends on the lateral hypothalamus for part of its anorectic action (10, 20). Recent developments in histochemistry in

Sweden by Ungerstedt (21) and others suggested to Eric Ahlskog in this laboratory that ascending noradrenergic pathways that pass through the lateral hypothalamus might be involved in appetite suppression. Figure 10 summarizes experiments in which 6-hydroxydopamine, which is toxic to norepinephrine and dopamine cells, was injected through implanted cannulas into the ventral or dorsal noradrenergic bundles in the midbrain. Note that the injection was made posterior to the origin of the dopamine pathway. Fluorescence histochemical analysis of serial sections of the brain confirmed that dopamine was not depleted by the neurotoxin. Norepinephrine was drastically depleted. In the left bar graph in Fig. 10, it is shown that ventral

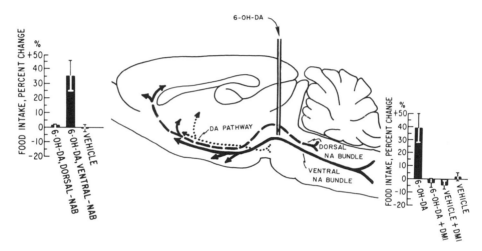

FIG. 10. Left: The selective neurotoxin 6-hydroxydopamine (6-OH-DA) depleted the brain of norepineph-rine and caused hyperphagia, but only when injected into the ventral, not dorsal, noradrenergic bundle; Middle: Side view of the brain showing the ventral and dorsal noradrenergic (NA) bundles and the dopamine (DA) nigrostriatal pathway. (After Ungerstedt, ref. 21.) Right: Hyperphagia was prevented by pretreatment with desmethylimipramine (DMI) which protected the ventral noradrenergic bundle from 6-OH-DA. (From Ahlskog and Hoebel, ref. 22, and Ahlskog, ref. 25.)

bundle injections caused hyperphagia. The right graph confirms that the loss of norepinephrine neurons was responsible for hyperphagia. Pretreat-ment with desmethylimipramine to block uptake of the neurotoxin into noradrenergic neurons thereby prevented destruction of noradrenergic neu-rons and prevented hyperphagia. All of these results were confirmed by neurochemical assay as well as histochemistry. Therefore we conclude that norepinephrine pathways ascending from the midbrain serve a satiety func-tion in the intact animal (22).

One qualification is necessary. Epinephrine neurons form a pathway that runs along with the ventral norepinephrine bundle (23). Epinephrine was probably depleted by our procedures and could be involved in the hyper-phagia phenomenon.

These hyperphagic rats have several interesting characteristics. Insulin-induced feeding is normal (24), but amphetamine loses much of its anorectic potency (22, 25). Figure 11 shows that the amphetamine dose-response curve was shifted to the right by lesions or by 6-hydroxydopamine treatment to destroy the ventral noradrenergic bundle. It is conceivable that the diminished anorexia to amphetamine might result from the general increase in feeding, not from norepinephrine depletion per se. However, this is unlikely because in a replication of this study rats that showed reduced anorexia to amphetamine also showed enhanced anorexia to fenfluramine (26). A nonspecific hunger effect would have attenuated fenfluramine

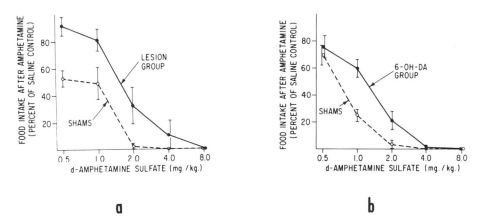

FIG. 11. Lesions or 6-OH-DA injection in the vicinity of the ventral noradrenergic bundle attenuated amphetamine-induced anorexia. Food consumption after amphetamine is expressed as a percent of the previous day's intake following saline injection (±SEM). a: Electrolytically lesioned rats versus sham controls. b: 6-OH-DA-injected animals compared to their control group. (From Ahlskog, ref. 25.)

anorexia like amphetamine anorexia, but to the contrary fenfluramine gained potency after norepinephrine loss. Therefore attenuation of amphetamine anorexia by intramesencephalic 6-hydroxydopamine was probably the specific result of depletion of the necessary neurotransmitter. We conclude that one way amphetamine normally causes appetite suppression is by the release of norepinephrine or epinephrine from ascending neurons.

Kapatos and Gold (27) produced hyperphagia using lesions and knife cuts to interrupt ascending pathways. Gold (28) proposed that hypothalamic lesions that cause hyperphagia, including their knife cuts which traced the effect back to the level of the mammilary bodies, are effective to the extent that they destroy the ventral noradrenergic bundle or its projections. Thus the more damage a medial hypothalamic lesion does to this pathway, the greater will be the tendency to overeat.

We find the symptoms of classical hypothalamic hyperphagia involve more than just norepinephrine depletion, however. There are two distinct syndromes, one produced by midbrain destruction of the ventral noradrenergic bundle, the other by localized lesions of the ventromedial region of the hypothalamus. The effects of the two procedures on amphetamine anorexia are different. Ventromedial hypothalamic lesions tend to enhance amphetamine anorexia (10), whereas norepinephrine depletion tends to diminish anorexia, as described above and in Fig. 11 (22, 25).

It has been shown that hypophysectomy does not prevent classic hypothalamic hyperphagia (29) but does prevent hyperphagia after norepinephrine depletion (30). This was shown in an experiment with four groups of rats; 6-hydroxydopamine or its vehicle was injected after complete or incomplete hypophysectomy. Only the group receiving 6-hydroxydopamine plus incomplete hypophysectomy became hyperphagic and obese. They ate 5 g of food per day more than the others. By contrast, the group with 6-hydroxydopamine after complete hypophysectomy showed minimal changes in eating and weight, which were no different than the controls. Complete hypophysectomy was verified by observing lower preoperative body weight and postoperative loss of adrenal and ovary weight, and of course, a missing pituitary gland. We have not been able to identify the role of the pituitary in norepinephrine-depletion hyperphagia. Removing the adrenals does not have the same effect, and growth hormone replacement therapy does not totally reinstate hyperphagia. Perhaps the pituitary plays a permissive role in this hyperphagia phenomenon rather than being directly involved in the induction of overeating. In any case, classic hypothalamic hyperphagia is different because it persists in spite of hypophysectomy. This could be because hypothalamic hyperphagia is a bigger effect and therefore harder to prevent, or it could be that the two syndromes are basically quite different.

The third point of comparison is taste hyperactivity, known as finickiness. It should be noted here that classic hyperphagia after medial hypothalamic lesions is itself not a unitary phenomenon. Beven (31) confirmed Graff and Stellar's (32) observation that some lesions cause hyperphagia with finickiness, some cause hyperphagia without finickiness, and some cause finickiness alone. Some studies also suggest that finickiness is a function of the body weight, not the lesion (33, 34). Unfortunately many aspects of the surgical and posttesting and pretesting procedures influence what will be observed, as I have reviewed earlier (6). Details aside, it seemed clear on the basis of Beven's study, which varied lesion placement, that finickiness and overeating could be dissociated anatomically (31). A logical problem was to see if they could be dissociated neurochemically.

Ahlskog found that norepinephrine-depleted hyperphagic rats were not finicky. Their response to high-fat diet that was made especially palatable with sacharine or cheese, or less palatable with quinine, was the same as that of control rats (24). Although this was admittedly a negative result, it confirmed in a new way the dissociation of finickiness and hyperphagia.

Social psychologists, Schachter (35) and some of his former students, have noted striking similarities between hypothalamic hyperphagic rats and obese people who weigh more than the national average for their sex, age, and height. This has led to useful descriptions of personality types based on the tendency to respond to external as opposed to internal stimuli. Overweight people seem to be externally oriented. As Nisbett notes, however, Teitelbaum and I (7) demonstrated that medial hypothalamic rats can be over the average weight for rats of a given sex and strain and yet be underweight relative to the individual's preferred obese plateau. This is shown in Fig. 12; the rat on a starvation diet is over its original weight but under its preferred weight. Thus there is a debate as to whether externality is associated with

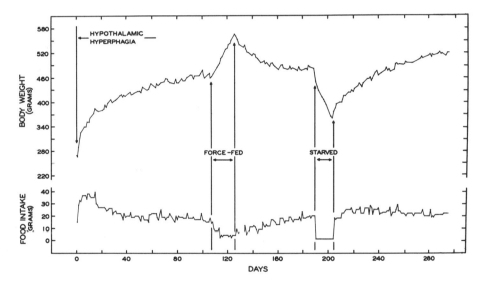

FIG. 12. Effects of force-feeding and starvation on food intake and body weight of a rat with ventromedial hypothalamic lesions. (From Hoebel and Teitelbaum, ref. 7.)

overweight or underweight (36). It is also not yet clear whether overweight people show externality because they have a weight problem of some kind or whether they have a weight problem because they are externally oriented.

We must add one more complication to the social psychologist's story. It is now possible to make rats obese without the usual signs of finickiness or externality by producing restricted, precisely localized hypothalamic lesions (31), or by norepinephrine deficits (24, 37). In this regard, an interesting distinction between increased appetite and decreased satiety has recently been emphasized by Sclafani and Kluge (38). Some obese rats may exhibit one and not the other. Since obesity has a variety of etiologies and symptomatology in rats, there are surely differences to be expected among overweight humans.

A fourth major difference between the new syndrome of hyperphagia and the old, perhaps the most telling, is the time of day at which rats exhibit hyperphagia. Le Magnen (39), Becker and Kisseleff (40), and others have shown that ventromedial hypothalamic rats overeat extensively in the day-time instead of sleeping, so that they lose the circadian rhythmicity of their feeding patterns. The 6-hydroxydopamine-treated rats, on the other hand, overate only at night (Fig. 13) (41).

When 6-hydroxydopamine-injected rats were compared to hypothalam-ically lesioned animals, it was clear that the classic lesion techniques gave a bigger overall effect on daily food intake. This comparison is made in Fig. 14A. The hypothalamic animals showed greater hyperphagia, but they were not depleted of norepinephrine at all. On the other hand, the 6-hydroxy-dopamine injections reduced norepinephrine to 6% of normal and caused relatively modest hyperphagia.

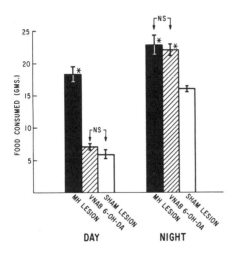

FIG. 13. Right: At night rats with ventral norad-renergic bundle (VNAB), 6-hydroxydopamine (6-OH-DA) lesions and rats with medial hypo-thalamic (MH) lesions were equally hyperphagic. Both were significantly different (asterisks) from the sham lesion controls (*), but were not differ-ent from each other (NS). Left: During the day, the VNAB animals ate normally while the MH rats continued to display marked hyperphagia (astericks, $p < 0.001$). (From Ahlskog et al., ref. 41.)

Apparently there are at least two kinds of hyperphagia following brain damage. If so, they might be additive, Ahlskog reasoned. If, on the other hand, norepinephrine depletion is tantamount to a medial hypothalamic lesion, then combined lesions would simply substitute for each other. There-fore rats were prepared with a combination of discrete lesions in the hypo-thalamus that did not affect norepinephrine levels plus 6-hydroxydopamine lesions in the ascending norepinephrine pathways.

Fig. 14B shows that the combined lesions were additive. Hypothalamic lesions in the prior obese, norepinephrine-lacking animals produced a dramatic second increment in food intake. Apparently the ventromedial hypothalamus contains satiety functions that act in addition to mesencephalic noradrenergic or adrenergic influences (41). This may well explain why Gold's (28) rats with large medial hypothalamic lesions showed progres-sively greater hyperphagia with progressively larger lesions in the region of noradrenergic projections and yet gave greater hyperphagia than we ob-served after nearly total norepinephrine depletion alone.

If there is another major satiety system in addition to the one destroyed by intramesencephalic 6-hydroxydopamine, what is it? The evidence points to a serotonergic system. I mentioned at the outset of this neurochemical section that fenfluramine, unlike amphetamine, produced enhanced anorexia after norepinephrine depletion (26). This amphetamine-fenfluramine dichotomy was also seen by Fibiger et al. (42) after depleting catecholamines with 6-hydroxydopamine injected in the substantia nigra or ventricles, by

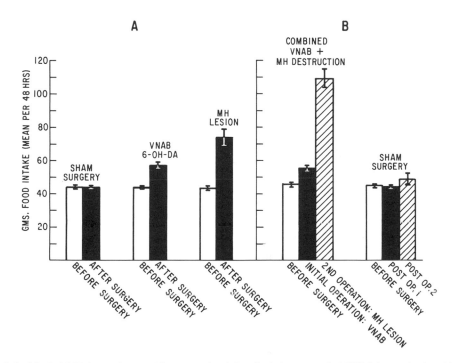

FIG. 14. A: VMH hyperphagia without norepinephrine depletion exceeded VNAB hyperphagia with nearly complete norepinephrine depletion. B: The two techniques for producing hyperphagia added to each other rather than substituting for each other. (From Ahlskog et al., ref. 41.)

Clineschmidt (43) after catecholamine synthesis block, and by Blundell and Leshem (44) after lateral hypothalamic lesions. Our study (26) produced the effect by norepinephrine depletion with no appreciable change in dopamine or serotonin levels; both were at about 92% of normal, so norepinephrine would seem to be responsible. However, considerable evidence suggests that there is a central antagonism between norepinephrine and serotonin, and fenfluramine is known to act on serotonergic systems, as reviewed elsewhere (17). It is therefore quite likely that norepinephrine depletion disinhibited a serotonergic substrate for fenfluramine anorexia.

If there is, in fact, a serotonergic satiety system, then a treatment known to deplete serotonin should cause hyperphagia. A logical drug to use is paracholorophenylalanine (PCPA). Many have tried and not observed a clear hyperphagic effect. Stuart Breisch, in this laboratory, noted that **PCPA** injected systemically seemed to fail because it made the animals sick. He then tried it intraventricularly and found clear hyperphagia that reached a maximum on the 4th day and returned to normal in about 2 weeks (45). The rats were also mildly hyperactive in tilt cages. Serotonin assays on such animals are not yet complete, but it would appear from the time course of the effect that serotonin depletion might be responsible for the behavioral changes (45).

Intraventricular **PCPA** clearly prevents the action of some feeding suppression system. This effect is probably not specific to feeding because activity also increases, and systemic PCPA is known to disinhibit numerous other behaviors. Nonetheless the feeding-suppression system revealed in this study could be one of the nonnoradrenergic satiety influences we were seeking to explain the difference between classic hyperphagia and norepinephrine-depletion hyperphagia.

Since norepinephrine-depleted rats were hyperphagic at night, **PCPA** rats might be hyperphagic in the daytime. Our most recent study supports this idea; the PCPA-treated rats were hyperphagic primarily during the day. Perhaps classical hypothalamic hyperphagia results from one or both effects depending on the size and placement of the lesion.

In summary I suspect that serotonergic neurons in the medial hypothalamus suppress feeding in the daytime and form a substrate for fenfluramine anorexia. Opposing this system are noradrenergic or adrenergic neurons arising in the midbrain that have as one of their functions the inhibition of feeding when the rat displays satiety at night. This is the substrate by which amphetamine and possibly phenylpropanolamine inhibit spontaneous feeding and probably electrically elicited feeding as well. The same mechanism apparently inhibits self-stimulation at feeding-reward sites. At least the same drug, phenylpropanolamine, does so. But inhibition, or lack of approach behavior, is only half of the story, because satiety engendered by food intake, excess body weight, or phenylpropanolamine, all increased stimulation-escape responding. It is as if hypothalamic stimulation represented food to the animals and was largely pleasurable until satiety factors or an anorectic drug shifted the balance in the direction of aversion. The fact that phenylpropanolamine can cause decreased food intake and weight loss in humans raises the possibility of a similar mechanism for homeostatic hedonism in people's approach to or withdrawal from food.

ACKNOWLEDGMENTS

Research from the author's laboratory reported here was supported by U.S. Public Health Service Grant MH-08493, National Science Foundation Grants GB-8431 and GB-43407, the Alleghany Pharm. Co., and a Spencer Foundation Neuroscience Training Grant.

REFERENCES

1. Olds, J. (1958): *J. Comp. Physiol. Psychol.*, 51:320–324.
2. Margules, D. L., and Olds, J. (1962): *Science*, 135:374–375.
3. Blundell, J. E., and Herberg, L. J. (1968): *Nature*, 219:627–628.
4. Hoebel, B. G., and Teitelbaum, P. (1962): *Science*, 135:375–377.
5. Hoebel, B. G., and Thompson, R. D. (1969): *J. Comp. Physiol. Psychol.*, 68:536–543.
6. Hoebel, B. G. (1975): In: *Nebraska Symposium on Motivation*, edited by J. K. Cole.
7. Hoebel, B. G., and Teitelbaum, P. (1966): *J. Comp. Physiol. Psychol.*, 61:189–193.
8. MacNeil, D. (1974): *Physiol. Psychol.*, 2:51–53.
9. Hoebel, B. G. (1971): *Ann. Rev. Physiol.*, 33:533–568.
10. Epstein, A. N. (1959): *J. Comp. Physiol. Psychol.*, 52:37–45.
11. Stein, L., and Wise, C. D. (1970): In: *Psychotomimetic Drugs*, edited by D. H. Efron, pp. 123–149. Raven Press, New York.
12. Hoebel, B. G., and McClelland, S. J.: *Submitted for publication.*
13. Kornblith, C. (1974): Paper Presented at Eastern Psychological Association Meeting.
14. Hoebel, B. G., Hernandez, L., and Thompson, R. D.: *J. Comp. Physiol. Psychol., in press.*
15. Stark, P., Totty, W., Turk, J. A., and Henderson, J. K. (1968): *Am. J. Physiol.*, 214:463–468.
16. Devor, M. G., Wise, R. A., Milgram, N. W., and Hoebel, B. G. (1970): *J. Comp. Physiol. Psychol.*, 73:226–232.
17. Hoebel, B. G. (1975): In: *Handbook of Psychopharmacology*, edited by L. L. Iversen, S. D. Iversen, and S. H. Snyder.
18. Hoebel, B. G., Krauss, I. K., Cooper, J., and Willard, D.: *Obesity Bariatr. Med., in press.*
19. Jordan, H. A., Wieland, W. F., Zebley, S. P., Stellar, E., and Stunkard, A. J. (1966): *Psychosom. Med.*, 28:836–842.
20. Carlisle, H. J. (1964): *J. Comp. Physiol. Psychol.*, 58:47–54.
21. Ungerstedt, U. (1971): *Acta Physiol. Scand. Suppl.* 367(b).
22. Ahlskog, E., and Hoebel, B. G. (1973): *Science*, 182:166–169.
23. Hokfelt, T., Fuxe, K., Goldstein, M. and Johansson, O. (1974): *Brain Res.*, 66:235–360.
24. Ahlskog, J. E.: *Submitted for publication.*
25. Ahlskog, J. E. (1974): *Brain Res.*, 82:211–240.
26. Ahlskog, J. E., Randall, P. K., and Hoebel, B. G.: *Submitted for publication.*
27. Kapatos, G., and Gold, R. M. (1973): *Pharmacol. Biochem. Behav.*, 1:81–87.
28. Gold, R. M. (1973): *Science*, 182:488–490.
29. Cox, V. C., Kakolewski, J. W., and Valenstein, E. S. (1968) *J. Comp. Physiol. Psychol.*, 65:145–148.
30. Ahlskog, J. E., Hoebel, B. G., and Breisch, S. T. (1974): *Fed. Proc.*, 33:463.
31. Bevan, T. E. (1973): Ph.D. dissertation. Princeton University.
32. Graff, H., and Stellar, E. (1962): *J. Comp. Physiol. Psychol.*, 55:418–424.
33. Teitelbaum, P. (1955): *J. Comp. Physiol. Psychol.*, 48:156–163.
34. Franklin, K. B. J., and Herberg, L. J. (1974): *J. Comp. Physiol. Psychol.*, 87:410–414.
35. Schacter, S. (1971): *Am. Psychol.*, 26:129.
36. Nisbett, R. E. (1972): *Adv. Psychosom. Med.*, 7:173–193.
37. Ahlskog, J. E., and Hoebel, B. G. (1972): *Fed. Proc.*, 31:377.
38. Sclafani, A., and Kluge, L. (1974): *J. Comp. Physiol. Psychol.*, 86:28–46.
39. Le Magnen, J., Devos, M., Guadilliere, J. P., Louis-Sylvestre, J., and Tallon, S. (1973): *J. Comp. Physiol. Psychol.*, 84:1.
40. Becker, E. E., and Kissileff, H. R. (1974): *Am. J. Physiol.*, 226:383–396.

41. Ahlskog, J. E., Randall, P. K., and Hoebel, B. G.: *Submitted for publication.*
42. Fibiger, H. C., Zis, A. P., and McGeer, E. G. (1973): *Brain Res.,* 55:135–148.
43. Clineschmidt, B. V., McGuffin, J. C., and Werner, A. B. (1974): *Eur. J. Pharmacol.,* 27:313–323.
44. Blundell, J. E., and Leshem, M. B. (1974): *Eur. J. Pharmacol.,* 28:81–88.
45. Breisch, S. T., and Hoebel, B. G. (1975): *Fed. Proc.,* 34:296.
46. Sheard, M. (1969): *Brain Res.,* 15:524–528.
47. Hoebel, B. G. (1969): *Ann. N.Y. Acad. Sci.,* 157:758–778.

Hunger: Basic Mechanisms and Clinical Implications,
edited by D. Novin, W. Wyrwicka, and G. Bray.
Raven Press, New York © 1976.

Neuroanatomy of Food and Water Intake

Sebastian P. Grossman

Department of Behavioral Sciences, University of Chicago, Chicago, Illinois 60637

This volume may well signal the end of an era that began with Hetherington and Ranson's (1) demonstration in 1940 that lesions in the ventromedial hypothalamus (VMH)[1] of the rat produced hyperphagia and obesity and Anand and Brobeck's (2) discovery 11 years later that lesions in the lateral hypothalamus (LH) resulted in aphagia and adipsia. On the basis of these and related observations, Stellar (3) promulgated a hypothalamic theory of appetitive motivation, which has had enormous heuristic influence on the research and thinking of the past decades. It has only been in recent years that fundamental questions have been raised concerning the nature and indeed the very existence of the hypothalamic influences that such a model proposes.

THE LH

Much of the support for the hypothalamic model of food and water intake regulation derives from the observation that lesions in the dorsolateral hypothalamus produce aphagia and adipsia, whereas electrical stimulation of this region elicits ingestive behaviors. However, the area is traversed by numerous fiber systems, including components of the medial forebrain bundle, afferent and efferent connections of the striatum, amygdalofugal and -petal projections, and several major sensory pathways. It is becoming increasingly clear that at least some of the effects of lesions or stimulation in this area may be caused by effects on fibers of passage and that sensory and motor disturbances may play a more important role in the etiology of some of the lesion effects than has generally been assumed.

That the effects of LH lesions might be due to an interruption of fibers of passage was first suggested by Morgane (4) almost 15 years ago when he discovered that lesions in the globus pallidus (GP) reproduced the disturbances in ingestive behavior previously observed after LH damage. Gold (5) supported Morgane's interpretation by showing that aphagia and adipsia could also be produced by tegmental lesions and that the relatively mild effects of a unilateral lesion in that area summed with those of a contralateral

---

Abbreviations used in this chapter: **VMH,** ventromedial hypothalamus; **LH,** lateral hypothalamus; **GP,** globus pallidus; **ZI,** zona incerta; **VMN,** ventromedial nucleus.

lesion in the LH to produce persistent effects on food and water intake. More recently, Ungerstedt (6) has shown that chemical or electrolytic lesions of the substantia nigra (SN), which projects to the striatum by way of the dorsolateral hypothalamus also result in aphagia and adipsia.

We have found that an interruption of the fibers that enter or leave the hypothalamus laterally reproduced the effects of LH lesions on food and water intake in every detail (7, 8), even though the retractable tungsten wire knife used in these experiments produced little or no damage to cellular components of the LH itself. A cut along the medial border of the internal capsule produced persisting aphagia and adipsia, which in many cases could not be reversed in 90 to 120 days of concerted efforts to wean the animals to a palatable diet. Animals that did recover voluntary ingestive behavior after weeks or months of aphagia and adipsia showed the gradual recovery process described by Teitelbaum and Epstein (9) for rats with LH lesions. These animals eventually consumed adequate amounts of a pellet diet and were, in fact, hyperphagic when offered highly palatable liquid foods. They remained hypersensitive to the sensory qualities of their diet and refused powdered or quinine-adulterated foods, which were readily accepted by control animals. Like rats that have recovered voluntary intake after LH lesions, our rats did not eat in response to insulin or 2-deoxy-D-glucose and even failed to adjust food intake in response to variations in environmental temperature, the only regulatory response that appears to be intact after LH lesions (10). Even after recovery, our rats consumed water only in order to facilitate the ingestion of dry food. Water intake fell to zero during periods of food deprivation and there was no response to experimental treatments that result in cellular dehydration or extracellular hypovolemia.

We have attempted to specify more precisely those fibers responsible for these effects (7; also Alheid and Grossman, *unpublished observations*). These experiments demonstrated that the effectiveness of the transection (i.e., the duration of aphagia and adipsia and the severity of the persisting deficits) declined sharply as the plane of the cuts was moved either laterally or medially and that shorter or shallower cuts in the same parasagittal plane as the long cuts, found to be maximally effective in the earlier experiments, produced shorter and less severe effects on ingestive behavior. The pattern of effects observed in these experiments permits several tentative conclusions concerning the distribution of fibers that appear to contribute to the aphagia and adipsia syndrome. (a) Since parasagittal cuts lateral to the hypothalamus and cuts that interrupted only the connections of the anterior half or two-thirds of the hypothalamus produced only mild and transient effects on ingestive behavior, amygdalofugal (and -petal) projections or other direct interconnections between the brainstem and temporal lobe do not appear to be responsible for the observed effects. (b) Since cuts that spared a relatively small percentage of the lateral connections of the hypothalamus at any anterior-posterior plane produced only transient effects on food intake (persisting deficits in body water regulation were often seen even after smaller cuts), it seems likely that the aphagia component of the syndrome may be caused by the near-complete interruption of a diffuse fiber system that crosses the lateral border of the hypothalamus along its entire length.

Attempts to specify the course of this fiber system further with cuts in the coronal plane have suggested that they may ascend (or descend) for only a short distance in the postero-LH and then sharply turn in a dorsal direction. Kent, Rezak, and I (11) have observed persisting aphagia and adipsia (>30 days) after a small cut in the coronal plane just anterior to the rostral tip of the substantia nigra. McDermott and I (*unpublished observations*) have found that a similar cut as little as 0.5 mm anterior to the plane of the effective coronal cuts produced little or no effect on food and water intake. Even extensive cuts in the coronal plane that transected all ascending or descending fibers in an area bounded medially by the fornix and mamillary tract, laterally by the medial edge of the internal capsule, ventrally by the base of the brain, and dorsally by the ventral edge of the zona incerta, produced only transient (<6 days) aphagia. Since parasagittal cuts lateral to the region that separates the effective and ineffective coronal cuts did not result in long-lasting aphagia and adipsia, it appears likely that the critical fibers turn in a dorsal direction at this point in their course.

These considerations suggested an investigation of the region just dorsal to the LH, which has led us to the conclusion that the apparently permanent loss of regulatory control over water intake, which is such a prominent part of the LH lesion syndrome, is probably the result of damage to tissues of the immediately adjacent zona incerta (ZI) or, perhaps, to an interruption of fibers of passage that project to or from the ZI. Walsh and I (12–14) have observed that lesions restricted to the anterior aspects of the ZI of the rat resulted in a syndrome of effects on food and water intake that is remarkably similar to that observed in rats "recovered" from LH lesions. *Ad libitum* water intake was only slightly reduced and food intake essentially normal, but water intake fell to near zero levels during periods of food deprivation and the animals failed to eat in response to 2-deoxy-D-glucose, which elicits feeding in the intact animal. Surprisingly rats with ZI lesions ate normally in response to insulin, suggesting that 2-deoxy-D-glucose and insulin may not act on common glucoreceptor mechanisms in the brain. Alheid and I (*unpublished observation*) have recently observed a similar loss of response to 2-deoxy-D-glucose in animals with coronal cuts in the ventral midbrain that produced no reliable change in *ad libitum* food or water intake and also did not impair the feeding response to insulin.

Our rats with anterior ZI lesions also showed markedly impaired responses to hypertonic saline challenges that induce cellular dehydration [even the delayed reaction which Stricker and Wolf (15) have observed in rats with LH lesions were affected by these lesions]. Drinking after polyethylene glycol injections that result in extracellular hypovolemia, on the other hand, was not reduced. The apparently selective impairment in the animals' response to cellular dehydration is of particular interest in view of Blass and Epstein's (16) report of a similar pattern of effects after lesions in the lateral preoptic region.

The ZI is surrounded by structures that have been related to the regulation of food and water intake, and Walsh and I (13) have made some attempts to investigate the possible relationships with neighboring areas by transecting their connections with the ZI by means of a fine retractable tungsten wire knife that produces little direct damage to cellular components of the area of the cut. These experiments have demonstrated that a transection of the direct connections between the ZI and preoptic region decreased (but did not abolish) water intake during periods of food deprivation, but had no reliable inhibitory effects on water intake in response to hypertonic saline or polyethylene glycol treatments. Semicircular cuts beneath the ZI that interrupted its connections with the LH and lower brainstem not only reproduced the effects of ZI lesions in abolishing regulatory drinking and the response to cellular dehydration but also impaired or abolished drinking in response to extracellular hypovolemia, which had been spared by electrolytic lesions in the anterior ZI. This interesting pattern of effects suggests that pathways that may be specifically related to the regulation of extracellular fluids enter or leave the posteroventral aspects of the ZI, whereas pathways that contribute to the regulation of cellular hydration project to or from its anterior aspects. A separate projection of these two pathways was further indicated by the effects of semicircular cuts above the ZI, which resulted in a small but consistent impairment in the response to extracellular hypovolemia but had no effect on water intake in response to hypertonic saline treatments.

Walsh and I (13) also obtained evidence suggesting that at least some of the osmo- or sodium receptors, which are believed to monitor the state of cellular hydration, may be located in the ZI. Blass and Epstein (16) previously reported that microinjections of hypertonic saline or hypertonic sucrose into some sites in the lateral preoptic region elicited drinking in sated rats. Peck and Novin (17) have noted similar effects in the rabbit. Walsh and I (13) obtained marked drinking from injections of hypertonic saline into the ZI, but did not observe reliable drinking in response to hypertonic sucrose in these experiments. This pattern of effects suggests that the ZI may contain receptors that may be selectively stimulated by sodium. Andersson (18) has recently argued that such sodium receptors may be important for the regulation of water intake.

It thus appears that most of the classic LH lesion syndrome, notably the complete and irreversible loss of regulatory water intake and, somewhat surprisingly, the persisting deficit in feeding in response to cellular glucoprivation, may be caused by incidental damage to tissues or fiber connections of the ZI. The only part of the syndrome that appears to be unique to the

LH (or pathways which course through it) is the sudden inhibition of feeding which characterizes animals with LH damage.

We have not, so far, been able to isolate the location of the fiber system that is responsible for this effect. A number of investigators have reported marked sensory and motor impairments in rats that are aphagic as the result of electrolytic or chemical lesions in the LH, GP, or SN (6, 19) and it is often suggested that an interruption of afferent or efferent connections of the striatum might be responsible for some or all of the disturbances in ingestive behavior. The results of our ZI lesions as well as the effects of our parasagittal or coronal knife cuts are compatible with such an interpretation, since many of these projections course through the subthalamus and ZI before turning laterally into the striatum. Alheid and Grossman (20) have attempted to study the role of the striatal projections further by examining the effects of semicircular cuts beneath large portions of this structure. Such cuts produce aphagia and adipsia which lasts for 6 to 8 days but surprisingly small persisting regulatory deficits (i.e., impaired reactions to hypertonic saline, polyethylene glycol, 2-deoxy-D-glucose, or insulin, and only prandial water intake), which are seen after other types of lesions that produce aphagia and adipsia.

Because microinjections of 6-hydroxydopamine into the SN, LH, GP, or ventricular system produce aphagia and adipsia as well as many persisting regulatory deficits (e.g., 6, 19, 21), it is widely believed that the effects of LH lesions on ingestive behavior may be the direct result of an interruption of the dopaminergic nigrostriatal projections (see Stricker, *this volume,* for further discussion). I would like to take this opportunity to briefly discuss some observations from my own as well as other laboratories that suggest that this may not be the complete story.

The aphagia and adipsia which characterizes rats often for as long as 3 to 6 months after LH lesions are seen only transiently (often only a few days) in most experiments which use 6-hydroxydopamine to deplete striatal dopamine (e.g., 6, 21, 22). Stricker and Zigmond (21) have argued that more persistent effects can be obtained with treatments that result in a depletion of 90 to 95% of striatal dopamine and Marshall et al. (19) have reported reliable correlations between the duration of aphagia and the degree of dopamine depletion. However, we (Alheid, McDermott, Halaris, and Grossman, *unpublished observations*) have observed only very transient (<6 days) aphagia and adipsia in some animals with small parasagittal cuts along the LH, which produced depletions of up to 98% of striatal dopamine. Aphagia and adipsia of similar duration were also produced by cuts beneath the striatum, which depleted striatal dopamine by only 40 to 50%.

A look at long-term regulatory deficits after 6-hydroxydopamine treatments also does not support the hypothesis very well. Many investigators have observed a loss of feeding in response to 2-deoxy-D-glucose (e.g., 19, 21), but this may not reflect a dysfunction of nigrostriatal projections since we

(Alheid, McDermott, Halaris, and Grossman, *unpublished observations*) have observed a loss of feeding to 2-deoxy-D-glucose after coronal cuts in the midbrain that did not deplete striatal dopamine. Other persisting regulatory deficits have been seen after severe striatal dopamine depletion but the effects have often been small (e.g., 21, 23), and attempts to correlate their magnitude with the severity of the dopamine depletion have not been successful (19). Although the picture is as yet far from clear, it appears likely that the relatively acute aphagia and adipsia that is seen after LH lesions may represent an anatomically and, perhaps, neurochemically different phenomenon than the persisting regulatory deficits that remain after voluntary ingestive behavior has returned, and the relationship of either of these phenomena to striatal dysfunction remains to be elucidated.

THE MEDIAL HYPOTHALAMUS

It has long been known that hypothalamic lesions that result in hyperphagia and obesity need not involve the ventromedial nucleus itself and that the most effective lesions are located lateral and somewhat ventral to it (24, 25). Since hyperphagia can be produced by lesions caudal to the ventromedial nucleus, Brobeck (25) suggested, many years ago, that the overeating might be due to an interruption of projections to or from the lower brainstem. Several recent observations have reawakened interest in this possibility.

Several years ago I (26) observed that knife cuts in the coronal plane just behind the ventromedial nucleus that did not produce significant damage to cellular components of the area resulted in hyperphagia and obesity. Hennessy and I (*unpublished observation*) have recently investigated the effects of these cuts in greater detail because Sclafani (27), working in my laboratory, did not observe hyperphagia after cuts directly behind the ventromedial nucleus (VMN). We found that only cuts that transect fibers that ascend or descend in the area ventral or lateral to the VMN consistently produced hyperphagia and obesity. This is in good agreement with Gold's (28) report that electrolytic lesions in this portion of the mediolateral hypothalamus, but not damage to the VMN itself, were effective in producing overeating. Hennessy and I also noted that the effects of cuts on food intake and body weight were pronounced only in female rats. Males showed only small and transient effects, which might easily escape detection. This observation may account for a report by Paxinos and Bindra (29) that coronal cuts behind the ventromedial hypothalamus (VMH) of male rats did not produce hyperphagia or obesity.

It is interesting to note that even in the female rat, the effects of cuts behind the VMN were smaller and less persistent than those typically seen after electrolytic lesions. Immediately after surgery, the hyperphagia was pronounced but the effect rarely lasted longer than 4 to 5 weeks and did not result in the excessive deposition of body fat often seen in rats with electrolytic lesions in the VMH. The animals also showed a mild and transient hyperdipsia (i.e., the water-food ratio was increased and water intake during periods of food deprivation exceeded that of controls).

Males with similar cuts overate only slightly shortly after surgery but consumed spectacular quantities of water for months afterward. Even though their infundibulum was typically intact, these animals displayed many of the dysfunctions commonly seen in diabetes insipidus, indicating that the excessive water intake may have been secondary to an interference with pituitary functions (Grossman, Hennessy, and Kanner, *unpublished observation*). However, in some animals, water intake promptly fell to or below normal levels during periods of food deprivation, suggesting that other factors may contribute to the hyperdipsia. Kent and I (*unpublished observation*) have recently observed transient hyperdipsia after coronal knife cuts in the mesencephalon. We have not yet tested kidney functions in these animals and thus cannot rule out a possible contribution of hormonal dysfunctions. However, our lesions are several millimeters behind the infundibular stalk and do not transect any known connections of the pituitary gland. These observations suggest that a pathway, which normally exerts inhibitory influences on water intake, may course through the medial portions of the brainstem.

A review of the literature that describes the effects of coronal knife cuts rostral to the VMN suggests that satiety-related pathways may ascend or descend for some distance in the medial half of the anterolateral hypothalamus. Sclafani (27), working in my laboratory, as well as others (30, 31) have reported that small cuts immediately ahead of the VMN itself do not significantly modify food intake or body weight. I (26) have observed transient hyperphagia and mild obesity after larger cuts which extended into the anterolateral hypothalamus. Several investigators have replicated this observation in male (29) as well as in female (31) rats.

Sclafani and I (32) as well as others (33, 34) have also observed hyperphagia following parasagittal knife cuts lateral to the VMN. Sclafani (27) performed a detailed analysis of these parasagittal cuts and concluded that the most effective ones involved the area lateral to the anteriormost portion of the VMN. Gold (34) reported similar observations and has more recently shown that a unilateral cut in this region (which produced only small and transient increases in food intake) resulted in significant hyperphagia when combined with a contralateral electrolytic lesion in the mamillary region behind the VMN (35). These observations suggest that parasagittal cuts lateral to the VMN, coronal cuts behind it, and electrolytic lesions lateral or caudal to it may all interrupt the same neural system.

Whether this satiety-related neural system has synapses in the medial hypothalamus is not, at this time, clear. Ahlskog and Hoebel (36) have reported hyperphagia after brainstem lesions, which depleted hypothalamic norepinephrine, and Gold (28) has argued that the most effective hypothalamic lesion sites may involve rostral projections of the ventral noradrenergic bundle. Microinjections of noradrenergic compounds into the hypothalamus elicit feeding in sated rats (37, 38, 39), and this has been interpreted in terms of an inhibitory drug action on medial satiety mechanisms (40). To be consistent with the lesion data, such a model implies that all of the knife cuts that result in hyperphagia are downstream from the noradrenergic synapse (an interruption of afferents to this synapse should produce opposite, inhibitory effects on food intake). Such a picture is not readily congruent with commonly held preconceptions concerning the role of the hypothalamic satiety mechanisms, but there is little empiric evidence that could not be accommodated by this model. However, such a mechanism can, at best, be part of a more complex satiety system since the effects of noradrenergic bundle lesions (41) as well as intrahypothalamic norepinephrine injections (Leibowitz, *This Volume*) are prevented by hypophysectomy, which does not prevent or abolish the hyperphagia that occurs after electrolytic lesions in the VMH. Here, as in the case of the lateral hypothalamic pathways, more information is needed before we can construct a useful working model of hypothalamic influences on food and water intake.

REFERENCES

1. Hetherington, A. W., and Ranson, S. W. (1940): *Anat. Rec.,* 78:149–172.
2. Anand, B. K., and Brobeck, J. R. (1951): *Yale J. Biol. Med.,* 24:123–140.
3. Stellar, E. (1954): *Psychol. Rev.,* 61:522.
4. Morgane, P. J. (1961): *Am. J. Physiol.,* 201:420–428.
5. Gold, R. M. (1967): *Physiol. Behav.,* 2:211–220.
6. Ungerstedt, U. (1971): *Acta Physiol. Scand.,* 367:95–122.
7. Grossman, S. P., and Grossman, L. (1971): *J. Comp. Physiol. Psychol.,* 74:148–156.
8. Grossman, S. P., and Grossman, L. (1973): *J. Comp. Physiol. Psychol.,* 85:515–527.
9. Teitelbaum, P., and Epstein, A. N. (1962): *Psychol. Rev.,* 69:74–90.
10. Epstein, A. N., and Teitelbaum, P. (1967): *Am. J. Physiol.,* 213:1159–1167.
11. Kent, E. W., Rezak, M., and Grossman, S. P. (1973): *Abstr. Soc. Neurosci.*
12. Walsh, L. L., and Grossman, S. P. (1973): *Physiol. Behav.,* 11:885–887.
13. Walsh, L. L., and Grossman, S. P. (1974): *Proc. Soc. Neurosci.,* 4:464 (Abstr.).
14. Walsh, L. L., and Grossman, S. P. (1975): *Physiology and Behavior, in press.*
15. Stricker, E. M., and Wolf, G. (1967): *Proc. Soc. Exp. Biol. Med.,* 124:816–820.
16. Blass, E. M., and Epstein, A. N. (1971): *J. Comp. Physiol. Psychol.,* 76:378–394.
17. Peck, J. W., and Novin, D. (1971): *J. Comp. Physiol. Psychol.,* 74:134–147.
18. Andersson, B. (1973): In: *The Neuropsychology of Thirst,* edited by A. N. Epstein, H. R. Kissileff, and E. Stellar, pp. 113–118. Winston and Sons, Washington, D.C.
19. Marshall, J. F., Richardson, J. S., and Teitelbaum, P. (1974): *J. Comp. Physiol. Psychol.,* 87:808–830.
20. Alheid, G., and Grossman, S. P. (1974): *Proc. Soc. Neurosci.,* 4:115 (Abstr.).
21. Stricker, E. M., and Zigmond, M. J. (1974): *J. Comp. Physiol. Psychol.,* 86:973–994.
22. Zigmond, M. J., and Stricker, E. M. (1972): *Science,* 177:1211–1213.
23. Fibiger, H. C., Zis, A. P., and McGeer, E. G. (1973): *Brain Res.,* 55:135–148.
24. Hetherington, A. W., and Ranson, S. W. (1942): *J. Comp. Neurol.,* 76:475–499.

25. Brobeck, J. R. (1946): *Physiol. Rev.,* 26:541–559.
26. Grossman, S. P. (1971): *J. Comp. Physiol. Psychol.,* 75:23–31.
27. Sclafani, A. (1971): *J. Comp. Physiol. Psychol.,* 77:70–96.
28. Gold, R. M. (1973): *Science,* 182:488–490.
29. Paxinos, G., and Bindra, D. (1972): *J. Comp. Physiol. Psychol.,* 79:219–229.
30. Palka, V., Coyer, D., and Critchlow, V. (1969): *Neuroendocrinology,* 5:333–349.
31. Storlien, L. H. M., and Albert, D. J. (1972): *Physiol. Behav.,* 9:191–197.
32. Sclafani, A., and Grossman, S. P. (1969): *Physiol. Behav.,* 4:533–538.
33. Albert, D. J., and Storlien, L. H. (1969): *Science,* 165:599–600.
34. Gold, R. M. (1970): *J. Comp. Physiol. Psychol.,* 71:347–356.
35. Gold, R. M., Quakenbush, P. M., and Kapatos, G. (1972): *J. Comp. Physiol. Psychol.,* 79:210–218.
36. Ahlskog, J. E., and Hoebel, B. G. (1973): *Science,* 182:166–168.
37. Grossman, S. P. (1960): *Science,* 132:301–302.
38. Grossman, S. P. (1962a): *Am. J. Physiol.,* 202:872–882.
39. Grossman, S. P. (1962b): *Am. J. Physiol.,* 202:1230–1236.
40. Leibowitz, S. F. (1970): *Proc. Nat. Acad. Sci.,* 67:1063–1070.
41. Ahlskog, J. E., Hoebel, B. G., and Breisch, S. T. (1974): *Fed. Proc.,* 33:463 (Abstr.).

Hunger: Basic Mechanisms and Clinical Implications,
edited by D. Novin, W. Wyrwicka, and G. Bray.
Raven Press, New York © 1976.

The Relation Between Alimentary and Emotional Amygdalar Regulation

Elzbieta Fonberg

Department of Neurophysiology, Nencki Institute, Warsaw, Poland

Changes in the amount of food intake and concomitant changes of body weight are not dependent on a single mechanism but consist of multiple factors. Most attention has been concentrated on one level of hunger, but this may not be the most important factor.

Various brain areas are involved in the central control over the alimentary mechanisms. The most important are the hypothalamus, amygdaloid complex, and midbrain. The main problem is how these various structures interact with each other and how the control of various alimentary mechanisms is divided among them.

Impairment of the hypothalamus was known long ago from clinical observations as the structure responsible for both cachexia and obesity syndromes. Starting with Hetherington and Ranson (28) and Anand and Brobeck (1), numerous experimental investigations proved that both excitatory (lateral hypothalamus; LH)[1] and inhibitory (ventromedial hypothalamus; VMH) mechanisms of feeding are integrated by the hypothalamus. Although there is general agreement on the main aspect of this division and the prominent role of the hypothalamus in alimentary regulation, there are several controversies. They concern more detailed problems, such as relations between feeding and reward, sensory and motor components of feeding, and neurochemical regulation. Many intriguing hypotheses explaining the basic mechanisms underlying the behavioral effects have been presented in the last few decades. Since there are several excellent recent reviews on this (6, 9, 30, 40, 41, 58), I shall not review the literature here.

Another structure that also has great importance in alimentary mechanisms, comparable to the hypothalamus, is the amygdaloid complex (for review see Fonberg, ref. 20). The problem arises as to how those hypothalamic and amygdalar influences are intermixed and in what respect they are separate. Is the amygdaloid complex a driver and controller of the hypothalamus, or is it a duplicate?

---

[1] Abbreviations used in this chapter: **LH,** lateral hypothalamus; **VMH,** ventromedial hypothalamus; **DMA,** dorsomedial amygdada; **LA,** lateral amygdala; **CSi,** conditioned stimuli; **ST,** striaterminalis; **VAF,** ventroamygdalofugal system; **VM,** ventromedial nucleus.

SIMILARITIES BETWEEN AMYGDALAR AND
HYPOTHALAMIC SYNDROMES

Dorsomedial Amygdala and Lateral Hypothalamus

Our experiments on dogs showed that the amygdaloid complex exerts both facilitatory (dorsomedial amygdala; DMA) and inhibitory (lateral amygdala; LA) control over feeding; these effects are comparable to those of the hypothalamus (15, 20). Thus lesions localized in the dorsomedial part

FIG. 1. Dogs after DMA (A) LA (B) lesions, and LA lesion performed subsequently after DMA damage (C). Notice the differences in their behavior and posture.

of the amygdaloid complex produced aphagia with adipsia, lasting no more than 21 days (usually 5 to 10 days), but followed by long-lasting hypophagia, finickiness, vomiting, and decrease of body weight (10, 14).

The most interesting changes, however, occurred in other aspects of the dogs' behavior. Their outlook and behavioral patterns were completely changed. They were generally apathetic and motionless, did not explore the surroundings as they used to do before the operation; they stood motionless, mostly in one spot, and were not responsive to most of the external signals (Fig. 1A). They lost their friendly relations with technicians who fed them, seemed not to recognize well-known persons, did not come when called by name, and abandoned all their previous skills and habits. The technicians also judged the dog as "not the same one." On the other hand, these dogs were not completely unreactive. They withdrew from the food bowl, resisted feeding, ran away quickly, even through obstacles, and with great force opposed being led by leash and other manipulations, and showed this negativistic attitude in most instances.

Their instrumental responses to conditioned stimuli (CSi), trained before operation, were either completely abolished or impaired and fluctuating (10, 20). The same concerns postoperative training (14). Also, the classic salivary responses trained preoperatively were greatly decreased (35). The changes in the general emotionality and behavioral signs of apathy, indifference, and on the other hand negativism were for us the most striking symptoms. The changes in feeding were similar to those described by other authors for LH-lesioned animals. Therefore the question arose as to whether the emotional changes are specific for the amygdalar syndrome.

Those kinds of reactions are more difficult to detect in rats, in which most of the work on the hypothalamus has been performed; therefore we decided to repeat the lateral hypothalamic syndrome on experiments on dogs. Strikingly, we observed exactly the same behavioral effects after the lesion of the LH as had been observed after lesions of the DMA, with regard not only to feeding but also there were changes in general behavior, emotionality, and in instrumental and classic responses (15, 49, 50).

Aphagia in LH-lesioned dogs lasted no longer than 26 days, and was also followed by hypophagia, finickiness, vomiting, decrease of body weight, and prominent changes in the general behavior of the dogs. Although the individual subjects varied in the intensity of postoperative symptoms, there were no differences between amygdalar and hypothalamic groups in total. Behaviorally, one could not recognize whether a certain dog had lesions in the

TABLE 1. Comparison of the DMA and LH Syndromes in Dogs

DMA	LH
Aphagia 1 to 21 days followed by hypophagia	Aphagia 1 to 23 days followed by hypophagia
Finickiness	Finickiness
Vomiting	Vomiting
Decrease of body weight	Decrease of body weight
Atrophic changes in skin and hair	Atrophic changes in skin and hair
Decrease of classical salivary responses	Decrease or abolishment of classical salivary responses
Impairment of instrumental alimentary responses	Impairment of instrumental alimentary responses
Decreased motility	Decreased motility
Changes in posture:	Changes in posture:
Ears hanging down	Ears hanging down
Legs bent, tail under	Legs bent, tail under
Cataleptic-like postures	Cataleptic-like postures
Apathy and indifference	Apathy and indifference
Lack of friendliness	Lack of friendliness
Negativistic responses	Negativistic responses

lateral hypothalamus or the dorsomedial amygdala. Even the general appearance of the dogs—eyes sad and expressionless, ears hanging, tail under, legs slightly bent, hair thin and dull—was similar in both LH- and DMA-lesioned dogs. Table 1 shows these similarities.

Lateral Amygdala and Ventromedial Hypothalamus

Lesions of the lateral amygdala produced a quite opposite syndrome. The dogs became hyperphagic, voracious, interested in food and in all objects in the environment. They were running around and sniffing the area. They

TABLE 2. Comparison of LA and VMH Syndromes in dogs

LA	VMH
Hyperphagia (weeks)	Hyperphagia (weeks)
Increase of body weight	Increase of body weight
Growth of hair	No changes in hair
Disinhibition of alimentary instrumental responses to nonreinforced stimuli and during intertrial intervals	Disinhibition of instrumental and classical responses to nonreinforced stimuli and during intertrial intervals
Increased motility	Increased motility before meals decreased thereafter
Playfulness	No changes in social behavior
Friendliness	

were, in general, very lively and mobile. They became more affectionate toward the technicians: jumping on them, licking their faces, asking for petting and for play (16, 20). Their body weight increased and continued to increase, even during a stage when the amount of food intake decreased and became stabilized (16). The instrumental responses to positive CSi were not changed, but they were slightly disinhibited to negative CSi, even during intertrial intervals (20).

The twin syndrome was obtained by the lesions of VMH, concerning all alimentary responses. However, it should be noted that the emotional changes observed after VMH lesions were less obvious. The social behavior of these dogs was not changed, they were more lively only before meals and quiet and sleepy thereafter (50, 51, 52). The main features of amygdalar and hypothalamic syndromes are compared in Table 2.

RELATIONS BETWEEN THE AMYGDALOID COMPLEX AND THE HYPOTHALAMUS

The similarities between the effects of lesions of amygdaloid and hypothalamic areas may be explained by the fact that there exist strong anatomical connections between these two structures and they therefore act as one physiologic system. The main efferent connections from amygdala and hypothalamus are the stria terminalis (ST) and the ventral amygdalofugal (VAF) system (23, 24, 27, 32, 36, 37, 60). ST derives mostly from the corticomedial area and VAF from basolateral nuclei. In dogs the stria terminalis may be divided into five components (33). The most interesting from our point of view would be the fibers going to the ventromedial nucleus (VM) and to anterior and lateral parts of the hypothalamus. By these routes the DMA may influence the LH facilitating its activity and VMH by inhibiting its neurons. Lesions of DMA cutting off these influences may produce a decrease in the activity of LH neurons and release ventromedial "satiation" mechanisms from inhibition.

The LA in contrast may exert an inhibitory influence on the LH and increase the activity of the VMH. Thus lesions of the lateral amygdala may enhance the activity of the LH and decrease that of the VMH. Recently, electrophysiological experiments have furnished strong support for such explanations (4, 5, 42–45).

There is evidence that ST and VAF also carry fibers from the hypothalamus to the amygdala (7, 26, 29, 34, 48). In this way the hypothalamus may directly influence amygdaloid activity. It is also possible that these last pathways may serve as routes for feedback of the amygdaloid action upon the hypothalamus.

Pure electrophysiological and anatomical evidence does not tell us, however, which kind of behavior is mediated in which way, what is inhibited, and what is facilitated. It is known that the amygdaloid complex, as well as alimentary mechanisms, also controls defensive, reproductive, and other functions. One possibility is that each particular function is mediated by separate neurons through separate fibers. On the other hand, it is also possible that amygdalar neurons play a general facilitatory (DMA) and inhibitory (LA) role upon various different functions.

From the observations of the behavior of our dogs after DMA lesions, the evidence was that not only food intake and other alimentary functions are decreased, but also the general activity of the dogs, their social relations, and response to different external stimuli. These dogs are in general depressed. However dogs with LA lesions became more mobile, social, and playful, besides being voracious.

One of the most tempting hypotheses is that the amygdaloid complex analyzes and evaluates the stimuli as to their rewarding values with respect to biologic needs and pleasure, and then creates positive or negative emotional states. Then the DMA would be activated by stimuli evaluated as pleasant and rewarding and thereafter send the activating impulses further to the other brain areas, the hypothalamus or the midbrain, which would in turn be responsible for activation of the mechanisms important for reacting toward the external environment and patterning the responses indispensable for getting the rewarding and pleasant stimuli. In the absence of DMA

mechanisms, on the one hand, the external stimuli would then lose their rewarding, pleasurable properties, and, on the other hand, the structures that
pattern behavior would not be driven any more (or at least less activated).
This would be reflected in the decrease of general activity, decrease of interest in the external stimuli, and emotional depression in respect to positive
emotions. This is exactly what we see in our dogs (Fig. 1A).

In contrast lesions of the LA, which normally have an inhibitory role (13,
16, 41, 44, 45, 53, 62, 63), would release LH and other brain structures
from the inhibitory influences, which are reflected by increased interest (Fig.
1B), voraciousness, and playfulness. According to this hypothesis, level and
direction of general emotional arousal are the most important factors in
producing all symptoms of DMA and LA syndromes; changes in alimentary
responses are secondary.

We have obtained evidence that, in fact, the role of DMA and LA consist
rather in exciting or inhibiting other brain structures than in patterning the
alimentary reactions.

LA DAMAGE REVERSE THE SYNDROMES OF APHAGIA

In dogs with previous lesions of the DMA, in which the whole syndrome
of aphagia with subsequent hypophagia, impairment of instrumental performance and general depression, indifference and loss of friendliness toward
humans was observed, the subsequent damage of LA was performed in
various stages of postoperative period after DMA operation. It was found
that independently of the period of time in which this operation was done,
the subsequent lesion of LA abolished all the symptoms produced by the
first operation, and resulted in the quick recovery of functions damaged by
the first operation, i.e., the dogs again became lively, interested in their
surroundings, friendly to the technicians, and playful (Fig. 1C). They returned to their old habits, and their negativism disappeared. Their food intake increased to the level seen before the two operations (18, 19). Their
instrumental performance, which was not improved between the two operations, but fluctuated from session to session, now became gradually, but
increasingly improved (Fig. 2).

The fact that it is possible to restore by lesioning LA the functions impaired by DMA damage seems to demonstrate that the effect of DMA lesions is not produced by the damage of neurons patterning these alimentary
and other functions, since in this last case they would not be restored shortly
after the LA operation. It seems, rather, that both DMA and LA areas play
upon other structures of the brain in which the most important is the hypothalamus. The preliminary experiments show that the LA syndrome is also
reversed by DMA damage, which suggest reciprocal antagonistic relations
between these two amygdalar areas. It supports my previous hypothesis concerning the functional division of the amygdalar complex (13, 15).

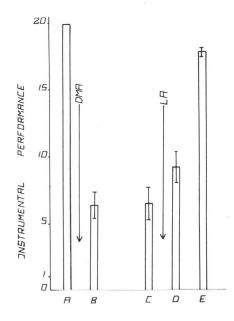

FIG. 2. Impairment of the instrumental performance after DMA damage and improvement by
subsequent LA damage on six dogs. Bars represent mean for 10 days of performance (200
trials). A, normal state before operation; B, after
DMA damage; C, 6 weeks later, before LA operation; D, after LA damage. Note: Six weeks
elapse between periods B and C; only 10 days
elapse between A and B or C and D.

Our other experiment showed that it is possible to restore the functions impaired by the lesions of the LH by subsequent damage of the LA (15). This might be explained in this way: now that DMA is released from inhibition, it may compensate for functions of LH, acting directly or indirectly, but not only through the already damaged LH, on the third important locus which is probably the midbrain (31, 47, 48, 55, 56, 65).

Further proof of the importance of a third locus in addition to the hypothalamus and the amygdala is that LA lesions were able to restore partially even the food intake and alimentary instrumental performance abolished completely for 2.5 months by damage of both LH and DMA (18, 20). On the other hand, the fact that the general arousal and emotional behavior of the dog was in these last cases not restored may prove that the midbrain centers are important only for alimentary reactions, but not for emotional behavior. This would fit well with our previous assumption about the main emotional factor in amygdala functions.

METABOLIC CHANGES PRODUCED BY AMYGDALA LESIONS

On the other hand, it is well known that stimulation and lesions of the amygdala influence various autonomic functions. It should be noted that in our experiment DMA lesions also produced obvious metabolic changes reflected by the decrease of body weight in spite of forced feeding of sufficient amounts of food, thin and dull hair, and thin skin, susceptibility to wounds and infection. These symptoms speak for deep multifactor metabolic disturbances. All these changes were also reversed by the subsequent lesions. Body weight increased; hair became thick and shiny.

Recently it was found that lesions of the DMA in rabbits also produce a few days of aphagia and a further decrease of food intake (22). Furthermore we found that intraduodenal injections of glucose in these subjects did not decrease food intake (tested in the period when the food intake was restored to at least 50% of preoperative level). This effect is similar to that obtained on LH-lesioned rats in contrast with normal rabbits that show marked decreases in food intake after intraduodenal glucose infusions (38, 61). This fact suggests that DMA similar to LH, is involved in short-term alimentary regulation. The role of both these structures in the regulation of satiation mechanisms in response to glucose proves one more similarity of the functions of DMA and LH, supporting the previous assumption (15, 20).

On the other hand, subcutaneous injection of insulin produced no effect in LH-lesioned rats, whereas DMA-lesioned rabbits reacted as the normal ones did; i.e., insulin injections produce an increase of food intake. Therefore, at least in this respect, there exist differences between LH and DMA, which show that the amygdala plays a less important role in the metabolic regulation of feeding than does LH.

The same conclusion might be drawn from our observations on the classical salivary reflexes in LH- and DMA-lesioned dogs. Although in both groups of dogs the salivary reflexes, conditioned as well as unconditioned, were greatly impaired, this impairment, however, was much more pronounced in LH-lesioned dogs, in which the salivary responses were completely abolished in the postoperative period (50), whereas in the DMA-lesioned dogs they were only decreased or fluctuating (35).

Although the metabolic changes produced by the lesions of DMA are undeniable, it remains unexplained whether all the various effects produced by DMA lesions are independent or whether they are all derivatives of one causative factor. Any of the observed symptoms may be produced by different causes. For example the decrease of food intake may be caused by a low level of hunger drive. But it may also be evoked by changed perception of taste or smell of food, which consequently may lower the rewarding properties of food. On the other hand, the dogs may not eat because of nausea or changes in stomach contractions (the fact that the dogs often vomited supports this last explanation) (12) or because of metabolic disturbances that made the animal sick or poisoned. Therefore, the problem arises whether the metabolic and neurohormonal changes are primary, thus affecting the emotional behavior, or whether the emotional changes affect secondarily metabolism and functions of internal organs.

DMA DEPRESSION

The decrease of food intake, as well as other symptoms, observed in the DMA syndrome may be caused by a decrease in general arousal of the dogs. The general activation factor in food intake was demonstrated by Wolgin et al. (*This Volume*). Our dogs, in addition to being hypophagic, also were less mobile, apathetic, and indifferent. Moreover what struck everyone who had the opportunity to observe these dogs was that they were also so "sad" and "depressed" that it reminded the observer of human depression. If we assume that the primary factor may be the same in both cases, we would be able to explain most of the symptoms produced both by LH and DMA lesions. Even changes in digestion and other metabolic disturbances may be easily explained this way, as it is well known that depressive states and other emotional disturbances produce changes in functioning of various internal organs and result in severe neurohumoral dysfunction (3). Changes in hair and skin, similar to that observed on our dogs, were also observed in neurotic states both in humans and animals (see also the review by Fonberg, ref. 17).

Going further we may hypothesize that the main cause of all DMA symptoms is similar, as it has been assumed in endogenous human depression, i.e., the depletion of monoamines (2, 39). Hall and Geneser-Jensen (25) found that this part of amygdala stains for monoamine oxidase (whereas the lateral part stains for acetylcholinesterase). Other recent findings support the assumption that some neurons of the DMA region may be involved in monoamine production or storage. After amygdala lesions, reductions in the level of monoamines (norepinephrine and dopamine) may produce all the symptoms of depression observed in DMA-lesioned dogs. Stricker and Zigmond (59) furnish further evidence for such an assumption.

EFFECT OF ANTIDEPRESSIVE DRUGS IN DMA- AND LH-LESIONED DOGS

Starting from the above assumption, that causes of the hypothalamic and amygdalar depression are comparable and might be produced by similar factors as human depression, we were interested in investigating the effect of tricyclic antidepressive drugs (which seem to be the most efficient in treatment of human depressive states) on those dogs who showed a long-lasting syndrome of postoperative depression.

In recent experiments performed together with my coworkers (21), an injection of either imipramine or amitriptyline were administered subcutaneously on eight dogs with lesions of both the DMA and the LH. All these dogs showed symptoms of apathy and depression, as described above. The antidepressant was administered in increasing doses from 10 to 50 mg. After a few days of the drug administration, the dogs became more lively, mobile, and social, but still much more depressed than preoperatively. For example dog Okon, which before antidepressive treatment did not react at all, now reacted to calling by name by turning the head, and he walked himself to the experimental chamber, whereas before the treatment he had to be carried in. The instrumental responses reappeared, although not in perfect form, but before treatment he did not react at all during many weeks of observations. Similar effects were observed on other dogs. In some of them, however, only the number of intertrial responses increased, and the instrumental responses to CSi were not improved. In one dog within this group his unconditioned response (food intake from the feeder) was postoperatively greatly diminished in the experimental situation. The administration of amitriptyline in this dog increased food intake from 30% to 100%, i.e., he consumed now all out of 20 usual portions presented during experiments. This last case gives some evidence that in the decrease of food intake emotional depression may play an essential role.

The effect of antidepressants in some dogs ceased immediately after removal of the drug; in the others it lasted for some days or weeks and gradually decreased (Fig. 3). These results seem to show that it is possible to improve the functions impaired by DMA or LH lesions by the administrations of antidepressants, which may indicate that the underlying mechanisms are similar in depressive states produced by neurosis or endogenous factors as produced by brain lesions.

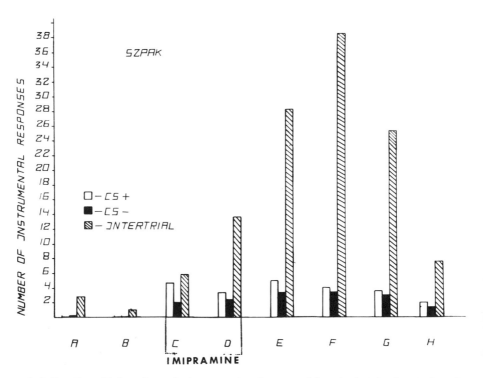

FIG. 3. The effect of imipramine on the instrumental performance of the individual dog Szpake. Bars denote mean number of responses, letters subsequent weekly periods of observations. Notice the appearance of response to positive CS (*open bars*) as well as to nonreinforced CS (—) (*solid bars*) and increase of intertrial movements.

On the other hand, the effect of these drugs was much lower than the effect of LA lesions, although acting in a similar way. There is, however, some evidence that antidepressive drugs in intact brain act directly on the amygdaloid complex. If this is the case, the drugs administered to DMA-lesioned dogs would act only on the remnants of the amygdala, as the main locus of their action would have been removed, which may explain why we did not get the full effect.

The next step to elucidate this mechanism would be to compare whether the effect of antidepressant will be different in the syndromes produced by separate damage of the LH or the DMA from those in neurotic dogs.

AGGRESSION AND REWARDING MECHANISMS

Five out of eight dogs treated by antidepressive drugs showed increased aggressiveness (Fig. 4). Four of these dogs were never aggressive before. In the one which was aggressive before, aggressiveness increased and became more goal directed.

As one may recall from the previous description, our dogs after DMA and LH lesions were not completely unreactive. They showed strong negativistic responses, whereas they did not react either spontaneously or by cooperation with humans. It is probable that both in LH and DMA syndromes the emotional balance between positive and negative evaluation of external stimuli is shifted toward the negative side. Thus, discomfort, disgust, sadness, hostility is increased, and the value of all rewards decreased. This is reflected in low activity because all responses are rather punished than rewarded (57), diminished friendliness, and also decrease of food intake. The external signals like smell, taste, and sight of food might be underestimated in such a case. According to Schachter (54), obese people may overeat because they overestimate these signals. The same may be true for our LA-lesioned dogs. In contrast DMA-lesioned dogs indicate that food is for them aversive and feeding unpleasant. They would withdraw from the food bowl, spit the food out, run away from the feeding place, and resist with great strength being led to food. They oppose all other demands for action also, which shows that aversiveness is not limited to food but is more generalized. Because of apathy and atony, they do not react by overt aggression; when aroused by administration of antidepressive drugs, in cases where the structure that normally mediates the positive emotional response, is damaged by lesion, negative reactions are the only ones to appear when activity increases.

We should, however, take into account that the DMA is also mediating fear-defense mechanisms (8, 11, 13, 29); therefore these responses should also be lowered. The increase of free norepinephrine as a result of administration of tricyclic antidepressants may partly explain the increased aggressiveness. The action of antidepressants may be on hypothalamic centers of aggression, which were not damaged in these dogs.

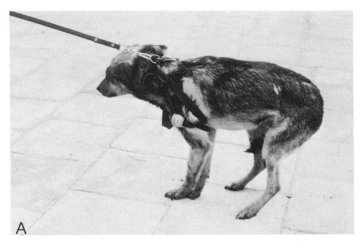

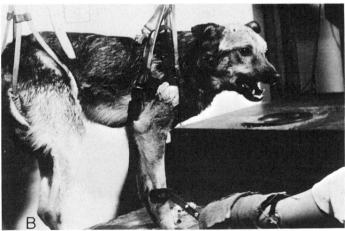

FIG. 4. Dog with both amygdalar and hypothalamic damage. A: Before drug administration. B: During treatment by amitriptyline. Notice the aggressive display and postural changes as the effect of antidepressant.

SUMMARY AND CONCLUDING REMARKS

It was found in dogs that lesions localized in the dorsomedial part of the amygdaloid complex produced aphagia and adipsia that lasted several days and was followed by long-lasting hypophagia, finickiness, decrease of body weight, and decrement of alimentary performance. On the other hand, lesions localized in the lateral part of the amygdala produced opposite effects, i.e., hyperphagia, increase of body weight and disinhibition of alimentary responses.

The antagonistic effects of DMA and LA damage were, however, not limited to alimentary reactions. The dorsomedial dogs were generally de-

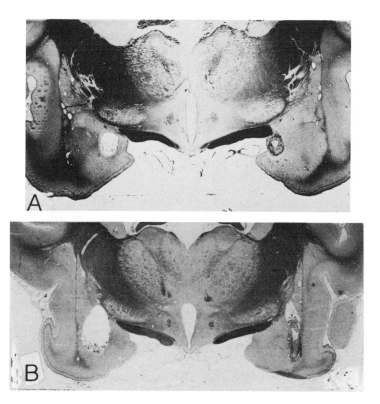

FIG. 5. Histological slides of typical localization for DMA syndrome (A) and LA syndrome (B).

pressed and less motile than normal dogs, and they lost their friendly attitude toward humans and interest in the environment, whereas lateral amygdalar dogs became more lively, playful, and friendly.

Those facts speak for the close relations between alimentary mechanisms and emotional states. The problem arises whether the changes in alimentary behavior are primary, i.e., caused by the impairment of hunger and satiation mechanisms and metabolic disregulation. In view of our results, it seems probable that changes in food intake and other alimentary reactions may be secondary, reflecting the general emotional state. Depression and a lowered level of reward mechanisms in general may produce decreases in alimentary motivation, whereas a highly aroused state may augment the reward values of food and thus evoke an increase of food intake. The obvious changes in metabolism in amygdalar dogs may be explained by the well-known fact that changes in emotional state exert an influence on the functions of the digestive system and metabolic turnover.

The elucidation of this problem may explain the role of amygdala in the mechanism of psychogenic anorexia (anorexia nervosa) and neurotic obesity. It is worthwhile to note that depression and changes in the emotional expression of DMA-lesioned dogs were removed by subsequent damage of the LA. This effect, similar to lesioning of the LA on the dorsomedial syndrome, was also produced by the administration of antidepressive drugs (imiprimine and amitryptiline). These drugs are effective in the treatment of human endogenic depression and suggest the existence of similar mechanisms for both syndromes.

ACKNOWLEDGMENTS

This investigation was supported by funds of Project 0.9.4.1 of the Polish Academy of Sciences, Foreign Research Agreement 05.275.2 of the U.S. Department of Health, Education and Welfare under PL480, and fellowship of Foundation's Fund for Research in Psychiatry and Prof. Novin's Grant.

Figures 3 and 4 are from experiments of Fonberg, Golebiewska, Kasicki, Korczynski, and Zagrodzka.

REFERENCES

1. Anand, B. K., and Brobeck, J. R. (1951): *Yale Biol. Med.*, 24:123–140.
2. Bunney, W. E., and Davis, J. M. (1965): *Arch. Gen. Psychiat.*, 13:483–494.
3. Cannon, W. B. (1953): *Bodily Changes in Pain, Hunger, Fear and Rage.* Branford, Boston.
4. Dreifuss, J. J. (1972): *Adv. Behav. Biol.*, 2:295–317.
5. Dreifuss, J. J., Murphy, J. T., and Gloor, P. (1968): *J. Neurophysiol.*, 31:237–248.
6. Epstein, A. N. (1971): In: *Progress in Physiology and Psychology*, Vol. 4, edited by E. Stellar and J. Sprague, pp. 263–317. Academic Press, New York.
7. Fernandez de Molina, A., and Garcia Sanches, J. L. (1967): *Physiol. Behav.*, 2:225–227.
8. Fernandez de Molina, A., and Hunsperger, R. W. (1962): *J. Physiol.*, 160:200–213.
9. Fitzsimons, J. T. (1972): *Physiol. Rev.*, 2:468–511.
10. Fonberg, E. (1966): *Bull. Acad. Pol. Sci.* [*Biol.*], 4:719–722.
11. Fonberg, E. (1967): *Acta. Biol. Exp.*, 27:303–318.
12. Fonberg, E. (1968): *Proceedings of the XXIV Congress on Physiological Science* (Washington), 416.
13. Fonberg, E. (1968): *Progr. Brain Res.*, 22:273–281.
14. Fonberg, E. (1969): *Physiol. Behav.*, 4:739–743.
15. Fonberg, E. (1969): *Acta Biol. Exp.*, 29:335–358.
16. Fonberg, E. (1971): *Acta Neurobiol. Exp.*, 31:19–32.
17. Fonberg, E. (1971): *Neuroses Omega*, pp. 1–189. Wiedza Powszechna, Warsaw.
18. Fonberg, E. (1972): In: *Physiology, Emotions and Psychosomatic Illness*, edited by R. Porter and J. Knight, pp. 131–161. Elsevier Amsterdam.
19. Fonberg, E. (1973): *Acta Neurobiol. Exp.*, 33:449–466.
20. Fonberg, E. (1974): *Acta Neurobiol. Exp.*, 34:435–466.
21. Fonberg, E., Golebiewska, M., Kasicki, S., Korczynski, R. and Zagrodzka, J. (1974): *Proceedings of the XXVI Congress on Physiological Science*, New Delhi, India 0857.
22. Fonberg, E., Schneider, K., and Novin, D. (1975): *Fed. Proc.*, (*Abstr.*)
23. Fox, A. C. (1940): *J. Comp. Neurol.*, 79:277–295.
24. Hall, E. A., et al. (1963): *Am. J. Anat.*, 113:139–151.
25. Hall, E. A., and Geneser-Jensen, F. A. (1975): *J. Zellforsch. Mikrosk. Anat.*, 120:204–221.
26. Happel, L. T., and Bach, L. M. N. (1970): *Fed. Proc.*, 29:392.

27. Heimer, L., and Nauta, W. J. H. (1969): *Brain Res.*, 13:284–297.
28. Hetherington, A. W., and Ranson, S. W. (1942): *Am. J. Physiol.*, 136:609–617.
29. Hilton, S. M., and Zbrozyna, A. W. (1963): *J. Physiol.*, 165:160–173.
30. Hoebel, B. (1971): *Ann. Rev. Physiol.*, 33:533–568.
31. Huang, Y. H., and Mogenson, G. J. (1972): *Exp. Neurol.*, 37:269–286.
32. Johnston, J. B. (1923): *J. Comp. Neurol.*, 35:337–481.
33. Kosmal, A. (1972): *Proceedings of the XII Congress of the Polish Physiological Society*, Olsztyn, p. 119.
34. Kraczun, G. P. (1970): *Z. Vyssh. Nerv. Deyat. A. N. USSR*, 22:130–138.
35. Lagowska J., and Fonberg, E. (1972): *Proceedings of the XII Congress of the Polish Physiological Society*, Olsztyn, p. 150.
36. Nauta, W. J. H. (1961): *J. Anat.*, 95:515–531.
37. Nauta, W. J. H. and Haymaker, W. (1969) In: *The Hypothalamus*, edited by W. Haymaker, E. Anderson, and W. J. H. Nauta, pp. 136–209. Charles C. Thomas. Springfield, Ill.
38. Novin, D. (1975): *This Volume*.
39. McKinney, W. T., Suomi, S. J., and Harlow, H. F. (1971): *Dis. Nerv. Syst.*, 32:735–741.
40. Mogenson, G. J., and Huang, Y. H. (1973): *Prog. Neurobiol.*, 1:55–83.
41. Morgane, P. J., and Jacobs, H. L. (1969): In: *World Rev. Nutr. Diet.*, 10:100–213.
42. Murphy, J. T., and Renaud, L. P. (1969): *J. Neurophysiol.*, 32:85–102.
43. Oniani, T. J., and Naneishvili, T. L. (1968): In: *Problems of Physiology of the Hypothalamus* (in Russian), pp. 89–99. University of Kiev, Kiev.
44. Oomura, Y., Ooyama, H., Yamamoto, T., Naka, T., Kobayashi, N., and Ono, T. (1967): *Prog. Brain Res.*, 27:1–33.
45. Oomura, Y., Ono, T., and Ooyama, H. (1970): *Nature*, 228:1108–1110.
46. Papez, J. W. (1937): *Arch. Neurol. Psychiatry*, 38:725–749.
47. Parker, S. W., and Feldman, S. M. (1967): *Exp. Neurol.*, 17:313–326.
48. Rolls, E. T. (1972): *Brain Res.*, 45:365–381.
49. Rozkowska, E., and Fonberg, E. (1970): *Acta Neurobiol. Exp.*, 30:59–68.
50. Rozkowska, E., and Fonberg, E. (1971): *Acta Neurobiol. Exp.*, 31:351–364.
51. Rozkowska, E., and Fonberg, E. (1972): *Acta Neurobiol. Exp.*, 32:711–722.
52. Rozkowska, E., and Fonberg, E. (1973): *Acta Neurobiol. Exp.*, 33:553–562.
53. Scalfani, J., Beluzzi, J. D., and Grossman, S. P. (1970): *J. Comp. Physiol. Psychol.*, 72:394–403.
54. Schachter, S. (1967): In: *Neurophysiology and Emotions*, edited by D. C. Glass, pp. 117–144. Rockefeller University Press, New York.
55. Skultety, M. F. (1966): *Arch. Neurol.*, 14:670–690.
56. Skultety, M. F., and Gary, T. M. (1962): *Neurology*, 12:394–401.
57. Stein, L., and Wise, C. D. (1969): *J. Comp. Physiol. Psychol*, 67:189–198.
58. Stevenson, J. A. F. (1969): In: *The Hypothalamus*, edited by W. Haymaker, E. Anderson, and W. J. H. Nauta, pp. 524–621. Charles C. Thomas, Springfield. Ill.
59. Stricker, M., and Zigmond, M. J. (1975): *This Volume*.
60. Valverde, S. (1965): pp. 1–131. Harvard Press, Cambridge, Mass.
61. Vanderweele, D. A., Novin, D., Rezek, M., and Sanderson, J. D. (1974): *Physiol. Behav.*, 12:467–473.
62. White, N. M. (1973): *Physiol. Behav.*, 10:215–219.
63. White, N. M., and Fisher, A. P. (1969): *Physiol. Behav.*, 4:199–205.
64. Wyrwicka, W., and Doty, R. (1966): *Exp. Brain Res.*, 1:152–160.

Hunger: Basic Mechanisms and Clinical Implications,
edited by D. Novin, W. Wyrwicka, and G. Bray.
Raven Press, New York © 1976.

Increased Feeding in Rats in a Low Ambient Temperature

F. Scott Kraly* and Elliott M. Blass

Department of Psychology, Johns Hopkins University, Baltimore, Maryland 21218

Enhanced feeding is one of a variety of responses mobilized by mammals in defense against cold stress. Its occurrence has been documented in many mammalian orders including primates (man, 14), carnivores (dog, 6), ungulates (goat, 3), lagomorphs (rabbit, 7), and rodents (rat, 4; mouse, 18). Moreover enhanced feeding occurs following a relatively brief exposure to cold stress. For example rats markedly increase food intake during the first 24 hr of cold (8°C) exposure (12).

Yet the mechanisms that control this behavioral adaptation remain poorly understood. Andersson and Larsson (2) were the first to suggest that thermosensitive elements in the anterior hypothalamic and anterior preoptic areas were involved in the control of feeding at low ambient temperature. Decreasing anterior hypothalamic temperature by 3 to 4°C increased feeding in goats, the converse holding for increased hypothalamic temperature. This suggestion has been questioned on a number of grounds. For one, Hamilton and his colleagues (13, 22) have reported that more modest increases in hypothalamic temperature enhanced feeding in rats, a response possibly related to the lowering of skin temperature following hypothalamic heating.

Abrams and Hammel (1) have also questioned the contribution of temperature-sensitive elements in either the initiation or termination of feeding. Abrams and Hammel (1, see also 10, 17), did not find any correlation between changes in hypothalamic temperature (T_h) and meal onset in rats. They did find, however, a slight rise in T_h during feeding, but this rise occurred well in advance of metabolic changes; indeed it was also seen when rats ate a nonnutritive cellulose meal. Abrams and Hammel (1) concluded that the rise in T_h was owing to heat from the muscular movements involved in feeding.

The contribution of deep core temperature as a feeding control has been minimized by Brobeck (5), the leading proponent of the "thermostatic control of feeding." Brobeck's view is that core temperature is well defended, and any transients that may occur are sufficiently small and slow to preclude

* Present address: Edward W. Bourne Behavioral Research Laboratory, Department of Psychiatry, New York Hospital, Cornell Medical Center, Westchester Division, White Plains, New York 10605.

a major influence by core temperature on feeding. Altered metabolic rate has also been dismissed in the short-term control of food intake for much the same reasons.

In summary a number of mechanisms have been brought forth and dismissed as mediators of enhanced feeding in the cold. Accordingly we sought to identify some of the mechanisms through which these alterations in feeding behavior are mediated in laboratory rats. Three specific, conceptually distinct, hypotheses that could account for enhanced feeding in the cold were evaluated. The first hypothesis, and most logical from a homeostatic point of view, proposes that increased food intake occurs in response to the enhanced energy expenditure that maintains normal core temperature in the cold. That is, enhanced feeding should follow energy depletion and thereby operate to restore normal energy balance. Alternatively feeding may be enhanced by the cold temperature stimulus *per se*. This hypothesis predicts that food intake is enhanced by the peripheral sensation of cold, independent of previous energy commitment. The third hypothesis proposes that feeding is increased secondarily to an alteration in gastric function induced by the cold environment. Stomach motility, and hence clearance of food from the stomach into the intestine, may be increased in the cold (20). Food intake in the cold may, therefore, increase in advance of increased energy output, but subsequent to gastrointestinal adaptation(s) to the cold.

We will show that a low ambient temperature *per se* is sufficient for increased food intake and that rats eat more in the cold by increasing meal frequency and not by eating larger meals. Two mechanisms have been identified that may help account for the elevated food intake. First, the stomach empties more quickly in the cold. Second, rats appear to be more motivated to eat in the cold, as inferred from elevated operant rates on a variable-interval, 30-sec schedule of reinforcement and from a greater resistance to quinine adulteration of a liquid diet.

DETERMINANTS OF FEEDING IN THE COLD

Although it is well known that feeding increases in the cold, it is not known whether feeding is in response to the heightened loss of energy or to the cold stimulus *per se*. In order to help choose between these alternatives, 18 adult female albino rats (Sherman strain) were deprived, in a large temperature and humidity controlled chamber, of liquid diet but not water for 24 hr at either 5 or 22°C and were then allowed to eat and drink for 6 hr at either 5 or 22°C. Liquid diet and water intakes were recorded every 2 min during the initial 30 min, at 5-min intervals during the next 30 min, and at 30-min intervals thereafter. Tests were balanced across rats and each rat served in each of the four possible conditions: deprived (dep) 5°C—eat 5°C; dep 5°C—eat 22°C; dep 22°C—eat 22°C; dep 22°C—eat 5°C. Tests were separated by a minimum of 4 days. Liquid diet and tap water were available continuously during the interval and ambient temperature was 22°C.

Figures 1 and 2 suggest that the "cold as a stimulus to eat" hypothesis more accurately predicts feeding behavior in this specific experimental situation. Figure 1 shows that a mean of 24.6 ml was eaten in 6 hr at 5°C as opposed to 21.2 ml at 22°C [$F(1,17) = 9.4, p < 0.01$]. The differences in intake are apparent at 30 min and attain statistical significance by 2 hr. Figure 2 makes it clear that the temperature in which deprivation occurred did not influence

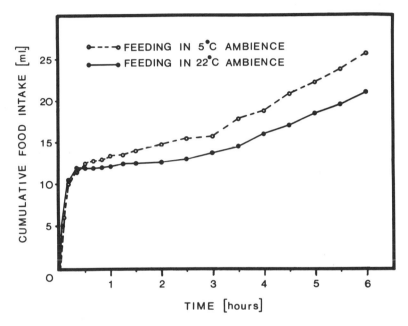

FIG. 1. Effects of ambient temperature during feeding on food intake following 24 hr of food deprivation ($n = 18$).

subsequent feeding. Mean 6-hr intake following 24-hr food deprivation at 5°C did not differ statistically from that following deprivation at 22°C [$F(1,17) = 0.9, p > 0.20$].

It is not likely that the taste of the cold diet enhanced feeding. This possibility, which runs counter to human preferences for soups and warm drinks in winter, may also be rejected empirically. In a separate experiment, six, 24-hr food-deprived rats were allowed to eat, at either 5 or 22°C, a liquid diet that was kept at either 5 or 22°C by replacing the diet every 30 min with diet maintained at the appropriate temperature. Rats always ate more in the cold than when in the thermoneutral ambience, regardless of diet temperature, and intake of the 5°C diet did not differ from that of the 22°C diet, regardless of ambient temperature. There were therefore no interactions between diet and ambient temperatures.

How was feeding enhanced? Did the rats eat larger meals, did they eat more frequently, or was there an interaction between meal size and frequency? These possibilities were evaluated in seven rats that had reliably increased feeding in the cold in the original experiment. This series was repeated. Test conditions differed only in that the amount and duration of each meal and the duration of each intermeal interval were recorded for

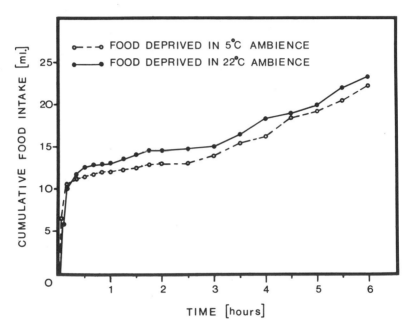

FIG. 2. Effects of ambient temperature during 24 hr of food deprivation on subsequent 6-hr food intake (n = 18).

each rat on all tests. A meal was defined as an episode of feeding separated from all other feeding episodes by at least a 4-min interval of nonfeeding.

The relationship between meal size and frequency for individual rats deprived at 22°C and eating at either 5 or 22°C are presented in Fig. 3. The major finding here (and it also holds for rats food deprived at 5°C) is that rats eat more in the cold by increasing meal frequency and not, with the exception of the initial meal, by increasing meal size. Possible bases for these behaviors will be described below.

In summary, under the specific experimental regimen used here, albino rats eat more in response to low ambient temperatures *per se* and not in response to being deprived in the cold. There were no interactions among deprivation and feeding conditions and diet temperature was not a deter-

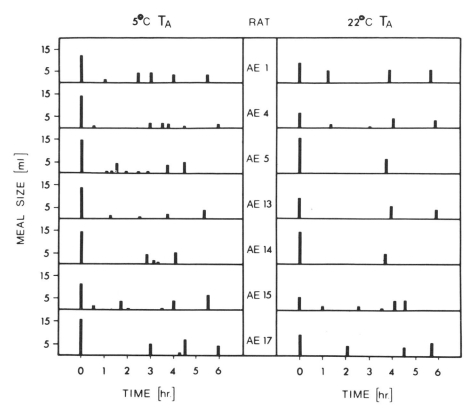

FIG. 3. Meal patterns of individual rats during a 6-hr test in a 5°C (*left*) or 22°C (*right*) environment following 24-hr of food deprivation in a 22°C environment. Individual rats are identified in the *center;* a horizontal row presents the meal patterns for one rat. T_A = ambient temperature.

mining factor. Six-hour food intake was increased by virtue of eating more frequently and not, excepting the initial meal, by eating larger meals.

RATE OF STOMACH CLEARANCE IN THE COLD

Two possible candidates for increased feeding in the cold are enhanced rate of stomach clearance and increased hunger. Each alteration could, by itself account for the increased intake and the changes in meal patterns described above. Rate of clearance was determined in eight naive female rats equipped with stainless-steel stomach fistulae (16, 19). Rats were maintained for 2 weeks postoperatively on tap water and Purina Laboratory pellets. Testing proceeded as follows: rats were deprived of pellets but not water at 22°C for 24 hr, at which time a collecting tube was connected to the fistula and the stomach contents were evacuated by gentle flushing with isotonic saline. The rats were then placed in an ambient temperature of either 5 or 22°C for 1 hr and were then allowed to eat 5 ml of the standard liquid diet.

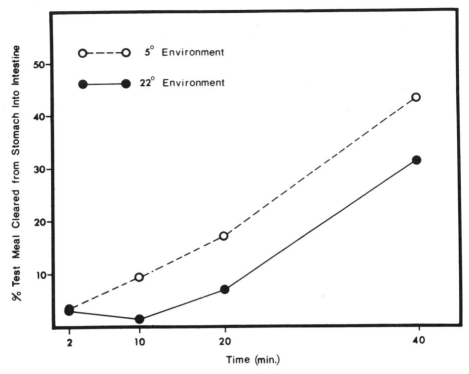

FIG. 4. Cumulative mean percent of a 5-ml liquid diet meal cleared from the stomach into the intestine.

The rats ate avidly and continuously. Food was removed from the stomach at either 2, 10, 20, or 40 min after meal completion. Each rat was tested eight times (two ambient temperatures × four delay conditions) using a Latin Square design. At least 2 days intervened between deprivation experiences.

Stomach clearance was determined by subtracting the dry weight of food recovered from the stomach from the dry weight of the 5-ml meal. Figure 4 shows that stomach clearance was enhanced in the cold, $F(1,7) = 19.1$, $p < 0.005$). Low environmental temperature, therefore, increased stomach clearance of a 5-ml meal in rats deprived of food for 24 hr. The effect is reliable, as it was seen in all eight rats. The gastrointestinal adjustment is fairly rapid as it was seen within 20 min postprandially in rats that had been in the cold for less than 1.5 hr.

INCREASED HUNGER IN THE COLD

We have just raised the possibility that increased feeding in the cold was secondary to altered gastric motility. The cold may also directly influence the urge to eat. The following two experiments assess this suggestion.

Changes in Operant Rate on a VI 30-Schedule of Food Reinforcement

Operant rate was determined in 5 and 22°C ambient temperatures in rats that were equipped with reversible stomach clamps (11). The clamp, designed by W. G. Hall in our laboratory, consists of nylon fishing leader that is placed about the pylorus. The nylon line is sheathed in P.E. 50 tubing, which is threaded subcutaneously to emerge out of a stab wound between

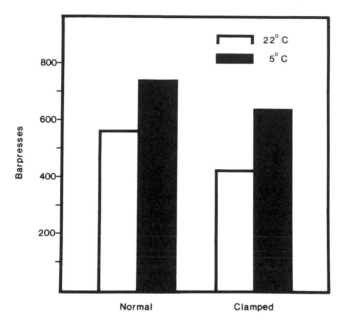

FIG. 5. Mean number of lever presses in 1 hr by 24-hr food-deprived rats, working on a VI 30-sec schedule of reinforcement, in a 5 or 22°C environment. Left: Pylorus in normal position. Right: Pylorus clamped.

the scapulae. The stomach is clamped simply by drawing the nylon line and is reopened by pushing the line to its normally open position.

Twelve rats were deprived of food but not water at 22°C for 24 hr at which time they were handled, weighed, and when appropriate the clamp was drawn closed. The rats were tested in an operant box that was equipped with two levers. One delivered 45 mg Noyes pellets on a VI 30-sec schedule of reinforcement; the other did not and was used as an index of noncontingent operant rate. The operant tests were 1 hr in duration and took place in an ambient temperature of either 5 or 22°C.

Operant rate for food differed markedly between temperature conditions (Fig. 5). It was considerably higher at 5°C than at 22°C both when the stomach was open and when clamped. Increased operant rate was probably specific to food as there was no increase in pressing the noncontingent lever; indeed the modal response was zero. Response rates in both ambient temperatures were reduced by clamping the stomach.

It is of interest that the amount of food eaten did not differ between ambient temperatures and clamping the stomach reduced intake equally. The solid diet used in this experiment may have contributed to this finding. A solid diet needs to be churned and mixed in the stomach before it can be cleared into the intestine (23). However, the liquid diet used in the previous experiments, not needing to be ground or mixed, was probably cleared more readily. Hence, increased feeding of a liquid diet might appear earlier than increased feeding of a solid diet, since a meal of solid food would remain in the stomach longer than a liquid meal of comparable size. In short, the inhibitory properties of solid food in the stomach may have dampened the stimulating effect of the cold environment upon food intake. This idea is supported by the finding that clamping the pylorus reduced food intake, although the rats did not appear satiated. They did not sleep following termination of feeding. Rather they groomed and remained relatively active. Perhaps postabsorptive signals are necessary for the satiety marked by the tranquility and sleep that typically follows feeding.

In any event the enhanced operant rates at 5°C suggest that measures other than total intake may be more sensitive indices of hunger under these circumstances. In accord with the idea of using multiple measures of motivation (15) we compared the resistance to quinine adulteration of liquid diet in rats eating in the 5 and 22°C environments.

Effects of Quinine Adulteration on Food Intake in the Cold

Six naive adult rats were trained to eat their entire daily food ration in 6 hr starting at 0900. After food intake of a liquid diet and body weights stabilized (8 days were required) three rats ate at 5°C, the others at 22°C. The rats were housed at 22°C with water continuously available during the food deprivation. After intake had again stabilized, the liquid diet was made bitter by adding 0.02 g of quinine hydrochloride to 100 ml of diet for 2 days. Ambient temperatures were then reversed and the experiment repeated. Three days after the second quinine presentation, the rats were housed continuously at 22°C, and were maintained on the same test schedule. However, the diets were maintained at approximately 5°C by changing the diet at 30-min intervals.

Figure 6 shows that intake of the unadulterated liquid diet did not differ between temperature conditions on the limited access schedule, possibly because eating was at its maximum. Ambient temperature did, however, markedly affect intake of the adulterated diet. Food intake at 22°C was significantly depressed on both days of quinine adulteration. In contrast feeding in the cold was only slightly depressed on the 1st day of quinine

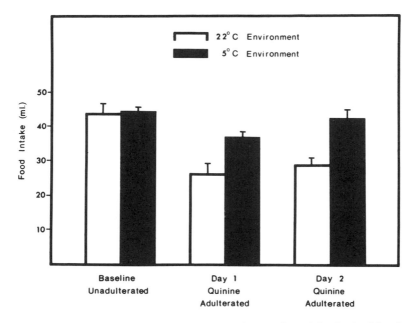

FIG. 6. Mean (±SE) 6-hr total daily food intake of an unadulterated liquid diet for the 3 baseline days (*left*) immediately prior to quinine adulteration, for day 1 of 0.02% quinine adulteration of diet (*middle*), and for day 2 of quinine adulteration (*right*) n = 6.

adulteration and not at all on the 2nd day. The depression was not due to the 5°C adulterated diet being more palatable than the 22°C adulterated diet because, when housed at 22°C, rats did not eat more of the 5°C adulterated diet than they did of the 22°C adulterated diet.

Taken together, these data support the idea that rats in the cold are more motivated to eat than rats living in a thermoneutral ambience and that the peripheral sensation of cold is the sufficient stimulus.

GENERAL DISCUSSION

These experiments have identified some of the mechanisms through which a cold ambient temperature could enhance food intake in laboratory rats. They suggest that the temperature in which rats eat influences the amount of food eaten. Food-deprived rats eat more in the cold and do so primarily by increasing the frequency of eating and not by increasing meal size. Increased meal frequency may be caused in part by the more rapid clearance of food from the stomach into the intestine, which would lead to a more rapid dissipation of the inhibitory signals that arise from stomach stretch receptors (21), and from the upper gastrointestinal tract through the release of the gut hormone cholecystokinin (8, 9).

In addition to enhancing the clearance of food from the stomach, the cold appears to directly increase the urge to eat. The operant and quinine adulteration experiments support this idea. In short the accelerated rate of stomach clearance and the increase in motivation for food help account for enhanced feeding at low ambient temperatures.

Caution must be exercised in generalizing these findings. These experiments were conducted using relatively brief exposures to the cold, as little as 1 hr in some cases. It remains an open issue, therefore, whether the mechanisms identified in the present circumstances are the ones that manage enhanced feeding in animals living in the cold for more sustained periods of time.

Second, the phenomenon was obtained using a liquid diet that is cleared more readily from the stomach than solid diets. In the one experiment where a solid diet was utilized feeding was not enhanced in the cold even though the operant rate was. Although rats do eat more solid diet during the first 24 hr of cold exposure, the mechanisms may differ with the role of accelerated stomach clearance being diminished. It is also worth noting in this regard that cold did not enhance the food intake of rats on a restricted diet, even though rats were more resistant to quinine adulteration when eating at 5°C.

These exceptions point to the complexity of the mechanisms that control food intake at lower ambient temperatures. They point to the conclusion that temperature-related factors, other than increased stomach clearance and enhanced motivation must be taken into consideration when accounting for increased food intake in the cold.

Finally one must ask how these findings relate to normal spontaneous feeding in thermoneutral environments. Are these thermostatic controls involved in normal spontaneous feeding or are they activated in a stepwise manner? The present experiments, which must be viewed as a start toward clarifying the influence of low ambient temperatures on feeding, do not allow us to choose between these alternatives. Additional research is clearly called for.

ACKNOWLEDGMENT

This research was supported by U.S. Public Health Service Grant NS09305 to EMB from the Institute of Neurological Diseases and Stroke.

REFERENCES

1. Abrams, R., and Hammel, H. T. (1964): *Am. J. Physiol.,* 206:641–646.
2. Andersson, B., and Larsson, B. (1961): *Acta. Physiol. Scand.,* 52:75–89.
3. Appleman, R. D., and DeLauche, J. C. (1958): *J. Anim. Sci.,* 17:326–335.
4. Brobeck, J. R. (1948): *Yale J. Biol. Med.,* 20:545–552.
5. Brobeck, J. R. (1960): In: *Recent Progress in Hormone Research,* edited by G. Pincus, pp. 439–466. Academic Press, New York.

6. Durrer, J. L., and Hannon, J. P. (1962): *Am. J. Physiol.*, 202:375–378.
7. Gasnier, A., and Mayer, A. (1939): *Ann. Physiol. Physicochim. Biol.*, 15:186–194.
8. Gibbs, J., Young, R. C., and Smith, G. P. (1973): *J. Comp. Physiol. Psychol.*, 84:488–495.
9. Gibbs, J., Young, R. C., and Smith, G. P. (1973): *Nature*, 245:323–325.
10. Grossman, S. P., and Rechtschaffen, A. (1967): *Physiol. Behav.*, 2:379–383.
11. Hall, W. G. (1973): *Physiol. Behav.*, 11:897–901.
12. Hamilton, C. L. (1967): Alimentary canal. In: *Handbook of Physiology*, Vol. 1, edited by C. F. Code. American Physiological Society, Washington, D.C.
13. Hamilton, C. L., and Ciaccia, P. J. (1971): *Am. J. Physiol.*, 221:800–807.
14. Johnson, R. E., and Kark, R. M. (1947): *Science*, 105:378–379.
15. Miller, N. E. (1957): *Science*, 126:1271–1278.
16. Paré, W. P. (1972): *J. Comp. Physiol. Psychol*, 80:150–162.
17. Rampone, A. J., and Shirasu, M. E. (1964): *Science*, 144:317–319.
18. Sealander, J. A. (1952): *J. Mammalogy*, 33:206–218.
19. Setler, P. E., and Smith, G. P. (1969): *Am. J. Dig. Dis.*, 14:137–142.
20. Sleeth, C. K., and Van Liere, E. J. (1937): *Am. J. Physiol*, 118:272–275.
21. Snowdon, C. T. (1970): *J. Comp. Physiol. Psychol.*, 71:68–76.
22. Spector, N. H., Brobeck, J. R. and Hamilton, C. L. (1968): *Science*, 161:286–288.
23. Thomas, J. E. (1967): In: *The Stomach*, edited by C. Thompson, D. Berkowitz, E. Polish, and J. Mayer. Grune and Statton, New York.

Hunger: Basic Mechanisms and Clinical Implications, edited by D. Novin, W. Wyrwicka, and G. Bray. Raven Press, New York © 1976.

Interactions of Glucostatic and Lipostatic Mechanisms in the Regulatory Control of Feeding

Jacques Le Magnen

Laboratoire de Neurophysiologie Sensorielle et Comportementale, Collège de France, 75231 Paris Cedex 05, France

Basic mechanisms of the control of food intake are being increasingly investigated and must be studied as a part of the overall neurometabolic mechanisms involved in the regulation of body energy balance and body composition. The three classic terms of the body energy balance are (a) the energy outflow as heat and work, (b) the energy inflow by feeding, (c) the body substances as potential energy. The last term can be usefully divided into two compartments: (i) the energy content of body substances immediately mobilizable as fuel, essentially carbohydrates and fats, and (ii) the energy content of other body substances, essentially the lean body mass. A body energy balance, considered in such terms, implies that the body energy content, its output, and its input are really balanced; in other words, there are some mechanisms to be identified by which the outflow equals the inflow and by which the body energy content is kept constant. This assertion raises two classic questions: What is regulated and, if something is regulated, what is doing the regulating?

BASIC ASSESSMENT OF THE BODY ENERGY BALANCE . IN THE DIURNAL CYCLE OF RATS

The experimental investigation of an answer to these questions and on the part played in this regulatory system by the control of food intake required the technical possibility of performing a simultaneous measure of the evolution of the three terms, that is (a) the momentary evolution of energy expenses of a freely moving and feeding animal at a given ambient temperature (the energy outflow); (b) the momentary and cumulative *ad libitum* or schedule feeding pattern (the energy inflow); and (c) the body weight and some indices of intermediary metabolisms providing a measure of the body energy content and of its repartition in various types of body substances.

We have undertaken 10 years ago to fit this requirement by pairing our previous technique of the momentary recording of the free-feeding pattern with a continuous measure of respiratory exchanges of a freely moving rat (1). In an individual rat so recorded for 2 consecutive days, the consideration of the oxygen consumption and of the concomitant meal pattern led to the following basic observations.

1. At the short time scale level (here, 10 min), energy expenses were not constant. They fluctuated over time in a relatively large range. Out of the steady state condition here realized, energy expenses through exercise and heat production may vary in peak of expense in a range of 1 to 8 or 10.

2. The energy inflow by food intake was essentially discontinuous. It was a pattern of meals, and meal-to-meal intervals.

3. This discontinuous outflow rate and all-or-none feeding rate were not synchronous (Fig. 1).

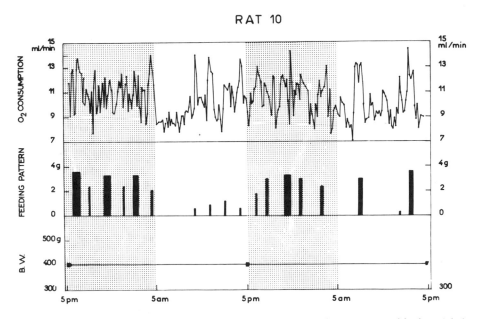

FIG. 1. Continuous recordings of concomitant oxygen consumption, feeding pattern, and body weight in the same rat during 2 consecutive days.

Considered at the 12-hr time scale in the same rat and in others, a large discrepancy of concomitant feeding rate and metabolic rates was obvious in the two parts of the diurnal cycle. Rats ate about two times their caloric expenses at night. The opposite was observed in daytime (Fig. 2).

4. The imbalance within the 12 hr between inflow and outflow was associated, respectively, with increases or decreases of body substances. Excesses of inflow were associated with fat synthesis and body weight gain at night, deficits in daytime with fat mobilization and body weight loss (Fig. 3).

5. These moment-to-moment and 12-hr to 12-hr discrepancies between inflow and outflow of energy were in fact regulated by a common factor within 24 hr or more. In this rat (Fig. 1) and in the average of 30 rats, the cumulative daily caloric input has been equal to the daily caloric output and, as a

RAT 10

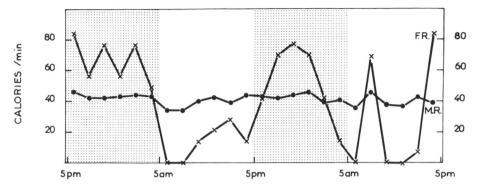

FIG. 2. Concomitant feeding and metabolic rates during 2 consecutive days.

result of this balance, the body weight was shown constant from day to day with an accuracy of less than 0.5%.

Preliminary conclusions and suggestions might be drawn from these basic observations:

1. The current metabolic output (basal metabolism, exercise, and so on) and the inflow by feeding are not dependent on each other.

2. Their respective and independent control mechanisms are related to a common control system, which acts to insure the long-term constancy of the body energy content and the constant balance of outflow and inflow.

What is regulated? It is, of course, what is found effectively constant over time, i.e., the body energy content and particularly the content of immediately

RAT 10

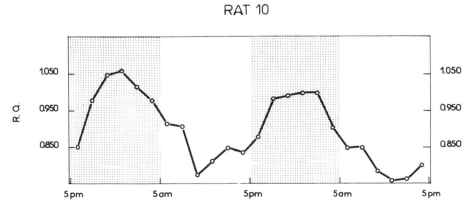

FIG. 3. Diurnal variations of the respiratory quotient during 2 consecutive days in an ad libitum fed rat indicating the diurnal cyclicity of fat synthesis and fat mobilization.

available sources of expendable energy (glucose and fats). Such regulation of the body energy content will be demonstrated only if an answer is given to the other and decisive question: What is doing the regulating and how?

Theoretically, two alternatives exist. Either excesses or deficits of bodily sources of available energy, resulting from a nonregulatory food intake, act through feedback mechanisms to augment or to reduce metabolic expenses. Or the same excesses and deficits of potential energy in the body, resulting from independently regulated metabolic expenses, act through feedback mechanisms on a regulatory control of food intake. Before discussing these alternatives further, the endogenous neuroendocrine mechanisms by which the glucose availability and the fat content are kept constant must be considered.

ENDOGENOUS MECHANISMS OF GLUCOSTASIS AND LIPOSTASIS

The existence of glucostatic and connected lipostatic systems is well established in physiology. Their experimental study has been, and still is, developed independently of studies on the possible role of the same or other systems in the command of feeding responses.

The regulation of blood glucose level is achieved through a glucostatic mechanism. In this glucoregulatory system, the blood glucose load and the constant level of its availability to cell oxidation are performed by the alternate synthesis and mobilization of the limited carbohydrate stores. Beyond this endogenous glucostasis, the glucostatic system is completed at the expense of the constancy of the body fat mass by fat synthesis in excesses of glucose, by fat mobilization in glucopenia. Two well-known antagonist neuroendocrine mechanisms are involved in this regulatory removal and supply of available sources of energy in the blood. The elevation of the blood glucose level, acting both peripherally and centrally, causes insulin release. The pancreatic hormone fills at first the carbohydrate stores. Furthermore, if an elevated blood glucose level persists as a result of the imbalance between the entry and clearance of glucose, the stimulated insulin release brings about the triglyceride synthesis and the fat deposition. The fall of the blood glucose level, mainly through the hypophyseo-medullo-adrenal mechanism, stimulates the opposite and successive metabolic processes of glycogenolysis and lipolysis.

However, there is a purely endogenous lipostatic mechanism that tends to limit this regulation of the glucose load by variations of body fats. Various evidences for such a primary lipostatic mechanism have been provided. In the chronic condition, *ad libitum* fed rats display a sustained fat synthesis during the dark period. Synchronized with the light onset, 12 hr of lipolysis in daytime compensate at the end of the 24-hr cycle for the preceding nocturnal fat synthesis (1). When, out of this physiological condition, weight gain is forced by various means (forced feeding, insulin administration, lateral hypothalamic (LH) stimulation), the cessation of the treatment is associated with the occurrence of a strong lypolysis until the return to the initial body weight. When, conversely, lowered body weight is realized by food restriction, a compensatory lipogenesis is induced at the restoration of the *ad libitum* feeding condition. The exact mechanism of such a functional lipostasis is poorly documented. On the side of excesses and lipogenesis, the increasing insulin resistance of adipose tissue, as a result of the elevation of fat mass and of the adipocyte size, is obviously a part of this mechanism (2).

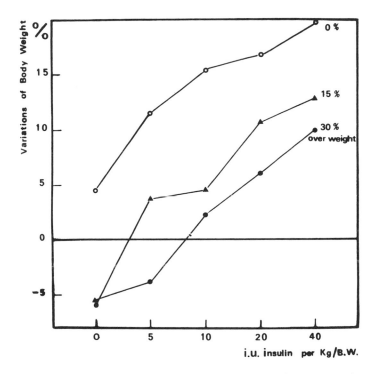

FIG. 4. Body weight dependence of the dose response effectiveness of insulin to promote the weight gain in three groups of rats treated at 0, 15, and 30% of their normal body weight.

In three groups of tube-fed rats, tested respectively at 0, 15, and 30% increases of their initial body weight with five doses of insulin, the efficiency of the hormone to stop the weight loss or to promote a further weight gain was found to be body weight dependent (Fig. 4) (3).

In addition to this decrease with increasing body fat mass of the efficiency of the lipogenetic hormone, the strong lipolysis and rapid weight loss of overweight animals at the end of the treatment suggest that the sensitivity of adipose tissue to lipolytic agents increases with the body fat mass. On the side of underweight, it may be presumed that opposite variations with decreasing body fat mass and adipocyte size of the respective sensitivity to lipolytic and lipogenetic agents occur.

Such a lipostatic mechanism would not imply a participation of afferent signals to and efferent feedbacks from the central nervous system (CNS). However, a complementary mechanism in which a neural control is certainly involved seems to result from the glucose–free fatty acid (FFA) cycle of Randle et al. (28). The FFA mobilization induced by a preceding lipogenesis acts to reduce the sensitivity of target tissues to insulin and the glucose utilization. Conversely, the lipogenesis subsequent to lipolysis has the opposite effect of enhancing the insulin sensitivity. This complementary mechanism is clearly at work in the diurnal metabolic cycle of rats. At night, as in a postfasting lipogenesis, the insulin responsiveness measured by the K coefficient of the glucose tolerance test, is high. In daytime, insulino-secretory responses and glucose utilization contemporary with the prevailing lipolysis are lowered (4–7). Through positive feedbacks, this mechanism leads to a regulatory facilitation of lipogenesis below and of lipolysis above the set point of body fats.

Much evidence has been provided that hypothalamic gluco- or liporeceptors do exist and that they are functioning in the glucoregulatory weight gain–weight loss system. Basic questions are raised about their identity and about their difference and relations with possible receptors involved in the control of feeding.

METABOLIC AND BEHAVIORAL FEEDBACKS

The performance of this purely endogenous glucolipostatic mechanism is limited. Against a persistent positive or negative balance, the regulatory correction may only result from feedbacks by which the glucose and fat content acts either to augment the metabolic expenses or to repress feeding in the condition of a positive balance, either to reduce the energy output or to stimulate food intake in the opposite condition. It is impossible to review here all the arguments supporting the second alternative, i.e., that the behavioral energy input is the main regulator of the body energy balance. Forced feeding is required to induce obesity, and food restriction to induce leanness. When obesity and leanness are realized, a modulation of the energy outflow seems to play a minor role in their subsequent correction, which is operated, foods being available, through feedbacks acting to counteract or to stimulate feeding.

Therefore, in their necessary framework, two classic questions posed by investigators of feeding behavior, may be asked. Do glucopenia and lipopenia and their neuroendocrine correlates stimulate eating, and how? Do elevated blood glucose and body fat loads and their neuroendocrine correlates inhibit or delay eating, and how?

ACUTE AND CHRONIC CONDITIONS

An important distinction must be made between, on one hand, the acute condition realized by food deprivation or a peak of expenses and, on the other hand, the chronic and steady-state condition of rats fed *ad libitum* or on a familiar feeding schedule. Two different control systems are obviously involved in the two conditions. This distinction has been generally overlooked because most experimental feeding tests are limited to a single meal. Consideration only of the occurrence of a meal and of its size, in satiated or food-deprived subjects, provides very poor information and may be misleading. A full study of the response to a given prefeeding condition or manipulation requires the recording over time of the subsequent meal pattern, and of its two parameters, meal sizes (MS) and meal-to-meal intervals (MMI).

The observation of relations of MS to MMI in acute, compared to chronic, conditions of feeding leads to a preliminary suggestion of the role of two different control systems. The MS to MMI relations prevailing in the chronic *ad libitum* fed rats, are well known (8–11). MS is not correlated with the length of free premeal intervals but determines the length of the postmeal interval terminated by the onset of a new meal. By contrast, when at night, the free intermeal interval was extended in successive tests by 4, 6, 8, and 10-hr delays in access to the food, the size of the first meal became positively correlated with the length of these premeal durations of food deprivation. After this first meal, and 6 hr of deprivation prior to feeding, the MS–postmeal interval relationship disappeared (Fig. 5) (12). After 24 hr of fasting or more, and after the very high first meal, the subsequent meals progressively decreased in size, whereas their interval increased (13).

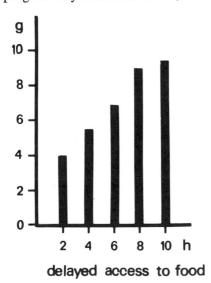

FIG. 5. Sizes of the first meal plotted against the duration of free or extended premeal intervals.

Thus, after the acute food deprivation, the regulatory response is performed through a relative variation of the two parameters of the cumulative intake exactly opposite to that occurring in the regulatory pattern observed in the free feeding condition. An old and already published experiment illustrated the change in the same rats from the acute to the chronic conditions of the characteristics of the meal size-interval relationships. The simple procedure also displayed the main feature of the chronic condition of feeding that is the fact (below developed) that in these conditions the amount of food eaten in each meal is an anticipatory feeding.

Rats were given, three times daily, a 1-hr access to the food. These three scheduled meals were identically separated by 7 hr. After habituation to the schedule and the stabilization of amounts taken in each meal, one meal was suddenly eliminated and the effect of the new gap of 15 hr between meals was observed. During the first 3 days, the meal after the gap was increased. Later, and increasingly over time, the meal prior to the 15-hr interval was augmented. After 18 days 75% of the previous consumption in the suppressed meal were added, as an anticipatory response, to the meal preceding the long interval of no access to the food.

HUNGER AROUSAL OF EATING IN ACUTE CONDITION

Food deprivation, for a time longer than the free MMI, or a sudden high level of energy expense (exercise or thermogenesis) introduces the acute condition of eating. In this condition of natural hunger, the food made available is readily accepted, the size of the first meal is augmented and the subsequent meal pattern modified as mentioned above. The metabolic correlates of this acute condition of energy deficit are: (a) the partial or total exhaustion of carbohydrate stores leading to a tendency of the blood glucose level to fall under the set point of the blood glucoregulatory system; (b) the high level of plasma FFA and the reduction of fat stores below normal levels preventing through the same glucoregulatory system a sharp and lethal fall of the blood glucose. The two sets of correlates, which both have been studied and suggested as signals in the endogenous glucolipostatic systems, are also old candidates as signals of the complementary feeding mechanism.

As recalled above, the role of the glucose level as a stimulus of the glucoregulatory system is not questionable. The same role of the glucose availability as a stimulus for the mobilization of the feeding system is still questioned. Is it questionable?

The fact that the glucoprivic condition produced by insulin and 2-deoxyglucose (2-DG) administrations may stimulate eating, in the absence of a current energy deficit, could be taken as sufficient evidence. The disappearance of this feeding response to insulin in LH-recovered rats (14) and to 2-DG after discrete lesions in the LH areas (15–17) suggested, as in the glucoregulatory system, the involvement of diencephalic receptors.

The opposite effect of glucose overload acting to delay or suppress eating is generally not understood. The caloric compensation by a variation of the subsequent free-feeding pattern after an intragastric load of glucose in normal rats and its absence in diabetic rats suggested the role of the systemic glucose repletion in satiety (18). But such a condition of satiety or delayed feeding does not argue for an active inhibition by a humoral glucose stimulus. Such an inhibition is only provided in the satiation process through peripheral (oral and gastric) or peripherally generated feedbacks. The caloric compensation after the gastric load proves only that, through this route of administration, glucose realizes or prolongs the condition of no hunger in the free-feeding situation. However, it is difficult to make this finding and its interpretation compatible with other evidence that, in the acute condition of food deprivation, an intravenous glucose injection or infusion is not able to suppress the stimulation to eat (19, 20).

However, arguments have been presented recently against a major contribution of a glucoprivic system in the regulatory control of feeding. Some central lesions suppress the feeding response to 2-DG and insulin but preserve a current feeding as well as some feeding responses to regulatory challenges (21). This fact could be explained by the hypothesis that the exogenous insulin and glucose analogue administrations in nondeprived rats stimulate eating in an unphysiological condition through an emergency high-threshold system. Its destruction by central lesions would leave intact a distinct low-threshold mechanism, active in acute and chronic regulatory responses.

In fact, the demonstration that the glucoprivic condition produced by insulin and 2-DG mimics all the characteristics prevailing in natural hunger, is still lacking. The second component of the metabolic pattern of fasting (the high plasma FFA level and loss of body fats) is not reproduced by 2-DG and insulin administrations. The role of a lipopenic system in the short-term stimulation of eating although reasonably plausible, has been rarely considered and studied. The hyperphagia of diabetic rats provides a presumption of its physiological role. This hyperphagia may be interpreted as a permanent result of the deficient glycolysis and of the exhaustion of body fats similar to the condition of fasting in normal rats but uncorrected by foods in diabetics. Further experimental evidence for this short-term lipoprivic stimulus will be provided by the study of concomitant diurnal feeding and metabolic cycles in chronically fed rats. Rats are hyperphagic at night and behave somewhat as acutely food-deprived rats. At the same time, the metabolic and endocrine pattern indicates that they are under the current set point of their body fats. In daytime, rats are as hypophagic as sated rats. At that time, the concomitant lipolysis occurring above the set point of fat stores, contrary to the night condition, does not readily stimulate but instead delays eating (1, 4). This fact may indicate that the low threshold system of responding to the glucoprivic stimulus is dependent on a modulated sensitization of glucoreceptors due, through the Randle mechanism (28), to the level of fat supply for cell oxidation. Such a receptor sensitization, not reproduced by the effect of insulin and 2-DG administrations, would be maximal after an acute condition of natural hunger.

THE REGULATORY FEEDING PATTERN AND ITS STIMULI
IN A CHRONIC CONDITION

The free-feeding pattern in chronic conditions is characterized by several things. (a) Its discontinuity contrasts with the concomitant continuous energy expenses. In rats, 10 to 25% of the daily energy inflow is taken in discrete meals of 15- to 30-min durations, separated from each other by intervals of no feeding also called ambiguously "satiety." The free-feeding pattern in chronic conditions is also characterized by (b) the typical relations of the amount eaten in each meal (MS) to the length of these free intervals of no feeding preceding and following the meal, by (c) the difference of these relations in the two parts of the diurnal cycle producing the fundamental diurnal cyclicity of the chronic free feeding pattern, and by (d) quantitative relations between the cumulative intake in these two parts of the diurnal cycle.

The fact that, contrary to the acute condition, the food consumption within a meal is not dependent on the length of the premeal interval proves that some factors prevailing at the end of this interval are sufficient to start the meal but not to determine the size of the meal, as a graded response to a level of energy imbalance. Other and presumably only peripheral factors (which will not be discussed here) determine in this condition the size of the meal. The fact that the amount of calories taken in at each meal affects the length of the postmeal interval or may be affected by a fixed MMI proves that this intake is an "anticipatory feeding." It is not the response to the deficit (glucose and fat levels) present at the start of the meal, but rather it is an orogastric overload of energy anticipating the subsequent energy expenses. The length of each postmeal interval will thus depend on the balance between the size of this overload and the expenses or disposal of energy during that interval. It was shown that a continuous (22) or a single intragastric load of glucose (23) without changing the meal size, prolonged postmeal intervals. In some rats, the caloric adjustment to diluted food is entirely performed by the relative shortening of the MMI (24).

Thus it is clear that the value of the ratio of MS to the duration of the postmeal interval and its variation with the metabolic background will be indicative of the conditions present before the onset of the meal and, therefore, will offer a possibility of identifying the nature of the stimulus to eat in the chronic condition.

In normal rats, kept in a 12-hr dark 12-hr light cycle, it was found that the ratio of meal size in calories to the expenses of energy during the postmeal interval (measured by the oxygen consumption) was very different in dark and light periods, and roughly equaled 2 at night and 0.5 in the day. This ratio was very constant and highly significant from meal to meal at night and was less constant and significant in the day. As already mentioned, the respiratory quotient (RQ) and plasma FFA level revealed at night a strong and sustained lipogenesis, whereas in daytime they revealed a strong and sustained lipolysis. Using a ^{14}C-labeled food eaten at night, it was shown by measuring the $^{14}CO_2$ output that fats synthesized at night were utilized as fuel for energy metabolism during the day and increasingly at the end of each MMI. As the weight loss and fat mobilization in daytime compensate for and were proportional to the weight gain and fat synthesis the preceding night, it was shown that the cumulative intake of food at night was negatively correlated to the intake in daytime.

Note that all these cyclic features of metabolism and feeding disappeared in hypothalamic hyperphagic rats that exhibited, during the day as well as at night, exaggerated forms of all the symptoms prevailing only at night in normal rats.

From these and other data, the respective and interacting role of the glucose and body fat levels in the stimulation to eat in the chronic condition may be inferred. A fall of the oxygen consumption, which is not observed at the start of the meal, cannot be a stimulus. At least it is not apparent as such in a measure of the whole body. The role of the glucose availability and of a glucoprivic condition in starting the meal and the difference of this effectiveness at night and during the day would require a long discussion. That this glucoprivic condition, active on some differentiated targets, takes part in the stimulation to eat in the chronic condition is not doubtful. In normal rats, the blood glucose level falls progressively from the end of a meal to the onset of the following one, started in daytime, at 110 mg% (25). When, during the day, rats received a continuous intravenous infusion of insulin (2,800 μU/min), the MMI were dramatically shortened; in other words, the occurrences of successive meals were precipitated (26).

But this effectiveness of a glucose stimulus appears to be affected and completed by the endogenous lipostatic system through two different mechanisms displayed by the comparison of metabolic and feeding patterns during the night and day. Much evidence has been obtained recently that at the beginning of the active part of the diurnal cycle (night in rats, day in humans) and through the action of the neural efferent control by the CNS of the islets of Langerhans, the insulin secretory response to glucose in the blood is enhanced. In contrast, the insulin secretory responsiveness is lowered at the beginning of the nonactive phase of the cycle. This pattern in fed rats is primarily responsible for the lipogenesis observed at night and lipolysis observed during the day. By diversion of ingested metabolites toward lipogenesis, fat storage at night, and supply from fat stores of FFA to the pool of metabolites in daytime, the net intake available for the lean tissue is reduced and then elevated. Much evidence exists that, by this first effect, the occurrence of a critical deficit of readily available energy able to start a meal is precipitated at night and slowed in daytime. The suppression of lipolysis in daytime produced by either insulin or deprivation of food on the preceding night induced immediately in this period a feeding pattern identical to that normally seen at night (1, 27).

A second effect of the same metabolic pattern on the feeding mechanism is suggested. The hyperinsulin secretion in response to food during the nocturnal period and the opposite train in daytime producing the successive fall and elevation of the plasma FFA level, give rise, during the 24 hr, to a 12/12 glucose FFA cycle. As shown by Randle et al. (28) and already mentioned, this cycle is associated with the alternate increase and decrease of the insulin sensitivity and glucose utilization of target tissues. Inasmuch as these target tissues are represented by specific glucoreceptors, this process must lead to an increase of their receptivity at night and to a decrease during the day. This direct effect on the feeding mechanism could contribute to hyperphagia at night and to hypophagia in the subsequent part of the diurnal cycle. The combination of these two mechanisms would be the source of a positive feedback between hyperphagia and lipogenesis at night, to a negative feedback between hypophagia and lipolysis during the day, which seems to correspond to the observed facts.

Finally a common underlying factor seems to be the variations of the set point of regulation of the body fat mass driven by the central control of involved neuroendocrine systems. At night, the metabolic and feeding pattern of rats is that of rats below an elevated set point; during the day of rats above a lowered set point.

Thus the endogenous neuroendocrine lipostatic mechanism would be indirectly and directly the source of feedbacks active to stimulate or to repress the responsiveness of the specific feeding system. It is now quite evident that the ventromedial nucleus and lateral area of the hypothalamus play a major role in the central command of this neuroendocrine mechanism and that perturbations of food intake produced by their lesion or stimulation are partly or entirely due to the disturbance of that mechanism.

Through the balance over time of these oscillating mechanisms, the permanent adjustment of the inflow and outflow of energy and the constancy of the body energy content are realized from day to day, or over longer time periods.

SUMMARY

By measuring over time energy expense, feeding patterns, and body weight in rats, it was observed that, despite a momentary and 12-hr to 12-hr asynchrony of the energy outflow and inflow, the body energy balance is realized and body weight kept constant from day to day. These and other facts suggest that the body energy balance is achieved by mechanisms that maintain constant the body content of sources of readily available energy, glucose and fats. These mechanisms at first include an endogenous gluco- and lipostatic regulatory system. The evidence from such a system and its neuroendocrine mechanisms is classically investigated independently of the role of glucose and fat availability in the control of food intake. The effective role of the glucose and fat levels and of their interactions in the control of a regulatory meal pattern is emphasized.

The study of the relations between parameters of this meal pattern in acute versus chronic conditions of feeding leads to the distinction of these two conditions and to the suggestion of a different action of the gluco- and lipostatic mechanism. In the acute condition of food deprivation, it may be argued that the role of a glucoprivic stimulus in hunger arousal of eating is modulated by and added to the effect of a lipoprivic stimulus. Evidence is provided that in the chronic conditions each meal is an anticipatory feeding. Nevertheless it is revealed by the study of the diurnal metabolic and free-feeding pattern that the glucose and fat disposals and their interactions govern the time of the meal onset and thereby the day-to-day energy balance.

REFERENCES

1. Le Magnen, J., and Devos, M. (1970): *Physiol. Behav.*, 5:805–814.
2. Cuatrecasas, P. (1972): *Proc. Natl. Acad. Sci. USA*, 69:318–322.
3. Le Magnen, J., Devos, M., and Tallon, S. (1975): *unpublished data.*
4. Le Magnen, J., Devos, M., Gaudillière, J. P., Louis-Sylvestre, J., and Tallon, S. (1973): *J. Comp. Physiol. Psychol.*, 84(1):1–23.
5. Gagliardino, J. J., and Hernandez, R. E. (1971): *Endocrinology*, 88(6):529–531.
6. Aparicio, N. J., Puchulu, F. E., Gagliardino, J. J., and Ruiz, M.D. (1974): *Diabetes*, 23:132–137.
7. Malherbe, C., De Gasparo, M., De Hertog, R., and Hoet, J. J. (1969): *Diabetologia*, 5:397–404.
8. Le Magnen, J., and Tallon, S. (1963): *J. Physiol.* (Paris), 55:286–287.
9. Le Magnen, J., and Tallon, S. (1966): *J. Physiol.* (Paris), 58:323–349.
10. Snowdon, C. T. (1969): *J. Comp. Physiol. Psychol.*, 69:91–100.
11. Thomas, D. W. (1966): *Ph.D. Thesis*, Tufts University.
12. Le Magnen, J., and Tallon, S. (1975): *unpublished data.*
13. Le Magnen, J., and Tallon, S. (1968): *J. Physiol.* (Paris), 60:143–154.
14. Epstein, A. N. and Teitelbaum, P. (1967): *Am. J. Physiol.*, 213:1159–1167.
15. Nicolaïdis, S., and Meile, M. J. (1972): *J. Physiol.* (Paris), 65:151A.
16. Miselis, R., and Epstein, A. N. (1970): *Physiologist*, 13:262.
17. Kanner, M., and Balagura, S. (1971): *Am. Zool.*, 11:30.
18. Booth, D. A. (1972): *Physiol. Behav.*, 8:801–806.
19. Smith, M. (1966): *J. Comp. Physiol. Psychol.*, 61:11–14.
20. Campbell, S., and Davis, J. D. (1974): *Physiol. Behav.*, 12:374–384.
21. Blass, E. M., and Kraly, F. S. (1974): *J. Comp. Physiol. Psychol.*, 86:676–692.
22. Thomas, D. W., and Mayer, J. (1968): *J. Comp. Physiol. Psychol.*, 66:642–653.
23. Booth, D. A. (1972): *J. Comp. Physiol. Psychol.*, 78:412–432.
24. Le Magnen, J. (1969): *Ann. N.Y. Acad. Sci.*, 157:1126–1127.
25. Steffens, A. B. (1969): *Physiol. Behav.*, 4:215–225.
26. Steffens, A. B. (1969): *Physiol. Behav.*, 4:823–828.
27. Le Magnen, J., and Devos, M. (1975): *unpublished data.*
28. Randle, M. J., Hales, C. N., Garland, P. B., and Newsholme, E. A. (1963): *Lancet*, 1:785–789.

Hunger: Basic Mechanisms and Clinical Implications,
edited by D. Novin, W. Wyrwicka, and G. Bray.
Raven Press, New York © 1976.

Protein and Amino Acids in the Regulation of Food Intake

A. E. Harper

Departments of Nutritional Sciences and Biochemistry, University of Wisconsin, Madison, Wisconsin 53706

The protein content and the amino acid composition of the diet are two of many variables that can influence food intake and food selection. Food intake is depressed when the protein content of the diet is very low (1–3) or very high (4–6), when the proportions of amino acids in the diet deviate appreciably from the proportional amino acid requirements of the organism (6, 7), or when the diet is deficient in an indispensable amino acid (6, 8). Animals will also select quite distinctly between two diets that differ substantially either in protein content (7, 9) or the proportions of amino acids they contain (6, 7).

These observations indicate that the amino acid composition of the food ingested is monitored by the body. They suggest that, when the dietary amino acid pattern changes enough to cause deviations in the amino acid content or pattern of body fluids from some standard state, a signal is initiated that elicits a response from a food-intake-regulating center and that, when the degree of deviation exceeds what is tolerable, food intake is curtailed and food rejection occurs if an alternative diet with a balanced pattern of amino acids is available (6, 7). It is questionable whether or not the relationship between the amino acid needs of an organism and its amino acid intake is of importance in regulating food intake generally when the diet is adequate and the amino acid pattern is reasonably well balanced. Nevertheless, other mechanisms by which food intake is regulated become subsidiary to those responsive to amino acid supply when the protein content of the diet is inadequate or excessive or when the proportions of amino acids in the diet deviate substantially from the proportions of the amino acid requirements.

Effects on food intake of changes in the dietary proportions of amino acids have been studied more extensively than have effects of changes in the protein content of the diet (9). As our investigations have been concerned mainly with effects of amino acid imbalances, I devote most of this chapter to some of our observations on this subject and then present some thoughts on the general significance of dietary protein and amino acids in the regulation of food intake.

First, it is important that we agree on the use of the term amino acid imbalance. In general, amino acid imbalances result from additions to a low-protein diet of one or more amino acids, other than the one that is growth-limiting, in amounts that individually are not toxic. They cause depressions in food intake and growth that are readily prevented by a supplement of the growth-limiting amino acid (7). Also, when the rat is offered a choice, it will reject a diet with an amino acid imbalance and select a protein-free diet or one with a balanced pattern of amino acids (10). Although the severity of the food intake depression differs, depending on which amino acid is growth-limiting, and varies with the degree of disproportion in the amino acid pattern of the diet (11), amino acid imbalance is a general phenomenon; it has been demonstrated with a variety of combinations of amino acids and with several species of animals (12).

We have selected as a model for most of our studies an amino acid imbalance created by adding a mixture of amino acids devoid of histidine to a diet containing 6% casein supplemented with methionine and threonine (13). For studies of the effect of the imbalance on food intake and growth, we have used weanling rats fed *ad libitum*. For most of the biochemical studies, animals of approximately 100 g body weight have been trained to eat a single meal daily so they will eat a meal of at least 5 g in a short time to magnify any effects of the diet on body fluid amino acid concentrations.

The rapidity with which food intake depression occurs after ingestion of a diet with an amino acid imbalance is striking (6, 7, 14). Changes in food consumption can be detected within 4 hr. The falling food intake is associated with depression of the plasma concentration of the amino acid that is growth-limiting and elevations of the plasma concentrations of those added to create the imbalance (6, 7). This plasma amino acid pattern resembles that observed in animals fed an amino acid-deficient diet (9). The association between alterations in both food intake and plasma amino acid concentrations led to the development of the hypothesis that the signal for regulation of food intake in response to altered dietary patterns of amino acids was mediated in some way by the altered blood amino acid pattern.

We have vacillated in our views on the basis for the signal. Initially, we were struck by the change in the ratio of the plasma concentrations of amino acids added to create the imbalance to that of the limiting amino acid in the diet (15). Subsequently, we focused more on the low plasma concentration of the limiting amino acid (16). The importance of this for regulation of the intake of both imbalanced and deficient diets has since been established by Leung and Rogers (17). Later, however, we returned our attention to the amino acids in excess in the plasma, because this seemed to be a common feature among animals fed amino acid-imbalanced diets, high-protein diets (5), amino acid-deficient diets (8), and diets containing an excess of a single amino acid (7), all of which cause food intake depression (6, 7). The importance of the high plasma concentrations of amino acids in excess in the diet now also seems evident (13); I elaborate on the relationship between the changes in plasma concentrations of the growth-limiting amino acid and those in excess in the diet.

First, I shall emphasize some basic observations made by Rogers and Leung (6), who demonstrated that injection of a small amount of the limiting amino acid into the carotid artery of intact rats fed a diet with an amino acid imbalance prevented food-intake depression, whereas a similar injection into the jugular vein did not. Subsequently, Rogers and Leung observed that rats with bilateral lesions in the ventromedial hypothalamus or the amygdala responded to ingestion of an imbalanced diet with a reduction in food intake, just as did the intact rat. However, the food intake of rats with bilateral lesions in the prepyriform cortex was not depressed when they were fed amino acid-deficient or -imbalanced diets. These observations indicated that a center in the brain other than the classically recognized satiety center in the ventromedial hypothalamus was involved in regulation of the food intake of animals fed a diet with a drastically altered amino acid pattern. They suggested that changes in the concentrations of amino acids in blood and body fluids impinged upon the brain to create a signal that elicited the food-intake depression. It should be noted, however, that rats with lesions in the prepyriform cortex, which failed to respond to amino acid imbalances and deficiencies with depressed food intake, still responded as did intact rats to a large excess of one amino acid or to a high-protein diet (6). Consequently, still other signals and monitors must be involved in regulation of the intake of dietary surpluses of one or more amino acids.

Examination of the relationship between plasma and brain amino acid concentrations (Fig. 1) in rats fed a histidine-imbalanced diet (13) revealed that the brain concentration of histidine fell more rapidly and more drastically than that in the plasma and that elevations of the amino acids added to the diet to create the imbalance were much less in brain than in plasma. These observations corresponded well with those of Rogers and Leung (6) on the responsiveness of a food-intake-regulating center to a deficit of the growth-limiting amino acid and indicated that the imbalanced plasma amino acid pattern of rats fed a histidine-imbalanced diet was associated with a low concentration of the growth-limiting amino acid in brain. They left open the question, however, as to why the degree of food-intake depression in rats consuming diets with equal quantities of the growth-limiting amino acid tended to be proportional to the amount of imbalancing amino acid mixture added to the diet and why the concentration of the growth-limiting amino acid in brain should fall more rapidly and more drastically than it did in the plasma. The observations on the relationship between plasma and brain amino acid concentrations in rats fed a diet with a histidine imbalance suggested that the amino acids in surplus in the plasma might compete with histidine for entry into brain (13).

To examine in more detail the probability of competition between the limiting amino acid and amino acids in surplus in plasma for entry into brain, we conducted experiments *in vitro* using brain slices incubated in media containing amino acids in concentrations approximately equivalent to those

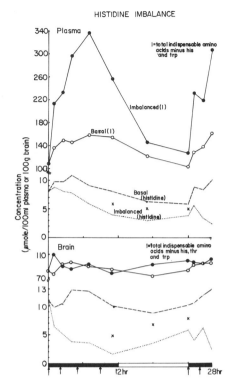

FIG. 1. Effect of force-feeding at times indicated by arrows at base (6% casein plus 0.3% methionine and 0.2% threonine) or histidine-imbalanced (basal plus 6% amino acid mixture minus histidine) diet on free histidine and total indispensable amino acids minus histidine and tryptophan of plasma and cerebrum of rats.

found in plasma (18). We then studied the uptake of ^{14}C-labeled histidine using concentrations of histidine in the medium that also simulated the concentrations found in plasma (13). Uptake is expressed in terms of the distribution ratio, i.e., the ^{14}C-histidine content of the tissue water divided by the ^{14}C-histidine content of the medium.

$$\text{Distribution ratio} = \frac{\text{dpm/ml total tissue water}}{\text{dpm/ml medium}}$$

Table 1 shows that incubation of brain slices in a medium containing a mixture of amino acids in concentrations (3.6 mM) equivalent to those encountered in the plasma of rats fed the basal diet suppressed histidine uptake by brain slices. A mixture of amino acids added to the medium in concentrations (5.0 mM) simulating those present in plasma of rats fed the histidine-imbalanced diet suppressed histidine uptake significantly more than did the mixture simulating the plasma amino acid composition of rats fed the basal diet.

When amino acids were tested individually or in small groups (Fig. 2), it is evident that a mixture of lysine and arginine had relatively little effect on histidine uptake, indicating that the basic amino acids compete relatively little with histidine for entry into brain slices. Threonine, a small neutral amino

TABLE 1. *Distribution ratios (DR) and accumulation of [U-14C]-L-histidine in rat brain slices incubated in media containing basal or unbalanced amino acid mixtures*

Addition	DR	^{14}C-histidine (μmoles/g)
No amino acids	8.6	1.43
Basal mixture (3.6 mM)	4.6	0.86
Unbalanced mixture (3.6 mM)	4.4	0.81
Unbalanced mixture (5.0 mM)	3.9	0.74

(After Lutz, Tews, and Harper, ref. 18.)

acid, exerted some inhibition; but the aromatic, the branched-chain amino acids, and methionine were by far the most effective inhibitors of histidine uptake.

The pattern of inhibition of histidine uptake from increasing increments of amino acid mixtures simulating the amino acid composition of plasma from rats fed the basal diet is shown in Fig. 3. Inhibition of ^{14}C-histidine uptake increased in more or less exponential fashion as the concentration of the inhibiting amino acids in the medium was increased. A mixture of the large neutral amino acids inhibited histidine uptake more than an equivalent concentration of the entire mixture and a mixture of the small neutral, hydroxy;

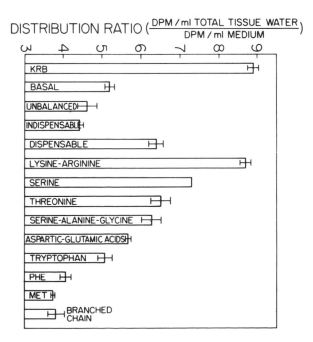

FIG. 2. Inhibitory effects of various amino acids on histidine uptake by rat brain slices.

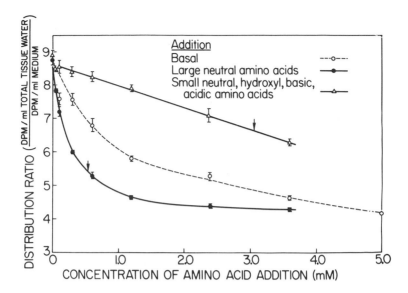

FIG. 3. Influence of concentration of basal amino acid mixture on histidine uptake by rat brain slices.

and basic amino acids inhibited uptake much less at all concentrations tested. Calculated values for ^{14}C-histidine uptake paralleled those for the distribution ratio.

Figure 4 shows that inhibition of histidine uptake by the imbalanced mixture was greater when histidine concentration in the medium was only 0.05 mM than when it was 0.1 mM. Histidine concentrations in the former range occur in plasma of rats fed the imbalanced diet. Relatively low concentrations of the inhibitory amino acid mixtures (less than 1.0 mM) depressed histidine uptake by brain slices, suggesting that inhibitory effects from the surplus of amino acids in the plasma of rats fed the imbalanced amino acid mixture would occur over much of the time required to clear them from the blood after ingestion of a meal (from 3 to 8 hr, depending on the size of the meal).

If these observations on competition for uptake of histidine by brain slices *in vitro* apply to competition for uptake of histidine by brain *in vivo,* and if the low concentration of histidine in brain is the signal initiating food-intake depression, then one would predict that a mixture of lysine and arginine, which has relatively little inhibitory effect on histidine uptake by brain, would have relatively little effect on food intake when added to a diet in which histidine was the limiting amino acid; however, a mixture of the branched chain and aromatic amino acids, which exerts a strong inhibitory effect on histidine uptake by brain, would depress food intake substantially.

In a trial designed to test these predictions, addition of a mixture of lysine and arginine at the level of 4.5% in the basal low-histidine diet depressed food intake and growth very little, whereas the same amount of a mixture of the

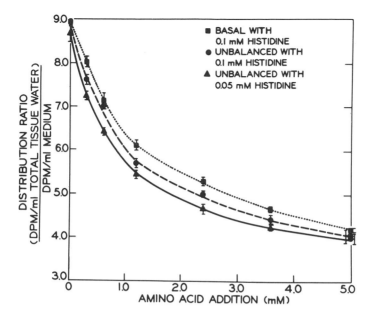

FIG. 4. Effects of basal and unbalanced amino acid mixture additions and initial histidine concentration on histidine uptake by rat brain slices.

large neutral amino acids caused a marked depression of food intake and growth (Table 2). These results correspond well with the predicted response. However, the basis for the response is probably more complex than simple competition among amino acids of the same transport group for entry into brain, as the *in vitro* studies suggest. In many experiments *in vivo*, food-intake depression depends on supplementation of the diet with a quantity (sometimes a small one) of the amino acid that is second limiting for growth (12). The addition of the second limiting amino acid evidently stimulates protein synthesis, especially in the liver, resulting in increased utilization of the limiting amino acid for this purpose and, hence, in an inordinate fall in its concentra-

TABLE 2. Effect of dietary additions of amino acids on food intake and weight gain of rats

	Average daily food intake	Average weight gain (2 weeks)
Control (6% casein)	12.1 ± 0.5	53 ± 5
C + 4.5% (lys and arg)	11.4 ± 0.5	48 ± 2
C + 4.5% (BCAA, met, phe, tyr)	7.8 ± 0.4	24 ± 2

(Y. W. Lee and A. E. Harper, *unpublished*.)

tion in blood and body fluids (7). The effects of elevated concentrations of other amino acids that compete with it for uptake would then be magnified. In the study reported here, the mixture of branched-chain and aromatic amino acids includes both the amino acids that become limiting for growth next after histidine, as well as the amino acids that compete most strongly with histidine for transport. However, with other imbalances the situation may be much more complex, with the limiting and competing amino acids being in different transport groups. One can then envision that prediction of food intake and growth responses from *in vitro* observations may be less reliable. More extensive studies of this phenomenon will be required before general conclusions about the phenomenon can be justified.

The observations reported here and those of others cited by Harper et al. (7), Rogers and Leung (6), and Peng et al. (17) demonstrate quite clearly that the rat responds with depressed food intake when the amino acid composition of the diet is unbalanced or deficient or when dietary protein content is excessively low or high; however, the question remains as to the significance of such responses in day-to-day regulation of food intake.

Regardless of the failure so far to identify the signal and the monitor, when the protein content of the diet (and hence protein intake) is increased suddenly, food intake (and hence energy intake) are depressed (5). However, the depression is only transitory and within a few days food intake and growth rate increase to near "normal" (5). Evidently then, the ability of the rat to dispose of a surplus of amino acids becomes limiting under these conditions but it adapts rapidly to the higher protein intake. This adaptation is associated with increased activities of many amino-acid-degrading enzymes and with an increased ability to clear amino acids and ammonia from the blood. As the adaptation occurs, energy intake rises until within a few days food intake has returned to normal but with a much higher intake of protein (5). This, together with observations that, apart from the transitory effect of a high-protein diet on food intake, animals do not show appreciable differences in intake of diets with differing protein content over a considerable range (10 to 40%) on either side of the amount required to meet amino acid requirements (9), suggests that responsiveness to alterations in the protein content of the diet is not a basic component of regulation of food intake.

This conclusion is also supported by observations on the food intake of animals fed a low-protein diet. Food intake of young animals fed a low-protein diet is depressed, yet the weight gained by rats fed a low-protein diet is disproportionately high in fat (9). This suggests that such animals do tend to increase their food intake in order to compensate for an inadequate supply of protein; however, their ability to do so is very limited. On the other hand, if the food is diluted with inert material, if the environmental temperature is lowered, or if energy expenditure is increased through forced exercise, food intake increases (7, 9). Thus, even in this situation, food intake is regulated primarily by the ability of the animal to dissipate energy and only indirectly by amino acid supply. The low food intake of animals fed a low-protein diet can be considered a protective mechanism since a high intake of energy in relation to the intake of utilizable protein tends to increase the severity of the adverse effects of an inadequate protein intake.

If the consequences for man of having food consumption controlled by a regulatory system based on maintenance of balance between amino acid needs and amino acid intake are examined, it becomes evident that evolution of such a system would be contrary to biological wisdom, as it would not contribute to overall homeostasis of the body. This is most obvious, as was mentioned, in connection with regulation of intake of a low-protein diet. To meet amino acid requirements from a protein-deficient diet, it is necessary to consume an excess of energy that, in the growing organism in particular, exacerbates the effects of protein deficiency.

For the adult, it is almost impossible to devise a diet from natural foods that would not meet the protein requirement when energy requirement was met, unless the diet consisted mainly of cassava or some comparable root crop. With a diet composed of foods of this type, regulation of food intake through a mechanism based on meeting amino acid needs would ensure continued energy storage and obesity.

With a diet composed of foods such as the cereal grains or other food mixtures with unbalanced amino acid patterns, total nitrogen requirement would be met before the requirements for some of the individual amino acids. This would require a monitoring system whereby those amino acids or nitrogen in surplus would not elicit a satiety signal but would respond when the requirement for the amino acid in least amount in the diet in relation to the requirement had been met. This would be the reverse of the type of system that suppresses consumption of diets with deficiencies or imbalances of amino acids. If, on the other hand, the diet were rich in indispensable amino acids (as is the case with diets composed largely of animal products and even for most mixed diets), amino acid requirements would be met before the requirement for total nitrogen. This would require a monitoring system whereby individual amino acids in surplus would not elicit a satiety response but would respond when the requirement for total nitrogen had been met. With control by total nitrogen supply, intake of diets with a low content of indispensable amino acids would be curtailed before either individual amino acid requirements or energy requirement had been met; with control by amino acid supply, intake of diets with high-quality protein would be curtailed before either energy or nitrogen requirements had been met. It is difficult to envision effective control of food consumption by an amino acid-responsive mechanism without envisioning a complex feedback system involving interactions among individual amino acids, nitrogen, and energy and a separate amino acid-responsive system that would act in the opposite direction if the diet were more than marginally deficient in an amino acid.

On the other hand, a monitoring system that responded to the balance between energy needs and energy intake would also provide reasonable assurance that protein needs were met from most diets without complex monitoring of either amino acids or nitrogen. Subsidiary systems that would suppress food intake if protein synthesis was curtailed by an inadequate supply of nitrogen or amino acids or if ingestion of a surplus of amino acids led to some undesirable effect such as accumulation of deleterious end products, would make it improbable that an excess of energy would be consumed when protein supply was inadequate and would protect against ingestion of excessive amounts of amino acids.

Thus, although an aminostatic mechanism involved in regulation of food intake seems to be well established, it appears likely from consideration of the available information that it is subsidiary to regulatory systems based on maintenance of energy balance. Nevertheless, it is important to emphasize that, besides the protective value of such a system, the food preference response of the rat to an amino acid imbalance is more sensitive than the food-intake response. Acquisition of high sensitivity to an unbalanced dietary pattern of amino acids during the course of evolution could have considerable survival value in assuring that the organism would select from among the available foods those with a well-balanced amino acid pattern, even if this mechanism is not involved in food-intake regulation generally.

In summary, food intake is influenced by both the proportions of amino acids in the diet and the dietary content of amino acids and protein. The signal leading to depressed food consumption by animals fed a diet with an amino acid imbalance would appear to arise not only from the low blood concentration of the growth-limiting amino acid but also as a result of competition between amino acids in surplus and those in deficit in the blood for entry into the brain, and to be monitored in the prepyriform cortex. The mechanisms responsive to changes in total protein or amino acid content of the diet have not been identified but would, like those responsive to amino acid imbalances and deficiencies, appear to have evolved as protective mechanisms that prevent excessive consumption of diets that can cause adverse effects rather than as mechanisms involved generally in regulation of food intake.

ACKNOWLEDGMENTS

This work was supported by the College of Agricultural and Life Sciences, University of Wisconsin, Madison, Wisconsin, and by U.S. Public Health Service grant AM 10747 from the National Institute of Arthritis and Metabolic Diseases.

Unpublished observations included in the paper are from the M.S. thesis of Josephine Lutz, Department of Biochemistry, University of Wisconsin, and from a manuscript by Lutz, Tews, and Harper (18).

REFERENCES

1. Meyer, J. H. (1958): *Am. J. Physiol.*, 193:488–494.
2. Meyer, J. H., and Hargus, W. A. (1959): *Am. J. Physiol.*, 197:1350–1352.
3. Peng, Y. S., Meliza, L. L., Vavich, M. G., and Kemmerer, A. R. (1974): *J. Nur.*, 104:1008–1017.
4. Mackay, E. M., Bonds, R. H., and Carne, H. O. (1941): *Am. J. Physiol.*, 135:193–201.
5. Anderson, H. L., Benevenga, N. J., and Harper, A. E. (1968): *Am. J. Physiol.*, 214:1008–1013.
6. Rogers, Q. R., and Leung, P. M-B. (1973): *Fed. Proc.*, 32:1709–1719.
7. Harper, A. E., Benevenga, N. J., and Wohlhueter, R. M. (1970): *Physiol. Rev.*, 50:428–558.
8. Frazier, L. E., Wissler, R. W., Stefler, C. H., Woolridge, F. L., and Cannon, P. R. (1947): *J. Nutr.*, 33:65–83.
9. Harper, A. E. (1967): In: *Handbook of Physiology,* Sec. 6, Vol. I, Chapter 29. American Physiological Society, Washington, D.C.
10. Leung, P. M-B., Rogers, Q. R., and Harper, A. E. (1968): *J. Nutr.*, 95:483–492.
11. Harper, A. E., and Rogers, Q. R. (1965): *Proc. Nutr. Soc.*, 24:173–190.
12. Harper, A. E. (1958): *Ann. NY Acad. Sci.*, 69:1025–1038.
13. Peng, Y., Tews, J. K., and Harper, A. E. (1972): *Am. J. Physiol.*, 314–321.
14. Simson, P. C., and Booth, D. A. (1974): *Br. J. Nutr.*, 31:285–296.
15. Sanahuja, J. C., and Harper, A. E. (1963): *Am. J. Physiol.*, 204:686–690.
16. Harper, A. E., Leung, P., Yoshida, A., and Rogers, Q. R. (1964): *Fed. Proc.*, 23:1087–1092.
17. Leung, P., and Rogers, Q. R. (1969): *Life Sci.*, 8:1–9.
18. Lutz, J., Tews, J. K., and Harper, A. E. (1975): *Am. J. Physiol.*, 229–234.

Hunger: Basic Mechanisms and Clinical Implications,
edited by D. Novin, W. Wyrwicka, and G. Bray.
Raven Press, New York © 1976.

Possible Interrelationship Between Metabolite Flux and Appetite

Ann C. Sullivan and Joseph Triscari

Roche Research Center, Hoffman-La Roche Inc., Nutley, New Jersey 07110

The regulation of food intake represents a complex physiological process involving the recognition and integration of many different types of signals. Estimations of the extent of the contribution of peripheral metabolic factors to this regulatory system have been attempted by many investigators. Blood glucose (1–3), insulin (4), glucagon (5), free fatty acids (6), and amino acids (7, 8) have been postulated to be peripheral sensors because (a) their levels fluctuated according to the metabolic state and/or (b) altering their concentrations in the circulation evoked changes in feeding behavior. It is possible that the rate of change of metabolites rather than their absolute levels may be a more sensitive index in attempting to demonstrate a relationship between peripheral metabolism and food intake regulation.

(—)-Hydroxycitrate was utilized in these experiments to examine the possible interrelationship between metabolite flux and appetite. This compound is a potent competitive inhibitor of ATP citrate lyase, the enzyme catalyzing the extramitochondrial cleavage of citrate to acetyl coenzyme A (CoA) (9). During nutritional conditions of high-carbohydrate feeding, ATP citrate lyase apparently supplied most of the acetyl CoA for lipid biosynthesis (10, 11). Our previous investigations in the rat demonstrated that the administration of (—)-hydroxycitrate (orally, intraperitoneally, or intravenously) significantly inhibited *in vivo* rates of fatty acid and cholesterol synthesis in the tissues which serve as sources of newly synthesized lipid, i.e., liver, adipose tissue, and small intestine (12–14). Additionally, the chronic oral administration of a nontoxic dose of (—)-hydroxycitrate significantly reduced appetite (14, 15). This (—)-hydroxycitrate-induced anorexia produced a reduction in body weight gain which was reflected in significant decreases in total body lipid (14, 15). When food intake was restricted to that consumed by the (—)-hydroxycitrate-treated rats, normal rates of hepatic fatty acid synthesis were observed in these pair-fed rats, whereas the (—)-hydroxycitrate group demonstrated significantly reduced lipogenic rates (13).

The present experiments were designed to analyze quantitatively the effect of (—)-hydroxycitrate on the flux of nutrients. Carbon flux from dietary carbohydrate and its metabolites into hepatic lipids and glycogen was determined in relation to plasma levels of glucose, insulin, and free fatty acids at 2-hr intervals during the 24-hr experimental period.

MATERIALS AND METHODS

Female rats of the Charles River CD strain weighing 175 to 185 g were trained to consume a high carbohydrate meal during a single 3-hr period. This feeding regimen was essential for the quantitative determination of carbon flux from dietary nutrients. Rats were housed individually in wire-bottomed cages in a temperature regulated (22°C) light-controlled room (12-hr light, 6 A.M. to 6 P.M., and dark, 6 P.M. to 6 A.M.). Water was available *ad libitum*. Rats were prefasted for 2 days, then meal-fed a single meal daily from 8 to 11 A.M. consisting of a 70% glucose, 23% protein, 1% corn oil diet (G-70 diet) for 5 to 8 days as described previously (16).

The effects of (—)-hydroxycitrate on lipogenesis and appetite were determined in an experimental system in which rats were administered saline or varying doses of (—)-hydroxycitrate, trisodium salt orally by intubation immediately before feeding. Following the 3-hr meal, rats received intravenously 0.25 ml of a saline solution containing 1 mCi ^3H_2O, 12.3 mg alanine, 30.6 mg α-ketoglutarate (as an amine acceptor for transaminase), and 5 μCi ^{14}C-alanine. ^3H_2O was utilized to determine the total rate of lipogenesis since tritium was incorporated into fatty acids independent of the source of carbon precursors of acetyl CoA (17). ^{14}C-Alanine was employed as a specific carbon precursor of acetyl CoA. Experiments indicated that ^{14}C-alanine was equivalent to either ^{14}C-pyruvate or ^{14}C-lactate as a carbon precursor for lipogenesis. Rats were killed 30 min later by decapitation and *in vivo* rates of hepatic fatty acid synthesis were determined as described previously (12, 13). Food intake and body weight gain were measured during the feeding period.

Carbon flux from dietary carbohydrate and its metabolites was analyzed in an experimental design in which rats received saline or (—)-hydroxycitrate, trisodium salt (2.63 mmoles/kg) orally by intubation immediately before feeding. To normalize any effects on metabolite flux due to caloric intake, all rats received an amount of food (8.7 g) equivalent to that consumed after the administration of 2.63 mmoles/kg of (—)-hydroxycitrate. At 2, 4, 6, 8, 10, 12, 15, 18, 21, and 24 hr after the initiation of the 3-hr meal, rats (10 control and 10 treated per time point) received an intravenous injection of ^3H_2O and ^{14}C-alanine as described above. *In vivo* rates of hepatic fatty acid synthesis were determined as described above. Liver glycogen was isolated by standard procedures (18, 19) and the rates of glycogenesis were determined by oxidizing the purified glycogen to $^{14}CO_2$ and ^3H_2O in a tissue oxidizer. Plasma concentrations of insulin were evaluated by radioimmunoassay (20), of glucose by a standard glucose oxidase method, and of free fatty acids by colorimetry (21).

RESULTS

When (—)-hydroxycitrate was administered orally immediately before feeding, a dose-related reduction in both food intake and *in vivo* rates of

TABLE 1. *Effect of the acute administration of (−)-hydroxycitrate on appetite and in vivo lipogenesis*[a]

Treatment	Dose (mmoles/kg body weight)	Food intake[b]		Fatty acid synthesis[c]			
		G	control (%)	μmoles ³H-converted/ G_s/30 min[d]	control (%)	nmoles ¹⁴C-converted/ G_s/30 min[d]	control (%)
Saline	—	12.1 ± 0.9	100	42.3 ± 6.7	100	631 ± 52	100
(−)-Hydroxycitrate	5.26	8.6 ± 0.8[e]	71	12.0 ± 1.0[f]	28	104 ± 9[f]	17
(−)-Hydroxycitrate	2.63	9.6 ± 0.5[e]	79	14.8 ± 1.2[f]	35	145 ± 16[f]	27
(−)-Hydroxycitrate	1.32	9.9 ± 0.9	82	17.5 ± 5.0[e]	41	226 ± 91[f]	36
(−)-Hydroxycitrate	0.66	9.8 ± 0.8	81	27.2 ± 4.5	64	415 ± 105	66

[a] Rats were fasted 48 hr, then meal-fed a 3-hr meal for 5 to 8 days. On the last day, (−)-hydroxycitrate was administered by stomach gavage immediately before feeding, and livers were assayed immediately after the 3-hr feeding period.

[b] Ten rats per group.

[c] Five rats per group.

[d] Data are expressed as μmoles ³H₂O converted into fatty acids/g liver/30 min, and nmoles ¹⁴C-alanine converted into fatty acids/g liver/30 min.

[e] $p < 0.05$.

[f] $p < 0.01$.

hepatic lipogenesis was observed (Table 1). The inverse relationship between food consumption and dose was significant at (—)-hydroxycitrate levels of 5.26 and 2.63 mmoles/kg; in addition to these concentrations, 1.32 mmoles kg (—)-hydroxycitrate significantly inhibited fatty acid synthesis.

The effect of (—)-hydroxycitrate on carbon flux from dietary carbohydrate and its metabolites was examined. To normalize any effects on metabolite flux due to differences in caloric intake between treated and control animals, all rats received an identical quantity of food during the 3-hr meal. The rate at which control rats converted dietary carbohydrate and its metabolites into fatty acids increased to a maximum at 3 to 5 hr after the initiation of the meal and declined subsequently to a minimum at 24 hr (Fig. 1). In contrast to this result, (—)-hydroxycitrate produced a significant inhibition of the *in vivo* rate of hepatic lipogenesis (53% from ^3H_2O and 69% from ^{14}C-alanine) during the first 8-hr period when control animals were synthesizing fatty acids at an elevated rate. Rates of lipogenesis were similar in treated and control animals during the last 14 hr of the experiment. Figure 2 demonstrates the apparent rates of *in vivo* hepatic glycogenesis in the same animals. The

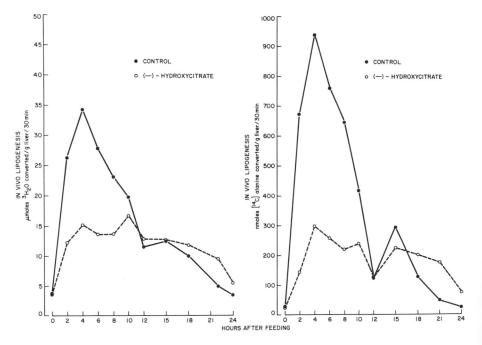

FIG. 1. Effect of oral administration of (—)-hydroxycitrate on the *in vivo* rate of hepatic lipogenesis determined over a 24-hr period. Rats were prefasted 48 hr, then meal-fed the G-70 diet for 6 days. On day 7, rats were given either saline or (—)-hydroxycitrate (2.63 mmoles/kg) by gastric intubation immediately before receiving 8.7 g of food. The *in vivo* rate of lipogenesis was determined using the ^3H_2O and ^{14}C-alanine pulse at the indicated times (eight to 10 rats per point). The animals were killed 30 min after pulse administration. The μmoles ^3H_2O and nmoles ^{14}C-alanine converted into fatty acids in the (—)-hydroxycitrate-treated rats were significantly less than controls at 2, 4, 6, and 8 hr ($p < 0.05$).

incorporation of radioactivity into glycogen was greater in the (—)-hydroxy-citrate-treated rats during 4 to 10 hr when ^3H_2O was the source of isotope and during 4 to 6 hr when ^{14}C-alanine was the radiolabeled precursor. A significantly greater conversion of ^3H_2O (2.9-fold) and ^{14}C-alanine (3.7-fold) was observed in the (—)-hydroxycitrate group relative to the controls 6 hr after feeding. The conversion of ^3H_2O into glycogen was still significantly elevated 1.8-fold compared to controls at 8 hr. From 12 to 24 hr, the rates of glycogenesis were indistinguishable in control and treated animals.

The (—)-hydroxycitrate-mediated increase in apparent rate of glycogenesis was reflected in a significant elevation of liver glycogen content (Fig. 3). The treated animals demonstrated a significantly greater amount of glycogen (~20%) from 6 to 10 hr after feeding. At other time intervals, glycogen levels in control and treated rats were similar.

Although significant differences in the characteristics of metabolite flux (as demonstrated by the *in vivo* rates of hepatic lipogenesis, glycogenesis, and glycogen levels) were produced by (—)-hydroxycitrate administration, no significant effects on plasma glucose, insulin, or free fatty acid concentration were observed (Fig. 4). Glucose levels increased following the initiation of the meal to a maximum at 3 to 5 hr and subsequently returned to prefeeding

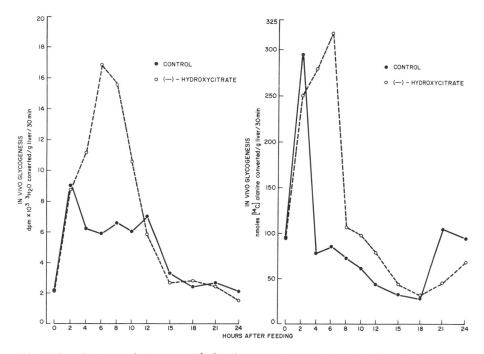

FIG. 2. Effect of the oral administration of (—)-hydroxycitrate on the *in vivo* rate of hepatic glycogenesis determined over a 24-hr period. (See Fig. 1 legend for experimental details.) The dpm ^3H_2O and nmoles ^{14}C-alanine converted into glycogen in the (—)-hydroxycitrate-treated rats (five rats per point) were significantly greater than controls at 6 and 8 hr (^3H_2O), and 6 hr (^{14}C-alanine) ($p < 0.01$).

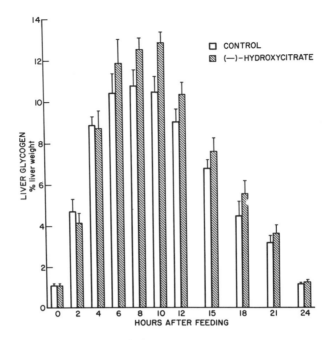

FIG. 3. Effect of the oral administration of (—)-hydroxycitrate on hepatic glycogen content determined over a 24-hr period. (See Fig. 1 legend for experimental details.) Hepatic glycogen was isolated at the indicated times (10 rats per group). The amount of glycogen in (—)-hydroxycitrate-treated rats from 6 to 10 ﬁr was significantly greater than controls (p < 0.05).

levels near hour 10 (Fig. 4A). Recall that fatty acid synthesis from both precursors decreased to a slow rate at 10 to 12 hr suggesting that lack of availability of substrate accounted for the diminished synthetic rate. No significant differences in plasma glucose levels were observed in treated animals compared to controls. These data suggested that the rates of absorption of carbohydrate from the gut and utilization of glucose by tissues were unaffected by (—)-hydroxycitrate.

Changes in plasma insulin levels (Fig. 4B) paralleled those observed for glucose, i.e., increased following initiation of feeding and decreased to prefed values near hour 10. No significant differences in circulating insulin levels were observed between control and treated rats, although the mean plasma insulin values of control animals appeared to be greater than those in (—)-hydroxycitrate-treated rats at the 2-hr period.

Changes in free fatty acid levels were inversely correlated to alterations in levels of plasma glucose, i.e., levels decreased after the initiation of feeding, returned to prefeeding values at 6 hr, and subsequently continued to rise slowly (Fig. 4C). However, no significant differences in free fatty acid concentrations between control and treated animals were observed at any time point.

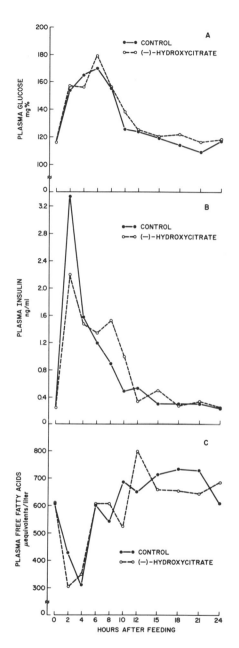

FIG. 4. Effect of the oral administration of (—)- hydroxycitrate on plasma levels of glucose (A), insulin (B), and free fatty acids (C).(See Fig. 1 legend for experimental details.) Plasma glucose (seven to eight rats per point), insulin (seven to eight rats per point), and free fatty acids (nine to 10 rats per point) were determined at the indicated times. No significant differences were observed in treated rats compared to controls.

DISCUSSION

(—)-Hydroxycitrate significantly reduced food consumption (Table 1) and concomitantly altered the metabolic flux of dietary nutrients by diverting carbohydrate and its metabolites from lipid biosynthesis in the liver (Fig. 1). Some of these diverted carbons were apparently channeled into hepatic glycogen since significant increases in both glycogen content and the conversion of radiolabeled isotopes into glycogen were observed (Figs. 2, 3). No significant differences in plasma levels of glucose, insulin, or free fatty acids were detected in (—)-hydroxycitrate-treated rats relative to controls (Fig. 4A–C). These data suggest that peripheral metabolism, defined in the present context as metabolite flux, may be involved in appetite regulation, but whether this interaction is causative or correlative is unknown.

That the anorexia produced by (—)-hydroxycitrate was not due to an adulteration of taste, toxicity, or to a general feeling of malaise was suggested by the following observations:

1. (—)-Hydroxycitrate reduced food intake equivalently when given as a dietary admixture, or injected intragastrically or intraperitoneally (15; *unpublished observations*).

2. (—)-Hydroxycitrate reduced food intake to the same extent after acute or chronic administration (compare Table 1 with Table 1 in ref. 15).

3. Citrate administered as a dietary admixture (*unpublished observations*) or orally by intubation at equimolar concentrations compared to (—)-hydroxycitrate produced no anorexia (15). These data argued against a nonspecific tricarboxylate effect on appetite.

4. The acute LD_{50} values obtained after oral and intraperitoneal administration of citrate and (—)-hydroxycitrate to mice and rats were essentially identical (*unpublished observations*).

5. (—)-Hydroxycitrate did not affect water consumption (*unpublished observations*). Further experiments designed to examine the effects of (—)-hydroxycitrate on taste preferences and other behavioral parameters are in progress.

Our observations that (—)-hydroxycitrate increased hepatic glycogen synthesis and levels and concomitantly reduced food intake are consistent with the hypothesis that information regarding liver carbohydrate metabolism is involved in appetite regulation. Russek (22) postulated the existence of hepatic glucoreceptors which modulated food intake in the following manner: a decrease in glucose concentration in hepatic cells would produce hunger signals, whereas an increase in glucose levels would terminate these signals. This theory was developed from experiments in rats in which changes in food intake were inversely correlated with changes in hepatic concentrations of reducing sugars but not related to sugar levels in blood, muscle, or adipose tissue (22). Experiments using amphetamine suggested that the stimulus for these hepatic glucoreceptors could be the rate of glucose change in the liver cell rather than the actual glucose concentration (22). Additional supporting evidence for hepatic glucoreceptors was derived from studies in which the intraportal injection of glucose to a 22-hr fasted dog produced an anorexia equivalent to approximately 1 hr, whereas the intraportal injection of saline or intrajugular injection of an equivalent dose of glucose produced no effect (23).

Further evidence suggesting the involvement of hepatic glucoreceptors in the regulation of food intake was provided by Niijima (24) who demonstrated the existence of glucose-sensitive fibers in the vagus nerve using an isolated perfused liver preparation. The importance of vagally mediated glucoreceptors was also apparent in the experiments of Novin et al. (25) in which the intraportal injection of 2-deoxyglucose (to block glucose utilization) to normal free-feeding rabbits increased eating to a greater degree and with a shorter latency than equivalent intrajugular injections or intraportal injections of 2-deoxyglucose to vagotomized rabbits. However, other studies in the same laboratory using glucose infusions in free-feeding rabbits suggested that glucoreceptors in the duodenum rather than the liver may be more important in controlling food intake (26), since the duodenal infusion of glucose rather than hepatic intraportal perfusion had a greater effect on subsequent food consumption. This duodenal-based satiety was apparently mediated by the vagus.

Changes in hepatic glycogen levels were also associated with alterations in feeding behavior in an unusual model system in which rat adipose tissue was enriched with odd-chain fatty acids. When rats (27, 28) or dogs (29) were fed a diet containing triundecanoin for prolonged periods, the adipose tissue fatty acids became enriched with undecanoate. During prolonged starvation (48, 96, and 144 hr), liver glycogen and serum glucose levels in the odd-enriched rats were significantly greater than even-enriched controls, presumably due to the potentially gluconeogenic 3-carbon units produced during the terminal step of β-oxidation of the odd-chain fatty acids (27). Behavioral studies comparing these two groups after a 48-hr fast demonstrated that the undecanoate-enriched rats exhibited a significantly reduced drive for food, possibly due to a lower threshold for satiety (30).

Booth (31, 32) postulated that food intake was controlled by the metabolism of energy-yielding nutrients from normally ingested food and that energy supply was the single basic factor controlling feeding. He visualized that food intake was regulated by energy flow to a receptor system and developed a computer model that predicted meal patterns and cumulative food intake for normal and ventromedial hypothalamus (VMH)-lesioned rats (31, 32). If we substitute metabolite flow for energy flow, then the interrelationship between an energy flow receptor system and our quantitative analysis of lipid and carbohydrate flux becomes apparent. Since energy supply at any time point represents a complex summation of dietary nutrients and their metabolites distributed throughout the body in various tissues and pools, an alteration in metabolite flux might be expected to alter the receptivity of an energy flow receptor system. For instance, if glycogen represents a more energy-rich nutrient than lipid, i.e., produces a greater signal in a satiety:energy receptor system or a dampened signal in a hunger:energy receptor system, then the (—)-hydroxycitrate-induced increase in glycogen levels could decrease food intake.

It is possible that (—)-hydroxycitrate produces anorexia by altering metabolite flux in the central nervous system directly. In recent experiments designed to ascertain the metabolic fate of ^{14}C-(—)-hydroxycitrate in the rat, we have detected ^{14}C in the brain and hypothalamus. If (—)-hydroxycitrate were transported into the brain as these preliminary data suggested, then changes in carbohydrate and lipid metabolism in neural tissue similar to those reported here in liver could occur. If the neurosecretory cells were undergoing alterations in metabolite flux of carbohydrate and its metabolites, these changes could influence cAMP and Ca^{2+} levels thus affecting secretory activity and, ultimately, physiological function. If ATP citrate lyase supplied most of the acetyl CoA in brain (33) as it apparently does in liver (10, 11), then inhibition of this enzyme by (—)-hydroxycitrate should result in some change in the rate and/or extent of production of acetylcholine. Cholinergic mechanisms have been implicated in the regulation of hunger and satiety (34, 35).

The model described here represents a useful tool to increase our understanding of the involvement of metabolite flux in the regulation of food intake at both the peripheral and central levels. Results obtained in these studies can be used to design experiments in genetically obese hyperphagic rodents, VMH-lesioned, and lateral hypothalamus (LH)-lesioned animals. The latter studies will permit us to more clearly evaluate the involvement of metabolite flux in the regulation of food intake.

REFERENCES

1. Van Itallie, T. B., Beaudoin, R., and Mayer, J. (1952): *Am. J. Clin. Nutr.,* 1:208–217.
2. Mayer, J. (1953): *N. Engl. J. Med.,* 249:13–16.
3. Mayer, J. (1955): *Ann. NY Acad. Sci.,* 63:15–43.
4. Kumaresan, P., and Turner, C. W. (1965): *Proc. Soc. Exp. Biol. Med.,* 120:828–831.
5. Penick, S. B., and Hinkle, L. E. (1961): *N. Engl. J. Med.,* 264:893–897.
6. Penick, S. B., Prince, H., and Hinkle, L. E. (1966): *N. Engl. J. Med.,* 275:416–419.
7. Mellinkoff, S. M., Frankland, M., Boyle, D., and Greipel, M. (1956): *J. Appl. Physiol.,* 8:535–538.
8. Mellinkoff, S. M., Frankland, M., and Greipel, M. (1956): *J. Appl. Physiol.* 9:85–87.
9. Watson, J. A., Fang. M., and Lowenstein, J. M. (1969): *Arch. Biochem. Biophys.,* 135:209–217.
10. Spencer, A. F., and Lowenstein, J. M. (1962): *J. Biol. Chem.,* 237:3640–3648.
11. Srere, P. A., and Bhaduri, A. (1962): *Biochim. Biophys. Acta,* 59:487–489.
12. Sullivan, A. C., Hamilton, J. G., Miller, O. N., and Wheatley, V. R. (1972): *Arch. Biochem. Biophys.,* 150:183–190.
13. Sullivan, A. C., Triscari, J., Hamilton, J. G., Miller, O. N., and Wheatley, V. R., (1974): *Lipids,* 9:121–128.
14. Sullivan, A. C. (1975): In: *Modification of Lipid Metabolism,* edited by E. G. Perkins and L. Witting. Academic Press, New York.
15. Sullivan, A. C., Triscari, J., Hamilton, J. G., and Miller, O. N. (1974): *Lipids,* 9:129–134.
16. Sullivan, A. C., Miller, O. N., Wittman, J. S., and Hamilton, J. G. (1971): *J. Nutr.,* 101:265–272.

17. Jungas, R. L. (1968): *Biochemistry,* 7:3708–3717.
18. Good, C. A., Kramer, H., and Somogyi, M. (1933): *J. Biol. Chem.,* 100:485–491.
19. Wittman, J. S., and Bawin, R. R. (1972): *Biochim. Biophys. Acta,* 273:119–121.
20. Hales, C. N., and Randle, P. J. (1963): *Biochem. J.,* 88:137–146.
21. Dalton, C., and Kowalski, C. (1967): *Clin. Chem.,* 13:744–751.
22. Russek, M., and Stevenson, J. A. F. (1972): *Physiol. Behav.,* 8:245–249.
23. Russek, M. (1970): *Physiol. Behav.,* 5:1207–1209.
24. Niijima, A. (1969): *Ann. NY Acad. Sci.,* 157:690–700.
25. Novin, D., Vanderweele, D. A., and Rezek, M. (1973): *Science,* 181:858–860.
26. Vanderweele, D. A., Novin, D., Rezek, M., and Sanderson, J. D. (1974): *Physiol. Behav.,* 12:467–473.
27. Pi-Sunyer, F. X. (1971): *Diabetes,* 20:200–205.
28. Campbell, R. G., and Hashim, S. A. (1972): *Proc. Soc. Exp. Biol. Med.,* 141:652–655.
29. Campbell, R. G., and Hashim, S. A. (1969): *Am. J. Physiol.,* 217:1614–1618.
30. Quartermain, D., Judge, M. E., and Van Itallie, T. B. (1973): *Proc. Soc. Exp. Biol. Med.,* 143:929–931.
31. Booth, D. A., and Toates, F. M. (1974): *Bull. Psychon. Soc.,* 3:442–444.
32. Toates, F. M., and Booth, D. A. (1974): *Nature,* 251:710–711.
33. Sollenberg, J., and Sorbo, B. (1970): *J. Neurochem.,* 17:201–207.
34. Oomura, Y., Ooyama, H., Yamamoto, T., Oto, T., and Kobayashi, N. (1969): *Ann. NY Acad. Sci.,* 157:642–665.
35. Soulairac, A. (1969): *Ann. NY Acad. Sci.,* 157:934–961.

Hunger: Basic Mechanisms and Clinical Implications,
edited by D. Novin, W. Wyrwicka, and G. Bray.
Raven Press, New York © 1976.

Control System for Hunger and its Implications in Animals and Man

D. A. Booth, F. M. Toates,* and S. V. Platt

Department of Psychology, University of Birmingham, Birmingham B15 2TT, England and *Psychology Division, Preston Polytechnic, Preston, England

METABOLIC INFLUENCE ON HUNGER

The current multifactor approach to the explanation of hunger includes a role for influences of bodily metabolism. The most widely favored idea appears to be that metabolism of glucose in a specialized part of the central or peripheral nervous system produces short-term inhibitory effects, and some representation of adipose triglyceride stores produces adjustments in food intake which promote the long-term precision of energy regulation.

These metabolic hunger signals are unlikely to be identified without techniques to separate normal metabolic influences on feeding from confounding nonmetabolic effects. The remarkable fact is that, in the 20 years of the glucostatic and lipostatic theories, there has been no proof that metabolism of ingested food affects hunger at all, let alone an experimental paradigm in which metabolic factors could be studied in isolation.

Postabsorptive Satiation

The first such proof and paradigm was reported in Cambridge in 1971 (Fourth International Conference on the Regulation of Food and Water Intake; see Introduction in ref. 1) and is at last due to be published in full (2). It depends on the very simple maneuver of waiting for all the ingested food to be absorbed in an otherwise little-deprived rat and then testing for a residual inhibitory effect on feeding. Under conditions of fast absorption (by night in the rat), hunger is lessened for 1 hr or more after all the original load has passed from the stomach and intestine. The effect does not depend on the nutrient having passed the mouth, nor on the release of intestinal hormones during absorption. The strength of the effect appears to relate to the speed with which an absorbed nutrient is used for energy by the liver— fructose given intraportally being more effective than glucose, and galactose being ineffective.

In retrospect, it is unfortunate that experimenters have generally used starved animals, hypertonic hydrolyzed nutrients, unnatural routes and rates of administration, and the drastic metabolic insults resulting from large doses of insulin or 2-deoxyglucose. An insistence on arbitrary criteria of good experimental control—large effects, small variance—has only served to obscure the important phenomena. If what matters is the normal satiating effect of food, then one will use animals that are at most mildly deprived, administer chow or its major components (i.e., starch, with some protein), and expect changes in food intake similar in size to the imposed variation in nutrient input. A proportionately small, fairly variable effect will then (if statistically reliable) have some chance of being relevant to normal hunger control.

Ventromedial Hypothalamus is Not the Metabolic Satiety Center

One application of the postabsorptive satiation paradigm to scientific problems of obesity would be to test the hypothesis that metabolic influences on feeding act via receptors in the ventromedial hypothalamus (VMH). If that were so, the rat with bilateral VMH lesions should fail to suppress food intake following complete absorption of a nutrient load.

The notion that the VMH is the satiety center has recently been strongly challenged on a number of grounds (3–5). Nevertheless, such an experiment is crucial because the existing literature fails to show whether or not tissue in the VMH is important in the inhibition of feeding specifically by metabolism. Earlier experiments in which VMH rats show no deficit did not look at normal metabolic influences on hunger, but either at the colligative effects of concentrated solutions in the gut or at the cellular glucopenic stimulus, which is thought not to have a role in normal feeding. Abnormalities in responses to nutrients have been reported but they are attributable to taste hypersensitivity (6), to overreactivity (7) during stress induced by intraperitoneal glucose (8), or to hormonal deficits crucial under extended deprivation (4).

The postabsorptive satiety effect of a meal-sized load of chow or starch in intact rats was suitably small—approximately the size of the load (Table 1). Rats with ventromedial lesions showed normal suppression of food intake following absorption. These were bilateral anodal lesions (0.5 to 1.1 mA, 15 to 30 sec) which completely destroyed the VMH nuclei and generally damaged tissue laterally and dorsally out to the fornix and ventrally to the base of the brain. Rats with similar size lesions dorsal and lateral to the fornix showed satiety deficits. The extensive anterior elaboration of this critical area will be reported in detail elsewhere. If there are diencephalic metabolic receptors controlling feeding, they may be perifornical, like the tissue mediating endocrine responses to cellular glucopenia (9).

Postabsorptive Satiety in Man

We are much further from proving the existence of metabolic satiation in man, but we do have a satiety effect which is harder than most to attribute to

TABLE 1. *Inhibition of food intake following absorption of loads*

Group	Mean food intake in 2 hr test					Satiety effect					
	Body weight gain (g)	after nothing (g)	after saccharin (g)	after 1 g starch (g)	after 2 g chow (g)	nothing minus starch		saccharin minus starch		nothing minus chow	
						SEM	p	SEM	p	SEM	p
Intact	57	7.71	7.93	6.52	6.21	0.32	0.01	0.28	0.001	0.64	0.1
Ventromedial lesion	178	6.48	6.62	6.55	4.58	0.12	0.001	0.26	0.01	0.14	0.001
Dorsolateral lesion	51	6.45	6.36	6.46	6.51	0.09	>0.1[a,b]	0.07	>0.1[a]	0.22	>0.1[b]

Maintenance chow powder was removed for 5 hr in the dark phase. Loads taken voluntarily 2 hr before refeeding, leaving time for complete absorption (2). There were four male and four female rats in each group. No dorsolateral rat had been aphagic. Satiety effect differs from that in [a]intact group and [b]ventromedial group by Mann-Whitney U test (p < 0.05).

p-values, mean difference from zero by correlated t test.

preabsorptive mechanisms. It too correlates with rapid absorption of ready energy.

In 1970, we reported that the 50-g load of glucose typically given in glucose tolerance tests had a suppressant effect on food intake in man not dependent on its sweet taste (10). Shortly after that work, we found that the same amount of starch, which has negligible osmotic effects in the lumen of the gastrointestinal tract, had indistinguishable suppressant effects on intake of ordinary foods in undeprived human subjects. The maximum effect was also delayed by 10 to 20 min in many subjects. When the concentrated starch load was given by stomach tube to remove mediation by taste, blood glucose concentration started to rise within 5 min of intubation. The rise over the first 20 min was so fast that it overtook the more rapidly initiated hyperglycemia resulting from a gastric load of the same amount and concentration of glucose. Most of the starch load but less of the glucose load was lost from the stomach within 10 min of loading. The same lag in digestion which delayed the onset of hyperglycemia presumably delayed the onset of appropriately strong inhibition of gastric evacuation by the action of starch-derived glucose on the duodenal osmoreceptors.

The contrast in satiating effects between starch and carboxymethylcellulose in suitably disguised concentrated loads provides a suitable manipulation for sensitivity training in people who seem insufficiently aware of postingestive satiation.

QUANTITATIVE MODEL OF METABOLIC CONTROL OF FEEDING

Once having proved that metabolism can affect feeding, we became increasingly impressed with the way intermeal intervals, the amount taken in meals, and the cumulative total intake all respond rapidly to suitably moderate imposed variations in energy input of any sort (1, 11). Even the less direct influences of conditioning or learning on the control of food intake were strikingly dependent on effects that seemed likely to be metabolic (12–14).

At times, multifactor theorizing seemed to be little more than the trivial assertion that feeding can be affected by almost anything. It was a tempting strategy to reject that orientation and to erect an alternative working hypothesis that the single basic controlling influence was energy supply. Russek (15) tried to explain all hunger phenomena by a hepatic glucoreceptor and many of his arguments could be transferred to an energostatic theory. The plethora of glucostats, aminostats, thermostats, and lipostats could be unified by the biochemically obvious step of invoking the Krebs cycle and cellular respiration (16). The long-standing biochemical concept that the liver uses any available energy substrate to spare the supply of glucose for the brain (and the pancreas) could point to a link between peripheral energy metabolism and central or local glucoreceptor systems. With such a control mecha-

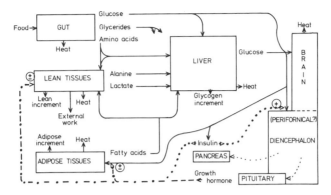

FIG. 1. Some major energy flows between tissues in the laboratory rat and their hormonal modulation.

nism, there would be no need for biochemically separate representation of fat metabolism in the brain.

A crude abstract of current views on the metabolite transfers and conversions between and within the organs of the body is given in Fig. 1. By coincidence or by confluence of thought, data have recently become available providing a bare minimum for even cruder estimates of the division of metabolizable energy supply between tissues similar to the hunger receptor and dissimilar tissues.

Absorption

By far the largest and most variable energy supply is absorption from the intestine. In the rat, this is considerably faster by night than by day (Fig. 2). The clearance function in spontaneously feeding rats appears to be similar to that more easily measured in mildly deprived and refed animals (Fig. 2, dark phase). Probably because under our conditions there is sufficient food in the duodenum to keep gastric evacuation under normal control, we do not find the inordinate rush of food to the intestine which is seen immediately after a meal in starved rats (17). Nevertheless, the stomach is emptying much faster at that stage, and so digestive enzyme secretion must be fast and anticipatory.

Our data on the clearance of glucose loads, either mixed with chow (11) or not (2; see also Fig. 2), and of chow meals (Fig. 2) are linearized better by square-root functions than by exponentials. Furthermore, when we substitute the best-fit exponential functions for the square-root gut-clearance functions in Mark 1 of our energy flow model of feeding control (18), the meal pattern predictions are wildly unrealistic, especially in the dark phase (Table 2). Hopkins (19) pointed out that a square-root relationship would be expected if the fundal-duodenal pump were controlled by a balloon-like response of the antrum to its volume of contents. However, we should not wax too meta-

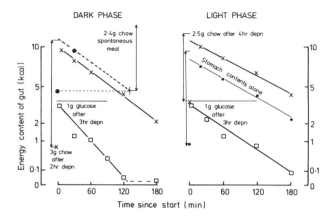

FIG. 2. Energy absorption from gut—metabolizable energy equivalent of dry weight recovered from stomach and small intestine of the rat (two to three rats per point). X, food-deprived rats permitted to consume a fixed amount of maintenance chow (vertical bar); ● (dark phase only), gut contents at start of spontaneous meal in freely fed rats, and 30 min later (clearance line by extrapolation to the mean inter-meal interval of 130 min); □, clearance of a glucose load (2). Note that gut contents are given on a square-root scale.

physical about the square-root function. In other circumstances, exponential or even linear equations might fit better.

Laboratory chow is typically half starch, one-fifth to one-quarter protein, and a very few percent triglyceride and other fats. In our initial model, to transform our glucose clearance data into estimates of chow clearance, we ignored the fat content of chow (Fig. 1) and took starch and protein to be calorically equivalent to glucose. However, not only do we have some chow clearance data but also Hunt and Stubbs (20) have argued (from a collation of data on human gastric emptying) that the characteristics of the controlling duodenal receptors are such that the stomach clears and absorption proceeds according to energy yield independently of the proportions of carbohydrate, protein, and fat. If this generalization proves sufficiently robust and precise, then we will need details of the time-course of clearance for only one representative dietary mixture.

TABLE 2. Gut clearance function (Mark I)

	Square root	Exponential
Light phase		
Amount eaten (g)	7.6	5.1
Number of meals	3	5
Mean meal size (g)	2.6	1.0
Dark phase		
Amount eaten (g)	13.0	12.7
Number of meals	7	22
Mean meal size (g)	1.9	0.6

Circadian Variation in Energy Storage and Expenditure

We allowed for the circadian rhythm in fat deposition and mobilization in the earlier versions of the model (18, 21). The heat production rhythm is estimated on the basis of metabolic rate values in the current version (Fig. 3). We used the 2-hr averages estimated from respiratory data for 10 rats by Le Magnen and Devos (22). Le Magnen et al. (23) give RQs and metabolic rates based on 20 rats and we now use values calculated from their Fig. 2 using the earlier equations (22); this gives a lower metabolic rate and a much less marked lipogenesis-lipolysis cycle. Note that such data serve the model as interim estimates of energy diverted away from (and fed to) the receptor system by consumption in different types of tissue. The lipid function is not total energy storage, which would include growth in lean mass. Also, metabolic rate is not used to model total energy flow between the organism and the environment.

Shorter-term variations in energy disposition will be incorporated into later versions of the model. We shall have to use respiratory data initially, although they are subject to activity artifacts under such conditions. The small change in metabolic rate around meals (22, 24), and many other types of experi-

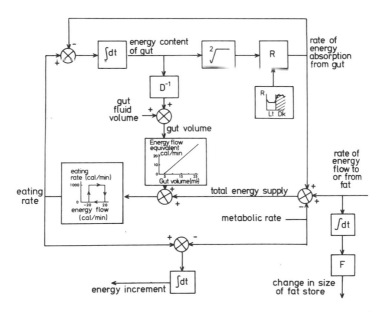

FIG. 3. Feeding model Mark 2D. The system is mathematically determinate and all functions and values are specified by physiological measurements. R, gut clearance rate constant (usually a large fraction of unity); D, energy density of food (cal/g); F, energy density of fat. The integrals are in fact programmed as successive additions, e.g., at 10-sec intervals. The model will predict temporal patterns of feeding bouts, gut contents, actual or virtual inhibition or facilitation of feeding by energy supply, change in total body energy.

ments, clearly indicate large changes in net metabolite flows into adipose tissue, liver, and muscle in parallel to absorption. Eventually it should be possible to model the control of these energy distributions at the level of interactions between absorption and hormone secretion in the way that blood glucose has been modeled.

Hunger and Satiety Thresholds

From gut clearance rates at the start and finish of meals (Fig. 2) and from hepatic portal infusion rates that just fail to prevent the release of feeding and just succeed in suppressing feeding altogether (25), we estimated absorption rates at which feeding was switched on or off in the rat with continuous access to a single familiar diet. Allowing for a metabolic rate of approximately 40 cal/min in Mark 2 (Fig. 3), the threshold values we used in Mark 1 (18, 21) become approximately −20 and +20 cal/min. This symmetry, and rounding to the decade, is well within the error limits on the absorption threshold data. As long as data do not preclude the notion, we like the idea of only one receptor system which operates with a null point of zero net energy flow and has a detection problem approximately equal for energy consumption and energy excess. The predictions of the model are not highly sensitive to the value of symmetrical thresholds in the 15 to 25 cal/min range. Asymmetry is more serious, especially for the energy increment predictions (*in preparation*).

Nearly all receptors respond to a flux of material or energy or to a partial pressure (concentration, force). The adequate stimulus to the metabolic hunger receptor may prove to be concentration of glucose at the neuronal membrane or of some metabolite within the cell, but the necessary combination of neurophysiology, biochemistry, and behavior to elucidate the matter is still some way off. Even then, the functional stimulus could still be the speed at which energy is being supplied. Engineers find proportional control very useful to add to the stability of a control system. If a flow rate is tightly coupled to the quantity held in a source (e.g., as with gut clearance in the model), control according to instantaneous flow rate will stabilize quantity in the absence of any set point for amount in the system. Our provisional commitment to a rate-sensing system was clinched by the fact that approximate estimates of the major variations in energy flow are currently practicable, whereas data on quantities of crucial metabolites or body constituents are not as readily available.

Distension at Large Gut Volumes

When we modeled the diabetic rat as having insensitive energy flow receptors (21), meals large enough to burst the stomach were predicted in the absence of inhibition from distension. Unfortunately, we cannot locate useable rat data on distension receptors, and none of the electrophysiological work is directly related to behavior. We therefore use Paintal's (25) data on the effects of antral distension on vagal firing rate in the cat. The volumes are divided by 10, scaling down relative to body weight. Complete inhibition purely from distension is set at the physical limit of rat stomach volume (40 ml). In Mark 2 with distension (Mark 2D, Fig. 3), this inhibition is calculated as a virtual energy flow. It could be a real energy flow if distension inhibits via a glycogenolytic reflex (15). Gut volume is calculated by multiplying the energy content of the gut by the reciprocal of the energy density of food and adding an equal volume of fluid, which is what drinking, salivation, and gastrointestinal secretion are attuned to do (27).

Eating Rate

We model the food energy input rate as either zero or constant. Under some conditions, eating rate at the beginning of a meal shows a transient acceleration as a joint function of dietary palatability and duration of prior food deprivation. This has been interpreted as reflecting a positive feedback mechanism, serving to lock the animal into persistent feeding activity. Also, it is widely supposed that ingestion rate steadily goes down toward the end of a bout, although this impression may largely be an artifact of grouping data from animals or occasions when bouts at nearly constant rate end at different times. In our experience of rats with continuous access to chow a mouthful at a time (28, 29), these accelerative and decelerative phases are relatively short and often undetectable. Immediately graspable pellets of normal palatability are taken at approximately 300 mg/min, which (at an energy density of 3.4 kcal/g) gives the modeled rate of 1 kcal/min.

Predictions from the Model

The above hypothetical system generates predictions of feeding behavior and body energy increments solely on the basis of interacting physiological components whose functions and values have been specified by experimental data. Earlier feeding models have not achieved this empirical reduction. We believe physiologizing in psychology to be more often pernicious than helpful. Nevertheless, in this case it works.

Intact Freely Fed Rat

The predictions of *ad libitum* feeding from Mark 2D, using the same data as Mark 1, are almost identical to those of the model without distension and the small circadian heat output cycle (21). Using the more recent data on gut clearance and respiration specified above, phasing the slowing of clearance immediately after dawn, and setting chow at 3.2 kcal/g for Le Magnen's laboratory, the model predicts real behavior quite precisely: night intake 13 g and day intake 3.8 g [14 g and 3.5 g observed (23)].

A determinate model with stationary physiological functions naturally predicts unrealistically low variance. Feeding is subject to competition from other activities and motivations. In most laboratory conditions, feeding is also subject to facilitation by random arousing exogenous stimuli. Noise in the feeding onset threshold would roughly model these influences until there are useable theoretical accounts of them. Variation also enters the feeding offset threshold by learning (see below). These additions to the model (creating Mark 3) should produce realistic variability in feeding parameters with little alteration in the already realistic mean values.

Feeding Following Food Deprivation

Unfortunately, there are no respiratory data for rats unexpectedly deprived of food. After 12 hr of daytime deprivation, lipolysis should be substantial, perhaps 10 cal/min. Onset of feeding very rapidly builds up lipogenesis—linearly over 25 min to a value of 35 cal/min—which persists for some time. Mark 2D (Fig. 3) predicts a meal of 4.0 g on refeeding at the start of the dark phase, and an interval of 116 min to the next meal. Values of 4.0 g and 110 min have been reported for real rats (30).

In the model, distension contributes to satiety onset with a meal of that size, although metabolism still has some influence. The size of the first meal on refeeding increases rapidly with recycling through a deprivation schedule (30). Learned desatiation (see below) would explain this, perhaps also with gastric adaptation. When the Mark 2 model allows merely for the metabolic adaptations (23), it does not predict the very large meals observed. Extended prior deprivation eliminates the satiating metabolic effects of recently ingested nutrient (2; see above). It is eccentric (31) to extrapolate to reasonably nourished rats the results of experiments in rats adapted to recovery from starvation.

The model quantitatively substantiates some of Le Magnen's (23) suggestions about the effectiveness of lipolysis at inhibiting hunger. The peak of lipolysis during the day in the freely fed rat is indeed sufficiently high on the earlier data (22) to suppress hunger until the gut is nearly empty and even then to permit only a small meal. An otherwise normal rat chronically force-fed and then left, loses fat at a rate of more than 20 cal/min. Even if metabolic rate remains as high as 40 cal/min, this abnormal lipolysis is sufficient to keep energy flow above the threshold for feeding onset in the model. Thus energy flow explains the anorexia after fattening by insulin, electrical stimulation, or tubing. It could also explain much of cachexic anorexia (32).

VMH Lesions

Mark 1 of the model qualitatively predicted many of the features of feeding behavior in the dynamic and static phases of VMH obesity (18). Mark 2D predicts similar behavior when recently reported respiratory data (23) are substituted for the assumed lipogenesis values of Booth and Toates (18). The onus of proof is now placed on any claim that ventromedial hyperphagia is entirely a behavioral abnormality. However, we lack sufficient physiological data for the model to determine if the food intake changes can be entirely accounted for by physiological consequences of the autonomic and endocrine effects of the lesions. Circadian metabolic variations can be estimated from Le Magnen's respiratory data (23), but nobody yet has gut clearance functions for VMH preparations. When normal gut functions are assumed (18), neither Mark 1 (18) nor Mark 2D predicts as extreme an increase in food intake and precisely the same distortion in meal pattern as generally seen. According to the model, abnormalities in sensory reactivity (as expressed in changed feeding rate) do not produce sufficiently dramatic differences in intake. Sensory-dependent hormonal effects are already allowed for by the metabolic data. The evidence is against substantial changes in feeding offset thresholds (see above). We predict that one of the next primary effects of VMH lesions to be discovered will be abnormal gastrointestinal control, even when weight and feeding pattern are normalized. Mark 2D with respiratory values from VMH rats (23) and the same clearance rate by day as by night (0.8) predicts a realistic 15 g daytime intake in much more realistic 2.5 g meals (2.7 g with no distension loop) at 122-min intervals.

This discussion illustrates an important merit of quantitative control theory —reciprocal feedback interactions are mechanically calculated. Verbal theorizing about the effects of feeding on lipid metabolism and the effects of lipid metabolism on feeding can sound circular. Intuitions on the net properties of the hypothetical system are easily doubted. Computer models are neither an entertaining luxury nor a fearful bogey in physiology and psychology. They will increasingly become a necessity in theory construction and testing.

Long-Term Regulation of Energy Exchange

The predicted energy increment varies little from day to day in the present model, and the cumulative average daily increment is highly stable. The value of the average increment would be further stabilized if the net energy supply to the receptor system controlling feeding was even weakly coupled to the size of the body energy store or in particular to the amount of triglyceride in adipose tissue. If, for example, large cells leaked glycerol faster or if as triglyceride content rose above a certain level insulin became rapidly less effective at reversing lipolysis, the present model would adjust food intake to limit adiposity. The characteristics of this long-term regulation cannot of course be stated until such a physiological mechanism has been identified in a form that can be modeled and the relevant computations run; yet the qualitative tendency is clear.

Note that such a system does not rely on an accurate signal of fat store size. Neither stability nor precision requires a signal to the nervous system which is independent of the general metabolic signal reflecting net energy flow to receptor-like tissues.

Regulation with No Set-Point Mechanism

The stability of such a system of fat store size could be mathematically equivalent to a set-point function, but there is no set-point mechanism involved, no receptor specific to a signal from the fat store, no system to generate a precise reference value, and no comparator mechanism to compute the error value. If stable or defended value is meant, the term set point should not be substituted because presuppositions from engineering then encourage experimenters to look for unnecessarily complex systems in biology. To regulate body weight, a male rat would need a clock to say what age it was, a map of its proper growth curve (yet to be satisfactorily described mathematically!), a sensor—in the soles of its feet (33)?—of its current body weight, and a reading mechanism to compare them all. There is no evidence for regulation in this sense. Simple physical properties of different parts of the body can readily maintain the powerful observable homeostasis and homeorhesis. For example, if the rate of intestinal absorption of an unmetabolized substance is a decreasing function of its blood concentration and the rate of renal excretion is an increasing function of blood concentration, then blood concentration of that substance will return rapidly and precisely to a preferred value determined by those transport characteristics at widely separated sites, with no receptors and no communication—let alone comparison and error-correcting feedback.

The productive question is likely to be how the metabolite flow into and out of adipose tissue is influenced by the amount of triglyceride in the tissue, not how the brain could build a precise representation of the amount of fat in the body and adjust behavior according to some standard. An energy flow theory can, for example, explain the VMH syndrome without any body-weight set point, let alone two set points and postulated splits of a unitary system into drive and incentive components (34, 35). Energy flow into fat because of taste-triggered endocrine reactions would explain short latencies and large meals on palatable food *ad libitum*. Energy flow from fat during acute deprivation would explain poor motivation (see deprived rat, above) and its normalcy in slimmed VMH rats.

INDIRECT METABOLIC CONTROL

Functional analysis of the asymptotic performance of a fully adapted system tells us little of the processing or structure which directly controls behavior. The relative success of the feeding model for rats adapted to a single familiar diet is not evidence that hunger is under direct instantaneous control by variations in current energy supply to tissues. Such close adaptation to current supply could be achieved by behavior that depends on interpretation of present events according to past experience of their consequences for energy flows.

Acquired Sensory Control of Energy Intake Rate

Long-established conditioned or learned reactions to orosensory cues in anticipation of energy yield could be a major determinant of chow-eating rate. Ingestion of solids in the infant (14), adult taste preferences (12) and aversions (13, 36, 37), and the operant or adjunctive lever-press to feed intravenously (38) all appear to be acquired largely by energy yields conditioning the reactions of the rat to sensory or internal sensations. There is some relation between the two-stimulus preference for a diet and the rate of ingestion of that diet alone (39, 40). This effect may not greatly influence single-diet intake rate, except at extremes of palatability. When a choice of foodstuffs is provided, however, energy-conditioned preferences would strongly influence the average rate of energy intake during the meal. In the model, a change in energy input rate has definite although small effects on meal size and other variables.

Acquired Sensory Control of Satiety Threshold

One of the most remarkable statements in the model is that the major contribution to the inhibition of feeding that ends a meal *ad libitum* comes from the energy flow of absorption. It has often been assumed that gastric clearance and intestinal digestion are too slow for absorbed nutrients to make any contribution to the onset of satiety. This alternative extreme is certainly false. Relevant findings in man have already been mentioned. Radioactivity from starch taken on an empty stomach has begun to be digested, absorbed, and transported into the rat brain in much less than 5 min from the start of ingestion (41). With some food from the previous meal still in the stomach, at least the initial parts of the new meal mostly pass immediately into the intestine, which contains abundant enzymes under those conditions.

Thus absorption starts very early and can gather pace extremely rapidly. Nevertheless, the physics of transporting energy from the mouth to a receptor tissue would impose a delay of many seconds between final ingestion and peak absorption, even if the biochemistry and physiology did not expand it to 2 to 10 minutes. Introducing such a lag into the absorption loop of the model would produce much larger meals.

If the success of the model truly reflects the ultimate controlling factor in feeding, real rats must be anticipating peak energy absorption. Engineers use acceleration rather than rate, a principle that has been suggested for satiety

(15, 42). The initial pulse of insulin secretion could amplify the submaximal flow of glucose at an insulin-sensitive receptor. What certainly does occur in the rat is the acquisition and maintenance of oral sensory control of the end of a meal, reinforced or conditioned by the eventual rate of carbohydrate absorption (13, 37). The effect may be purely central or it could be mediated by conditioned oral control of insulin secretion (43).

Addition to Feeding Model

The phenomenon could be represented in the model as a sensory driving of a reduction in the off-threshold by the amount that peak absorption exceeded 20 cal/min on previous occasions following ingestion of food having that sensory quality. Meal size would then approach that producing a peak absorption of 20 cal/min after some delay (Mark 3).

Acquired Sensory Satiety in Man

People also rapidly acquire feeding offset differentiation according to previous experience of the after effects of ingesting food of a particular flavor (44). Differential aftereffects were generated by disguised starch loads immediately before the otherwise normal sandwich lunches. Most of the acquired sensory control of meal size was vested in the unfamiliar flavor possessed by a slightly modified yogurt dessert (Fig. 4). The response was not deliberate, even if it was instrumental: conditioned subjects did not seem to be aware of their differentiation of behavior, nor did they consistently report any perception of the dessert or the starch load which could account for the anticipatory use of the flavor cue. Nevertheless, such differentiation is likely to enter awareness in some cases or in due course, and we would not doubt that an element of thought and calculation can and often does enter the control of human feeding.

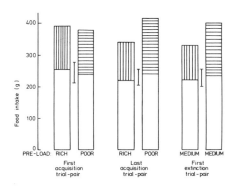

FIG. 4. Acquired oral control of satiation in man (44). Each column is mean lunch size under one condition (n = 8). A load which was rich, poor, or medium in starch content was given immediately before lunch. Vertical hatching, intake of dessert of a flavor following the rich load during acquisition; horizontal hatching, flavor paired with poor load; vertical line, SD of difference in amounts of dessert taken (this difference and total meal size difference at last acquisition lunches and first extinction lunches, p < 0.01).

The sensitivity of these people's feeding behavior to postprandial consequences was sufficient to establish an anticipatory response difference almost equal in energy to the energy difference imposed in the starch loads. Clearly, this behavior cannot coherently be described as a straight summation of internal (or drive) influences and external (or incentive) influences. The two are in continuous cognitive interaction, in or out of awareness. Systematic training according to this acquired sensory satiation paradigm could be at least as helpful in weight control as the use of direct subjective effects of starch loads suggested earlier. Anticipatory control of feeding offset may be particularly important for man in societies like ours, because other behavioral mechanisms for regulating energy balance have little chance to operate— social factors largely determine feeding onset and the size of a meal is often fixed at its beginning when the plate or tray is filled.

EXTENSIONS OF THE PHYSIOLOGICAL CONTROL THEORY

This simplified quantitative theory, particularly when elaborated to include learning and other refinements of the sensory control of feeding, may be applicable to economically or clinically important problems.

Ruminant Model

Physiological data on gut contents and the energy flow from absorption of short-chain fatty acids are available for sheep and other economically important ruminants. The thus far successful inclusion of a distension loop in Mark 2 for the rat encourages the hope that these theoretical principles will prove to be applicable with the diets of low-energy density common in animal production (45–47).

Human Model

It is ethically and technically feasible to obtain estimates of energy flows in lean or obese subjects that would provide a data base homologous to that used in the rat model. The physiological reduction of human hunger could then be attempted. Given the data and arguments on human feeding presented in this chapter, it is quite conceivable that some realistic predictions will be possible, at least in lean subjects, from a model that allows for indirect as well as direct metabolic control, and specifies many social factors as limits on the availability of food. The model could well give the most illuminating account yet of the unfortunate and complex interactions between behavior and physiology in the obese subject. In principle, it might provide an individually tailored specification for an optimum and stable feeding schedule at which behavior modification could be aimed.

ACKNOWLEDGMENTS

This work was supported by the British Nutrition Foundation, the U. K. Medical Research Council, and the European Training Programme for Brain and Behaviour Research.

REFERENCES

1. Booth, D. A. (1972): *Physiol. Behav.,* 9:199–202.
2. Booth, D. A., and Jarman, S. P. (1976): *J. Physiol. (Lond.) (In press.)*
3. Grossman, S. P. (1968): *Fed. Proc.,* 27:1349–1355.
4. Panksepp, J. (1971): *Physiol. Behav.,* 7:381–384.
5. Rabin, B. R. (1972): *Brain Res.,* 43:317–325.
6. Sclafani, A. (1973): *Physiol. Behav.,* 11:771–780.
7. Grossman, S. P. (1966): *Physiol. Behav.,* 1:1–10.
8. Reynolds, R. W., and Kimm, J. (1965): *J. Comp. Physiol. Psychol.,* 60:438–440.
9. Himsworth, R. L., Carmel, P. W., and Frantz, A. G. (1972): *Endocrinology,* 91:217–226.
10. Booth, D. A., Campbell, A. T., and Chase, A. (1970): *Nature,* 228:1104–1105.
11. Booth, D. A. (1972): *J. Comp. Physiol. Psychol.,* 78:412–432.
12. Booth, D. A., Lovett, D., and McSherry, G. M. (1972): *J. Comp. Physiol. Psychol.,* 78:485–512.
13. Booth, D. A., and Davis, J. D. (1973): *Physiol. Behav.,* 11:23–29.
14. Booth, D. A., Stoloff, R., and Nicholls, J. (1974): *Physiol. Psychol.,* 2:313–319.
15. Russek, M. (1971): *Neurosci. Res.,* 4:213–282.
16. Ugolev, A. M., and Kassil, V. G. (1961): *Uspekhi. Sov. Biol.,* 51:352–368.
17. Wiepkema, P. R., Prins, J., and Steffens, A. B. (1972): *Physiol. Behav.,* 9:759–763.
18. Booth, D. A., and Toates, F. M. (1974): *Bull. Psychon. Soc.,* 3:442–444.
19. Hopkins, A. (1966): *J. Physiol. (Lond.),* 182:144–149.
20. Hunt, J. N., and Stubbs, D. F. (1974): *J. Physiol., (Lond.),* 245:209–225.
21. Toates, F. M., and Booth, D. A. (1974): *Nature,* 251:710–711.
22. Le Magnen, J., and Devos, M. (1970): *Physiol. Behav.,* 5:805–814.
23. Le Magnen, J., Devos, M., Gaudilliere, J. P., Louis-Sylvestre, J., and Tallon, S. (1973): *J. Comp. Physiol. Psychol.,* 84:1–23.
24. Morrison, S. D. (1968): *J. Physiol. (Lond.),* 197:305–323.
25. Campbell, C. S., and Davis, J. D. (1974): *Physiol. Behav.,* 12:377–384.
26. Paintal, A. S. (1954): *J. Physiol. (Lond.),* 126:255–265.
27. Oatley, K., and Toates, F. M. (1969): *Psychon. Sci.,* 16:225–226.
28. Booth, D. A. (1972): *J. Comp. Physiol. Psychol.,* 80:238–249.
29. Booth, D. A., and Campbell, C. S. (1975): *J. Physiol. (Paris),* 58:143–154.
30. Le Magnen, J., and Tallon, S. (1968): *J. Physiol. (Paris),* 58:143–154.
31. Young, R. C., Gibbs, J., Antin, J., Holt, J., and Smith, G. P. (1974): *J. Comp. Physiol. Psychol.,* 87:795–800.
32. Theologides, A. (1974): *Ann. NY Acad. Sci.,* 230:14–22.
33. Johnsen, S. G. (1973): *Ugeskrift Laeger,* 135:2751–2754.
34. Sclafani, A. (1974): *J. Comp. Physiol. Psychol.,* 86:28–46.
35. Franklin, K. B. J., and Herberg, L. J. (1974): *J. Comp. Physiol. Psychol.,* 87:410–414.
36. Booth, D. A. (1972): *Physiol. Behav.,* 8:891–899.
37. Booth, D. A. (1972): *J. Comp. Physiol. Psychol.,* 81:457–471.
38. Holman, G. L. (1969): *J. Comp. Physiol. Psychol.,* 69:432–441.
39. Young, P. T., and Trafton, C. W. (1964): *J. Comp. Physiol. Psychol.,* 58:68–75.
40. Davis, J. D. (1973): *Physiol. Behav.,* 11:39–45.
41. Pilcher, C. W. T., Jarman, S. P., and Booth, D. A. (1974): *J. Comp. Physiol. Psychol.,* 87:56–61.

42. Nicolaidis, S., and Rowland, N. (1974): *Personal communication.*
43. Woods, S. C., and Porte, D. (1974): *Physiol. Rev.,* 54:596–619.
44. Booth, D. A., Lee, M., and McAleavey, C. (1975): *Br. J. Psychol. (In press.)*
45. Monteiro, L. S. (1972): *Anim. Prod.,* 14:263–281.
46. Baumgardt, B. R. (1970): In: *Proc. Third Internat. Symp. Physiology of Digestion and Metabolism in Ruminants,* pp. 235–253. Oriel Press, London.
47. Baile, C. A., and Forbes, J. M. (1974): *Physiol. Rev.,* 54:160–214.

Hunger: Basic Mechanisms and Clinical Implications,
edited by D. Novin, W. Wyrwicka, and G. Bray.
Raven Press, New York © 1976.

Significance of Glucose, Insulin, and Free Fatty Acid on the Hypothalamic Feeding and Satiety Neurons

Yutaka Oomura

Department of Physiology, Faculty of Medicine, Kyushu University, Fukuoka, 812, Japan

Mammalian feeding behavior is governed by the lateral hypothalamic (LH) area, the feeding center, and the ventromedial hypothalamus (VMH), the satiety center. When simultaneous recordings are made from these two locations during feeding behavior, it is found that one increases while the other decreases, in a reciprocal manner (1). Similar reciprocal activity can be observed during various other states such as sleep, arousal, and searching. Signals resulting from neuronal activity within these two areas are transmitted to other areas through the medial forebrain bundle and the dorsal longitudinal fasciculus. Signals from the LH and VMH intermingle in the midbrain reticular formations, then proceed to the motor nucleus of the vagus and to the trigeminal nucleus. However, both signals are also controlled by the amygdaloid nucleus (2), the globus pallidus along with other extrapyramidal systems (3), and the frontal cortex (4). In addition, the network receives somatosensory and proprioceptive signals from peripheral areas (5) via the reticular formation and the basal ganglia (6). Consequently, elicitation of precise feeding behavior is controlled by an extremely complex correlation between the feeding and satiety centers and other structures.

What source of activity in the feeding and satiety centers ultimately leads to appetite-associated behavior? Rats control caloric consumption at a relatively constant level regardless of caloric content of their food (7, 8), whether food intake is completely oral or partly supplied by a feeding tube (9). Such materials as glycine, ammonium sulfate, and ammonium content of amino acids are known to be anorexigenic. Consideration of abdominal organs as the source of such directives can be discounted since sectioning of the abdominal vagi, coelial ganglia, and all other nerves which could be found emanating from the liver and intestines resulted in only a temporary reduction of food intake, not complete aphagia (10, 11). Rats maintain their caloric input even after vagotomy prevents transfer of information from the stomach and liver glucoreceptors. When blood from a satiated rat was injected into a fasted rat, food intake of the latter was suppressed. When the process was repeated 5 hr after satiation, the acceptor rat increased its food intake (12). These facts expostulate the existence of an appetite control center that receives information from sources other than the gastrointestinal system and its associated organs, and which acts independently of such a system. It has been shown that certain chemical substances found in the blood will modify the spontaneous discharge rate of certain neurons in the LH and VMH. These chemosensitive neurons react to both the presence and the level of concentration of various chemicals in the blood to initiate feeding behavior.

It has been shown that glucose has a stimulating effect on about 30% of VMH neurons and 16% of LH neurons, whereas it has an inhibitory effect on approximately 30% of LH neurons (13). It has also been shown that insulin application along with glucose generally enhances the effect of glucose on VMH neurons, even though it tends to reverse the effects of glucose on LH neurons (13, 14). In light of subsequent verification of important parts of these data, there is no longer any doubt that certain VMH and LH neurons are able to discriminate blood composition both qualitatively and quantitatively, and respond to the analysis. Much work has been done on the relative effects of glucose and insulin on neurons in these two areas and any connections that they might have with hunger and satiety. To date, no clear-cut correlation between glucose level, its effects on neuronal activity, hunger, and overt manifestation of hunger has been demonstrated.

In the presence of hunger, the free fatty acid (FFA) concentration of blood increases. FFA has been tested on LH and VMH neurons and has elicited neuronal activity consistent with what is known of the connections between LH and VMH activity, and hunger satiety. The intent of this chapter is presentation of data and conclusions, which will demonstrate a close relation between blood concentration of FFA, effects of FFA on neuronal activity, and effects of neuronal activity on observable hunger-alleviating behavior.

Early investigations disclosed that injected glucose generally increased VMH activity and decreased LH activity (15). These effects were later verified by others. Because of the reciprocal relationship between the LH and the VMH, however, the primary effect on each was not clear. The answer to this question required direct application of glucose to the neuron being tested.

TECHNIQUES AND DEVICES

Electroapplication from a glass micropipette fulfills the requirement for direct application. A direct electric current through such a pipette will cause electrophoretic application of ionized chemicals or electroosmotic application of nonionized chemicals such as glucose, insulin, or FFA. In these experiments, multibarreled pipettes having seven barrels were used. These were made by drawing all seven pipettes simultaneously to an overall outside tip diameter of less than 1 μm. If the tip opening of any one barrel is too large, it becomes necessary to apply a backing current to the pipette to prevent spontaneous chemical leakage. Each pipette was filled with a different chemical solution for administration to the subject neuron. Using a binocular microscope, a recording electrode was cemented to the multibarreled electrode with its tip extending 10 to 30 μm beyond the multibarrel tip. The recording electrode was filled with 3 M KCL or 4 M NaCl. With the recording tip extending beyond the pipette tips, it becomes possible to record intracellularly while applying chemicals extracellularly.

Including the electrode and the organic matter in the circuit, it is not uncommon for the resistance to change during current flow. The tendency for resistance to increase is especially great when using nonionized chemicals. If this resistance change should cause a current change, it would be impossible to ascertain the exact amount of chemical released. To overcome such a problem, a constant current supply was employed to dispense the chemicals. The diagram of a constant current supply is shown in Fig. 1. Since this device has a maximum available output voltage of 120 V, a constant current of 0 to 120 nA can be supplied to any circuit with resistance, fixed or variable, up to a maximum of 10^9 Ω. All solutions were dissolved in 0.15 M/liter NaCl solution. The amount of chemical dispensed is then dependent on current $\times$ time (coulombs) only and is independent of concentration.

Wistar rats were used under urethan anesthesia (1.5 g/kg). Single neuronal discharges were recorded from the VMH and LH in the same frontal plane.

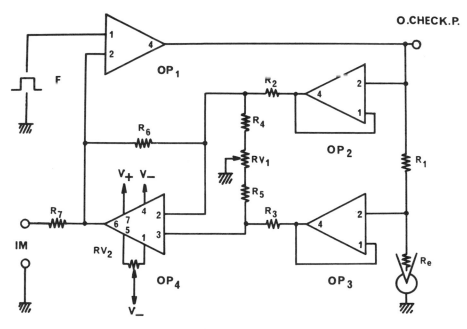

FIG. 1. Circuit diagram of constant current device for supplying constant d.c. current through very high resistance load. E, command voltage, controls constant current value; O.CHECK.P., this point should be zero, when input 2 of OP_3 is grounded and E = 0; RV_2, zero adjust for O.CHECK.P.; RV_1, common mode rejection balance to maximize constant current and allowable load resistance; IM, current monitor; OP_1, OP_2, OP_3, B-B IC 3460; OP_4, B-B 3500 C; R_1, 100 MΩ; R_2, R_3, 500 kΩ; R_4, R_5, 2 kΩ; RV_1, 500 Ω; R_6, 15 kΩ; RV_2, 2 kΩ; R_7, 50 kΩ.

EFFECT OF CHEMICALS

Amount of glucose applied was determined by using ^{14}C-glucose to calibrate the dispensing electrode in terms of amount of glucose expelled per unit of current. The average value found, for the pipettes used, was 5×10^{-12} M/μcoul of charge. The chemical effect of interest must be isolated and differentiated from the current and from the osmotic effects. The current effect is identified by its lack of latency at both onset and termination compared to the 500 to 1,000 msec latency of the chemical effect. Susceptibility of the involved neuron to nonspecific osmotic effects was determined by testing with NaCl or sucrose, for example. L-Glutamic acid, a nonspecific facilitating agent, was always applied first to confirm functioning of the entire system, including the subject neuron and the recording electrode.

Application of insulin was accomplished in a manner similar to that used for glucose, with ^{125}I-insulin used as the calibrating agent. Average emitted values of insulin were found to be 5×10^{-8} IU/μcoul.

Glucose and Insulin Effect

Glucose tends to increase the frequency of discharge of approximately ⅓ of the VMH neurons in a dose-response manner and to decrease the discharge frequency of glucose-sensitive neurons in the LH.

The taste equation describes the relationship between receptor sites on the tongue and molecules of taste stimulant (16). Assuming that the same relation exists between sites in the VMH or LH and glucose or insulin, respectively, the taste equation was applied to the dose-response data obtained for these chemicals. If R is the magnitude of response, R_s is its maximum value, and C is a measure of concentration, then the slope of a plot of $R/(R_s - R)$ against C should divulge the ratio of stimulus units per response site. Plots of these values for glucose and insulin both had slopes of 1:1; it therefore seemed reasonable to conclude that one molecule of glucose reacts with one glucoreceptor site and one molecule of insulin reacts with one insulin receptor site (14). The dose-response rate was such as to indicate one molecule uptake per glucoreceptive membrane site. The threshold level of glucose concentration was 2 mM (13) comparable to the normal rat blood glucose level of 5.5 mM.

Insulin alone tended to inhibit VMH neuronal discharge, but it enhanced the effects of glucose when both were applied simultaneously. In the LH, only glucose-sensitive neurons were affected by insulin, and they were excited in a dose-response manner which indicated a reaction for one molecule per receptor site. The threshold level for insulin effect was approximately 5×10^{-9} IU.

The effects of glucose, insulin, and glucose plus insulin are summarized in Fig. 2. Inhibition by insulin might be explained in terms of membrane hyper-

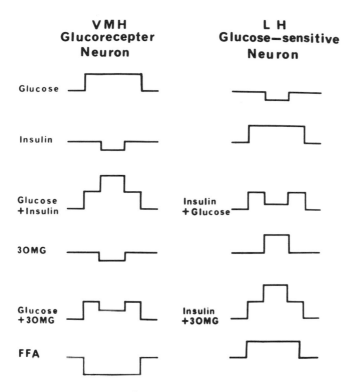

FIG. 2. Schematic representation of the effects of glucose, insulin, glucose analogue, FFA, and their combined effects on rat neuronal discharge frequency. Left: Glucoreceptor VMH neuron. Right: Glucose-sensitive LH neuron. Upward deflection, discharge frequency increase.

polarization. Insulin is known to cause such hyperpolarization in muscle membrane by causing increased electrogenic Na-pump activity combined with intracellular K accumulation (18, 19). The above explains inhibition by insulin, but not stimulation by glucose or enhancement by glucose plus insulin. It is possible that insulin may increase assimilation or neuron uptake of glucose at the specific neuronal glucoreceptive membrane as it does in the fat cell membrane. Among the glucose analogues, 2-DG (2-deoxy-D-glucose) produces no distinct response, whereas 3-OMG (3-O-methyl-glucose) clearly shows an inhibitory effect on VMH neurons. Figure 2 shows the inhibitory effect of 3-OMG alone, and its suppression of glucose-induced activity when used in combination with glucose.

Although it is possible to conceive certain models to help explain the reasons for the effects of glucose on VMH neurons, it is still impossible to determine with certainty if simple binding of the glucose molecule to the receptor is adequate or if assimilation and metabolism of the molecule by the neuron is necessary to produce the observed results.

Since, in the LH, most of the neurons that responded to glucose by increasing activity also responded the same way to osmosis, it appears that there are few if any glucoreceptors in the LH, but that those neurons that do respond to glucose are glucose-sensitive. Intracellular recording of neuronal activity distinctly shows approximately 5 mV hyperpolarization of the membrane (20). At the same time, the absence of change in membrane conductance is also obvious. Since this glucose sensitivity can be diminished by cardiac glycosides or antimetabolites, which inhibit extrusion of intracellular Na by the sodium-pump, it is apparent that glucose operates by membrane hyperpolarization which, in turn, is caused by activation of the energy-dependent Na-pump, not by permeability change.

The functioning of insulin is caused by the presence of insulin receptors on the glucose-sensitive neurons. The decrease of insulin effect by glucose is probably caused by the hyperpolarization mentioned above, whereas the enhancement of the insulin effect by glucose analogues is probably the result of depolarization resulting from slowing of the Na-K pump, perhaps because of partial interruption of cellular metabolism.

Effect of FFA on the LH and VMH Neurons

FFA was extracted from 30-hr deprived and normal rats using Doles extraction mixture (17). Dispensing electrode rate was calibrated using ^{14}C-palmitic acid, a major component of FFA. The application rate averaged 2.5×10^{-12} M/μcoul.

When FFA, prepared and administered in this manner, was applied to a glucose-sensitive neuron in the LH, it was a powerful excitant of the neuron. FFA extracted from fasted or normal rats yielded no significant difference in results. Figure 3A illustrates a typical result of application of FFA to a glucose-sensitive neuron in the LH. In the beginning, the spontaneous activity was near zero. Introduction of FFA increased the discharge rate to 50 impulses/sec with a few second latency when applied with +25 nA. The first application was from a fasted rat, the second from a normal rat. The effect usually persisted for several seconds after termination of the current. The discharge frequency of this cell was increased by application of acetylcholine (ACh). After increasing the frequency with several applications of L-glutamic acid, glucose caused complete suppression of activity with less than 10-sec latency. Full recovery occurred 20 sec after current termination. After recovery to a normal spontaneous discharge rate, application of Na had no effect. When glucose was applied during FFA excitation, a small dose diminished the excitation and a large dose, as shown in Fig. 3, completely suppressed the activity. The threshold for FFA application was below 10 nA for 10 sec with saturation occurring at 70 nA for 10-sec duration. This threshold dose amounts to 1.3×10^{-13} Equ or approximately 1 mEqu/liter, which is comparable to the normal FFA level in rat blood of about 0.75

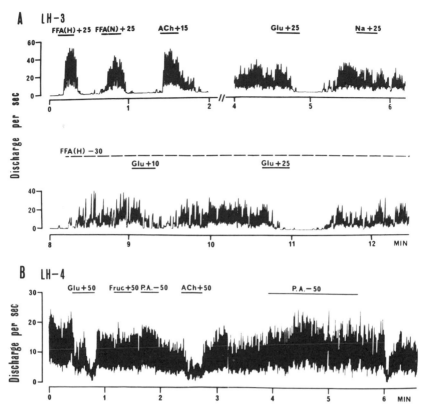

FIG. 0. Effect of FFA on glucose-sensitive rat LH neurons. Rate-meter plot. A: *Upper:* FFA(H)+25 (FFA extracted from blood of fasted rats applied at +25 nA for period indicated by an underscore) increased discharge from almost zero level. FFA(N)+25 (FFA extracted from normal rat, otherwise as above) had similar but slightly less effect than FFA(N). ACh applied at +15 nA caused nearly instantaneous discharge increase. Because of rare spontaneous firing, L-glutamate was applied several times at closer proximity to increase discharge (not illustrated). After increase of spontaneous firing by this maneuver, glucose applied at +25 nA inhibited discharge. Na had no effect. *Lower:* Interaction between glucose and FFA effects. Continuous application of FFA(H) at −30 nA gradually increased firing frequencies. FFA activity facilitation partially inhibited by glucose at 10 nA, completely with 25 nA. B: Effect of palmitic acid (P.A.) on a glucose-sensitive rat LH neuron. Activity was suppressed by glucose (+50 nA) but not by fructose (+50 nA). P.A. (−50 nA) increased discharge rate slightly at the first application, greatly at the second. ACh (+50 nA) inhibited activity between P.A. applications. (17)

mEqu/liter. Table 1 summarizes the results of tests on 140 neurons. Of these, 43 (31%) were glucose-sensitive, 68 (49%) were nonglucose-sensitive, and 29 (21%) were osmosensitive. Of the 43 glucose-sensitive neurons, 41 were subjected to FFA application. Of these 41, 22 (54%) were excited by FFA, 4 (10%) were inhibited, and 15 (37%) showed no response. Of the 22 excited by FFA, 10 were checked for osmosensitivity. None of these responded positively, whereas two showed negative response to sucrose. Of 49 nonglucose-sensitive neurons tested with FFA, only 12% were excited, none of these being osmosensitive. The difference in effect of FFA on glucose-sensitive and nonglucose-sensitive neurons was significant by the X^2-test ($p < 0.005$).

To determine the relative effectiveness of the components of FFA, palmitic and oleic acids (which together comprise approximately 70% of the FFA in rat blood) were tested separately. Both showed effects on glucose-sensitive neurons that were similar to the effects of complete FFA. This is illustrated in Fig. 3B with palmitic acid as the example. Checking for normal functioning with glucose, fructose, and ACh, palmitic acid yielded increased discharge rates in each of two applications, the second showing slightly greater effect. These results clearly demonstrate the specificity of facilitation of activity in glucose-sensitive neurons by FFA.

TABLE 1. FFA effect on LH neurons (17)

Glucose			FFA	Sucrose
		↑	11	4
↑ 29		↓	8	2
		no effect	9	2
		↑	6	0
NO 68		↓	8	0
		no effect	35	15
		↑	22	0
↓ 43		↓	4	2
		no effect	15	8

In the VMH, glucose and FFA reversed their relative functional roles from those exhibited in the LH. Figure 4 demonstrates a discharge increase caused by glucose being suppressed by FFA. After FFA suppression, the neuron was again facilitated by glucose and then allowed to recover to normal, after which it was again inhibited by application of FFA. The lower portion of Fig. 4 shows the lack of effect by application of growth hormone. Since growth hormone as well as FFA increased its concentration in the blood during hunger, growth hormone was tested for its effect on glucoreceptor neurons in the VMH to either verify or dismiss its contribution to neuronal action. As seen in the response pattern of Fig. 4, growth hormone had no effect, either excitatory or inhibitory, on a glucoreceptor neuron of the VMH. The glutamate application was made to verify functioning of the system and to present a basis of comparison. The FFA effect is shown schematically in Fig. 2.

To date, 122 neurons have been tested for effects of glucose and FFA (Table 2). Of the neurons tested with glucose, 42 (34%) were glucoreceptors, 73 (60%) were nonglucoreceptors, and seven (6%) were glucose-

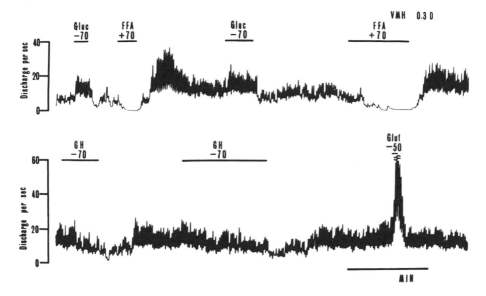

FIG. 4. Effect of FFA on rat glucoreceptor neurons. Top: Glucose applied at −70 nA during period under-scored increased discharge frequency and FFA applied at +70 nA almost completely inhibited the neuronal activity. Bottom: The same neuron. Growth hormone had no effect. Time calibration, 1 min.

sensitive. The glucose-sensitive neurons were recorded at 0.2 mm dorsal from the VMH in the zona incerta. All of the glucoreceptors and glucose-sensitive neurons were also tested with FFA. Of the 42 glucoreceptors, 18 (43%) were suppressed by FFA, whereas 15 (36%) were not affected by FFA. Of these last 15, the seven tested also showed no response to sucrose. Of the seven glucose-sensitive neurons, four were facilitated by FFA, one was in-hibited, and two showed no response. Among 52 nonglucoreceptors, 10 (19%) were inhibited by FFA.

From these data, it is apparent that FFA, when it affects VMH neurons, is

TABLE 2. FFA effect on VMH neurons

Glucose			FFA	Sucrose
↑ 42	↑		9	0
	↓		18	0
		no effect	15	7
NO 73	↑		2	0
	↓		10	0
		no effect	40	8
↓ 7	↑		4	0
	↓		1	0
		no effect	2	3

mostly suppressive in its effect on both glucoreceptors and nonglucoreceptors. In the LH, we concluded that FFA functionally affected the uptake of glucose by the neuron (21). In the VMH, it appears that the FFA may be acting in any one or more of several different ways. FFA may (a) interfere with the take-up of glucose by the neuron, (b) inhibit binding of the glucose molecule to the receptor site, (c) reduce glucose metabolism by the neuron, and/or, (d) induce hyperpolarization or inhibit the depolarization which is normally caused by the glucose molecule when it attaches to the receptor site. The occurrence of complete suppression implies existence of hyperpolarization. Therefore, it is probable that (d) most certainly happens. The most plausible prospect, in fact, is that (a), (b), and (c) all occur to some extent, the consequence of which is the occurrence of (d).

SIGNIFICANCE OF FFA EFFECTS

Figure 5 illustrates schematically the one difference between the glucoreceptor neurons occurring principally in the VMH, and the glucose-sensitive neurons, located primarily in the LH. The glucoreceptor neuron has glucose receptor sites, whereas the glucose-sensitive neuron has insulin receptor sites.

Food intake and body weight in mammals are closely correlated with lipogenesis and lipolysis. It has also been proposed that the VMH functions as a deterrent to an animal's addition of excess fat (22) and that the LH acts to conserve the animal's fat tissue (23). The roles of FFA and other metabolic substances in the regulation of food intake have been emphasized (22). Furthermore, it is supposed that (a) neurons that control appetite and maintain body weight will also detect the concentration of such metabolic sub-

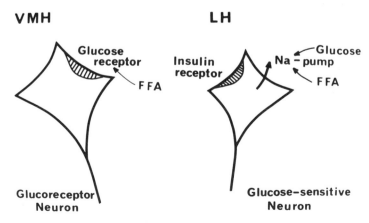

FIG. 5. Schematic illustration of glucoreceptor neuron in the VMH and glucose-sensitive neuron in the LH. Left: Glucoreceptor neuron has glucose receptor sites. FFA inhibits firing of this neuron by interposing between the glucose molecules and the receptor site, hence inhibiting binding or uptake of glucose by the neuron. Right: Glucose-sensitive neuron has insulin receptor sites. Na-pump action is accelerated by glucose but slowed by FFA.

stances, (b) as a result of constantly monitoring the level of FFA, glucose, insulin, growth hormone, adrenalin, and other blood chemicals, they will immediately be aware of changes, and (c) these neurons will be located in the LH and/or in the VMH. The remarkable sensitivity of the LH glucose-sensitive neuron to FFA is shown from past data (17). The present investigation presents additional data to demonstrate the effect of equal magnitude, but opposite sign, that FFA has on VMH glucoreceptor neurons. Efficient feeding behavior requires (a) an increase in the activity of glucose-sensitive neurons that respond to FFA, (b) a decrease in activity of neurons that would inhibit effective behavior or instigate counter behavior, and (c) animation of neuronal networks at the heads of which are the chemosensitive neurons. This experiment has demonstrated the effective functioning of FFA in the LH to accomplish the first and third of these requirements and its equally effective functioning in the VMH to meet the second and third.

There are variations of concentration of glucose and insulin in the blood as a function of hunger and satiation, but the effect is small from a relatively long time prior to just after initiation of eating (24). Consequently, explanation of hunger or the onset of eating under *ad lib* conditions may be difficult in terms of these substances alone.

On the other hand, FFA level falls shortly after the onset of eating and recovers as glucose and insulin decrease (24). During hunger, this level increases along with the decrease of glucose and insulin, but at a much higher relative rate. Simultaneously, growth hormone (25) and epinephrine increase (26). Liberation of FFA by these two substances is well known (27, 28). Thus glucose and insulin are both closely related to FFA, as are epinephrine and growth hormone, during the hunger stage. It is demonstrated in the present experiment that glucose-sensitive neurons in the LH, and glucoreceptor neurons in the VMH, both have, in reality, complex chemosensitivity to FFA as well as to glucose and insulin.

Obese subjects have high FFA levels (23). Diabetics, who are usually hyperphagic, have a high FFA blood level. Obesity is produced by VMH lesions which result in disinhibition of the LH. At that time, the levels of FFA and insulin in the blood are high (29) as is gastric acid secretion (29). Amino acid injections cause anorexia and lower FFA level in blood (23). These facts provide evidence of the relationship between FFA level and hunger-connected behavior. One of the actions of growth hormone is lipolysis, which results in increase of FFA level.

Increase of food intake has been induced by intravenous injection of FFA into the rat (30). Replication of this result has not always been successful, possibly because ready binding of the FFA to body tissue dispersed the injected excess before the circulatory system could transport it to the brain in sufficient quantity to be effective. Such dispersion could conceivably occur if the system were in a generally lipogenic state in contrast to lipolytic.

The ability of LH neurons to detect and discriminate blood-borne chemicals such as glucose, insulin, and FFA has been previously demonstrated. This experiment demonstrates a similar ability of VMH neurons. Relationships between the LH and the VMH, the LH and the frontal cortex, and other areas of the cortex have all been shown (4). Thus results of the chemical analyses performed by the LH and VMH are interchanged, and further exchange and integration occurs in connection with the frontal cortex. Furthermore, via the frontal cortex and the midbrain reticular formation, other somatosensory and proprioceptive signals are received by the center, processed, and then dispersed to control foraging or alimentary behavior to be performed by the organism. There are many neuronal networks, each having a chemosensitive neuron at its head. Each chemosensitive neuron has a different threshold level for excitation by, for instance, FFA. The lowest threshold concentration of FFA for firing a chemosensitive neuron in the LH is 1 mEqu/liter (17). Hence some neurons are fired as the concentration reaches a certain level, and some are not. As a network is activated, its output goes to the frontal cortex. That is the beginning of, for example, hunger which is initiated by FFA. As more and more neurons, activated by FFA, fire, the subject is motivated to behave in a manner intended to alleviate the hunger.

SUMMARY

FFA applied electroosmotically to glucose-sensitive neurons in the rat LH, and to glucoreceptor neurons in the rat VMH, facilitated the former and inhibited the latter. Approximately 50% of the glucose-responsive neurons tested responded in this manner to FFA. Glucose and FFA were applied through respective barrels of multibarreled micropipette. Extracellular recordings were made through a microelectrode attached to the micropipette. Results imply depolarization of LH and hyperpolarization of VMH. It is suggested that chemosensitive neuronal monitoring of increased level of FFA in the bloodstream causes simultaneous direct activation of LH, and disinhibition of LH by suppression of VMH, strongly motivating the animal to eat.

ACKNOWLEDGMENTS

This work has been done with Drs. Sugimori, T. Nakamura, and Y. Yamada. I deeply thank Prof. A. Simpson of Showa University for kind advice and help in preparation of this manuscript. This work was partly supported by grants 90958, 92455, 99054, 887010, 811022, and 844023 from the Ministry of Education and DA-CRD-AFE-S92-544-72-G177 and 73-G191.

REFERENCES

1. Oomura, Y., Ooyama, H., Naka, F., Yamamoto, T., Ono, T., and Kobayashi, N. (1969): *Ann. NY Acad. Sci.,* 157:666–689.
2. Oomura, Y., Ono, T., and Ooyama, H. (1970): *Nature,* 228:1108–1110.

3. Oomura, Y., and Nakamura, T. (1974): *XXVI Int. Cong.*, Abstr. 365, also *VI Int. Cong. Physiology of Food and Fluid Intake*, Abstr. 99.
4. Oomura, Y., and Takigawa, M. (1975): In: *Mechanisms in Transmission of Signals for Conscious Behavior*, edited by T. Desiraju. Elsevier, Amsterdam.
5. Marshall, J. F., and Teitelbaum. (1974): *J. Comp. Physiol. Psychol.*, 86:375–395.
6. Blatt, B., and Lyon, M. (1968): *Acta Neurol. Scand.*, 44:576–595.
7. Adolph, E. F. (1947): *Am. J. Physiol.*, 151:110–125.
8. Le Magnen, J., and Devos, M. (1969): *C. R. Acad. Sci. (Paris)*, 268:3107–3110.
9. Thomas, D. W., and Mayer, J. (1968): *J. Comp. Physiol. Psychol.*, 66:642–653.
10. Russek, M. (1971): In: *Neurosciences Research*, edited by S. Ehrenpreis and O. C. Solnitzky, vol. 4, pp. 213–282. Academic Press, New York.
11. Snowdon, C. T., and Epstein, A. N. (1970): *J. Comp. Physiol. Psychol.*, 71:59–67.
12. Davis, J. D., Campbell, C. S., Gallagher, R. J., and Zurakov, M. A. (1971): *J. Comp. Physiol. Psychol.*, 75:476–482.
13. Oomura, Y. (1973): In: *Advances in Biophysics, Vol. 5*, edited by M. Kotani, pp. 65–142. Tokyo University Press, Tokyo.
14. Oomura, Y., Sugimori, M., Nakamura, T., and Yamada, Y. (1975): In: *Neural Integration of Physiological Mechanisms and Behavior*, edited by G. J. Mogenson and F. R. Calaresu. Toronto University Press, Toronto.
15. Oomura, Y., Kimura, K., Ooyama, H., Maeno, T., Iki, M., and Kuniyoshi, M. (1964): *Science*, 143:484–485.
16. Beidler, L. M. (1971): In: *Handbook of Sensory Physiology, Vol. 4*, edited by L. M. Beidler. Springer-Verlag, Berlin.
17. Oomura, Y., Nakamura, T., Sugimori, M., and Yamada, Y. (1975): *Physiol. Behav.*, 14:483–486.
18. Creese, R., and Jenden, D. J. (1968): *J. Physiol.*, 197:255–278.
19. Zierler, K. L. (1966): *Am. J. Med.*, 40:735–739.
20. Oomura, Y., Ooyama, H., Sugimori, M., Nakamura, T., and Yamada, Y. (1974): *Nature*, 247:284–286.
21. Bornstein, J., and Park, C. R. (1953): *J. Biol. Chem.*, 205:503.
22. Kennedy, G. C. (1966): *Br. Med. Bull.*, 22:216–220.
23. Nisbett, R. E. (1972): *Psychol. Rev.*, 79:433–453.
24. Steffens, A. B. (1970): *Physiol Behav.*, 5:147–151.
25. Himthworth, R. L., Carmel, P. W., and Frantz, A. G. (1972): *Endocrinology*, 91:217–226.
26. McNew, J.J., Sabbot, I. M. et al. (1972): *Am. J. Physiol.*, 222:640–644.
27. Goodman, H. M. (1970): *Physiologist*, 13:75–88.
28. Goodner, C. J., Koerker, D. J., Werrbach, J. H., Toivola, P., and Gale, C. C. (1973): *Am. J. Physiol.*, 224:534–539.
29. Hongslo, C. F., Hustvedt, B. E., and Løvø, A. (1974): *Acta Physiol. Scand.*, 90:757–763.
30. Adair, E. R., Miller, N. E., and Booth, D. A. (1968): *Comm. Behav. Biol.*, 2:25.

Hunger: Basic Mechanisms and Clinical Implications,
edited by D. Novin, W. Wyrwicka, and G. Bray.
Raven Press, New York © 1976.

Hypothalamic Unit Activity Related to Lever Pressing and Eating in the Chronic Monkey

T. Ono,* Y. Oomura, M. Sugimori,* T. Nakamura, N. Shimizu,
H. Kita, and S. Ishibashi

*Department of Physiology, Faculty of Medicine, Kyushu University, Fukuoka 812, and *Department
of Physiology, Faculty of Medicine, Kanazawa University, Kanazawa 920, Japan*

Lesions in the ventromedial nucleus of the hypothalamus (VMH) cause hyperphagia; those in the rostrocaudal plane of the lateral hypothalamus (LH) cause aphagia (1). Electric stimulation of the rat LH elicits, and of the VMH suppresses, feeding behavior (2, 3). The VMH and LH are referred to as the satiety and feeding centers, respectively. The presence of specific glucose receptive neurons in the VMH has been suggested (4) and actually demonstrated by direct microelectroosmotic application of glucose (5, 6). Also, microelectroosmotic application of free fatty acid or insulin increases the excitability of glucose-sensitive neurons in the LH and decreases the excitability of glucoreceptor neurons in the VMH (7, 8). Levels of glucose, free fatty acid, insulin, other unknown substances, and the degree of stomach distension may be important intrinsic factors in eliciting feeding and satiation behavior. Inputs from vision, smell, taste, and other sensory systems might be important extrinsic factors.

It has been suggested that organization of feeding behavior is integrated between the closely correlated frontal cortex and the hypothalamus (9). The amygdala, part of the limbic system, also has significant influence on feeding. Food intake can be diminished by chronic electrical stimulation of the basolateral and anterior parts of the amygdala, and eating and chewing behavior will cease immediately with stimulation (10, 11). It has been shown that inhibition by the amygdala of the LH is due to direct inhibitory postsynaptic potentials (IPSPs) in rats (12). We can thus assume that the LH initiates hunger alleviating behavior after integration of information received from the intrinsic and extrinsic factors mentioned and from other related central structures. Ultimately, it motivates the animal to seek food, to put it into the mouth, to chew, and to swallow, i.e., the final commands to perform the chained behavior associated with feeding emanate from the LH.

A pattern of preperformance excitation and inhibition has recently been demonstrated in LH neuronal discharges from chronic cats trained to press a bar for food and water. This pattern was in the form of a short period of inhibition immediately prior to the bar press preceded by an occasional period of excitation. The excitation was random in duration and in time of occurrence. The occurrence was observed to have some crude relation to the position of the cat relative to the bar and was presumed to be associated in some way with hunger-induced motivation (9).

It is essential to ascertain, more precisely, the temporal and functional relationships between LH neuronal response and bar pressing for food, a hunger-induced behavior. Thus the present study, using chronic monkeys, delved into the activity of LH neurons before and after bar pressing for food and water. The results reported are mostly concerned with food intake. LH neuronal activity and its temporal relation to feeding behavior were also examined during stimulation of the basolateral amygdaloid nucleus (AL) and the frontoorbital cortex (FOB).

METHODS

Five 3 to 5 kg macaque monkeys (*Macaca mulatta*) were used. They were seated in primate chairs, facing a panel 30 to 60 cm away, as shown in Fig. 1. The panel had two bars 15 cm apart, each 2.5 cm $\times$ 3 cm in size. The left bar was for food and the right for water. The reward was one soy bean or a drop of water. The program was fixed ratio, adjustable, but never exceeding 5.

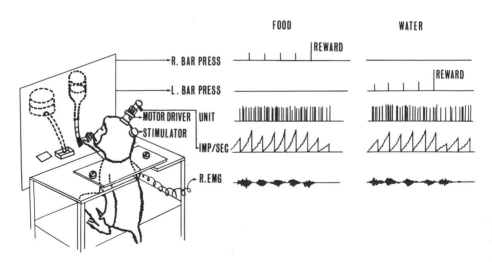

FIG. 1. Schematic diagram of experiment. Left: Monkey seated in primate chair facing panel 30 to 60 cm away. The panel has two bars 15 cm apart, each 2.5 cm $\times$ 3 cm. Left bar, food, right bar, water. A microelectrode positioner connected to motor driver head is attached to socket implanted on monkey. Stimulator is plugged into implanted stimulator socket connected to AL and FOB electrodes. Implanted constraining bolts not illustrated but similar to the preparation by Evarts (14). Signals from r. bar press or l. bar press with respective rewards, single unit discharges, and right triceps EMG (R. EMG) were recorded on seven-channel FM tape recorder. This information and unit discharge rate (imp/sec) were also monitored by ink-writing oscillograph.

Surgery

After lever training, surgical preparation for recording and stimulation was performed under phencyclidine hydrochloride anesthesia (approximately 1.5 mg/kg). In sterile conditions, the socket of a microelectrode positioner for recording unit discharges (13) and two stimulating electrodes were mounted on the head, positioned at the AL and FOB. Bolts and nuts for restraining the monkey's head were implanted (not illustrated in Fig. 1 but similar to the preparation by Evarts, ref. 14).

Recording and Data Analysis

During recording, the monkey was seated in a chair with its head rigidly constrained by the implanted bolts. A microelectrode positioner developed by Oomura et al. (13) was attached to the implanted socket, and a tungsten microelectrode insulated with polyurethane was inserted to the ventral part of the thalamus, nucleus of field of Forel, and the LH in 1 μm steps. A microelectrode positioner was adjusted to a standard point (A, 11.5; L, 2.2; H, 2.0) according to stereotaxic coordinates (15). The position of the microelectrode was changeable: ±2 for A, ±2 for L, and +5 to −3 for H. The electrode, having 15 to 30 MΩ resistance at 50 Hz, was connected to the FET input of a preamplifier having automatic negative capacitance compensation. The output was fed to another amplifier and to a rate meter to plot the unit discharge rate per second. The EMG of the triceps brachii was recorded through an a.c. amplifier (300 to 1,500 Hz; gain × 4,000). Single unit discharges, triceps EMG, and signals associated with bar press and reward were recorded on a seven-channel FM tape recorder. This information was also monitored by a nine-channel ink-writing oscillograph (Fig. 1).

To isolate single unit discharges from multiple-unit records, a window discriminator (Bur-Brown 4115/04) was utilized. The unit discharges, correlated with bar-press feeding and drinking behavior, were converted to before and after bar-press histograms by a minicomputer (YHP, 2100A), displayed on the screen of a Braun oscilloscope, and photographed. Usually data from 2 sec before and after bar press with τ of 50 and 100 msec was used.

Each histogram was an average of at least 20 pre- and post- bar-press trials. If there was a clear increase or decrease of the discharge rate during a given period, compared with the mean rate of spontaneous discharge, a significant change in discharge rate was said to have occurred. As an additional test of significance, it was required that the histogram obtained after complete shuffling of spike intervals show no such changes.

Stimulation

Stimulation was applied with concentric bipolar stainless steel electrodes insulated with varnish. The inner electrode of stainless wire protruded approximately 0.6 mm beyond the outer sheath of 25-gauge tubing. The coatings of both the outer tube and the inner wire were stripped back 0.3 mm with a sharp knife producing a pole separation of about 0.3 mm. The d.c. resistance of these electrodes measured in saline was about 70 kΩ. Stimuli were 0.01 msec pulses with adjustable intensity (0.05 to 1.0 mA) delivered through an isolation unit. The stimulating electrode tips were placed in the AL (A, 13.5; L, 7.8; H, −1.0) and in the FOB (A, 30.0; L, 8.0; H, +10.5), respectively, according to stereotaxic coordinates (15).

Anatomic Identification

The subject was anesthetized after the experiment. The recording electrode was then replaced by a steel electrode, inserted to the standard point and left in position. The stimulating sites were marked with 1 to 2 mA of d.c. for 10 sec and the electrodes left in position. Ringer solution was introduced through the left cardiac ventricle and the brain fixed by formalin perfusion. After removal, serial 40 or 50 μm sections of the brain were cut parallel to the plane of the stereotaxic coordinates and stained by cresyl violet showing a clear electrode tract. The position of each recorded neuron was plotted on the brain section with reference to the electrode tract.

RESULTS AND CONCLUSION

Sample Size and Spontaneous Discharge

Recordings were obtained from a total of 53 neurons: 26 in the LH and 27 in other sites (table in Fig. 4). Discharge rates were recorded from all these neurons before and after bar press for food or water.

The mean discharge rates of different LH neurons varied from 2 to 39/sec (14.8 ± 11.3, mean ±SD, $N = 26$). The rates of different neurons in other sites varied from 3 to 44/sec (17.8 ± 12.3, mean ±SD, $N = 27$). Discharge rates of interpositus and dentate neurons of cerebellum in the unanesthetized monkey were higher than 30/sec (16). Mean discharge rates of neurons inside and outside the LH were comparable to the mean of 5 to 15/sec reported for the dorsal medial nucleus of the thalamus (17) and up to 20/sec reported for the dorsolateral prefrontal cortex (18).

Unitary Response to Bar-Press Feeding

Using original and shuffled data, pre- and post-bar-press histograms were made for the neuronal discharges of 26 neurons in the LH and 27 neurons in other sites during alimentary behavior.

Examples of such histograms are shown in Figs. 2 and 3. In each histogram, the total number of discharges (ordinate) per τ of 50 msec is plotted against pre- and post-bar-press times (abscissa) of 2 sec each for the total number of trials. Zero indicates bar-press time. The mean discharge rates per

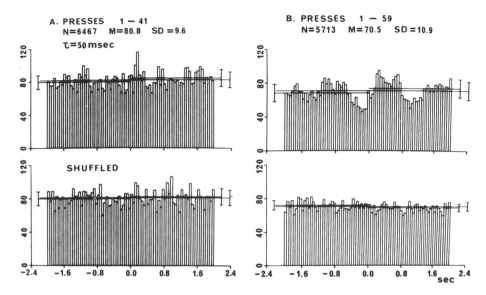

FIG. 2. Pre- and post-bar-press histograms of bar-press-associated discharges from ventral thalamus neuron (A) and LH neuron (B). A: *Upper:* From original data for series of 41 bar presses shows no significant change in discharge rate of thalamic neuron before and after bar press. *Lower:* Similar to upper but from shuffled data. B: *Upper:* From original data for series of 59 bar presses shows this LH neuron responding with excitation during interval 1.15 to 0.55 sec before bar press, inhibition from 0.55 to 0.05 sec before bar press, and excitation-inhibition in the post-bar-press periods 0.15 to 0.75 and 0.75 to 1.3 sec, respectively. This type of response with pre-bar-press excitation-inhibition and post-bar-press excitation-inhibition was classified type F_1 (Fig. 4). *Lower:* Histogram obtained from same data, shuffled, shows no significant changes during pre- and post-bar-press periods.

In all histograms shown, total number of spike discharges per τ of 50 msec (ordinate) is plotted against pre- and post-bar-press time (abscissa) of 2 sec each, for total of all trials. Mean discharge rate per τ of 50 msec before bar press (solid line, left), after bar press (solid line, right), and during the entire period (solid line, full length), for a given number of trials are also shown.

τ of 50 msec before bar press, after bar press, and during the entire period for the given number of trials are shown with solid line at left, right, and full length in each histogram.

Figure 2A shows an example of a ventral thalamus neuron (using 41 bar presses) that did not react to bar press. The lower histogram using the same data, after shuffling, shows no difference from the upper. The mean discharge rates were 80 (38/sec) for pre-bar-press and 83 (41/sec) for post-bar-press during each 50 msec accumulation, averaging 81 (39/sec) for an entire period of 41 bar presses. It is clear that this thalamic neuron did not respond to bar-press feeding. Twenty-six of 27 neurons (see table in Fig. 4) in sites outside the LH responded, in the manner of Fig. 2A, with no reaction.

Only one neuron showed a significant reaction, which was classified as F_1 (Fig. 4). The response was relatively small compared with reactions of LH neurons.

Figure 2B shows a histogram recorded from a LH neuron for 59 bar presses. In contrast to the thalamic neuron, the LH neuron responded with

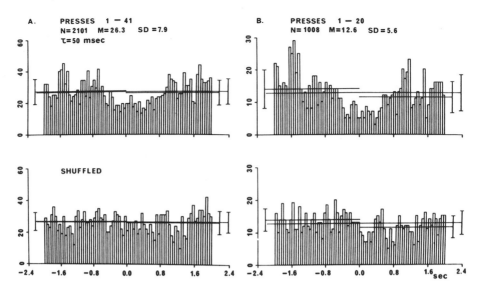

FIG. 3. Response histograms of different LH neuron for bar press feeding. A: *Upper:* Obtained from original data for 41 bar presses, shows this LH neuron responding with excitation from 1.65 to 0.55 sec before the bar press, inhibition until 0.95 sec after bar press, and slight excitation until 2 sec after the bar press. This type of response is classified as F_2 (Fig. 4). *Lower:* Same data after shuffling shows no such changes. B: Similar to A but for the first 20 of the 41 bar presses mentioned above. (See Fig. 2 for description of histogram features.)

excitation during the interval 1.15 to 0.55 sec prior to bar press followed by inhibition from 0.55 to 0.05 sec before the bar-press time with further excitation-inhibition in the periods 0.15 to 0.75 and 0.75 to 1.3 sec, respectively. The mean discharge rate for 59 trials was 68 per 50 msec interval (23/sec) for pre-bar-press period and 73 (25/sec) for post-bar-press period, averaging 71 (24/sec) for both periods. The respective maxima and minima were 86 (29/sec), 46 (16/sec), 95 (32/sec), and 50 (17/sec). This type of response (pre-bar-press excitation-inhibition, and post-bar-press excitation-inhibition) was classified type F_1 (Fig. 4). The response is significant since no equivalent change in spike discharge can be seen in the lower histogram using the same data after shuffling.

Figures 3A and B show more pre- and post-bar-press histograms for a different LH neuron. A is the histogram for 41 bar presses and B, for the first 20. In A (upper) there is excitation from 1.65 to 0.55 sec before bar press followed by inhibition continuing until 0.95 sec after, followed in turn by slight excitation until 2 sec after bar press. The mean rate is 26 spikes per 41 periods of 50 msec each (13/sec) with respective maxima and minima of 46 (23/sec), 15 (7/sec), 45 (22/sec). The lower histogram with the same data, but after shuffling, did not show such changes. In B, the response was similar to that of A, but each response was larger; these changes are also significant. This type of response is classified as F_2 (Fig. 4).

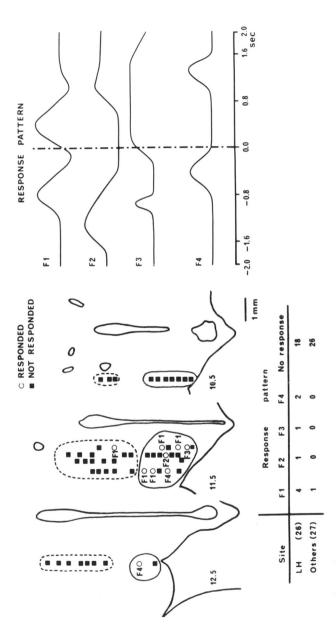

FIG. 4. Schematic summary of text. Left: Top: Locations of neurons tested. Solid enclosures, LH; dotted enclosures, ventral part of thalamus, nucleus of field of Forel. The three portions labeled 10.5, 11.5, and 12.5 are the respective anterior-posterior planes. Solid squares (■), nonresponsive sites; open circles (○), sites which showed reaction. Each F number with open circle specifies response pattern shown by respective neuron. Bottom: Table summarizing responses by site. Right: Graphs illustrating general excitation-suppression pattern versus pre- and post-bar-press time.

Figure 4 is a summary of the present study. At the right, the four types of response pattern are tentatively classified. The pre- and post-bar-press histograms in which LH neurons displayed response pattern F_3 and F_4 are not presented in this chapter. However, the neuron classified as F_3 responded with short-lasting excitation from 1.2 to 0.8 sec prior to bar press with a second excitation from 0.3 sec before until 2 sec after bar press.

The neuron classified as F_4 responded with excitation starting at 0.8 sec before bar press and ending near bar-press time. This neuron was also excited in the period from 0.95 to 1.6 sec after bar press. Activation of all responding LH neurons occurs at some time during the period 1.7 to 0.8 sec prior to bar press.

It is notable that a slowly increasing surface negative readiness potential distributed over the cortex starts 850 msec (SD 308 msec) before movement and increases until engagement (19). Evarts (20), studying primate pyramidal tract neuron activity in a simple visual reaction test, found that the pyramidal tract neurons responded to a light signal beginning 100 to 200 msec preceding a key release by contraction of the extensor digitorum communis muscle of the hand. Following lamp signals, visuokinctic units in the dorsolateral prefrontal cortex responded an average of 160 msec earlier than EMG onset and 200 msec earlier than hold-key release (18). It is impossible, in this study, to estimate timing of onset of impulse for bar-pressing behavior only, and to compare these latencies with ours. However, activation of LH neurons is at least 0.6 sec earlier than activation of visuokinetic units in the dorsolateral prefrontal cortex (18). The activation of LH neurons 1.7 to 0.8 sec prior to bar press strongly indicates that the LH initiates hunger-alleviating behavior after integration of information received from the intrinsic and extrinsic factors and from other related central structures.

The inhibition, preceded by initial excitation, in LH neurons showing response patterns F_1 and F_2 is assumed to originate in the frontal cortex. This suggests that the frontal cortex may inhibit LH activity. This conclusion is based on studies of other investigators associating frontal cortex activity with inhibition of feeding behavior. Accelerated neural discharges just before bar press for food have been shown in the caudate nucleus (21), which has a direct connection with the frontal cortex (22). The inhibition may imply a specific phenomenon observed in the hypothalamus. It has been reported that the frontal cortex inhibits on-going behavior associated with food intake (23), hunger induced arousal (24), and bite-attack behavior provoked by LH stimulation (25). Eating and drinking behavior has been elicited by arrival of a spreading depression wave at the frontal cortex (26). Frontal cortex lesion has resulted in increased bar-press rate in a fixed ratio program for food (27), and increased running wheel activity over an extended time (28). Demonstrating the importance of the anatomic connection is the failure to inhibit behavior via the frontal cortex until 3 weeks of age, before which time the connection had not matured (24). The existence of a direct anatomic connection from frontal cortex to LH has been established (29), as has a similar connection from LH to frontal cortex (30). Unit activity within the frontal cortex, and in no other brain location, is enhanced by stimulation of the effective site for self-stimulation (31). Further correlation is demonstrated by the diminishing or discontinuing of self-stimulation to the LH following application of procaine to the frontal cortex (32).

In a recent neuroelectrophysiological study, mutual frontal cortex and LH interconnection was established by stimulating one while recording from the other. According to Oomura et al. (9), LH neurons directly project axons that terminate on and excite frontal cortex neurons. Excitatory and inhibitory interneurons located within the ventral LH, but not in the dorsal LH, may result in a modulating effect caused by frontal cortex stimulation. This modulation appears as an excitation-inhibition pattern in the dorsal LH, with inhibition only in the ventral LH.

The above citations clearly point out both anatomic and functional connections between the frontal cortex and the LH. It is thus suggested that the inhibition, preceded by excitation, of LH neurons prior to bar press is due, at least in part, to frontal cortex activity, and that it has important significance in emanation from the LH of signals leading to hunger alleviating behavior (motivation). Response components other than the initial excitation followed by inhibition may also have meaning in feeding behavior, but there is, so far, no known explanation. A possible explanation may be the feedback reflected by these response components on LH neurons by way of a direct linguo-hypothalamic or linguocerebrohypothalamic system. This concurs with the speculation that the cerebral cortex receives taste information from the tongue and passes enhancing or inhibiting effects to the positive or negative reinforcement area in the hypothalamus (33). Some responses might be related to movement associated with ingestion, such as putting food into the mouth, chewing, and swallowing.

In Fig. 4, positions of 53 neurons tested are plotted on the frontal section of the brain (A: 12.5, 11.5, and 10.5). F_1, F_2, F_3, and F_4 next to the open circles correspond to the response patterns F_1, F_2, F_3, and F_4, which are schematically presented at the right.

The significance of the response patterns of LH neurons cannot yet be explained in terms of relevance to feeding. It is not known whether different response patterns are due to differences between .the neurons themselves or result from temporal differences in excitation. It is also possible that these differences may depend on position of a neuron within a neural network during on-going feeding behavior.

Effects of Stimulation of the Basolateral Amygdaloid Nucleus and Fronto-orbital Cortex on Spontaneous Activity and Feeding

Of 17 LH neurons tested, four were clearly inhibited by AL and FOB stimulation. Stimulation of the AL and FOB were applied at various intensities and rates of 1 or 2/sec. Examples are shown, in Fig. 5, of LH neuronal

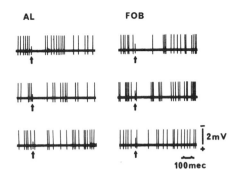

FIG. 5. Effects of AL and FOB stimulation on LH single-unit discharge of *Macaca mulatta*. Stimulation (arrow) applied 1/sec. Driven discharges followed by inhibition shown in bottom trace of AL and lower two traces of FOB. Inhibition periods shown: 162 msec min, 240 msec max.

response to stimulation of the AL and FOB applied 1/sec at relatively high stimulus intensity. The arrow below each record and the small deflection in each record indicate stimulus time.

To the left, stimulation of the AL produces complete inhibition of spontaneous discharge lasting 188 (top), 200 (middle), and 175 (bottom) msec, respectively. The record at the bottom also shows an initial driven discharge with a latency of about 25 msec.

At right is shown the same neuron which responded to FOB stimulation with complete suppression of spontaneous discharges. A stronger stimulus intensity was used for the FOB than for the AL. Inhibition lasted for 240 (top), 200 (middle) and 162 (bottom) msec. In the middle and bottom records, there are initial driven discharges with latency of about 20 msec. Driven discharges produced by AL and FOB stimulation are not always consistent. Threshold current intensity for AL inhibition was usually lower than that for FOB stimulation in the present study. Stimulation of either the AL or the FOB also sometimes inhibited feeding behavior.

Neurophysiological effects of stimulation of the AL and FOB on LH neurons, and consequent feeding behavior changes, have yet to be analyzed in detail. However, the marked inhibition of LH neurons observed when stimulating the AL and FOB confirmed the results reported by many of the investigators cited in this chapter, thus substantiating the strong influence by these two central structures on LH neuronal activity as well as LH elicited behavior.

The results of this study appear to verify our assumption that hunger-alleviating behavior is initiated in the LH after integration of information received from intrinsic and extrinsic factors and from the other central structures, at least from the basolateral amygdaloid nucleus, a part of the limbic structure, and from the frontal cortex.

SUMMARY

Single unit discharges were recorded from LH, ventral part of the thalamus, and nucleus of field of Forel of five macaque monkeys. Recordings were made from 53 neurons: 26 in the LH and 27 in other sites. Discharge rate changes were recorded before and after bar press for food or water, and presented as histograms relating single unit discharge to time.

Of 26 LH neurons, eight showed significant variation of discharge rate before and after bar press in four categories, classified F_1, F_2, F_3, and F_4. All responding LH neurons increased activity during the period 1.7 to 0.8 sec before bar press perhaps indicating motivation of hunger-alleviating behavior. All responding neurons had two separate periods of excitation: the initial response and a post-bar-press response. In some (types F_1 and F_2), there was a period of suppression below mean discharge level and in one type (F_1), there was a second suppression period after the second excitation. Only one of 27 neurons tested in other sites responded significantly.

Of 17 LH neurons tested, the spontaneous discharge of four were clearly inhibited for 100 to 300 msec by stimulation of basolateral amygdaloid nucleus and frontoorbital cortex. Inhibition was often preceded by initial driven discharge with a latency of 15 to 30 msec. Inhibition of LH neurons was sometimes associated with inhibition of feeding.

Results of this study appear to verify our assumption that hunger-alleviating behavior is initiated in the LH after integration of information from intrinsic and extrinsic factors and other central structures, at least from the basolateral amygdaloid nucleus, a part of the limbic structure, and from the frontal cortex.

ACKNOWLEDGMENTS

We thank Prof. A. Simpson, Showa University, for help in preparation of this manuscript; and Prof. K. Kubota, Primate Research Institute, Kyoto University, for his invaluable advice and suggestions while conducting these experiments. This work was partly supported by grants 887010 and 844023 from the Ministry of Education.

REFERENCES

1. Anand, B. K., and Brobeck, J. R. (1951): *Yale J. Biol. Med.*, 24:123–140.
2. Larsson, S. (1954): *Acta Physiol. Scand. (Suppl. 115)*, 32:1–63.
3. Miller, N. E. (1960): *Fed. Proc.*, 19:846–854.
4. Mayer, J., and Marshall, N. B. (1956): *Nature*, 178:1399–1400.
5. Oomura, Y., Ono, T., Ooyama, H., and Wayner, M. J. (1969): *Nature*, 222:282–284.
6. Oomura, Y., Ooyama, H., Sugimori, M., Nakamura, T., and Yamada, Y. (1974): *Nature*, 247:284–286.
7. Oomura, Y., Nakamura, T., Sugimori, M., and Yamada, Y. (1975): *Physiol. Behav.*, 14:483–486.
8. Oomura, Y. (1973): In: *Advances in Biophysics, Vol. 5*, edited by M. Kotani, pp. 65–142. Univ. Tokyo Press, Tokyo.
9. Oomura, Y., and Takigawa, M. (1975): In: *Mechanism in Transmission of Signals for Conscious Behavior*, edited by T. Desiraju. Elsevier, Amsterdam.
10. Fonberg, E., and Delgado, J. M. R. (1961): *J. Neurophysiol.*, 24:651–664.

11. Oomura, Y., Ooyama, H., Yamamoto, T., Naka, F., Kobayashi, N., and Ono, T. (1967): In: *Progress in Brain Research,* edited by W. R. Adey and T. Tokizano, *Vol. 27,* pp. 1–33. Elsevier, Amsterdam.
12. Oomura, Y., Ono, T., and Ooyama, H. (1970): *Nature,* 228:1108–1110.
13. Oomura, Y., Ono, T., and Sugimori, M. (1975): *Physiol. Behav., in press.*
14. Evarts, E. V. (1968): *J. Neurophysiol.,* 31:14–27.
15. Snider, R. S., and Lee, J. C. (1961): *A Stereotaxic Atlas of the Monkey Brain (Macaca mulatta).* University of Chicago Press, Chicago.
16. Thach, W. T. (1970): *J. Neurophysiol.,* 33:527–536.
17. Fuster, J. M., and Alexander, G. E. (1973): *Brain Res.,* 61:79–91.
18. Kubota, K., Iwamoto, T., and Suzuki, H. (1974): *J. Neurophysiol.,* 37:1196–1212.
19. Deecke, L., Scheid, P., and Kornhuber, H. H. (1969): *Exp. Brain Res.,* 7:158–168.
20. Evarts, E. V. (1966): *J. Neurophysiol.,* 29:1011–1027.
21. Buser, P., Pouderoux, G., and Mereaux, J. (1974): *Brain Res.,* 71:337–344.
22. Tigner, J. (1974): *Physiol. Behav.,* 12:13–17.
23. Siegel, J., and Wang, R. Y. (1974): *Exp. Neurol.,* 42:28–50.
24. Moorcroft, W. H. (1971): *Brain Res.,* 35:513–522.
25. Siegel, A., Edinger, H., and Lowenthal, H. (1974): *Brain Res.,* 66:467–479.
26. Huston, J. P., and Bures, J. (1970): *Science,* 169:702–704.
27. Manning, F. J. (1973): *Physiol. Behav.,* 11:563–569.
28. Lynch, G., Ballentine, P., and Campbell, B. A. (1971): *Physiol. Behav.,* 7:737–741.
29. Leonard, C. M. (1969): *Brain Res.,* 12:321–343.
30. Nauta, W. J. H. (1972): *Acta Neurobiol. Exp.,* 32:125–140.
31. Rolls, E. T., and Cooper, S. J. (1973): *Brain Res.,* 60:351–368.
32. Rolls, E. T., and Cooper, S. J. (1974): *Physiol. Behav.,* 12:563–571.
33. Kawamura, Y., Kasahara, Y., and Funakoshi, M. (1970): *Physiol. Behav.,* 5:67–74.

Hunger: Basic Mechanisms and Clinical Implications,
edited by D. Novin, W. Wyrwicka, and G. Bray.
Raven Press, New York © 1976.

Hypothalamic Glucoreceptor Response—Biphasic Nature of Unit Potential Changes

Mary Ann Marrazzi

Department of Pharmacology, Wayne State University School of Medicine, Detroit, Michigan 48201

Hypothalamic glucoreceptors are operationally defined as neurons that change their rate of firing in response to modified blood glucose. Such units have been found in the ventromedial hypothalamus (VMH) and lateral hypothalamus (LH) (i.e., the respective presumed satiety and feeding centers) leading to the proposal that these units are the specific functional entities of Mayer's hypothalamic glucostat theory for the hypothalamic control of food intake.

Another potential role of hypothalamic glucoreceptors in a direct regulation of metabolic homeostasis, through autonomic and/or endocrine control, would also reflect itself in the regulation of food intake.

Existence of hypothalamic glucoreceptors has been described by several different groups (1–8), especially those of Oomura and Anand. They used a variety of species (including rat, rabbit, cat, and dog) and changed the blood glucose by a variety of methods (intravenous, intracarotid, or electroosmotic glucose administration, intracarotid 2-deoxyglucose injection, starvation, or intravenous insulin injection). The electrical response was monitored extracellularly using either multi- or single-unit recording. Oomura et al. (9) have recently done intracellular recording from these units.

We have recorded hypothalamic glucoreceptor activity in a preparation suitable for studies in which function and the local microchemistry can be correlated by utilizing a combination of electrophysiological monitoring and Lowry microchemical techniques (10).

However, before I discuss that, let me note that localized biochemical studies of glucose or energy metabolism in these hypothalamic nuclei are largely limited to two early studies. In 1954, Forssberg and Larsson (11) showed that $^{32}P_i$ (inorganic phosphate) and ^{14}C-glucose uptake in an area including the VMH and LH increase in starvation. There was an increase in acid-soluble, acid-labile phosphate, which they presume to be adenosine triphosphate (ATP) and phosphocreatine (PCr). However, the area included both of the two nuclei thought to act in a reciprocal manner and was without the benefit of more specific assays for ATP and PCr now available. In 1961, Anand et al. (12) found oxygen and glucose consumption to be 10 to 20% greater in tissue slices of the VMH than the LH in the fed state and the converse in the starved state. We plan to reapproach the biochemical studies with Lowry microchemical techniques.

A gallamine-immobilized rat preparation is used for VMH recording. For a variety of reasons, including the relative ease of achieving the necessary quick freezing for microchemistry, the rat was selected for these studies. Male Sprague Dawley rats, 290 to 320 g, were used. After an initial induction dose of thiopental, the rat is switched over to local lidocaine anesthesia and gallamine neuromuscular block to avoid the complication of a general anesthesia. Blood pressure, EKG, and rectal temperature are continuously monitored routinely.

Glucose is administered by close-arterial injection into the carotid artery. In this way, it is delivered by the natural blood-borne route, but its principal effects are localized to the central nervous system, since peripheral effects will be largely avoided by the reduction in peripheral dose resulting from the dilution in the general circulation. A gradual build-up of hypothalamic glucose and recovery is thus achieved and the effect is continuously monitored electrically. Furthermore, distributing the glucose *throughout* the hypothalamus has two advantages for our project. First, we are able to compare the local microchemistry of firing neurons, which behave as glucoreceptors, with controls that have simultaneously been exposed to this same sugar concentration without change in their rate of firing in response to the same stimulus. Second, we can activate a population of hypothalamic glucoreceptors which must act in concert to produce a neuronal control of food intake. Thus we can correlate the electrical response with its regulatory physiological roles, such as control of appetite.

The intracarotid injection is achieved with a polyethylene cannula in the external carotid pointing in the retrograde direction with its tip near the bifurcation. Thus blood flow from the common carotid washes the injection into the brain via the internal carotid artery without ever interrupting blood flow to the brain.

A femoral artery cannula with its tip near the iliac artery provides for uniform (microliter size) blood sampling. Blood sugar is monitored by "on-the-spot" Dextrostix-reflectance meter[1] readings, with more detailed analysis by enzymatic fluorometric assay (13) done later. Fasting is used to stabilize blood sugar.

A tungsten microelectrode with an 8μm tip is directed stereotaxically to the point given in the Pellegrino atlas (14) as $+5.8$ A-P, -1.0 L, and -3.0 to -4.0 H, from ear bar zero. The multiunit recording achieved with this relatively broad electrode tip was chosen so that a small population of units could be monitored without averaging the more massive effects entering into field potentials. We plan to correlate such function with the local microchemistry of the small group of cells immediately surrounding the microelectrode tip from

---

[1] Ames Eyetone meter.

which we just recorded and hence in a known functional state at the time of sampling. Lowry microchemical techniques (15) are sensitive assays which can monitor energy metabolism in 0.01 μg samples, the size of large single neurons, or in this case of a small group of small neurons. The sample sizes for the electrical and chemical measures will match better with multiunit monitoring.

With this preparation, we have confirmed the increased firing of rat hypothalamic glucoreceptors in the VMH activated by locally applied glucose of Oomura et al. (4). Continuous monitoring during and subsequent to hypothalamic glucose changes from external carotid infusion enabled detection of a regularly biphasic response not previously reported.

Three different doses in three different rats are shown. In Fig. 1, strip 1 shows the control rate of firing. Glucose injection is started between strips 1 and 2, with strips 1, 2, and 3 continuous in time. Strip 2 shows an excitation or increased rate of firing including the appearance (increase over zero) of a new unit of larger amplitude. Strip 3, in this case while glucose is still on, shows a post excitatory depression or decreased rate of firing to below control level. Strip 4 shows the return to control level.

Characteristic all-or-none amplitudes can be used to identify individual units in the multiunit recording. In Fig. 2 each different bar designates a

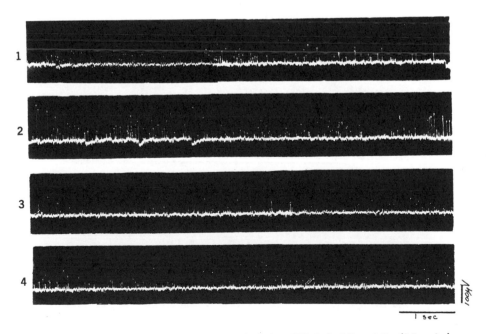

FIG. 1. Intracarotid glucose given as a constant speed infusion of 17 μl of a 0.5 M solution (8.5 μmoles) was started at time zero and completed in 24 sec. Times for the records shown are 1: control, −8 to 0 sec; 2: after glucose, 0 to +8 sec; 3: postexcitatory depression, 8 to 16 sec; 4: recovery, 32 to 40 sec.

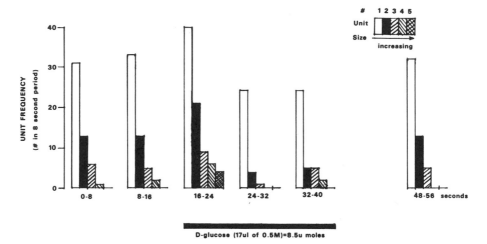

FIG. 2. 16 sec in this notation by 8-sec epochs corresponds to zero time of Fig. 1.

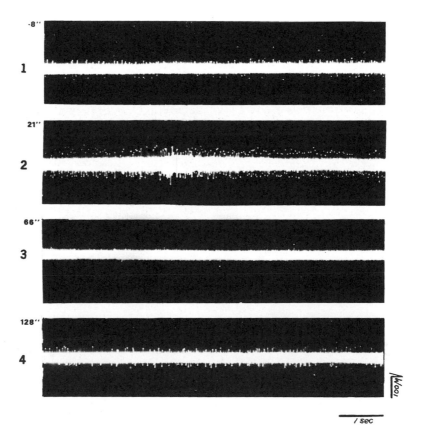

FIG. 3. Intracarotid glucose given as a constant speed infusion of 43 μl of 0.5 M solution (12.7 μmoles) was started at time zero and completed in 21 sec. Times for the records shown are 1: control, -8 to 0 sec; 2: after glucose, 21 to 29 sec; 3: postexcitatory depression, 66 to 74 sec; 4: recovery, 128 to 136 sec.

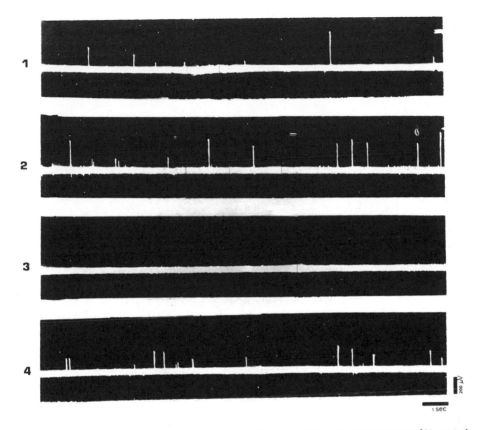

FIG. 1. Intracarotid glucose given as a constant speed infusion of 120 μl of a 0.5 M solution (60 μmoles) was started at time zero and completed in 40 sec. Times for the records shown are 1: control, −150 to −135 sec; 2: after glucose, 46 to 61 sec; 3: postexcitatory depression, 118 to 133 sec; 4: recovery, 214 to 229 sec.

separate unit (in order of increasing size) and frequency in spikes/8 sec is plotted against time in 8-sec epochs. All of the units shown demonstrated a glucoreceptor response, but to varying degrees. Perhaps the clearest is the solid black bar. The double cross-hatched bar in period 3 shows the appearance of the new larger unit.

Figure 3 shows the same biphasic pattern for a lower amplitude higher frequency firing pattern. The biphasic pattern for a single unit recording is shown in Fig. 4. To eliminate the possibility of an osmotic effect, the lack of effect of an equiosmolar saline control injection on the same unit immediately following the glucose record is shown in Fig. 5.

The lack of osmotic effect is to be expected. The glucose (given as a 0.5 M solution) must be diluted less than one to two on injection (into the carotid circulation) to be isotonic. Novin and Durham (16) and Hayward (see ref. 17), for example, have shown that a three-fold hypertonicity is needed to activate osmoreceptors in the neighboring supraoptic nucleus and that glucose is less effective than saline (18). In accord with this, Oomura et al. (4) reported

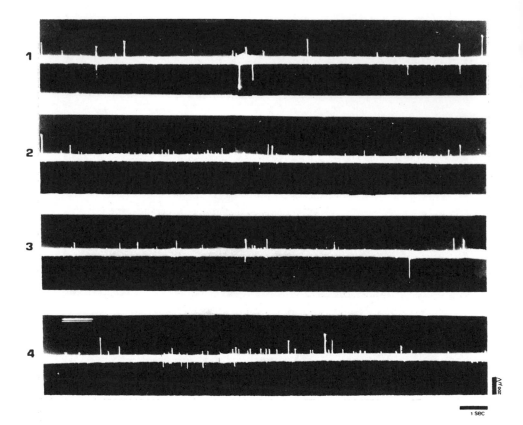

FIG. 5. Saline in a solution equiosmolar (0.25 M) with that of the glucose in Fig. 4 was given under the same conditions immediately following the glucose record in Fig. 4 without moving the electrode placement. Records for the corresponding time periods are shown.

that none of the glucose-sensitive units in the VMH were responsive to saline, even with electroosmotic application.

The biphasic nature of the unit potential changes was found for every glucoreceptor response. Specificity of the glucoreceptor response is suggested because only about 25% of the spontaneously firing units tested were responsive to glucose.

Previous studies have, on the whole, described most glucoreceptors in the VMH to be excited by increased glucose but a few to be inhibited and the converse in the LH. The biphasic response described here raises the possibility that there is just one type of hypothalamic glucoreceptor with a range of thresholds. Thus a fixed dose of glucose not continuously monitored but sampled at one instant or brief period would show only one phase of the response, with the particular phase seen for a given unit depending on its threshold. Thus the system appears not to be critically damped, as is true of many other homeostatic systems.

The mechanism of the postexcitatory depression remains to be elucidated. Three possibilities come to mind. First, it represents a fatiguing of some component of the neural conduction or transmission mechanisms. Second, the high intracarotid glucose, seen by the brain, triggers a central regulatory mechanism to lower the blood glucose subsequently reaching the brain. Although this cannot be eliminated at present, the rapid time course and preliminary blood glucose measurements make this unlikely. Third, a variety of neuronal and/or endocrine feedback loops, including, for example, responsiveness to insulin, may be the mechanism accounting for the apparent postexcitatory depression. We plan to use blocks of these possible mechanisms, including formation of a hypothalamic island, to determine the role of negative feedback. Such biphasic responses have similarly been described for a variety of synaptic activations of neuronal activity (19).

We believe the description of this biphasic response not previously reported demonstrates the potential of this system to look at hypothalamic glucoreceptor function. Our data lead us to the relevant study of hypothalamic local or neural micrometabolism to clarify the operation of hypothalamic glucoreceptors. Lowry microchemical methods are appropriately sensitive monitors of glucose metabolism, and we are adapting them to a special technique that will sample the cells generating the potential recorded by the microelectrode.

This progress report is an introduction to attacking questions concerning the nature of the receptor and transduction mechanism and the control mechanisms mediated by these glucoreceptor units. Perhaps better understanding of these glucoreceptors will lead to a new basis for the design of anorexics.

ACKNOWLEDGMENT

This research was supported by NINDS Postdoctoral Fellowship NS53397–02 and NIH General Research Support Grant RR05384.

REFERENCES

1. Anand, B. K., Chhina, G. S., Sharma, K. N., Dua, S., and Singh, B. (1964): *Am. J. Physiol.*, 207:1146.
2. Desiraju, T., Banerjee, M. G., and Anand, B. K. (1968): *Physiol. Behav.*, 3:757.
3. Chhina, G. S., Anand, B. K., Singh, B., and Rao, P. S. (1971): *Am. J. Physiol.*, 221:662.
4. Oomura, Y., Ono, T., Ooyama, H., and Wayner, M. J. (1969): *Nature*, 222:283.
5. Oomura, Y. (1973): *Adv. Biophys.*, 5:65.
6. Brown, K., and Melzack, R. (1969): *Exp. Neurol.*, 24:363.
7. Krebs, H., and Bindra, D. (1971): *Nature*, 229:178.
8. Kotlyar, B. I., and Yeroshenko, T. (1971): *Physiol. Behav.*, 7:609.
9. Oomura, Y., Ooyama, H., Sugimori, M., Nakamura, T., and Yamada, Y. (1974): *Nature*, 247:284.
10. Marrazzi, M. A. (1974): *Fed. Proc.*, 33:294.
11. Forssberg, A., and Larsson, S. (1954): *Acta Physiol. Scand. (Suppl. 115)*, 32:41.
12. Anand, B. K., Talwar, G. P., Dua, S., and Mhatre, R. M. (1961): *Ind. J. Med. Res.*, 49:725.

13. Lowry, O. H., Passoneau, J. V., Hasselberger, F. X. and Schulz, D. W. (1964): *J. Biol. Chem.*, 239:18.
14. Pellegrino, L. J., and Cushman, A. J. (1967): *A Stereotaxic Atlas of the Rat Brain.* Appleton-Century-Crofts, New York.
15. Lowry, O. H. (1962): *Bull. NY Acad. Med.*, 38:789.
16. Novin, D., and Durham, R. (1969): *Ann. NY Acad. Sci.*, 157:740.
17. Hayward, J. N., and Jennings, D. P. (1973): *J. Physiol.*, 232:545.
18. Hayward, J. N., and Jennings, D. P. (1973): *Brain Res.*, 57:467.
19. Marrazzi, A. S. (1975): In: *Legacies in the Study of Behavior: The Wisdom and Experience of Many,* edited by Joseph W. Cullen. C. C Thomas, Springfield, Ill.

Hunger: Basic Mechanisms and Clinical Implications,
edited by D. Novin, W. Wyrwicka, and G. Bray.
Raven Press, New York © 1976.

The Role of Activation in the Regulation of Food Intake

D. L. Wolgin, J. Cytawa, and P. Teitelbaum

Department of Psychology, University of Illinois, Urbana-Champaign, Illinois 61801 and Department of Physiology, Gdansk School of Medicine, Gdansk, Poland

For several years, analysis of the recovery from the aphagia and adipsia produced by lateral hypothalamic (LH) damage (the LH syndrome) has focused on the deficits in homeostasis that occur in the later stages of recovery. This work has shown, for example, that so-called "recovered lateral" rats do not respond normally to thirst challenges like cellular dehydration (1) or hypovolemia (2), and so drink only prandially (i.e., when they eat) (see refs. 1, 3). Furthermore, although such animals do eat more in the cold, they do not eat more in response to lowered blood glucose availability produced by 2-deoxy-D-glucose (4–6), or by insulin (7).

In spite of these deficits, however, the recovered LH-damaged rat eats relatively normal quantities daily and regulates its body weight remarkably well, even if the set point for such regulation appears lower than normal (8, see also ref. 9). This means that the later deficits in homeostasis cannot be responsible for the failure to eat seen in the early stages of recovery. Therefore, our more recent analyses have focused on the nature of the deficits in Stage I (aphagia) and Stage II (anorexia). Our work suggests that two kinds of nonhomeostatic impairments contribute to the disturbances in feeding in these early stages. One of these is multimodal sensory neglect (10, 11); the other, only recently appreciated (12–14), is the loss of endogenous activation.

SENSORY NEGLECT

Flynn and his collaborators have shown that the hypothalamus can exert a profound effect on the sensorimotor integration involved in such instinctive motivated acts as attacking, killing, and eating prey (see ref. 15 for a recent review). Electrical stimulation of sites in the cat's hypothalamus evokes a quiet biting attack on a rat. If the cat's body is restrained during unilateral hypothalamic excitation and the contralateral snout region is touched, the cat reflexively turns its head toward the touch (ipsilateral touch is ineffective). Increasing the intensity of hypothalamic excitation causes the sensory field for this reflex to expand posteriorly along the snout. Similarly, touch of the contralateral lip during hypothalamic excitation elicits jaw opening, and sight of a mouse in the contralateral visual field elicits lunging. Therefore, the hypothalamus facilitates killing by opening up sensory fields for specific stimuli that release the patterned reflexes involved in attack behavior.

The loss of similar sensorimotor reflexes of orientation and ingestion contributes to the aphagia of Stage I of the LH syndrome (10, 11). Thus, following LH lesions, rats show severe deficits in orientation to visual, olfactory, and tactile stimuli associated with food. After unilateral damage, they neglect such stimuli on the contralateral side of the body and preferentially take food from the ipsilateral side. Furthermore, after bilateral damage, the initial recovery of feeding (i.e., the transition from aphagia to anorexia) coincides with the return of orientation to olfactory stimuli and to whisker touch. Therefore, the feeding deficits in the first stage of the lateral hypothalamic syndrome are intimately tied to specific sensorimotor impairments.

LOSS OF ENDOGENOUS ACTIVATION

Along with neglect, rats with large LH lesions display somnolence, catalepsy, and akinesia (11, 12, 16). As we show, manipulations that counteract these states also counteract aphagia. As shown by Levitt and Teitelbaum (12), early in Stage I these rats remain in a somnolent stupor from which they can be aroused only momentarily by sufficiently intense stimuli, such as a tail pinch. When the stimulus ceases, the animals return to their somnolent state. Gradually, somnolence gives way to a state of akinesia in which the rats remain in a standing position but show no spontaneous locomotion. Such rats are also cataleptic. They allow their limbs to be placed in awkward positions of abduction that are not tolerated by normal rats, and they cannot extricate themselves when draped over obstacles. They do show some behaviors, however. A variety of stereotyped motor automatisms, like grooming, teeth chattering, and scratching, can be readily elicited even though more complex self-initiated or self-guided patterns, like walking or orienting, are totally lacking.

These deficits in wakefulness and spontaneity seem to be caused by a persistent lack of endogenous activation, perhaps related to damage to the reticular activating system which runs through the LH (17, 18). Consistent with this interpretation is the finding that intense stimuli can momentarily activate many behavior patterns that do not otherwise appear (12). For example, when placed in a tank of lukewarm water, LH-lesioned rats sink to the bottom. However, when the water is colder, they swim quite vigorously. In one striking case, an otherwise akinetic rat swam rapidly across the tank, climbed up on the edge, leaped to the floor, ran a quarter of a meter, and then lapsed back into immobility. Such phenomena suggest that the lack of voluntary behavior in the early stages of recovery is due to deficits in the tonic activating system that is necessary to maintain the normal spontaneity of behavior.

Many of these phenomena can be seen even more dramatically in the cat, an animal whose sensorimotor coordination is exquisitely developed. Wolgin and Teitelbaum (14) have found that as in the rat, LH lesions in the cat produce aphagia and adipsia, followed by recovery in the same four stages. Therefore, the stages of recovery are intrinsic to the phenomenon, and are not an artifact of the species used previously. In the early stages, the deficits in orientation to sensory stimuli and in arousal are particulary striking. In the immediate postoperative period, the cats are somnolent. They typically sit in a hunched posture with ther heads touching the floor (Fig. 1a). It is generally difficult to arouse such animals, even with nociceptive stimuli (tail pinch, pin prick), and initially at least, the only stimulus to which they will respond is a loud noise. As shown in Fig. 1b–d, the cat then raises its head very slowly, and then lets it subside just as slowly, until it once again comes to rest on the floor.

After a brief period of recovery, somnolence gives way to a period characterized by catalepsy, akinesia, and bilateral neglect of visual, tactile, and olfactory stimuli. By catalepsy we mean the tendency to maintain awkward postures spontaneously assumed and to retain postures imposed by the experimenter. For example, when such a cat is placed on a vertical support, e.g., the back of a chair, it develops strong flexion tone in its forelimbs and clings tenaciously for long periods of time. In contrast, a normal cat quickly jumps to the floor or climbs over the top of the chair.

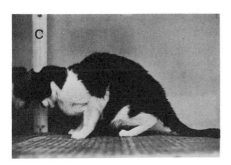

FIG. 1. a: Somnolent, akinetic, and aphagic LH-lesioned cat (Stage I). (b–d): In response to noise, the cat rises, then slowly subsides.

ACTIVATION AND AGGRESSIVE BEHAVIOR

As might be expected, these impairments severely disrupt all voluntary behavior, not only feeding. However, the deficits in attack behavior are particularly instructive. In the early postoperative period, a cat with LH lesions will
not spontaneously attack a mouse. Even if the mouse is pressed against its
snout, the cat will not kill the mouse. At best, it will hold the mouse in its
teeth and then fall asleep with the mouse dangling from its jaws (Fig. 2).
Thus, in the early stages, the patterned reflexes normally activated by the sight,

FIG. 2. Top: Normal cat attacking a mouse. Bottom: When a mouse is pressed against the snout of LH
lesioned cat, it grasps the mouse in its jaws and then falls asleep.

smell, and touch of a mouse, and which are controlled by the hypothalamus, are severely impaired. However, later in recovery, some of these reflexes reappear. At first, the cat will track a mouse only with its eyes. Later in recovery, it will stalk the mouse and try to trap it with its forepaws, but makes no attempt to bite it. Still later in recovery, it will stalk, pounce on, and trap the mouse but, instead of making the killing bite, it makes a "killing kiss," i.e., it lowers its head as though to bite, but then merely touches the mouse with its closed mouth. This is similar to a phenomenon reported by MacDonnell and Flynn (19) that when the sensory branches of the trigeminal nerve are sectioned, cats that had attacked and killed a rat during electrical stimulation of the LH no longer make the killing bite when they catch the rat. Instead, they too seem to kiss the rat. This suggests that, like sensory denervated cats, the cat with LH lesions is unable to use the sensory information from the snout necessary for the normal act of killing. A similar role for trigeminal input in feeding in the rat has been demonstrated by Zeigler and Karten (20). However, we have recently found that with sufficient activation, many of the patterned reflexes involved in attack can be reinstated in the LH-lesioned cat (see also ref. 21). Thus, when its tail is pinched, a cat that had been totally unresponsive will orient briskly to tactile stimulation of the head and body. When its snout is touched, it will lunge toward the stimulus and snap at it. When presented with a mouse, it quickly pounces on it, kills it with a vicious bite, and then devours it. These are the same patterned reflexes that are elicited in the normal cat by LH stimulation. Therefore, the sensorimotor mechanisms that are involved in attack have not been abolished by the lesions. Instead, the lesions have impaired a system that controls the activation of those mechanisms.

ACTIVATION OF FEEDING

Like the deficits in attack, all of the phenomena that accompany aphagia (i.e., somnolence, catalepsy, and akinesia) may be considered manifestations of deficient endogenous activation, and all can be counteracted by stressful stimuli, e.g., pain or cold (12, 22). In the same way, a lack of activation seems also to be a contributing factor in the lack of interest in food. We have therefore tried to promote feeding in cats in Stage I by placing a painful clamp on their tails. This usually elicits a brief, very slow bout of locomotion and, if food is placed immediately in front of the cat, prompts reflexive licking, chewing, and ingestion with little or no overt signs of pain or rage that would be elicited in a normal cat. Later in recovery, when the cat eats limited quantities of palatable food spontaneously, the phenomenon can be seen more clearly. Thus, in Stage II, activation by tail clamp prompts voluntary approach to the food and such vigorous feeding that the cat may gain weight for the first time since surgery. For example, a cat that ate only 18 g of food overnight, ate four times that amount in 15 min with the clamp. However, they are still quite finicky; even with the clamp the cats do not eat dry chow or drink water, even if these are the only substances available.

The activating effect of pain might well be due to its effect on the damaged reticular activating system. If so, then pharmacological activation of this system should also promote feeding. Amphetamine, a potent pharmacological stimulant, is well known for its antinarcoleptic and anticataleptic properties (23–26). As shown in Fig. 3, we have found that we can activate feeding and increase body weight dramatically in the anorexic cat (Stage II) by an injection of *d*-amphetamine sulfate (2 mg/kg). The same dose given to normal cats almost totally inhibits food intake and causes a sharp drop in body weight.

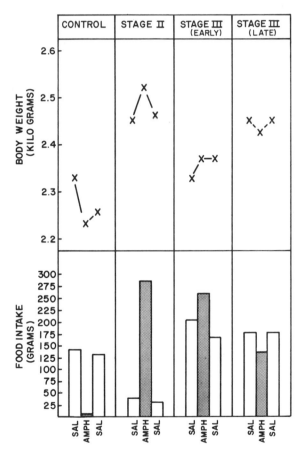

FIG. 3. Control: 2 mg/kg *d*-amphetamine sulfate in the normal cat greatly depresses the amount of food eaten in a daily 3-hr feeding period, with consequent weight loss. Stage II: Paradoxically, the same dose of amphetamine injected into an anorexic LH-lesioned cat, which otherwise eats very little in its 3-hr feeding periods, causes it to eat a very large amount of food and gain weight. Early Stage III: When the cat eats enough to gain weight steadily, the anorexic action of amphetamine begins to recover, nearly balancing its activating effect on feeding. Late Stage III (and thereafter): The anorexic action of amphetamine is predominant, but less effective than in the normal cat.

Similar results have recently been reported in rats with electrolytic lesions in the LH or following intraventricular injection of 6-hydroxydopamine (13). This hyperphagic effect of amphetamine in the LH-lesioned cat demonstrates that the drug has two effects with respect to feeding: first, its well-known anorexigenic effect, which is usually prepotent; and second, an activating effect, which is normally inhibited. When the anorexigenic effect is abolished, as with LH lesions, the activating effect is unmasked. Liebowitz (27) has shown a similar fractionation of the effects of intrahypothalamic amphetamine in the neurologically intact rat pretreated with LH injection of propranalol, a beta-adrenergic blocker.

As is also shown in Fig. 3, with recovery of spontaneous feeding the anorexic action of amphetamine returns, passing through a phase of equal balance between activation and anorexia (early Stage III, Fig. 3), where amphetamine seems to have little effect on eating, through a phase of sub-normal anorexia (late Stake III, Fig. 3), the effect which is well-known in LH-lesioned animals (28–30). This change in the apparent effect of amphetamine on feeding underscores the fact that each stage of recovery represents a different level of nervous control over feeding. (It also suggests that the recovering brain-damaged animal is an excellent preparation for fractionating, and thereby analyzing, the multiple effects of psychoactive drugs.) The activating effect in the early stages lends strong support to the view that aphagia and anorexia, like somnolence, catalepsy, and akinesia, all result in large part from a chronic deficit in endogenous activation.

ACTIVATION BY SENSORY STIMULI

In the course of recovery, sensory stimuli begin to activate feeding just as do pain and amphetamine. For example, when the cats recover to the point that they orient to visual and tactile stimuli, they begin to approach the feeding dishes and to eat limited quantities of palatable foods. This transition to Stage II, the stage of anorexia, is controlled primarily by visual stimuli. If opaque contact occluders are placed in their eyes, the cats do not approach the food, and will not eat it even if it is held directly in front of their mouths (Fig. 4, Bottom). In contrast, a normal cat with occluders readily eats food that is held near its face or placed randomly around its cage (Fig. 4, Top). Therefore, in Stage II, feeding is activated by sight of the food.

Even with vision, however, cats in Stage II do not eat enough to regulate their body weight. The transition to Stage III, when weight regulation on palatable food returns, is marked by the emergence of olfactory control over feeding; that is, once the cats regain the ability to localize food by olfaction alone, with their eyes occluded, a new level of control is reached. Food intake and body weight take a dramatic turn upward, and the cat begins to regulate its weight on palatable food. This suggests that smell is also an activating stimulus. Indeed, the general activating effect of smell can be isolated in the

FIG. 4. Top: Normal cat with opaque occluders in its eyes orients to food and begins to eat it. Bottom: Anorexic lateral hypothalamic cat (Stage II) does not orient to food when its eyes are occluded and does not eat even when food is held near its face.

course of recovery: when the eyes are occluded, smell first activates excited random searching; then, later in recovery, it helps in localization. Therefore, in addition to their directing and reinforcing properties, sensory stimuli also have an activating component which energizes the animal and helps maintain the act of feeding.

LOSS OF ACTIVATION AFTER POSTERIOR HYPOTHALAMIC LESIONS

The role of activation in the control of feeding can be seen even more clearly following damage to the posterior hypothalamus. As is well known

(31–37), lesions of the posterior hypothalamus produce severe deficits in arousal with attendant aphagia and adipsia. We have found that rats with such lesions are somnolent for more than 1 week and remain akinetic and cataleptic for several months. As are rats with LH lesions, such animals have deficits in initiating voluntary movements (e.g., walking and swimming) even though more stereotyped automatic movements (e.g., grooming) remain relatively unimpaired. Thus, when placed in a tank of warm water, these animals sink to the bottom and, at the same time, may engage in vigorous face grooming (37). We have found that the aphagia and adipsia that accompany such deficits typically last for about 1 week, during which time the rat's body weight may drop by as much as 30%. However, unlike rats with LH lesions, these rats do not display sensory neglect; that is, they respond quite normally to sensory stimuli. As a result, some of the residual deficits that seem to contribute to aphagia in the LH-lesioned rat can be seen much more clearly in rats with posterior lesions. For example, such rats have difficulties biting, licking, and using their paws to hold food. We have occasionally seen similar deficits in rats with LH lesions, but they are much more short-lived and difficult to assess because they are masked by the accompanying deficit of sensory neglect.

Because they lack neglect, rats with posterior lesions are also more responsive to external activation than animals with LH lesions. For example, in the immediate postoperative period when the rats are extremely somnolent, feeding can be activated by relatively innocuous stimuli, such as dripping water on the snout. In response to such activation, the rat typically begins to groom and then gradually redirects its activity to the food. This activational spread to related instinctive activities (i.e., from grooming to feeding) is similar in many respects to the neurological phenomenon of the spread of allied reflexes. For example, in the human, a mild nociceptive stimulus to the foot may elicit a withdrawal reflex involving only the toes (the Babinski reflex) but, with a more intense stimulus, the reflex spreads to include flexion withdrawal of the ankle, knee, and thigh. In a similar way, a drop of water on the snout of the rat with posterior lesions first elicits grooming. The rat methodically wipes its face with its paws, licks them, and then wipes its face again. As additional drops of water land on its snout, the pattern becomes increasingly more vigorous until at last the rat appears to be caught up in a frenzy of paw licking and face wiping. At this point, if the rat comes into contact with a dish of food, it will begin to lick and nibble the dish. However, the amplitude and vigor of these reflexive acts are very weak. Then, as it tastes the food, the licking and biting become more rapid and vigorous until finally the rat appears to be engaged in relatively effective feeding, using its paws to hold the food, biting off bits of pellets, and chewing normally. At this point, grooming has spread to feeding. However, such feeding is critically dependent on external activation and is therefore much more reflexive than in the normal rat. Thus, when the steady stream of droplets stops, feeding gradually wanes and the rat lapses

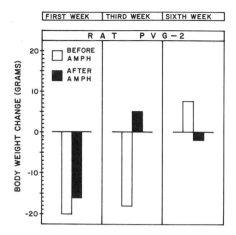

FIG. 5. Body weight changes before and after 2 mg/kg d-amphetamine sulfate in a posterior hypothalamic rat. First Week: In the early postoperative period, amphetamine has little effect on feeding. Third Week: Later in recovery, amphetamine promotes a large increase in food intake, resulting in weight gain. Sixth Week: When the rat begins to eat enough to gain weight, the anorexic effect of amphetamine returns.

back into somnolence. If left to itself without activation, such a rat may remain aphagic for several days. More prolonged activation can be effected pharmacologically. As in the cat, *d*-amphetamine promotes dramatic increases in food intake and body weight in these rats early in recovery (Fig. 5, first and third weeks). Later in recovery, the activating effect diminishes and the anorexic effect returns, but always in subnormal degree (Fig. 5, sixth week).

SUMMARY AND CONCLUSIONS

In summary, then, we believe that several important generalities emerge from the present work. The somnolence, catalepsy, and akinesia that appear in the early stages of recovery suggest that a major effect of LH lesions is a loss of endogenous activation. Because of this, intense stimuli (e.g., pain) or stimulant drugs (e.g., amphetamine) are necessary to energize behavior, presumably by their strong action on the damaged reticular system. Similar phenomena can also be seen following damage to the nigrostriatal bundle (38), posterior hypothalamus (31), or retromammillary region (32), or after circumsection of the hypothalamus (21, 39).

Heilman et al. (40) recently suggested that sensory neglect may also be caused by deficient endogenous activation. They note that neglect is found following damage to the frontal lobes (41–43), parietal lobes (44–48), cingulate gyrus (49), subthalamus (50, 51), and mesencephalic reticular formation (42, 52), all of which are part of a corticolimbic reticular activating system. Therefore, neglect may be caused by a loss of reticular activation produced by a disconnection of this system. The reinstatement of orientation to somatosensory stimulation and of attack that we observed in our cats following a tail pinch is consistent with this view.

The lack of tonic arousal also exaggerates the importance of the activating component of sensory stimuli. This can be seen most clearly in the cat in the case of olfaction: when orientation to smell is impaired, there is minimal intake of food; when this orientation has recovered, there is the return of regulation. This role of activation in the control of feeding represents a departure from the current emphasis on homeostatic views in which intake is thought to occur solely in response to internal signals arising from the depletion of body nutrients. According to this view, sensory stimuli (e.g., smell) may be involved in the detection of food, but should have nothing at all to do with regulation. Instead, our data strongly suggest that sensory stimuli are enormously important for regulation. They provide the background activation which maintains feeding behavior.

In a sense, homeostatic regulatory behavior involves two kinds of variables: (a) those involved in detecting physiological changes in the internal environment (the traditional view of homeostasis) and (b) those variables involved in reacting to the external environment which enable the animal to approach and ingest the food needed to counteract the changes in the internal environment. We can conceive of the stages of the LH syndrome as revealing differentially the variables involved in each of these aspects of homeostatic behavior. The later stages (Stage III and Stage IV) reveal very clearly the deficits involved in internal homeostasis; the early stages (Stage I and Stage II) reveal most clearly the variables involved in the action required to obtain food.

ACKNOWLEDGMENT

This work was supported by a Postdoctoral Fellowship from the Institute on Neurological Sciences, University of Pennsylvania, School of Medicine, U.S. Public Health Service Grant 5 T01 NS 05273, to David L. Wolgin, and by U.S. Public Health Service Grant R01 NS 11671 to Philip Teitelbaum, University of Illinois.

REFERENCES

1. Epstein, A. N., and Teitelbaum, P. (1964): Severe and persistent deficits in thirst produced by lateral hypothalamic damage: In: *Thirst,* edited by M. J. Wayner, pp. 395–410. Pergamon Press, Oxford.
2. Stricker, E. M., and Wolf, G. (1967): The effects of hypovolemia on drinking in rats with lateral hypothalamic damage. *Proc. Soc. Exp. Biol. Med.,* 124:816–820.
3. Kissileff, H. R., and Epstein, A. N. (1969): Exaggerated prandial drinking in the "recovered lateral" rat without saliva. *J. Comp. Physiol. Psychol.,* 67:301–308.
4. Kanner, M., and Balagura, S. (1971): Loss of feeding response to 2-deoxy-D-glucose by recovered lateral hypothalamic rats. *Am. Zool.,* 11:624.
5. Miselis, R. R., and Epstein, A. N. (1971): Preoptic-hypothalamic mediation of feeding induced by cerebral glucoprivation. *Am. Zool.,* 11:624.
6. Wayner, M. J., Cott, A., Millner, J., and Tartaglione, R. (1971): Loss of 2-deoxy-D-glucose induced eating in recovered lateral rats. *Physiol. Behav.,* 7:881–884.
7. Epstein, A. N., and Teitelbaum, P. (1967): Specific loss of the hypoglycemic control of feeding in recovered lateral rats. *Am. J. Physiol.,* 213:1159–1167.

8. Powley, T. L., and Keesey, R. E. (1970): Relationship of body weight to the lateral hypothalamic feeding syndrome. *J. Comp. Physiol. Psychol.,* 70:25–36.
9. Mufson, E. J., and Wampler, R. S. (1972): Weight regulation with palatable food and liquids in rats with lateral hypothalamic lesions. *J. Comp. Physiol. Psychol.,* 80:382–392.
10. Marshall, J. F., Turner, B. H., and Teitelbaum, P. (1971): Sensory neglect produced by lateral hypothalamic damage. *Science,* 174:523–525.
11. Marshall, J. F., and Teitelbaum, P. (1974): Further analysis of sensory inattention following lateral hypothalamic damage in rats. *J. Comp. Physiol. Psychol.,* 86:375–395.
12. Levitt, D. R., and Teitelbaum, P. (1973): Somnolence, akinesia and sensory activation of motivated behavior in the lateral hypothalamic syndrome. Paper presented at the meetings of the Eastern Psychological Association in Washington, D.C.
13. Stricker, E. M., and Zigmond, M. J. (1976): Recovery of function following damage to central catecholamine-containing neurons: A neurochemical model for the lateral hypothalamic syndrome. In: *Progr. Phychobiol. Physiol. Psychol.,* Vol. 6.
14. Wolgin, D. L., and Teitelbaum, P. (1974): The role of activation and sensory stimuli in the recovery of feeding following lateral hypothalamic lesions in the cat. Paper presented at the meetings of the Eastern Psychological Association in Philadelphia.
15. Flynn, J. P., Edwards, S. B., and Bandler, R. J. (1971): Changes in sensory and motor systems during centrally elicited attack. *Behav. Sci.,* 16:1–19.
16. Balagura, S., Wilcox, R. H., and Coscina, D. V. (1969): The effect of diencephalic lesions on food intake and motor activity. *Physiol. Behav.,* 4:629–633.
17. Anchel, H., and Lindsley, D. B. (1972): Differentiation of two reticulohypothalamic systems regulating hippocampal activity. *EEG Clin. Neurophys.,* 32:209–226.
18. Macadar, A. W., Chalupa, L. M., and Lindsley, D. B. (1974): Differentiation of brain stem loci which affect hippocampal and neocortical electrical activity. *Exp. Neurol.,* 43:499–514.
19. MacDonnell, M., and Flynn, J. P. (1966): Sensory control of hypothalamic attack. *Anim. Behav.,* 14:399–405.
20. Zeigler, H. P., and Karten, H. J. (1974): Central trigeminal structures and the lateral hypothalamic syndrome in the rat. *Science,* 186:636–638.
21. Ellison, G. D., and Flynn, J. P. (1968): Organized aggressive behavior in cats after surgical isolation of the hypothalamus. *Arch. Ital. Biol.,* 106:1–20.
22. Wagner, H. N., and Woods, J. W. (1950): Interruption of bulbocapnine catalepsy in rats by environmental stress. *Arch. Neurol. Psychiatry,* 64:720–725.
23. Fog. R. (1972): *On Stereotypy and Catalepsy.* Munksgaard, Copenhagen.
24. Prinzmetal, M., and Bloomberg, W. (1935): The use of benzedrine for the treatment of narcolepsy, *JAMA,* 105:2051–2054.
25. Lutz, E. G. (1973): Narcolepsy. *Clin. Med.,* 80:14–19.
26. Zarcone, V. (1973): Narcolepsy. *N. Engl. J. Med.,* 288:1156–1166.
27. Leibowitz, S. F. (1970): Amphetamine's anorexic versus hunger-inducing effects mediated respectively by hypothalamic beta- versus alpha-adrenergic receptors. *Proc. 78th Ann. Conv. APA,* 813–814.
28. Carlisle, H. J. (1964): Differential effects of amphetamine on food and water intake in rats with lateral hypothalamic lesions. *J. Comp. Physiol. Psychol.,* 58:47–54.
29. Panksepp, J., and Booth, D. A. (1973): Tolerance in the depression of intake when amphetamine is added to the rat's food. *Psychopharmacologia,* 29:45–54.
30. Russek, M., Rodriguez-Zendejas, A. M., and Teitelbaum, P. (1973): The action of adrenergic anorexigenic substances on rats recovered from lateral hypothalamic lesions. *Physiol. Behav.,* 10:329–333.
31. Anand, B. K. (1955): Somnolence caused by destructive lesions in the hypothalamus in cat. *Ind. J. Med. Res.,* 43:195–199.
32. Ingram, W. R., Barris, R. W., and Ranson, S. W. (1936): Catalepsy: An experimental study. *Arch. Neurol. Psychiat.,* 35:1175–1197.
33. Lindsley, D. B., Schreiner, L. H., Knowles, W. B., and Magoun, H. W. (1950): Behavioral and EEG changes following chronic brain lesions in the cat. *EEG Clin. Neurophysiol.,* 2:483–498.

34. McGinty, D. J. (1969): Somnolence, recovery and hyposomnia following ventromedial diencephalic lesions in the rat. *EEG Clin. Neurophysiol.,* 26:70–79.
35. Nauta, W. J. H. (1946): Hypothalamic regulation of sleep in rats. An experimental study. *J. Neurophysiol.,* 9:285–316.
36. Ranson, S. W. (1939): Somnolence caused by hypothalamic lesions in the monkey, *Arch. Neurol. Psychiatry,* 41:1–23.
37. Robinson, T. E., and Whishaw, I. Q. (1974): Effects of posterior hypothalamic lesions on voluntary behavior and hippocampal electroencephalograms in the rat. *J. Comp. Physiol. Psychol.,* 86:768–786.
38. Marshall, J. F., Richardson, J. S., and Teitelbaum, P. (1974), Nigrostriatal bundle damage and the lateral hypothalamic syndrome. *J. Comp. Physiol. Psychol.,* 87:808–830.
39. Ellison, G. D., Sorenson, C. A., and Jacobs, B. L. (1970): Two feeding syndromes following surgical isolation of the hypothalamus in rats. *J. Comp. Physiol. Psychol.,* 70:173–188.
40. Heilman, K. M., Watson, R. T., and Schulman, H. M. (1974): A unilateral memory deficit. *J. Neurol. Neurosurg. Psychiatry,* 37:790–793.
41. Heilman, K. M., and Valenstein, E. (1972): Frontal lobe neglect in man. *Neurology,* 22:660–664.
42. Reeves, A. G., and Hagamen, W. D. (1971): Behavioral and EEG asymmetry following unilateral lesions of the forebrain and midbrain in cats. *EEG Clin. Neurophysiol.,* 30:83–86.
43. Welch, K., and Stuteville, P. (1958): Experimental production of unilateral neglect in monkeys. *Brain,* 81:341–347.
44. Critchley, M. (1953): *The Parietal Lobes.* Arnold, London.
45. Denny-Brown, D., and Chambers, R. A. (1958): The parietal lobe and behavior. *Res. Publ. Assoc. Res. Nerv. Ment. Dis.,* 36:35–117.
46. Heilman, K. M., and Valenstein, E. (1972): Auditory neglect in man. *Arch. Neurol.,* 26:32–35.
47. Heilman, K. M., Pandya, D. N., and Geschwind, N. (1970): Trimodal inattention following parietal lobe ablations. *Trans. Amer. Neurol. Assoc.,* 95:259–261.
48. Eidelberg, E., and Schwartz, A. S. (1971): Experimental analysis of the extinction phenomenon in monkeys. *Brain,* 94:91–108.
49. Watson, R. T., Heilman, K. M., Cauthen, J. C., and King, F. A. (1973): Neglect following cingulectomy. *Neurology,* 23:1003–1007.
50. Adey, W. R., Walter, D. O., and Lindsley, D. F. (1962): Subthalamic lesions. *Arch. Neurol.,* 6:194–207.
51. Hess, W. R. (1943): Induzierte Storungen der Optischen Wahrnehmung. *Nervenarzt,* 16:57–66.
52. Watson, R. T., Heilman, K. M., Miller, B. D., and King, F. A. (1974): Neglect after mesencephalic reticular formation lesions. *Neurology,* 24:294–298.

Hunger: Basic Mechanisms and Clinical Implications,
edited by D. Novin, W. Wyrwicka, and G. Bray.
Raven Press, New York © 1976.

Feeding and Drinking in Suckling Rats

Alan N. Epstein

Institute of Neurological Sciences and Department of Biology, University of Pennsylvania, Philadelphia, Pennsylvania 19174

The suckling of the infant mammal is the simplest of ingestive behaviors. The animal utilizes a single behavior to ingest a single fluid. The behavior is largely reflexive, or consumatory[1] in Craig's sense (1), and the fluid, both food and water, is provided by the dam as part of the life-support system on which the suckling depends as a virtual parasite. But the suckling period is brief, only 3 weeks in the rat, and (with the exception of the precocial species) the infant mammal must cope with the crisis of weaning. As it becomes a free-foraging adult, appetitive behaviors precede ingestion, and ingestion itself is no longer a simple act. It is differentiated into feeding and drinking, necessitating the search for, the selection of, and the separate regulations of food and free water.

Very little is known about the developmental process that permits the transition from suckling to weanling to be made with such obvious success. Our ignorance is the result of the peculiar difficulties that have obstructed the study of feeding and drinking behavior in the suckling, the most obvious of which is the frailty of the infant mammal and its complete dependence on the litter environment. Typically, newborn mammals are incapable of appetitive behavior and can not be studied in adult test circumstances. In addition, because milk is both food and water to the neonate, hunger and thirst have not been studied separately in the suckling period. Recently, my students (K. A. Houpt and J. B. Wirth) and I have overcome these obstacles and we can report (2, 3) that the suckling is amply prepared at the time of weaning for adult ingestive behavior. The crisis of weaning is met by a developmental process that is sequential and remarkably precocious. It begins before birth, continues throughout the suckling period, and culminates on the eve of weaning.

METHODS

Subjects

Both sucklings and weanlings of the Charles River strain were used. They were born in the laboratory of timed-pregnant females. Adults of both sexes

---

[1] I use consumatory here as a special case (i.e., referring to consumption) of Craig's more general term, consummatory (i.e., leading to consummation).

(of the same strain) were also used. Animals were not used more than once in any experiment.

Procedures

Studies of Sucklings

The methods for the studies of the feeding behavior of sucklings are described in detail by Houpt and Epstein (2). Essentially, the ingestion of mother's milk was measured by weight differences. Pups remained in their natural litters for short periods (usually 4 hr) after manipulations that were expected to increase their intake. Increases in weight were measures of increased milk intake. Two challenges were studied in detail. First, pups were deprived by removal to nonlactating foster dams. The mechanisms controlling the response to deprivation were studied with intragastric injections that were made with a miniaturized conventional technique requiring no anesthesia. Second, glucoprivation was studied with subcutaneous injections of 2-deoxy-ᴅ-glucose (2DG) made under the skin between the scapulae while the pups were gently hand held. Again, anesthesia was not used.

Studies of the drinking behavior of sucklings require their removal from the litter. The methods are described in full by Wirth and Epstein (3). Just before testing, litters of eight were removed from the dam for 2 hr and then returned to her for 1 hr 45 min of nursing. The one pup of each sex that gained least was excluded. This was done to assure that all experimental pups were maximally fed just prior to thirst testing. The recently fed litter of six (three males, three females) was then removed from the dam for a second and final time, weighed to the nearest 0.01 g, subjected to thirst challenge by subcutaneous injection, and transferred to a small box lined with paper towels and heated under a 25-W tungsten lamp (skin temperature maintained at 32°C). During the next 2 hr, each pup was held onto the outlet of a syringe for 15 sec every 15 min (nine bouts of testing for each pup) while water was infused into its mouth by a Harvard infusion pump. The suckling was held on the spout for the entire 15-sec period whether it licked, struggled, or was inactive. Water was infused into its mouth at a rate of 0.763 ml/min. At the end of the 2-hr test period, the pups were weighed again and water intake calculated by the following formula:

$$\frac{100 \times \text{weight gain during the test period}}{\text{body weight before nursing}}$$

This eliminates the weight of the milk taken during the nursing period. Other sources of weight loss can be neglected. Young pups do not defecate or micturate spontaneously and pulmocutaneous losses are neglible for periods of only 2 hr.

This method circumvents the obstacles to the study of drinking in suckling rats by (a) inserting a water spout directly into the suckling's mouth to provide it with water instead of milk and to make appetitive behavior unnecessary and (b) by holding the pup onto the spout during the test of ingestion thereby taking advantage of its well-developed consumatory reflexes.

Thirst challenges were (a) subcutaneous hypertonic saline (0.39 to 5.00 mOsm/100 g), (b) subcutaneous polyethylene glycol (PEG) (1.25ml/100 g of 10, 20, and 40% by volume in isotonic saline), (c) subcutaneous isoproterenol (100 to 2,000 μg/kg), (d) skin temperature elevation to 35 $\pm$1°C throughout the test period, and (e) overnight deprivation from nursing. The polyethylene glycol was given before the final nursing period. The overnight deprivation test omitted the final nursing period.

Litters were tested from the day of birth (day 0) until the day after thirst responding appeared. Naive litters were used for each challenge at each age. On the day of maximum responsiveness to each of the thirst challenges, litters of the same age were challenged and offered Esbilac (Borden's artificial bitch's milk) to determine if the responding was specific for water. In addition, litters were tested for responsiveness· to water during nonspecific arousal produced by chemical irritation of the skin of the back (silver nitrate cautery applied over a depot of isotonic saline).

Studies of Weanlings

Studies of the feeding and drinking behavior of weanlings began at 14 to 15 days of age, the earliest age at which infant rats can be tested as if they were miniadults. They were isolated in individual wire-mesh cages, given commercial diets (Purina pellets available on the floor of the cage) and free water and then subjected (usually the next morning) to challenges known to provoke either food or water intake in adult rats. Animals were studied at increasing ages up to adulthood. Sixteen- and 20-day-old rats lived, while individually caged, in an incubator heated to 30°C. In addition, the 16-day-olds had the benefit of a low-walled glass dish instead of the conventional spouted-graduate as the reservoir for their water. Groups of adults (more than 3 months of age) were also tested. Each rat (adults and weanlings) was weighed before the test. The tests lasted 4 to 6 hr. Water and food intakes were measured directly.

RESULTS

The results of the Houpt and Epstein study can be briefly summarized. Deprivation emptied the stomach and induced increased milk intake from the day of birth. The increased feeding was satiated by fullness of the upper gastrointestinal tract whether produced by clay (Kaolin) or milk. Water which empties rapidly from the stomach did not produce satiation. At birth, the fullness or emptiness of the upper gut controls feeding behavior. Evidently, the pup roots and suckles to fill a gastric void and the nutrient quality

of the fluid in the gut plays no detectable role. Sleep is the pup's dominant behavioral state. The pup seems to be aroused by signals from an empty stomach. Then, aided by the dam, it suckles, performing the only ingestive
behavior for which it is fully competent, and, having filled the upper gastrointestinal tract, it lapses back into sleep.

Glucoprivation, on the other hand, had no effect on the feeding of the
suckling or indeed on that of the early weanling even when excessive doses
were used (up to 2,000 mg/kg). The adult response of increased food intake
did not occur until the week after natural weaning. And this was true of
animals that had been weaned prematurely at 14 days of age and had been
eating pellets for a week or more before injection with 2DG. The delayed
appearance of the glucoprivic control of feeding was not the result of insensitivity of the brain to decreased glucose utilization. The hyperglycemic
response was evoked by 2DG in suckling rats as early as the third day after
birth, and we now have a confirmation of this finding (4).

Other controls of food intake were not studied in the Houpt and Epstein
work. There may be a long-term effect of stored nutrient or of some blood-
borne agent. Although the sucklings clearly ate more in response to deprivation, the weight loss incurred during the deprivation was not fully repaired
during the first refeeding period. The deprived sucklings returned to their
expected weight by a slow adjustment over the many feedings that occurred
in the 20 to 24 hr that followed the deprivation. Something other than gastrointestinal bulk is operating here, and it must relate to the total nutrient content of the suckling's body.

The major results of Wirth's study can also be quickly summarized. They
are a clear and striking reemphasis of the principles of precocity and sequence
in the development of ingestive behavior. Responsiveness to three specific
thirst challenges appeared in the first week of postnatal life, and they did so
in succession. In our test of consumatory behavior, pups ingested water to
cellular dehydration (NaCl) at 2 days of age, to hypovolemia (PEG) at 4
days of age, and to beta-adrenergic activation (isoproterenol) at 6 days of
age. Skin temperature elevation provoked excess water intake but only in the
immediate neonatal period. This interesting finding was not pursued. In addition, the pups responded vigorously at 1 day of age to overnight deprivation
from mother's milk, but the interpretation of this result is ambiguous. The
pups could have been drinking in response to hunger. This ambiguity does
not plague the interpretation of the increased water intake provoked by the
other challenges for the following reasons: first, because they were not studied
after deprivation from nursing; second, because they were accompanied by
changes in distribution of body water that were quite consistent with the
physiologic mechanisms that underlie the dipsogenic effect of each challenge
in the adult rat; third, because excess water intake was not provoked by mere
arousal and irritation of the skin; and finally, because the responses were
specific for water. When the pups were given milk after the challenges, they

did not consume more. Interestingly, when drinking to thirst challenge, the pups licked the spout. They did not suckle it. They were, perhaps, demonstrating the precocity of their drinking behavior by using the adult rather than the neonatal response.

The results for the early-weaned pups, tested as miniadults, were equally clear. At 20 days of age (that is, just before weaning would have occurred), the animals responded to all thirst challenges (deprivation, cell dehydration, hypovolemia, and beta-adrenergic activation) when tested in adult circumstances. The rat pup is therefore ready at weaning to drink like an adult. Appetitive responsiveness to deprivation and cellular dehydration were in fact present at the earlier age (16 days) as was the strong suggestion of competence for responding to hypovolemia. Successful responding to thirst challenges at both 16 and 20 days of age depended on the maintenance of a warm ambient temperature (30°C minimum) not only during the test but throughout the time from isolation to the completion of the experiment. This prevents the hypothermia and consequent immobilization to which pups are subject when isolated from the litter. In addition, the youngest weanlings were aided in their access to the water by use of shallow cups. Without these concessions to the frailties of the early weaned rat, their well-developed capacities for appetitive responsiveness to thirst challenges could not have been expressed.

DISCUSSION

Clearly, the simplicity of the suckling period is only apparent. It masks a complex process whereby the mechanisms of food and water intake follow an ontogenetic timetable that culminates in competence for adult ingestive behavior on the eve of weaning. Ingestion is therefore not different from other behaviors or indeed from other physiological phenomena. It is the result of a precocious and sequential developmental process. In the rat the process is marked by early competence for consummatory responses of sufficient complexity to assure optimal nutrition on the day of birth. These include avidity for some tastes and avoidance of others (5) as well as the upper gastrointestinal control emphasized above. These must have matured *in utero*. Other consummatory capacities are added in the first postnatal week, increasing the diversity of the controls of ingestive behavior. These include a variety of controls of water intake, despite the fact the free water will not be available to the pup until 2 weeks later. By the second week after birth the pup is equipped with an impressive complement of controls of ingestion. The fact that controls for both food and water are operating at such an early age despite the fact that the animal can ingest only mother's milk suggests that both hunger and thirst may control milk intake.

In the second week of the suckling period, physiological competence for thermoregulation, locomotion, sustained wakefulness, and use of distance senses improve and the animal begins to show some mastery of its habitat.

Appetitive behaviors are now possible. By 14 to 15 days after birth, the animal can, in fact, be forcibly weaned. But natural weaning is delayed for at least another week assuring maximal success in the transition to the more independent life of the free-foraging adult. Like birth, weaning is delayed well beyond the developmental age at which survival is merely possible.

The developmental process for ingestive behavior continues beyond the time of weaning well into the juvenile period. We have shown that the glucoprivic control does not reach competence for the arousal of feeding until at least the fourth week after birth, and it is in this early juvenile period that the pups develop the nocturnal periodicity of ingestive behaviors (6) and become socialized to select the diet preferred by their parents (7). When it is completely understood, we may find, as Kennedy (8) suggested some years ago, that the ontogeny of ingestive behavior is not complete until puberty.

This work clarifies a conflict in the most recently published studies of the ontogeny of drinking behavior. Friedman and Campbell (9) demonstrated early responsiveness (16 days of age) only to hypovolemia, and then only when it was induced by polyethylene glycol. Drinking to cellular dehydration was unusually delayed in their study appearing reliably only at 30 days of age. On the other hand, Almli (10) reported prompt and avid drinking in 14-day-old pups in response to cell dehydration.

Early weaned pups are difficult subjects for the study of ingestive behavior. They appear unable to sustain appetitive behavior for more than a minute or two. In Wirth's experiments, they slept through at least two-thirds of the test period; this has been noted previously (11). When they awakened, they explored the cage and, if they encountered it, they attempted to ingest the water by chewing, pawing, and licking, but they did so only briefly, soon returning to sleep in a corner of the cage. The tendency to sleep and lack of persistence in ingestion were not signs of satiation. Pups that had left the spout avidly and persistently consumed water when they were treated like sucklings, that is, when water was placed directly into their mouths by dropper or infusion pump. Sleep apparently took precedence over requirements for water, as it may for milk in the suckling dog (12). In addition, early-weaned pups do not approach the water directly from a distance when aroused by a thirst challenge. They often require experience licking water from their paws and body surface, after an accidental encounter, before they make a prompt and direct approach to it when in water need. And lastly early weaned rats cannot maintain their body temperature when isolated from their littermates (13) in a cage at room temperature. They become hypothermic and are inactivated.

In Wirth's and in Almli's experiments, these obstacles to appetitive behavior were avoided. The ambient temperature was elevated, in our work, from isolation to the completion of the testing. In addition, we placed the water in an open dish in the center of the cage to give the 16-day-olds easy access to it. Almli's method approximated that used by us for the suckling. His pups were

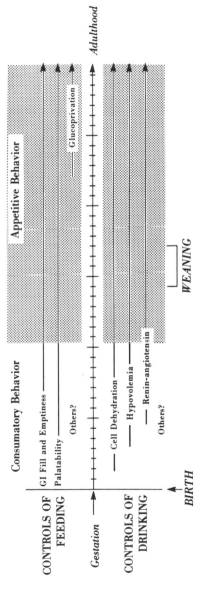

FIG. 1. The timetable of development of the controls of ingestive behavior in the rat, emphasizing the recent work of Houpt and Epstein (2) and Wirth and Epstein (3). A calendar, marked off in days and weeks, runs through the center from gestation to adulthood. Above, timetable for feeding; below, timetable for drinking. Note (a) the presence at birth of controls of food intake exercised by the upper GI tract, (b) the sequential appearance within the first postnatal week of three controls of water intake, and (c) the delayed appearance of the glucoprivic control of feeding. Capacities for mastery of the habitat appear at the end of the second week. These include improved locomotion, use of distance senses, and some competence for thermoregulation. Appetitive behaviors are now added to the neonatal capacity for consumatory behaviors and weaning ensues. The timetable is not complete. The appearance in ontogeny of other controls of both modes of ingestion is predicted. For feeding, these may be the demands of thermoregulation, the influence of stored nutrients, and the effect of blood-borne agents including hormones. For drinking, these may be deprivation from water and ambient temperature.

tested at 14 days of age in a container lined with paper towels and positioned under a heat source, and he held the water spout close to the animal's mouth. The 14-day-old pups responded well to cellular dehydration. He did not study other thirst challenges. The obvious lesson here is that conclusions about capacities for adult drinking behavior cannot be drawn from studies of the early-weaned pup, unless it is given the environmental support it must have to mobilize sustained appetitive behavior. The early-weaned suckling will drink water under control of the physiological systems that have matured in the first week of postnatal life, but it cannot do so if it is soporific and hypothermic.

Figure 1 illustrates the major theme of this chapter. It is a first draft for the rat of the timetable of appearance of the controls of ingestive behavior. Time advances through the middle of the figure from emergence into postnatal life to commencement into adulthood. The days are counted from birth and accumulate into weeks that provide a convenient calendar for the suckling and weanling period. What we know of the timetable for the controls of feeding is sketched above the time line, and a similar sketch for the controls of drinking is given below the line. Emphasis is placed on the information generated by the works of Houpt and Wirth.

The physiological mechanisms for ingestive behaviors mature early and in sequence. Both feeding and drinking are under complex control during the first week of life. But the controls can operate only on consumatory behavior. The development of motivated behavior awaits the appearance of capacities for sustained appetitive behavior. These are added in the last week of the suckling period and the animal is weaned, ready for its debut as a miniadult.

SUMMARY

The timetable of development of the controls of feeding and drinking behavior was examined in the neonatal rat. Feeding of mother's milk was studied in pups within natural litters. Drinking was studied in sucklings by hand-holding pups while they received automatic oral infusions of water, thus capitalizing on their vigorous consumatory reflexes and minimizing appetitive responding. Weanlings of 16 days or older were aided in their drinking by ambient warmth and optimal access to the water source.

The controls of ingestive behavior were found to be precocious and sequential in their ontogeny. Deprivation stimulated feeding from the day of birth. Gastric loads of milk or kaolin depressed subsequent intake quantitatively as early as the fourth day of age, but water, which empties rapidly from the stomach, did not. On the other hand, glucoprivation produced by 2DG did not increase intake in sucklings 2- to 21-days-old despite its effectiveness in stimulating hyperglycemia, nor did it increase feeding in 21-day-old weanlings (weaned at 14 days) despite the effectiveness of deprivation at that age. The feeding response to glucoprivation did not mature until the fourth to fifth week of age. From the outset, upper gastrointestinal fill and emptiness control feeding, but the glucoprivic control does not appear until after weaning.

Responsiveness to the following specific thirst challenges appeared in the suckling rat with a clear timetable: cellular dehydration at 2 days of age, hypovolemia induced by colloid dialysis at 4 days, and beta-adrenergic activation at 6 days. Water drinking in response to deprivation from mother's milk was vigorous at the earliest day tested (2 days) but could not be distinguished from hunger. Rats weaned prematurely and then isolated and tested as mini-adults responded appetitively to thirst challenges as early as 16 days of age. But they required a warm environment, optimum access to the water source, and sufficient time to respond.

As revealed by consumatory responding, the physiological controls of feeding and drinking mature early and in sequence, the controls of drinking reaching competence weeks before they can be employed in behavior. The physiological controls await the maturation of capacities for sustained appetitive behavior. These appear in the last week of the suckling period yielding animals that are prepared for adult-motivated ingestive behavior on the eve of weaning.

ACKNOWLEDGMENTS

This work was supported by U.S. Public Health Service grants NDS 03469 to Alan N. Epstein and GM-281 to the Institute of Neurological Sciences.

REFERENCES

1. Craig, W. (1918): Appetites and aversions as constituents of instincts. *Biol. Bull.,* 34:91–107.
2. Houpt, K. A., and Epstein, A. N. (1973): Ontogeny of controls of food intake in the rat: GI fill and glucoprivation. *Am. J. Physiol.,* 225:58–66.
3. Wirth, J. B., and Epstein, A. N. (1975): The ontogeny of thirst in the infant rat. *Am. J. Physiol. (In press.)*
4. Gil-Ad, I., Udeschini, D., Cocchi, D., and Müller, E. E. (1975): Hyporesponsiveness to glucoprivation during postnatal period in the rat. *Am. J. Physiol. (In press.)*
5. Jacobs, H. L. (1964): Observations on the ontogeny of saccharine preference in the neonate rat. *Psychon. Sci.,* 1:105–106.
6. Stern, J. M., and Levin, R. Ontogeny of nursing and feeding rhythms in the rat. *J. Comp. Physiol. Psychol. (In Press.)*
7. Galef, B. G., and Clark, M. M. (1972): Mother's milk and adult presence: Two factors determining initial dietary selection by weanling rats. *J. Comp. Physiol. Psychol.,* 78:220–225.
8. Kennedy, G. C. (1969): The relation between the central control of appetite, growth, and sexual maturation. *Guys Hosp. Rep.,* 118:315–327.
9. Freidman, M., and Campbell, B. A. (1974): Ontogeny of thirst in the rat: effects of hypertonic saline, polyethylene glycol and vena cava ligation. *J. Comp. Physiol Psychol.,* 87:37–46.
10. Almli, C. R. (1973): Ontogeny of onset of drinking and plasma osmotic pressure regulation. *Dev. Psychobiol.,* 6:147–158.

11. Bolles, R. C., and Woods, P. J. (1964): The ontogeny of behavior in the albino rat. *Anim. Behav.,* 12:427–444.
12. Satinoff, E., and Stanley, W. C. (1963): Effects of stomach loading on suckling behavior in neonatal puppies. *J. Comp. Physiol. Psychol.,* 56:66–68.
13. Gulick, A. (1937): The development of temperature control in infant rats. *Am. J. Physiol.* (Abstr.), 119:322.

Hunger: Basic Mechanisms and Clinical Implications,
edited by D. Novin, W. Wyrwicka, and G. Bray.
Raven Press, New York © 1976.

The Problem of Motivation in Feeding Behavior

Wanda Wyrwicka

Department of Anatomy and the Brain Research Institute, University of California School of Medicine,
Los Angeles, California 90024

The organism must obtain food to provide for metabolic needs and to ensure survival. A number of empirical findings suggest, however, that the physiological need for nutrition is not the immediate motive leading the animal to eat. Jacobs and Sharma (10) compared the intake of 2.8% lactose solution approximately as sweet as mother's milk, with the intake of 0.1% saccharin in neonate rats. They observed that young rats in the first 2 days of life drank more saccharin solution than lactose solution. Only when the lactose solution was made much sweeter (17%) did its intake significantly increase. The authors concluded that the neonate rats were responding on the basis of taste and not on the basis of calories; if their intake had been based on calories, they should show maximum preference for the 2.8% lactose solution as a result of the learned association between taste and calories of mother's milk.

Valenstein (22) studied preference for various solutions in rats. He found that when they were offered 6.5% glucose and 0.25% saccharin solution, they preferred glucose to saccharin both when they were hungry and when they were satiated. However, when 3% glucose solution and 0.25% saccharin solution were offered, the rats preferred saccharin even when they were hungry. Their choice, therefore, depended on the sweetness rather than on the nutritive value of the solution.

Kennedy and Baldwin (11) observed that pigs preferred sucrose, glucose, or saccharin solution to plain water. By using a special experimental method in which the animal had to respond once for the first portion, twice for the second, and three times for the third, the authors demonstrated a consistent tendency in the pigs toward higher ratios of responding at the higher concentrations of sweetness in solution. Ernitz and Corbit (4) reported that rats not deprived of water or food drank large amounts of water when it was sweetened with saccharin, glucose, or sucrose, whereas they drank much less when weak sodium chloride solution was available under the same conditions. Obviously, in these experiments, pigs as well as rats were drinking sweet solutions to obtain desired sensory oral input rather than to satisfy thirst.

Likewise, Corbit and Stellar (1) demonstrated that not only hypothalamic obese but also normal rats ate more when a high-fat diet was offered than when only a standard powdered diet was available. The importance of taste in feeding was also shown in the experiments of McGinty et al. (15) who studied intragastric feeding in rats with the use of the technique developed by Epstein (3). These authors found that normal rats easily fed themselves by pumping liquid food straight into their stomach; when these rats were made hyperphagic after the hypothalamic lesions, they refused to press for intragastric food (although they would overeat when given food orally). When a drop of saccharin solution was offered to these rats to lick each time they pressed a lever, however, vigorous pumping was observed. Evidently, the rats pressed the lever for oral pleasure and not for the intragastric nutrition.

In other, more dramatic experiments, the animals refused to eat the food necessary for survival when that food supposedly did not provide oral satisfaction. For instance, in the early experiments of Kon (12), rats were given a choice of foods in a "cafeteria." The author found that in these conditions the rats ate mostly sucrose (90%) and only very little purified casein (6.5%), the only source of protein; as a result, these animals lost much weight and some died. Scott (19) observed that rats fed in a cafeteria consumed only fat until all of them died. In more recent experiments by Hogan (7), 3-day-old chickens started to recognize and consume mealworms; when another food, presumably less palatable, was substituted for mealworms, the chicks refused to eat it, and all of them died from starvation within a few days.

To better understand the mechanisms responsible for the above findings, several experimental studies (below) have been carried out in our laboratory.

ELECTRICAL BRAIN STIMULATION AS A REWARD IN FOOD CONSUMPTION

The purpose of this study (27) was to answer the question of whether or not artificial sensory input, not directly related to food, can serve as a reward in feeding. The experiments were performed on cats. These animals first learned to self-stimulate, i.e., to press a lever and obtain electrical stimulation within the lateral hypothalamus or septum through previously implanted monopolar electrodes. The lever was then removed from the experimental compartment; the cats, when moderately hungry, were allowed to drink a mixture of milk and broth from either of two identical feeders. Drinking from one of these feeders was rewarded by electrical stimulation (ESB), whereas drinking from the other feeder was never rewarded by ESB. As a result, the cats drank only from that feeder where electrical stimulation of the brain was delivered. When stimulation was transferred to the other feeder, the animals also switched feeders (Fig. 1). When stimulation reward was withheld, the animals walked away from both feeders within a few minutes.

These results indicate that the animals clearly chose to consume the food that provided additional, although nonoral, sensations which were evidently desired by the animal (just as previously the cat pressed a lever to receive the same stimulation). In this case, the act of consumption appeared to be an

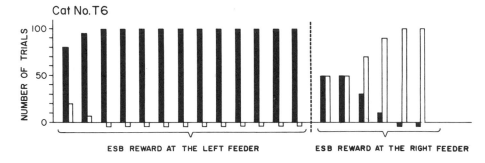

FIG. 1. A diagram showing the effect of rewarding ESB for drinking a milk/broth mixture. Each pair of bars corresponds to the number of consumption trials during successive sessions. Filled bars, number of consumption trials at the left feeder; empty bars, number of consumption trials at the right feeder; small bar below 0 level, no drinking occurred from the corresponding feeder; vertical broken line, time of transferring the ESB from the left to the right feeder. At the beginning of training, the animal drank from both feeders, but spent more time at the left feeder where the consumption was rewarded by ESB. Starting from the third session, the cat drank exclusively from the left feeder. When, after 13 sessions, stimulation was transferred to the right feeder, the animal initially drank from both feeders alternatively, then switched completely to drink only from the right feeder.

instrumental response which served to provide desirable sensory input. ESB therefore proved to be an effective reward in food intake.

EATING OF PRIMARILY NONPREFERRED FOOD
FOR BRAIN STIMULATION REWARD

A question arose as to whether or not the animal would eat previously rejected food to get desirable brain stimulation. To answer this question, the following study was carried out (26). Monopolar electrodes were implanted in the lateral hypothalamus of seven cats (six females, one male). A reference electrode was placed in the skull bone over the frontal sinus. After recovery, each cat was taken to the experimental compartment to be tested for self-stimulation. Each of these cats learned to press a lever to obtain ESB which consisted of a 0.5-sec train of 100/sec 2 to 3 V pulses of 1 msec duration per pulse. The post-mortem examination of the brains of four of these cats showed that the tips of the effective electrodes were located in the lateral hypothalamus (Fig. 2).

During the second self-stimulation session, a container filled with meat pellets (the standard diet for these cats) was introduced into the compartment at a distance of 10 cm from the lever to allow the animals to eat if they wanted to do so. The cats were always moderately hungry, as they were fed only once a day after the session. The animals seemed to ignore the meat pellets, however, and continued to press the lever for ESB.

After three to five sessions, when the self-stimulation behavior seemed to be firmly established, the lever was removed from the experimental compart-

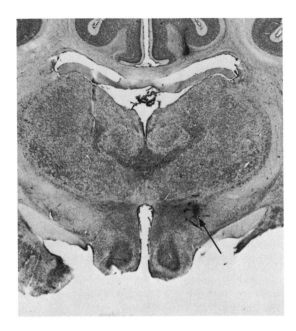

FIG. 2. A microphotograph of a frontal section of the hypothalamus, showing the site of the rewarding stimulation.

ment and, instead, two kinds of food were offered to the cats in separate, identical familiar containers. One of these foods was standard meat pellets, the usually well-accepted food which the cats obtained daily in their home compartments. The other, considered nonpreferred, was pieces of peeled bananas. In a preliminary test in the home compartment, the cats completely ignored the banana. In the previous study, the cats refused to eat banana during ESB of the lateral hypothalamic feeding area, whereas they voraciously ate the standard diet (28).

When banana pieces and meat pellets were presented to the cat, the animal usually started to eat meat pellets, ignoring banana. During pauses in eating, however, the cat occasionally moved close to the banana container. In such moments, ESB was given. This resulted in approaching and sniffing banana which was followed each time by ESB. Finally, the cat began to lick the banana and then actually to consume it by vigorous licking or biting a small piece of it and chewing it, while being regularly rewarded by ESB. When the placement of both containers was reversed, the cats followed the banana container. At the same time, the animal began to ignore meat pellets and concentrated only on eating banana (Fig. 3). It was found that banana consumption already occurred in the first session in five cats, whereas two other cats started to eat banana only after a few sessions of exposure to both foods.

The amount of consumption of banana gradually increased during the train-

FIG. 3. A view of the experimental situation: a hungry cat eating banana in the presence of meat pellets.

ing, averaging 26.5 g and 18 g in two of the cats and somewhat less in the other five cats. There were 200 trials in each session, i.e., ESB was given 200 times for consumption of banana. The frequency of reward depended on the cat's behavior. Usually, the ESB was given in intervals of a few seconds; however, longer intervals in reacting, between 1 and 3 min, were observed during the session.

Acute Extinction

When the ESB reward was withheld during one of the sessions, the animals still continued to consume banana for the first 10 to 60 sec (or a few minutes in one cat). Their behavior then started to change. Typically, the cat looked and sniffed around, returned to lick banana pieces for a few seconds, then stopped licking, became restless, and finally, 5 to 10 min after withholding ESB, walked away from the banana container. Some cats went to the meat pellet container and started eating pellets. Then, after a 15-min withholding period when the cat was away from the meat container, the ESB was given free a few times. As a result, the cat resumed eating banana pieces.

Test in the Home Cage

To determine if the preference for banana in the experimental compartment could influence food preference in another situation (without ESB), the following test was performed. After approximately 10 training sessions, the two containers previously used in the experimental compartment were presented to the cats just before the usual feeding time, one filled with meat pellets and the other filled with pieces of banana. All cats reacted similarly: after a brief orienting reaction, they came to sniff and even briefly lick the banana pieces while ignoring the meat pellets. All cats seemed very excited during the 10-min test and their general motor behavior resembled that observed during the session. However, no significant consumption of banana was observed.

Discussion

The above experiments provided evidence that the previously nonpreferred food may become a preferred one when its consumption is associated with desirable sensory input, in this case provided directly to the brain. The fact that the cats recognized and strongly reacted to banana pieces presented to them in the home cage suggests that the sight and smell of banana acquired the property of a conditioned stimulus. The conditioned stimulus, however, could maintain the reaction of consumption of banana only when this reaction was followed by a brain-stimulation reward, suggesting that the act of eating banana pieces should be treated here as an instrumental response.

The results of this experiment may help us to better understand the neural organization of food consumption. That the cats were eating the banana for nonoral reward suggests that eating may take place for nonoral satisfaction as well. When the animal is hungry, it may eat in order to escape gastric pangs and other undesirable sensations of hunger; in that case, the oral rewards are secondary. In fact, Miller (16) reported that the amount of quinine in food necessary to inhibit eating increased considerably during the 54 hr of food deprivation in rats; this suggests that food-deprived animals can eat food that is less tasty than that normally accepted.

Simple observations also prove that eating frequently occurs as an escape from stress or boredom. Eating in the company of good friends may also provide sensory satisfaction that counts much more than oral pleasure alone. In general, the act of eating can therefore be considered an instrumental reaction which is performed either to (a) escape an undesirable sensory state produced by either food deprivation or other factors, (b) to obtain desirable oral satisfaction related to the food consumed, or (c) to obtain other sensory satisfaction not necessarily related to the food eaten.

Considering the act of eating an instrumental reaction is in accord with the observation that eating and drinking activities develop gradually from reflexes such as sucking in mammals or pecking in birds. Hunt and Smith (9), for instance, observed that naive 2- to 5-day-old chickens that had been neither watered nor fed, learned to drink water only gradually. Initially, they pecked at the drops of water but could not hold it in their beaks; active drinking started only when they accidentally discovered that they must lift their heads to hold water in the beak and swallow it. Likewise, Hogan (8) found that newly hatched chickens first pecked indiscriminately at sand and food; pecking frequency increased when some food was ingested as a result of pecking. Similarly, Kovach and Kling (13) reported that naive, 2- to 5-day-old kittens, separated from their mother, sucked both a nonnutritive and a nutritive nipple and only gradually increased the amount of time spent at the nutritive nipple while decreasing the amount of time spent at the nonnutritive one. These experiments indicate that eating or drinking are reactions based on simple reflexes that become instrumentalized by learning.

As discussed elsewhere (24, 25), the elicitation of these reactions depends not only on the presence of the external stimuli associated with the particular food (or liquid), such as the sight of this food, but also on the sensory state produced by conditions of the internal environment. The state of satiation, for instance, increases the threshold for elicitation of eating reaction, whereas deprivation lowers this threshold. It was also found that animals deprived of a specific ingredient in the diet (e.g., salt or thiamine) select food containing the lacking ingredient (see reviews by Denton, ref. 2, Lat, ref. 14, and Rozin, ref. 17). According to the observations of Lat (14), however, the selection of the proper diet from among other available foods was never immediate and usually occurred after a period of a few days of exposure to that diet. This indicates that the animal learned to recognize that diet because of its delayed beneficial effect. Similarly, rats learned to avoid a poisoned food after consuming it and probably experiencing gastric pains (18). To obtain a delayed effect of food, however, the animal had to consume it first. When the animal refused to eat the proper diet, as had happened in the experiments of Kon (12) and Scott (19), it never could learn about the beneficial effects of that diet. This suggests that the internal environmental (or metabolic) control of food selection can take place only after the food has been ingested at least once. This control can, therefore, be exerted only through the behavioral reactions directed by "memories" of the delayed sensations associated with the given food. These memories can, however, be formed only on condition that oral sensations related to that food are desirable, thus leading to the ingestion of the food; a proper nutritious diet can be selected only if it is tasty enough to be accepted.

EFFECT OF MOTHER'S FOOD PREFERENCE ON THE CHOICE OF FOOD BY THE YOUNG

Derived from the above experiments was another study which, however, involved a new problem not directly related to the topic thus far discussed herein; namely, we asked if a mother cat induced by ESB reward to eat a banana will influence her kitten to do the same.

It has been observed that the behavior of the young is strongly influenced by the parents or adults of the same species. Hogan (8) observed a strong influence of a mother hen on the choice of food by chickens: they pecked significantly more at the kind of grain chosen by the mother. Likewise, in the experiments of Turner (21), 1-day-old chickens were offered artificially colored orange and green grain. When a cut-out model of a hen was placed nearby and made to peck only at one color grain (e.g., orange), the chicks pecked at grain of that color twice as much as at the grains of a different color. Galef and Clark (6) observed that when young rats were offered a choice of food in the absence of adults, they did not start to eat solid food until they reached a mean age of 25.4 days; when, however, the choice of food was offered in the presence of adult rats, the pups started to eat solid food much earlier, at a mean age of 19.9 days. In another experiment, the same authors observed that rat pups did not eat food which was avoided by adult rats as a result of previous poison experience (5).

In the present experiments, two monopolar electrodes were implanted in the lateral hypothalamus in a female cat in an early stage of pregnancy. Six weeks after the delivery, the mother was tested for self-stimulation. When the cat learned to press a lever to obtain hypothalamic stimulation, she was offered two kinds of food: meat pellets and banana pieces each in separate containers, as in the previously described experiments. Consuming banana was rewarded by the desired stimulation, whereas eating pellets was never associated with ESB. As with the aforementioned animals, this cat easily learned to eat banana only and to ignore the meat pellets. Meanwhile, at the home compartment, her three 2-month-old kittens were suckling only occasionally and began to eat solid food such as meat pellets or canned tuna.

After several sessions during which the mother cat consumed 20 to 30 g of banana daily, one of her kittens was introduced to the experimental compartment together with the mother. During the first few sessions, the kitten occupied itself examining the environment and playing and did not seem to be interested in the mother's behavior. During the fourth session, however, the kitten approached a piece of banana which had fallen out of the container and was lying on the floor, and started first to sniff it and then to lick and actually eat it. The eating of banana by the kitten was even more intensive during the following sessions. The kitten consumed an average of 2 to 3 g (occasionally as much as 5 g) of banana during each session.

The kitten seemed to ignore meat pellets, as did the mother. When a few meat pellets were placed on the floor close to a piece of banana (a distance of 2 cm), the kitten still ate only banana and evidently did not pay any attention to the meat pellets (although this kitten had been observed nibbling at the pellets in the home compartment).

When the kitten was either introduced alone to the experimental compartment or left there alone, it did not accept banana. In fact, it did not eat the meat pellets either, but concentrated on attempts to leave the compartment or to play with various objects in the cage.

The experiments with the mother and kitten continued for several weeks until the kitten was 4 months old. At that time, the kitten started to pay less attention to the mother (whose electrically induced behavior of eating banana was unchanged) and to banana pieces, and became interested mostly in playing, jumping, and scratching on the walls. Since this behavior disturbed the mother's feeding reactions, the experiment was then discontinued.

Two other kittens were also tested for feeding behavior in the presence of their mother. Each kitten was separately introduced to the experimental compartment together with the mother. It was observed that after a few sessions, each started to sniff and occasionally lick banana pieces placed near the banana container from which the mother was eating. These experiments were not, however, conducted as systematically as those with the first kitten.

Discussion

The above preliminary results of the study fully confirm the observations made by other investigators (5–8, 21) that the mother's behavior strongly influences the choice of food of the young. In addition, the results suggest that when a mother makes her choice under abnormal conditions, the young make a similar choice, even if the food chosen is bizarre for that species.

As is well known, the phenomenon of imitation in feeding among animals is not limited to imitation of the mother or other adults by the young. For instance, Weiskrantz and Cowey (23) observed that monkeys rapidly increased their intake of a commercial food when they saw other monkeys consuming that food. Tolman (20) reported that chicks reared in pairs ate significantly more than isolated chicks, as indicated by greater weight gains. It may be, therefore, that the observed influence of the mother on the feeding behavior of her young represents a case of a general tendency of animals to imitate one another.

The phenomenon of imitation in feeding cannot be easily explained. Imitative activity does not seem to be controlled by the same basic laws which govern instrumental behavior. In imitative activity, there is only a stimulus (usually visual) and the reaction, which occurs regardless of the reward. If the food consumed brings some desirable sensory input, the reaction may be changed into a typical instrumental response rewarded by sensory satisfaction. But the imitative activity may occur for a long time without such a reward and even when unpleasant feelings develop as a result of the response. Smoking cigarettes by children only because their parents do so is an example of the imitative behavior which has been maintained without obtaining desirable sensations.

Since the phenomenon of imitation appears to be a powerful mechanism in feeding behavior, it deserves special attention in future research.

SUMMARY AND CONCLUSIONS

Experimental data suggest that the metabolic need for nutrition is, in many cases, overcome by other motives which lead to selection of food according to taste rather than to nutritional value, even when such choices may be fatal.

The present experiments were designed to explore several motives responsible for overriding metabolic needs in feeding. It was found that (a) cats drank milk and broth mixture only from that of the two feeders when they obtained desirable ESB as a reward; (b) hungry cats ate banana, a non-preferred food under natural conditions, in the presence of meat pellets when eating banana was rewarded by ESB and eating meat pellets was not; (c) a young kitten imitated its mother in whom banana-eating was induced by ESB, and consumed banana when accompanying the mother during the experimental sessions.

It is concluded that the act of eating in general should be considered an instrumental reaction performed to obtain either oral or nonoral sensory satisfaction. The elicitation of the reaction of eating depends not only on the external stimuli associated with the food but also on the state of the internal environment; e.g., satiation increases the threshold for elicitation of this reaction, whereas food deprivation decreases this threshold. The reaction to the particular food is influenced by the memories of the delayed nonoral sensations related to this food. If these sensations were undesirable, the food may be rejected even though it once provided oral satisfaction. The eating of a particular food can also be evoked by the mechanism of imitation, especially imitation of the mother by the young, presumably without special sensory reward.

ACKNOWLEDGMENT

This research was supported by U.S. Public Health Service grants MH 13958 and AM 17328.

REFERENCES

1. Corbit, J. D., and Stellar, E. (1967): *J. Comp. Physiol. Psychol.,* 58:63–67.
2. Denton, D. A. (1967): Alimentary canal. In: *Handbook of Physiology. Vol. 1,* pp. 433–459. American Physiology Society, Washington, D.C.
3. Epstein, A. N. (1960): *Science,* 131:497–489.
4. Ernitz, T., and Corbit, J. D. (1973): *J. Comp. Physiol. Psychol.,* 83:27–31.
5. Galef, B. G., Jr., and Clark, M. M. (1971): *J. Comp. Physiol. Psychol.,* 75:341–357.
6. Galef, B. G., Jr., and Clark, M. M. (1972): *J. Comp. Physiol. Psychol.,* 78:220–225.
7. Hogan, J. A. (1971): *Behaviour,* 39:128–201.
8. Hogan, J. A. (1973): In: *Constraints on Learning,* edited by R. A. Hinde and J. G. Stevenson-Hinde. pp. 119–139. Academic Press, London.
9. Hunt, G. L., and Smith, W I. (1967): *J. Comp. Physiol. Psychol.,* 64:230–236.
10. Jacobs, H. L., and Sharma, K. N. (1969): *Ann. NY Acad. Sci.,* 157:1084–1125.
11. Kennedy, J. M., and Baldwin, B. A. (1972): *Anim. Behav.,* 20:706–718.
12. Kon, S. K. (1931): *Biochem. J.,* 25:473–481.
13. Kovach, J. K., and Kling, A. (1967): *Anim. Behav.,* 15:91–101.
14. Lat, J. (1967): Alimentary Canal. In: *Handbook of Physiology.* Vol. 1, pp. 367–386. American Physiology Society, Washington, D.C.
15. McGinty, D., Epstein, A. N., and Teitelbaum, P. (1965): *Anim. Behav.,* 13:413–418.

16. Miller, N. E. (1956): *Ann. NY Acad. Sci.,* 65:318–333.
17. Rozin, P. (1967): *Alimentary Canal,* In: *Handbook of Physiology.* Vol. 1, pp. 411–431. American Physiology Society, Washington, D.C.
18. Rzoska, J. (1953): *Br. J. Anim. Behav.,* 1:128–135.
19. Scott, E. M. (1946): *J. Nutr.,* 31:397–406.
20. Tolman, C. W. (1964): *Anim. Behav.,* 12:245–251.
21. Turner, E. R. A. (1964): *Behaviour,* 24:1–46.
22. Valenstein, E. S. (1967): *J. Comp. Physiol. Psychol.,* 63:429–433.
23. Weiskrantz, L., and Cowey, A. (1963): *Anim. Behav.,* 11:225–234.
24. Wyrwicka, W. (1969): *Physiol. Behav.,* 4:853–858.
25. Wyrwicka, W. (1972): *The Mechanisms of Conditioned Behavior.* C C Thomas, Springfield, Ill.
26. Wyrwicka, W. (1974): *Physiol Behav.,* 12:1063–1066.
27. Wyrwicka, W., and Chase, M. H. (1972): *Physiol. Behav.,* 9:717–720.
28. Wyrwicka, W., and Doty, R. W. (1966): *Exp. Brain Res.,* 1:152–160.

Hunger: Basic Mechanisms and Clinical Implications,
edited by D. Novin, W. Wyrwicka, and G. Bray.
Raven Press, New York © 1976.

Facilitation of Feeding in Aphagic Cats by Rewarding Brain Stimulation

Michael H. Chase and Wanda Wyrwicka

Departments of Physiology and Anatomy and the Brain Research Institute, University of California, Los Angeles, California 90024

As presented in the previous chapter, rewarding electrical stimulation of the brain (ESB) can serve to maintain food consumption in satiated cats. It was clear from those experiments that ESB is a powerful reinforcer for the ingestion of food. Consequently, we were interested in determining if ESB would be effective in initiating and maintaining food consumption in an animal that refused to eat, specifically in cats that were made aphagic by bilateral destruction of the anterior or lateral hypothalamus.

Previous studies have demonstrated that a number of procedures can accelerate the course of recovery of hypothalamic-lesioned animals. These procedures typically include special methods of feeding, such as intragastric intubation of milk or forced feeding with highly palatable food (1–3). In the adipsic cat, water may be consumed to avoid a nociceptive electrical shock (4). In carrying out the present investigation, we were interested in obtaining information relating to the processes underlying both ESB and aphagia as well as determining if the drive initiated by the former mechanisms might ameliorate the latter syndrome.

All experiments were carried out on freely moving adult cats. Each animal was initially anesthetized with sodium pentobarbital (Nembutal®) for the permanent implantation of electrodes. Bipolar electrodes for ESB were placed in the septum (A14–16, L1–2, H + 4; septal cats) and/or the ventral midbrain tegmentum (A3–5, L3, H-4; tegmental cats) (Fig. 1). Monopolar electrodes were placed in the anterior or lateral hypothalamus to deliver a lesioning current. Other electrodes were implanted to record the EEG to monitor the general state of the animal.

After recovery from these procedures, the animals were trained to press a lever for ESB. The lever was then removed and the animals were conditioned to consume a milk and broth mixture from a feeder to receive ESB. A bowl containing the identical mixture was placed next to the feeder to control for consumption in the absence of ESB. Experiments were carried out on alternate days until the animals were overtrained at the criterion level of performance (after approximately 15 days), which consisted of the successful completion of 100 trials (i.e., the consumption of 0.5 ml of a milk and broth mixture from the feeder in conjunction with ESB).

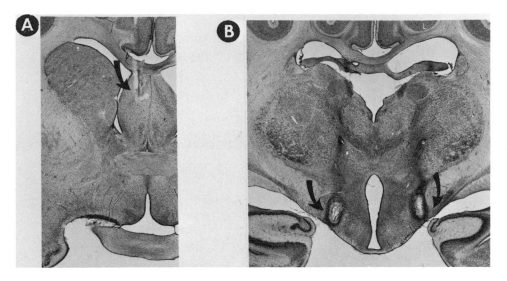

FIG. 1. Frontal section of cat brain showing a representative site of one of the septal electrodes used to induce rewarding ESB (A) and a typical lesion of the lateral hypothalamus which resulted in aphagia (B). (Reproduced from Chase and Wyrwicka, ref. 6.)

Subsequently, bilateral lesions were made in the lateral hypothalamus through previously implanted electrodes by passing 2-mA direct current for 90 sec bilaterally. Observations were made on six animals, one with an ESB electrode in the septum (and a lateral hypothalamic lesion) and five with ESB electrodes in the tegmentum (of which two had anterior and three had lateral hypothalamic lesions). The animals' consumption of food, EEG, and general behavior were monitored. A representative pattern was displayed by the cat whose daily record is presented as Table 1. In general, all lesioned cats initially consumed less of the mixture than they did during the prelesion period. In the first few postlesion days, ESB was able to maintain a rather weak pattern of consumption. Thereafter, the prelesion pattern and rate of consumption returned. As in the previous experiment, tests for extinction were performed (5). We found that food consumption ceased when it was not rewarded by ESB and returned with the resumption of ESB.

These results clearly indicate that ESB can remain an effective reinforcer for food consumption in the aphagic cat. Moreover, the conditioned behavioral pattern of ESB-rewarded food consumption was maintained after hypothalamic destruction. This indicates that the functional integrity of ESB is not dependent on lateral or anterior hypothalamic mechanisms. In addition, it appears that aphagic animals are capable, at least within the experimental paradigm of the present study, of consuming food. Although we have provided no information as to the underlying basis of the aphagic syndrome, we can state that whatever the causes may be, they can be overridden by the drive produced by ESB.

TABLE 1

PATTERN OF FOOD CONSUMPTION AFTER A BILATERAL HYPOTHALAMIC LESION

Home cage		Experimental cage	
Consumption of		Consumption of milk/broth	
Dry food	Milk/broth	Bowl (without stimulation)	Feeder (with stimulation)
3/16 ∼	∼	∼	∼

Commentary: Bilateral lesion of the lateral hypothalamus (2 ma for 1.5 min).

3/17 None	None	None	5 Trials (2-min duration)

Commentary: There was a general depression of motor activity; slow movements predominated. The cat ignored the mixture in the large bowl, drank from the feeder for about 2 min, and then ceased consumption.

3/19 None	None	None	3-5 Trials

Commentary: Following stimulation the cat licked a little of the mixture from the feeder but did not sustain the conditioned behavior of food consumption.

3/26 None	None	None	120 Trials

Commentary: Initially the cat was quiet, indifferent, drank a few times from the feeder (reinforced with electrical stimulation of the brain), and then stopped drinking. Four "free" rewards (electrical stimulation) were given. The cat then returned to the feeder and drank without hesitation. At no time did he consume the mixture from the bowl which was adjacent to the feeder.

3/31 None	20 ml	None	108 Trials

Commentary: The cat did not spontaneously approach the feeder; after 8 min, "free" stimulation was given several times; the cat then went immediately to the feeder and drank repeatedly. There was no consumption of mixture from the large bowl.

4/2 None	30 ml	None	Extinction experiment

Commentary: The cat ignored the bowl with the mixture; he drank repetitively from the feeder where stimulation occurred after consumption. After 5 min of food consumption, stimulation was withheld (test for extinction). The cat stopped drinking after two to three unrewarded trials, searched around the chamber, and then went to a far corner and sat down. After a few minutes, stimulation was given "free." The cat then slowly approached the feeder and started to drink. This process of extinction was repeated once more with similar results.

4/7 None	40 ml	None	100 Trials

Commentary: The cat ignored the bowl and drank only from the feeder. After 100 trials, he was returned to his home cage.

(Reproduced from Chase and Wyrwicka, ref. 6.)

We hope that the present study will provide a model for further exploration of the aphagic syndrome. Until now, the study of this behavior has been hampered because lesioned animals exhibit little or no motor activity and, of course, do not consume food in any predictable, regular fashion. By employing ESB, it should be possible to determine the extent to which the destruction of motor activity interferes with food consumption. It should also be possible to examine food preferences in aphagic animals by determining the response rate for the consumption of different meals to a fixed level of ESB. These and other studies, including those dealing previously with ESB, should extend our knowledge of the basic mechanism underlying food consumption and its disruption by hypothalamic destruction.

ACKNOWLEDGMENTS

This research was supported by U.S. Public Health grants MH 13958 and MH 10083 from the National Institute of Mental Health. Bibliographic assistance was received from the Brain Information Service.

REFERENCES

1. Balinska, H. (1963): *Acta Biol. Exp.,* 23:115–124.
2. Teitelbaum, P., and Epstein, A. N. (1962): *Psychol. Rev.,* 69:74–90.
3. Teitelbaum, P., and Stellar, B. (1954): *Science,* 120:894–895.
4. Williams, D. R., and Teitelbaum, P. (1959): *J. Comp. Physiol. Psychol.,* 52:458–465.
5. Wyrwicka, W., and Chase, M. H. (1972): *Physiol. Behav.,* 9:717–720.
6. Chase, M. H., and Wyrwicka, W. (1973): *Exp. Neurol.,* 40:153–160.

Hunger: Basic Mechanisms and Clinical Implications,
edited by D. Novin, W. Wyrwicka, and G. Bray.
Raven Press, New York © 1976.

Spontaneous Activity and Meal Patterns

Ilene L. Bernstein

Department of Psychology, University of Washington, Seattle, Washington 98195

The characterization of spontaneous meal patterns of rats has been of interest to those investigating the physiological determinants of feeding. When food is available at all times, rats take frequent meals at irregular intervals. There is a strong influence of diurnal cycling with large meals with short intermeal intervals in the dark, and small meals with long intermeal intervals in the light. This diurnal cycling probably contributes the greatest source of variability to meal pattern data (4, 9).

A high correlation between meal size and length of the postmeal interval has been reported to be characteristic of free-feeding patterns by LeMagnen and others (1, 4, 6). On the other hand, a correlation between the length of the premeal interval and meal size has not been found. Thus the larger the meal a rat eats, the longer it waits before eating again. These results have recently been questioned by Panksepp (9, also *This Volume*). He has questioned the validity of the statistical procedures employed and has noted that some investigators are unable to obtain a significant correlation. An evaluation of these problems follows.

Panksepp (9) has argued persuasively that the positive correlation between meal size and postmeal interval may be a statistical artifact of pooling data since he failed to obtain it when calculations were performed on raw data. He has suggested that circadian signals are largely responsible for how satiating a meal is and that any other meal-to-meal regulation is accomplished by corrections of some unspecified error signal. Perhaps in response to this criticism, investigators have now been calculating the meal size–postmeal interval correlations from raw data (7, 11). Significant positive correlations between meal size and postmeal interval have still been observed.

There are considerable differences in the magnitude of the correlations observed by different investigators using different diets and feeding situations. Some investigators have not observed the correlation. Levitsky (7) has attempted to reconcile much of the conflicting data in this area by varying the accessibility of meals. He found that under freely accessible feeding conditions, rats ate numerous very small meals and had no significant meal size–postmeal interval correlation. As food became less accessible (or more palatable), meals became larger and less frequent, and a significant positive correlation between meal size and postmeal interval appeared. Therefore, differences in diet delivery and diet content may account for earlier failures to observe significant meal size–postmeal interval correlations (8–10). Levitsky further suggested that meal sizes of at least 7 calories were needed to obtain a significant meal size–postmeal interval correlation in normal rats. Panksepp noted that any manipulation that reduces the diurnal difference of intake and, hence, the variability of meal sizes, tends to inflate the correlation. However, along with reducing the variability, these manipulations increase the average calories per meal. If, as Levitsky suggests, there is a minimum number of calories necessary to exert a gastrointestinal satiety effect, then whether or not significant correlations between meal size and postmeal interval are observed may be directly related to physiological mechanisms of intake regulation and not to statistical coincidence.

It is clear that the contribution of the diurnal cycle in determining meal size and intermeal interval is substantial. It should also be recognized that the circadian effects on meal patterns directly oppose the positive meal size–postmeal interval correlation (small meals with long intermeal intervals in the light, and large meals with short intermeal intervals in the dark). If one is to ascertain if there are significant physiological determinants of meal onset over and above this circadian rhythmicity, efforts must be made to look at meal patterns with this source of variance held constant. Under these conditions, the basis for the meal size–postmeal interval correlation may be revealed.

LeMagnen and Devos (4) suggested that the depletion of energy content of meals may be the factor causing the initiation of the next feeding. If the basis of the high correlation between meal size and postmeal interval is that meals provide the nutrients for energy in the postmeal interval, such that when they are depleted a new meal begins, a high correlation between meal size and total activity within the postmeal interval would be expected. However, the metabolic events occurring at the onset of a daytime meal (lipolysis) are entirely different, according to LeMagnen, from those coinciding with the onset of a nighttime meal (lipogenesis). Yet high meal size–postmeal interval correlations have been reported for both phases of the light cycle. This has been explained by the suggestion that the detector mechanism which initiates a meal has different sensitivity during the day than during the night. Another possibility, of course, is that metabolic depletion is not the basis of this correlation.

The purpose of the present study was to evaluate the degree of correlation between meal size and total activity within the postmeal interval. This was done by recording levels of general activity concurrently with food intake of rats. Each postmeal interval was partitioned to determine the amount of activity and rest that occurred during that interval. The degree to which total activity or minutes of rest in the postmeal interval correlate with size of the corresponding meal was investigated.

METHOD

Four female and five male Wistar rats were maintained on a 12-hr light/ 12-hr dark schedule. Recordings of activity and food intake were done in circular stabilimeter cages. The sensitivity of this apparatus was sufficient to detect moderate grooming activity. Data were collected on a cumulative recorder. In the stabilimeter, 45 mg Noyes pellets were available from a metal bin suspended from the cage. The rats obtained these pellets by pushing open the door and closing a mercury switch. Contacts from the activity recorder caused the upper pen of the cumulative recorder to step. Meal onset reset this pen and the lower pen recorded each food door opening. The number of pellets taken could therefore be counted. A meal was defined as the taking of at least 10 pellets, preceded and followed by 30 min of no eating. Activity scores were obtained by measuring the length of all reset lines for each inter-meal interval. Rest periods were scored as the total of 5-min periods or longer in which no activity was recorded.

For each meal, there were three scores obtained: number of minutes until the next meal, total general activity in that interval, and total rest in that interval.

Day and night meals were analyzed separately. The rationale for this was that although a main source of variance is the diurnal cycle, other factors may also influence feeding patterns. Correlation coefficients were calculated for individual subjects from the raw data.

RESULTS

A total of 292 meals were analyzed. As indicated in Table 1, most but not all subjects had a significant positive correlation between meal size and the

TABLE 1. Correlation of meal size to postmeal interval, activity, and rest

Correlation of meal size to:	Correlation (mean)	Animals showing significant correlation (%)
Nighttime		
Postmeal interval	+0.60	88
Activity	+0.21	22
Rest	+0.42	66
Daytime		
Postmeal interval	+0.45	50
Activity	+0.27	34
Rest	+0.40	50

length of the postmeal interval. Table 1 also contains the correlations of meal size with activity and rest during the postmeal interval. Both sets of correlations are smaller than those based solely on the length of the interval. In other words, time alone provides a stronger correlation with meal size than behavioral indices during the same interval. The correlation of meal size with activity in the postmeal interval was quite low: only two animals had a significant correlation. The correlation of meal size with rest was significant in six of nine animals during the night. In all but two animals, the correlation of meal size with amount of rest was higher than the correlation with activity.

DISCUSSION

This work was done to investigate the possibility that metabolic exhaustion of a meal signals the onset of the next meal. This suggestion implies that a measure of energy expended during a postmeal interval should account for a considerable amount of variability of patterns of eating. Yet activity and meal size are not strongly correlated. Therefore, these data do not support the idea that exhaustion of nutrients through general activity is related to meal onset.

It is surprising that amount of inactivity or rest in the postmeal interval showed a greater degree of positive correlation with meal size than did amount of activity. This observation warrants speculation. Nutritive material provided by a meal has a number of effects. One of these effects is the inhibition of motivated activity for a time period following a meal. It is known, for example, that nutritive material in the stomach (either orally ingested or directly injected) is capable of eliciting activity suppression (3) and EEG synchronization (2). If the extent of this behavioral suppression and cortical modification were proportional to the size of a meal, this could account for the finding that the amount of rest in the postmeal interval is better correlated with meal size than is amount of activity. Activity suppression could be only one consequence of a meal, and this consequence may be the basis of the correlation between meal size and postmeal interval.

REFERENCES

1. Balagura, S., and Coscina, D. V. (1968): Periodicity of food intake in the rat as measured by an operant response. *Physiol. Behav.*, 3:641–643.
2. Bernstein, I. I., (1974): Post-prandial EEG synchronization in normal and hypothalamically lesioned rats. *Physiol. Behav.*, 12:535–545.
3. Finger, F. W. (1951): The effect of food deprivation and subsequent satiation upon general activity in the rat. *J. Comp. Physiol. Psychol.*, 44:557–564.
4. LeMagnen, J., and Devos, M. (1970): Metabolic correlates of the meal onset in the free food intake of rats. *Physiol. Behav.*, 5:805–814.
5. LeMagnen, J., Devos, M., Gaudillière, J., Louis-Sylvestre, J., and Tallon, S. (1973): Role of a lipostatic mechanism in regulation by feeding of energy balance in rats. *J. Comp. Physiol. Psychol.*, 84:1–23.

6. LeMagnen, J., and Tallon, S. (1966): La périodicité spontanée de la prise d'aliments ad libitum du rat blanc. *J. Physiol.*, 58:323–349.
7. Levitsky, D. A. (1974): Feeding Conditions and intermeal relationships. *Physiol. Behav.*, 12:779–787.
8. Levitsky, D. A., and Collier, G. (1968): Effects of diet and deprivation on meal eating behavior in rats. *Physiol. Behav.*, 3:137–140.
9. Panksepp, J. (1973): Reanalysis of feeding patterns in the rat. *J. Comp. Physiol. Psychol.*, 82:78–94.
10. Premack, D., and Kinsch, W. (1970): A description of free responding in the rat. *Learning Motiv.*, 1:321–326.
11. Snowdon, C. T., and Wampler, R. S. (1974): Effects of lateral hypothalamic lesions and vagotomy on meal patterns in rats. *J. Comp. Physiol. Psychol.*, 87:399–409.

Hunger: Basic Mechanisms and Clinical Implications,
edited by D. Novin, W. Wyrwicka, and G. Bray.
Raven Press, New York © 1976.

Weight Regulation in Hamsters and Rats: Differences in the Effects of Exercise and Neonatal Nutrition

Katarina Tomljenović Borer

Neuroscience Laboratory, University of Michigan, Ann Arbor, Michigan 48104

Two features of rodent body weight stand out: (a) its relative stability in adulthood in the face of environmental challenges and (b) its vulnerability to neonatal nutritional manipulations. Adult rats maintain stable weight levels and body composition over large portions of their lifespan. If their weight is disturbed by lack of food (43), lack of water (12), caloric overload (8), or exercise (7), adult rats restore it to its original level after the cessation of disturbance, indicating that body weight in the adult rat is regulated. Similar challenges applied to newborn or rapidly growing animals generally produce lasting changes in adult weight levels and body composition. For instance, neonatal food restriction by means of increased litter size (20, 22, 42), acute fluid restriction (12), or forced exercise (9) slows down the growth of suckling rats and mice (35) and permanently reduces their adult body size, adiposity (18, 22, 31, 32), and certain organ size (44, 45). Conversely, an increase in calories available to suckling rats and mice by reduction in litter size (20, 22, 42), by cross-fostering of mice pups to lactating rat dams (36), or by supplementary force-feeding (10) accelerates their rate of weight gain and permanently elevates their adult body size, percentage of body fat (18, 22), and size of certain organs (46).

The magnitude of neonatal nutritional influence over adult body weight is related to age and to the rate of growth of the animals at the time nutritional challenge is applied. Largest reductions in adult body weight are obtained when the caloric restriction is applied during the first 3 days of life in the rat (21, 43, 45), at which time the rate of growth is also at its maximum. Incurred weight deficits are more completely compensated for as the caloric restriction is applied at progressively later ages to less rapidly growing animals (43, 45). Kennedy (20, 21) concluded that the concurrent cessation of rapid growth and onset of weight regulation in rats are under separate neural controls. He suggested that their interaction is limited to the early period of rapid growth when the endocrine sequelae of growth interfere with the lipostatic regulation of body weight. As growth slows down, hypothalamic restraint over food intake starts to operate (20, 21).

A recent finding suggested the possibility of continuous interdependence of mechanisms of growth and of adult weight regulation. It was found that during, and for some time following, voluntary activity on horizontal disks, adult female hamsters show an accelerated weight gain (3, 4) and accelerated linear growth (Fig. 1). During exercise-induced weight gain, regulation of body weight appeared impaired. Weight displacements were not corrected for following the termination of exercise (3, 4). The magnitude of final weight displacements (3, 4) and, for a limited period, the percentage of body fat (3) were susceptible to environmental variables of the length of exposure to disk activity and the availability of calorically concentrated food (3). Regulatory defenses in response to a 20% weight loss could again be demonstrated in the retired exercised hamsters once the rates of their linear growth and weight gain returned to low control levels (4). The percentage of body fat was found to be appropriate to the new body size (4) 90 days following the retirement from disks.

Vulnerability of both body weight and composition to environmental variables of food availability and caloric density during the periods of rapid growth in either young rodents or adult exercising hamsters suggest that, in rodents, mechanisms of weight regulation and growth suppression are closely interrelated. The present experiment addresses itself to the question of whether or not weight regulation in adult rats and hamsters is influenced in any way by alterations in adult body size and composition resulting from different rates of early growth. The experiment consisted of the manipulation of early growth and adult body size by neonatal over- and undernutrition of

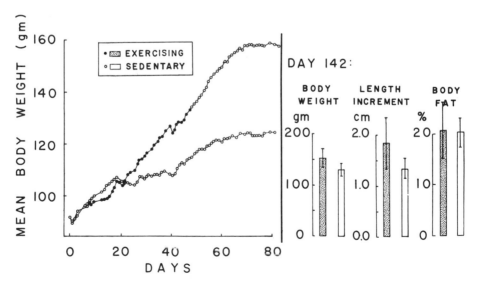

FIG. 1. Left: Weight changes in adult female hamsters as a function of sedentary existence (*n* = 10) or voluntary disk exercise (*n* = 12). Right: Mean body weight, length increments, and percentage of body fat in 12 exercised (stippled bars) and 10 sedentary (open bars) adult female hamsters 94 days following the termination of exercise. Vertical bars, 1 SD. (Modified after Borer and Kooi, ref. 4, with permission from Academic Press.)

hamsters and rats and of challenges to their adult body weight with circumstances known to induce weight changes.

METHOD

Animals

Rats

To insure genetic homogeneity in this experiment, in which the survival of all underfed (UF) animals was not likely, two strains of highly inbred rats were used. Rats derived from the Wistar albino (University of Michigan, Department of Pathology) and brother-sister mated for about 75 generations were bred in the laboratory. Pregnant Buffalo albino rats, brother-sister mated for approximately 25 generations, were obtained from the breeder (Simonsen Laboratories, Gilroy, California). Only female pups were kept for these studies because of the early cessation of growth and early onset of weight regulation in the female rat (40).

Hamsters

Pregnant golden Syrian hamsters (*Mesocricetus auratus*) were obtained from the breeder (Con Olson, Madison, Wisconsin). Hamsters of both sexes were used because gonadal hormones have been reported to have little influence over the growth and body weight of hamsters (18). All animals were maintained at 20°C on a 12-hr light:12-hr dark light cycle. After weaning on day 28, animals were housed individually in 18-cm wide, 24-cm long, and 18-cm deep suspended cages, except where specified otherwise.

Neonatal Nutritional Manipulations

Rats

Since neonatal undernutrition by increased litter size does not produce lasting weight changes in adult female rats (20, 21, 42), a more vigorous method of nutritional deprivation (5) was used in this experiment. Rat pups were removed from the lactating dam to an incubator maintained at 38°C for a total of 200 hr distributed in deprivations, which increased from 6 to 12 hr/day over a 21-day period. Lactation was maintained in the dams of neonatally UF pups by maintaining three to 10 male pups in the litter in addition to the three female UF pups. Because some weanlings initially failed to drink enough water, between days 28 and 42 the pellet diet of UF rats was supplemented with a 50% mixture of powdered Purina rat chow and water. Neonatal overnutrition was encouraged by reducing the litter size to four pups and by offering on days 14 to 42 a mixture, in equivalent proportions, of sweetened condensed milk (Borden's Eagle brand), water, and powdered Purina rat chow. Subsequent to day 42, both the neonatally overfed (OF) and UF rats were maintained on rat pellets and water except when specified otherwise.

Hamsters

Neonatal undernutrition was induced by artificially increasing the litter size to 11 pups. Neonatal overnutrition was encouraged by reducing the litter size to three pups and by offering sunflower seeds on days 14 to 42. Subsequent to day 42, both UF and OF hamsters were maintained on pellets and water, supplemented occasionally with apples, until the start of adult weight challenges.

Diets

Standard diet was Purina laboratory rat chow. In some experiments, rats were offered a high-fat diet (HFD), which was prepared by blending 60% solid shortening (Crisco) and 40% powdered rat chow. The fat and protein content of sunflower seeds is very similar to the composition of rat HFD (3). Estimates of caloric content of pellets, HFD, and sunflower seeds were based on their composition (3), and values of 3.61, 6.96, and 6.84 kcal/g, respectively, were used.

Activity Devices

In the hamster experiments, plastic vertical wheels (Hykro, Denmark, local pet stores) were attached to the side wall of suspended home cages. The wheels measured 15 cm in diameter, 7 cm in width, and had 0.4 cm steps spaced 0.4 cm apart. These wheels were not equipped with counting devices. Rats were given access to horizontal, slightly inclined Plexiglass disks, 30 cm in diameter, in Plexiglass boxes 35-cm wide, 40-cm long, and 42-cm deep. Except for the difference in the diameter, these disks were comparable to the exercisers that induce in freely running adult hamsters increases in linear growth and permanent upward weight displacements (3). Disk revolutions tripped a microswitch and were recorded on electronic counters.

Measurements

Weight measurements were taken once a week from birth until the start, and some time following, the termination of adult weight-challenge experiments. During the experimental challenge of adult weight, animals were weighed daily. In the instances where food intake was measured, the amount consumed was determined by subtracting the weight of spilled and remaining food from the weight of food left 24 hr beforehand. Body length measurements were taken in anesthetized, prone animals between the snout and tail tip in hamsters and between the snout and anus and the anus and tail tip in rats. Body fat measurements were generated indirectly from the body water content, which bears a constant relationship of 72.3% to the lean body mass in hamster (23), rat, and a variety of other animals (33). Body water content was determined by drying carcasses in an oven at 60 to 90°C until a constant weight has been reached.

Data Analysis

Student's *t*-test was used for data comparisons involving two independent treatment groups. In experiments involving multiple comparisons among groups of animals subjected to different treatments, Duncan's multiple range test was used.

RESULTS OF RAT EXPERIMENTS

A total of 18 OF rats (10 Buffalo, 8 Wistar) and 17 UF rats (6 Buffalo, 11 Wistar) were used. Neonatal nutritional manipulations were more effective

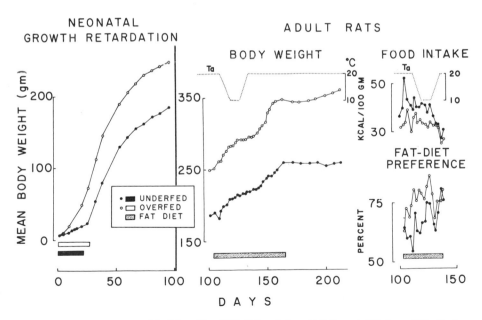

FIG. 2. Left: Weight changes of six OF and five UF Buffalo rats from birth through 100 days of life. Center: Weight changes of the same rats in response to introduction of HFD and to 10°C ambient temperature (T_a). Right: Caloric intake/100 g weight/day (*top*) and percent preference for HFD (*bottom*) by the OF and UF rats during exposure to cold.

in Buffalo strain where OF and UF rats weighed at weaning 70.8 ± 4.1 g and 23.0 ± 2.5 g, respectively, than in the Wistar strain where the same manipulation resulted in OF and UF rats weighing 58.4 ± 13.1 g and 32.8 ± 8.3 g, respectively. The growth curves of six OF and five UF Buffalo rats from birth until the start of Experiment 1 are presented in Fig. 2.

Three experiments were performed challenging the regulatory defenses of adult body weight. Experiment 1 examined the effect of HFD in conjunction with the lowering of the ambient temperature from 20 to 10°C on the body weight levels of OF and UF rats in adulthood. Experiment 2 examined the influence of voluntary disk exercise on adult body weight of OF and UF rats. Experiment 3 examined the ability of OF and UF rats to compensate for a 42-day-long reduction of body weight to 70% of the starting level.

Experiment 1

Procedure

Between days 103 and 163, six OF and five UF Buffalo rats were offered HFD in addition to pellets. Between days 110 and 132, rats were housed in a room with controlled temperature. Temperature was lowered in 3.3°C steps every 2 days to 10°C, maintained at 10°C for 10 days, and then returned to 20°C at the same rate. Food intake was measured between days 98 and 138.

Results

Body weight changes after the introduction of HFD and of cold are presented in Fig. 2. The presence of HFD stimulated comparable rates of weight gain in OF rats (2.37 ± 0.69 g/day) and UF rats (2.0 ± 0.70 g/day). During the 22-day cold exposure, there was a comparable reduction in the daily weight gain in OF and UF rats (0.14 ± 0.23 g versus 0.38 ± 0.25 g/day, respectively). Following exposure to cold, OF rats gained weight significantly faster than the UF rats (2.61 ± 0.97 g versus 1.48 ± 0.58 g/day, respectively, $p < 0.05$), increasing the weight difference between the two groups from 60 to 70 g at the start of the experiment ($p < 0.001$) to about 100 g by the end of the experiment ($p < 0.001$).

Caloric intake per 100-g body weight was significantly greater in UF rats than in OF rats (Fig. 2) both at room temperature (by 10.7 kcal/100 g/day, $p < 0.01$) and in the cold (by 5.4 kcal/100 g/day, $p < 0.01$). Under the same circumstances, the UF rats appeared to select less HFD than the OF rats (Fig. 2), but the differences were not statistically significant.

Discussion

Similar weight changes were seen in adult OF and UF rats when offered HFD with or without concurrent 10°C reduction in ambient temperature.

Reasons for greater caloric intake of UF rats and for their failure to resume rapid weight gain in the presence of HFD following a 3-week exposure to cold are not clear. A lowered resistance of UF rats to a prolonged cold challenge could have resulted from a poorer body insulation or compromised endocrine function (2, 37), which are known to result from neonatal undernutrition. The challenge of the adult body weight with HFD and exposure to cold did not reveal a fundamental difference in the weight regulation of rats of significantly different sizes induced by different neonatal nutrition.

Experiment 2

Procedure

Eight OF and eight UF rats were matched by their adult weight and litter origin and assigned to either the sedentary condition or to exercise. Four OF and four UF rats were given a 55- to 62-day exposure to disk exercisers at ages 110 days (1 OF, 1 UF), 150 days (2 OF, 2 UF), and 240 to 280 days (1 OF, 1 UF), whereas their matched controls remained sedentary.

Results

The activity levels of OF and UF rats rose from about 2,000 and 600 revolutions per day (RPD), respectively, during the first 10 days to different levels

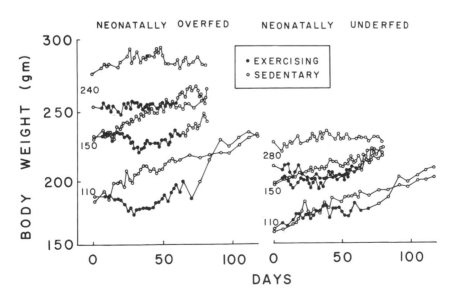

FIG. 3. Body weight changes in response to exercise and sedentary condition in four OF and four UF adult rats in each treatment group. Numbers in the figure, starting age of rats in days. Average weights were presented for the two 150-day-old rats in each group.

related to their age. Highest activity levels, 22,000 to 31,000 RPDs, were reached by the two 110-day-old rats and by one 150-day-old OF rat. Three remaining 150-day-old rats ran between 13,000 and 18,000 RPDs, one 280-day-old UF rat generated up to 12,000 RPDs, and the one 240-day-old OF rat did not run at all. Figure 3 presents the weight changes. Voluntary exercise induced a 20 to 30 g weight loss in the three OF rats that ran and in the heaviest, 280-day-old UF rat. The three younger and lighter UF rats lost only 5 to 10 g in the course of voluntary activity. Following the termination of exercise, the weight of retired exercised rats returned to the weight level of their sedentary controls.

Discussion

OF and UF rats responded in a comparable way to voluntary exercise. There was an initial weight loss and a reduction in weight level that was corrected after the termination of exercise. Comparable weight changes have been reported in rats freely exercising in vertical wheels (7). There was no indication of acceleration in the rate of weight gain or of growth during the 8 to 9 weeks of voluntary disk activity in OF and UF rats in a manner displayed by freely exercising hamsters (3, 4). Body length measurements of four exercised rats (2 OF, 2 UF) did not differ at the end of the experiment from the body lengths of four sedentary rats (2 UF, 2 OF, 21.6 ± 0.66 versus 21.2 ± 0.40 cm, respectively).

Experiment 3

Procedure

Twelve OF and 11 UF rats were subjected to a 30% weight reduction over a 52-day period. Ten OF and six UF rats were of Buffalo strain, 210-days-old at the start of the experiment, and all but 1 OF and 1 UF rat were used in Experiment 1. The remaining rats were of the Wistar strain and 160- (OF) and 196- (UF) days-old at the start of the experiment. Animals were assigned to weight reduction groups (7 OF, 6 UF) and control groups (5 OF, 5 UF) on the basis of their similarity by weight, strain, and litter origin. Food intake was measured during the 15 days following reintroduction of unlimited food to weight-reduced rats.

Results

A 30% weight loss was induced in all weight-reduction rats by restricting their food to 3 to 4 g of pellets daily over 22 to 23 days (Fig. 4). Food intake was subsequently limited to 5 to 11 g/animal/day to maintain their body weight at the 70% of the starting level over 32 more days. The slow weight

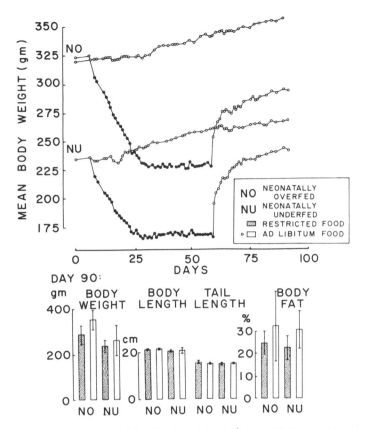

FIG. 4. Top: Weight changes of seven OF and six UF adult rats during a 52-day weight restriction and of their five UF, five UF nondeprived controls. Bottom: Mean body weights, body and tail lengths, and percentages of body fat in the weight-reduced and control rats on the last day of the experiment. Vertical bars, 1 SD.

gain of 0.4 g/day in the two control groups increased the weight deficit of weight-reduced relative to control rats from 30.4 to 34.4% in OF rats and from 31 to 37.5% in UF rats by the end of the restriction period. On reintroduction of an unlimited supply of food, the OF and UF rats displayed comparable increases in caloric intake and initially comparable weight changes. During the first, second, and third consecutive 5-day blocks following reintroduction of unlimited food, the refed OF rats increased their caloric intake by 17, 11.5, and 9 kcal/100 g/day above their baseline food intake of 19 kcal/100 g/day. The comparable increases of the refed UF rats were 17.7, 11, and 6 kcal/100 g/day, respectively, above a baseline intake of 21 kcal/100 g/day. There was a large weight increase during the first day of refeeding in both OF and UF rats (27 and 30 g, respectively). Over the following 4 days, the rates of weight gain in OF and UF rats were 5.75 g and 5.50 g/day, respectively. During the remaining 10 days, before the rates of weight gain of OF and UF rats returned to control levels of 0.4 g/day, the UF rats gained twice as fast (2.0 g/day) as OF rats (1.0 g/day). As a result of this differential rate of compensatory weight gain, OF rats failed to make up for 18% of the weight deficit separating them from their nonreduced controls ($p < 0.05$), whereas UF rats compensated for all but 11% of the weight deficit relative to their controls ($p > 0.1$). At the time of sacrifice (Fig. 4), the formerly weight-reduced OF rats still weighed significantly less than their nonreduced controls ($p < 0.05$), but the adult weight challenge had no other lasting consequence. In contrast, a lasting influence of neonatal nutrition was evident as a significant difference in body length of OF and UF rats (22.2 ± 0.2 cm versus 21.4 ± 0.5 cm, $p < 0.001$), which persisted to the end of the experiment.

Discussion

The timing and the pattern of feeding and weight changes following a prolonged weight-reduction challenge was very similar in adult OF and UF rats. A quantitative difference appeared that consisted of the failure of OF rats to sustain as high a rate of catch-up weight gain during the last 10 days of compensation for weight reduction as was seen in UF rats. As a consequence adult OF rats failed to compensate for all of the weight deficit incurred during the prolonged weight reduction, whereas adult UF rats succeeded in completely correcting theirs.

RESULTS OF THE HAMSTER EXPERIMENT

Procedure

OF and UF hamsters were reared on two occasions. At the time adult weight-challenge experiments were started, 34 OF hamsters (19 males, 15 females) and 41 UF hamsters (20 males, 21 females) were 135-days-old, whereas 5 OF (two males, three females) and 9 UF hamsters (five males, four females) were 180-days-old. The 39 OF and 50 UF hamsters were matched by weight and balanced by sex, age, and litter origin and assigned to four equivalent OF groups and five equivalent UF groups of 9 to 10 animals each. An OF and UF group, each, were assigned to the following four treatments: control animals with pellets *ad libitum* (C), weight reduction group maintained at 87% of the control group body weight through food restriction (R), seed group with unlimited access to pellets and sunflower seeds (S), and exercise group with access to vertical wheels in their home cages (X). The fifth UF group (SX) had access to pellets, seeds, and activity wheels. Adult challenges were applied for 52 days.

Results

The course of weight changes from birth through day 135 or 180 in the two groups of OF and UF hamsters is presented in Fig. 5. At weaning, the weights of UF and OF hamsters were 51.6 ± 7.0 g and 63.8 ± 7.4. There were no sex differences in body weight at weaning, and data analysis by sex was not further pursued. The course of weight changes in response to adult weight challenges is presented in Fig. 6. Although all hamsters were

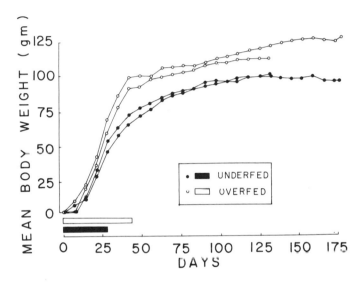

FIG. 5. Neonatal growth retardation. Weight changes of 39 OF and 50 UF hamsters from birth until the start of adult weight-challenge experiments.

observed to engage in running in the activity wheels and to eat sunflower seeds, the availability of exercise and of sunflower seeds had no effect on the body weight of OF hamsters. As a consequence, none of the OF hamster groups differed from one another at the end of the treatment period except for the R group whose weight was significantly lower than the weight of OF controls ($p < 0.01$). The same type of treatment, as well as the combination of the two had an accelerating effect on the rate of weight gain of UF hamsters. As a result one of the two exercising UF groups (SX) became indistinguishable by weight from all OF groups by the end of the challenge period, and X caught up in weight to OF controls (Fig. 6). Sunflower seeds augmented the weight gain of UF exercising hamsters, although presented alone they did not induce significant weight change. Because of an unexplained decline in the weight of UF group C, there was no significant weight difference between

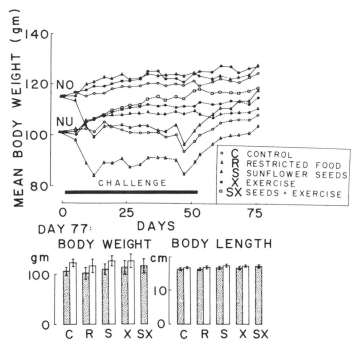

FIG. 6. Top: Weight changes of adult hamsters as a function of neonatal overfeeding, underfeeding, and weight-challenge stimuli. Bottom: Mean body weights, body lengths, and percentages of body fat in the OF and UF hamster groups 22 days after the termination of various challenges. Vertical lines, 1 SD.

them and the R hamsters. After the termination of challenges the two R groups engaged in compensatory weight gain during the remaining 22 days of the experiment. Both the OF and the UF R hamsters caught up to the weight level of their unreduced controls by the last day of the experiment. The weight relationships of UF hamsters established during the challenge period persisted to the end of the experiment. Adult weight challenges also had an effect over the final body length of UF groups. One exercised UF group (SX) was indistinguishable in its final length from all of the OF groups, whereas the other X and the UF S group caught up in length with all but the heaviest of OF groups (S). The lengths of the four OF groups did not differ from each other, whereas the length of UF hamsters in groups SX and S exceeded the length of UF control hamsters significantly ($p < 0.01$ and $p < 0.05$, respectively).

Discussion

The display of weight regulation in adult hamsters was dependent on their neonatal nutritional experience and the type of regulatory challenges used. Hamsters showed compensation for weight deficits incurred through caloric restriction regardless of their neonatal nutritional treatment. Differences in responses with respect to rats and related to neonatal manipulations of growth were seen when adult hamsters were presented with the opportunity to exercise and eat high-fat diets. These two challenges had no effect over the adult body weight of OF hamsters in contrast to the opposite effects they had over body weight of rats. The same two challenges led to accelerated weight gain and growth in length in UF hamsters. Neonatal growth retardation in UF hamsters was associated with failure to regulate weight in adulthood when presented with the opportunity to exercise and eat calorically concentrated food. Instead, these challenges were associated with a reinstatement of rapid linear growth and with partial or total compensation for deficits in body size and length generated during the neonatal growth retardation. Since the activity and feeding rates were not measured in this experiment, it is not possible to determine whether this outcome resulted from the OF hamsters' failure to engage in exercise and seed consumption to the same degree as UF hamsters.

DISCUSSION

The present study addressed itself to the question of possible interaction between the rate of early growth and the regulation of body weight in adult rats and hamsters of different body size. The goal of the study was to determine whether different rates of growth during the neonatal period predominantly influenced adult body size without an effect on regulation of body weight or whether body size and the rate of preceding growth influenced in some way the operation of weight regulatory mechanisms in adult rodents. The study uncovered a species difference between the hamster and the rat in the interaction of neonatal growth and adult weight regulation and provided additional data that support the hypothesis that active suppression of growth may play an integral part in the mechanism of weight regulation in adult rodents.

In the present experiment, the variation in the size of litter between three and 11 pups was sufficient to produce significant weight differences in hamsters of both sexes. A more vigorous deprivation in the form of restricted access to lactating dam was necessary to produce lasting weight differences in female rats. After the age of 100 days, when the rate of weight gain in both OF and UF rats and hamsters had subsided, the animals were presented with the opportunity to exercise, a choice of calorically concentrated diet, a prolonged weight reduction, or exposure to cold, and their weight or feeding responses were observed for evidence of an interaction between neonatal growth and adult weight regulation.

Weight regulation of adult rats was largely uninfluenced by their body size and neonatal growth manipulations. Large neonatally overfed female rats defended their weight against the challenges of weight loss, increased caloric density of food, exposure to cold, and voluntary exercise in a comparable way to small neonatally underfed rats. The two exceptions to this generalization that emerge represent a quantitative difference in the degree of regulatory responses. Neonatally overfed rats failed to correct for all of the weight deficit when the restraint over their food intake was removed after a prolonged weight reduction. After a prolonged cold exposure, the UF rats failed to restore a rapid rate of weight gain, which they originally maintained when given a choice of pellets and HFD. No explanation for these differences can be offered at the present time. They may be related to differences in body composition (18, 21, 22, 32) or endocrine function (2, 37), which can result from early nutritional manipulations of the kind used in this study. Both instances of incomplete weight regulation involved a failure to recover lost weight or a previously higher rate of weight gain. No challenge used in this study was effective in restoring the rapid growth rate of the neonatal period in the rat. Unlike the situation in adult hamsters, voluntary exercise on horizontal disks did not reinstate rapid growth and induce upward weight displacements in adult rats regardless of their early history. It only induced transient weight losses comparable to weight changes observed in rats exercising in vertical wheels (7). Owing to the apparent impossibility of reinstating with natural stimuli rapid linear growth in the adult rat, the interrelationship between the low rate of growth in adulthood (11, 13) and the regulation of body weight is not apparent. Instead, according to the current view (20, 21, 40, 41), the control of growth and the regulation of body weight represent independent processes under separate neural control. Their interaction is seen to be limited to the inhibition by anterior pituitary hormones of the weight regulatory mechanism during the early phase of rapid growth in the rat.

The nature of the weight challenge influenced the type of response exhibited by adult hamsters. In response to prolonged weight restriction adult hamsters corrected all of the incurred weight deficit regardless of their early nutritional history. In this respect adult hamsters displayed equivalent weight regulatory ability to that of rats or possibly even a superior one. Neonatal growth manipulations did not interfere with the complete compensation for weight losses in the hamster as they did in OF rats. Responses of adult hamsters to challenges of exercise and HFD were different from those seen in rats and were greatly influenced by neonatal nutritional manipulation. The weight of large OF hamsters remained stable during the exposure to exercise or to HFD in contrast to transient weight losses and gains seen in rats subjected to corresponding challenges. As a consequence the weights and lengths of experimental and control OF hamsters remained comparable throughout the experiment.

Neonatally underfed hamsters did not defend their body weight when given the opportunity to run in the activity wheels or eat sunflower seeds. Instead they responded to both challenges with increased linear growth and with permanent weight elevations. The opportunity for voluntary exercise, alone or accompanied with a diet of seeds, led in UF hamsters to partial or complete correction of the weight and length deficits incurred during the neonatal period. In the hamster the onset of weight regulation appears to be contingent on the attainment of some body size or on the execution of a certain amount or rate of growth. Because of the ease with which voluntary exercise reinstates rapid linear growth in adult hamsters, the reciprocity of growth and weight regulation is readily observable. Periods of rapid growth in either the newborn hamster or in the exercising adult are characterized by disturbances in weight regulation. Increases in body size generated during such periods of rapid growth are permanent and subject to great modification by external influences, such as availability, caloric density of food, and duration of disk exercise (3, 4, and present experiment). Regulatory defenses of body weight and composition are seen only during the periods of low linear growth (4). Voluntary exercise represents an exceptional situation, which appears to interfere with the neural controls over the growth rate and with the regulation of body weight. Neonatal growth retardation appears to make adult hamsters more susceptible to this type of interference.

Although no known environmental stimulus will reinstate rapid linear growth in adult rats, slow skeletal growth is maintained throughout their life span (11, 13), and their capacity to engage in rapid linear growth is evident following some types of interference with the integrity of their neuroendocrine systems. Temporary reinstatement of rapid growth occurs in adult female rats following ovariectomy (19). Concomitant absence of weight regulation can be seen in permanent upward weight displacements (38) and in lasting changes in the percentage of body fat (24). Disconnection of medial basal hypothalamus from the anterior telencephalic structures leads to a reinstatement of rapid skeletal growth and to accumulation of body fat in adult female rats (28, 29, 34). This disconnection leads to rapid growth and to disturbance in weight regulation only after female rats exceed the age of 40 to 50 days (15). Individual components of adult rat's weight regulatory mechanism such as estrogenic suppression of weight and feeding (41) and responsiveness to glucoprivic stimuli (17) appear at about the same age. The reciprocity of growth and weight regulation before and after this critical age as well as in adult female rats with disconnection of medial basal hypothalamus from anterior neural influences support the hypothesis that a common neural mechanism is responsible for both events. Common involvement of a number of brain areas in both the control of growth and the regulation of weight or feeding lend further credence to this notion. Medial basal hypothalamus is the effector area for behavioral (30) and metabolic (47) processes of weight regulation as well as for the release of growth hormone (14, 25, 26). In addition neocortex and amygdala have been strongly implicated both in growth hormone release (25–27) and in feeding or weight regulation (6, 16, 39). The stability and defense of adult body weight in rodents probably depend in part on maintenance of a low rate of skeletal growth. Mechanism of weight regulation in rodents may involve an active suppression of skeletal growth and adjustments in caloric intake, caloric expenditure, and endocrine secretions for maintenance of low growth rate and for the defense of body structure and composition at a given body size. The adult hamster may be the model of choice in studies of the interrelationship of neural controls of growth and weight regulation because of the ease with which availability of disk exercise can alternate the states of weight-regulation-suppressed growth and unregulated weight-rapid growth.

ACKNOWLEDGMENTS

This work was supported in part by grants from the Department of Research Development and Administration, University of Michigan, and from the Weight Watchers Foundation, Inc. to the author and by the National Institute of Mental Health Grant MH-20811 to E. S. Valenstein. I wish to acknowledge the technical assistance of Louise Braisted, Pam Forbeck, and Alice A. Kooi and the helpful suggestions for the improvement of the manuscript from E. S. Valenstein and S. M. Garn.

REFERENCES

1. Bernardis, L. L., and Skelton, F. R. (1965): *Neuroendocrinology,* 1:265–275.
2. Blackmore, D. (1973): *Biol. Neonate,* 23:359–365.
3. Borer, K. T. (1974): *Physiol. Behav.,* 12:589–597.
4. Borer, K. T., and Kooi, A. A. (1975): *Behav. Biol.,* 13:301–310.
5. Cheng, M. -F., Rozin, P., and Teitelbaum, P. (1971): *J. Comp. Physiol. Psychol.,* 76:206–218.
6. Collier, B. D., and Gault, F. P. (1969): *Psychon. Science,* 17:41–42.
7. Collier, G. H. (1970): *Trans. NY Acad. Sci.,* 32:557–576.
8. Cohn, C., and Joseph, D. (1962): *Yale J. Biol. Med.,* 34:598–607.
9. Crews, E. L., Fuge, K. W., Oscai, L. B., Holloszy, J. O., and Shank, R. E. (1969): *Am. J. Physiol.,* 216:359–363.
10. Czajka-Narins, D. M., and Hirsch, J. (1974): *Biol. Neonate,* 25:63–67.
11. Dawson, A. B. (1925): *Anat. Record,* 27:202.
12. Detieux, Y., Dutillet, B., and Picard, D. (1974): *Annee Endocrinol.,* 35:11–119.
13. Donaldson, H. H., and Conrow, S. B. (1919): *Am. J. Anat.,* 26:237–314.
14. Frohman, L. A., Bernardis, L. L., and Kant, K. J. (1968): *Science,* 162:580–582.
15. Gold, R. M., and Kapatos, G. (1975): *J. Comp. Physiol. Psychol.,* 88:202–209.
16. Grossman, S. P., and Grossman, L. (1963): *Am. J. Physiol.,* 205:761–765.
17. Houpt, K. A., and Epstein, A. N. (1973): *Am. J. Physiol.,* 225:58–66.
18. Johnson, P. R., Stern, J. S., Greenwood, M. R. C., Zucker, L. M., and Hirsch, J. (1973): *J. Nutr.,* 103:738–743.
19. Kakolewski, J. W., Cox, V. C., and Valenstein, E. S. (1968): *Psychol. Rep.,* 22:547–554.
20. Kennedy, G. C. (1957): *J. Endocrinol.,* 16:9–17.
21. Kennedy, G. C. (1967): Alimentary Canal In: *Handbook of Physiology, Vol. 1, Control of Food and Water Intake,* edited by C. F. Code, pp. 337–351. American Physiology Society, Washington, D.C.
22. Knittle, J. L., and Hirsch, J. (1968): *J. Clin. Invest.,* 47:2091–2098.
23. Kodama, A. M. (1971): *J. Appl. Physiol.,* 31:218–222.
24. Leshner, A. I., and Collier, G. (1973): *Physiol. Behav.,* 11:671–676.

25. Martin, J. B. (1972): *Endocrinology*, 91:107–115.
26. Martin, J. B. (1973): *N. Engl. J. Med.*, 288:1384–1393.
27. Martin, J. B., Kontor, J., and Mead, P. (1973): *Endocrinology*, 92:1354–1360.
28. Mitchell, J. A., Smyrl, R., Hutchins, M., Schindler, W. J., and Critchlow, V. (1972): *Neuroendocrinology*, 10:31–45.
29. Mitchell, J. A., Hutchins, M., Schindler, W. J., and Critchlow, V. (1973): *Neuroendocrinology*, 12:161–173.
30. Mogenson, G. J. (1974): In: *Recent Studies of Hypothalamic Function*, edited by K. Lederis and K. E. Cooper, pp. 268–293. Karger, Basel.
31. Oscai, L. B., Babirak, S. P., Dubach, F. B., McGarr, J. A., and Spirakis, C. N. (1974): *Am. J. Physiol.*, 227:901–904.
32. Oscai, L. B., Babirak, S. P., McGarr, J. A., and Spirakis, C. N. (1974): *Fed. Proc.*, 33:1956–1958.
33. Pace, N., and Rathbun, E. N. (1945): *J. Biol. Chem.*, 158:685–691.
34. Palka, Y., Liebelt, R., and Critchlow, V. (1971): *Physiol. Behav.*, 7:187–194.
35. Parkes, A. S. (1926): *Ann. Appl. Biol.*, 13:374–394.
36. Parkes, A. S. (1929): *Ann. Appl. Biol.*, 14:171–173.
37. Sobotka, T. J., Cook, M. P., and Brodie, R. E. (1974): *Brain Res.*, 65:443–457.
38. Tarttelin, M. F., and Gorski, R. A. (1973): *Acta Endocrinol.*, 72:551–568.
39. Teitelbaum, P. (1971): *Prog. Physiol. Psychol.*, 4:319–350.
40. Wade, G. N. (1972): *Physiol. Behav.*, 8:523–534.
41. Wade, G. N., and Zucker, I. (1970): *J. Comp. Physiol. Psychol.*, 70:213–220.
42. Widdowson, E. M., and McCance, R. A. (1960): *Proc. R. Soc. Lond. (Biol.)*, 152:188–206.
43. Widdowson, E. M., and McCance, R. A. (1963): *Proc. R. Soc. Lond. (Biol.)* 158:329–342.
44. Williams, J. P. G., Tanner, J. M., and Hughes, P. C. R. (1974): *Pediat. Res.*, 8:157–162.
45. Winick, M., and Noble, A. (1966): *J. Nutr.*, 89:300–306.
46. Winick, M., and Noble, A. (1967): *J. Nutr.*, 91:179–182.
47. Woods, S. C., Decke, E., and Vaselli, J. R. (1974): *Psychol. Rev.*, 81:26–43.
48. Zucker, I., Wade, G. W., and Ziegler, R. (1972): *Physiol. Behav.*, 8:101–112.

Hunger: Basic Mechanisms and Clinical Implications,
edited by D. Novin, W. Wyrwicka, and G. Bray.
Raven Press, New York © 1976.

The Role of the Lateral Hypothalamus in Determining the Body Weight Set Point

Richard E. Keesey, Peter C. Boyle, Joseph W. Kemnitz, and Joel S. Mitchel

University of Wisconsin, Madison, Wisconsin 53706

A primary role for the lateral hypothalamus (LH) in determining the maintenance level or set point for body weight was first suggested by the observation that animals with lesions of this area display a reduced level of weight maintenance (1); that is, the weight that LH-lesioned animals lose during the postlesion periods of aphagia and anorexia is not recovered. Instead, body weight is maintained at a level significantly lower than that maintained by control animals. This effect is illustrated in the weight functions of LH-lesioned and control animals presented in Fig. 1 (2). During the postlesion periods of aphagia and/or anorexia, the LH-lesioned animals represented in Fig. 1 lost approximately 75 g. Food intake then returned to levels sufficient for weight maintenance and the normal pattern of slow weight gain reappeared. Body weight, however, not only remained at a level significantly below control, but was maintained at this lower level in a quite regular fashion. For example, if expressed as a percentage of the control level, the weight maintenance level of the LH-lesioned group varied by only a few percentage points ($86.4 \pm 2.3\%$) from the third-week postlesion until the end of the 24-week observation period. Nor did the average weekly variation in the body weight of individual LH-lesioned animals differ from that of the controls except during the first few weeks postlesion. Thus the maintenance of body weight at a reduced level by LH-lesioned animals appears to be not only chronic but quite precise.

A lower level of body weight, even if precisely and persistently maintained, is not, of course, evidence in itself of an altered regulation level or set point. Either general insult or more specific impairments in systems directly concerned with food intake might also lead to a chronically lower level of body weight. For these reasons, we have conducted a series of experiments over the past several years in which the LH-lesioned animal's new level of maintained body weight was challenged in various ways. The aim of these experiments was to determine whether this reduced weight level could and would be defended. Our purpose in this chapter is to review this work and to evaluate the accumulated evidence relevant to the question of whether the reduced level of body weight in the LH-lesioned animal does indeed represent an altered set point.

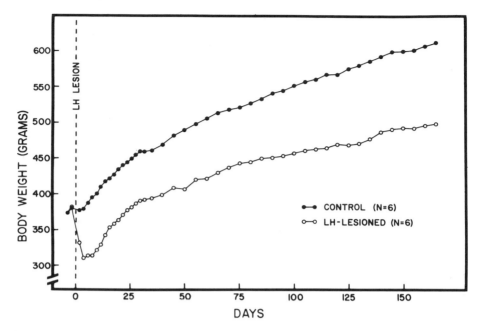

FIG. 1. Body weight functions of control and LH-lesioned rats over a 24-week period following surgery.

TESTS INVOLVING DIETARY MANIPULATIONS

The experiments we have undertaken in dealing with this issue have followed several general approaches. One has been to observe the LH-lesioned animal's defense of its lowered weight maintenance level and to compare it to that of normal animals when challenged by various dietary manipulations. In one of our earliest efforts of this type (1), we presented LH-lesioned animals with a highly palatable eggnog diet after they had been maintained for many months postlesion on a diet of regular laboratory chow and water. We subsequently varied the caloric density of this eggnog diet by progressively diluting it with water. The effects of these manipulations upon the control and LH-lesioned animals' maintained level of body weight are shown in Fig. 2.

When the eggnog diet is first introduced, the body weight of both the LH-lesioned and control animals can be seen to increase markedly. Eventually, however, the weight of both stabilizes at a higher level. This new level was then maintained by both groups throughout the series of progressively more dilute eggnog solutions, even though it was necessary for the animal to more than double its previous daily intake. Finally, when presented with a less palatable diet of wet mash, the weights of both groups declined to a lower maintenance level. Thus the weight adjustments of the LH-lesioned animals to these dietary changes parallel almost exactly that of the normals. In fact,

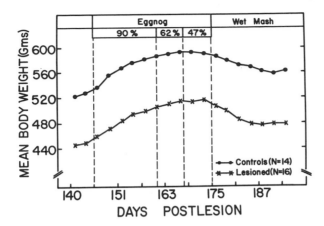

FIG. 2. Body weight of control and LH-lesioned animals as a function of both diet variation and diet dilution.

across the 50-day period of diet manipulations, the mean body weight of the lesioned animals, expressed as a percentage of control animals' weight, varied by no more than 1.2% from the mean value of 86%.

We have obtained similar results when quinine was added to the diet of LH-lesioned and control animals as a challenge to their level of weight maintenance (3). Animals receiving LH lesions and then maintained on a wet mash diet first reduced and then maintained their body weight at 90% of the control level. When the diet was adulterated with quinine, an additional 12.8% reduction in maintained body weight was observed. This quinine-induced reduction in the lesioned animals' weight was nearly identical to that (12.3%) seen in control animals when quinine was added to their diet.

Further work of this sort (4) was prompted by the report of Mufson and Wampler (5) that LH-lesioned rats, if fed a palatable high-fat diet, failed to display the reduced level of body weight that we have reported. Although such a result was inconsistent with our own experience with dietary manipulations of this sort, we had not tested the particular diet used by these investigators; we therefore undertook to assess the effects of this diet upon the weight maintenance level of LH-lesioned animals. Starting with groups of LH-lesioned and control animals maintained upon our regular wet mash diet, we first ascertained that the LH animals displayed the expected pattern of weight maintenance at a reduced level. In this case, the LH level was 89% of control. Giving the high-fat diet to half of the animals in both the control and LH-lesioned groups did not, however, cause the level of maintained body weight of either group to be altered. Both the control and LH-lesioned animals remained at essentially the same body weight on the high-fat diet as those continuing to receive the wet mash diet. These results failed to confirm the findings of Mufson and Wampler (5) concerning the effects of this dietary condition upon the weight maintenance level of LH animals. It is unclear to us what factor(s) may account for the different results. It may be significant, however, that Mufson and Wampler did not employ a control group to demonstrate that their LH-lesioned animals would have maintained a lower weight level on the wet mash diet. Thus the possibility exists that their lesions may not have initially produced the effect (i.e., a reduced weight level of weight maintenance on a wet mash diet) that their high-fat diet was presumed to eliminate.

In summary, our results to date indicate that the response of the LH-lesioned animal to various dietary challenges is neither qualitatively nor quantitatively different from that of the control. The only significant difference is that the weight adjustments that LH-lesioned animals make to these challenges take place around a reduced rather than a normal level of body weight. In addition to providing support for the view that LH lesions alter the set point for body weight, such results also speak to the general issue raised by others (e.g., refs. 5, 6) concerning the role of finickiness in the LH syndrome. The LH-lesioned animals we have studied display essentially normal adjustments in body weight to variation in diet palatability. This is not to deny that other lesions involving the lateral hypothalamus and/or other surrounding structures can produce a hyperreactivity to the sensory properties of a diet. Rather, it is to say that the LH lesions we have used in our work do not cause finickiness, and that the reduced level of maintained body weight that we see in LH animals is not due to an exaggerated responsiveness to unpalatable diets.

TESTS INVOLVING MANIPULATIONS OF BODY WEIGHT

In another series of experiments, we attempted to assess the LH animal's ability to defend its subnormal weight maintenance level by observing what happens when its body weight is experimentally displaced. One such experiment, the results of which can be seen in Fig. 3, compares the postlesion adjustment in body weight by LH animals lesioned at a normal body weight with that seen in animals lesioned while at a reduced weight level (1). Two groups of animals received either a 7-sec or 4-sec lesion while at an *ad lib* weight level. Both displayed postlesion aphagia (3.2 and 1.0 days, respectively) and anorexia (2.1 and 1.8 days, respectively) before finally regulating their body weight at a reduced percentage of the control level (88% and 93%, respectively). Two other groups receiving equivalent lesions, but after having their body weight reduced to 80% of the normal level, displayed quite a different postlesion pattern. Those receiving a 7-sec lesion displayed only 0.2 days of aphagia and 1.3 days of anorexia before assuming a level of food intake that served to bring their body weight to a maintenance level of 88%. Animals receiving the 4-sec lesion while at an 80% weight level displayed an even greater departure from the typical pattern. Not only were

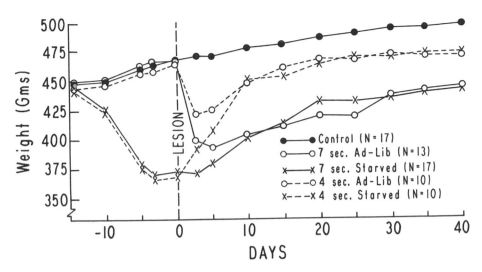

FIG. 3. Body weight of control and LH-lesioned rats as a function of lesion parameters and weight at the time of lesioning. The 4 sec and 7 sec refer to the duration of the 1 m/g electrolytic lesion. The body weight of the starved groups was reduced to 80% of control by partial starvation prior to lesioning. *Ad lib* groups were allowed to feed without restriction.

they not aphagic or anorexic following lesioning, but they ingested food at supranormal levels and gained an average of 50 g during the first week postlesion. They then maintained their body weight at 93% of the control level. The point is that the postlesion feeding behavior of the LH-lesioned animals in this experiment was appropriate to the achievement of the new level of weight maintenance. If lesioned at a normal body weight, they were aphagic and anorexic, and thereby achieved this new maintenance level by the loss of body weight. But, if lesioned while below their new level of weight maintenance, they were hyperphagic and displayed a rapid weight gain to reach this new level. In both cases, the primary effect of the LH lesion appears to be that of setting a new level of weight maintenance, while the adjustments in feeding behavior are apparently secondary to the achievement of this reduced level.

Two experiments in which force-feeding was used to alter the LH-lesioned animal's body weight add further support to the above conclusion. In the first (7), the results of which are presented in Fig. 4, two groups of rats were given LH lesions but one was force-fed for the first week postlesion. The group not force-fed was aphagic and/or anorexic for approximately 1 week postlesion before achieving a new level of weight maintenance (81%). During this same period, the weight of the other group was held at the level of control animals by force-feeding. When the force-feeding was discontinued, however, the body weight of this group declined until reaching the same stable maintenance level of 81% of control.

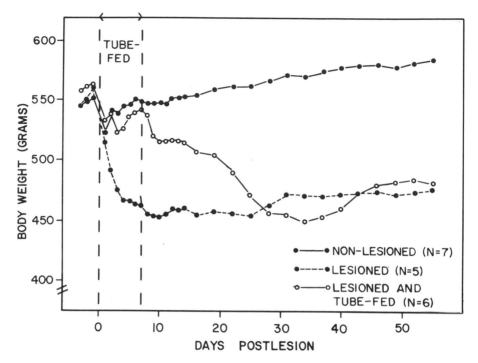

FIG. 4. The effect of force-feeding on the duration of anorexia in LH-lesioned rats. Force-feeding was used to maintain the weight of the lesioned and tube-fed group at a control level for the first week following surgery. This group was then permitted to feed *ad lib.* The nonlesioned and lesioned groups were permitted to feed *ad lib* throughout the experiment.

In a second experiment (8), we used force-feeding to raise the weight of an LH-lesioned animal from its lowered maintenance level. Figure 5 shows the weight functions of a group of control animals and a group of LH animals. The latter, having been lesioned some time previously, display the typical pattern of weight maintenance at a lower level (79%). An animal selected from the LH-lesioned group was then force-fed until its body weight had been increased to approximately that of the control group at which time it was again permitted to feed *ad lib.* Note that this animal was anorexic after force-feeding until its weight had returned to the level of the LH group from which it was originally selected. Thus force-feeding immediately after lesioning impedes the loss of body weight and has the effect of prolonging the postlesion period of anorexia. Once a reduced level of weight maintenance has been achieved, however, causing the weight of an LH-lesioned animal to be elevated to control levels by force-feeding reinstates this anorexia. Thus the primary effect of the LH lesions in these animals again appears to be upon a mechanism setting the level of maintained body weight, whereas the changes in feeding behavior can be viewed as secondary to the achievement of this level.

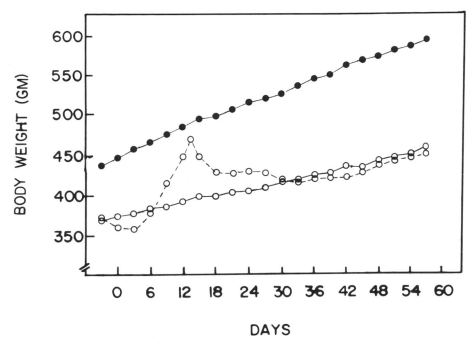

FIG. 5. Reinstatement of anorexia in a LH-lesioned rat by force-feeding. An animal selected from the lesioned group (open circles) was force-fed until its body weight approached that of the control group (closed circles). It was then returned to a regular *ad lib* feeding regimen.

Some of the most compelling data in favor of the argument that LH lesions reduce the set point for body weight comes from an experiment we have only recently completed (9). In this work, one group of rats was first given LH lesions and then observed for 1 month postlesion. At the end of this period, the lesion group was maintaining its weight at 86% of the control level. Some of the LH-lesioned animals were then placed upon a restricted feeding schedule until they reached a weight level that was 80% that of the LH animals remaining on an *ad lib* feeding regimen. The same procedure was followed with some of the animals in the nonlesioned group. Both deprived groups were then returned to *ad lib* feeding conditions, and their body weight and daily food intake were carefully monitored.

When permitted to feed *ad lib,* the deprived groups, whether lesioned or not, quickly returned to the weight levels of their nondeprived controls (see Fig. 6). Of special significance, however, is how closely the pattern of weight recovery in the lesioned group paralleled that of the nonlesioned animals. Both gained nearly identical percentages of the lost weight per day and took nearly an identical number of days to reach the levels of their nondeprived controls. A similar parallel was seen in the food-intake data. Upon being returned to an *ad lib* feeding schedule, the deprived LH-lesioned and non-

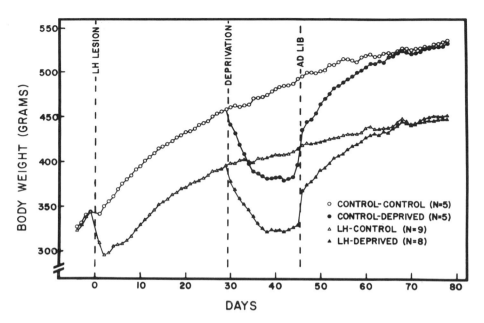

FIG. 6. Recovery of body weight in LH-lesioned and control animals following a period of food restriction. The body weight of the LH-deprived and control-deprived groups was first reduced to 80% of the value each normally maintained and then returned to an *ad lib* feeding regimen.

lesioned groups elevated their daily food intake above control levels by nearly identical amounts. As their weight subsequently increased to the level of their nondeprived controls, however, the daily intake levels gradually declined until finally returning to the control level of daily intake. Thus LH-lesioned and -nonlesioned animals not only display a rapid recovery to their appropriate weight levels following weight loss but also adjust their food intake in a virtually identical way in doing so. In fact the only difference to emerge between the LH-lesioned and normal animals in these experiments is in the level of body weight each is prepared to defend.

OTHER TESTS AND CONTROLS

Several experiments have been prompted by criticisms or reactions of others to our work. Cox and Kakolewski (10), for example, reported that they were unable to obtain a chronically lower level of weight maintenance in LH-lesioned female rats. Rather, their animals quickly recovered the weight lost in the first few days postlesion and eventually displayed a level of weight maintenance at or above the normal control level. Since we have generally used male rats in our experiments, these results raised the possibility of a sex difference in the weight effects of LH lesions. Thus we (11) conducted an experiment designed specifically to compare the effects of LH lesions upon

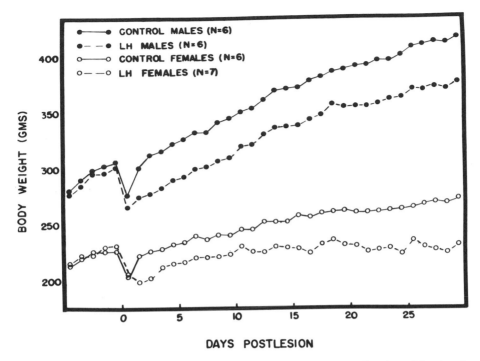

FIG. 7. The effect of LH lesions on the level of maintained body weight in both male and female rats.

the weight maintenance levels of male and female rats. The results of this work, shown in Fig. 7, do not confirm the earlier observations of Cox and Kakolewski (10). Both sexes displayed a postlesion pattern of weight maintenance at a reduced level and showed nearly identical percentage reductions in body weight. We are reluctant, however, to come to any firm conclusions regarding this issue until it has been examined more thoroughly. One reason for this is that the number of females we have studied is still too small to say whether the female effect is quantitatively the same as that seen in the male. Second, we have not studied the female's defense of this lower weight maintenance level in any of the ways we have in the male and therefore are unable to say how the female responds to such challenges. Finally, we too have observed in some females a postlesion pattern of weight decline and recovery similar to that reported by Cox and Kakolewski. Thus we wish only to make the point here that a lower level of weight maintenance following LH lesions can be demonstrated in both male and female rats. Questions such as whether the effect is quantitatively similar in the two sexes, or whether the female effect is complicated by factors not operating in the male, cannot be answered adequately at this time.

In another instance, we were led to reexamine the issue of whether adipsia, which is commonly a consequence of LH damage, may play a role in lowering the weight maintenance level of LH rats. Although we (1) had considered this matter earlier, and had demonstrated that neither the continued use of hydrated diets, nor repeated intubation of water caused the level of maintained body weight to be altered, we were prompted to reconsider it when Mufson and Wampler (5) suggested that, if LH animals are stimulated to ingest high levels of fluid by such sweetening agents as saccharin or sucrose, their weight may be caused to return to normal levels. We have now completed an experiment (4) in which the same saccharine solution employed by Mufson and Wampler (5), as well as a more palatable sucrose-saccharine solution, were given to LH animals lesioned according to our usual procedures. The results did not reveal any significant effect of these drinking solutions upon the level of maintained body weight. In spite of the fact that the lesioned animals drank copious quantities of these sweetened fluids, their weight maintenance level remained at the same reduced value throughout the entire test series. Thus we would like to reaffirm our earlier conclusion that the reduced levels of weight maintenance in LH-lesioned animals are not secondary to a dehydration anorexia.

Another matter deserves brief comment in this section. Several investigators have indicated that their attempts to eliminate LH aphagia and/or anorexia by our procedure (1) of reducing body weight prior to lesioning have been unsuccessful. It must first be noted in this regard that the new weight maintenance level of an LH-lesioned animal is an inverse function of the lesion size (1). In fact a continuous distribution of weight maintenance levels ranging from just below 100% to approximately 60% of normal can be generated by increasing the amount of a critical LH area that is destroyed (12). Thus, should one wish to eliminate the usual periods of LH aphagia and anorexia by reducing body weight prior to lesioning, it is important that both the lesion parameters and prelesion weight conditions be carefully chosen. For example, if our procedure of reducing prelesion body weight to 80% of normal is used, care must be taken to ensure that the lesion parameters will yield a postlesion weight maintenance level somewhat above 80%. Only under these conditions can the postlesion aphagia be eliminated and a postlesion hyperphagia be seen. The larger lesions frequently used in LH work are thus inappropriate to such a demonstration, since they will produce a new weight maintenance level even lower than that to which the animal has already been starved. We might also suggest that taking care to lesion the LH area found by Powley (12) to be critical to weight regulation will also facilitate such investigations.

CONCLUSIONS AND IMPLICATIONS

We might summarize the results of the preceding experiments in the following manner. First, rats with LH lesions not only maintain their body weight at a reduced level, but also defend this new level with essentially the same precision as a nonlesioned animal displays in defending a normal weight level.

If challenged by changes in a diet's palatability, caloric density, and/or composition, the LH and control animal display adjustments in body weight that are nearly identical. The same result obtains when body weight is experimentally altered by force-feeding or partial starvation, i.e., the LH and the control animals restore their initial weight levels in the same manner. The only difference between the LH-lesioned animal and control animals that does emerge from these experiments is that the LH-lesioned animal maintains and defends a weight level substantially below that of the control. Other work (12) indicates that this new maintenance level is an inverse function of the degree of LH damage.

It is principally upon these observations that we have based our argument that a direct or primary effect of LH damage is to lower the set point for body weight. This is not to say that a shift in the set point is the sole, or even the major, consequence of damage to the lateral hypothalamus. Indeed, the syndrome resulting from LH lesions can be quite complex, involving components not discussed in this presentation (see ref. 13). For this reason we have continued to give careful consideration to these other aspects of this syndrome, particularly with a view toward assessing their possible contribution to the weight effects that we are studying. In general, however, we have found either that these other components exert little influence upon the normal long-term regulation of body weight, or that effective procedures can be devised so as to minimize or eliminate their influence. As an example of the former circumstance, consider the lack of hypoglycemic control that many investigators have noted in the LH-lesioned animal. Certainly there is considerable evidence that the normal feeding response to insulin or to 2-deoxy-D-glucose is impaired in the LH-lesioned animal (13). Yet the indication that LH-lesioned animals still display essentially normal adjustments in food intake and body weight when challenged is most consistent with the view that this mechanism is one that is called into play only under emergency circumstances, rather than being one upon which the animal normally relies to control its food intake and regulate body weight (14, 15).

Adipsia, which is commonly a consequence of LH damage, offers an example of the second sort. Were care not taken to ensure that the LH-lesioned animal is adequately hydrated, anorexia and weight loss secondary to dehydration would almost certainly confound the weight effects we see in LH-lesioned animals. However, by providing hydrated diets, by demonstrating that LH-lesioned animals can concentrate their urine (1), and by conducting the various other tests that have been detailed earlier (4), we feel we have been able to avoid such a confounding and have strengthened our argument that the weight changes are direct or primary effects of LH damage.

Another matter deserving consideration is the role played by primary feeding impairments in the LH syndrome. Our work has focused upon the effects of LH lesions on the level of regulated body weight and the role played by feeding behavior in the achievement of this new weight maintenance level. We are convinced that our LH lesions produce no major or lasting effects upon the animal's ability or capacity to feed. Our observations of hyperphagia and rapid weight gain in LH animals starved to a body weight below their new maintenance level support this conviction (1, 9). At the same time, the lesions traditionally used in this type of work have tended to be substantially larger than those we use. It is, therefore, not uncommon for these lesions to damage systems lying adjacent to the lateral hypothalamus proper. We are thus led to believe that the severe sensorimotor deficits that others (e.g., 16, 17) have reported are caused by damage to structures not ordinarily included in our LH lesions. The nigrostriatal system would appear to merit prime consideration in this regard (18, 19), although the striatopallidal system may also be involved (20). However, whatever the anatomic basis of these sensorimotor impairments, there are two points we should like to emphasize. First, since our own lesions appear not to produce any serious feeding deficits, we feel that the aphagia and anorexia that we see can properly be regarded as secondary to a reduced body weight set point. Second, it seems reasonable to expect that, even though larger LH lesions may produce primary feeding impairments, such lesions will also cause the regulated level of body weight to be reduced. Thus caution must be exercised in drawing any firm conclusions from such lesions as to whether aphagia and anorexia are caused by direct damage to a feeding system or are secondary to a lowered set point for body weight.

In concluding we would like to caution that these effects of LH lesions upon the level of maintained body weight have yet to be demonstrated in other species of laboratory animals. Unlike the ventromedial hypothalamic syndrome, which has been observed in many species, including man, our current understanding of the LH involvement in determining the body weight set point is based primarily upon the rat. One encouraging indication, however, can be found in a recent report of a multiple sclerosis patient with confirmed bilateral LH damage who displayed a syndrome bearing certain compelling similarities to that seen in the LH-lesioned rat (21). Still, questions related to the generality of this syndrome, as well as to its potential for aiding in our ability to understand and devise strategies for dealing with various clinical aspects of weight control, will necessarily depend upon the success with which the present results can be extended to other species, particularly to the primates.

ACKNOWLEDGMENT

Much of the research reported in this paper was supported by National Institute of Mental Health grant MH-08909.

REFERENCES

1. Powley, T. L., and Keesey, R. E. (1970): Relationship of body weight to the lateral hypothalamic feeding syndrome. *J. Comp. Physiol. Psychol.*, 70:25–36.

2. Mitchel, J. S., and Keesey, R. E. (1974): The effects of lateral hypothalamic lesions and castration upon the body weight and composition of male rats. *Behav. Biol.,* 11:68–82.
3. Keesey, R. E., and Boyle, P. C. (1973): Effects of quinine adulteration upon body weight of LH-lesioned and intact male rats. *J. Comp. Physiol. Psychol.,* 84:38–46.
4. Boyle, P. C., and Keesey, R. E. (1975): Chronically reduced body weight in rats sustaining lesions of the lateral hypothalamus and maintained on palatable diets and drinking solutions. *J. Comp. Physiol. Psychol.,* 88:218–223.
5. Mufson, E. J., and Wampler, R. S. (1972): Weight regulation with palatable food and liquids in rats with lateral hypothalamic lesions. *J. Comp. Physiol. Psychol.,* 80:382–392.
6. Teitelbaum, P., and Epstein, A. N. (1962): The lateral hypothalamic syndrome. *Psychol. Rev.,* 69:74–90.
7. Keesey, R. E., Powley, T. L., and Kemnitz, J. W. (1975): Prolongation of lateral hypothalamic anorexia by tube feeding. *(In preparation.)*
8. Keesey, R. E., and Kemnitz, J. W. (1975): *Unpublished observations.*
9. Mitchel, J. S., and Keesey, R. E. (1975): Defense of lowered weight maintenance levels in lateral hypothalamically lesioned rats: Evidence from a starvation-refeeding regimen. *(In preparation.)*
10. Cox, V. C., and Kakolewski, J. W. (1970): Sex differences in body weight regulation in rats following lateral hypothalamic lesions. *Comm. Behav. Biol.,* 5:195–197.
11. Kemnitz, J. W., and Keesey, R. E. (1975): *Unpublished observations.*
12. Powley, T. L. (1970): Reduction of body weight set-point by lateral hypothalamic lesions: Implications for an analysis of the lateral hypothalamic feeding syndrome. Ph.D. dissertation, University of Wisconsin, Madison, Wisconsin.
13. Epstein, A. N. (1971): The lateral hypothalamic syndrome: Its implications for the physiological psychology of hunger and thirst. In: *Progress in Physiological Psychology,* edited by E. Stellar and J. M. Sprague, pp. 263–317. New York.
14. Smith, G. P., Gibbs, J., Strohmayer, A. J., and Stokes, P. E. (1972): Threshold doses of 2-deoxy-D-glucose for hyperglycemia and feeding in rats and monkeys. *Am. J. Physiol.,* 222:77–81.
15. Blass, E. M., and Kraly, F. S. (1974): Medial forebrain bundle lesions: Specific loss of feeding to decreased glucose utilization in rats. *J. Comp. Physiol. Psychol.,* 86:679–692.
16. Marshall, J. F., Turner, B. H., and Teitelbaum, P. (1971): Sensory neglect produced by lateral hypothalamic damage. *Science,* 174:523–525.
17. Balagura, S., Wilcox, R. H., and Coscina, D. V. (1969): The effects of diencephalic lesions of food intake and motor activity. *Physiol. Behav.,* 4:629–633.
18. Ungerstedt, U. (1970): Is interruption of the nigro-striatal dopamine system producing the "Lateral Hypothalamic Syndrome"? *Acta Physiol. Scand.,* 80:354–364.
19. Marshall, J. F., Richardson, J. S., and Teitelbaum, P. (1974): Nigro-striatal bundle damage and the lateral hypothalamic syndrome. *J. Comp. Physiol. Psychol.,* 87:808–830.
20. Levine, M. S., and Schwartzbaum, J. S. (1973): Sensorimotor functions of the striatopallidal system and lateral hypothalamus and consummatory behavior in rats. *J. Comp. Physiol. Psychol.,* 85:615–635.
21. Kamalian, N., Keesey, R. E., and ZuRhein, G. M. (1975): Lateral hypothalamic demyelination and cachexia in a case of "malignant" multiple sclerosis. *Neurology,* 25:25–30.

Hunger: Basic Mechanisms and Clinical Implications,
edited by D. Novin, W. Wyrwicka, and G. Bray.
Raven Press, New York © 1976.

Neural and Hormonal Determinants of Sex Differences in Food Intake and Body Weight

Dwight M. Nance, Roger A. Gorski, and Jaak Panksepp*

*Department of Anatomy, University of California, Los Angeles, California 90024 and * Department of Psychology, Bowling Green State University, Bowling Green, Ohio 43403*

Beginning approximately at puberty, male rats weigh and eat more than do female rats of the same age; this sex difference becomes more pronounced with age. This sexual dimorphism is a result of the early organizational effects of androgens on neonatal sexual differentiation of the brain (1, 2). Male rats exposed to endogeneous androgens and female rats exposed to exogeneous testosterone both typically weigh and eat more than do neonatally castrated male and normal female rats. Although the mechanism underlying this organizational difference in energy regulation has not been defined, it is clear that sex-specific gonadal hormones further modulate this basic difference such that postpubertal body weight and food intake is augmented by testicular hormones (androgens) and depressed by ovarian hormones (estrogens). Sensitivity to these gonadal hormones is permanently altered by neonatal presence or absence of androgens as shown by the behavioral sensitivity of normal female and neonatally castrated male rats to estrogens and their insensitivity to the behavioral effects of androgens. Early exposure to androgens results in the opposite condition, decreased sensitivity to estrogens, and enhanced behavioral responsiveness to androgens (3, 4).

In approaching the question of what physiological mechanism underlies this sexual dimorphism in body weight and food intake, we have extended the observations of Kennedy (5), who noted that body fat is not as closely regulated in male rats as in normal females. Upon reaching a body weight of about 200 g, males have more body fat, on the average, than do females, and become ". . . more sensitive to what I have called secondary appetite factors" (5). He goes on to state that ". . . male rats, in fact, represent an intermediate stage of regulation between normal females and hypothalamic obese rats."

By placing emphasis on possible regulatory differences between male and female rats, Kennedy (5) has also provided an experimental approach to the physiologic mechanisms underlying sex differences in feeding behavior. If for example on a variety of regulatory challenges male rats regulate their food intake and body weight more like animals with lesions in the ventromedial hypothalamus (VMH) than do female rats, we could reasonably hypothesize that the degree of VMH control over energy balance may differ between male and female rats. Extending this approach we could utilize animals with lesions in the lateral hypothalamus (LH) as a reference point and test whether female rats regulate their food intake and body weight more like animals with LH lesions than do male rats. We have, in fact, done exactly this, and have utilized the known behavioral effects of VMH and LH lesions on the regulation of food intake and body weight of rats as end points along a continuum on which possible sex differences in hypothalamic regulation can be assessed (2). The results of the present series of sex comparisons in terms of various regulatory challenges suggest that the mechanism underlying the elevated body weight and food intake of male rats, relative to females, does indeed simulate the regulatory pattern leading to the elevated food intake and body weight found in animals with VMH lesions.

EXPERIMENT 1A

Sex Differences in Taste Preference for Saccharin Solutions

Valenstein et al. (6) found that with increasing concentrations of saccharin, male rats began to reject saccharin for water at a concentration of 0.75%, whereas female rats continued to show a preference for saccharin over water. Zucker (7) and Wade and Zucker (8) have also shown that female rats show a higher preference for an 0.75% saccharin solution than do male rats. Furthermore ovariectomy, which increases food intake and body weight, was found to decrease the preference of female rats for 0.75% saccharin.

In terms of the effects of hypothalamic lesions on saccharin preference, Storlien and Albert (9) found that relative to their controls, animals with lesions in the VMH showed a suppression in daily intake of a liquid diet that was adulterated with saccharin or quinine. They concluded that their 0.50 and 1.00% concentrations of saccharin, which is comparable to the 0.75% saccharin solution used by Wade and Zucker (8), were aversive and decreased the diet's palatability by making it too sweet. Conversely, Wyrwicka and Clemente (10) have reported that animals with lesions in the LH show an increased acceptance of extremely high concentrations of saccharin. The present experiment shows that the sex difference in saccharin preference is a function of saccharin concentration and the direction of this sex difference is consistent with the hypothesis that relative to each other, male rats are similar to animals with VMH lesions and female rats are similar to animals with LH lesions. That this sexual dimorphism in taste preference is related to the process of sexual differentiation is shown by the masculinized pattern of saccharin preference exhibited by androgenized female rats.

Method and Results

Six 90- to 100-day-old Sprague-Dawley male, six female, and six androgen sterilized (AS) female rats (animals were injected with 100 μg testosterone propionate at 5 days of age) were maintained in individual stainless steel cages with a pair of calibrated Richter drinking tubes mounted on the front of each cage. Animals were given six 12-hr two-bottle preference tests with six different concentrations of saccharin (0.009 to 2.250% weight/volume) which were paired with distilled water. Preference tests were conducted during the dark phase of the illumination cycle, and a 12-hr, distilled water only, maintenance period separated each test period. Positions of the bottles were counterbalanced across days, and Charles River Formula Rat Chow was available *ad lib* throughout the experiment.

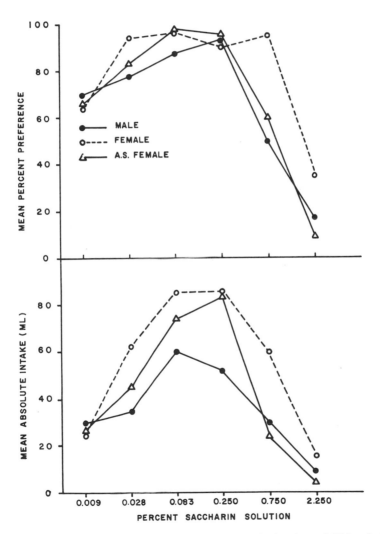

FIG. 1. Mean percent preference and absolute intake of adult male, female, and AS female (100 μg testosterone propionate day 5) rats for six saccharin solutions (0.009 to 2.25%) during six 12-hr two-bottle preference tests (saccharin versus distilled water). Percent preference computed as (intake saccharin/ intake saccharin + distilled water) × 100 for each of the six concentrations.

Preference for saccharin was computed as a percent (saccharin intake/ saccharin + water intake × 100) at every concentration for each animal. Figure 1 shows the mean percent preference and mean absolute intake of male, female, and AS female rats, plotted as a function of saccharin concentration. Female rats show a significantly ($p < 0.05$) higher preference for saccharin over water than male and AS female rats only at the 0.75% concentration. However, relative to the males, absolute saccharin consumption is elevated in females for all concentrations between 0.028 and 0.750%. The mean absolute saccharin intake for the AS female group is intermediate between male and female rats for the 0.028 to 0.250% concentrations, but drops to male levels for the two highest concentrations.

EXPERIMENT 1B

Sex Differences in Response to Quinine Adulteration

Results of experiment 1A indicate that it is along the aversive limb of the saccharin preference-aversion curve that sex differences in saccharin preference become most apparent. In the present experiment we tested whether this aversive limb of the saccharin preference-aversion curve could be duplicated by gradually adulterating the highly preferred 0.250% saccharin solution with quinine sulfate (bitter).

Method and Results

Six adult male and six female rats (matched for age) were given three successive daily 24-hr two-bottle preference tests. A 0.250% saccharin solution was adulterated with 0.0000, 0.0025, and 0.0050% quinine sulfate on days 1, 2, and 3, respectively. Distilled water was always available in the other tube. Food was available *ad lib* and the position of the bottles was randomized across days.

Figure 2 shows the mean percent preference for 0.250% saccharin plotted as a function of quinine adulteration. Male rats show significantly ($p < 0.05$, $p < 0.01$) lower preference (greater aversion) for both the 0.0025 and 0.0050% levels of quinine adulteration than do female rats.

Discussion

Experiment 1A showed that a significant sex difference in saccharin preference is a function of saccharin concentration, and is associated with the more concentrated solutions. This sex difference in saccharin preference is due to some aversive properties associated with saccharin solutions as sug-

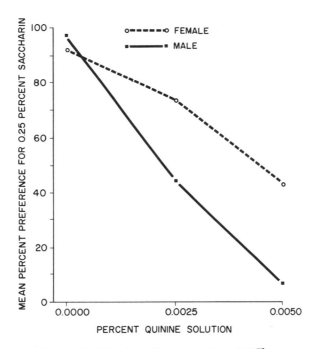

FIG. 2. Mean percent preference of adult male and female rats for an 0.25% saccharin solution which was adulterated with 0.0000, 0.0025, or 0.0050% quinine over distilled water. Percent preference computed as (intake test solution/intake test solution + distilled water) × 100.

gested by the results of Experiment 1B, in which male rats show greater rejection (lower preference) for a quinine adulterated 0.250% saccharin solution than do female rats.

This sex difference in saccharin preference is also related to the process of sexual differentiation of the brain. Female rats treated neonatally with a single injection of testosterone propionate show a saccharin preference-aversion curve that is comparable to normal male rats. However, because these AS females are exposed to a hormone environment different from that of the normal cycling female, saccharin preference could also reflect this difference. In additional experiments (2), it was found that, whereas gonadectomy almost completely attenuates the sex difference in absolute intake of saccharin, significant sex differences in mean percent preference for the 0.750% saccharin solution remained. Thus the sex difference in taste preference for saccharine-quinine solutions is viewed as a reflection of possible sex differences in hypothalamic regulation. The aversion to a concentrated saccharin solution shown by male rats relative to females is similar to the results reported for animals with VMH lesions (9). The elevated saccharin preference, and greater tolerance for quinine adulteration shown by female rats, relative to males, is similar to data reported for animals with lesions in the LH (10). Thus sex differences in taste preference may reflect sex differences in the hypothalamic regulation of feeding behavior. Subsequent experiments will bear directly on this latter point.

EXPERIMENT 2

Sex Differences in Caloric Intake as a Function of Different Diets

The importance of palatability on the food intake of animals with VMH lesions has been well documented. Typically, animals with VMH lesions overeat on a palatable high-fat diet and a 50% dextrose diet, yet undereat on a salt adulterated diet (11, 12). These results are consistent with the notion that animals with VMH lesions have a deficit in long-term regulation resulting in their greater reliance upon short-term factors, such as palatability, for regulating feeding behavior. If, as we propose, male rats are more similar to animals with VMH lesions than are female rats, their food intake should be more dependent upon the diet palatability than female rats. This possibility was tested in the present experiment. In addition the effects of gonadectomy and VMH lesions were also examined.

Method and Results

Six age-matched adult Sprague-Dawley male and six female rats were maintained in individual stainless steel cages and given *ad lib* access to powdered Purina Rat Chow. During a 2-week adaptation period, food intake was measured daily to the nearest 0.1 g. After this baseline period, animals were given 24-hr access to one of three diets in a counterbalanced order. The diets consisted of (a) powdered chow, which was adulterated with 20% NaCl, (b) high fat chow which consisted of powdered chow and Crisco in a ratio of 2:1, and (c) powdered chow with a 50% sucrose solution available at the front of the cage. The various diets were presented at 5-day intervals with powdered chow available *ad lib* between each test. After being tested with the three diets, all animals were gonadectomized, and beginning 1 month after surgery, retested with the three different diets using the same procedure. Animals were then given anodal electrolytic lesions (2 mA/20 sec) in the VMH, and again retested with the different diets.

Results of the sex comparison in response to the various diets are shown in Table 1. Since no significant differences within each of the three treatment conditions were found for the 3 days immediately prior to each test diet presentation, these data were pooled and are represented as baseline in Table 1. During the baseline period (powdered chow), intact male rats consume significantly ($p < 0.01$) more calories per day than intact female rats. However, when presented with the 20% NaCl diet, males consume slightly fewer calories/day than female rats, resulting in a significantly ($p < 0.05$) larger absolute and relative decrease in caloric intake for intact male than for intact female rats. When given 24-hr access to a concentrated 50% sucrose solution, intact male rats showed a small but statistically significant ($p < 0.05$) increase (5%) in caloric intake, whereas the intact female rats showed a small (-3%) decrease in caloric intake. When given the 33% fat-diet, intact male rats showed a very reliable ($p < 0.01$) increase ($+15\%$) in daily caloric intake. While intact female rats did show a 7% increase in caloric intake on the high-fat diet, this increase was not statistically significant.

Following gonadectomy, sex differences in caloric intake during the baseline period was attenuated, due exclusively to an increase in the daily caloric intake in ovariectomized female rats above their intact levels. After gonadectomy, male and female rats show a comparable decrease in caloric intake on

TABLE 1. Mean daily caloric intake of intact male and female rats fed powdered rat chow (baseline) and when given 24-hr access to either a 20% salt-adulterated diet, a 33% fat diet (chow and Crisco in a ratio of 2:1), or the availability of a 50% sucrose solution

Groups	n	Baseline calories	20% NaCl calories	50% Sucrose calories	33% Fat calories
Intact male	6	105.4	29.5 (-73)	111.7 ($+$ 5)	121.8 ($+$ 15)
Intact female	6	79.8	32.9 (-59)	77.9 ($-$ 3)	85.8 ($+$ 7)
Gonad-X male	6	108.5	38.8 (-65)	121.7 ($+12$)	133.1 ($+$ 22)
Gonad-X female	6	93.9	39.2 (-59)	91.0 ($-$ 4)	106.8 ($+$ 13)
VMH lesion Male	3	84.2	23.4 (-73)	119.9 ($+42$)	162.3 ($+$ 92)
VMH lesion Female	3	79.6	22.7 (-72)	124.9 ($+56$)	173.3 ($+117$)

Percent change from baseline is shown in parentheses.

Also shown is the mean daily caloric intake after gonadectomy and after VMH lesions. Tests with the various diets were separated by 5 days of baseline.

the salt-adulterated diet, but sex differences in response to the two palatable diets are still present. Gonadectomized male rats still increase their caloric intake when given a 50% sucrose solution, whereas female rats again show a small decrease in daily caloric intake. Both male and female rats significantly ($p < 0.01$ and $p < 0.05$, respectively) increase their caloric intake on the high-fat diet after gonadectomy, but as in the intact condition, males show a larger relative increase ($p < 0.05$) than do female rats. After receiving lesions in the VMH, sex differences in response to all the diets were virtually eliminated. The relative decrease in baseline caloric intake following VMH lesions may reflect a lesion-induced finickiness that is precipitated by the animal's prior experience with more palatable diets. As would be expected, the largest absolute and relative increase in daily caloric intake was found with the highly palatable 33% fat diet.

In order to facilitate a more direct comparison between male and female rats under the various treatment and diet conditions, the ratio of male/female is shown in terms of mean daily caloric intake in Table 2. Ratios greater than one indicate the relative extent to which male rats eat more than do female rats, whereas a ratio less than one (see intact-NaCl-diet results) would indicate the opposite. Briefly, the ratio is greater than one for the baseline, sucrose and high fat diets under both the intact and gonadectomized conditions, but the relative difference between male and female rats was reduced by gonadectomy (decrease in ratio toward 1.0). Furthermore, this analysis clearly indicates how the relative difference between male and female rats, both intact and gonadectomized, depends upon the type of diet. For example, gonadectomized males consumed 16% more calories per day than females on powdered chow, but 34% more when access to a 50% sucrose solution was

TABLE 2. *Ratios of male/female in terms of mean daily caloric intake for intact, gonadectomized, and VMH lesion male and female rats as a function of different diets*

Groups	n	Baseline	20% NaCl	50% Sucrose	33% Fat
Intact	6	1.32	0.90	1.43	1.42
Gonad-X	6	1.16	0.99	1.34	1.25
VMH-X	3	1.06	1.03	0.96	0.94

allowed. VMH lesions eliminated all sex differences in response to different diets.

Discussion

Results of Experiment 2 show that as reported for animals with VMH lesions (11, 12), male rats are more susceptible to alterations in diet palatability than are female rats. Relative to daily caloric intake on powdered rat chow, male rats show a larger decrease and increase on unpalatable and highly palatable diets, respectively, than do female rats. As shown by the male/female ratios (Table 2), this sexual dimorphism in response to different diets was attenuated by gonadectomy, and virtually eliminated by VMH lesions. These results provide additional support for the hypothesis that male and female rats differ in terms of the hypothalamic regulation of feeding behavior and furthermore, suggest that the VMH is a critical neural site for the elaboration of sex differences in feeding behavior. The next experiment indicates that similar to animals with VMH lesions, male rats make relatively slower metabolic (long-term) adjustments in feeding behavior than do female rats.

EXPERIMENT 3

Sex Differences in Response to Two Glucose Solutions

Booth et al. (13) found that, when rats are simultaneously offered two glucose solutions of different concentrations, they initially show equal or greater preference for the higher concentration. However, across several days, the animals display a gradual reversal in preference such that the lower concentration is preferred over the higher concentration. Panksepp (14) found that animals with VMH lesions do not make this type of metabolic adjustment in feeding behavior but, rather, they persist in consuming glucose primarily from the more concentrated glucose solution. These results suggest that the VMH is involved in the modulation of glucose consumption, and also provide us with the prediction that relative to female rats, and similar to animals with VMH lesions, male rats will take longer to exhibit this change in glucose preference.

Method and Results

Nine adult Sprague-Dawley male and nine female rats, matched for age, and given *ad lib* access to Charles River Formula Rat Chow, were maintained in individual stainless steel cages with two graduated Richter drinking tubes attached to the front. After a 1-week adaptation period, animals were given continuous access to two concentrations of glucose (10% and 50%) for 5 days. Fluid intakes were measured daily at the start of the dark phase of the illumination cycle.

Results are illustrated in Fig. 3, which show the mean percent preference for 10 over 50% glucose for male and female rats plotted as a function of days. Percent preference for 10 over 50% glucose was computed daily for each animal according to the formula: intake 10%/total intake × 100. Mean percent preferences greater than 50% indicate the relative preference for the

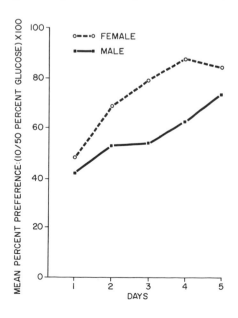

FIG. 3. Mean percent preference of adult male and female rats for 10 over 50% glucose solutions as a function of days. Percent preference computed as (intake 10%/intake 10 + 50%) × 100.

lower glucose solution over the higher. As shown in Fig. 3, female rats show a more rapid rise in preference for the 10 over the 50% glucose solution than male rats. This sex difference was statistically significant on days 3 and 4 ($p < 0.05$).

Discussion

These results show that as predicted from the data reported for animals with lesions in the VMH, male rats take longer than female rats to display a metabolic adjustment in feeding behavior when presented with two glucose solutions. This sex difference in the rate of making a long-term adjustment in feeding behavior provides further support for the hypothesis that male rats rely more than do female rats upon short-term factors (e.g., taste or palatability) in overall control of feeding behavior.

EXPERIMENT 4

Sex Differences in Response to Chronic Insulin Injections

In the last experiment we compared male and female rats in terms of another long-term regulatory challenge, chronic insulin injections, which has also been shown to differentiate between normal and VMH lesion rats (15). Although animals with VMH lesions do show a normal increase in food intake in response to an acute (short-term) insulin challenge (16), Panksepp and Nance (15) found that VMH-lesioned animals show a deficit in response to repeated daily injections of protamine zinc insulin (PZI), a long-term regulatory challenge. Whereas control animals exhibited hyperphagia and dramatic weight gain in response to PZI, the VMH-lesioned animals were much less responsive to the chronic PZI regimen and across days exhibited significantly lower weight gains and food intake. From the present perspective, if male rats are more similar to animals with VMH lesions than female rats, they should exhibit less hyperphagia and weight gain during chronic PZI treatment than females, though possibly showing a normal short-term response to the insulin. These predictions were supported in the following experiment.

Method and Results

Adult Sprague-Dawley male (12) and female (12) rats, matched for age, were divided into two groups and maintained *ad lib* on powdered Purina Rat Chow. Following a 1-week baseline period, the two groups of animals were injected twice daily at the start and the end of a 12-hr illumination period with either saline or else increasing units of PZI for a total of seven days. The insulin regimen consisted of 4, 4, 6, 6, 8, 8, and 8 units of PZI/day for the 7 day chronic treatment period, and the daily dose of PZI was administered as two equal injections spaced 12 hr apart. Food intake was measured 6 hr after the initial injection of PZI (two units at the start of the light period) and daily thereafter for 7 days. Body weight was also determined daily at the same time the daily food intake was measured (at the start of the light period).

Illustrated in Fig. 4 are the short- and long-term effects of PZI injections on the food intake of male and female rats. Both male and female rats show a significant ($p < 0.01$) increase in food intake 6 hr after the administration

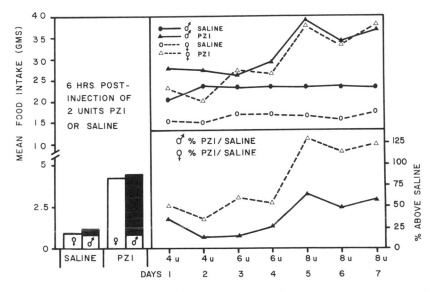

FIG. 4. Acute (6 hr after the initial injection) and chronic effects of daily injecting either increasing units of protamine zinc insulin (PZI) or saline on the food intake of adult male and female rats. Also shown is the relative percentage increase in food intake for the PZI over the saline-treated male and female rats.

of two units PZI, relative to saline injected control animals and there was no sex difference in response to this short-term regulatory challenge. In terms of the daily food intake, the saline injected male rats consumed significantly ($p < 0.01$) more chow than the saline-injected female group across the entire 7 days of the experiment. Significant ($p < 0.05$) sex differences in daily food intake for the animals receiving chronic PZI injections were found only for the first 2 days of treatment. However, from day 3 to the end of the experiment the chronic PZI treatment eliminated sex differences in food intake. Female rats receiving PZI consumed significantly ($p < 0.01$) more chow than saline-injected female rats on all 7 injection days. However, the male-

PZI group ate significantly ($p < 0.05$ to 0.01) more food, relative to the saline-injected male group, only on days 1, 4, 5, 6, and 7. On days 2 and 3, although the PZI-male group ate more than the saline male group, this difference was not statistically significant.

In order to facilitate a relative sex comparison of the effects of chronic PZI injections on food intake, plotted in Fig. 4 is the percentage increase in food intake for the PZI-treated male and female groups, relative to their respective saline control groups. This index clearly shows that the chronic PZI regimen produced a more sustained and dramatic degree of hyperphagia in female than in male rats. This sex difference in PZI-induced hyperphagia is

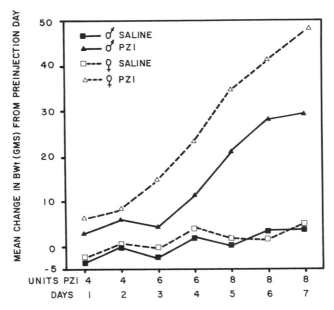

FIG. 5. Mean change in body weight from the preinjection day of adult male and female rats treated daily with either increasing units of protamine zinc insulin (PZI) or saline.

directly reflected in the significantly ($p < 0.01$) larger weight gains exhibited by female than by male rats shown in Fig. 5.

Discussion

Results of Experiment 4 indicate that relative to female rats, and as predicted by the results found for animals with VMH lesions (15), male rats show a normal response to an acute injection of PZI, but are behaviorally less responsive to chronic PZI injections. Again the same regulatory challenge that differentiates between normal and hypothalamic-lesioned rats also differentiates between male and female rats.

GENERAL DISCUSSION

Whereas the present series of experiments involve a wide variety of variables, all are related to the suggestion of Kennedy (5) that male rats regulate their feeding behavior more like animals with VMH lesions than do normal female rats. These experiments are all consistent with this hypothesis and also provide a basis on which a tentative model to account for sex differences in feeding behavior has been proposed (see ref. 2).

Briefly, the model states that, analogous to the regulation of gonadotropins and sex behavior (3), there is initially a sexually bipotential neural substrate for the regulation of body weight and food intake. During a neonatal (and possibly prenatal) critical period, exposure to androgens results in an irreversible sexual differentiation of the brain, which is functionally expressed in terms of a masculine pattern of reproduction and as we propose here, a male pattern of energy regulation. The absence of early exposure to androgens is associated with a feminine reproductive capacity and a proposed female pattern of energy regulation. Again as with the regulation of gonadotropins and sex behavior, sex-specific gonadal hormones secondarily reinforce and activate the full expression of this sexual dimorphism in energy regulation. Sexual differentiation of the regulation of body weight and food intake can be conceived as occurring along a continuum, the two ends of which are delimited by animals with VMH lesions and animals with LH lesions. The position of an individual animal between these two extreme poles, then, would presumably reflect the degree of dominance of one or the other of these two brain areas. Conceptually, because of the process of sexual differentiation of the brain, male rats are displaced toward the VMH lesion end of this continuum, with female rats positioned more toward the LH lesion end. Estrogen has the effect of shifting the female even further toward the LH regulatory pole. As a result of occupying different regulatory positions, male rats show greater dependence upon short-term factors for controlling feeding behavior, whereas females rely more on long-term factors. Thus, the same overall regulation of energy balance that results in elevated food intake and body weight in animals with VMH lesions is the same regulatory pattern (but to a much lesser degree) that results in male rats having a higher body weight and food intake than female rats.

Current evidence for the model is primarily based upon the fact that the same regulatory challenges and variables that differentiate between male and female rats are exactly the same ones that differentiate between normal and hypothalamic lesioned animals. Whereas these sex differences are generally not as dramatic as the differences between lesioned and control animals, they are consistent and thus far have proven to be predictable from the model. For example the observation that, relative to females, male rats show an attenuated diurnal feeding pattern (17) is consistent with the data that VMH lesions produce an attenuation in the diurnal feeding patterns of rats (17,

18). Also, as has been reported for LH lesions, an exaggeration in the diurnal distribution of feeding in female rats is associated with high endogenous estrogen titers (Nance and Gorski, *unpublished data*). These data are consistent with the effects of estrogen on lowering the set point for body weight regulation and in terms of the model, an estrogen-dependent shift toward the LH lesion end of our continuum. In addition the observation that female rats generally exhibit a more dramatic hyperphagia following VMH lesions than do male rats, relative to their respective controls (19), is consistent with the suggestion that the hypothalamic restraint on feeding behavior via the VMH is greater in female than in male rats (or, more simply, males already show a regulatory pattern similar to VMH lesion animals and as a result show less dramatic effects following VMH lesions than do female rats). The consistent failure to replicate the effects of LH lesions on lowering the set point for body weight regulation (20, 21, 22) with female rats has yet to be explained. If, however, sex differences in hypothalamic regulation of feeding behavior are controlled neurally by the VMH, then the bias of female rats toward more precise long-term regulation (mediated by the VMH) could mediate their increased capacity to recover normal body weight. The fact that chronic food deprivation (23) and chronic insulin injections (24), both of which are long-term regulatory challenges, facilitate recovery of feeding in male rats following LH lesions suggest that indeed, the VMH may be involved in behavioral recovery following LH lesions.

In final consideration of the possible importance of the VMH in the mediation of sex differences in energy regulation, experiments utilizing direct intracranial implants of testosterone into neonatal rats have shown that the VMH-arcuate region is an effective neural site for androgenization (25, 26). Also, sex differences in the morphology of the VMH have been reported for the rat and detectable histological changes are reported to occur in the VMH as a function of neonatal exposure to androgens (27). From the present behavioral data, it seems that the process of androgenization reduces the ability of VMH regulatory circuits to maintain precise control over body energy balance. Although this speculative model of the regulation of feeding behavior is only a working hypothesis at present, the fact that it already has been shown to have predictive value illustrates its potential usefulness.

ACKNOWLEDGMENT

Research supported by U.S. Public Health Service grant 5 T01 MH-10625 from the National Institute of Mental Health, and grants 00282 HD 01182 from the National Institutes of Health.

REFERENCES

1. Wade, G. N. (1973): *Physiol. Behav.*, 8:523–524.
2. Nance, D. M. (1975): In: *Advances in Psychobiology, Vol. 3*, edited by G. Newton and A. H. Riesen. John Wiley & Sons, Inc., New York.

3. Gorski, R. A. (1971): In: *Frontiers in Neuroendocrinology,* edited by L. Martini and W. F. Ganong, pp. 237–290. Oxford University Press, New York.
4. Bell, D. D., and Zucker, I. (1971): *Physiol. Behav.,* 7:27–34.
5. Kennedy, G. C. (1969): *Ann. NY Acad. Sci.,* 157:1049–1061.
6. Valenstein, E. S., Kakolewski, J. W., and Cox, V. C. (1967): *Science,* 156:942–943.
7. Zucker, I. (1969): *Physiol. Behav.,* 4:595–602.
8. Wade, G. N., and Zucker, I. (1969): *J. Comp. Physiol. Psychol.,* 69:291–300.
9. Storlien, L. H., and Albert, D. J. (1971): *Physiol. Behav.,* 9:191–197.
10. Wyrwicka, W., and Clemente, C. D. (1973): *Exp. Neurol.,* 40:367–376.
11. Graff, H., and Stellar, E. (1962): *J. Comp. Physiol. Psychol.,* 55:418–424.
12. Corbit, J. D., and Stellar, E. (1964): *J. Comp. Physiol. Psychol.,* 58:63–67.
13. Booth, D. A., Lovett, D., and McSherry, G. M. (1972): *J. Comp. Physiol. Psychol.,* 78:485–512.
14. Panksepp, J. (1973): *Behav. Biol.,* 9:65–79.
15. Panksepp, J., and Nance, D. M. (1972): *Physiol. Behav.,* 9:447–451.
16. Epstein, A. N., and Tietelbaum, P. (1967): *Am. J. Physiol.,* 213:1159–1167.
17. Balagura, S., and Davenport, L. D. (1970): *J. Comp. Physiol. Psychol.,* 71:357–364.
18. Kakolewski, J. W., Deaux, E., Christensen, J., and Case, B. (1971): *Am. J. Physiol.,* 221:711–718.
19. Valenstein, E. S., Cox, V. C., and Kakolewski, J. W. (1969): *Ann. NY Acad. Sci.,* 157:1030–1048.
20. Cox, V. C., and Kakolewski, J. W. (1970): *Commun. Behav. Biol.,* 5:195–197.
21. Mufson, E. J., and Wampler, R. S. (1972): *J. Comp. Physiol. Psychol.,* 80:382–392.
22. Balagura, S., and Harrell, L. E. (1974): *Physiol. Behav.,* 13:345–347.
23. Powley, T., and Keesey, R. (1970): *J. Comp. Physiol. Psychol.,* 70:25–36.
24. Balagura, S., Harrell, L., and Ralph, T. (1973): *Science,* 182:59–60.
25. Nadler, R. D. (1973): *Neuroendocrinology,* 12:110–119.
26. Hayashi, S., and Gorski, R. A. (1974): *Endocrinology,* 94:1161–1167.
27. Döiner, G., and Staudt, J. (1969): *Neuroendocrinology,* 5:103–106.

Hunger: Basic Mechanisms and Clinical Implications,
edited by D. Novin, W. Wyrwicka, and G. Bray.
Raven Press, New York © 1976.

Insulin and the Set-Point Regulation of Body Weight

Stephen C. Woods and Daniel Porte, Jr.

Departments of Psychology and Medicine, University of Washington, and the Seattle Veterans Administration Hospital, Seattle, Washington 98195

Kennedy (1), in his introduction of the lipostatic hypothesis of the regulation of body weight, stated that some correlate of long-term adipose stores
within the body must have an integral role in governing food intake and
therefore in the maintenance of body weight. Although this is generally held
to be true, the nature of the signal to the central nervous system that both
correlates with adipose stores and influences feeding behavior has not been
identified (e.g., see ref. 2). The development of specific assays for metabolically active hormones over the last 15 years has enabled researchers to determine the relationship between body weight and several of these hormones.
One of these hormones, insulin, has been shown to correlate well with body
weight[1] given certain conditions. We present here a theory about the role of
insulin in the regulation of body weight and present preliminary evidence to
support our contentions.

CORRELATION BETWEEN INSULIN AND BODY WEIGHT

Insulin is a peptide hormone secreted from the B-cells of the islets of
Langerhans of the pancreas. Although it is secreted continually in basal
amounts (i.e., in the absence of any known secretagogues), a major stimulus
for increases from basal secretion is the presence of the products of digestion,
i.e., digested carbohydrates (principally glucose), fats (free fatty acids), and
proteins (amino acids); all have the ability to elicit insulin secretion directly
at the B-cells. Therefore, insulin secretion is directly stimulated by products
of digestion. One of the major actions of this insulin is to enable the various
tissues of the body to utilize and/or to store these fuels. In the absence of
sufficient insulin (as in diabetes mellitus), these processes become relatively
inefficient. Insulin can therefore be considered a hormone which signifies the
sated state and one which is anabolic in nature. For a review of these well-
documented actions of insulin or of the circumstances of its secretion, the
interested reader is referred to the recent volume by Steiner and Freinkel (3).

The amount of insulin in the blood in the basal or unstimulated state is
positively correlated with body weight (4–6). The leaner an individual, the

---

[1] Changes of body weight refer to changes of adipose mass of the animal.

lower his basal insulin, and vice versa. This relationship has also been shown to occur in every commonly used model of altered body weight, including animals with bilateral electrolytic lesions of the ventromedial hypothalamic (VMH) nuclei (e.g., refs. 7–9), rats with bilateral electrolytic lesions of the ventrolateral hypothalamic (VLH) nuclei (10), genetically obese rodents (11), and overfed humans (12). In fact, the relationship is sufficiently robust that it exists in the presence of widespread metabolic disorder, such as in diabetes mellitus (13), i.e., obese diabetics have elevated basal insulin levels in proportion to their body weight. We have recently extended these findings to include rats maintained at different proportions of their normal weights through twice daily intragastric feedings (14). In short, there are no known major exceptions to this correlation.

INSULIN AND THE REGULATION OF BODY WEIGHT

The strict relationship between insulin in the basal state and body weight is depicted in Fig. 1. Because the effective amount of insulin can be modified

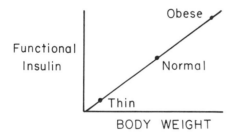

FIG. 1. Diagrammatic relationship between functional or effective insulin and body weight.

by the relative amounts of other hormones (such as steroids and/or growth hormone), the ordinate of the figure is labeled functional insulin. This relationship was the basis of a recent theoretical statement by Woods et al. (15, 16), in which it was postulated that the brain could use basal insulin levels as an index of the amount of fat in the body. It was further postulated that the brain has the ability to modify body weight through appropriate reflex activity of the ventral hypothalamus. The influence of the VMH and VLH on food intake is well documented (e.g., see ref. 2). In particular, the VLH is often called the eating center of the brain because stimulation there elicits feeding, and because lesions there lead to hypophagia and a subsequent reduction of body weight. The VMH, on the other hand, is often called the satiety center of the brain because stimulation there suppresses ongoing feeding and because lesions there cause hyperphagia and eventual obesity.

More recently, it has also been shown that lesions of the ventral hypothalamus also elicit chronic changes of basal insulin. Rats with lesions of the VMH have elevated insulin levels (7–9, 15), a finding often interpreted as being secondary to the increased meal size that also occurs after the lesions (e.g., refs. 7, 8). However, there is overwhelming evidence that the observed hyperinsulinemia of VMH-lesioned rats is a primary effect of the lesion. First, weanling rats with VMH-lesions do not overeat, yet they have elevated insulin levels (17, 18). Furthermore, preventing the hyperphagia of adult lesioned rats by yoking their food intake to that of nonlesioned controls does not prevent the hyperinsulinemia (19, 20). In fact, Hustvedt and Lovo (21) reported that they could predict the subsequent gain of weight of VMH-lesioned rats from the increase of basal insulin that occurred after the lesions but before hyperphagia was allowed. Similarly, we have observed an increase of insulin that occurs within 3 min of the administration of a small quantity of sodium pentobarbital to the cerebrospinal fluid (CSF) of rats (22). This procedure appears to produce a central effect on eating similar to that seen after VMH lesioning (23, 24). We also observed an increase of food intake, but an increase of insulin level occurred inde-

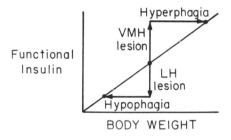

FIG. 2. Diagrammatic relationship between functional insulin and body weight following lesions of the VMH and the ventrolateral hypothalamic nuclei.

pendently of this eating. Therefore, a lesion of the VMH results in an increase of insulin, which is accompanied by an increase of feeding and an eventual gain of body weight. That the obesity of VMH-lesioned animals depends on the integrity of the B-cells has been demonstrated by experiments in which rats rendered diabetic prior to or following VMH lesions did not become obese (25, 26). Further support for the importance of insulin in the obesity of VMH-lesioned rats is the observation of Powley and Opsahl (27) that cutting the vagus nerves eliminates the obesity. One of the organs innervated by the vagus nerves is the pancreas. A review of the nature of the influence of the central nervous system upon insulin secretion has recently been made (28). Figure 2 depicts our conception of the events that occur following lesions of the ventral hypothalamus.

These experiments strongly suggest that the brain has the ability to influence the amount of insulin secreted by the pancreas and that experimental alterations of the ventral hypothalamus can lead to permanent changes of the normal input to the pancreas. The net result is that the animal alters its meal size until its body weight aligns with the new level of insulin (Fig. 2). Support for this contention are the observations of Hoebel and Teitelbaum (29) and Powley and Keesey (30) that when rats are brought to a new weight prior to receiving a lesion of the ventral hypothalamus, they do not necessarily undergo an alteration of feeding. Rather, their meal sizes correspond well with their already attained weights. Stated another way, lesions of the ventral hypothalamus appear to alter the set-point weight which is being maintained by the animal, such that it now maintains its weight at a different level from that of the unlesioned control.

Of particular interest is the nature of the brain's influence on insulin secretion. Although the experimental stimulation of the vagus or mixed pancreatic nerves has been shown to elicit insulin secretion (31, 32), it is unlikely that there is continuous input to the islet in the fasted animal since section of the vagus nerves or the administration of atropine causes no deficit of insulin secretion (32, 33). A second possibility is that the neural input to the pancreas modifies the response of the B-cells to their normal secretagogues. In particular it has been shown that the ability of parasympathetic input to the pancreas to elicit insulin secretion is a function of the amount of glucose present (34, 35), i.e., the more glucose present, the greater the influence of parasympathetic stimulation of the B-cells. In this light, the nervous system can be visualized as altering the gain of the B-cells to glucose and other substrates. Therefore, although a slight increase of insulin occurs as a result of a lesion of the VMH and prior to any overeating, it is not until the animal has consistently overeaten that its insulin levels attain their final value. Insulin levels would therefore increase initially after a VMH lesion, but the major change is to magnify the normal responses to food ingestion as a function of hyperphagia and developing obesity.

INSULIN AND THE CSF

Assuming body weight to be a regulated parameter, a lingering question concerns the mechanism by which the brain is able to detect the amount of fat in the body so as to regulate appropriately the size of meals and the input to the pancreas. As reviewed above, there is almost a one-to-one correspondance between basal insulin levels and body weight (see Fig. 1). However, the term basal implies absence of external signals for insulin secretion. The only way to obtain basal blood samples is to fast and relax an animal for a prolonged interval (at least 12 hr) prior to taking the sample. Since the level of insulin in the blood of nonfasted animals is continually fluctuating, it is unlikely that the brain could derive much useful information regarding body weight from the level of insulin in the blood. However, some integral of total daily insulin secretion which would be correlated with basal secretion might serve as a useful signal for the degree of adiposity. One possible signal that we have considered is the insulin within the CSF. It has been reported that the CSF normally contains around 25% of the level found in the plasma (36, 37). When plasma insulin is altered via a continuous infusion of insulin intravenously, CSF insulin values are reportedly changed appropriately after a lag of 15 to 30 min (37). We have found that when insulin is injected as a single pulse into the veins of dogs there is only a small change of CSF insulin even though plasma insulin may be increased by a factor of 50 (38). In other words, when insulin levels were maintained at an elevated level (37), CSF insulin levels followed them; on the other hand, when plasma insulin levels were only transiently elevated but to a greater absolute level (38), the CSF insulin still changes very slowly. This suggests that the mechanism by which insulin enters the CSF is an integral of plasma insulin. If plasma insulin is constant (such as in the basal state or following a prolonged intravenous infusion), CSF insulin aligns upon it; if plasma insulin is rapidly changing (such as following a meal or an intravenous injection), the changes are markedly damped in the CSF. The following preliminary experiment was designed to test this hypothesis.

METHOD

Male mongrel dogs were fasted for at least 12 hr and anesthetized with sodium pentobarbital. They were maintained in a sitting position with the ears elevated and the nose pointing down for the duration of the experiment so that a spinal needle could be inserted into the cisternum magnum and left in place for several hours. Cannulae were inserted into a vein on each of two limbs and were kept patent by means of a slow infusion of physiological saline. Blood and CSF samples could therefore be obtained at desired intervals throughout the experiment. All samples were collected over ice and frozen until assayed. Immunoreactive insulin determinations were made by a previously described technique (39).

In the same dogs on different days, insulin or glucose was administered intravenously as either a single pulse or a prolonged infusion. All blood samples were obtained from the limb opposite to that receiving the administered glucose or insulin.

RESULTS

Although this experiment is still in progress, the data presently available appear to support the hypothesis. Figure 3 depicts the results of a dog which received a pulse of 0.2 U/kg of regular injection pork insulin intravenously. Although plasma insulin was increased more than 100 times, there was only a doubling of CSF insulin. Figure 4 depicts the results from the same dog 1 week later. In this experiment, the same dose of insulin (0.2 U/kg) was administered, but was infused over a period of 60 min. Plasma insulin was increased by a factor of eight or nine times for a 1-hr interval, and CSF insulin was increased by a factor of 3 to 5 times over the same interval. In both experiments, the dose of insulin was the same; the only difference was the time span over which it was administered. Figure 5 depicts the results

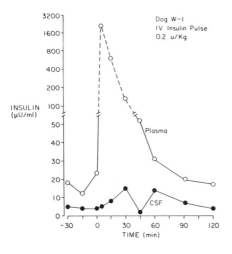

FIG. 3. Plasma and CSF insulin levels following an intravenous injection of insulin to an anesthetized dog.

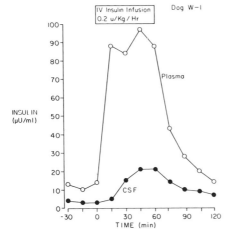

FIG. 4. Plasma and CSF insulin levels before, during, and after a 1-hr infusion of insulin into the vein of an anesthetized dog.

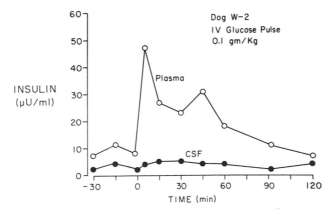

FIG. 5. Plasma and CSF insulin levels following an intravenous injection of glucose to an anesthetized dog.

from a dog receiving an intravenous pulse of glucose, a situation designed to simulate more closely a likely physiological event. Insulin in the plasma increased by a factor of six and decreased thereafter. There was no change of CSF insulin.

DISCUSSION

The results at hand support the hypothesis that CSF insulin responds slowly to changes of plasma insulin rather than reflecting the moment-to-moment changes of level that occur in response to food ingestion. A 100-fold increase of plasma insulin was barely manifest in the CSF (see Fig. 3), whereas a much smaller but sustained increase of plasma insulin in the same dog was reflected by a maintained increase of CSF insulin (see Fig. 4). This experiment therefore supports the findings of both previous experiments of a similar nature (37, 38).

Since basal insulin levels correlate so well with body weight, our contention is that CSF insulin reflects body weight as well, although data bearing on this have never been reported. The CSF is appropriate as a vehicle for the heretofore elusive messenger, which informs the brain as to the amount of fat in the body since it comes in contact with the ventral hypothalamus in the floor of the third ventricle. We are presently testing the further implications of this relationship.

ACKNOWLEDGMENTS

The studies reported here were supported by U.S. Public Health Service grants AM 05498, AM 12829, and AM 17112 from the National Institute of Arthritis and Metabolic Diseases.

REFERENCES

1. Kennedy, G. C. (1953): *Proc. R. Soc. (Biol.)*, 140:578–592.
2. Hoebel, G. B. (1971): *Ann. Rev. Physiol.*, 33:533–568.
3. Steiner, D. F., and Freinkel, N. (Eds.) (1972): *Handbook of Physiology*, Sec. 7, Vol. 1. American Physiology Society, Washington, D.C.
4. Bagdade, J. D., (1968): *Lancet*, 2:630–631.
5. Decker, T., and Hagerup, L. (1967): *Acta Med. Scand.*, 182:225–232.
6. Kreisberg, R. A., Boshell, B. R., DiPlacido, J., and Roddam, R. F. (1967): *N. Engl. J. Med.*, 276:314–319.
7. Hales, C. N., and Kennedy, G. C. (1964): *Biochem. J.*, 90:620–624.
8. Steffens, A. B., Morgenson, G. J., and Stevenson, J. A. F. (1972): *Am. J. Physiol.*, 222:1446–1452.
9. Hamilton, C. L., Kuo, P. T., and Feng, L. Y. (1972): *Proc. Soc. Exp. Biol. Med.*, 140:1005–1008.
10. Chlouverakis, C., and Bernardis, L. L. (1972): *Diabetologia*, 8:179–184.
11. Bray, G. A., and York, D. A. (1971): *Physiol. Rev.*, 51:598–646.
12. Sims, E. A. H., and Horton, E. S. (1968): *Am. J. Clin. Nutr.*, 21:1455–1470.

13. Bagdade, J. D., Bierman, E. L., and Porte, D., Jr. (1967): *J. Clin. Invest.*, 46:1549–1557.
14. Bernstein, I. L., Kulkosky, P. J., Lotter, E. C., Porte, D., Jr., and Woods, S. C. (1975): *Proc. Soc. Exp. Biol. Med.* (*In press.*)
15. Woods, S. C., Decke, E., and Vasselli, J. R. (1974): *Psychol. Rev.*, 81:26–43.
16. Woods, S. C., Kaestner, E., and Vasselli, J. R. (1975): *Psychol. Rev.*, 82:165–168.
17. Martin, J. M., Konijnendijk, W., and Bouman, P. R. (1974): *Diabetes*, 23:203–208.
18. Tannenbaum, G. A., Paxinos, G., and Bindra, B. (1974): *J. Comp. Physiol. Psychol.*, 86:404–413.
19. Frohman, L. A., and Bernardis, L. L. (1968): *Endocrinology*, 82:1125–1132.
20. Han, P. W. (1967): *Fed. Proc.*, 26:316.
21. Hustvedt, B. E., and Lovo, A. (1972): *Acta Physiol. Scand.*, 84:29–33.
22. Kulkosky, P. J., Porte, D., Jr., and Woods, S. C. (1975): *Experientia.* 31:123–124.
23. Feldberg, W. (1958): *J. Physiol.* (*Lond.*), 140:20–21P.
24. Epstein, A. N. (1960): *Am. J. Physiol.*, 199:969–974.
25. Young, T. K., and Liu, A. C. (1965): *Chin. J. Physiol.*, 19:247–253.
26. York, D. A., and Bray, G. A. (1972): *Endocrinology*, 90:855–894.
27. Powley, T. L., and Opsahl, C. A. (1974): *Am. J. Physiol.*, 226:25–33.
28. Woods, S. C., and Porte, D., Jr. (1974): *Physiol. Rev.*, 54:596–619.
29. Hoebel, G. B., and Teitelbaum, P. (1966): *J. Comp. Physiol. Psychol.*, 61:189–193.
30. Powley, T. L., and Keesey, R. E. (1970): *J. Comp. Physiol. Psychol.*, 70:25–36.
31. Porte, D., Jr., Girardier, L., Seydoux, J., Kanazawa, Y., and Posternak, J. (1973): *J. Clin. Invest.*, 52:210–214.
32. Frohman, L. A., Ezdinli, E. Z., and Javid, R. (1967): *Diabetes*, 16:443–448 .
33. Hakanson, R., Liedberg, G., and Lundquist, I. (1971): *Experientia*, 27:460–461.
34. Iversen, J. (1973): *J. Clin. Invest.*, 52:2102–2116.
35. Bergman, R. N., and Miller, R. E. (1973): *Am. J. Physiol.*, 225:481–486.
36. Owen, O. E., Reichard, G. A., Jr., DiTullio, N. W., and Shuman, C. R. (1970): *Diabetes*, 19:397.
37. Margolis, R. U., and Altszuler, N. (1967): *Nature*, 215:1375–1376.
38. Woods, S. C., Chen, M., and Porte, D., Jr. (1974): *Diabetes*, 23: 341.
39. Porte, D., Jr., Graber, A. L., Kuzuya, T., and Williams, R. H. (1966): *J. Clin. Invest.*, 45:228–236.

Hunger: Basic Mechanisms and Clinical Implications,
edited by D. Novin, W. Wyrwicka, and G. Bray.
Raven Press, New York © 1976.

Appetite and Hunger in Experimental Obesity Syndromes

Anthony Sclafani

Department of Psychology, Brooklyn College of the City University of New York, Brooklyn, New York
11210

Adult animals normally regulate their body weight at relatively stable
levels by controlling their food consumption and energy expenditure. Various
experimental procedures, however, can produce overeating and obesity. The
changes in food motivation associated with this overeating have been extensively analyzed only in the case of obese animals with hypothalamic
hyperphagia, although recent studies have examined other forms of experimentally induced obesity. This chapter reviews the current motivational research on experimental obesity in rodents and analyzes the findings using a
dual lipostat model of body weight regulation.

Basic concepts must first be defined. A distinction is often but not always
made between the terms hunger and appetite (1). Hunger is defined here as
the drive for food aroused by internal stimuli which accumulate during food
deprivation and body weight loss. Appetite, on the other hand, is defined as
the incentive to eat aroused by external food-related stimuli, e,g., taste.
Satiety refers to the absence of appetite and hunger. Postprandial satiety,
however, may result from an active inhibitory reflex elicited by ingested
foods (2) and thus may represent a state distinct from appetite and hunger.

HYPOTHALAMIC OBESITY

Electrolytic lesions or knife cuts in the ventromedial hypothalamus
(VMH) can produce voracious eating and extreme obesity, but their effects
on food motivation are less obvious. Miller et al. (3) originally reported that
VMH lesions, although producing hyperphagia, appear to reduce the animal's hunger drive; that is, VMH-lesioned rats were less willing to work for
food or eat a bitter diet than were intact controls. These findings were confirmed in later experiments (4, 5), and it was proposed that decreased satiety
rather than increased hunger is responsible for hypothalamic hyperphagia.
The view that VMH damage impairs postprandial satiety became widely accepted, although several recent findings now question its validity (6–9).

Recent studies also indicate that a reevaluation of the motivational con-
comitants of hypothalamic hyperphagia is in order. This author (10, 11)
reported that VMH lesions or knife cuts that produce hyperphagia and obesity
do not significantly reduce bar pressing for food on VI or FR schedules

when the subjects are tested at 80 or 90% of their preoperative body weights (see Fig. 1). Similar results have also been obtained in several other laboratories (12–17). Hyperphagic rats tested at a percentage of their obese weights, on the other hand, work less for food compared to controls (10, 11, 14, 16, 18–20). These findings indicate that obesity, but not VMH damage *per se,* suppresses behavior motivated by food deprivation and body weight loss.

Factors other than obesity must also be involved, however, since several experimenters have reported reduced bar pressing performance in nonobese hyperphagic subjects (3, 5, 21, 22). Sclafani and Kluge (11) proposed, on the basis of earlier knife cut findings (23, 24), that the lateral extent of VMH damage may be an important factor influencing its motivational effects. This view is supported by the recent observations that damage to the lateral perifornical region, which often occurs with large VMH lesions, significantly depresses food motivated bar pressing, whereas damage restricted to the medial hypothalamus does not (25, 26). It has also been postulated that the hyperemotionality of VMH-lesioned subjects interferes with their performance of food motivated tasks. This is based on the findings that preoperative bar press training eliminates the postoperative depression in food

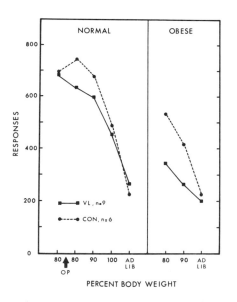
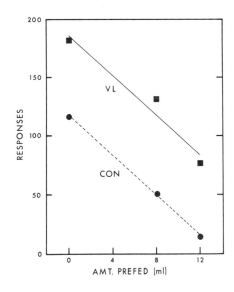

FIG. 1. *Left:* Mean bar-pressing responses of hypothalamic hyperphagic rats (VL knife cuts) maintained at different percentages of their normal (preoperative) and obese weights compared to control subjects. (From Sclafani and Kluge, ref. 11.) *Right:* Mean bar-pressing responses of nondeprived hypothalamic hyperphagic (VL knife cuts) and control rats prefed varying amounts of milk diet 10 min prior to testing. The hyperphagic rats were in the dynamic stage, although their body weights were significantly greater than control weights at time of testing. (From Sclafani and Schacher, *unpublished.*) In both experiments, subjects were tested on a VI 1-min schedule during daily 30-min sessions for sweetened condensed milk diet.

motivated bar pressing otherwise displayed by VMH-lesioned animals (20, 27). Training before surgery is not always necessary, however, to prevent postoperative deficits (10), and it does not eliminate the motivational depression displayed by obese hyperphagic rats (20). Thus, under appropriate conditions, hypothalamic hyperphagia is accompanied by normal hunger-motivated behaviors, whereas in other cases, owing to either obesity, lack of preoperative training, or lateral hypothalamic (LH) damage, it is associated with below normal performance.

The finding that nonobese hyperphagic rats may display normal hunger drive when deprived of food does not, of course, explain why they overeat under *ad lib* conditions, but evidence is now available that such animals may have increased appetitive motivation. Sclafani and co-workers (10, 28) observed that hyperphagic rats have significantly reduced latencies to eat in a novel environment compared to controls. Since the hyperphagic rats did not display these reduced latencies to eat when tested with less palatable foods or when deprived of food, Sclafani (29) proposed that enhanced appetite rather than increased hunger was responsible. It should be noted, however, that the latency-to-eat findings are open to other interpretations (30), and brain lesions that do not produce overeating may also reduce the latencies to eat (31, 32).

Consistent with an enhanced appetite interpretation, Sclafani and Kluge (11) observed that nonobese hyperphagic rats, while working at normal rates when food deprived, bar press more than controls for palatable foods when nondeprived. We have recently confirmed this finding (Sclafani and Schacher, *unpublished*) and further observed that the appetite of the hyperphagic rat for a palatable milk diet, as measured by their bar-pressing performance, declines at the same rate as that of controls when the subjects are prefed before testing (Fig. 1). Thus hyperphagic rats appear normally sensitive to the satiety effects of food, but eat more than normal because their appetite is increased. Unlike rats in the dynamic stage of hyperphagia, obese animals do not bar press significantly more for milk than do controls, and, in fact, work less than controls when tested under food-deprived conditions (11). On the basis of these findings, Sclafani and Kluge (11) proposed that obesity reduces the appetite of hyperphagic animals to normal levels, whereas it suppresses the hunger drive to below normal levels. Results consistent with this view have been obtained in other laboratories (18).

Peters and co-workers (13, 15) reported results similar to those of Sclafani and Kluge (11) but concluded that hyperphagic rats have increased hunger drive. The discrepancy betweeen their interpretation and that of Sclafani and Kluge may only be semantic since Peters et al. did not distinguish between hunger and appetite. An advantage of such a distinction is that it can explain why VMH-damaged rats may work more for food than do controls when nondeprived, but fail to do so, or even work less, when food deprived; that is, increased appetite and normal or decreased hunger may coexist. The most dramatic example of this is the hyperphagia-aphagia syndrome displayed by rats with both medial and LH damage (10, 23, 33). Such animals overeat palatable foods but refuse to eat unpalatable foods.

Wampler (26) also has proposed that VMH lesions enhance the hunger drive. This conclusion was based on his finding that four hyperphagic rats increased their bar pressing for food following surgery when body weights were maintained at 85% of preoperative levels. However, no operated controls were used and the significance of this increase is difficult to assess since control rats have been observed in other studies (11) to increase their bar pressing following sham surgery. Furthermore, Wampler also reported that nine other hyperphagic rats showed either no change or a decrease in their postoperative bar-pressing performance. The decrease in bar pressing was attributed to LH damage. Finally, lesioned rats that did not become hyperphagic displayed either increased, decreased, or unchanged bar-pressing behavior. Thus, rather than supporting the interpretation that hypothalamic hyperphagia is the result of increased hunger drive, Wampler's data appear more compatible with the view expressed above that hypothalamic hyperphagia is associated with either normal or reduced hunger motivation, depending on lesion placement and other factors.

HYPOTHALAMIC FINICKINESS

The degree of hyperphagia and obesity produced by medial hypothalamic damage is highly dependent on the palatability of the diet. In fact, VMH-lesioned rats have been found to undereat if the diet is adulterated with quinine, salt, or cellulose (3, 4, 34). This finickiness has been interpreted as additional evidence that VMH lesions impair the hunger drive. The findings that hyperphagic rats are finicky to quinine adulteration of water as well as food (35, 36) and overreact to increased as well as decreased diet palatability (4) has suggested that hypothalamic finickiness may represent a more basic change in the animals' taste or sensory reactivity (37). This interpretation is questioned, however, by more recent studies of hypothalamic finickiness.

New findings confirm earlier results that obesity increases the hyperphagic rat's rejection of unpalatable diets (4, 34) and further indicate that excessive weight is the major cause of this finickiness. As depicted in Fig. 2, Sclafani et al. (38) observed that hypothalamic rats, who overate and became obese on a high-fat diet, underate and rapidly lost weight when given quinine-adulterated food. The hypothalamic rats stopped losing weight when they reached control levels, however, and continued to maintain themselves at control body weights even when the quinine concentration of the diet was increased fourfold. Similar results have been obtained in other laboratories using different procedures (39, 40) and they agree with the earlier view of Kennedy (34, 41) that VMH damage does not alter the lower limit of body weight.

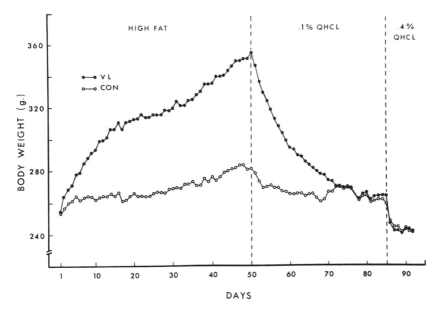

FIG. 2. Mean body weights of hypothalamic hyperphagic (VL knife cuts) and control rats maintained on high-fat (33%), 0.1% quinine, and 0.4% quinine hydrochloride diets. (From Sclafani, Springer, and Kluge, ref. 38.)

Nevertheless, other findings indicate that hypothalamic damage may produce quinine finickiness independent of obesity (3, 42). Sclafani et al. (38) found, for example, that hypothalamic knife cuts decreased the food intake and body weight of rats maintained on very bitter quinine diets, whereas the cuts produced hyperphagia and obesity when the subjects were later switched to a more palatable diet (see Fig. 5). The hyperphagia and quinine finickiness, however, appear to represent independent effects of the knife cuts. Rats with cuts lateral to the fornix lost more weight on the quinine diet and gained less weight on the high-fat diet than did rats with more medial transections. Thus, as in the case of bar-pressing behavior, the lateral extent of VMH damage appears to be an important variable affecting quinine aversion.

Diet palatability not only determines the food intake and body weight of hyperphagic rats, but it also influences their meal-taking patterns. Sclafani and Berner (9) observed that reducing the palatability of the diet decreases the meal size, but not the meal frequency of hyperphagic rats. Furthermore, when the daily food intakes of hyperphagic and control rats are equated by adjusting diet palatability, the meal sizes of the hyperphagic rats are no greater than those of the controls. Thus the frequently observed increased meal sizes of hyperphagic animals (43) may result from enhanced appetite rather than from a postprandial satiety deficit.

The increased appetite of the hyperphagic animal for palatable foods does not appear to generalize to palatable low or no calorie solutions. In numerous experiments performed in this laboratory, VMH lesions or knife cuts were found not to increase responsivity of the rat to dilute sugar or saccharin solutions and, in fact, often reduced the intakes of such solutions (24, 38, 44–46). Other investigators have also found that hyperphagic rats fail to show enhanced preferences for palatable solutions of low caloric value in a variety of test situations (18, 47, 48). The increased appetite of hyperphagic rats for palatable foods, therefore, does not appear to result from a general increase in their reactivity to taste. The finickiness to quinine-adulterated water also may not be the result of enhanced sensory reactivity. VMH lesions (49) and knife cuts (24) impair thirst regulation, and hypothalamic obesity appears to suppress thirst drive (11). Thus motivational rather than sensory reactivity changes may be responsible for the hyperphagic animal's rejection of unpalatable solutions.

DUAL LIPOSTAT MODEL

The above findings indicate that a basic deficit produced by VMH damage in rats is the reduced ability to limit appetite and body weight when palatable diets are available. To explain this deficit as well as the effects of the resulting obesity, Sclafani and Kluge (11) proposed a dual lipostat model of body weight regulation which represents an elaboration of earlier lipostatic inter- pretations of the hyperphagic syndrome (34, 50). The model postulates that separate lipostatic mechanisms control the upper and lower limits of body weight; that is, one lipostat controls hunger drive and protects against body weight loss when weight declines to a lower set point level due to food scarcity or unpalatability. The second lipostat prevents excessive weight gain by inhibiting appetite when, as the result of an abundance of highly palatable foods, weight increases to an upper set point level. Sclafani and Kluge (11) proposed that it is the second upper set point that is elevated by VMH dam- age allowing the animal to overeat and become obese on good-tasting diets.

A revised and more detailed version of this model is outlined in Fig. 3. This version preserves the concept of separate upper and lower lipostats but includes the possibility that one rather than two set points exist. That is, the same set point may serve as an input to both the upper and lower lipostatic mechanisms. When body weight rises above the set point the upper lipostat inhibits appetite, and when it falls below the set point the lower lipostat stimulates the hunger drive. According to this model VMH damage does not elevate the set point but rather interferes only with the upper lipostatic mechanism reducing its inhibitory output. The advantage of this single set point–dual lipostat model is that it more readily explains the effects of other physiologic interventions that, unlike VMH damage, appear to alter both the upper and lower limits of body weight. LH lesions, for example, are thought to lower the body weight set point and equally reduce the upper and lower limits of weight as revealed by the responses to altered diet palatability (51, 52).

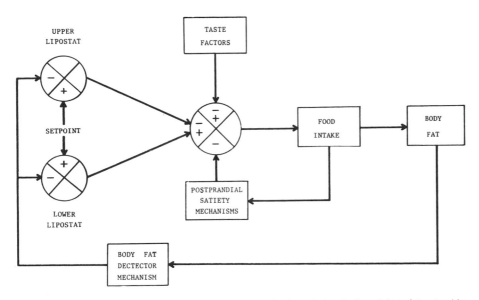

FIG. 3. Dual lipostat model of food intake and body weight (fat) regulation. Body weight is determined by the set point and diet palatability, as well as other factors not included in the model. When weight is above the set point, the output of the upper lipostat inhibits feeding by depressing appetite; when weight is below the set point, the output of the lower lipostat facilitates feeding by stimulating hunger. Postprandial satiety is thought to provide only a temporary inhibition of feeding and does not significantly influence body weight.

In the model proposed in Fig. 3, body weight is determined not only by the set point, but also by diet palatability. (This interpretation is favored over the alternative that palatability changes the set point.) Thus, when offered a very unpalatable diet, taste assumes a negative value and the animal undereats until its body weight falls sufficiently below the set point such that the excitatory output of the lower lipostat equals the inhibitory effect of the diet. The animal will then maintain this new body weight and even defend it under some conditions (53). Similarly, if the animal is given a very tasty diet it will overeat until its weight is sufficiently above the set point such that the inhibitory output of the upper lipostat equals the excitatory effect of the diet.

The overeating of palatable foods by VMH-damaged rats appears to result primarily from a reduction in lipostatic inhibition, rather than from an exaggeration of the taste input. This is suggested by the normal or subnormal responsivity of hyperphagic rats to palatable solutions, as previously discussed, as well as the finding that VMH lesions may increase body weight even when rats are feeding themselves intragastrically (54). Nevertheless a reduction in lipostatic inhibition makes taste a very important factor determining the degree of obesity displayed by the hyperphagic animal. The undereating of an unpalatable diet by obese hyperphagic rats also need not represent an exaggerated taste input, but rather results, according to the dual lipostat model, because their supra-set-point body weight does not produce an excitatory output from the lower lipostat to counteract the negative effect of the diet. When their weight falls to control levels the hyperphagic rats display normal or near-normal intakes of adulterated foods (38, 40) as well as normal bar pressing for food (11).

The dual lipostat model, therefore, provides a framework to explain many of the effects of VMH damage on food intake and body weight, and it may also be useful in the analysis of the other obesity syndromes to be discussed next. The model remains speculative, however, since the exact means by which body weight is regulated remains unclear. In particular, although weight may be regulated by a lipostatic feedback mechanism that monitors body fat content, as suggested by the model, it is also possible that weight is regulated indirectly by a mechanism that monitors some other body nutrient or process related to the body fat stores.

DIETARY OBESITY

Normal neurologically intact rats, although less responsive than VMH-damaged animals, are not immune to the appetizing effects of food. In fact, several studies have demonstrated that normal animals gain excessive weight when fed very palatable highly caloric diets (55, 56), although little behavioral research has been conducted on dietary obesity (48). Sclafani and Springer (57) have recently observed that giving adult female rats an assortment of palatable supermarket foods, such as cookies, candy, salami, banana, and sweetened condensed milk, along with lab pellets, is an especially effective means of producing dietary obesity (Fig. 4). Weight gains displayed by the rats offered this diet ranged between 80 and 233 g in 60 days compared to the 25- to 71-g gains shown by the control rats fed only lab pellets. Since the dietary obese rats were able to choose among the supermarket foods and lab pellets their overeating and overweight appear to result from the appetizing effect of the diet rather than from any nutritional deficiencies.

While the dietary obese rats maintained elevated body weights when palatable foods were freely available, Sclafani and Springer found that they did not defend their weights when forced to work for food, or to eat less palatable diets (Fig. 4). The dietary obese animals also failed to show the increase in spontaneous activity that normally occurs during food deprivation. These responses resemble, of course, those displayed by hypothalamic obese animals. The similarities between the two obesity syndromes may be interpreted according to the dual lipostat model. That is, both dietary and hypothalamic obesity may result from enhanced appetite because of increased diet palatability or decreased lipostatic inhibition, rather than from an elevation in the set point. The obese animals display subnormal food motivation when faced with unfavorable feeding conditions, therefore, because their body weights, being far above the set point, do not activate the lower lipostatic mechanism

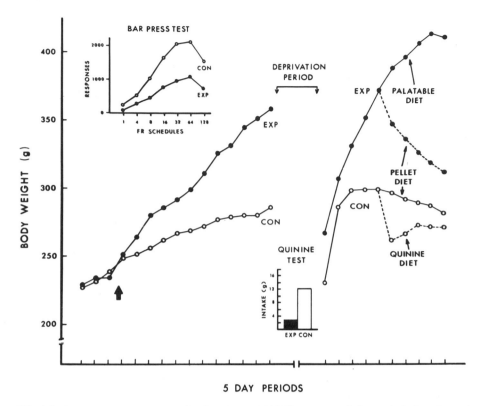

FIG. 4. Body weights of experimental (EXP) and control (CON) rats across 5-day periods. Experimental group was given an assortment of palatable supermarket foods in addition to Purina pellets at the point indicated by arrow; the control group was maintained on Purina pellets. *Lower middle inset:* After 60 days on these diets, the subjects were given a 0.1% quinine diet for 3 days and their food intakes were measured. *Upper left inset:* The subjects were then food deprived to 80% of their normal or obese weights and their bar press response for food was measured on various FR schedules. Following this test, the rats were returned to their respective diets for 20 days. Half of the experimental group was then given only pellets to eat; half of the control group was given a 0.4% quinine diet during the next 25 days. The remaining animals in each group continued on their original diets. (From Sclafani and Springer, *unpublished.*)

controlling the hunger drive. The hypothesis that it is the discrepancy between the obese weight and the set point, rather than excessive weight *per se,* that is responsible for the reduced hunger drive is given some support by the findings, to be discussed below, that not all forms of obesity are associated with decreased hunger motivation.

OVARIAN OBESITY

Another obesity syndrome that has been related to hypothalamic obesity is that produced by ovariectomy in female rats. It has been suggested, for example, that ovarian atrophy produced by VMH lesions contributes to hypothalamic obesity (58), whereas other data indicate that the VMH mediates the suppressive effects of estrogen on food intake and body weight (59). However, recent work questions this view and indicates that hypothalamic and ovarian obesity are separate syndromes. Several studies have found that VMH lesions do not always produce ovarian atrophy (60, 61), that ovariectomy and VMH lesions have additive effects on body weight (62, 63), and that VMH damage does not prevent the weight suppressive effects of estrogen injections (62–64).

Further evidence for the independence of hypothalamic and ovarian obesity is provided by recent findings of Gale and Sclafani (*unpublished*). As depicted in Fig. 5, maintaining rats on a quinine-supplemented diet was found to completely block hypothalamic obesity, but did not prevent the obesity produced by ovariectomy. A second experiment revealed that ovariectomy produced excessive weight gains even in quinine-fed rats previously given VMH knife cuts, which had reduced their body weight. Figure 5 also illustrates that the presentation of a high-fat diet greatly increased the weight gains of the hypothalamic rats, but did not potentiate the obesity displayed

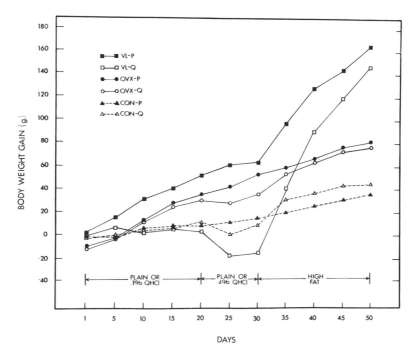

FIG. 5. Postoperative body weight gains of hypothalamic (VL knife cuts), ovariectomized (OVX), and control (CON) rats as a function of days and diet condition. During the first 30 postoperative days, the subjects were maintained on either quinine-adulterated diets (VL-Q, OVX-Q, CON-Q) or a plain Purina diet (VL-P, OVX-P, CON-P). During the next 20 days, all subjects were given a high-fat diet (33% Crisco fat, 67% Purina). Note that on the 0.4% quinine diet, the body weight gain of the VL-Q group was significantly less than that of the CON-Q group. (From Gale and Sclafani, *unpublished*.)

by the ovariectomized subjects. Ovarian obesity, therefore, is relatively un-affected by changes in diet palatability which is in marked contrast to the hypothalamic syndrome. One explanation of this finding is that ovariectomy and hypothalamic damage differentially affect taste reactivity (70). Gale and Sclafani observed, however, that ovariectomized and VMH-damaged rats display similar aversions to quinine adulterated water. These investigators also found that food-deprived ovariectomized rats, unlike hypothalamic sub-jects, bar press more for food on demanding FR schedules than do operated controls suggesting that ovariectomy increases hunger drive. Ovariectomized animals further differ from hypothalamic rats in that they do not display reduced latencies to eat in a novel environment. Finally, another distinction between the ovarian and hypothalamic obesity syndromes recently reported by Powley et al. (66) is that, whereas subdiaphragmatic vagotomy completely reverses hypothalamic obesity, it is without effect on ovarian obesity.

Thus several different lines of evidence indicate that the hyperphagia and obesity produced by ovariectomy is distinct from that produced by medial hypothalamic damage. Previous investigators have proposed that ovarian obesity results from an increase in the body weight set point (65, 67), and the results of Gale and Sclafani are consistent with this view. In terms of the dual lipostat model, ovariectomy, by raising the set point, would elevate both the upper and lower body weight limits and this would explain why ovariec-tomized rats gain excessive weight on both palatable and unpalatable diets. (More appropriately, perhaps, it should be stated that ovariectomized rats behave as if their set point is elevated since ovariectomy may produce its effects by reducing the negative feedback from body fat, or by otherwise altering the error signals from the lipostats without directly changing the set point.) The differences between the behavioral effects of ovariectomy and VMH damage, as well as the additivity of these effects, may result, therefore, because ovariectomy raises the set point either directly or functionally, whereas VMH damage does not alter the set point but affects only the upper lipostatic mechanism.

GENETIC OBESITY

Several different forms of genetically transmitted obesity have been identi-fied in rodents (68, 69). Only recently, however, have the motivational aspects of genetic obesity been analyzed. Sclafani and Griffo (*unpublished*) have compared the food motivation of genetically obese (ob/ob) mice with that of electrolytically lesioned (VMH) or goldthioglucose-lesioned (GTG) hypothalamic mice. When maintained on quinine diets for 2 weeks, the genetically obese mice showed greater reductions in their food intake and body weight (body weight change $= -9.9\%$) than did lean controls (body weight change $= -3.6\%$), but not as great compared to hypothalamic obese mice (body weight change, VMH $= -22.1\%$, GTG $= -12.4\%$). The increased aversion to bitter diets, relative to controls, of the ob/ob mice is consistent with the earlier findings of Fuller (69, 70). Sclafani and Griffo further observed that both genetically obese and hypothalamic obese mice bar pressed less for food on high FR schedules compared to the controls (Fig. 6). These findings suggest that genetically obese ob/ob mice suffer weight regulatory impairments similar to the hypothalamic obese animal (see also 68), but conflicting results have been reported. Singh et al. (71) observed that ob/ob mice worked significantly more for food on high FR schedules than did either controls or GTG mice; the latter two groups did not significantly differ. The reason for this discrepancy is unclear and we are currently examining this problem. It should be noted that Greenwood et al. (19), in a study of a different form of genetic obesity, found that yellow obese mice (aA^y) bar pressed more for food on high FR schedules than did controls, whereas consistent with our results, GTG mice worked less than did controls.

Greenwood et al. (19) and Cruce et al. (72) also studied genetically obese Zucker fatty rats (fa/fa) and found that not only do they eat more food than controls but they also work more for food on FR schedules and tolerate quinine adulteration of their diet as well as do controls. VMH-lesioned rats, on the other hand, displayed a hyperphagia and obesity similar to that of the fatty rat, but bar pressed less for food, and ate less quinine diet compared to the genetically obese and control rats. A further difference between genetically obese and hypothalamic obese rats is that vagotomy does

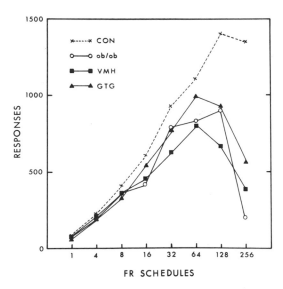

FIG. 6. Mean bar-pressing responses of genetic obese (ob/ob), control (CON), and two groups of hypothalamic obese (VMH and GTG) mice as a function of FR schedules. Subjects were tested during 30-min sessions for 20 mg Noyes pellets. (From Sclafani and Griffo, *unpublished*.)

not eliminate the excessive adiposity of the fatty rat as it does in the VMH-lesioned animal (73).

Thus, although some forms of genetic obesity (ob/ob mouse) may be similar to hypothalamic obesity, other forms (fa/fa rat, aA^y mouse) appear to be different. These results may be interpretable within the dual lipostat model, but further evidence is needed before specific hypotheses of genetic obesity can be offered.

SUMMARY AND CLINICAL IMPLICATIONS

This review of the motivational aspects of experimental obesity suggests that at least two different types of syndromes exist. Some forms of overweight (e.g., hypothalamic, dietary, and perhaps genetic obesity) appear only under favorable feeding conditions, whereas others (e.g., ovarian and some forms of genetic obesity) are displayed under all conditions. In terms of the dual lipostat model, the first type of obesity is associated with an elevation in only the upper limit of body weight due either to reduced inhibitory signals from the upper lipostat or increased excitatory signals from the diet. This obesity is accompanied by enhanced appetite, but reduced hunger motivation. In the second type of obesity, both the upper and lower limits of body weight are elevated. This may result from an increase in the body weight set point, or from some other change, such as reduced negative feedback from adipose tissue, which would have the same effect as a set point elevation. In this case, both appetite and hunger are elevated during the dynamic phase, and are normal during the static phase of the obesity.

In view of these behavioral differences between experimental obesity syndromes, it would appear likely that similar differences also exist between overweight humans. Some individuals may have an elevated body weight set point and thus regulate their weight normally but at above average levels, whereas other individuals may not have an increased set point and become obese only when feeding conditions are especially favorable. One must be cognizant of these possible differences in selecting the most appropriate animal model of human obesity.

Finally, although much of the experimental and clinical emphasis has been placed on the physiological and genetic disorders responsible for overweight, the occurrence of dietary obesity in normal rats demonstrates that environmental factors must not be ignored. In fact, the prevalence of human obesity in affluent supermarket societies may be directly related to the abundance of the highly palatable products of modern food technology. In light of the behavioral resemblances between dietary and hypothalamic obesity in rats, therefore, the reported similarities between overweight humans and hypothalamic rats may be less surprising (74, 75). The question remains, however: Why are some humans more susceptible than others to the appetizing effects of food?

ACKNOWLEDGMENTS

The research reported herein was supported by National Institute of Mental Health grant MH-21563 and by the Research Foundation of the City University of New York grant 10103.

REFERENCES

1. Cannon, W. B. (1934): In: *Handbook of General Experimental Psychology*, edited by G. Muchinson, pp. 247–263. Clark University Press, Worcester, Mass.
2. Smith, G. P., Gibbs, J., and Young, R. C. (1974): *Fed. Proc.*, 33:1146–1149.
3. Miller, N. E., Bailey, C. J., and Stevenson, J. A. F. (1950): *Science*, 112:256–259.
4. Teitelbaum, P. (1955): *J. Comp. Physiol. Psychol.*, 48:158–163.
5. Teitelbaum, P. (1957): *J. Comp. Physiol. Psychol.*, 50:486–490.
6. Panksepp, J. (1971): *Physiol. Behav.*, 7:381–384.
7. Panksepp, J. (1971): *Physiol. Behav.*, 7:385–394.
8. Liu, C. M., and Yin, T. H. (1974): *Physiol. Behav.*, 13:231–238.
9. Sclafani, A., and Berner, C. N. (1976): *Physiol. Behav., in press*.
10. Sclafani, A. (1971): *J. Comp. Physiol. Psychol.*, 77:70–96.
11. Sclafani, A., and Kluge, L. (1974): *J. Comp. Physiol. Psychol.*, 86:28–46.
12. Jaffe, M. L. (1973): *Physiol. Psychol.*, 1:191–198.
13. Kent, M. A., and Peters, R. H. (1973): *J. Comp. Physiol. Psychol.*, 83:92–97.
14. Marks, H. E., and Remley, N. R. (1972): *Behav. Biol.*, 7:95–111.
15. Peters, R. H., Sensenig, L. D., and Reich, M. J. (1973): *Physiol. Psychol.*, 1:131–138.
16. Porter, J. H., and Allen, J. D. (1972): *Psychon. Sci.*, 28:285–288.
17. Porter, J. H., Allen, J. D., and Arazie, R. (1974): *Physiol. Behav.*, 13:627–632.
18. Beatty, W. W. (1973): *Physiol. Behav.*, 10:841–846.
19. Greenwood, M. R. C., Quartermain, D., Johnson, P. R., Cruce, J. A. F., and Hirsch, J. (1974): *Physiol. Behav.*, 13:687–692.
20. Singh, D. (1973): *J. Comp. Physiol. Psychol.*, 84:47–52.
21. Panksepp, J., and Dickinson, A. (1972): *Physiol. Behav.*, 9:609–614.
22. Singh, D. (1970): *Psychon. Sci.*, 21:306–308.
23. Grossman, S. P., and Grossman, L. (1971): *J. Comp. Physiol. Psychol.*, 74:148–156.
24. Sclafani, A., Berner, C. N., and Maul, G. (1973): *J. Comp. Physiol. Psychol.*, 85:29–51.
25. Beven, T. E. (1973): Ph.D. dissertation, Princeton University, Princeton, N.J.
26. Wampler, R. S. (1973): *J. Comp. Physiol. Psychol.*, 84:275–285.
27. King, B. M., and Gaston, M. G. (1973): *Physiol. Behav.*, 11:161–166.
28. Sclafani, A., Belluzzi, J. D., and Grossman, S. P. (1970): *J. Comp. Physiol. Psychol.*, 72:394–403.
29. Sclafani, A. (1972): *Physiol. Behav.*, 8:977–979.
30. Grossman, S. P. (1972): *J. Comp. Physiol. Psychol.*, 78:274–283.
31. Davenport, L. D., and Balagura, S. (1971): *Science*, 171:744–745.
32. Neill, D. B., Ross, J. F., and Grossman, S. P. (1974): *Physiol. Behav.*, 13:297–305.
33. Williams, D. R., and Teitelbaum, P. (1959): *J. Comp. Physiol. Psychol.*, 52:458–465.
34. Kennedy, G. C. (1953): *Proc. Roy. Soc. [Biol.]*, 140:578–592.
35. Corbit, J. D. (1965): *J. Comp. Physiol. Psychol.*, 60:123–124.
36. Krasne, F. B. (1966): *Psychon. Sci.*, 4:313–314.
37. Grossman, S. P. (1966): *Physiol. Behav.*, 1:1–10.
38. Sclafani, A., Springer, D., and Kluge, L. (1976): *Physiol. Behav., in press*.
39. Ferguson, N. B. L., and Keesey, R. E. (1975): *J. Comp. Physiol. Psychol.*, 89:478–488.
40. Franklin, K. B. J., and Herberg, L. J. (1974): *J. Comp. Physiol. Psychol.*, 87:410–414.

41. Kennedy, G. C. (1969): *Ann. N.Y. Acad. Sci.,* 157:1049–1061.
42. Graff, H., and Stellar, E. (1962): *J. Comp. Physiol. Psychol.,* 55:418–424.
43. Teitelbaum, P., and Campbell, B. A. (1958): *J. Comp. Physiol. Psychol.,* 51:135–141.
44. Sclafani, A., and Grossman, S. P. (1971): *J. Comp. Physiol. Psychol.,* 74:157–166.
45. Sclafani, A. (1973): *Physiol. Behav.,* 11:771–780.
46. Sclafani, A., Gale, S. K., and Springer, D. (1975): *Physiol. Behav., in press.*
47. Mook, D. G., and Blass, E. M. (1970): *Psychon. Sci.,* 19:34–35.
48. Maller, O. (1964): *Life Sci.,* 3:1281–1291.
49. Stevenson, J. A. F. (1969): In: *The Hypothalamus,* edited by W. Haymaker, E. Anderson, and W. J. H. Nauta, pp. 524–621. Thomas, Springfield, Ill.
50. Hoebel, B. G., and Teitelbaum, P. (1966): *J. Comp. Physiol. Psychol.,* 61:189–193.
51. Powley, T. L., and Keesey, R. E. (1970): *J. Comp. Physiol. Psychol.,* 70:25–36.
52. Keesey, R. E., and Boyle, P. C. (1973): *J. Comp. Physiol. Psychol.,* 84:38–46.
53. Peck, J. W. (1974): Presented at the Fifth International Conference on the Physiology of Food and Fluid Intake, Jerusalem.
54. McGinty, D., Epstein, A. N., and Teitelbaum, P. (1965): *Anim. Behav.,* 13:413–418.
55. Ingle, D. J. (1949): *Proc. Soc. Exp. Biol. Med.,* 72:604–605.
56. Mickelsen, O., Takahashi, S., and Craig, S. (1955): *J. Nutr.,* 57:541–554.
57. Sclafani, A., and Springer, D. (1974): Presented at the Fifth International Conference on the Physiology of Food and Fluid Intake, Jerusalem.
58. Valenstein, E. S., Cox, V. C., and Kakolewski, J. W. (1969): *Ann. N.Y. Acad. Sci.,* 157:1030–1046.
59. Wade, G. N., and Zucker, I. (1970): *J. Comp. Physiol. Psychol.,* 72:328–336.
60. Kennedy, G. C., and Mitra, J. (1963): *J. Physiol.,* 166:395–407.
61. Wampler, R. S., and Gier, H. T. (1974): *J. Comp. Physiol. Psychol.,* 87:831–840.
62. Decke, E. (1974): Ph.D. Dissertation, Columbia University, New York.
63. King, J. M., and Cox, V. C. (1973): *Physiol. Psychol.,* 1:261–264.
64. Montemurro, D. G. (1971): *Can. J. Physiol. Pharmacol.,* 49:554–558.
65. Wade, G. N. (1975): In: *Advances in the Study of Behavior, Vol. 5,* edited by J. S. Rosenblatt, R. A. Hinde, E. Shaw, and C. G. Beer, Academic Press, New York.
66. Powley, T. L., Opsahl, C. O., and Van Den Pol, A. N. (1974): Presented at the Fifth International Conference on the Physiology of Food and Fluid Intake, Jerusalem.
67. Mook, D. G., Kenny, N. J., Roberts, S., Nussbaum, A. I., and Rodier, W. I., III (1972): *J. Comp. Physiol. Psychol.,* 81:198–211.
68. Bray, G. A., and York, D. A. (1971): *Physiol. Rev.,* 51:598–646.
69. Fuller, J. L. (1972): *Adv. Psychosom. Med.,* 7:2–24.
70. Fuller, J. L., and Jacoby, G. A., Jr. (1955): *Am. J. Physiol.,* 183:279–283.
71. Singh, D., Lakey, J. R., and Sanders, M. K. (1974): *J. Comp. Physiol. Psychol.,* 86:890–897.
72. Cruce, J. A. F., Greenwood, M. R. C., Johnson, P. R., and Quartermain, D. (1974): *J. Comp. Physiol. Psychol.,* 87:295–301.
73. Opsahl, C. A., and Powley, T. L. (1974): *Am. J. Physiol.,* 226:34–38.
74. Schachter, S. (1971): *Am. Psychol.,* 26:129–144.
75. Schachter, S., and Rodin, J. (1974): *Obese Humans and Rats.* Lawrence Erlbaum Associates, Potomac, Maryland.

Hunger: Basic Mechanisms and Clinical Implications,
edited by D. Novin, W. Wyrwicka, and G. Bray.
Raven Press, New York © 1976.

Situational Determinants of the Body Weights Defended by Normal Rats and Rats with Hypothalamic Lesions

Jeffrey W. Peck

Department of Psychology, University of Utah, Salt Lake City, Utah 84112

Three usages of the concept of defense of body weights and of the hunger for calories are presented in this chapter. Data are from normal rats, rats with ventromedial hypothalamic (VMH) lesions, and rats with lateral hypothalamic (LH) lesions and also suggest reinterpretation of the effects of those lesions. Subsequently, the distinctions are reduced to definitions and are incorporated into a fixed set-point model for the control of body weight to clarify both the definitions and the concept of set point. One possible clinical implication of this analysis is mentioned.

TASTE, REINFORCEMENT DENSITY, AND DEFENDED BODY WEIGHTS

The hunger for calories is usually said to result from energy deficits, even though rats do not always remain in energy balance. For instance, Corbit and Stellar (1) and Maller (2) showed that rats maintained different body weights depending on the diets chronically available to them. Adolph (3) and Kennedy (4) made similar observations, showing that rats maintained less than normal body weights on many diets. However, the bulk and taste of the diets the latter authors fed their rats were commonly assumed afterward to have reflected extremes that physically limited the amounts the rats could eat, so that maintenance of normal weight was not possible. That qualities of the diet or dietary regimen determined the weights rats actively sought to maintain was not given serious consideration. However, this is in fact the case.

Rats maintained different body weights depending on the palatability and reinforcement density of the only diets available to them over long periods of time (Fig. 1). Palatability was changed by adulterating a powdered diet with quinine sulfate. Reinforcement density was changed by forcing rats living in Skinner boxes to press a lever up to 256 times (FR 256) for each 45-mg Noyes pellet. A stable body weight on a given diet or dietary regimen was defended against changes in caloric requirements, even when body weights were much less than normal weight on pelleted diets (Fig. 2). Caloric requirements were decreased by giving a liquid diet by stomach tube, and increased by lowering the ambient temperature. Voluntary food

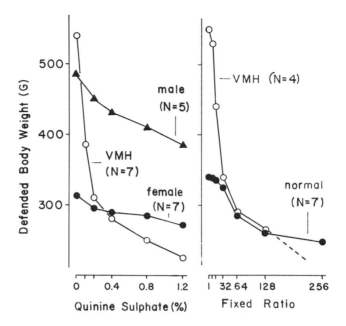

FIG. 1. Mean stable body weights successively reached by rats exposed to diets adulterated with quinine sulfate (QS) or available only on fixed ratio (FR) schedules of reinforcement. Rats exposed to QS diets were Long-Evans (LE) males and females, 10 to 15 months old. Rats exposed to FR schedules were LE and Sprague-Dawley (SD) females, 6 to 12 months old. All VMH-lesioned rats were females. Both food intake and body weight were stable for at least 8 days for each diet or schedule plotted. Many weeks or months on a given regimen may have elapsed before this criterion was reached and the rat was exposed to the next most adulterated diet or next higher schedule of reinforcement.

intake decreased or increased, respectively, by amounts sufficient to prevent both increases and decreases in body weight.

To understand these results requires distinguishing at least two definitions of hunger related to the defense of body weight. Traditionally, hunger or the defense of body weight was assessed by the degree to which rats "ate for calories" when faced with widely differing diets and dietary regimen. As will be developed later, the concept of defense of body weight against changed diet or dietary regimen remains useful. But as shown in Figs. 1 and 2, this concept must be distinguished from defense of body weight against changed caloric requirements.

To further complicate things, rats defending body weight against changed caloric requirements on a poor quality diet or dietary regimen nevertheless appeared hungry in still another sense. For example, rats that rummaged through the powdered quinine-adulterated diets did so to an extent (assessed by amount spilled each day when intakes and body weights had stabilized for that diet) that was directly proportional to the concentration of quinine sulfate in the diet, and thus to the amount the maintained body weights were below the rats' weights on plain mash. They spilled less when the

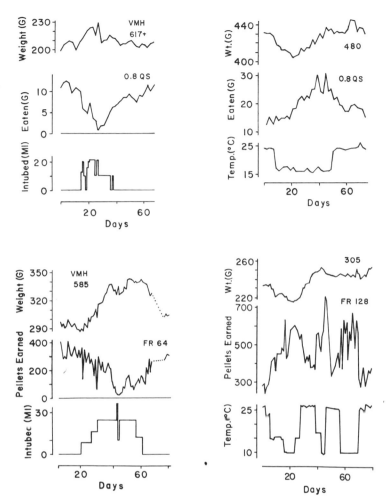

FIG. 2. Body weights and daily voluntary food intakes maintained by four representative rats during periods of supplemental intragastric feeding or exposure to decreased ambient temperatures. These results are selected from at least four normal and two VMH-lesioned rats for each condition. *Upper left:* VMH-lesioned LE female with 0.8 QS as sole food source. On subsequent exposure to unadulterated powdered diet, this rat reached 617 g. *Upper right:* LE male with 0.8 QS as sole food source. Body weight on unadulterated mash was 480 g. *Lower left:* VMH-lesioned LE female receiving 45 mg Noyes pellets on FR 64. The 50 g weight gain of this rat during intragastric feeding was the most extensive observed in these experiments, but the weight achieved (345 g) in no way approached the 585 g of this rat on FR 1 before, or 735 g after, the period illustrated. Dotted lines indicate a period of repeated apparatus failure. *Lower right:* SD female on FR 128 exposed to repeated fluctuations of ambient temperature between 26 and 10°C. This rat weighed 305 g on FR 1. Typically, both lesioned and normal rats gained about 15 to 20 g before voluntary intake was reduced to zero by intragastric intubations. Since succeeding meals do not entirely compensate for intragastric caloric loads, unless the loads are given just prior to a spontaneous meal (22), the weight gain observed here may reflect properties of the linkage between separate long-term and short-term controls over food intake (23).

concentration of quinine sulfate was decreased again and little or none of the plain powdered diet. Also, rats on high fixed-ratio schedules of reinforcement always ate a free Noyes pellet promptly, even after just terminating a spontaneous meal.

This last aspect of the behavior of rats conforms intuitively to an expectation derived from the notion of a fixed set point for body weight, as will be developed further in later sections. The point to be made here is that careful observation of the behavior of rats eating adulterated or poorly accessible diets on a chronic basis seems to demand distinguishing at least three senses in which food-seeking or food ingestion are related to body weight. Body weight, not energy balance, is the primary construct referred to because of the systematic influence of dietary quality on the body weights actively maintained (Figs. 1 and 2). It is hard to conceive how these results could be obtained without rats being responsive to some correlate of body weight, since intakes of a given adulterated diet and lever-pressing for Noyes pellets on a given schedule of reinforcement increased or decreased with changed caloric requirements by amounts appropriate to prevent large changes in body weight. Stable body weights could not have been a function of rats simply ingesting as much of the adulterated diet as they could stand or lever-pressing as much as they were able.

DEFENDED BODY WEIGHT AND VMH LESIONS

As is apparent from Fig. 2, rats with VMH lesions defend body weights against changed caloric requirements (see 5, 6). However, the change in the body weight so defended is much greater for VMH-lesioned rats than for normal rats, for any given change in diet or dietary regimen (Fig. 1). Thus the finickiness of obese VMH-lesioned rats represents an exaggeration of the control that dietary regimen exerts over body weight for all rats. VMH-lesioned rats have presented the paradox of rats that ate more, despite appearing to be less hungry than normal rats (7). The definition of hunger assumed in this paradox was strictly homeostatic, i.e., that food intake should be determined by events internal to the body only. In effect, the results described in the previous section showed that hunger cannot be treated entirely within the framework of homeostasis, but several definitions of hunger must be distinguished. The effects of VMH-lesions on hunger according to these various definitions will be discussed in more detail later.

DEFENDED BODY WEIGHT AND LH LESIONS

The LH is often called the hunger center. If, as suggested above, there is more than one definition of hunger, then this description of the LH is no longer adequate. In fact, when large electrolytic lesions were placed in the far LH, several patterns of body weight control were evident after recovery (Fig. 3). The patterns discussed here are referred to as LH-types I–III. LH is

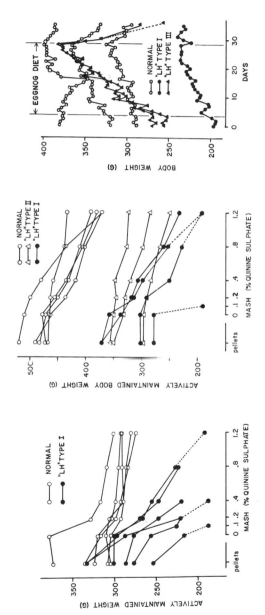

FIG. 3. *Left and center:* Dietary determination of the body weights defended against decreased caloric demands by individual Long-Evans rats. *Left:* Females. *Center:* Males. Rats were 12 to 18 months old when tested here, and 8 to 14 months postlesion if LH-lesioned. Not indicated is the difficulty a given rat experienced in adapting to the diets in successive steps, from left to right as indicated on the x-axis. LH-type I rats characteristically experienced great difficulty. Normal rats and LH-type II rats characteristically did not. *Right:* The exaggerated weight gain on egg nog diets that defined LH-type III rats. A LH-type I rat is also shown for comparison. Rats were female, Sprague-Dawley, 8 to 12 months old, with chronically implanted electrodes if LH-lesioned.

in quotes in Fig. 3 because the lesions were large and invaded the internal capsule and subthalamic regions, as well as the lateral hypothalamus. Histologic analysis is incomplete. That several neuronal systems may be involved in the LH syndrome is evident from the work of others in this volume.

The feature distinguishing LH-type I rats is that they defended body weight poorly against decreases in dietary palatability (Fig. 3, left and center). On a pelleted diet, the body weights of LH-type I rats were often, but not always, below preoperative weights or the weights of unlesioned controls. Transition from the pelleted diet to a powdered diet, and from this diet to quinine-adulterated diets, usually was accomplished with much difficulty. A month or more of trying, with and without cumulative severe losses of body weight, did not accomplish this for many rats. (The dotted lines in Fig. 3 indicate failures to adapt, with and without body weight losses to the extent indicated.)

If body weights did stabilize on any given diet, then these weights were defended against increases during periods of intragastric intubation of an untasted liquid diet. Thus the finickiness of LH-type I rats represented not a failure to control body weight, but an exaggerated control by dietary quality over the body weight maintained in the face of decreased caloric demands. However, these rats were fragile in addition; they adjusted to new diets with difficulty and only slowly recovered voluntary caloric intake to levels adequate to maintain body weight when intragastric intubations were terminated. The finickiness seemed unidirectional, since LH-type I rats did not gain more weight than normal rats when palatable eggnog diets replaced the pelleted diet (Fig. 3).

LH-type II rats maintained body weights on pellets or plain mash that were below both preoperative weights and the body weights of unoperated controls. In contrast to LH-type I rats, the body weights of LH-type II rats decreased only by amounts comparable to control rats upon adulteration of the diet (Fig. 3, center). These weights were defended against intragastric intubations and increased only by amounts comparable to control rats on exposure to eggnog diets.

The pattern of body weight control by LH-type II rats after recovery confirms Powley and Keesey (80) and Keesey and Boyle (9), who found that LH lesions decreased body weight without increasing finickiness. However, although weight reduction was an integral part of the syndrome of LH-type II rats, simple loss of weight did not explain the pattern of recovery from the syndrome, as it did for Powley and Keesey's (8) rats. Many of these rats were maintained by intubation for weeks or even months at body weights subsequently found to be lower than the weights the rats maintained after recovering voluntary food intake. Furthermore the body weights at which rats first accepted palatable diets were not greater than the body weights subsequently maintained on pellets after recovery. I emphasize that the present lesions were not confined to the lateral hypothalamus. The lesions made by Powley and Keesey (8) were more discrete and more medial.

Unlike LH-type I and II rats, but like VMH-lesioned rats, LH-type III rats after recovery greatly increased body weights upon exposure to eggnog diets (Fig. 3, right). When pellets and water replaced the eggnog, LH-type III rats either failed to adjust and died, or lost most of the gained weight before stabilizing. The behavior of LH-type III rats on quinine-adulterated diets was not assessed.

DEFINITIONS OF DEFENSE OF BODY WEIGHT (HUNGER FOR CALORIES)

1. The stable body weight reached when a specified diet has been available on a specified regimen is defended against changed caloric demands. Definitions of hunger cannot be made by reference to energy deficits or caloric balance unless the diet and dietary regimen are specified. For the present, this definition assumes that intragastric intubation of untasted diet can be treated as simply decreasing caloric requirements, and cold stress as simply increasing caloric requirements. Caloric density and cold may be shown on finer analysis to affect body weight as well.

With the possible exception of LH-type III, the hypothalamic lesions described in the previous sections did not degrade or enhance the defense of body weight by Definition 1 (Table 1). Definition 1 corresponds to how well-plotted points in Figs. 1 and 3 predict body weight on any given day, given the diet as specified, but allowing caloric demands to vary at will. Poor defense by Definition 1 will mean that the point as plotted will represent only a sample from a range of weights on that diet.

2. Body weight is defended against changes in diet and dietary regimen. Implicit in Definition 2 is that voluntary caloric intake tends to remain the same despite changes in diet and dietary regimen, so long as caloric demands remain constant; this is hunger definition 2. Definition 2 describes the control by dietary quality of body weights defended in the sense of Definition 1. Thus Definition 2 corresponds to the slopes of the curves of body weight plotted against dietary quality in Figs. 1 and 3. The steeper the slope, the poorer the defense of body weight (definition 2).

The body weights of LH-type II rats are well below those of normal rats for all diets; but since these body weights are no more affected by changes in dietary quality than are the body weights of normal rats, LH-type II rats

TABLE 1. *Changes in the defenses of body weight following hypothalamic lesions*

| Definition of defense | Lesions | | | |
	VMH	LH-type I	LH-type II	LH-type III
Against changed caloric demands	none	none	none	decrease?
Against changed diet	decrease	decrease	none	decrease
Normal weight on normal diet	increase	decrease or none	decrease	decrease?

are not deficient in defending body weight by definition 2. On the other hand, the body weights of VMH-lesioned and LH-type I rats change drastically as a result of changes in dietary regimen, so these rats are deficient by Definition 2 (Table 1).

3. A diet of sufficient quality for maintaining normal body weight is sought when body weight is less than normal. Definition 3 does not refer directly to defense of body weight by altering ingestion; since dietary quality determines the actively maintained body weight, the animal must first seek for diets under which normal body weight can be achieved. The dual considerations of a normal weight and of seeking a normal diet, yield hunger definition 3.

This peculiar definition is based on several features of the results previously described. First, normal rats defending (Definition 1) a lean body weight on a poor dietary regimen appeared hungry. They did not appear hungry by the same criteria when defending normal weight on plain mash or on pellets. Second, LH-type II rats exhibited decreased maintained body weights over all diets without the increased importance of dietary quality for determining body weights seen in LH-type I or VMH-lesioned rats. Thus, the normal weight of LH-type II rats seems to have been decreased. Third, increased importance of the dietary regimen for determining the maintained body weight resulted in obesity on exposure to palatable diets for VMH-lesioned rats, but not for LH-type I rats. It seems that normal body weight was increased for VMH-lesioned rats, but not for LH-type I rats. A summary of how the three definitions of body weight may apply to behavioral changes produced by VMH or LH lesions is provided in Table 1.

Since Definition 3 must imply a normal diet, if it is to specify a normal body weight, Definition 3 probably corresponds to the body weight on pellets in Figs. 1 and 3, and would be the y intercept of the curve whose slope is described by Definition 2 and whose stability is described by Definition 1. These definitions specify the extent to which rats are motivated to be leaner when the fare is poor, motivated to find better fare when lean (even when underutilizing the available food source), and motivated to be fatter when the fare is good.

The definitions above describe the weekly or monthly food consumption of adult rats. What other considerations are relevant for encompassing growing rats is unknown. To describe the actual food intake of adult rats, one must recognize that rats (and humans) take food in meals and thus are only intermittently hungry. Mechanisms determining meal-taking will be incorporated in the model in the next section.

SET POINT(S) AND CONTROL THEORY MODELS

The concepts of defended body weight elaborated in hunger Definitions 1 and 2, and even the normal body weight in Definition 3, were not equated with the set point for body weight. To make clear why this was so requires describing the kind of control system to which the concept of set point makes analogy. A generalized control system with a fixed set point is diagrammed in Fig. 4. The comparison between the set-point signal and the feedback signal gives an error signal. The error signal is translated by the controller into an output for driving the controlled system. After combination with the reference value signal, this output is now the output of the controlling system and is called the output-forcing function. When the controlled system operates against the load assumed by the reference value, the steady-state feedback signal will exactly equal the set-point signal. For all other loads, the system will stabilize at values of the feedback signal that differ from the set-point signal, and the error signal and output-forcing function will fluctuate about some value other than zero.

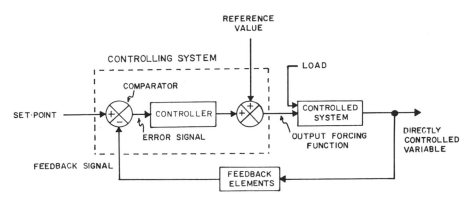

FIG. 4. A control system with a fixed set point and reference value.

This generalized system may be translated into a system controlling body weight (Fig. 5). In this translation, the output of the controlled system is voluntary caloric intake (the directly controlled variable), which is accomplished through specific activities of ingestion (the indirectly controlled variable). The first key feature of the model is that feedback from adipose tissue mass is assumed to exist in parallel to postingestional feedback signals (GI distension, GI hormones, and duodenal or portal metabolites) determining meal patterns. Since taste and reinforcement density determine the body weight defended against changed caloric requirements, there seems no way to avoid the addition of feedback from adipose tissue to any model of long-term controls over caloric intake. Hervey's (10) experiments on parabiotic rats provided one reason for postulating that this lipostatic feedback is hormonal, although cumulative effects of a hormonal signal terminating meals could also explain Hervey's results.

The second key feature of the model is that taste and reinforcement density are treated as loads on the controlled system. For reasons already discussed, these are not loads in the intuitive sense of physically restricting the amounts rats can ingest, so that increased ingestion is impossible. Increased ingestion

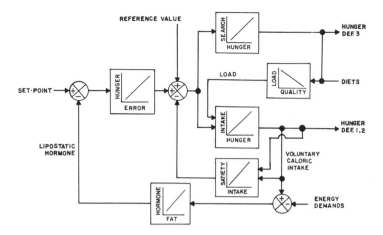

A FIXED SET-POINT MODEL OF BODY WEIGHT CONTROL

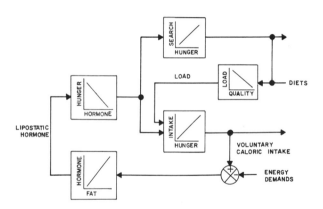

BODY WEIGHT CONTROL WITHOUT SET-POINT

FIG. 5. Hypothetical regulators for controlling body weight in adult rats by controlling caloric intake, with (above) and without (below) a set point for body weight. Above: Hunger definitions shown at the points where measurements are taken to infer them. Below: Analysis is exactly the same. Voluntary caloric intake represents hunger definition 1 when the diet is fixed and energy demands are varied and hunger definition 2 when energy demands are fixed and the diet varied. The transfer functions drawn should be taken to indicate only that the functions are monotonic in the direction indicated. Feedback both from caloric intake and other postingestional consequences determining the size and timing of individual meals is included as postingestional satiety in the model with set point. This feedback is omitted from the model without set point for reasons of simplicity and clarity only.

was possible, when cold ambient temperatures demanded it to maintain body weight. Hence taste *per se* and reinforcement density *per se* are the loads. Caloric requirements are shown subtracted elsewhere.

The alternative to treating taste and reinforcement density as loads applied to a fixed set-point system for controlling body weight is to assume that taste and reinforcement density change the set point for body weight directly. A variable set-point conceptualization for controls over body weight has the intuitive value of maintaining an identity of defended body weight (at least by one definition) with set point. However, this advantage is negated by the many advantages of the alternative in Fig. 5. Four of these advantages are discussed below.

Advantage 1

When a load is applied to the controlled system, there is a steady-state error signal and a steady-state value of the output-forcing function, neither of which is zero. In the model in Fig. 5, changed caloric requirements are assumed not to change the load, and voluntary caloric intake varies with the lipostatic feedback signal to maintain a stable body weight, although with a constant error that depends on the load. Hence, when the dietary regimen (the load) is fixed and caloric demands vary, voluntary caloric intake corresponds directly to hunger definition 1.

One evidence for hunger definition 3 was that rats appeared hungry while defending stable lean body weights against changed caloric requirements, when eating adulterated or poorly accessible diets. The worse the diet, the less the rats weighed, and the hungrier they appeared. Thus hunger definition 3 parallels the steady-state values of the error signal and output-forcing function. In Fig. 5, hunger definition 3 is shown as inferred from the activity of a search mechanism in parallel to the mechanism determining caloric intake. The object of the search mechanism is reducing the load on the caloric intake mechanism (so that normal body weight may be attained). Since no load is assumed to act on the search mechanism, its activity corresponds to the value of the output-forcing function.

In a variable set-point model, taste and reinforcement density are assumed to modify the set-point of the system, and there is no simple schematic correlate distinguishing hunger definition 3 from hunger definition 1. The treatment of taste and reinforcement density as loads on the controlled system provides this distinction.

Advantage 2

How well a closed-loop regulatory control system does its job can be described by the concept of minification. If loads change the steady-state value of the feedback signal greatly, then the system regulates poorly. Conversely, if approximately the same value of the feedback signal is maintained over many values of the load, the system regulates well. In effect minification describes the slope of a plot of steady-state error against the load, which is equivalent to hunger definition 2. Hunger definition 2 is inferred from voluntary caloric intake and stable body weight when diet (the load) is changed and energy demands remain constant. The behavior of LH-type I rats (Fig. 3)

seems consistent with a circuit for controlling body weight with poor minification.

In a variable set-point model, taste and reinforcement density are assumed
to change the set point of the system for controlling body weight, and an
equation of hunger definition 2 with minification would not apply.

Advantage 3

The reference value defines the load condition under which body weight
will be equal to the set point for body weight. If the load applied by dietary
quality to the system is somehow less than that reference value, the system
will actively maintain body weights greater than set point, which seems to
reflect what is meant by dietary obesity (2). Defense of dietary obesity
against changed caloric requirements has not been demonstrated, but would
be predicted by the model in Fig. 5. Similarly VMH-lesioned rats could become fat either because their set points for body weight have been raised or
because the reference value has been increased so that on normal diets body
weights greater than set point will be maintained. In support of the latter possibility, VMH-lesioned rats feeding themselves intragastrically did not become markedly obese unless palatable (but nonnutritive) taste cues were
provided (11). Conversely, by this model LH-type II rats may have either
lowered set points for body weight, or decreased reference values so that on
normal diets body weights less than the set point will be maintained.

Normal body weight is determined both by the set point and by the reference value. VMH lesions produce direct hormonal changes (12, 13) and
increased meal sizes (6). These changes cannot cause obesity in VMH-
lesioned rats, since under appropriate dietary conditions VMH-lesioned rats
defend a lean body weight perfectly well against changed caloric requirements
(Figs. 1 and 2), and so do not lack some essential control over food intake.
However, these changes could represent what is meant by changes in the
reference value or in the set point.

A reference value is not important for a variable set-point model, where
taste and reinforcement density are not treated as loads.

Advantage 4

LH (14) and nigrostriatal (15) lesions cause sensorimotor dysfunctions,
recovery from which parallels recovery from aphagia. Marshall and Teitelbaum (14, 15) mean by sensorimotor dysfunctions something more than
reflexive adjustment and different from unmotivated in the sense of totally
lacking motivation. In fact indices of hunger can be dissociated from caloric
intake in LH-lesioned rats. For instance I have observed that many such rats
are often more active, the lower is the body weight maintained by intubation
during Stages I and II of recovery. The model in Fig. 5 makes clear that

such a statement does not deny that there is an impaired motivation for food in LH-lesioned rats: hunger definitions 1 and 2 can be distinguished from hunger definition 3. Hunger definitions 1 and 2 reflect the motivation to consume the particular diets available. The importance of taste and availability in the food intake of LH-lesioned rats during recovery is well known (16). The treating of taste and reinforcement as loads applied to the system translating hunger to caloric intake seems particularly appropriate for incorporating both the enhanced importance of dietary regimen and the sensorimotor dysfunctions following LH lesions into a single mechanism.

CONCLUSIONS

A fixed set-point model of the control of caloric intake and body weight incorporates the various definitions of the hunger for calories and the various meanings of defense of body weight that these definitions serve, and many of the effects of VMH and LH lesions in addition. Elaboration of the model makes clear that every change in stable body weight need not imply a change in the set point for body weight. A control system with fixed set point is stable at many values of the feedback signal, depending on the load and/or reference value.

The fact that defense of body weight cannot be equated with the set point for body weight in models like this removes a good deal of the utility of the set-point concept for explaining results of brain and other manipulations. The concept of set point applied to body weight does allow ease of discussion, but is not demanded by the evidence. Figure 5 diagrams a regulatory circuit without set point, which also will actively maintain stable body weights at various values depending on the load. The transfer functions between hunger, caloric intake, and the lipostatic feedback determine the stable operating values of the system. Dietary obesity and the effects of LH and VMH lesions would be incorporated by discussing transfer functions directly. This may be preferred by those who rebel at the thought of the defense of body weights greater than or less than set point.

The strictly analogical nature of the models in Fig. 5 should be stressed. They have not been mathematically modeled. Furthermore, a general criticism of them is that they do not translate readily into known neuronal pathways. But they are not meant to as yet. To date brain manipulations have provided inadequate evidence for assigning functions to structures. First, many effects of brain manipulations (especially lesions) may depend on peripheral consequences secondary to them. For instance, the prandial drinking characteristic of recovered LH-lesioned rats depends on functional desalivation that accompanied the lesions (17). Second, functions cannot be assigned to neuronal pathways with confidence, if the functions spoken of provide inadequate descriptions of behavior. For instance, I have tried to present evidence in this paper that the unqualified use of the construct hunger is inadequate. Several such constructs, previously confounded, must be distinguished. Presumably these distinctions represent separable brain mechanisms. Third, when lesions are made, the behavior that results is a property of the rest of the organism. One cannot infer the function of a brain region from the inabilities of the organism lacking that region. In terms of an example already mentioned, the function of the lateral hypothalamus is not to inhibit prandial drinking. In this sense, models not referring directly to brain mechanisms may actually help in avoiding pitfalls of the premature assigning of specific functions to specific neural substrates.

CLINICAL IMPLICATIONS

There is space to indicate only one possible clinical implication. This implication takes the analogy between situational determinants of body weight for humans and for rats literally. Such determinants may not be so restricted in humans.

Nisbett (18) predicted the failure of psychological treatment programs for obesity, starting from Schachter's (19) analogy between obese humans and VMH-lesioned rats. Nisbett's (17) analysis assumed a single defended body weight, equated with set point, which individuals would try to attain no matter what the diet. In the present analysis, what body weight is defended is under the systematic control of the external environment. Thus programs for treating obesity now conceptualized in terms of operant conditioning (e.g., ref. 20) could succeed in fact because these programs make food preparation and ingestion tedious by removing social reinforcements from eating. That behavioral modification programs are effective for some obese patients, but that the majority of patients drop out is predictable, since both normal and VMH-lesioned rats defending lean body weights nevertheless appeared hungry (definition 3). But what body weight is sought (hunger definition 3) may be a product of developmental history as well as of genotype. If so, culturally selected meal patterns and foods, and perhaps activity (21), may contribute to the selection and prevention of obesity. The lack of novelty of these conclusions should not prevent serious consideration of them.

ACKNOWLEDGMENTS

The author's research was supported by the University Research Committee, University of Utah, and by U.S. Public Health Service Biomedical Sciences Support grant RR07092 to the University of Utah. Some of this research had origin in experiments done for other reasons at the suggestion of Alan N. Epstein, during the author's tenure as U.S. Public Health Service postdoctoral fellow MH 24,556 at the University of Pennsylvania, and supported by grant NDS 03469 to A. N. Epstein. I am grateful for this opportunity to acknowledge my debt to A. N. Epstein.

REFERENCES

1. Corbit, J. D., and Stellar, E. (1964): *J. Comp. Physiol. Psychol.*, 58:63–67.
2. Maller, O. (1964): *Life Sci.*, 3:1281–1291.
3. Adolph, E. F. (1947): *Am J. Physiol.*, 151:110–125.
4. Kennedy, G. C. (1950): *Proc. Roy. Soc. [Biol.]*, 137:535–549.
5. Hoebel, B. G., and Teitelbaum, P. (1966): *J. Comp. Physiol. Psychol.*, 61:189–193.
6. Thomas, D. W., and Mayer, J. (1968): *J. Comp. Physiol. Psychol.*, 66:642–653.
7. Miller, N. E., Bailey, C. J., and Stevenson, J. A. F. (1950): *Science*, 112:256–259.
8. Powley, T. L., and Keesey, R. E. (1970): *J. Comp. Physiol. Psychol.*, 70:25–36.
9. Keesey, R. E., and Boyle, P. C. (1973): *J. Comp. Physiol. Psychol.*, 84:38–46.
10. Hervey, G. R. (1959): *J. Physiol. (Lond.)*, 145:336–351.
11. McGinty, D., Epstein, A. N., and Teitelbaum, P. (1965): *Anim. Behav.*, 13:413–418.
12. Powley, T. L., and Opsahl, C. A. (1974): *Am. J. Physiol.*, 226:25–33.
13. Woods, S. C., Decke, E., and Vasselli, J. R. (1974): *Psychol. Rev.*, 81:26–43.
14. Marshall, J. F., and Teitelbaum, P. (1974): *J. Comp. Physiol. Psychol.*, 86:375–395.
15. Marshall, J. F., Richardson, J. S., and Teitelbaum, P. (1974): *J. Comp. Physiol. Psychol.*, 87:808–830.
16. Teitelbaum, P., and Epstein, A. N. (1962): *Psychol. Rev.*, 69:74–90.
17. Epstein, A. N. (1971): *Prog. Physiol. Psychol.*, 4:263–317.
18. Nisbett, R. E. (1972): *Psychol. Rev.*, 79:433–453.
19. Schachter, S. (1971): *Am. Psychol.*, 26:129–144.
20. Stuart, R. B., and Davis, B. (1972): *Slim Chance in a Fat World*. Research Press, Champaign, Ill.
21. Mayer, J., Marshall, N. B., Vitale, J. J., Christensen, J. H., Mashayekhi, M. B., and Stare, F. J. (1954): *Am. J. Physiol.*, 177:544–548.
22. Quartermain, D., Kissileff, H., Shapiro, R., and Miller, N. E. (1971): *Science*, 173:941–943.
23. Mayer, J. (1953): *Physiol. Rev.*, 33:472–508.

Hunger: Basic Mechanisms and Clinical Implications,
edited by D. Novin, W. Wyrwicka, and G. Bray.
Raven Press, New York © 1976.

Autonomic Components of the Hypothalamic Feeding Syndromes

Terry L. Powley and Charles A. Opsahl

Department of Psychology, Yale University, New Haven, Connecticut 06520

The hypothalamus is generally characterized as the area preeminently involved in the integration of autonomic, endocrine, and somatic responses. It can be viewed as the neural area which simultaneously performs autonomic, endocrine, and somatic regulatory adjustments (15). Destruction or stimulation of different hypothalamic regions almost invariably produces complex changes in all three of these systems. However, in spite of the widespread recognition of the integrated nature of hypothalamic responses, the various feeding perturbations produced by hypothalamic lesions and stimulation have been discussed largely in terms of somatic or behavioral disturbances. Autonomic and endocrine adjustments that might represent concomitant or even mediating mechanisms have been far less completely studied.

Even with this relative lack of attention, a variety of studies do suggest that the autonomic nervous system may play a central role in the metabolic and hormonal adjustments associated with the ventromedial hypothalamic (VMH) syndrome, the lateral hypothalamic (LH) syndrome, and LH stimulation-induced feeding. First, numerous studies have shown that neither preventing changes in feeding by experimentally controlling food intake nor eliminating pituitary influences by hypophysectomy abolishes the metabolic and endocrine adjustments characteristic of the ventromedial hypothalamic syndrome (e.g., refs. 9, 10, 11). Second, a variety of metabolic and visceral adjustments produced by hypothalamic manipulation are eliminated by sectioning appropriate sympathetic and parasympathetic nerves (e.g., ref. 24). In particular, several experiments suggest that the vagus nerve may play a central role in such hormonal and metabolic adjustments. For example, Booth et al. (4) have shown that stimulation through LH electrodes, which will produce feeding, also produces a biphasic hyperglycemia, part of which is eliminated by vagotomy. (The other component of the glycemic function is eliminated by removing the sympathetic adrenal medulla.) LH stimulation that induces feeding also produces changes in gastric motor activity (8), and this hypothalamic influence on gastric activity is eliminated by vagotomy (7). The increased gastric acid secretion elicited from the LH by 2-deoxy-D-glucose (2-DG) or by electrical stimulation is also abolished by vagotomy (5, 14). Evidence also indicates that afferent information concerning gastric distension that modulates VMH activity is carried by the vagus nerve (1). Finally the vagus modulates the splanchnic nerve afferent activity projected to the LH (25).

In view of this evidence, suggesting that the various hypothalamic syndromes may have autonomic components, we have examined the role of the vagus nerve in various hypothalamic feeding disturbances. Our experiments indicate that the obesity and related physiological disturbances associated with VMH lesions and the feeding induced by stimulation of the perifornical LH are dramatically altered, even eliminated, by vagotomy. In addition lowered gastric acid secretion produced by LH lesions is returned to control levels by vagotomy, whereas the lowered body weight set point characteristic of the LH syndrome is further reduced by vagotomy.

VMH OBESITY AND VAGOTOMY

In an earlier study, we reported that subdiaphragmatic vagotomy eliminated the obesity induced by VMH lesions (21). In that study, male albino rats were first made obese with bilateral electrolytic lesions (1 mA for 12 sec) of the VMH area. Forty days postlesion some of the VMH-lesioned animals and some of the nonlesioned control animals were bilaterally vagotomized by removing a section of the vagus on either side of the esophagus immediately below the diaphragm. At the termination of the experiment, as in all the experiments reported here, completeness of the vagotomy procedure was assessed by comparing stomach secretion of hydrochloric acid at rest and during periods of electrical stimulation of the cervical vagus. (Details of the surgical and test procedures can be found in refs. 19 and 21.)

The basic results are reproduced in Fig. 1. Complete bilateral vagotomy reversed the VMH lesion-induced obesity and lowered body weights of VMH animals to vagotomized control levels. Vagotomy also reduced the basal hypersecretion of gastric acid characteristic of VMH rats to the level of non-lesioned controls with vagotomies. In addition, when the animals in this experiment were maintained on a high-fat diet, the consumption data suggested that VMH finickiness, as defined by overconsumption of a high-fat diet, was spared by vagotomy.

In another recent study, we have extended these results by examining the effect of vagotomy on female rats with VMH lesions (22). In this case, female rats were first lesioned in the VMH area or sham operated. After 42 days animals were then subjected to either vagotomy or sham vagotomy. The results of this experiment indicate that VMH obesity is also eliminated in female rats by vagotomy. The weight gain characteristic of the VMH syndrome remained abolished when all the animals were maintained for 8 weeks on an eggnog diet used to maximize palatability and minimize the problems of reduced gastrointestinal motility (one of the consequences of vagotomy). Once again, finickiness, defined this time as overconsumption of eggnog,

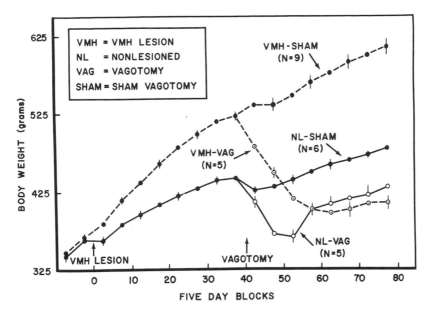

FIG. 1. Mean body weights (g ± SEM) of male rats receiving VMH lesions (or nonlesioned) on day 0 and subdiaphragmatic vagotomy (or sham vagotomy) on day 40.

was observed in the lesioned animals with vagotomies as well as in the lesioned animals with sham vagotomies.

One of the major questions these experiments raise regards the specificity of the effect of vagotomy. Vagotomy clearly reduces gastrointestinal motility and stomach emptying time as well as basal levels of a variety of gastrointestinal hormones and enzymes (12). Given these considerations, it is conceivable that subdiaphragmatic vagotomy has its effect by introducing a rate-limiting step in the animal's ability to digest foodstuffs or pass food through its digestive tract. Several control experiments that we have performed suggest, however, that vagotomy does not produce a general debilitation severe enough to restrict all weight gains or all obesities. That is to say, the effect of subdiaphragmatic vagotomy upon the VMH syndrome appears to be selective.

In one experiment that was addressed to this question, we found another rodent obesity, that of the genetically obese Zucker fatty rat, was spared by vagotomy (19). Male and female fatty rats lost no greater a percentage of their weight following subdiaphragmatic vagotomy performed at 150 days of age than did nonobese siblings. Inspection of gastrointestinal tract contents indicated that the obese Zucker rats with vagotomy had the typical increase in stomach contents usually associated with this operation. Clearly, then, the fatty rat is able to support elevated weight levels and food intake in the face of the general reduction in gastrointestinal motility.

In another experiment we have examined whether the weight increase produced by ovariectomy is eliminated by vagotomy (22). In this experiment female rats were first ovariectomized and then subsequently subjected to our usual vagotomy procedure. The weight gain and adiposity induced by castration were spared by vagotomy. (In other groups of animals that had received VMH lesions or ovariectomy plus VMH lesions in this study, vagotomy again eliminated the weight increases produced by the VMH lesions.) The finding that the body weight increase due to ovariectomy is spared by vagotomy suggests, too, that the effect of vagotomy on VMH obesity cannot be attributed to a general limitation of the processing of foodstuffs that affects all weight gains or obesities in the same nonspecific way.

We have more recently examined this issue of specificity in another way. To convince ourselves that the effect of vagotomy on VMH obesity was not due to a ceiling, dictated by reduced motility, in the amount of foodstuffs that animals could ingest, we performed an experiment using bulk dilutions of a wet mash diet. (Note: if this "ceiling" explanation were correct, then the vagotomized animals maintained on the calorically dense high-fat and egg-nog diets should have been able to support substantially higher weight levels than they did.) For this dilution experiment, we maintained separate groups of male rats with VMH lesions, VMH lesions plus bilateral subdiaphragmatic vagotomies, sham lesions, or sham lesions plus bilateral subdiaphragmatic vagotomies on our basic wet mash diet. This diet consists of 30% dry ground Purina chow and 70% water by weight. After 2 weeks, we diluted this diet by adulterating the dry ground chow portion with 10% cellulose by weight. After 2 weeks at this 10% dilution, we increased the dilution to 20% of the dry weight for 2 weeks and then to 30% of the dry weight for 2 more weeks. All animals, including those vagotomized, exhibited compensatory increases in food intake. For the 2 weeks at the 30% dilution in the diet, the two groups with vagotomy took 137% more food than they had taken when maintained on unadulterated mash. (Perfect compensation would have been

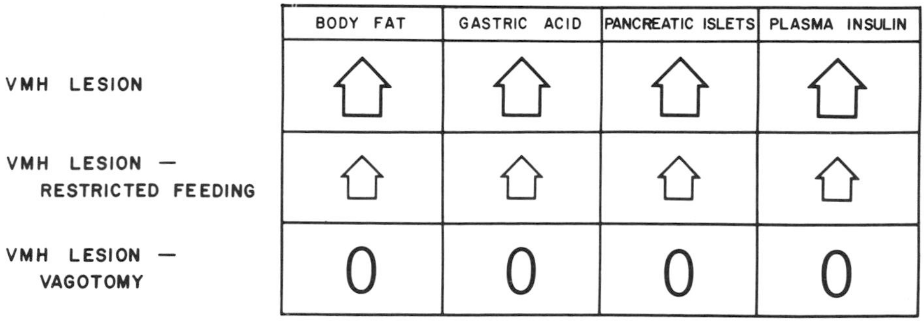

	BODY FAT	GASTRIC ACID	PANCREATIC ISLETS	PLASMA INSULIN
VMH LESION	⇧	⇧	⇧	⇧
VMH LESION — RESTRICTED FEEDING	⇧	⇧	⇧	⇧
VMH LESION — VAGOTOMY	0	0	0	0

FIG. 2. Comparison of the effects of restricted feeding and subdiaphragmatic vagotomy on several physiological parameters associated with the VMH syndrome. Arrows, increase in the parameter as compared to nonlesioned control values; relative size of arrows indicates relative magnitude of increase. Zeros, value of the parameter does not differ from that of nonlesioned controls.

a 130% increase in overall wet mash intake.) These results rather strongly argue that the VMH-lesioned rats with vagotomy eat less bulk than they are capable of processing after vagotomy and hence that they may be actively regulating their weights at normal levels.

In these several experiments examining the role of the vagus nerve in the VMH syndrome, we have made another type of observation that bears on the question of specificity. Previous research has shown that limiting food intake of VMH-lesioned rats by restricted feeding, pair feeding, or intubation reduces but does not eliminate the increases in body fat (9), gastric acid secretion (23), pancreatic islet mass (11), and plasma insulin levels (10) characteristic of the VMH syndrome. These observations are summarized in the first two rows of Fig. 2. These findings can be interpreted to mean that the lesion-induced increase in each of these parameters is not secondary to overeating but rather may reflect part of the primary disturbance of the VMH syndrome. Each of these disturbances could, in fact, be explained as a lesion-

TABLE 1. Mean values[a] for the carcass lipid content, fasting gastric acid secretion, pancreatic islet size, and plasma insulin levels in rats with VMH lesions (or nonlesioned) and subdiaphragmatic vagotomy (or sham operation)

Group	Body fat (g $\pm$ SEM)	Gastric acid (μEq H$^+$/ 30 min $\pm$ SEM)	Pancreatic islets (mm^2 $\pm$ SEM)	Plasma insulin (μU/ml $\pm$ SEM)
VMH lesion				
Sham vagotomy	193.10 $\pm$ 8.80	13.12 $\pm$ 3.10	9.83 $\pm$ 1.51	66.44 $\pm$ 10.21
Vagotomy	78.60 $\pm$ 23.16	2.59 $\pm$ 0.81	4.48 $\pm$ 0.91	19.33 $\pm$ 4.00
Nonlesioned				
Sham vagotomy	126.60 $\pm$ 16.06	6.73 $\pm$ 2.20	5.19 $\pm$ 0.75	31.50 $\pm$ 4.70
Vagotomy	72.80	3.86 $\pm$ 1.00	4.40 $\pm$ 0.50	10.0

Body lipid content was determined by measuring the number of grams of ether-extractable fat in the decapitated carcass. Fasting gastric acidity was measured under pentobarbital anesthesia by saline perfusion through a duodenal catheter. Pancreatic islet size was estimated by determining the total islet area of 6-μm sections of tissue sampled at 312-μm intervals through the pancreas. Plasma insulin levels were measured with an immunoreactive insulin assay after a 24-hr fast.

[a] $\pm$SEM.

induced alteration of vagal tone. At any rate, as summarized in Fig. 2, we have found in our experiments that vagotomy, unlike restricted feeding, eliminates the increases in each of these parameters: body fat (22), gastric acid (21), pancreatic islet mass (18), and plasma insulin levels (22). The actual values obtained in these experiments are presented in Table 1. These observations suggest again that the effect of vagotomy is not merely equivalent to surgically restricting the lesioned animals' food intake.[1]

---

[1] It is, of course, possible that the differences between restricted feeding and vagotomy are only ones of degree and not ones of kind. In this vein, Slaunwhite et al. (27) have found that severe food restriction, which prevents a VMH-lesioned animal from even maintaining its weight, eliminates the increase in several metabolic and hormonal parameters.

STIMULATION-INDUCED FEEDING AND VAGOTOMY

Stimulus-bound or stimulation-induced (28) feeding is, of course, another major experimental feeding syndrome associated with hypothalamic manipulation. Ball (3) has reported that feeding elicited by lateral hypothalamic stimulation is "markedly" inhibited by vagotomy. We have recently examined this effect (20). Male and female rats were implanted at 125 days of age with a single indwelling bipolar electrode (Plastic Products, Roanoke, Virginia) aimed for the perifornical LH. After a minimum of 1 week for recovery from surgery, all animals were tested for the reliable display of stimulation-induced behaviors. The test stimulus was a 30-sec train of 0.2-msec biphasic pulses at 50 Hz provided by a Grass S48B stimulator with an isolation unit. Voltage could be continuously varied between 0 and 61 V. For testing purposes, animals were placed in a test chamber that had fresh wood blocks, water, and wet mash made with Purina chow continuously available. All three of these test stimuli were also continuously available in the home cage throughout the experiment. Those animals that were reliable stimulation-induced feeders (eating wet mash) and those that were reliable stimulation-induced gnawers (gnawing wood blocks) were selected for the experiment. All such animals were then given a minimum of three training sessions of exposure to the threshold procedure for induced behaviors and three sessions of self-stimulation testing. Thresholds for eliciting the test behavior were determined on odd days for each animal using a method-of-limits procedure. On even days, rate of self-stimulation at a fixed voltage at the same electrode was determined for each animal. For the self-stimulation tests, animals were placed in a second test chamber equipped with a bar that delivered 0.5-sec trains of current. Food, water, and wood blocks were not available during these tests. After completing the training procedures, prevagotomy behavioral thresholds and self-stimulation rates were determined for each animal over a 6-day period. All animals were then subjected to subdiaphragmatic vagotomy or to a sham operation and returned to their cages to recover for 1 month. After the recovery period, each animal was again retested to determine the threshold for the stimulation-induced behavior and the rate of self-stimulation. In the case of the behavioral threshold tests, voltage levels were increased until a behavior was displayed or until agitation incompatible with organized behavior occurred.

The basic results are summarized in Fig. 3. For the vagotomized animals, individual animal data are indicated with broken lines. Vagotomy clearly had a severely disruptive effect upon stimulation-induced feeding. In four of the seven vagotomized animals, feeding to stimulation was eliminated by vagotomy. In two of the four animals where feeding was abolished, only agitation could be elicited after vagotomy. In the other two animals where feeding was eliminated, only gnawing could be elicited after vagotomy. In contrast three of the animals continued to display reliable stimulation-induced feeding following vagotomy.

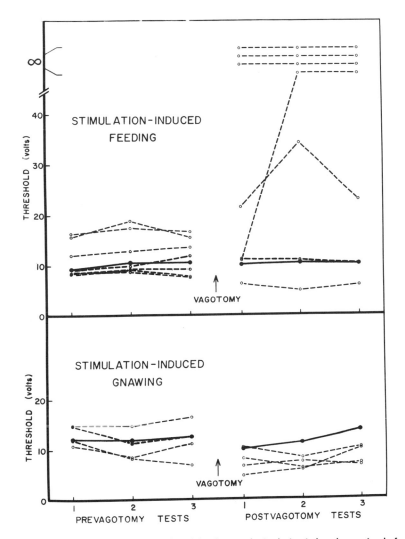

FIG. 3. Thresholds (volts) for stimulation-induced feeding and stimulation-induced gnawing before and after vagotomy. Solid lines with stippled surrounding areas, mean thresholds (± SEM) for grouped non-vagotomized control animals; dashed lines with open circles, thresholds for individual vagotomized animals; infinity symbol, no feeding behavior could be elicited.

These results require some caution in their interpretation. Grouping these data for vagotomized animals indicates a dramatic overall effect of vagotomy on stimulation-induced feeding behavior and summarizes the basic conclusion of the present experiment. Still it is necessary to recognize that this conclusion may underestimate the importance of the role of the vagus in stimulation-induced feeding. Grouping the data of the vagotomized animals would fail to indicate that in the present experiment vagotomized feeders apparently fall into two discrete groups, a group where feeding is eliminated and a group where feeding is intact although possibly elevated. This pattern is similar to that obtained by Ball, in which two of his five vagotomized animals ceased to feed in response to stimulation, whereas the other three responded at some threshold value (3). If this apparent difference in response to vagotomy is produced by sampling two discrete populations, then it might be explained as due to two species of stimulation-induced feeding or to two species of vagotomy (or a combination of both). Since we know of no information that would really suggest such qualitative differences in stimulation-induced feeding but much information suggesting that there are qualitative differences in vagotomy, we currently favor the hypothesis that the different responses of stimulation-induced feeders to vagotomy may be caused by differences in the nature of the vagal interruption. In fact, this hypothesis receives some support from our histological analysis of the vagal trunks of the animals in this experiment.

Throughout the series of experiments summarized here, we have defined completeness of vagotomy on the basis of the stomach secretory response to direct electrical stimulation of the cervical vagus. Although this procedure is probably the best physiological test for our purposes (21), all the available criteria for completeness of vagotomy, including this test, still remain somewhat problematic (2, 16). Even if the secretory test was totally reliable, however, in the final analysis it can only inform one as to whether the vagal innervation of the gastric parietal cells is eliminated. Interruption of the vagal innervation of the pancreas, liver, gall bladder, bile duct, and stomach musculature as well as the afferent vagal supply will certainly be correlated with interruption of the efferents controlling parietal cell release of acid, but only correlated. There must inevitably be some errors of inclusion when a complete truncal vagotomy is assumed on the basis of a test that only establishes that the parietal cells are completely vagotomized. To the extent that the effect of vagotomy on a given feeding syndrome is caused by alteration of gastric secretion, the predictive power of the secretory test will be excellent. To the extent that other vagal systems are responsible for mediating an effect, say the elimination of stimulation-induced feeding, the predictive power of the secretory test will be less. This point is raised because a histological analysis of the vagus nerve trunks for the animals in the present experiment suggests that those animals that continued to feed after vagotomy had larger nerve trunks remaining. At the termination of the physiological test for completeness, we prepared all esophagi, with investing tissues in place, using a Bodian stain for unmyelinated nerve fibers. We then measured the cross-sectional area of each vagal trunk proximal to the stump and a fixed distance below the diaphragm. Using this measure, the three stimulation-induced feeders that still displayed feeding after vagotomy had the three largest vagal trunks in the vagotomized group. Assuming that there were two different groups of vagotomized animals, this outcome would occur only three times in 100 on the basis of chance (Mann-Whitney U). In a similar vein, Ball's data might be considered a conservative estimate of the role of the vagus in

TABLE 2. Mean self-stimulation rate[a] for vagotomized and sham-vagotomized rats in the stimulation-induced feeding and gnawing groups

	Prevagotomy tests			Postvagotomy tests		
	1	2	3	1	2	3
Feeders						
Sham vagotomy	44.90 ± 4.61	50.88 ± 6.76	55.28 ± 7.06	57.00 ± 7.68	56.52 ± 10.16	62.48 ± 10.91
Vagotomy	48.83 ± 7.65	45.55 ± 8.58	52.88 ± 9.70	65.13 ± 9.33	61.42 ± 8.70	65.55 ± 8.50
Gnawers						
Sham vagotomy	29.43 ± 5.87	24.73 ± 1.22	29.05 ± 7.53	31.03 ± 1.53	27.06 ± 9.57	29.45 ± 10.08
Vagotomy	39.08 ± 5.16	49.40 ± 8.91	51.23 ± 8.26	39.39 ± 5.88	84.88 ± 9.00	74.39 ± 11.10

[a] Bar presses/min ± SEM.

stimulation-induced feeding. Ball based his estimate of complete vagotomy only on visual inspection of the esophagus, a procedure that is generally found to be unreliable. Furthermore Ball only indicated that he "could not find any significant bundle of fibers" projecting to the stomach. It is conceivable that hepatic or pancreatic branches of the vagus or fascicles to the stomach rated insignificant might in fact explain the savings of the three animals with detectable thresholds for feeding following vagotomy. Thus, on the basis of both our work and that of Ball, it would appear that the integrity of the vagus is of considerable importance in the expression of stimulation-induced feeding. The conclusion is underscored by the fact that both of these experiments may, indeed, underestimate the role of the vagal system in this behavior.

As in the case of the VMH syndrome, a major question concerns the specific susceptibility of stimulation-induced feeding to vagotomy. Our results indicate that, as with VMH obesity, the effect of vagotomy on stimulation-induced feeding is specific. As can be seen in the bottom part of Fig. 3, the threshold for gnawing elicited from the same perifornical region is unaffected, or even slightly lowered, by vagotomy. Also suggesting that gnawing is spared by vagotomy, as noted above, some feeders when vagotomized actually switched to gnawing. In addition vagotomy had no detectable effect on the self-stimulation rate at the same electrode tip where feeding behavior was typically lost (see Table 2).

LH WEIGHT SET POINT AND VAGOTOMY

Since the integrity of the vagus nerve seems to be of great importance in the VMH obesity syndrome and in stimulation-induced feeding, we have also investigated its role in the LH lesion syndrome of body weight loss (17). Insofar as the LH syndrome is often thought of as the converse of VMH obesity we were interested in the weight-modifying effect of vagal section in rats regulating body weight at chronically lowered levels. In this experiment 80 male albino rats of the Sprague-Dawley strain were used. After 10 days of recording baseline body weights, approximately 50% of the animals were anesthetized and given bilateral electrolytic lesions of the LH (1 mA for 9 sec). The remaining animals were similarly anesthetized on day 0 but received no lesions. All lesioned rats were given (in addition to pellets and water) the wet mash diet consisting of 30% ground Purina chow and 70% tap water in order to insure adequate hydration. Lesioned rats which failed to lose a significant amount of weight because of poor electrode placement were deleted from the study after 20 days and the remaining LH-lesioned animals were matched according to body weight loss and assigned to vagotomy or sham vagotomy groups. Nonlesioned rats were also matched for body weight change and assigned to vagotomy or sham vagotomy groups. On day 30 postlesion, all animals were anesthetized and subdiaphragmatic vagotomies or sham operations were performed on the appropriate rats. The wet mash dietary supplement was given to all animals for 5 days postoperatively. Body weights were measured every other day for the next 2.5 months, and on day 105 the animals were anesthetized and prepared for the vagotomy completeness test. Basal levels of gastric acid secretion were measured for all rats, and vagotomy completeness tests were performed on vagotomized animals.

As shown in Fig. 4, LH lesions significantly lowered the level at which lesioned animals regulated their body weight ($p < 0.01$). LH-lesioned rats regulated their body weights at approximately 87% of nonlesioned controls. Vagotomy produced the typical reduction in nonlesioned animals' levels of weight regulation and a somewhat larger decrease in the level at which LH-lesioned rats regulated their body weight. These observations are reflected in the fact that not only was the effect of vagotomy on body weight significant ($p < 0.01$) but the interaction between vagotomy and LH lesion was also significant ($p < 0.01$). Nonlesioned vagotomized rats maintained their body weights at about 93% of the nonlesioned-sham vagotomy group, and LH-vagotomy rats regulated at approximately 82% of the LH-sham vagotomy group. Thus body weight levels of LH rats were more depressed by vagotomy than were body weight levels of nonlesioned animals. Rather than ameliorating or abolishing the body weight set point change produced by LH lesions, vagotomy apparently added to the observed weight loss.

Since changes in gastric acidity have been proposed to play a part in the

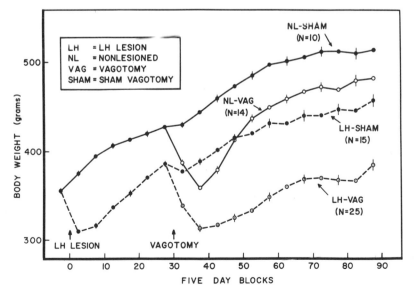

FIG. 4. Mean body weights (g ± SEM) of male rats receiving LH lesions (or nonlesioned) on bay 0 and subdiaphragmatic vagotomy (or sham vagotomy) on day 30.

etiology of VMH obesity (23), and since increases in this measure have been elicited by stimulation of the LH (5, 14), we measured baseline fasting acid levels in the present experiment as well (for procedure see 22). Animals with LH damage secreted significantly less gastric acid during the first baseline hour of vagotomy completeness testing than did nonlesioned rats ($p <$ 0.05). In addition, vagotomy tended to reverse this basal hyposecretion since LH-vagotomy animals (mean basal secretion = 5.16 μEqu H$^+$/30 min $\pm$ 0.59 SEM) secreted significantly more acid ($p < 0.05$) than did LH-sham vagotomy rats (mean basal secretion = 2.90 μEqu H$^+$/30 min $\pm$ 0.79 SEM). Neither the LH-vagotomy group nor the nonlesioned-vagotomy group (mean basal secretion = 5.99 μEqu H$^+$/30 min $\pm$ 0.79 SEM) differed significantly from the nonlesioned-sham vagotomy animals (mean basal secretion = 6.88 μEqu H$^+$/30 min $\pm$ 2.38 SEM). Thus, LH lesions appear to tonically reduce gastric acid secretion, a reduction that can be reversed by vagotomy. This result is certainly reminiscent of the gastric acid normalizing effect of vagotomy in the VMH preparation. The crucial difference, however, is that whereas both gastric acidity and the level of body weight regulation increase in VMH animals and both gastric acidity and level of body weight regulation decrease in LH-lesioned animals, vagotomy reverses both parameters in VMH obesity but only reverses the gastric acid response in the LH preparation. It appears, then, that some factor other than low levels of gastric secretion is responsible for the chronic reduction in the level of body weight regulation seen in the LH rat.

GENERAL DISCUSSION

The experiments reviewed here indicate that the obesity associated with VMH lesions and the feeding induced by LH stimulation are eliminated or, in the case of feeding, at least severely disrupted by subdiaphragmatic vagotomy. In addition the elevated levels of gastric acid secretion characteristic of the VMH syndrome and the reduced levels of gastric acid secretion produced by LH lesions are both reversed or normalized by vagotomy. The increases in body fat, pancreatic islet area, and plasma insulin levels associated with VMH lesions are also abolished by vagotomy. In contrast, the weight regulation alterations associated with LH lesions are aggravated by vagotomy. These several effects of vagotomy seem to be selective or specific in so far as the obesity of the Zucker rat, the weight gain produced by ovariectomy, and the gnawing induced by LH stimulation are not substantially affected by vagotomy. In the aggregate, these results suggest two different types of interpretation. On the one hand, they raise the possibility that alterations of vagal (or, more generally, autonomic) mechanisms may represent part of the physiological basis of the hypothalamic feeding syndromes. On the other hand, several components of the hypothalamic feeding syndromes may simply be particularly susceptible to the general disruptive consequences of vagotomy. Each of these possibilities will be briefly considered.

In the first view, the VMH syndrome might be due in part to lesion-induced changes in vagus nerve-mediated control over metabolism. We have recently reviewed some of the evidence consistent with such a hypothesis and discussed some of the possible forms such a mechanism might take (21). In brief, VMH lesions might alter parasympathetic tone maintained over a variety of metabolic and hormonal mechanisms and hence produce the altered fat metabolism and storage that ultimately result in obesity. The effect of vagotomy on VMH obesity might also be due to an interruption of afferent feedback. In a related manner, stimulation-induced feeding may require vagal mobilization of visceral reflexes in order to find expression. Alternatively, it could be that vagotomy has its effect on stimulation-induced feeding by interrupting afferent information necessary for the performance of the response. With respect to this possibility, one is reminded of MacDonnell and Flynn's finding that interruption of trigeminal afferents severely attenuated (or even eliminated) hypothalamically elicited attack (13). In the case of the LH syndrome, it would appear that the reduced basal secretion of gastric acid may represent an alteration in the maintained parasympathetic tone on secretion. Since LH weight set point levels were not ameliorated by vagotomy, one might conclude that the vagus does not play a major role in this aspect of the LH syndrome. Other autonomic (or endocrine) pathways might be examined for a possible role in the LH syndrome.

A second possibility, which contrasts with the interpretation that some or all of the hypothalamic syndromes involve autonomic disturbances in their primary etiology, is the view that the disruptive effects of vagotomy on these syndromes are selective but still not indicative of a basic mechanism. Some or all of the consequences of vagotomy may simply be peculiarly effective in inhibiting various characteristics of the hypothalamic syndromes. The chronically full stomach of the vagotomized animal may be a particularly salient inhibitory signal for the VMH syndrome. Complementary to such a view are the classical observations concerning the unwillingness of the VMH-lesioned animal to defend its elevated weight level and the heightened reactivity that is associated with VMH lesions (e.g., 26). Similarly, vagotomy's selective effect upon stimulation-induced feeding might represent an exaggeration of the interactions of normal physiologic mechanisms with this electrically induced feeding response (6). On the contrary, normalization of the basal acid secretion of LH animals by vagotomy does not as readily fit a disruption or inhibition explanation since gastric acid output is corrected by an increase in basal levels following vagotomy.

Whether some or all of the hypothalamic feeding syndromes involve as part of their basic mechanism specific vagal systems or whether the hypothalamic syndromes are merely particularly susceptible to the general disruptive consequences of vagotomy is an empirical question. In either case, the results reviewed here justify, we feel, a thorough examination of the role of the autonomic nervous system in the hypothalamic feeding syndromes.

ACKNOWLEDGMENTS

We thank Elise Low, Jennifer Pollack, and Gloria Schoolfield for their excellent technical assistance. In addition, we thank Drs. Daniel Porte and Stephen Woods for kindly performing the insulin assays summarized in Table 1. This research was supported by U.S. Public Health Service grant AM 15511 and NSF grant GB-36983 to T. L. Powley and by NSF and NIH Predoctoral Fellowships to C. A. Opsahl.

REFERENCES

1. Anand, B. K., and Pillai, R. W. (1967): *J. Physiol. (Lond.)*, 192:63–77.
2. Bachrach, W. H. (1962): *Am. J. Dig. Dis.*, 7:1071–1085.
3. Ball, G. G. (1974): *Science*, 184:484–485.
4. Booth, D. A., Coons, E. E., and Miller, N. E. (1969): *Physiol. Behav.*, 4:991–1001.
5. Colin-Jones, D. G., and Himsworth, R. L. (1970): *J. Physiol. (Lond.)*, 206:397–409.
6. Devor, M. G., Wise, R. A., Milgram, N. W., and Hoebel, B. G. (1970): *J. Comp. Physiol. Psychol.*, 73:226–232.
7. Fennegan, F. M., and Puiggari, M. J. (1966): *J. Neurosurg.*, 24:497–504.
8. Glavcheva, L., Manchanda, S. K., Box, B., and Stevenson, J. A. F. (1972): *Can. J. Physiol. Pharmacol.*, 50:1091–1098.
9. Han, P. W. (1968): *Proc. Soc. Exp. Biol. Med.*, 127:1057–1070.
10. Han, P. W., and Frohman, L. A. (1970): *Am. J. Physiol.*, 219:1632–1634.
11. Han, P. W., Yu, Y., and Chow, S. L. (1970): *Am. J. Physiol.*, 218:769–771.
12. Kennedy, T. (1974): *Med. Clin. N. Am.*, 58:1231–1246.
13. MacDonnell, M., and Flynn, J. P. (1966): *Anim. Behav.*, 14:399–405.
14. Misher, A., and Brooks, F. P. (1965): *Fed. Proc.*, 24:406.
15. Nauta, W. J. H. (1972): In: *Limbic System Mechanisms and Autonomic Function*, edited by C. H. Hockman, pp. 21–39. C C Thomas, Springfield, Ill.
16. Nundy, S., and Baron, J. H. (1973): *Gut*, 14:665–668.
17. Opsahl, C. A. (1975): *Unpublished results.*
18. Opsahl, C. A., and Powley, T. L. (1973): *Unpublished results.*
19. Opsahl, C. A., and Powley, T. L. (1974): *Am. J. Physiol.*, 226:34–38.
20. Powley, T. L., MacFarlane, B. A., and Opsahl, C. A. (1974): *Unpublished results.*
21. Powley, T. L., and Opsahl, C. A. (1974): *Am. J. Physiol.*, 226:25–33.
22. Powley, T. L., Opsahl, C. A., and van den Pol, A. N. (1974): *Proceedings of the XXVI International Congress of Physiological Sciences, Jerusalem, Israel.*
23. Ridley, P. T., and Brooks, F. P. (1965): *Am. J. Physiol.*, 209:319–323.
24. Rostad, H. (1973): *Acta Physiol. Scand.*, 89:154–168.
25. Schmitt, M. (1973): *Am. J. Physiol.*, 225:1089–1095.
26. Sclafani, A., and Grossman, S. P. (1971): *J. Comp. Physiol. Psychol.*, 74:157–166.
27. Slaunwhite, W. R., Goldman, J. K., and Bernardis, L. L. (1972): *Metabolism*, 21:619–631.
28. Wise, R. A. (1974): *Brain Res.*, 67:187–209.

Hunger: Basic Mechanisms and Clinical Implications,
edited by D. Novin, W. Wyrwicka, and G. Bray.
Raven Press, New York © 1976.

A Conceptual Equation of Intake Control

Mauricio Russek

Departmento de Fisiología, Escuela Nacional de Ciencias Biológicas, Instituto Politécnico Nacional,
México, 17. D.F. México

It has been said that an equation is a device to hide our ignorance. I disagree with this statement. I think an equation is a device to express our ignorance in a formal, clear, and concise way. Instead of using several paragraphs or even pages to state our hypotheses, we can do the same thing in one line by using an equation. But the equation has the added advantage that it can be operated to obtain new "statements" whose plausibility or absurdity is a good test of the ideas of the authors. Moreover, one can obtain quantitative or qualitative predictions that, if confirmed experimentally, bring further support to the hypothesis expressed by the equation.

This chapter is the first trial to formulate an equation that would summarize my concepts about the control of food intake. No attempt was made to obtain the best fit to experimental data, but to express the influence of each factor in the simplest possible mathematical way. Therefore, nothing more than a qualitative fit with the experimental data should be expected; it reproduces the trend of the relation between each factor considered and food intake, but not necessarily the quantitative relations. Nevertheless it allows semiquantitative predictions of the changes in the action of one factor when the level of others is modified. It also allows the prediction of the influence of different lesions on the action of the factors considered.

The equation reflects our hypothesis that the main source of information on which the control of food intake is based is conveyed to the central nervous system by the hepatic glucoreceptors. The experimental data supporting this idea have been extensively reviewed (1–3), so only a very brief summary will be given here.

The existence of hepatic glucoreceptors was postulated (4), on the basis of a number of data obtained in our laboratory that could not be explained by the classic glucostatic hypothesis or any of the other current hypotheses (5, 6). A few years later their existence was confirmed electrophysiologically (7). The hepatic glucoreceptors might correspond to the nerve fibers running in the Disse spaces (1) and to the nerve endings described as intracellular by some authors (8, 9), and observed with the electron microscope to be "in direct contact with the hepatocyte membrane and sometimes surrounded by the hepatocyte" (10). If we postulate an electric synapse between the innervated hepatocytes and their nerve fibers and considering that there are gap junctions between adjacent hepatocytes (11), the discharge frequency of the fibers would be modulated by the hepatocytes average membrane potential. This membrane potential varies with the rate of glucose output, because of the outward current of potassium ions, which hyperpolarizes the membrane (12–14). This outward transport of potassium is dependent mostly on the intracellular concentration of glucose, which, in its turn, depends on the rate of glycogenolysis and gluconeogenesis, and these reflect the amount of glycogen and protein reserves. Therefore the discharge frequency of these receptors is actually coding the amount of glycogen and protein reserves available during the intermeal postabsorptive periods. Their discharges would only reach the hunger threshold when glycogen and protein reserves in the liver attain a certain minimum and less amino acids liberated by muscle are reaching the liver (which means that glycogen and protein reserves in muscle have also reached a certain degree of depletion). In this condition glucose output from the hepatocytes would reach a minimum, which would cause a decrease in membrane potential (depolarization) and an increase in the firing rate of the glucoreceptors (innervated hepatocytes). The membrane potential of all hepatocytes is bound to be very similar (2) because of the gap junctions between them, so a rather small number of fibers could sample some hepatocytes and inform about the average metabolic reserves of the whole liver.

The equation calculates the average speed of food ingestion, during the first 30 min of feeding, after a certain intermeal fasting period. Most of our experiments were performed on rats under a 24-hr feeding–24-hr fasting schedule, so the values used in the calculations were those corresponding to fasting rats.

The equation expresses the relations between this initial speed of feeding and the information originated in hepatic glucoreceptors (glycogenostatic control), central glucoreceptors of the lateral hypothalamus (LH) and ventromedial hypothalamus (VMH) (glucostatic control), thermoreceptors without implying localization (thermostatic control), osmoreceptors, also without any implications about its localization (osmostatic control), and the information about total amount of body fat (lipostatic control) without any assumption about the receptors that monitor it.

HEPATIC GLYCOGENOSTATIC COMPONENT

This portion of the equation reflects the highly significant inverse lineal correlation that has been observed between food intake and (a) the hepatic concentration of reducing sugars (15, Fig. 1), (b) concentration of liver glycogen (16; Figs. 1 and 2), and (c) hepatocyte membrane potential (2; Fig. 1). All these relationships would be based on the lineal correlation existing between glucose concentration (or transport through the membrane) and the discharge frequency of the hepatic glucoreceptors (7). The simplest way

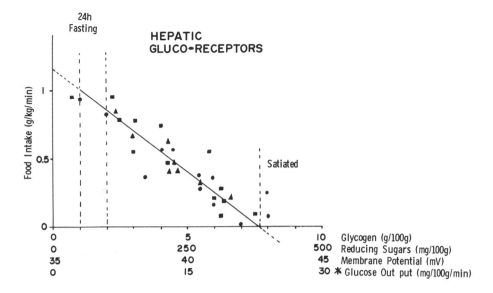

* Calculated from: Friedman et. al. Endoc, 81.
● Calculated from: Peret, C. R. Ac. Sc. (Paris), 274.
▲ Data from: Russek & Stevenson. Physiol & Behav, 8.
■ Data from: Russek & Grinstein. AAAS Meeting, Mexico.(in press)

FIG. 1.

of expressing the control exerted by the hepatic glucoreceptors on food intake is

$$F_1 = F_0 - k_0 \frac{dG}{dt},$$

where F_1 is the average food intake speed (g/min) during the first half
hour, F_0 the maximum food intake speed (produced by the maximum discharge frequency of the hepatic glucoreceptors), and dG/dt is the speed of
glucose output from the hepatocytes. Glucose output is very difficult to measure and no data on it related to feeding are available. Normally it is determined mainly by the concentration of glycogen and the concentration of
glycogenolytic substances in the hepatocyte, therefore, we can write

$$F_1 = F_0 - k_1 S_G G_y,$$

where S_G is the concentration (or logarithm of concentration) of a glycogenolytic substance and G_y the concentration of glycogen. When several
glycogenolytic substances are acting simultaneously, their effects are considered additive, therefore:

$$F_1 = F_0 - (k_1 S_1 G_y + k_2 S_2 G_y + \cdots + kn\ Sn\ G_y)$$

or

$$F_1 = F_0 - G_y(k_1S_1 + k_2S_2 + \cdots + kn\ Sn),$$

and this is the actual form used in all our calculations, as can be seen in the final equation: The glycogenolytic actions considered were those of glucagon (Gg), hypoglycemia (1/G), and epinephrine (E) when injected intraperitoneally (Fig. 7, bottom). We have already discussed elsewhere (2, 17, 18) the hypothesis that preabsorptive satiation could be due to the reflex secretion of epinephrine from intrahepatic chromaffin cells (17), produced by discharges originated in oropharyngeal and gastrointestinal receptors (anticipatory reflexes, 19). Perhaps the main information producing this intrahepatic liberation of adrenaline would be gluco- and amino acid receptors of the duodenum (20) and stomach (K. N. Sharma, *personal communication*). This agrees with the satiating effects obtained by intraduodenal infusions of glucose that are much stronger in *ad libitum* fed animals than in fasted ani-

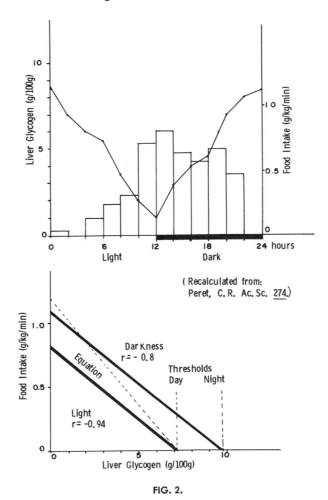

FIG. 2.

mals, whereas the reverse is true for the satiating effects of intraportal glucose (21–24). The *ad lib* animals have a much higher hepatic glycogen concentration than the fasting ones, so the glycogenolytic effect of preabsorptive intrahepatic secretion of epinephrine would be stronger; (the effects of i.p. epinephrine are much stronger in *ad lib* fed animals (25, see fig. 7); on the other hand, the amount of portal glucose uptaken by the fasting animals and transformed to glycogen would be much larger, and so would be the satiating effect, as compared to the *ad lib* situation.

The glycogenolytic effect of ammonia, which would account for the powerful satiating effect of amino acids (proteins) could also be included in the equation, but it was not used in any of the calculations performed so far, because we have no idea of its empiric coefficient (k_3 in the final equation).

Therefore, in all the calculations, only the glycogenolytic effects of glucagon and glycemia were included. The effects of circulating adrenaline are considered negligible (26, 27), so epinephrine was included only when the effect of i.p. injections (supposedly simulating preabsorptive satiation) was calculated (fig. 7, bottom).

The effects of glucagon and epinephrine were considered proportional to the logarithm of their concentration, whereas the effect of glycemia was considered proportional to the reciprocal of the concentration (hyperbolic relation).

When typical normal values for the hungry rat (Table 1) are given to the parameters of the equation, the relative contribution of the hepatic component in controlling the total intake is larger than that of all the other factors considered in the equation, as shown in Table 2.

The calculated relation between liver glycogen and food intake (Fig. 3, top) is between the actual relations obtained during the light and dark hours (Fig. 2, bottom), which should correspond to a fasted rat with low glycogen (like at the beginning of the night) but eating during the day. Thus it starts close to the night line, but, as it satiates, approaches the day line.

The difference in the nocturnal and diurnal relationships between food

TABLE 1. *Values of variables*

	Fasted	Satiated	
Gg	200	100	mg/100 ml
I	1	4	mμ/100 ml
G_1	1–2	7–8	g/100 g
A	0[a]	(preabsorptive satiation?)	
T_A	26	26	°C
G	80	120	mg/100 ml
U	1	1	
W	250	260	g
O	0.3	0.32	Osm.
(NH₄)	0[a]	(protein satiating power. starvation anorexia?)	

[a] Not considered in the calculations.

TABLE 2. *Predicted contribution of different factors to the ingestion of a normal rat on a 24-hr feeding 24-hr fasting schedule*

Factor	Food intake (g/kg/30 min)	%
Hepatic glucoreceptors	24.8	85
Central glucoreceptors	7.4	25
Temperature (neutral)	0	0
Lipostasis (on set point)	(×1)	0
Osmolarity	−3.2	−10
	30.0	100

intake and liver glycogen and also the circadian oscillations of both variables could easily be explained by assuming that the light produces a decrease in the sensitivity of the feeding integrating centers to the hunger signals from the hepatic glucoreceptors and maybe an increased preabsorptive intrahepatic secretion of epinephrine also (increased preabsorptive satiation). Therefore,

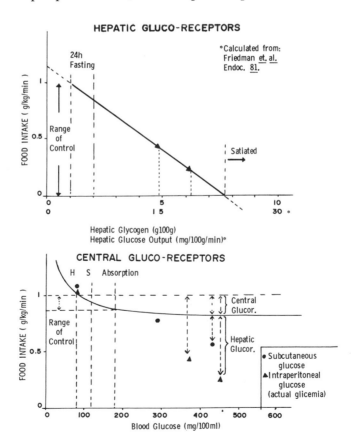

FIG. 3.

during the day the animal eats less for the same amount of liver glycogen (Fig. 2, bottom) and stops eating (by preabsorptive satiation) before it has ingested enough food to cover its metabolic needs (as was actually observed, 28). As a consequence, the average liver glycogen keeps falling during the whole light period, and lipolysis keeps increasing accordingly to fulfill the caloric requirements. During the night, the hepatic hunger signals become more effective and the preabsorptive reflexes become less intense, so the rat eats more than it needs, the liver glycogen begins to be restored and lipolysis decreases.

An animal that eats around the clock (and perhaps a rat subjected to continuous light or darkness) would not exhibit a circadian cicle of glycogen, but would exhibit smaller changes around the threshold for feeding, increasing above this concentration after each meal and decreasing gradually toward it during the intermeal period.

As the amount of glycogen stored after each meal depends on the size of the meal, and as the time taken to reach again the threshold of feeding depends on this amount, one would expect a correlation between size of the meal and the following intermeal period (which has been actually observed, 29). The amount eaten in a meal would be determined not only by the amount of glycogen present in the liver, but mainly by the strength of the preabsorptive reflex secretion of epincphrine, which might be subjected to various influences. Therefore no correlation would be observed between the size of a meal and the preceding intermeal period (29).

To simulate the effect of light and darkness in the equation, the slope of the relation between food intake and liver glycogcn should be slightly changed (by changing the coefficients of Gg and $1/G$), to adapt it to the relation obtain in darkness. Then the effect of light would be accounted for by the necessary decrease in F_0 (which would change the threshold of eating but not the slope of the curve) as is actually observed (Fig. 2, bottom).

CENTRAL GLUCOSTATIC COMPONENTS

My idea about the central glucoreceptors is that they might play an important role in the regulation of glycemia, by the control of glycogen and protein reserves, but that they play only a secondary role in the normal regulation of these reserves by the control of food intake. Only very marked hypoglycemia, or great reductions in glucose utilization (like the effect of 2-deoxyglucose) produce some increase in feeding, whereas large hyperglycemia produces only a mild satiation, and even this could be partially effected through the hepatic glucoreceptors (Fig. 3, bottom).

There are two components in the equation simulating the central glucoreceptors. Those in the lateral hypothalamus (LH) are considered to be the ones responding to absolute glycemia and to glucose utilization changes, giving a hyperbolic relation of the type

$$F_1 = F_0 + \frac{k_5}{uG},$$

where u is the utilization coefficient, normally taken as 1, and G is the glycemia.

To simulate the effect of insulin, another hyperbolic relation between its concentrations and glycemia is included (Fig. 6, top). This equation is

$$G_I = \frac{G_0}{1 + \log I},$$

where I is the insulin concentration.

The so called glucoreceptors of the ventromedial hypothalamus (VMH), for reasons too long to discuss here (30) are considered to be sensitive not to glycemia *per se* but to the relation between the concentrations of glucagon and insulin; the first hormone would decrease glucose entrance to the VMH, whereas the second would antagonize this action, that is, insulin would be needed for glucose penetration into the VMH, only in the presence of glucagon. This information would be very important in the regulation of glycemia by the control of these hormones (and perhaps others), but would have even less influence on food intake than the LH component.

The equation simulating the glucostatic influence of the VMH on food intake is:

$$F_1 = F_0 + \frac{\log Gg.}{1 + \log I} \cdot \frac{1}{\log G}$$

It can be seen that, in the complete equation, the glycemia has two opposing mild effects on feeding: one through the hepatic glucoreceptors and the other through the central glucoreceptors. The result is a hyperbolic relation (Fig. 3, bottom), exhibiting a rather small range of control on food intake for the normal limits of glycemia.

Insulin has three different effects in the equation: a rather small satiating effect through the VMH, some satiation through the effect of hypoglycemia on liver glycogenolysis, whose intensity depends on the amount of glycogen, and a predominant hunger effect by the action of hypoglycemia on the LH. This would agree with the fact that the actual increase in food intake is somewhat larger in the fasting (low glycogen) animals (Fig. 6, bottom).

The effect of low insulin levels (diabetes) is simulated in glycemia (Fig. 6, top) but not with respect to feeding. This is caused by the fact that the hyperphagia of the diabetic is obviously not due to the hyperglycemia that produces a slight hypophagia but, according to our hypothesis, would be the result of the decrease in liver glycogen, a chronic effect of insulin deficiency not simulated by the equation.

Glucagon would have two opposing effects in the equation: satiation through the hepatic glycogenolysis, dependent in its magnitude on liver glycogen concentration, and hunger through the VMH receptors. This might explain the small anorexia obtained in hungry rats (Fig. 7, top), and the rather strong anorexia described in *ad lib* humans (31, 32).

The VMH exerts a strong tonic inhibitory action on food intake, that might result from information about the amount of fat reserves. That is, it plays an important role in fixing the set point of body weight. The reduction of this information would be interpreted as a reduction of fat stores, thus increasing food intake (hyperphagia) and elevating the weight set point (33–35). This tonic information to the VMH might be achieved by accumulation of a certain fat metabolite (36, 37).

This inhibitory effect of the VMH was simulated by a coefficient of ½ multiplying the hepatic, glucostatic, and thermostatic components.

The Thermostatic Component

This part of the equation reflects the fact that, at neutral ambient temperature, there seems to be no influence of temperature on food intake (38),

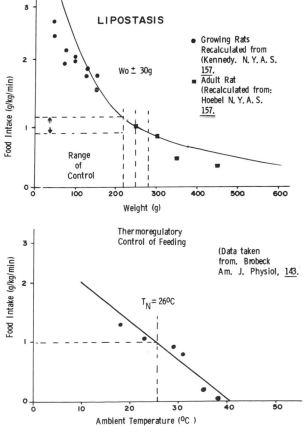

FIG. 4.

whereas during thermoregulatory reactions to heat or cold, there is an approximately linear relation between ambient temperature and feeding (39, Fig. 4, bottom). Thus the equation takes the following form:

$$F_T = F_0 + k_1(T_N - T_A),$$

where T_N is neutral temperature and T_A is ambient temperature. It is clear that, when $T_N = T_A$, $F_T = F_0$, and that the second term can be positive or negative, producing an increase or decrease of intake, inversely proportional to temperature.

The calculated effect of temperature on the relation between liver glycogen and food intake is similar to the real effect produced by light and darkness, that is, a change in threshold (and in maximum intake) without a change in slope (Fig. 5, bottom). This is a prediction to be confirmed experimentally. It was already discussed that this can be interpreted as a change in sensitivity of the integrating nervous centers to the hunger signals from the hepatic

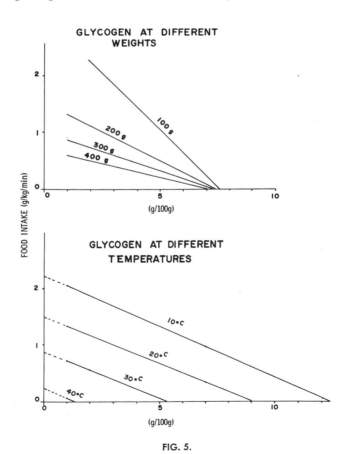

FIG. 5.

glucoreceptors. This same interpretation would apply to all factors that have an additive effect in the equation.

The Lipostatic Component

Some recent findings (40, 41) suggest that the regulation of weight (actually of fat reserves) is accomplished mainly by the control of energy *output* (activity and basal metabolism), and only secondarily by the control of energy input (food intake). Nevertheless there seems to be a certain modulation of feeding exerted by the lipostatic mechanism when the weight is outside the set point (42, 43). I have the intuition that this effect is not additive but multiplicatory, which would mean that it does not change the threshold of liver glycogen at which feeding starts, but it would change the slope of the relation between liver glycogen and food intake (Fig. 5, top). Again, this prediction should be confirmed experimentally. Therefore, the equation shows no effect of lipostasis when the animal is at its weight set point and a hyperbolic relation between weight and food intake, when the animal is thinner or fatter than its set point (Fig. 4, top):

$$F_1 = \frac{W_0}{W_1}(F_0 - \text{glycogenostatic} + \text{glucostatic} + \text{thermostatic})$$
$$\text{component} \qquad \text{component} \qquad \text{component}$$

where W_0 is the weight set point and W_1 is the actual weight.

This multiplicatory action could be interpreted as a nonlinear change in sensitivity of the effector (motor) mechanisms of feeding, without any influence on the triggering mechanism (threshold). The above agrees with the fact that rats, which reach quite low levels of liver glycogen during their circadian cicle, exhibit substantial changes in food intake when thinned or fattened (33, 43), whereas rabbits, who eat around the clock, and might be regulating glycogen close to the threshold, show a smaller change in intake when thinned, regaining weight by decreased metabolism (41).

The Osmostatic Component

Normal body fluid osmotic pressure is assumed to produce a small tonic inhibition on feeding, which increases exponentially with increased concentration. This is based on the fact that body dilution produces only a small increase in feeding (44), whereas concentrated saline produces strong anorexia (45). The equation would be of the form:

$$F_1 = F_0 - k_6 O^n$$

where O is osmotic pressure and n an exponent from 5 to 10.

Satiated Animal

When all the variables present in a satiated animal are given (Table 1), the equation gives a small negative number, which is a rather comforting result. Under these conditions, the equation will respond with a small increase in feeding to dilution of body fluids and to insulin, and with a substantial increase as a response to cooling (Fig. 8). All this corresponds to actual experimental findings (39, 44, 46).

The satiated equation also responds with a large increase in feeding, to a central glucoprivic effect ($u \rightarrow 0$), simulating the intracranial injections of 2-deoxyglucose (47). The hepatic glucoprivic effect of intraportal 2-deoxyglucose (48), can only be simulated by a decrease in liver glycogen, but its actual cause might be the blocking of hepatic glucose output by this substance. Therefore, the hyperglycemia produced by 2-deoxyglucose would be

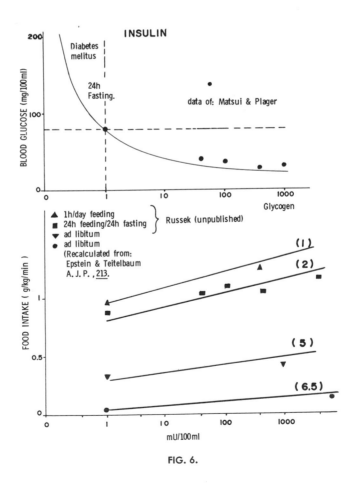

FIG. 6.

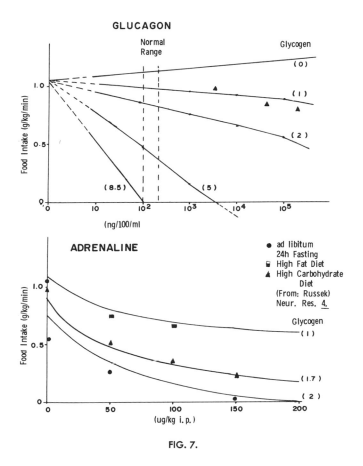

FIG. 7.

the consequence of a greater reduction in glucose utilization, than in glucose production (the same situation occurs in the diabetic animal, which is hyperphagic as a result of the low liver glucose output, and in spite of the hyperglycemia).

Effect of Epinephrine

The anorexigenic action of epinephrine is poorly represented by the equation because, for simplicity, only the glycogenolytic effect (elicited through beta adrenergic receptors) was taken into account. Thus the decrease in this anorexigenic effect observed in animals with reduced glycogen (15) is quantitatively simulated by the equation (Fig. 7, bottom), but as glycogen increases, the calculated effect becomes too large.

This is because the equation does not include the alpha-hyperpolarization,

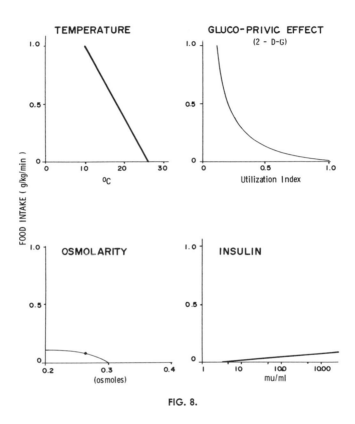

SATIATED ANIMAL

(Gg = 100 ; I = 4 ; G = 120 ; Gy = 7.5)

FIG. 8.

independent of glycogen that epinephrine produces (12, 13) and that, according to our hypothesis, would also reduce the hunger discharges from liver glucoreceptors (2). This effect might be a major component of epinephrine anorexia when liver glycogen is low, which means that its omission in the equation had to be compensated for by an exaggeration of the beta-glycogenolytic effect. Therefore a more accurate equation for the epinephrine effect on feeding is

$$F_A = F_0 - k_A A - k_B \ln A \; G_y$$

where A is intrahepatic epinephrine concentration. The alpha effect might be an important part of preabsorptive satiation, when liver glycogen is low, which would agree with the linearity of the initial satiation in rats under a 24-h feeding/24-hr fasting schedule (2).

The complete equation used to calculate all the graphs presented, was the following:

Conceptual equation of food intake

$$FI = k \left[F_0 - \left(\log Gg + \frac{k_2}{G} + k_3(NH_4) + k_4 \log \frac{A}{10} \right) Gy + (T_N - T_A) \right.$$

$$\underbrace{\hphantom{F_0 - \left(\log Gg + \frac{k_2}{G} + k_3(NH_4) + k_4 \log \frac{A}{10} \right) Gy}}_{\text{hepatic glucoreceptors}} \qquad \underbrace{\hphantom{(T_N - T_A)}}_{\substack{\text{tempera-}\\\text{ture}}}$$

$$+ \frac{k_5}{uG} + \left(\frac{\log Gg}{1 + \log I} \right)\left(\frac{1}{\log G} \right) \left] \left(\frac{1}{2} \right) \frac{W_0}{W_1} - k_{6(0)}{}^n \right.$$

$$\underbrace{\hphantom{\frac{k_5}{uG}}}_{\text{LH}} \qquad \underbrace{\hphantom{\left(\frac{\log Gg}{1 + \log I} \right)\left(\frac{1}{\log G} \right)}}_{\text{VMH}} \qquad \underbrace{\hphantom{\frac{W_0}{W_1}}}_{\substack{\text{li-}\\\text{po-}\\\text{stasis}}} \quad \underbrace{\hphantom{k_{6(0)}{}^n}}_{\substack{\text{osmo-}\\\text{larity}}}$$

$$\underbrace{\hphantom{\frac{k_5}{uG} + \left(\frac{\log Gg}{1 + \log I} \right)\left(\frac{1}{\log G} \right)}}_{\text{central glucoreceptors}}$$

$$G_I = \frac{G_0}{1 + \log I}$$

effect of insulin on glycemia

Variables		Parameters for rat	
FI—food intake	(g/kg/min)	(24 hr feeding–24 hr fasting schedule, first 30 min	
Gg—glucagon	(ng/100 ml)	of ingestion)	
I —insulin	(mU/100 ml)	$F_0 = 16$	
A —adrenaline	(μg/kg injected i.p.)		
Gy—glycogen	(g/100g)	$k_1 = \frac{1}{8}$; k_2 20; k_3?; $k_4 = 4$	
T_A —air temperature (°C)		$T_N = 26$ (neutral temperature)	
G —blood glucose	(mg/100 ml)	$K_5 = 200$	
u —glucose utilization by LH		$W_0 = 250$ (Weight set point)	
W_1—body weight (g)		$K_6 = \dfrac{105}{16}$	
O —osmolarity	(Osm)	$n = 10$	

LH Syndrome

The equation can simulate the effects of different lesions, by suppressing the corresponding components. In respect to LH lesions, our idea is that the aphagia is caused mainly by the impairment of pathways conveying information from the hepatic glucoreceptors, which is manifested in a lack of epinephrine anorexigenic effect during phase II (49). The recovery (phases III and IV), would be caused by the reestablishment of central pathways through which the hunger signals from the liver would again exert their influence, which is manifested by the reappearance of epinephrine anorexia (49). We could assume that during phase I, the pathways responsible for the thermostatic control of feeding are also temporarily impaired because of the effects of the closely located lateral lesion on the anterior hypothalamus.

Thus the equation in phase I (suppression of hepatic, LH, and temperature components) gives a negative value (satiation) and no factor is capable of eliciting feeding (Fig. 9). In phase II (reintroduction of the thermostatic component), the animal might start eating some food because of sporadic decreases in temperature (caused by critical reductions of metabolic reserves), as suggested by Teitelbaum and Epstein (50). The fact that it will only ingest very palatable foods might only indicate that the animal is almost satiated (the small temperature decrease produces a weak hunger drive). In

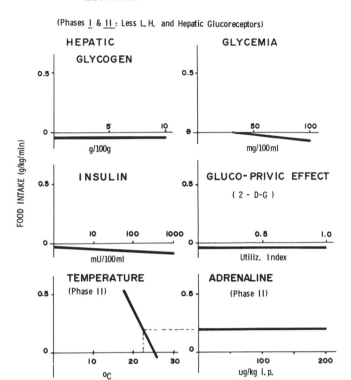

NON - RECOVERED
LATERAL   HYPOTHALAMIC
LESIONED

(Phases I & II : Less L. H. and Hepatic Glucoreceptors)

FIG. 9.

this phase the small amount ingested is not affected by epinephrine (Fig. 9, bottom). Only in phases III and IV (reintroduction of the hepatic component) can we observe the actual deficits caused by the permanent elimination of the LH glucoreceptors: no increase in food intake to hypoglycemia, even a decrease to insulin (hepatic and VMH anorexia), and no central gluco-privic effect (Fig. 10). Both have been observed experimentally (46, 51, 52).

Another characteristic of phases III and IV simulated by the equation is the slight increase in epinephrine anorexia (49), which is only a consequence of the relative increase in importance of the hepatic component, because of the reduction of the central glucostatic component. Finally the change in weight set point, which is supposed to be a chronic effect of the LH lesion (35), is also observed in the behavior of the lesioned equation (Fig. 10).

VMH Lesions

The suppression of the VMH component with its strong inhibitory effect represented by a coefficient of ½, obviously will produce a twofold increase

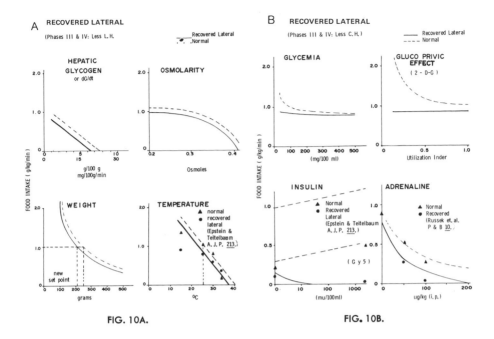

FIG. 10A.   FIG. 10B.

in food intake. But the interesting result is that this is manifested as an increase in the weight set point (Fig. 11), which is the interpretation given to the ventromedial syndrome by some authors (33, 34). Thus the dynamic phase, with a series of predictions to be confirmed experimentally, is simu-

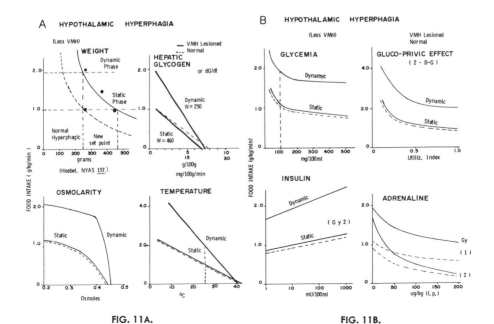

FIG. 11A.   FIG. 11B.

lated by the VMH-lesioned equation only while the weight (W_1) is close to the control. If W_1 is substituted by the new set point (the weight at which the new lipostatic curve gives a food intake equal to the normal animal, see Fig. 11), the behavior of the lesioned equation becomes quite close to the normal, which simulates the static phase.

Hepatic Deafferentation

The suppression of the hepatic component results in a great reduction but not complete suppression of food intake. This is what was actually observed in the peripheral aphagic syndrome produced by upper abdomen denervation (53), which is the closest to hepatic deafferentation that has been technically possible to achieve. The predictions obtained from the hepatic-deafferented equation, like the lack of epinephrine anorexia, the presence of insulin glucoprivic effects, etc. (Fig. 12), should be tested experimentally on animals with the above-mentioned syndrome or with autotransplanted livers.

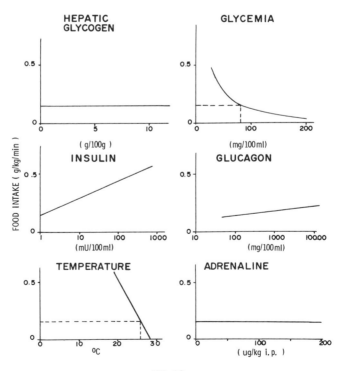

HEPATIC DE-AFFERENTATION
(Peripheral hypophagic syndrome)

FIG. 12.

I will take this opportunity to discuss the apparent lack of effect of liver transplantation on food intake (54–56) as this has been used as a strong criticism to the main concept on which this chapter is based. When we cut the vagii and splanchnic nerves in rabbits (53), some exhibited almost complete aphagia up to 2 weeks, others exhibited aphagia for a few days and then hypophagia of about 40 to 50% below the control for more than 40 days. This last effect was obtained also in one dog where the hepatic pedicle was peeled, as when the liver is prepared for a transplant, but without cutting any vessels. Both in the rabbits and the dog, the anorexia was apparent only if the amount eaten was measured and compared with the preoperative ingestion. The weight decreased about 20% in the first week and then it stabilized or even began to increase, in spite of the reduced intake (we think this is because of control of the energy output). Therefore just because an animal seems normal and does not lose any weight it does not mean he is eating the same as before the transplant.

About the possible reinnervation of the transplanted liver, one cannot say that it is "safe to assume it will take 6 to 9 months to be accomplished," as has been stated (57). First, the hepatic nerve fibers are so difficult to locate that until a few years ago whether the liver parenchyma was innervated at all was still questionable. Therefore it would be quite impossible to prove it is not innervated at some period after the transplant. Second, it has been shown that a piece of iris grafted in front of a sectioned nigrostriatal aminergic bundle is richly reinnervated by its fibers after 1 week (58). Much before we knew about this fact, we thought that part of the hepatic glucoreceptors extend into the splanchnics and may be the same noradrenergic effector sympathetic fibers acting by axon recurrent collaterals on ganglionic afferent interneurons (similar to the way the dorsal root afferent fibers act as antidromic vasodilators).

Third, it is not necessary that the whole liver be reinnervated for the hepatic glucoreceptors to regain control of food intake. If the glucoreceptors actually respond to the membrane potential of the hepatocytes (2), which vary very little from cell to cell because of gap junctions between them, there must be an enormous redundancy in their information. This, we think, is the reason why we failed to produce any effect in ⅓ of our denervated rabbits, as we may have spared a small proportion of the innervation.

Temporal Pattern of Feeding

A time course could be introduced into the equation, although it would greatly complicate it. In order to do this, one should start in the satiated state and introduce an output, which should gradually reduce liver glycogen in a lineal fashion. Then some sort of double threshold or hysteresis, like the one used by Booth (55), should be introduced, so the threshold of feeding would be at a lower liver glycogen than the threshold of satiation.

When the threshold of feeding is reached, intake would start, accumulating food in a simulated stomach and simultaneously producing intrahepatic epinephrine in proportion to the amount of food already accumulated. This epinephrine lineally reduces the intake speed (provided we have also introduced the alpha effect already discussed), until full preabsorptive satiation is achieved. Then liver glycogen would be restored in proportion to the amount of food ingested, producing postabsorptive satiation and the reinitiation of the cycle.

The change in both thresholds elicited by the alternation between light and darkness can also be introduced and then the circadian oscillations of liver glycogen and food intake are simulated.

All this may be tried in the future, but the main purpose of the equation up to the moment has been to synthesize our points of view about the multifactorial control of food intake and the relative importance of each factor.

REFERENCES

1. Russek, M. (1971): In: *Neurosciences Research,* edited by S. Ehrenpreis and O. C. Solnitzky, pp. 213–282. Academic Press, New York.
2. Russek, M., and Grinstein, S. (1974): In: *Neurohumoral Coding of Brain Function,* edited by R. D. Myers and R. R. Drucker-Colin, pp. 81–97. Plenum Press, New York.
3. Russek, M. (1975): In: *Stevenson's Memorial Book,* edited by G. Mogenson and F. Calaresu. Toronto University Press, Toronto.
4. Russek, M. (1963): *Nature,* 197:79.
5. Russek, M., Rodríguez-Zendejas., A. M., and Piña, S. (1968): *Physiol. Behav.,* 3:249.
6. Rodríguez-Zendejas, A. M., Vega, C., Soto-Mora, L. M., and Russek, M. (1968): *Physiol. Behav.,* 3:259.
7. Niijima, A. (1969): *Ann. NY Acad. Sci.,* 157:690.
8. Riegele, L. (1928): *Z. Mikrosk. Anat. Forsch.,* 14:73.
9. Nicolescu, J. (1958): *An Atlas Concerning Morphological Aspects of Visceral Nerve Endings.* Editura Medicala, Bucarest.
10. Tanikawa, K. (1968): *Ultrastructural Aspects of the Liver and Its Disorders,* p. 50. Igaku Shoin, Tokyo.
11. Kreutziger, G. C. (1968): In: *Proceedings of the XXVI Annual Meeting of the Electronmicroscope Society of America,* edited by C. J. Arseneaux. Claitor's Pub. Div., Baton Rouge,
12. Haylett, D. G., and Jenkinson, D. H. (1969): *Nature,* 224:80.
13. Daniel, E. E. Paton, P. M., Taylor, G. S., and Hodgson, B. J. (1970): *Fed. Proc.,* 29:1410.
14. Friedmann, N., Solyo, A .V., and Solyo, A. P. (1971): *Science,* 171:400.
15. Russek, M., and Stevenson, J. A. F. (1972): *Physiol. Behav.,* 8:245.
16. Peret, Y., Chanez, M., and Macaire, I. (1972): *C.R. Acad. Sci.* (Paris), 274:1562.
17. Russek, M., Racotta, R., and Martinez, I. (1974): *XXVI Int. Cong. Physiol. Sci., Jerusalem Satellite Symp.,* Oct. 1974:115.
18. Racotta, R., Vega, C., and Russek, M. (1972): *Fed. Proc.,* 31:309 Abstr.
19. Nicolaidis, S. (1968): *III Int. Conf. Regul. Food Water Intake,* Haverford, Pa., Sept. 1–3, 1968.
20. Sharma, K. N., and Nasset, E. (1963): *Am. J. Physiol.,* 202:725.
21. Russek, M. (1970): *Fed. Proc.,* 29:658.
22. Russek, M. (1970): *Physiol. Behav.,* 5:1207.

23. Vanderweele, D. A., Novin, D., Rezek, M., and Sanderson, Y. D. (1974): *Physiol. Behav.*, 12:467.
24. Novin, D., Sanderson, Y. D., and Vander Weele, D. A. (1974): *Physiol. Behav.*, 13:3.
25. Russek, M., Mogenson, G. J., and Stevenson, J. A. F. (1967): *Physiol. Behav.*, 2:429–433.
26. Shimazu, T., and Fukuda, A. (1965): *Science*, 150:1607.
27. Shimazu, T., Fukuda, A., and Ban, T. (1966): *Nature*, 210:1178.
28. Le Magnen, Y., and Tallon, S. (1966): *J. Physiol.* (Paris), 58:323.
29. Le Magnen, Y., and Devos, M. (1970): *Physiol. Behav.*, 5:805.
30. Racotta, R., and Russek, M. (1974): *XXVI Int. Cong. Physiol. Sci.*, New Delhi, Oct. 1974:1099.
31. Mayer, J. (1955): *Ann. NY Acad. Sci.*, 63:15.
32. Mayer, J. (1956): *Proc. Int. Physiol. Congr.*, 20:138.
33. Hoebel, B. G., and Teitelbaum, P. (1966): *J. Comp. Physiol. Psychol.*, 61:189.
34. Powley, T. L. (1971): *Int. Conf. Regul. Food Water Intake.*, Cambridge, England, Aug. 1971.
35. Powley, T. L., Keesey, R. E. (1970): *J. Comp. Physiol. Psychol.*, 70:25.
36. Panksepp, J. (1974): *XXVI Int. Congr. Physiol. Sci., Jerusalem Satellite Symp.*, 101.
37. Nicolaidis, S. (1974): *XXVI Int. Congr. Physiol. Sci., Jerusalem Satellite Symp.*, 97.
38. Rampone, A. J., and Shirasu, N. E. (1967): *Science*, 144:317.
39. Brobeck, J. R. (1945): *Am. J. Physiol.*, 143:1.
40. Apfelbaum, M., Bostsarron, J., and Lacatis, D. (1973): In: *Energy Balance in Man.* edited by M. Apfelbaum, pp. 71–81. Masson et Cie., Paris.
41. Levitsky, D. A., Faust, I., and Kratz, C. (1974): *XXVI Int. Cong. Physiol. Sci. Jerusalem Satellite Symp.*, 88.
42. Lepkowsky, S., and Furuta, F. (1971): *Poultry Sci.*, 50:573–577.
43. Hoebel, B. G. (1969): *Ann. NY Acad. Sci.*, 157:758.
44. Kakolewski, J. W., and Deaux, E. (1970): *Am. J. Physiol.*, 218:590.
45. McCleary, R. A. (1953): *J. Comp. Physiol. Psychol.*, 46:411.
46. Epstein, A. N., Teitelbaum, P. (1967): *Am. J. Physiol.*, 213:1159.
47. Novin, D. (1971): *IV Int. Conf. Reg. Food and Water Intake.* Cambridge, England.
48. Novin, D., Vander Weele, D. A., and Rezek, H. (1973): *Science*, 181:858.
49. Russek, M., Rodríguez-Zendejas, A. M., and Teitelbaum, P. (1973): *Physiol. Behav.*, 10:329.
50. Teitelbaum, P., and Epstein, A. N. (1962): *Psychol. Rev.*, 69:74.
51. Nicolaidis, S., Epstein, A. N., and Le Magnen, J. (1972): *J. Physiol.* (Paris), 65:150A.
52. Nicolaidis, S. and Meile, M. J. (1972): *J. Physiol.* (Paris), 65:151A.
53. Russek, M., and Racotta, R., (1971): *Proc. Int. Cong. Physiol. Sci.*, 25:485.
54. Calme, R. Y., Sells, R. A., Pena, J. R., Davis, D. R., Millard, P. R., Herbertson, B. M., Binns, R. M., and Davis, D. A. L. (1969): *Nature*, 223:472.
55. Calne, R. Y., Davis, D. R., Pena, J. R., Balner, H., de Vries, M., Herbertson, B. M., Joysey, V. S., Millard, P. R., Seaman, M. J., Samuel, J. R., Stibbe, J., and Westroek, D. (1970): *Lancet*, 1:103.
56. Slapak, M., Baddeley, M., Wexler, M., Saravis, C., Sise, H., Garcia, S., Giouard, M., and McDermott, W. V., Jr. (1971): In: *Medical Primatology, Proc. 2nd Conf. exp. Med. Sugarg. Primates.* New York, pp. 119–129. Karger, Basel.
57. Stephens, P. B., and Baldwin, B. A. (1974): *Physiol & Behav.*, 12:923.
58. Bjerre, B., Biörklund, A. and Stenevi, U. (1973): *Brain Res.*, 60:161.
59. Friedmann, B., Goodman, E. H., Jr., and Weinhouse, S. (1967): *Endocrinology*, 81:486.
60. Matsui, N., and Plager, J. E. (1966): *Endocrinolgy*, 79:737.
61. Kennedy, G. C. (1969): *Ann. NY Acad. Sci.*, 157.

Hunger: Basic Mechanisms and Clinical Implications,
edited by D. Novin, W. Wyrwicka, and G. Bray.
Raven Press, New York © 1976.

Cholecystokinin and Satiety: Theoretic and Therapeutic Implications

G. P. Smith and J. Gibbs

Department of Psychiatry, Cornell University Medical College and the Edward W. Bourne Behavioral Research Laboratory, New York Hospital, Westchester Division, White Plains, New York 10605

When a rat stops eating, we say that it is satiated for food. This remarkable change in behavioral responsiveness is called satiety. Since satiety in the rat occurs within minutes of beginning to eat, satiety must be due to rapid physiological consequences of eating. It is surprising that such an inviting problem has received so little experimental attention. After the early burst of experiments by Janowitz and Grossman (1) in the dog suggesting that bulk in the stomach or intestine inhibited eating by distending the wall of the gut, analysis of satiety has slowed to a trickle and focused on learned aspects (2) or postabsorptive effects of food that operate over hours (3); yet the mechanism of short-term satiety remained unexplored. One of the impediments to its analysis was that the usual behavioral expression of satiety was the cessation of feeding. But feeding stops for a variety of reasons: a predator appears, a sudden environmental stimulus occurs, or the available food tastes bitter. When none of these or other prepotent stimuli are known to be operating, the cessation of feeding is considered evidence for satiety. However, evidence arrived at by exclusion is weak because of the difficulty of proving the absence of competing stimuli.

We attempted to obtain a more restrictive definition of satiety by analyzing the behavior of rats during the interval in which they stop feeding. Using a time-sample technique, we described a behavioral sequence that characterizes satiety in the rat eating liquid food in its home cage (4). The sequence begins as the intake of food decreases. As the rat feeds less, it begins to groom, sniff, or move away from the food. After feeding stops, grooming, locomotion, rearing, or sniffing continue until the rat retreats to the rear of the cage and rests or sleeps. This sequence of feeding, nonfeeding activity, and rest has been observed before by Bolles (5) and Richter (6). It is characteristic of satiety in solitary rats with access to one food. When other foods are available, a rat samples them instead of resting after it stops eating its preferred food (7).

The behavioral sequence characteristic of satiety is more restrictive than the cessation of feeding as behavioral evidence of satiety. Antin et al. (4) demonstrated this by observing that rats stopped eating quinine-adulterated food, but they remained active when feeding stopped. Thus quinine stopped feeding but did not elicit the satiety sequence.

With this more restrictive behavioral expression of satiety, we began to analyze where food stimuli act to elicit short-term satiety. Since ingested food contacts the oral and gastrointestinal surfaces before it is digested and absorbed, we investigated the satiety effect of food stimuli acting at these surfaces.

To analyze the satiety effect of food stimuli on the oropharyngeal, esophageal, and gastric surfaces separate from their effect on the intestinal surface, we equipped rats with chronic gastric fistulas (8). When the fistulas were

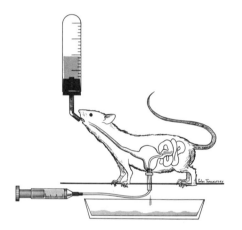

FIG. 1. A rat equipped with a chronic gastric cannula and duodenal catheter. When the cannula is open, ingested food drains out of the stomach and the rat sham feeds continuously (see Fig. 2). During sham feeding, the intestine can be perfused with liquid food through the duodenal catheter and then sham feeding stops (see Fig. 3).

opened, ingested liquid food drained outside the rat so that food did not pass into the intestine (Fig. 1). This form of sham feeding restricted liquid food to oropharyngeal, esophageal, and gastric surfaces. Food stimuli acting at these surfaces did not elicit satiety (Fig. 2). Although rats sham fed continuously in their first sham feeding test, the rate of ingestion decreased after the first 30 min. This decrease may be due to the effects of food stimuli in the upper gut which are subthreshold for satiety. We do not have data to decide this, but we do know that in subsequent sham feeding tests this decrease disappeared (8).

To analyze the satiety effect of food contacting the surface of the intestine as well as the surface of the upper gut, gastric fistula rats were equipped with chronic duodenal catheters (Fig. 1). When liquid food was infused through the catheter into the duodenum during sham feeding, sham feeding stopped and the complete behavioral sequence characteristic of satiety appeared (Fig. 3; see also ref. 9). This satiety effect was not mediated by gastric distention because the open gastric fistula prevented gastric distention.

It was possible that the rats stopped sham feeding because the duodenal infusion made them sick. If the infusion made them sick, then the infusion

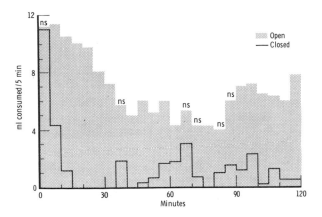

FIG. 2. Mean intake of liquid diet (milliliters per 5 min) when five rats ate liquid diet with the gastric fistula closed (solid line) and when they sham fed for the first time with gastric fistulas open (stippled area). Ns, those interval sham intakes not significantly larger than intake with gastric fistulas closed.

should serve as an unconditioned aversive stimulus for the formation of a conditioned aversion to a novel taste (10). Using an experimental design similar to that of Nachman (11), Liebling et al. (9) demonstrated that duodenal infusions that produced satiety did not function as unconditioned aversive stimuli. Liebling et al. (9) concluded that the inhibition of sham feeding produced by duodenal infusions reflected satiety, not sickness.

These results with duodenal infusions suggested that ingested food must contact the small intestine in order for satiety to occur when gastric distention was not present. Since the surface of the small intestine is studded with re-

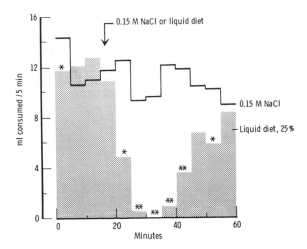

FIG. 3. Mean sham intake of liquid diet (milliliters per 5 min) after infusion of 6 ml liquid diet or 0.15 M NaCl. Six rats received both infusions. Infusions began at 17 min (arrow) and were given at the rate of 1 ml/min. *$p < 0.05$; **$p < 0.01$ by a matched pairs t test.

ceptors for the release of hormones (12) and the activation of nerves (13), we hypothesized that food in the intestine elicits satiety by activating neuroendocrine mechanisms. Aware that vagotomized animals showed satiety, we searched for a hormonal mechanism for the satiety effect of food in the intestine.

The search led to cholecystokinin (CCK), an intestinal polypeptide hormone containing 33 amino acids, which is named for its contractile effect on the gall bladder (14) and now known to stimulate pancreatic enzyme secretion and inhibit gastric emptying (15). An impure preparation of CCK (10% pure w/w, GIH Laboratories, Karolinska Institutet, Stockholm, Sweden) mimicked the effects of food in the intestine: CCK inhibited sham feeding (16), elicited the complete behavioral sequence of satiety (4), and did not serve as an unconditioned stimulus for the formation of a conditioned taste aversion (17, 18). The satiety effect of CCK was also obtained by equivalent

TABLE 1. Summary of satiety effect of gut hormones

Cholecystokinin	strong
Octapeptide of CCK	strong
Pentagastrin	weak
Gastrin I & II	weak
Secretin	no effect
Pancreatic glucagon	no effect

doses of the synthetic octapeptide (16, 17). This is strong evidence that the satiety effect is a new biologic action of the hormone because the octapeptide is the minimum fragment of the parent molecule with all the known actions of the parent molecule. Further evidence that the satiety effect is critically dependent on this structure is that removal of the sulfate group on the tyrosyl residue in the 7 position abolishes the satiety effect (16). This manipulation also markedly weakens or abolishes all other known biological actions of CCK. Furthermore, caerulein and gastrin (pentagastrin or a mixture of Gastrin I and II), which share a portion of the octapeptide sequence, also inhibit feeding (17, 19). Finally, secretin and pancreatic glucagon, which are structurally similar but lack the octapeptide sequence, did not elicit satiety under our conditions (17, 19; see also Table 1).

THEORETIC IMPLICATIONS

This work has several implications for any adequate theory of short-term satiety in the rat. First, the failure of rats to satiate the first time that they sham feed suggests that short-term satiety is critically dependent on negative-feedback mechanisms elicited by food ingested at that meal. Davis and Campbell (20) reached the same conclusion from their observations of sham feeding produced by gastric suction. We have considered these data evidence that short-term satiety in the rat is an inhibitory reflex (19). This suggestion runs counter to the ideas of Le Magnen (2) who has emphasized oral cues as conditioned stimuli for satiety. But Le Magnen has never tested the satiety power of such cues isolated from the other gastrointestinal consequences of ingested food. Under our conditions and those of Davis and Campbell (20), it is clear that such cues are not sufficient to elicit satiety when they act alone.

Second, the adequate stimuli for the intestinal inhibitory reflex for satiety is the chemical or colligative load or both of the intestinal fluid (9). Neither volume nor concentration of nutrient alone has been effective. This part of the work is in an early phase, but there is a biological advantage in having satiety mechanisms activated by chemical or colligative load or both rather than by volume or concentration alone: satiety mechanisms activated by load could solve the regulatory problem set by dilution of the diet, but mechanisms activated by volume or concentration alone could not. Furthermore, the primacy of intestinal load is consistent with our hypothesis that satiety elicited by food in the intestine is mediated by the release of CCK (at least, in part), because intestinal load of food stimuli is the critical parameter for the release of CCK (12).

Third, if endogenous CCK is released in sufficient amounts during spontaneous feeding to terminate that meal and elicit the satiety sequence (this critical test of our hypothesis has not yet been accomplished), it will be the first instance of a hormonal mechanism stopping a consummatory behavior.

THERAPEUTIC IMPLICATIONS

Whatever the fate of the hypothesis that endogenous CCK is a satiety signal under physiological conditions, the satiety effect of repeated administration of exogenous CCK has therapeutic implications. We tested this possibility by administering CCK to 17-hr deprived rats 15 min prior to a meal of solid food and water (17). CCK (5 to 40 U/kg, i.p.) inhibited food intake (Fig. 4). With the largest dose tested (40 U/kg), there was 50% inhibition of intake. The inhibition was restricted to the first 30 min of the test period. The CCK treated rats ate enough in the remaining 120 min of the test that their intake for the entire test period was equal to control.

This significant effect of CCK was consistently obtained over months with no sign of tachyphylaxis or toxicity (17). Equivalent doses of synthetic octapeptide produced equivalent satiety effects (17).

Gibbs et al. (21) recently extended this work to the rhesus monkey and obtained very similar results. Intravenous CCK (5, 10, or 20 U/kg) inhibited food intake and the inhibition was directly related to dose. The smallest dose (5 U/kg) reduced food intake 26% and the largest dose (20 U/kg) reduced intake 70%. Equivalent doses of octapeptide produced equivalent effects. Although the satiety effect was restricted to the first 15-min interval of feeding, monkeys differed from rats in that monkeys did not eat enough

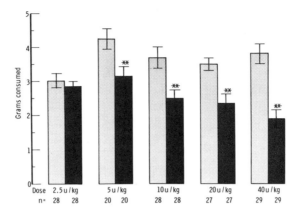

FIG. 4. Mean intake of pellets (g ± SEM) during first 30 min of test meal in 17-hr food-deprived rats. N, number of rats. Light stippled, intakes after saline injections; dark stippled, intakes after CCK in doses indicated. **$p < 0.01$ by a matched pairs t test.

in the remainder of the test to make up for the early inhibition of food intake. The satiety effect in monkeys did not show tachyphylaxis or toxicity.

These results in monkeys with exogenous CCK suggested to us that the endogenous CCK stored in the intestine could produce a similar satiety effect if it were released prior to a meal. The initial evaluation of this therapeutic mode was made by comparing the satiety effect of gastric preloads of *l*-phenylalanine and of *d*-phenylalanine. The isomers of phenylalanine were used because Meyer and Grossman (22) demonstrated in the dog that *l*-phenylalanine released CCK, but *d*-phenylalanine had only a very slight effect. The satiety effect of the preloads was consistent with their CCK releasing potency: *l*-phenylalanine elicited satiety in a dose-related manner, but *d*-phenylalanine had no significant effect (Table 2). Of course, these results do not prove that the satiety effect of *l*-phenylalanine was mediated by CCK, but they are consistent with our hypothesis. We believe this type of experiment should be pursued because it promises safe, inexpensive therapy for human hyperphagia

TABLE 2. *Satiety effect of intragastric preloads of l- or d-phenylalanine*

Preload (g/kg)	Percent inhibition of food intake	
	l-phenylalanine	*d*-phenylalanine
0.25	15	8
0.50	35[a]	18
1.00	73[b]	3

l-Phenylalanine (0.5 or 1.0 g/kg) significantly inhibited food intake; *d*-phenylalanine did not. [a] $p < 0.05$; [b] $p < 0.01$ by t test. At least five male rhesus monkeys were subjects for each preload.

and obesity unless such disorders reveal the lack of CCK or an insensitivity to its cellular effects.

ACKNOWLEDGMENTS

We thank our colleagues at the Bourne Laboratory for their assistance which made this review possible. Preparation of this manuscript was supported by U.S. Public Health Service Career Development Awards K04 NS38601 to G. P. S. and K02 MH70874 to J. G.

REFERENCES

1. Janowitz, H. D. (1967): *Alimentary Canal*. In: *Handbook of Physiology. Vol. I*, edited by C. F. Code, pp. 219–224, Williams and Wilkins, Baltimore.
2. Le Magnen, J. (1967): *Alimentary Canal*. In: *Handbook of Physiology. Vol. I*, edited by C. F. Code, pp. 11–30. Williams and Wilkins, Baltimore.
3. Booth, D. A. (1972): *Physiol. Behav.*, 9:199.
4. Antin, J., Gibbs, J., Holt, J., Young, R. C., and Smith, G. P. (1975): *J. Comp. Physiol. Psychol. (In press.)*
5. Bolles, R. C. (1960): *J. Comp. Physiol. Psychol.*, 53:306.
6. Richter, C. P. (1922): *Comp. Psychol. Monogr.*, 1:1.
7. Barnett, S. A. (1956): *Behaviour*, 9:24.
8. Young, R. C., Gibbs, J., Antin, J., Holt, J., and Smith, G. P. (1974): *J. Comp. Physiol. Psychol.*, 87:795.
9. Liebling, D. S., Eisner, J. D., Gibbs, J., and Smith, G. P. (1975): *J. Comp. Physiol. Psychol. (In press.)*
10. Garcia, J., Hankins, W. G., and Rusiniak, K. W. (1974): *Science*, 185:824.
11. Nachman, M. (1970): *J. Comp. Physiol. Psychol.*, 73:22.
12. Makhlouf, G. M. (1974): *Gastroenterology*, 67:159.
13. Sharma, K. N. (1967): *Alimentary Canal*. In: *Handbook of Physiology. Vol. I*, edited by C. F. Code, pp. 225–237. Williams and Wilkins, Baltimore.
14. Ivy, A. C., and Oldberg, E. (1928): *Am. J. Physiol.*, 86:599.
15. Jorpes, J. E., and Mutt, V. (1973): In: *Secretin, Cholecystokinin, Pancreozymin and Gastrin*, edited by J. E. Jorpes and V. Mutt, pp. 54–133. Springer Verlag, New York.
16. Gibbs, J., Young, R. C., and Smith, G. P. (1973): *Nature*, 245:323.
17. Gibbs, J., Young, R. C., and Smith, G. P. (1973): *J. Comp. Physiol. Psychol.*, 84:488.
18. Holt, J., Antin, J., Gibbs, J., Young, R. C., and Smith, G. P. (1974): *Physiol. Behav.*, 12:497.
19. Smith, G. P., Gibbs, J., and Young, R. C. (1974): *Fed. Proc.*, 33:1146–1149.
20. Davis, J. D., and Campbell, C. (1973): *J. Comp. Physiol. Psychol.*, 83:379.
21. Gibbs, J., Falasco, J. D., and McHugh, P. R. (1975): *Am. J. Physiol. (In press.)*
22. Meyer, J. H., and Grossman, M. I. (1972): *Am. J. Physiol.*, 222:1058.

Hunger: Basic Mechanisms and Clinical Implications,
edited by D. Novin, W. Wyrwicka, and G. Bray.
Raven Press, New York © 1976.

Visceral Mechanisms in The Control of Food Intake

Donald Novin

Department of Psychology and Brain Research Institute, University of California, Los Angeles,
California 90024

The primacy of visceral sensations in the subjective experience of hunger led early theorists to consider the gastrointestinal tract as important in the regulation of food intake. Cannon (6) argued that hunger pangs were the result of strong stomach contractions and that the vagus nerve monitored this peripheral activity. This hypothesis was supported in part by the observation that exogenous insulin produced both hunger and increased gastric contractions (33). Serious doubts were cast on this notion, however, by the observation that vagal transection below the diaphragm eliminated the gastric contractions (44) but not the hunger produced by insulin injection (16). Since the ability to regulate body weight and food intake appeared normal in man and animals subjected to vagotomy (15, 16, 23), sympathectomy (15), or gastrectomy (47), the importance of visceral signals was questioned.

With the development of stereotaxic techniques, manipulation of discrete sites deep within the central nervous system was possible. Because of the dramatic and seemingly irreversible alterations in feeding and energy balance that resulted from ventromedial hypothalamic (VMH) and lateral hypothalamic (LH) destruction these areas became the object of considerable research activity (1, 18). Evidence was also forthcoming that these same hypothalamic areas contained receptor sites capable of detecting changes in nutrient status or some correlate of energy balance (3, 4, 28). Thus the hypothalamus appeared as a self-contained unit that included both receptors and integrators and accounted for both excitation and inhibition of food intake. The elimination of peripheral information had already been shown to have apparently little effect on feeding and the periphery was therefore relegated to a position of little or no importance in the regulatory process.

For a variety of reasons, overlooking peripheral, especially visceral, control of feeding is not justified. The evidence, for example, that following recovery from visceral denervation food intake appears grossly normal is also true for recovery from lateral hypothalamic (LH) lesions (45). Moreover, whereas gross parameters of food intake recover in both cases, there are clearly alterations in feeding that persist and specific deficits that appear to be permanent. In fact, as is shown below, there are important similarities in the alterations produced by LH damage and visceral denervation that suggest a functional relation between vagal afferents and LH.

An alternative view of visceral mechanisms is that they are primarily involved in the short-term regulation of food intake. The fact that there is still regulation of food intake following such procedures as vagotomy is indicative of the redundancy of the system and the override by long-term control mechanisms that become especially clear in the absence of visceral inputs responsible for meal-to-meal regulation. The importance or, perhaps, the primary role that visceral organs, such as the liver and duodenum, and their neural innervations play in the short-term regulation of hunger and satiety mechanisms is what this paper will attempt to demonstrate.

VISCERAL EXCITATORY CONTROL OF FEEDING

The liver stores glucose in the form of glycogen, readily available to enter the metabolic pool and also be rapidly depleted (12). It would seem logical that the liver would have an early warning system for informing the brain that nutrients stores are being depleted. Niijima (24) has shown, in the isolated perfused guinea pig, that hepatic branches of the vagus have a discharge rate inversely proportional to the glucose concentration of the perfusate. Thus there is a neural substrate available that could serve to control food intake on the basis of changes in glucose availability or metabolism in the liver. The existence of liver glucoreceptors had already been postulated by Penaloza-Rojas and Russek (31) and Russek has since provided additional experimental evidence for their role in the regulation of hunger (37). That the vagus nerve might be involved in feeding has also been demonstrated by Russek and his colleagues using a d.c. current to block activity of the nerve (31), which had the effect of suppressing feeding in hungry cats.

Our work, I believe, provides a direct link among hepatic glucoreceptors, autonomic innervation, and feeding. In a recent experiment (27), we showed that blocking glucose utilization in the liver was a very effective stimulus to feeding in rabbits. Systemic infusions via the jugular vein of 2-deoxy-D-glucose (2-DG), an antimetabolite of glucose, were effective but much less so than hepatic-portal vein infusions in eliciting eating. In the vagotomized animal, hepatic-portal 2-DG still elicited feeding, but was now only as effective as were jugular vein infusions. We concluded that this was evidence for hepatic glucoreceptors, their vagal innervation, and this system's role in the activation of feeding.

Since then we (40) have looked at the effects of removal of coeliac and mesenteric ganglia to see if sympathetic denervation would have an effect on feeding induced by 2-DG. Visceral ganglionectomy reduced the 2-DG effect when portally-infused to the level where, in the first 2 hr postinfusion, there was no statistically significant difference between the effects of 2-DG and saline infusion in inducing food consumption. Only in the 3rd hour did the 2-DG infusions reliably increase food intake over control infusions. In comparison to vagotomy, ganglionectomy was more damaging to the 2-DG-elicited feeding response. Paradoxically ganglionectomy enhanced the effect 2-DG had on feeding when jugular vein infusions were used. Whereas the overall results suggest that sympathetic innervation of hepatic glucoreceptors may be more important than parasympathetic, the enhancement effect obviously complicates the interpretation. Ganglionectomy also eliminates important efferent effects of the sympathetic nervous system. Activation of central glucoreceptors by 2-DG is probably greater following jugular than hepatic-portal infusions. These central receptors may also be important in feeding, but their effects could be masked in the intact animal by the effects of general sympathetic arousal, which is known to result from 2-DG-induced central glucopenia (13).

VISCERAL SATIETY MECHANISMS

The liver is in a good position to assess the nutrient status of the organism in relation to food intake, since all ingested substances pass through its capillary bed before being distributed throughout the body. The same can be said of the small intestine, particularly the duodenal portion, where the majority of absorption of ingested material occurs. Very complex neural, endocrine, and enzymatic events are set off by the presence of ingesta in the alimentary canal, any one of which or all could be involved in the regulation of food intake. These considerations stimulated us to investigate and compare the roles of both the liver and small intestine in satiety. For this purpose, we cannulated the duodenum or hepatic-portal circulation of rabbits and compared the effects on food intake of infusions of glucose and equiosmotic saline solutions.

In our initial experiments (46), using rabbits on an *ad lib* schedule, we could find no effects of hepatic-portal infusions of glucose on feeding. Even highly concentrated glucose solutions (30% w/v) were ineffective. The result of duodenal glucose infusions were by comparison quite good. Small quantities (10 ml) of isotonic glucose-reduced food intake by half or more in the hour following the infusion. The reduction in food intake in the 3-hr observation period following infusion was, on a caloric basis, considerably greater than the calories gained from the small amount of infused glucose. The ratio of the caloric value of the infused glucose then to the caloric reduction in food intake was about 6:1. In free-feeding rabbits, it was clear that glucose had to pass through the duodenum before it would reliably suppress food intake.

This result was intriguing because there appeared to be a dichotomy of views in the literature as to whether or not gastrointestinal glucose infusions had any differential effects on feeding. Some investigators were able to demonstrate an effect (46), whereas others were not (5, 8). A similar controversy was also observed with respect to direct intravenous infusions of glucose. Here again there were proponents (37, 38, 42) and antagonists (5, 19).

In reviewing this literature, one variable appeared to be confounded and that seemed a possible explanation of the discrepancies. Duodenal or gastric glucose infusions were effective in experiments where animals were on a free-feeding schedule whereas intravenous effects were seen to suppress food intake in studies, where deprivation schedules were used.

A relatively simple experiment was done in which the duodenal or hepatic-portal infusions of glucose were performed in deprived or free-feeding rabbits (26). The results were quite clear. Hepatic-portal glucose was effective in reducing food intake in deprived rabbits but not in animals on a free-feeding schedule. In contrast duodenal infusions of glucose were effective in free-feeding animals but failed to reduce food intake when given in 24-hr deprived animals. The observation that duodenal infusions were ineffective in the deprived animal was surprising to us. If a hepatic satiety mechanism exists, we might expect that following duodenal absorption it would be rapidly activated since the glucose goes more or less directly into the liver. The failure of duodenal glucose to suppress food intake in deprived animals, however, might be explained by the fact that we were infusing relatively small amounts of glucose (10 ml of a 5% w/v) and were probably operating at or near threshold levels.

There appears to be at least two loci mediating satiety following carbohydrate loads, the liver and the gut. The gut appears to operate in situations where the animal is only minimally hungry and is ineffective when nutrient needs are greater, whereas the reverse is true of hepatic mechanisms. What mechanism switches the locus of satiety is presently under investigation. One possibility is hepatic glycogen levels and the hormones insulin and glucagon that control it. Preliminary results suggest that duodenal mechanisms lose effectiveness at deprivation intervals (2 to 4 hr) somewhat greater than the average intermeal interval, while the liver at this time is becoming effective. Forsgren (12) has shown that at 4 to 6 hr of deprivation the curve relating hepatic glycogen level to deprivation shows a steep decline. We are currently investigating further the possibility that there is a relation between hepatic glycogen and the locus of satiety.

SHORT-TERM SATIETY DEPENDS ON VAGAL INNERVATION

The results of our experiments suggest that both the gut and liver are importantly involved in mediating glucose-induced satiety. It now appears that this information reaches the brain uniquely through afferent vagal innervation of these organs. Our evidence for this is that glucose, which in intact animals reliably suppresses food intake, has no satiating effect in the vagotomized animal (26, 46). In fact, duodenal infusions of glucose in either deprived or free-feeding animals produced sizable increases in food intake and a smaller effect was obtained when the infusions were done in the hepatic-portal circulation of free-feeding animals. The only condition in

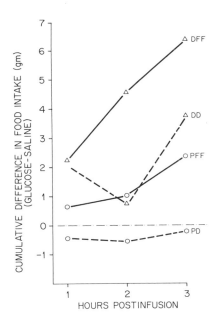

FIG. 1. The differences in food intake cumulated over 3 hr between infusions of 10 ml of a 5% (w/v) glucose solution and 10 ml of a 0.9% saline solution. DFF, duodenal infusions in free-feeding condition; DD, duodenal infusions after 24-hr deprivation; PFF, hepatic-portal vein infusions in free-feeding condition; PD, hepatic-portal vein infusions after 24-hr deprivation. The subjects were all rabbits tested after recovery of feeding following subdiaphragmatic vagotomy. Contrast this to Fig. 2 in ref. 26.

which glucose did not in fact increase food intake was when portal infusions were done in deprived animals (Fig. 1).

Do similar enhancement effects of glucose occur in vagotomized animals under more natural conditions? In order to determine this we gave vagotomized and intact rabbits glucose solutions to drink and observed subsequent food intake (Fig. 2). The results in the first 30 min postinfusion period showed that vagotomized animals ate significantly more food than intact animals did when both were given glucose to drink. It would seem as if glucose enhanced eating in vagotomized animals even when the glucose was ingested.

What is clear is that vagal mediation is necessary for small loads of glucose to suppress food intake whether the route of administration is directly into

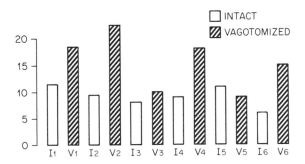

FIG. 2. Food intake (grams) in matched pairs of vagotomized or control laparotomized rabbits 30 min after the consumption of a glucose solution (35 ml, 5%).

the liver or through the small intestine. Why the effects of glucose in some cases are actually reversed, that is, enhance food intake in vagotomized animals, is not known.

We now have evidence suggesting that the efferent vagus is not involved in glucose-induced suppression of food intake. A recent experiment by Rezek (34) showed that glucose still suppresses subsequent food intake in the atropinized animal. The dose of atropin methyl nitrate used (0.25 mg/kg) was sufficient to inhibit the occurrence of stomach contractions induced by stimulation of the distal end of the cut vagus in acutely prepared rabbits for more than 1 hr. Thus, with the small doses of glucose used in our experiment, suppression of food intake depends upon the afferent vagus, because it still occurs even though efferent vagal effects are blocked, whereas it is eliminated by total abdominal vagotomy.

THE SPECIAL STATUS OF GLUCOSE

Glucose plays a unique role in satiety. This is apparent for at least two reasons. First, compared to the other nutrients we have used such as casein, glycerol, and individual amino acids, glucose is the only one clearly more effective when infused duodenally than when infused through the hepatic-portal circulation of free-feeding animals (34, 46). Second, the above-mentioned nutrients were still quite effective in suppressing food intake in vagotomized animals, whereas glucose failed to suppress food intake following vagotomy, as has been mentioned (34).

Glucose, it appears, acts on food intake through peripheral receptors innervated by the autonomic nervous system (and projecting to the LH, see below). The mechanisms by which other macronutrients effect feeding is unknown but they clearly do not involve vagal mediation (34). The fact that this visceral system only mediates carbohydrate-enhanced satiety should not mitigate against its importance, as in rabbits 60% of the typical diet is carbohydrate. Moreover our results of duodenal glucose infusions show that the satiating effect of glucose is greater proportionally than its caloric value.

CENTRAL REPRESENTATION OF VISCERAL SATIETY EFFECTS

In the course of our investigation on the role of the vagus in hunger and satiety we observed a number of similarities between the effect of vagotomy and LH lesions. Some of these are discussed in a previous publication (36). Table 1 outlines some of these similarities, which we have seen either in our own experiments or in the work of others.

Food intake can be increased or decreased by appropriate manipulations of LH (21) or vagus (30). More subtle effects on meal-patterns also show similarities (20, 39). There are similarities in their effects on insulin secre-

TABLE 1. *Effects on feeding and related phenomena following LH and vagal intervention: Similarities (mostly) and differences*

LH	Vagus
I. Electrical stimulation	
a. Increased food intake (21)	a. Increased food intake (30)
b. Increased insulin secretion (43)	b. Increased insulin secretion (49)
II. Destruction	
a. Initial decrease in food intake (45)	a. Initial decrease in food Intake (36)
b. Four-stage recovery pattern (45)[a]	b. 3 stage recovery pattern (36) [a]
c. Mitigates VMH-lesion induced hyperphagia and obesity (2)	c. Mitigates VMH-lesion induced hyperphagia and obesity (32)
d. Meal size/intermeal interval correlation is altered or disrupted (20)	d. Meal size/intermeal interval correlation is altered or disrupted (20)
e. Permanent deficits in thirst (9)[a]	e. No permanent deficits in thirst (36)
III. Chemical and nutrient administration	
a. Glucose infusions reduce electrical activity (4)	a. Glucose infusions reduce electrical activity (24)
b. Hyperphagic effect of 2DG and insulin are eliminated after LH-lesion (10)[a]	b. Hyperphagic effect of 2DG (27) is attenuated but insulin effect still present following vagal transsection (23)
c. The satiating effect of glucose but not other nutrients is eliminated by LH-destruction	c. The satiating effect of glucose but not other nutrients is eliminated by vagal transsection (34)
d. Duodenal glucose enhances food intake after LH lesion (25)	d. Duodenal glucose enhances food intake after vagal transsection (26,46)

[a] Comparisons where differences exist in the effects. (See text for discussion.)

tion (43, 49). In addition there is a large body of work showing evidence for a vagal-LH circuit for the control of gastrointestinal functions, which is not included in Table 1 (7, 11, 22).

There are also effects on alimentation that are either completely different or dissimilar enough to require explanations. In a previous experiment (36), we were unable to obtain complete aphagia following vagotomy as is seen in LH-lesioned rats. Thus, in Table 1 IIb, LH-lesioned rats are characterized by a four-stage, and vagotomized rabbits by a three-stage, recovery pattern in feeding behavior. This might be explained by entry IIe. Following vagotomy, water intake is affected only secondarily to food intake, whereas LH lesions cause permanent deficits in water intake. The initial adipsia could well contribute to the initial aphagia in LH-lesioned rats. Similarly the lack of primary effects on water intake following vagotomy could ameliorate the effects that manipulation might have on food intake.

The most puzzling difference, perhaps, is in IIIb. Two differences can be noted: First, LH lesions eliminate the hyperphagic effect of 2-DG and insulin, whereas vagotomy only reduces the effect of 2-DG. Second, vagotomy does not eliminate insulin-induced eating. The argument developed below that the

LH functions primarily to integrate visceral information does not exclude the possibility that the LH itself contains glucoreceptors, a contention for which there is considerable evidence (3, 4, 28). Vagotomy would leave these gluco-receptors still capable of detecting large changes in glucose availability and it would be expected then, that LH lesions would eliminate, whereas va-gotomy would only attenuate the feeding induced by hypoglycemia. Why insulin-induced eating is not affected by vagotomy is surprising but may be explained by the large doses used and the severe hypoglycemia that is pro-duced. This may so strongly activate central glucoreceptors that any effects because of a lack of innervation of visceral glucoreceptors is negligible. This, of course, is only speculation and needs considerable experimental work before it can be regarded seriously.

Notwithstanding the differences, Table 1 clearly shows a wide variety of similarities in the role of the two neural elements in the regulation of food intake. This led us to predict that we would see yet another similarity be-tween vagotomized and LH-lesioned animals. As shown above (see Fig. 1), vagotomized rabbits failed to suppress food intake when given glucose duo-denally. Indeed food intake was increased. The question we asked was what would happen to glucose-induced satiety in the LH-lesioned animals, that is, in an animal with destruction of the traditional feeding center. The experi-ments (25) were done in rats because we felt we could get more reliable lesions and also because the rat is the classic animal to show the LH-syndrome. When we administered glucose (3 ml, 5% w/v) duodenally to recovered LH-lesioned rats, not only was there no suppression of food intake but, in comparison to equiosmotic saline, there was a significant increase in food intake. Thus, with respect to glucose effects on feeding behavior, va-gotomy and LH lesions yield very similar results.

Preliminary work indicates that in the LH-lesioned animal, as following vagotomy, the deficit in response to satiety signal is specific to glucose or perhaps carbohydrate. (We are unsure about whether the specificity is for glucose or more generally for carbohydrate because we have not yet had a chance to experiment with carbohydrates other than glucose.) Other nutrients representing proteins and fats are as effective in suppressing food intake in LH-lesioned (and vagotomized) animals as they are in intact animals (14).

The fact that recovered LH-lesioned rats show a deficit in satiety in addi-tion to the well-known deficits in feeding makes the term feeding center for this hypothalamic region a clear misnomer. Our data strongly imply that at least one function of the LH is to receive (integrate and/or relay) informa-tion from the viscera conveyed over vagal afferents. Moreover, it is involved not only in the onset of feeding but in satiation. If we were to retain the classic dual center hypothesis, instead of a VMH satiety and LH hunger center a better dichotomy would be, perhaps, to identify the VMH with long-term and the LH with short-term regulations of feeding. However, that too is likely to be an over simplification.

GENERAL CONCLUSIONS

Visceral receptors sensitive to the colligative, volumetric, and chemical properties of ingested materials have been known for some time (17, 29, 41). There is growing evidence that these receptors are involved not only in digestive and metabolic reflexes but in the regulation of food intake itself. It would be logical to assume, and now seems supported by a large body of data, that the afferent neural innervation of these receptors is one and perhaps the primary way that this information reaches the brain.

The view that proposes that the autonomic innervation of the viscera is a primary mechanism in the regulation of feeding is reasonable, despite the wealth of evidence clearly demonstrating the ability in both animals and man to regulate food intake following visceral denervation procedures. For one, those studies looked at gross measures of behavior. A finer analysis would have revealed that there are clear differences in the short-term regulation of feeding on a meal to meal basis (39, see also Vander Weele and Sanderson, *this volume*). Second, it seems strange that recovery following visceral denervation procedures is used as an argument against the role of visceral input in feeding when much recovery is also seen following central destruction, yet the primary role of the hypothalamus in this regulation is not questioned on these grounds. Our results suggest that autonomic visceral innervation plays a very important role in the regulation of food intake and is primarily involved in short-term mechanisms. Overall daily food intake does in fact recover largely, but meal size, inter-meal intervals, and particularly the relation between these two parameters of food intake are considerably altered by vagotomy (39) and sympathetic denervation (35). LH lesions cause similar effects (20).

Several deficits in the regulation of feeding appear to be permanent following vagotomy. An attenuation of the response to 2-DG when infused through the hepatic-portal circulation is one deficit that occurs in vagotomized animals (27). More striking is the complete elimination of the ability of glucose infusions, whether duodenal or hepatic-portal, to suppress food intake (26, 46).

There are close parallels in the effects of LH lesions to those of vagotomy. Some of these have been outlined in Table 1 and in a previous publication (36). In addition LH lesions have been shown by other investigators to eliminate the effects of 2-DG on feeding (48). Even more interesting, perhaps, is that destruction of this supposed excitatory feeding center results in a permanent deficit in satiety that considerably resembles the deficiency following vagotomy. That is, glucose, which in the intact animal reduces subsequent food intake, when given duodenally increases food intake in the recovered LH-lesioned rat.

These results suggest a new interpretation of the role of the LH as part of the central representation for visceral afferents involved in the regulation of feeding. The old term feeding center must certainly be discarded since deficits in satiety are as clear a result of LH destruction as are deficiencies in the elicitation of feeding.

Finally, it appears that glucose (or more generally carbohydrates) has a specific role in the control of food intake. The mediation by vagal afferents of glucose-induced satiation and the greater potency when it was administered duodenally contrast sharply with the result observed when fats and proteins are administered. The effects of these other macronutrients do not depend on vagal mediation and hepatic-portal infusions are more effective in suppressing food intake. This suggests that different nutrients regulate feeding by very different mechanisms. Any scheme that attempts to explain the short-term regulation of food intake in a unitary fashion overlooking the diversity of mechanisms responsive to different nutrient portions of a meal is not likely to succeed.

ACKNOWLEDGMENTS

The work reported in this chapter was supported by U.S. Public Health Service Grant NS 07687 from the National Institute of Neurological Diseases and Stroke. I gratefully acknowledge the collaboration of Drs. M. Rezek, K. Schneider, and D. A. VanderWeele and Mr. M. Gonzales and Mr. J. D. Sanderson.

REFERENCES

1. Anand, B. K., and Brobeck, J. R. (1951): *Proc. Soc. Exp. Biol. Med.,* 77:323.
2. Anand, B. K., and Brobeck, J. R. (1951): *Yale J. Biol. Med.,* 24:123.
3. Anand, B. K., Chhina, G. S., Sharma, K. N., Dua, S., and Singh, B. (1964): *Am. J. Physiol.,* 207:1146.
4. Anand, B. K., Dua, S., and Singh, B. (1961): *EEG. Clin. Neurophysiol.,* 13:54.
5. Baile, C. A., Zinn, W., and Mayer, J. (1971): *Physiol. Behav.,* 6:537.
6. Cannon, W. B. (1929): *Bodily Changes in Pain, Hunger, Fear, and Rage.* Appleton-Century-Crofts, New York.
7. Colin-Jones, D. G., and Himsworth, R. L. (1970): *J. Physiol.,* 206:397.
8. Ehman, G. K., Albert, D. J., and Jamieson, J. J. (1971): *Can. J. Psychol.,* 25:147.
9. Epstein, A. N., and Teitelbaum, P. (1964): In: *Thirst,* edited by M. J. Wayner, pp. 395–406. Pergamon, Oxford.
10. Epstein, A. N., and Teitelbaum, P. (1967): *Am. J. Physiol.,* 213:1159.
11. Fennergen, F. M., and Puiggari, M. J. (1966): *J. Neurosurg.,* 24:497.
12. Forsgren, E. (1928): *Skand. Arch. Physiol.,* 53:137.
13. Frohman, L. A., Müller, E. E., and Cocchi, D. (1973): *Horm. Metab. Res.,* 5:21.
14. Gonzales, M., Novin, D., and Sanderson, J. D., *Unpublished.*
15. Grossman, M. E., Cummins, G. A., and Ivy, A. C. (1947): *Am. J. Physiol.,* 149:100.
16. Grossman, M. E., and Stein, I. F., Jr. (1948): *J. Appl. Physiol.,* 1:263.
17. Harding, R., and Leek, B. F. (1973): *J. Physiol.,* 228:73.
18. Hetherington, A. W., and Ranson, S. W. (1940): *Anat. Rec.,* 78:149.
19. Janowitz, H. D., Hanson, M. E., and Grossman, M. I. (1949): *Am. J. Physiol.,* 156:87.
20. Kissileff, H. R. (1970): *Physiol. Behav.,* 5:163.
21. Miller, N. E. (1960): *Fed. Proc.,* 19:846.

22. Misher, A., and Brooks, F. P. (1966): *Am. J. Physiol.*, 211:403.
23. Morgan, C. T., and Morgan, J. D. (1940): *J. Gen. Psychol.*, 57:143.
24. Niijima, A. (1969): *Ann. NY Acad. Sci.*, 157:690.
25. Novin, D., Gonzales, M., and Sanderson, J. D. *Unpublished.*
26. Novin, D., Sanderson, J. D., and VanderWeele, D. A. (1974): *Physiol. Behav.*, 13:3.
27. Novin, D., VanderWeele, D., and Rezek, M. (1973): *Science,* 181:858.
28. Oomura, Y., Ooyama, H., Yamamoto, T., Ono, T., and Kobayashi, N. (1969): *Ann. NY Acad. Sci.,* 157:642.
29. Paintal, A. S. (1957): *J. Physiol.,* 139:353.
30. Penaloza-Rojas, J. H., Barrera-Mera, B., and Kubli-Garfias, C. (1969): *Exp. Neurol.,* 23:378.
31. Penaloza-Rojas, J. H., and Russek, M. (1963): *Nature,* 200:176.
32. Powley, T. L., and Opsahl, C. A. (1974): *Am. J. Physiol.,* 226:25.
33. Quigley, J. P., Johnson, V., and Solomon, E. I. (1929): *Am. J. Physiol.,* 90:89.
34. Rezek, M. (1974): Ph.D., Dissertation, UCLA.
35. Rezek, M., Schneider, K., and Novin, D. (1975): *Physiol. Behav.*
36. Rezek, M., VanderWeele, D. A., and Novin, D. (1975): *Behav. Biol.*
37. Russek, M. (1970): *Physiol. Behav.,* 5:1207.
38. Russek, M., and Stevenson, J. A. F. (1972): *Physiol. Behav.,* 8:245.
39. Sanderson, J. D., and VanderWeele, D. A. (1975): *Physiol. Behav.*
40. Schneider, K., Rezek, M., and Novin, D. *Unpublished.*
41. Sharma, K. N., and Nasset, E. S. (1962): *Am. J. Physiol.,* 202:725.
42. Smith, M. H. (1966): *J. Comp. Physiol.,* 61:11.
43. Steffens, A. B., Mogenson, G. J. and Stevenson, J. A. F. (1972): *Am. J. Physiol.,* 222:1972.
44. Stein, I. F., Jr., and Meyer, K. A. (1948): *Surg. Gynecol. Obstet.,* 86:473.
45. Teitelbaum, P., and Epstein, A. N. (1962): *Psychol. Rev.,* 69:74.
46. VanderWeele, D. A., Novin, D., Rezek, M., and Sanderson, J. D. (1974): *Physiol. Behav.,* 12:467.
47. Wangensteen, O. H., and Carlson, A. J. (1931): *Proc. Soc. Exp. Biol. Med.,* 28:545.
48. Wayner, M. J., Cott, A., Millner, J., and Tartaglione, R. (1971): *Physiol. Behav.* 7:881.
49. Woods, S. C., and Porte, D. (1974): *Physiol. Rev.,* 54:596.

Hunger: Basic Mechanisms and Clinical Implications,
edited by D. Novin, W. Wyrwicka, and G. Bray.
Raven Press, New York © 1976.

On the Nature of Feeding Patterns—Primarily in Rats

J. Panksepp

Department of Psychology, Bowling Green State University, Bowling Green, Ohio 43403

The evolutionary heritage of each species dictates the behavioral tendencies and capacities of its members. So should feeding patterns be viewed as products of natural selection, as adaptive responses to environmental constraints. Animals that evolved within marginal subsistence environments should exhibit feeding patterns different from those that developed in the midst of abundance. The patterns of animals that subsist on calorically dilute foods should be different from those that live on heartier fare. Animals that expend much energy in short periods might reasonably have different feeding habits than those that live with more restraint. Those that live for a few summer days should respond to food differently than those that age across many winter years. Clearly, great diversity should exist in feeding patterns.

At the most general level, it might be useful to categorize feeding patterns in terms of complexity. One system which could be employed has been proposed by Mayr (1). He distinguishes genetically preordained behavior patterns which are modified little by the life experiences of an animal, called "closed programs," from those which are susceptible to considerable modification, the "open programs." This distinction could also apply in the physiological realm, since the resilience of metabolic adaptations may vary widely among species. By definition, animals with open energy regulatory systems would be capable of exhibiting greater flexibility in the face of environmental change and adversity than animals with closed systems.

Thus, in nature, some animals exhibit very stereotyped and inflexible feeding patterns, for example, aquatic filter feeders, many of which feed continuously and some of which exhibit little change in filtering rate as a function of ambient microorganism density (2). At a more sophisticated level, there are flies that eat when provoked by specific types and intensities of chemostimulation and stop when their guts are sufficiently distended, but pay little heed to the actual energy states of their bodies (3). At a more complex level, most vertebrates eat with great discretion. They have been liberated from the need for continuous fuel acquisition by being endowed with sizeable portable fuel tanks, and feeding need occur only when the tanks need to be filled to respectable survival levels. In such animals, feeding patterns could be controlled by open programs capable of exhibiting extensive adaptations to environmental variations. This, of course, could preclude the presence of systematic relationships in feeding patterns across members of a species.

During the past decade, an increasing emphasis has been placed on the analysis of feeding patterns in attempts to understand the nature of energy balance regulation in mammals, especially rats. Because of the limited yield of the approach, it is time to assess what kinds of information such techniques have provided and are capable of providing. The assumption widely held by psychobiologists, that the analysis of food intake on a meal-to-meal basis would shed light on the nature of mechanisms that permit animals to maintain stable body energy balance, has been forcefully challenged by those who recognize that feeding patterns may be more a reflection of the evolutionary adaptation of a species to its ecologic niche than a measure of an animal's momentary metabolic states (4, 5). From that perspective, a finer and finer analysis of feeding patterns might fail to clarify the underlying causes of energy balance regulation. In their most polar forms, the opposing sides of this controversy might be taken to insist that feeding patterns are closed systems, be it behavioral or physiologic. The ecologically minded would see feeding patterns as reflecting genetic imperatives that nicely fit the traditional food sources of an animal, whereas the metabolically minded would recognize only that feeding patterns are subservient to physiologic imperatives (states of body nutrient depletion and repletion) which dictate when, how much, and how fast the animal should eat. Obviously these viewpoints are exaggerations. Feeding patterns of all land-dwelling vertebrates are probably open systems to a large degree. Although feeding clearly has evolved to fulfill the energy needs of the animals, feeding patterns may be molded by life experiences as well as by the types of food and environmental and social stimuli to which the animals are exposed. Thus a considerable amount of feeding activity could be nonregulatory at the time it occurs, even though all the ingested calories ultimately tip the regulatory scales.

The aim of this chapter is to discuss how much and what kind of information an analysis of feeding patterns can provide and has provided, especially in the omnivorous laboratory rat. Although there is no reason to suppose that findings from the rat will illuminate the behavior of all other mammals, it should clarify general concepts and probably shed understanding on the feeding mechanisms of species that inhabit nearby ecologic niches, for instance, relentless omnivores such as man.

GENERAL NATURE OF ENERGY BALANCE REGULATION

It is reasonable to assume that an understanding of feeding patterns in omnivores will entail identification of mechanisms that evolved to keep the available fuel tanks (liver and fat) filled. Essentially this could have been accomplished in two separate ways. First, feeding patterns may be so designed that the likelihood of energy consumption would always tend to exceed needs, excess energy being spilled from the system by means such as thermogenesis. Alternatively, a metering system may have evolved to either directly assess the size of fuel stores or indirectly gauge how effectively the fuel stores were providing for the body's fuel needs and to adjust feeding accordingly. No doubt a composite mechanism actually evolved—overfilled animals dissipating extra energy as well as undereating, underfilled animals conserving energy while overeating. Probably the mechanisms were also designed with great inherent flexibility; so, if needed, one mechanism could be backed up by compensatory processes. The question which needs to be resolved is whether or not the ongoing process of body energy defense can be abstracted from the ongoing feeding patterns of animals, especially those having free access to food.

MEAL-TO-MEAL FEEDING PATTERNS OF RATS

Feeding behavior should be capable of being completely characterized in terms of feeding frequency, feeding duration, feeding rate, and feeding intensity. Although a criterion-free analysis of feeding patterns could be developed (e.g., a continuous measure of the rate of feeding), the visually apparent patterning of food intake as meals and intermeal intervals has favored the development of analyses based on discrete events. With ordinary dry laboratory chow, it has generally been found that bouts of food consumption exceeding approximately 0.5 g and separated from other bouts by at least 10 to 20 min serve fairly well to distinguish what appear to be discrete meals in normal rats.

In the only systematic study of criteria, Kissileff (6) has found that with intermeal interval criteria of 12 to 40 min, the distribution of meals remains stable in both the continuously reinforced lever press situation and the free-access eatometer condition. With shorter criteria (1 and 5 min), however, the frequency of scored meals increases in the lever-press situation but not in the eatometer condition. Kissileff concluded that intervals larger than 10 to 20 min constitute true intermeal intervals as opposed to within-meal pauses.

Using the conservative criterion of 40 min without eating to distinguish meals, Le Magnen and Tallon (7) originally described a mathematical relationship between the size of meals and duration of intermeal intervals in the freely fed rat. They found that the size of meals was reliably correlated to postprandial intervals but not to preprandial intervals, suggesting that the amount eaten each meal was not controlled by a simple time-dependent depletion signal, but that the amount eaten did determine how long hunger was quelled. Although this postprandial relationship has been replicated several times (8–10), its basic meaning has been questioned on statistical grounds. First, the original computations were not done on raw data but on meals pooled in a potentially biassing manner. Meals were rank ordered by size into deciles, and computations were done on the resulting means. Since no systematic pattern was thus forced on the corresponding intermeal intervals, this computational procedure tends to reduce the normal variability of inter-

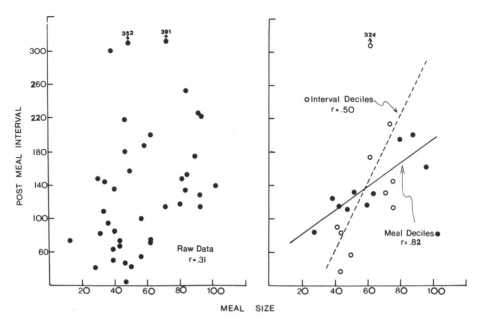

FIG. 1. Postprandial intervals (minutes) as a function of meal size (number of 45 mg Noyes pellets). *Left:* Raw data correlation = 0.31. *Right:* With data pooled into deciles according to meal sizes, the correlation is 0.82, and pooled according to intermeal intervals, it is 0.50.

meal intervals (11). As argued in (11) and indicated in Fig. 1, pooling procedures have marked effects of their own, and the reported positive results may have been wholly or partially due to the statistical bias rather than to an intrinsic relationship in the meal patterns. A second problem with the original procedures, more fully discussed by Hirsch and Collier (5), is that pooling was also performed across animals. Thus it is conceivable that the original correlations only indicated that some animals have frequent small meals with short intermeal intervals, whereas others have large meals with large intermeal intervals. In any case, a large number of investigators have now failed to find any systematic correlations between meals and intermeal intervals in the feeding pattern of rats (4, 11–13). For instance the average postprandial correlation computed on the raw data of 34 normal animals that have each been monitored for 4 successive days in our laboratory is 0.19, with 20% of the animals having statistically significant positive correlations. The average preprandial correlation for these animals is −0.08, with approximately 20% having significant negative values. Thus, we conclude that, in the daily feeding patterns of rats having free access to ordinary laboratory chow, no systematic relationships exist between the size of meals and intermeal intervals.

Still, it is worth considering why a small fraction of animals do exhibit reliable postprandial correlations, small as they may be. In terms of occurrence, the relationship appears to be clearly present when animals are maintained on liquid diets (1, 9), when animals are treated chronically with slow-acting forms of insulin (11), when animals are required to expend some moderate effort to obtain food (12), and possibly when rats are tested with high-fat diets (12) and possibly when only tested during the night phase of the diurnal cycle (8), although the evidence is ambiguous on this last point (15).

Because manipulations such as increasing the effort required to obtain food and diet concentration with fat can increase average meal sizes as well as postprandial correlations, Levitsky (12) suggested that manipulations that increase the size of meals beyond a critical level of 7 to 11 kcal will tend to yield significant postprandial correlations. Unfortunately this proposal does not generalize easily to other published data. Liquid diets increase the correlations, but they decrease the average caloric size of meals, while increasing daily meal frequency (14). Chronic insulin treatment produces similar effects with dry food (11). Conversely there are manipulations that increase meal size without increasing correlations. Diabetic animals eat meals twice as large as normal, but their postprandial correlations are only 0.25 as compared to 0.22 for controls ($n = 10$, per group) (16). Likewise, in yet to be published data, we have found that genetically obese Zucker rats also exhibit increased meal sizes with no increases in the postprandial correlations (fatty average $r = 0.12$, control $r = 0.09$).

Alternatively, I have proposed that the postprandial correlation may be characteristic of a depletion pattern of feeding (11). This is consistent with the insulin data, since that treatment appears to simulate a metabolic state of nutrient depletion. It can also potentially explain the results with liquid diets, since diet diluteness may enhance the likelihood of animals regulating at the depletion end of their normal regulatory range. Similarly, relative food scarcity, for instance, as when more effort is required to obtain food, might tend to shift the animal toward a depletion type of regulation. However, the finding that high-fat diets can also increase the relationship (12) is inconsistent with the depletion hypothesis, unless, of course, one assumes that the highly palatable diet is inducing the animal to regulate at a higher body weight, and accordingly the animal is temporarily in a relative state of depletion.

A third, although possibly not independent, explanation for the correlation is that any manipulation that tends to decrease the diurnal variability of feeding will tend to magnify the postprandial relationship. All of the above manipulations that increase correlations between meals and postmeal intervals also reduce differences between day and night feeding. The reason for the correlation may be the normalizing effect of this kind of feeding pattern on the typically bimodal distribution of intermeal intervals (11). This line of reasoning would also explain why postprandial correlations during the night phase might be more reliable than for the whole day.

But it may be academic to pursue this line of inquiry, for the correlations that do occur in occasional animals are quite small and there is as yet no evidence that they remain stable from day to day or week to week. A review of the literature indicates a value less than 0.4 is obtained when correlation coefficients from all individual animals that have been reported to exhibit reliable postprandial relationships are averaged. Hence the postprandial correlation begins to account for approximately 16% of the variance in one-third of the animals that have been tested. Although these few significant correlations do indicate that satiety can be correlated with amount ingested under restricted experimental conditions, the phenomenon is too weak to ascribe any important overall regulatory meaning to it. Certainly it cannot be used as a precise and reliable dependent measure in studies of energy balance regulation. Possibly a simple presentation of the diurnal distribution of meal sizes, intermeal intervals, and rates of feeding would suffice.

MODIFICATION OF FEEDING PATTERNS BY DIETARY CHANGE

Perhaps rats are capable of regulating energy intake with a variety of strategies, and no generally useful analytical procedure of meal patterns is possible. To demonstrate at least the feasibility of this extreme position, we have attempted to shift the rat's normal nocturnal mode of feeding to daylight

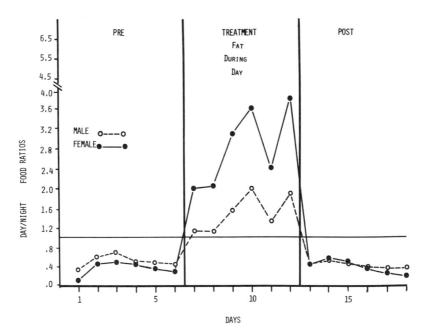

FIG. 2. Day/night food intake ratios of six male and eight female rats before, during, and after 6 experimental days of daytime access to a palatable high-fat diet. During the night, animals continued to receive their Purina maintenance chow.

hours by allowing access to a more palatable high-fat diet during those hours. As demonstrated in Fig. 2, this manipulation is very effective in reversing the animal's daily distribution of feeding. Whereas female rats normally consume about 80% of their food at night, they can be induced to consume 80% of it during the day without any change in the quality or availability of the night-time food. It is also noteworthy that females exhibit a larger reversal in feeding than males, all the more since they normally exhibit a more extreme diurnal distribution of feeding than males. Clearly, the feeding behavior of the rat can be labile to the extreme. Still this demonstration does not negate the possibility of finding a systematic regulatory pattern within the feeding pattern of rats when experimental conditions are maintained constant throughout the day.

AN ALTERNATIVE ANALYSIS OF FEEDING PATTERNS—A SIGNAL INTENSITY APPROACH

Merely because animals eat what appear to be discrete meals with intervening intervals, there are no *a priori* reasons for assuming that those events should be considered as the fundamental or optimal units by which feeding behavior should be analyzed. One could employ a variety of derived measures including ratios between meals and intervals. In fact, such measures, whether computed as satiety ratios (postmeal intervals/meal sizes) or deprivation ratios (meal sizes/premeal intervals), yield orderly circadian signals when plotted on the time axis as in Fig. 3. Moreover, since both functions wax and wane in phase, they probably reflect the operation of a unitary under-

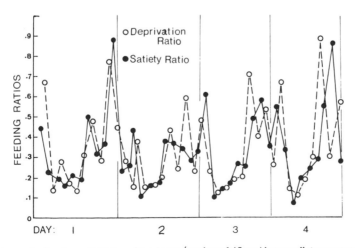

FIG. 3. Satiety ratios (postprandial interval in minutes/number of 45 mg Noyes pellets consumed per meal) and deprivation ratios (preprandial interval in minutes/number of 45 mg Noyes pellets consumed per meal) for one rat across 4 successive test days.

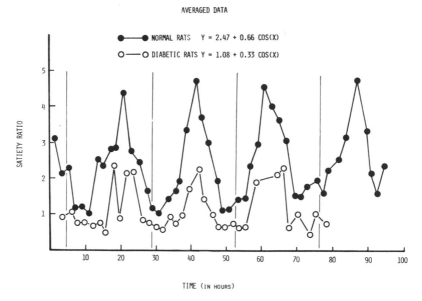

FIG. 4. Synchronously averaged curves of satiety ratios in 2-hr bins for 10 normal and 10 alloxan diabetic rats. The least squares equations of the form $Y = A + B \cos(X)$ for the two groups are indicated.

lying process, and this may be the long-term signal of body nutrient depletion-repletion by which body energy is stabilized (11).

In more recent work, we have analyzed this cyclic function in animals with different metabolic states, primarily experimental diabetes, and have found that the curves for these animals are distinguishable from control patterns (16). Figure 4 summarizes satiety-ratio curves for 10 normal and 10 diabetic animals that have been synchronously averaged. The diabetics exhibit a lower average level of satiety (lower d. c. level) and less systematic circadian variability around the mean level (lower a. c. level). To mathematize this behavior pattern, equations of the form $Y = A + B \cos(X)$ have been fit by least squares procedures to the sinusoidal functions. The procedure discriminates between groups in terms of both the magnitudes of the A(d. c. level) and B(a. c. level) coefficients. Since the curve fitting can be done on individual animals as well as the average groups curves, we have assessed the comparability of the various possible coefficients by (1) fitting each animal to its own best fitting curve, (2) fitting each animal to the average of the individual coefficients of the respective groups, and (3) fitting each animal to coefficients of the group average curve (data are summarized in Fig. 5). In agreement with mathematical requirements, the first procedure yielded the lowest average mean squared deviations. The other two techniques yielded somewhat higher deviations, but it is noteworthy that the coefficients of the average curve represented individual data as adequately as the average of individual coefficients. Furthermore, the procedures did discriminate between the two

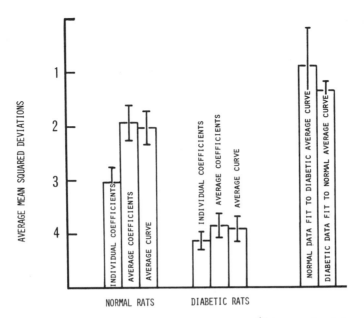

FIG. 5. Average mean squared deviations of individual animals from (1) their own best fitting curves of the form $Y = A + B \cos(X)$, (2) from a curve employing the average of individual coefficients of each group, and (3) from the average curves of each group depicted in Fig. 4. The rightmost histograms indicate deviations of animals in each group from the average curve of the other group. Standard errors of the mean are indicated.

groups since the deviations of individual animals from the averaged curves of the other group were reliably higher than any of the other comparisons (two right histograms of Fig. 3).

CRITIQUE OF THE SATIETY RATIO ANALYSIS OF FEEDING PATTERNS

From one perspective, these curve-fitting procedures may be more an academic exercise than an insightful analysis of a phenomenon. After all, the A coefficient, representing the average level of satiety, is a direct correlate of the average daily food intake of the animal, and the B coefficient, representing the circadian variability in satiety, must be related directly to average day and night food intakes. Thus it might be concluded that the rather laborious curve-fitting procedures have procured little insight into processes that control feeding.

Although the use of day-night feeding measures can provide a measure of the process that causes circadian fluctuation of satiety ratios, the mathematical analysis provides a finer focus on the underlying mechanisms. By using the proposed procedures, one can abstract all major information contained within feeding patterns into a simple mathematical function. Thus the procedure begins to delimit the minimum number of major processes that need to be understood in explaining feeding behavior (17). It also provides a more precise tool for correlating the cycle of energy regulation with physiological cycles that might be thought to mediate the regulation. Furthermore, by providing an on-line readout of the regulatory status of an animal, the procedures can be deployed under constant environmental conditions rather than being restricted to preselected illumination schedules. The data summarized in Figs. 3 and 4 were in fact collected from animals maintained under a continuous low level of illumination. This might be advantageous, since it is not clear what kind of illumination is ecologically most valid for the rat. Although diurnal lighting simulates the succession of day and night, it may not simulate a nocturnal animal's actual exposure to light in the real world. Rats may be entrained to but relatively unexposed to environmental light. In any case the use of unchanging illumination permits a clear analysis of circadian modulatory processes—a systematic bias that may arise from diurnal lighting conditions being eliminated.

Still, since the translation between the above mathematical analysis and a more simple diurnal analysis of feeding are straightforward, it is doubtful whether the technique does provide major empirical advantages, aside from completeness, over the simpler diurnal measurement procedures. More importantly, the procedure highlights the conceptual advantage of derived measures such as satiety ratios over simple measures of food intake. Indeed, it may be more informative to always describe feeding conjointly with the satiety that is produced. Maybe our basic units of feeding behavior should resemble the dynamic metabolic processes that are ultimately the basis for the energy intake of the organism. Clearly, this change of perspective reduces the urge to embark on potentially fruitless quests for privileged processes that control meal onsets and meal terminations. The sinusoidal form of successive satiety ratios suggests that discontinuities that are observed in feeding behavior may have no parallel discontinuities in underlying processes. Both meal initiation and meal termination may correspond to threshold levels on curves that relate metabolic processes to activity in neural circuits that control the rate of feeding. No doubt these threshold levels would be determined by levels of competing processes in the animal's life as well as by genetic prewiring. They may be open programs riding on a relatively closed program of physiological necessity.

These considerations highlight the need for an overall change in the types of measures that need to be used in feeding experiments, especially those that employ acute regulatory challenges. Most of the important information may be lost when feeding is measured only after predetermined intervals following the manipulations. In addition to food intake, it would be desirable to know how the satiating capacity of succeeding meals changes. Does a certain regulatory process require gradual readjustments in the satiating capacity of many meals or does a single meal suffice? Since this has never been done, all data that has been collected on feeding behavior is open to reanalysis.

FEEDING BEHAVIOR AND MODELS OF FEEDING BEHAVIOR

The signal intensity model of feeding patterns suggests that a confluence of factors converge to generate feeding behavior, with no privileged stimuli to initiate, maintain, and terminate meals. At the most fundamental level, the process of regulation is the result of the interplay of many conceptually and physiologically distinct processes interacting to yield an output that must reach threshold levels before activity in neural circuits that control feeding rate is increased to behaviorally observable levels. Presently the type of neural control model that serves as a theoretic base for our ongoing research is summarized in Fig. 6. On the basis of data, which has been reviewed elsewhere (17), it is believed that the medial hypothalamus elaborates a set-

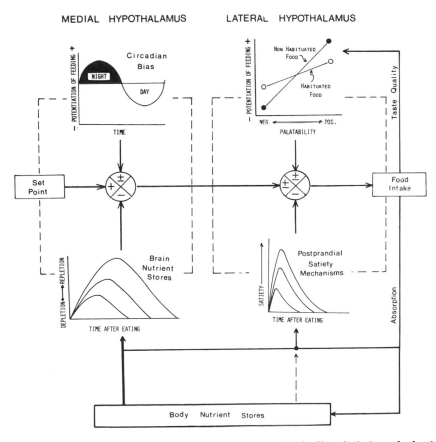

FIG. 6. A control system outline for hypothalamic control of energy intake. Hypothetical transfer functions are indicated for taste (it is proposed that the degree of gustatory influence is determined by the recent experiences of the animal with a certain food), short-term satiety processes operating relatively directly via LH circuits (the effects of three hypothetical meals of different sizes are indicated) and longer term signals of body nutrient repletion operating via the medial hypothalamus (the possible effects of these same three meals are indicated).

point process, a long-term error signal process, and an overriding circadian modulatory process, the interaction of which modulates activity of feeding circuits that course through the lateral hypothalamus, which themselves are more directly influenced by gustatory factors and short-term satiety signals. We have yet to empirically test the kind of output that this kind of model will generate, but we believe it will reasonably simulate the feeding patterns of rats as long as the short-term satiety process operating via lateral hypothalamic (LH) circuits is programmed to function as a threshold gate rather than a gradational interactive process.

This type of model further clarifies why strong systematic relationships between meals and intermeal intervals will not be forthcoming. However, it does predict certain changes in the magnitude of postprandial correlations, which should follow damage to hypothalamic subareas. Since the existence of a high postprandial correlation would require a reasonably good correspondence between the amount of ingested food and the duration of feeding inhibition, LH lesions, by attenuating the effect of a short-term proportional controller, would tend to decrease postprandial correlations. Recent data reported by Snowdon and Wampler (14) lends some support to this hypothesis. They observed that the average postprandial correlation dropped from a normal level of 0.36 to 0.32 after LH lesions, and to 0.06 after further imposition of bilateral vagotomy. The control group exhibited an initial correlation of 0.32, which rose to 0.52 after sham surgery and dropped only to 0.41 after vagotomy. Thus the LH lesion did contribute to the disappearance of the postprandial correlation, although vagotomy was necessary to amplify the deficit. In a preliminary series of four normal animals and four recovered LH-lesioned animals we have observed average postprandial correlations of 0.25 and 0.08, respectively. The changes, although by necessity small, have been in the predicted directions. It might also be noted that our animals with LH lesions exhibited on the average larger and longer meals (55 45-mg Noyes pellets/30 min) than did controls (44 pellets/7 min).

The model further predicts that after medial hypothalamic lesions, postprandial correlations would be increased because shorter term mechanisms operating via the LH area would dictate the control of feeding. Thomas and Mayer (10) have presented data consistent with this proposition.

Although it is certainly an oversimplification to assume that feeding control functions are as discretely localized as proposed in the model, existing data are compatible with the notion that these areas are major foci for the respective processes. In any case, the model is sufficiently precise to permit rigorous empirical tests and refutations.

CONCLUSIONS

Although the manner in which feeding patterns are controlled remains an intriguing psychobiological problem, there is presently no evidence that the simple analysis of meals and intermeal intervals has led to any valuable insights into the manner in which energy balance is regulated. Although an adequate understanding of body energy balance regulation will entail a thorough understanding of processes which control daily food intake, it does not follow that it shall also entail a thorough understanding of processes which control the patterns of food intake. When one considers the number of variables which could reasonably modulate the feeding pattern of an animal, the probability that measures of meal taking would be consistent and reliable indicators of regulation is remote. Among modulatory influences are taste, texture, caloric density, and nutritive quality of the food, types of food available, the state of body nutrient repletion of the animal, the degree of food availability, the effort required to obtain food, the metabolic rate of the animal, environmental temperature, environmental complexity, social setting, strength of competing motivations, activity level, general state of arousal, and health of the animal. Of course, this is not to say that a systematic regulatory pattern cannot be abstracted from meal-taking data. Indeed, with the use of derived measures such as satiety ratios and deprivation ratios, it becomes clear that a systematic correspondence occurs between feeding patterns and on-going body energy regulation. Still, because of the variety of influences that come to bear on the expression of regulation, it is unlikely that simple answers will be forthcoming to such questions as what initiates a meal, what terminates meals, and what determines how often animals eat each day. These behavioral events are not controlled by unitary physiological events, but rather by the converging influence of several concurrently operating mechanisms, some of which may exhibit intrinsic fluctuations during the course of the day.

It presently appears most plausible to conclude that although feeding is a relatively open behavioral system in rats, the physiological needs subserved are closed. Of course this is not to say the physiological substrate will never be modified by the animal's dietary experiences—permanent changes in weight regulation may occur with neonatal overfeeding, enzymes may be induced to cope with the types of food ingested, and endocrine exhaustion may be the consequence of dietary stresses. Furthermore, it must be remembered that, although rats regulate body energy balance, this regulation does not occur at some immutable level but within a range of values. Obviously, environmental influences will determine whether animals will regulate closer to the depletion end of the range or toward the repletion end. Furthermore, within the available range of normal regulation, there is probably more room on the repletion end when animals are fed ordinary rat chow. Surely, in the evolutionary history of each species, the danger of undereating must have been greater than the danger of overeating. Accordingly it is not surprising that body weight of animals will vary greatly depending on the types of foods to which they have access. It is also worth remembering that every regulatory system is subject to load errors. Even a thermostat-furnace heating system will not sustain the set-point temperature if the windows are opened on a cold winter day. There is no reason to expect that body weight will remain intact when animals are challenged with regulatory provocations such as extremely palatable foods. Furthermore, since feeding behavior may be ultimately controlled by the energy flux through certain parts of the visceral nervous system, body weight would have further opportunities to be dissociated from feeding behavior. Of course we will not know for sure until the exact mechanisms by which energy intake is regulated are more precisely identified.

ACKNOWLEDGMENTS

This work was supported by National Science Foundation grant GB-40150 and U.S. Public Health Service grant 1 R01 AM 17157–10 from the National Institute of Arthritis, Metabolism, and Digestive Diseases.

REFERENCES

1. Mayr, E. (1964): *Proc. Natl. Acad. Sci. USA*, 51:934–941.
2. Jorgensen, C. B. (1955): *Biol. Rev. Cambridge Phil. Soc.*, 30:391–454.
3. Dethier, V. G. (1967): In: *Handbook of Physiology, Sect. 6: Alimentary Canal, Vol. 1. Food and Water Intake.* edited by C. F. Code, pp. 79–96. American Physiological Society, Washington, D.C.
4. Collier, G., Hirsch, E., and Hamlin, P. H. (1972): *Physiol. Behav.*, 9:705–716.
5. Hirsch, E., and Collier, G. (1974): *Physiol. Behav.*, 12:239–249.
6. Kissileff, H. (1970): *Physiol. Behav.*, 5:163–173.
7. Le Magnen, J., and Tallon, S. (1966): *J. Physiol.* (Paris), 58:323–349.
8. Le Magnen, J., Devos, M., Gaudilliere, J. P., Louis-Sylvestre, J., and Tallon, S. (1973): *J. Comp. Physiol. Psychol.*, 84:1–23.
9. Snowdon, C. T. (1969): *J. Comp. Physiol. Psychol.*, 69:91–100.
10. Thomas, D. W., and Mayer, J. (1968): *J. Comp. Physiol. Psychol.*, 66:642–653.
11. Panksepp, J. (1973): *J. Comp. Physiol. Psychol.*, 82:78–94.
12. Levitsky, D. A. (1974): *Physiol. Behav.*, 12:779–787.
13. Premack, D., and Knisch, W. (1970): *Learn. Motivat.*, 1:321–326.
14. Snowdon, C. T., and Wampler, R. S. (1974): *J. Comp. Physiol. Psychol.*, 87:399–409.
15. Balagura, S., and Coscina, D. V. (1968): *Physiol. Behav.*, 3:641–643.
16. Panksepp, J., and Ritter, M. (1975): *J. Comp. Physiol. Psychol. (In press.)*
17. Panksepp, J. (1974): *Fed. Proc.*, 33:1150–1165.

Hunger: Basic Mechanisms and Clinical Implications,
edited by D. Novin, W. Wyrwicka, and G. Bray.
Raven Press, New York © 1976.

Peripheral Glucosensitive Satiety in the Rabbit and the Rat

Dennis A. VanderWeele and John D. Sanderson

Occidental College, Los Angeles, California 90041

The proposed existence of peripheral glucoreceptors active in the short-term control of food intake has received substantial support in recent experimentation. Interference with glucose utilization in the liver by direct intraportal infusion of 2-deoxy-*d*-glucose induces a greater hyperphagia with a shorter latency than that seen after general systemic infusion (1). Visceral vagal denervation results in hypophagia with subsequent recovery (2, 3), persistent alterations in the functioning of short-term feeding controls (3), and permanent deficits in peripheral glucose-induced satiety (4, 5). The concentration of sugars in the liver correlates inversely with feeding behavior in rats, whereas no such relationship exists between eating and sugar concentration in muscle, blood, and adipose tissue (6). When ingested nutrients are prevented from reaching the small intestine, an immediate and dramatic increase in food intake is observed (7). Electrophysiological investigation has provided support for the existence of glucosensitive receptors in hepatic (8, 9) and intestinal tissues (10).

In regard to satiety produced by the administration of glucose at peripheral sites, the literature contains conflicting reports. Infusions of glucose into the general circulation consistently failed to suppress food intake (11–14). Intraperitoneal, intragastric, intraduodenal, and intraportal glucose administration have been shown to inhibit food intake in some studies (5, 12, 13, 15, 16), but not in others (4, 5, 13, 17). One contributing factor to the discrepancy in results may be the nutrient state of the animal at the time the infusion is made. Novin et al. (4) have demonstrated that the locus of peripheral glucose-induced satiety is shifted when animals are subjected to 22 hr of food deprivation. Duodenal glucose infusions suppress food intake in free-feeding but not in food-deprived rabbits, whereas portal vein infusions are effective only in food-deprived animals. This shift may occur within as few as 4 hr of food deprivation (18).

Palatability of the test diet has also been shown to affect the appearance of satiety after duodenal glucose infusion. Campbell and Davis (19) found that intraduodenal glucose was an effective satiating agent in rats drinking a dilute glucose solution, but was ineffective when animals were tested with sweetened condensed milk, a highly palatable food for the rat.

Another variable which may contribute to the differing results in studies of satiety induced by peripheral nutrient administration is the temporality of infusion and its relationship to the spontaneous feeding pattern of the animal. Quartermain et al. (20) reported that intragastric infusion of a synthetic liquid diet programmed to approximate the natural feeding pattern of the rat is significantly more effective in suppressing oral intake than slow, continuous infusion of the same diet. Given 20 min before (17) or 4 hr after (21) a daily meal, intragastric loads of large amounts of nutrient are ineffective in reducing subsequent food intake in dogs. Even with daily injections of 175% of the normal caloric intake, no short-term effect is seen in that species (22). Similarly, Baile et al. (13) injected 25 g of glucose intragastrically in monkeys prior to a meal and found no effect on feeding. However, when they injected the same amount during the first 30 min of a meal, feeding was depressed by 60%. Premeal injection of glucose into jugular or mesenteric veins was also without apparent effect; they did not investigate the effects of glucose infusions during meals for these routes of entry. When infused slowly and continuously into the jugular vein, glucose has little effect on the food intake of rats (14).

The results of the experiments cited above suggested to us that the timing of peripheral glucose administration with respect to spontaneous meal taking may act to determine its effectiveness in suppressing food consumption. We have explored this notion by comparing the effects on feeding of small amounts of isotonic glucose infused into the hepatic-portal vein of rabbits and the duodenum of rabbits and rats either during or between spontaneous meals. Since the amounts of glucose infused were deliberately small and presumably of little significance in the total nutritive economy of the animal, we adopted a microanalytic approach in order to evaluate subtle, short-term changes in feeding behavior. Individual meal sizes, intervals between meals, and ratios of intermeal intervals to antecedent meal sizes (satiety ratios) were measured and compared to gross measurements of total consumption within preset periods of elapsed time. By using very small dosages of glucose we hoped to maximize any differences that might be revealed by our experimental conditions, and also to give us some impression of the sensitivity of the mechanisms involved. Two species whose feeding patterns differ quantitatively (rat, rabbit) were tested, as species differences are of obvious importance and could yield additional valuable information about interactions between exogenous glucose administration and natural feeding patterns.

METHODS

Female New Zealand rabbits, 2.7 to 3.4 kg at the time of surgery, were individually housed in cages 82 cm × 45 cm × 56 cm. Standard rabbit laboratory chow was offered during both testing and maintenance; no food or water deprivations were imposed except prior to surgery. Food was provided in glass histology dishes placed in a feeding box attached to the perimeter of the cage. The food was conveniently accessible from the cage interior and could also be removed for weighing through a hinged door on the outside of the feeding box. A photocell beam crossed the feeding box in a manner such that the animal interrupted it whenever eating. Visual output from the photocell was monitored on a 20-pen Esterline Angus event recorder in an adjacent room. Previous work has shown that rabbits adapt quickly to the measurement procedure and do not deviate from their normal feeding patterns (3).

Six rabbits were surgically implanted with an air-tight chronic infusion cannula whose tip rested in the hepatic-portal vein 1 to 2 cm from the liver (portals). Six rabbits were implanted with a cannula entering the gastric antrum and threaded through the pyloric sphincter to rest in the duodenal cap (duodenals). An additional eight rabbits were bilaterally vagotomized, subdiaphragmatically, four of which received duodenal cannulae, and four received portal cannulae at the time of surgery. Details of surgery and the method of verification of vagotomy are described in a previous paper (5).

Infusion and testing procedures were as follows. At the beginning of an experimental session, the animal's cannula was connected via counterweighted polyethylene tubing to a syringe driven by an infusion pump. The syringes were filled with 5-cc solutions of either 5.0% glucose or 0.9% saline. The weight of the food was recorded to the nearest 0.1 g and returned to the animal. At this time the experimenter left the room and tracked the spontaneous feeding behavior of the animal on the event recorder. The first meal that occurred during the experimental session was designated the criterion meal. Infusions were made either during the criterion meal (meal contingent infusions) or 12 min after the termination of that meal (postmeal infusion). All infusions were given at a constant rate of 1 cc/min. Meal contingent infusions were started 30 sec after the initiation of the first meal to assure that a meal was actually in progress. The first meal and each meal that occurred during the 2 hr that followed were measured 8 min after the meal ended. Intervals between meals were derived directly from the event recorder charts. Meals were defined as at least 1 min of feeding in which 0.8 g or more of chow was consumed, separated from other meals by at least 12 min. Meal contingent or postmeal infusions of saline or glucose were made during both the dark phase and light phase of the circadian feeding cycle, with each intact subject receiving two infusions in each condition; vagotomized subjects received three infusions in each condition. Differences between saline and glucose trials were determined with repeated measures t tests.

The second experiment employed 10 Long Evans hooded rats, implanted with duodenal cannulas. The animals were housed in operant chambers and trained to bar press for 45-mg Noyes pellets. The pattern of consumption was electronically displayed on an event recorder, and the number of pellets delivered recorded by relay counter. The infusions were similar to those described for the rabbit except that the volume of isotonic saline or glucose infused was 2 ml and was delivered at 0.4 cc/min. Meal contingent infusions were begun when either 10 bar presses or 1 min of sequential bar pressing had occurred, and postmeal infusions were started 55.5 min after the termination of the criterion meal. The definition of a meal in the rat was at least 10 consecutive bar presses within 1 min (the production of 0.45 g of food) separated from other clusters of bar presses by at least 3 min.

RESULTS AND DISCUSSION

Studies in Vagus-Intact Rabbits

Figure 1 graphically depicts the food intake pattern that follows meal contingent and postmeal glucose and saline infusions in intact rabbits. Isotonic glucose infused into the hepatic-portal vein during a spontaneous meal reduced the size of that meal by 24% ($p < 0.05$) in the light and 19% in the dark (these and all comparisons to follow are glucose versus saline controls). Note, however, that the duration of nonfeeding that follows a glucose-infused meal is reduced by 45% in the light and 48% in the dark phase ($p < 0.05$). Satiety ratios are actually significantly smaller when glucose is infused intraportally during the criterion meal (Table 1). Glucose infused into the portal vein after the criterion meal did not appreciably alter either the latency to the next meal or its size. Food intake measures based on the total 2-hour period did not differ substantially between glucose and saline infusions for the portal route of entry under either infusion condition (Table 2).

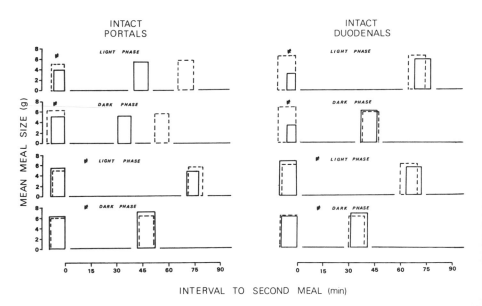

FIG. 1. Graphic representation of the effects of glucose (solid bars) and saline (dashed bars) infusions on the criterion meal, second meal, and interval between them in intact rabbits. Arrows, timing of infusion (meal contingent or postmeal).

TABLE 1. *Satiety ratios after infusion of isotonic glucose or saline at peripheral sites in intact and vagotomized rabbits*

Condition and solution	Intact		Vagotomized	
	Portals	Duodenals	Portals	Duodenals
Meal contingent				
glucose	11.4	24.0	23.7	7.7
light				
saline	17.0[a]	11.5[a]	17.6	13.6[a]
glucose	4.9	18.1	10.0	3.8
dark				
saline	10.9[a]	5.2[b]	8.6	7.1[a]
Postmeal				
glucose	15.2	16.5	16.2	12.2
light				
saline	24.4	14.0	14.6	11.3
glucose	8.9	5.2	11.4	4.9
dark				
saline	10.1	5.0	6.4	7.7

The satiety ratios (minutes nonfeeding/gram chow eaten) are in all cases based on the criterion meal and the intermeal interval that follows it. Only comparisons of glucose versus saline controls for identical conditions were made; no cross-condition or treatment comparisons were evaluated statistically.

[a] $p < 0.05$.
[b] $p < 0.01$.

TABLE 2. *Two-hour total food consumption in grams after infusions of isotonic glucose or saline at peripheral sites in intact and vagotomized rabbits*

Condition and solution	Intact		Vagotomized	
	Portals	Duodenals	Portals	Duodenals
Meal contingent				
glucose	14.5	9.8	8.9	16.1
light				
saline	11.6	13.8	10.5	12.6
glucose	18.3	15.0	14.6	29.6
dark				
saline	17.2	20.3	14.3	17.1[a]
Postmeal				
glucose	11.7	12.7	12.3	17.4
light				
saline	14.1	14.5	12.2	14.4
glucose	19.1	29.5	16.5	25.0
dark				
saline	17.6	22.0	19.3	18.4

Only comparisons of glucose versus saline controls for identical conditions were made; no cross-condition or treatment comparisons were evaluated statistically.

[a] $p < 0.05$.

Meal contingent glucose administered intraduodenally resulted in a 52% decrease in the size of the first meal in the light phase, and a 54% depression in the dark ($p < 0.01$), whereas subsequent intermeal intervals and second meal sizes are essentially the same as following saline infusions (Fig. 1). The resulting satiety ratios are more than doubled in magnitude in the light phase and more than tripled in the dark (Table 1). The reduction in food intake is still evident at the end of 2 hr, but the differences are not significant (Table 2). Intraduodenal glucose infusion in the postmeal condition fails to differ from control infusions on any of the measures.

Infused during a spontaneous meal, intraduodenal glucose effects an immediate and a lasting satiety, whereas the same amount infused 12 min after the end of a meal has no apparent effect. This finding parallels that of Quartermain et al. (20), who found significant differences between continuous gastric infusions of liquid diet and discrete infusions programmed to the animal's natural feeding pattern. This work also supports previous findings of a duodenally based satiety signal (5), and the microanalytic approach used here provides evidence that it functions rapidly in determining the size of meals or satiety onset. We have also observed an immediate feeding depression produced by hepatic-portal glucose infused during a meal, but the effect is far weaker than that seen after duodenal infusion. Also, the response to portally infused glucose includes a paradox: the small depression in meal size being more than compensated by a reduction in latency to the next meal. These results taken together suggest that hepatic glucoreceptors may participate in the induction of satiety, but that its maintenance may be dependent on events arising from the passage of nutrients across the intestinal wall.

The differing results reported here for the satiating action of glucose intraduodenally and intraportally has an interesting parallel in studies of glucose disappearance following its administration at different peripheral sites. The rate of removal of orally administered glucose from the blood is approximately three times as great as that following intravenous glucose (23), and similar differences are obtained when intestinal infusion is compared to the intravenous route (24). Scow and Cornfield (23) suggest that this is due to the increased hepatic removal of glucose from portal venous blood. They calculated that only 37% of the glucose leaving the intestine reaches the general circulation. Another relevant finding is that the presence of glucose in the gastrointestinal tract is able to stimulate the uptake of a load given intravenously (25). It is thus possible that glucose infused intraportally during a meal may contribute to the onset of satiety only because of the presence in the intestine of glucose arising from the meal being ingested concurrently (26). Experimental evidence that humoral substances arising from the intestinal mucosa participate substantially in the control of carbohydrate metabolism is accumulating, and considerable support has been gained for the concept of an enteroinsular axis whereby the absorption of nutrients is interfaced with its postabsorptive consequences (27). We propose that there is an orderly sequence of physiologic events that follows the ingestion of food, and that the sequence itself may be important in determining satiety. The behavioral observations from which we infer a state of satiety should not be considered the result of an interaction between ingested nutrient and a single receptor, but rather the reflection of a series of events taking place as food is taken, tasted, swallowed, digested, absorbed, transported, and metabolized.

Another point worthy of emphasis is the apparent sensitivity of the satiety mechanism rapidly responding to exogenous glucose. The actual dosages of glucose delivered in this study were 0.25 g in the rabbit and 0.1 g in the rat. For the rabbit, this amount of glucose contains less than 1 kcal, and yet the animal normally ingests over 400 kcal in a day, of which approximately two-thirds is derived from carbohydrate. The duodenal infusion of this small amount of glucose in an isotonic solution results in a 3 g decrease in the size of an ongoing meal, and yet is calorically equivalent to only approximately 10% of that amount of chow. It is obvious that under the conditions of this experiment, glucose administration stimulates satiety to a much greater degree than would be expected on the basis of its caloric significance alone.

Studies in Vagotomized Rabbits

As depicted in Fig. 2, no significant differences were observed between isotonic glucose and saline infusions for any of the measures in vagotomized rabbits when the route of entry was the hepatic-portal vein. There is, however, an apparent trend towards longer intermeal intervals and therefore larger satiety ratios (Table 1) after glucose for both infusion conditions. When infused into the duodenum of vagotomized animals, the effects of glucose are consistent and striking. Meal-contingent intraduodenal glucose infusion does not alter the size of the criterion meal as it does in intact animals. Rather than inducing satiety, the interval to the second meal is significantly shortened by 48% in the light and 41% in the dark phase ($p < 0.05$). Satiety ratios are significantly decreased (Table 1), reminiscent of the effects observed after meal contingent glucose in intact portally infused rabbits. Post-meal glucose infusions in vagotomized animals also tended to shorten slightly the latency to the next meal in the dark, but not the light phase. Two-hour totals also show increased feeding after glucose, significantly greater for meal contingent duodenal infusions in the dark phase (Table 2).

The satiety response that follows duodenal instillation of glucose during a meal requires an intact vagus nerve. Indeed, as we have seen here and in previous work, intraduodenal glucose can actually stimulate feeding in vagotomized animals. One tempting explanation of this result is the possibility of a positive-feedback mechanism operating at the visceral level that is revealed when the vagal limb of a peripheral glucosensitive satiety is eliminated. Recall the reduction in postprandial satiety seen with meal contingent

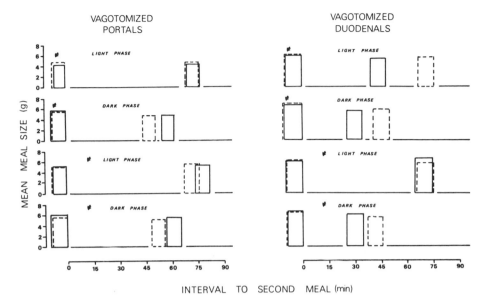

FIG. 2. Graphic representation of the effects of glucose (solid bars) and saline (dashed bars) infusions on the criterion meal, second meal, and interval between them in subdiaphragmatically vagotomized rabbits. Arrows, timing of infusion (meal contingent or postmeal).

infusion of small amounts of glucose intraportally in vagus-intact rabbits. It is interesting to note that both of these effects are clearly present only when the infusion is concurrent with a spontaneous meal, suggesting that the interruption in postprandial satiety results from an interaction between responses to ingested nutrient and infused glucose, probably in a synergistic fashion. The secretion of some of the humoral agents arising from the intestinal mucosa are impaired following truncal vagotomy (28), but the factors involved in the gastrointestinal response to insulin release are still operational. In fact, under some conditions, gastric or duodenal glucose administration is accompanied by high, rapid peaks in insulin release in vagotomized animals (29). This suggests the possibility that an insulin overreactivity is responsible for the disruption in satiety maintenance in vagotomized rabbits when given small amounts of glucose intraduodenally. This could also explain the satiety reduction seen in intact portals. Russek (30) has demonstrated that amounts of glucose comparable to those used in this study, when infused slowly into the portal vein of anesthetized cats, results in a substantial arterial hypoglycemia apparent 5 min and lasting more than 30 min after administration.

Studies in Rats

When duodenal infusions were made in rats feeding *ad lib* in an operant situation, the results differed somewhat from those reported for duodenally infused rabbits. Meal-contingent glucose did not significantly affect the criterion meal, but subsequent food intake was depressed, seen most markedly in a near doubling of the intermeal interval following the second meal. Postmeal or intermeal interval infusions of glucose increased the latency to the next meal by 52% and decreased the size of that meal by 24% ($p < 0.05$).

The rat, like the rabbit, is sensitive to the exogenous administration of small amounts of isotonic glucose delivered intraduodenally. In the experiment reported here, the food intake depression is accomplished by slightly different means: by a lengthening of subsequent intermeal intervals while meal size is

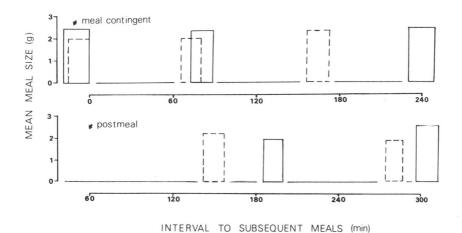

INTERVAL TO SUBSEQUENT MEALS (min)

FIG. 3. Effects of glucose infusions on meal-taking behavior in rats. Arrows, timing of glucose infusions occur either during (meal contingent) or 55.5 min after (postmeal) the criterion meal. Route of entry is through a chronic indwelling duodenal cannula.

unaltered. Levitsky and Collier (31) stated that meal initiation in the rat is a more immediate adjustment than meal duration to changes in nutritional status, a view that was supported by our results. Booth (15) has also demonstrated that gastric glucose intubation in rats, whose access to food is delayed for 1 hr, increased feeding latencies, whereas meal sizes were unchanged. Levitsky and Collier consider meal size to be a long-term adjustment to altered nutritional conditions.

The differences between rat and rabbit in these experiments may reflect differences in the testing situation rather than being attributable to species *per se*. Different dosages of glucose were delivered and the highly palatable Noyes pellets might limit duodenal glucosensitive satiety (19). Also the operant task performed by the rat may artificially limit meal size variance. A species difference in feeding patterns also exists in that the rabbit eats many more meals per day than does the rat. The metabolic flux that determines feeding frequency, by virtue of its greater periodicity, may make the rabbit responsive to small amounts of glucose.

SUMMARY AND CONCLUSIONS

Subtle differences in antecedent physiological and behavioral states can act to determine the outcome of experimental manipulations of visceral nutrient contents. The satiety that follows nutrient incorporation has an important temporal component in both rats and rabbits, and the sequence of alimentary events may itself determine to what extent ingested food inhibits further eating. A rapid and sensitive peripheral glucose-induced satiety that depends on an intact vagus nerve can be demonstrated in free-feeding rabbits, but no single organ or tissue, either peripherally or centrally located, can be characterized as the only locus of hunger or satiety. Food intake regulation is indeed multifactorial, involving complex physiological interplay at several sites. Simple conceptions of satiety as a hunger-free state or as the result of one particular food fraction acting on a single receptor are probably misleading. It may be more fruitful to consider a continuum of nervous, humoral, and metabolic events occurring during and between meals.

ACKNOWLEDGMENTS

We would like to express our appreciation to Sue Davison, Dennis Skoog, and Rick Smith for their able assistance during the conduction of the experiment. Experimentation with the rat was partially conducted by Kim Schiffer as an undergraduate thesis and we also express to her our appreciation. The experiments with rabbits were contained in a thesis submitted by John Sanderson to Occidental College in partial fulfillment of the requirement for the M.A. degree. Finally, this work was partially supported by U.S. Public Health Service Grant NS 7687 to Dr. Donald Novin.

REFERENCES

1. Novin, D., VanderWeele, D., and Rezek, M. (1973): *Science,* 181:858–860.
2. Rezek, M., VanderWeele, D., and Novin, D. (1975): *Behav. Biol.,* 14:75–84.
3. Sanderson, J., and VanderWeele D. (1975): *Physiol. Behav. (In press.)*
4. Novin, D., Sanderson, J., and VanderWeele, D. (1974): *Physiol. Behav.,* 13:3–7.
5. VanderWeele, D., Novin, D., Rezek, M., and Sanderson, J. (1974): *Physiol. Behav.,* 12:467–473.
6. Russek, M., and Stevenson, J. (1972): *Physiol. Behav.,* 8:245–249.
7. Davis, J., and Campbell, C. (1973): *J. Comp. Physiol. Psychol.,* 83:379–387.
8. Niijima, A. (1969): *Ann. NY Acad. Sci.,* 157:690–700.
9. Schmitt, M. (1973): *Am. J. Physiol.,* 225:1089–1095.
10. Sharma, K., and Nasset, E. (1962): *Am. J. Physiol.,* 202:725–730.
11. Janowitz, H., Hanson, M., and Grossman, M. (1949): *Am. J. Physiol.,* 156:87–91.
12. Russek, M. (1970): *Physiol. Behav.,* 5:1207–1209.
13. Baile, C., Zinn, W., and Mayer, J. (1971): *Physiol. Behav.,* 6:537–541.
14. Adair, E., Miller, N., and Booth, D. (1968): *Comm. Behav. Biol.,* 2:25–37.
15. Booth, D. (1972): *J. Comp. Physiol. Psychol.,* 78:412–432.
16. Yin, T., and Tsai, C. (1973): *J. Comp. Physiol. Psychol.,* 85:225–264.
17. Janowitz, H., and Grossman, M. (1948): *Am. J. Physiol.,* 155:28–34.

18. VanderWeele, D., and Novin, D. (1975): Presented at the proceedings of the Eastern Psychological Association in New York.
19. Campbell, C., and Davis, J. (1974): *Physiol. Behav.,* 12:377–384.
20. Quartermain, D., Kissileff, H., Shapiro, R., and Miller, N. (1971): *Science,* 173: 941–943.
21. Share, I., Martyniuk, E., and Grossman, M. (1952): *Am. J. Physiol.,* 169:229–237.
22. Janowitz, H., and Hollander, F. (1953): *Fed. Proc.,* 12:72.
23. Scow, R., and Cornfield, J. (1954): *Am. J. Physiol.,* 179:435.
24. McIntyre, N., Holdsworth, C., and Turner, D. (1965), *J. Clin. Endocrinol.,* 25: 1317–1324.
25. Conrad, V. (1955): *Acta. Gastroent. Belg.,* 18:655.
26. Steffens, A. (1969): *Physiol. Behav.,* 4:892–893.
27. Unger, R., and Eisentraut, A. (1969): *Arch. Intern. Med.,* 123:261–266.
28. Konturek, S., Becker, H., and Thompson, J. (1974): *Arch. Surg.,* 108:704–708.
29. Miller, R. (1970): *Endocrinology,* 86:642–651.
30. Rodriguez-Zendejas, A., Vega, C., Soto-Mora, L., and Russek, M. (1968): *Physiol. Behav.,* 3:259–264.
31. Levitsky, D., and Collier, G. (1968): *Physiol. Behav.,* 3:137–140.

Hunger: Basic Mechanisms and Clinical Implications,
edited by D. Novin, W. Wyrwicka, and G. Bray.
Raven Press, New York © 1976.

Peripheral Control of Meal Size: Interaction of Gustatory Stimulation and Postingestional Feedback

John D. Davis, Barbara J. Collins, and Michael W. Levine

University of Illinois, Chicago, Illinois 60612

Traditionally, peripheral theories of hunger have been concerned with the origin of the sensations of hunger, the preconditions assumed to motivate an organism to seek out and ingest food. Cannon's well-known theory (4), which ascribed these sensations to motility of the stomach, is the most recent example of a long line of speculation aimed at identifying the conscious expression of the sensations of hunger. These kinds of peripheral theories of hunger, while stimulating a great deal of research, have not been notably successful in describing the conditions that antedate the onset of a meal. More recently, however, the peripheral control of hunger has taken on a somewhat different meaning and with this change, perhaps because of it, more progress seems to be occurring. The field of the peripheral control of hunger seems now to be concerned less with identifying the source of the sensations that are believed to lead to the initiation of feeding and more with the variables that determine how much an animal will eat after the organism has made contact with food. We will focus our attention here on two types of these variables: gustatory stimulation and feedback from the gastrointestinal tract.

It has been recognized for some time that gustatory stimulation plays a central role in the control of feeding. High palatability stimulates feeding, and low palatability or adulteration by unpalatable substances such as quinine decreases intake. It has also been known for some time that the consequences of ingestion feedback to inhibit intake. Sham feeding studies (6, 12, 17, 27) are consistent in showing that when ingested food is not allowed to accumulate in the stomach, meal size increases dramatically. Many types of negative feedback signals that limit intake under normal conditions have been identified. Among these are an osmotic signal (14, 23, 21), gastric distention (6), hepatic glucoreceptor activity (19), chemospecific activity (22), and duodenal hormones (10, 24, 20), and it is likely that more will be identified in time. The research to be described here focuses on a negative feedback signal that has received little attention in the past. This signal we believe arises from the activation of tension receptors in the wall of the small intestine and is activated whenever the rate of ingestion and the rate of delivery of chyme from the stomach to the duodenum exceeds the rate of absorption from the intestine causing a net accumulation of fluid in the intestine. The results of the studies that have led us to this conclusion have been analyzed within the context of a quantitatively explicit feedback model. Therefore, before describing the results of our experiments, it will be necessary to describe the model.

The analysis of a system whose output influences its input by negative feedback has been developed in some detail in the field of engineering. This approach, known as control theory, has been applied with some success to physiologic systems (18) and recently to the study of animal behavior (15, 16). The relatively common use of the terms "short-term satiety signals" and "postingestional satiety signals" suggests that investigators have been talking in very general terms about the control of meal size within the context of control theory for some time. McFarland (15) has recently shown that the rather vague use of these terms can be made much more precise and that quantitatively explicit predictions can be made when control theory is applied to the analysis of meal size. Our model is similar to some of those he has developed.

Although we are fully aware of the fact that most biologic systems are nonlinear, our approach has nevertheless been to start with a linear model and then to introduce nonlinear components where they appear to be needed. The reason for this is that linear systems can be handled mathematically with relative ease (18) and sometimes are sufficiently close approximations to nonlinear systems to be useful as a first approximation to the final goal. The model described here is thus a linear one, and, as will be seen, does provide a reasonably good explanation of a substantial amount of data.

A fundamental assumption of the model is that there is an ingestion mechanism organized in the CNS whose output controls the musculature that is involved in the transfer of nutrients from the external to the internal environment. The input to this mechanism is a command signal, which represents the algebraic sum of those signals that activate the ingestion mechanism and those that inhibit it. This command signal is assumed to drive the ingestion mechanism, and thus the output, at a rate proportional to its magnitude. Thus the critical variable that determines at any moment the rate of drinking depends entirely on the magnitude of this systemic command signal, which in turn is a function of excitatory and inhibitory inputs.

The basic system is illustrated in Fig. 1 (top). The input to this system typically will represent all of the factors that can activate ingestive activity. The two most notable examples of these are food deprivation and palatability. Since in this paper we are concerned only with gustatory stimulation as an activator of ingestion the effects of deprivation on feeding are not included in this model. The box labeled d in the forward loop of the control system is a parameter that describes the properties of a CNS neural system that converts gustatory stimulation into a motor output (drinking rate). It is simply a convenient way of representing still another complicated control system.

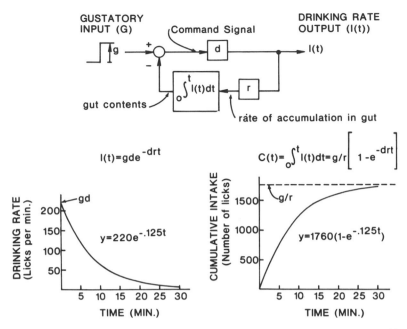

FIG. 1. *Top:* Schematic representation of the feedback model described in the text. *Bottom:* I(t) and its cumulative form C(t) along with representative graphs of these functions.

Considering just this forward loop and ignoring the negative feedback loop below it for the moment, the model indicates that the output (drinking rate) will be directly proportional to the product of the input, which is gustatory stimulation g, a variable which scales palatability, and the forward gain of the system d. In mathematical terms the output of this system under open loop conditions is gd ($I(t) = gd$), where I is the ingestion rate and t is time. Open loop performance of animals can be achieved by esophagotomy (17, 12) or approximated by brief contact drinking tests (2, 5, 26). The results of all of these studies are consistent in showing that open loop drinking rate is directly proportional to the type and concentration of carbohydrate used to stimulate drinking.

Figure 2 provides an example of the licking rate of rats in a brief contact test that approximates open loop performance. This figure summarizes the results of an unpublished experiment conducted in collaboration with Ann Rabinow. In this experiment the rats' rate of licking for 3 min in response to different concentrations of four different sugars was recorded. It is clear that licking rate under these conditions is directly related to both the concentration and nature of the sugar used to stimulate licking.

Under normal conditions the loop is closed and the consequences of ingestion feed back as an inhibitory signal to slow down drinking rate. The difference in performance between open loop and closed loop conditions in-

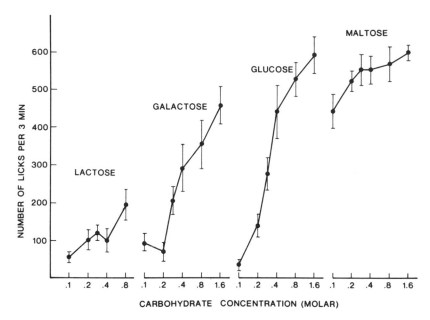

FIG. 2. Mean number of licking responses elicited by different concentrations of four sugars. The animals had daily 3-min exposures to each of the indicated concentrations of the sugars in the order of increasing concentration. The maximum concentration of lactose used was 0.8 M because of its limited solubility. Vertical bars, range of ± 1 SE.

dicates that some consequence of the introduction of fluid into the gut gives rise to this inhibitory signal. However, while the animal is drinking, fluid is being transferred from the stomach to the intestine, where it is absorbed. If absorption rate is greater than or equal to ingestion rate, there will be no net accumulation of fluid in the gut. However, if absorption rate is less than ingestion rate fluid will accumulate in the gut during drinking. This fact is incorporated in the model by defining a retention coefficient (r) that represents the modulation of absorption rate caused by the concentration and nature of the ingested substances.

The retention coefficient should be viewed as a mathematical fiction. We have found it convenient to think of it as a retention rate representing the ratio of volume absorption through the intestinal wall to the rate of inflow to the intestine (drinking rate). This yields an effective inflow rate that, when integrated over time, gives volume accumulated in the gut. Accumulation of gut contents can thus be represented mathematically as $r_0 \int^t I(t)dt$. This representation is a simplification of the real situation, in which volume contained within the intestine at any time is the difference between the time integrals of the influx (drinking rate) and the efflux (absorption rate). If efflux were a constant, this equation would be correct, but in fact it is some function of the instantaneous composition of the fluid in the intestine. What we have done is to model this subsystem with a simple multiplicative coefficient (r), whose value depends on the composition of the ingested fluid according to an empirically derived relationship.

In terms of the model, when an animal makes gustatory contact with a palatable solution, it is equivalent to introducing a step input of magnitude g proportional to the palatability of the solution. The behavior of the system in response to such a step input can be described by the function $I(t) = gde^{-drt}$, where g is proportional to palatability, d is the forward gain of the system, e is the base of the natural logarithms, r is the retention coefficient, and t is time in minutes (the derivation of this function is given in the appendix). Since intake is usually recorded cumulatively it is convenient to convert this function to a cumulative one. This can be accomplished by integrating $I(t)$ from 0 to t to give cumulative intake as a function of time, $C(t)$. This function is given to the right in Fig. 1 along with a representative curve for some specific values of the variables and parameters of the system.

Our model thus makes the following predictions about the amount of fluid consumed when g and r are variables: (1) the cumulative intake function will have the form of an exponential growth function; (2) the total amount drunk (g/r), which is the asymptote of $C(t)$, will be directly proportional to the palatability of the solution and inversely proportional to the retention coefficient; (3) the rate of approach to the asymptote (the inverse of the time constant) will be directly proportional to the product of the forward gain of the ingestion mechanism and the retention coefficient, and independent of palatability factors, since g does not appear in the exponent; (4) the initial rate of drinking (the value of $I(t)$ at $t = 0^+$) will be directly proportional to the product of the forward gain and palatability.

The experiment that led to the development of this model was designed specifically to vary the intestinal absorption rate while keeping gustatory stimulation constant. Since the concentration of the solution absorbed from the intestine is isotonic with the luminal contents of the intestine, absorption rate should be manipulable by introducing a nonabsorbable substance into the intestinal luminal fluid. Mannitol was used for this purpose because it is either not absorbed (9) or at most very slowly absorbed (8) by the intestine. Furthermore it tastes slightly sweet to humans, and we therefore assumed that it could be added in varying amounts to a very sweet solution without altering the palatability of the latter. The test solution to which mannitol was added was a mixture of saccharin and glucose (0.006 M Na saccharin $+0.1$ M glucose) which Valenstein, Cox, and Kakolewski (25) have shown stimulates a large amount of drinking.

Although we could not detect the presence of mannitol when it was added to the saccharin glucose solution, we could not be certain that it could not be detected or would not affect palatability for the rat. We therefore determined the effect of adding mannitol to the saccharin-glucose solution by determining the brief contact response to these solutions. The assumption was that if the addition of mannitol to the saccharin-glucose mixture affected palatability the licking rate would be increased or decreased in proportion to the amount of mannitol in the solution.

The subjects were seven male albino rats of the Sprague-Dawley strain. They were first adapted to a feeding schedule that gave them *ad lib* access to food except for a 7.5 hr period that began at 5 A.M. At that time food, but not water, was automatically removed. At 11 A.M. after 6 hr of food deprivation, the brief contact tests were begun. For this test the animal was placed in a small cage that contained a drinking spout and a phototransistor drinkometer which recorded each tongue contact made by the rat to the drinking spout. The animal remained in this drinkometer cage for 3 min from the time contact was first made with the drinking spout. A record was made of the total number of licks that occurred in each minute after the animal first made tongue contact with the drinking tube and the amount consumed in the 3-min period. After adaptation to the drinkometer using the saccharin-glucose mixture (0.006 M Na saccharin + 0.1 M glucose) mannitol was added to this solution and the tests were repeated. The concentrations of mannitol used were 0, 0.075, 0.1, 0.15, 0.2, 0.3, 0.4, and 0.5 M. The animals were offered each concentration for 3 days in the order of increasing concentration.

The results of this experiment were that there was a slight increase in licking rate with increasing concentrations of mannitol. However, the overall apparent upward trend in the data was not supported by statistical analysis ($F = 0.86$, $df = 7,16$). These results indicate that mannitol in these concentrations does not significantly affect the palatability of the test solution at least as measured by the brief contact response measure.

Our next experiment examined the effect of adding mannitol in varying amounts to the saccharin-glucose solution on the total amount drunk during a 30-min drinking period. The hypothesis was that the retention coefficient could be increased in proportion to the amount of mannitol added to the saccharin-glucose solution. According to the model this should have two effects. It should reduce the total amount ingested in proportion to the amount of mannitol in the test solution. This follows from the fact that the asymptote of $C(t)$, (g/r), is inversely proportional to r. It should also increase the magnitude of the exponent, dr, in direct proportion to the magnitude of the retention coefficient (i.e., decrease the time constant).

The subjects used in this experiment were the same ones used in the previous one. The feeding schedule and testing procedure were also the same as in the previous experiment except that the animals remained in the drinking test cages for 30 min after the first tongue contact with the drinking tube. Three daily consecutive test sessions with each of the concentrations of mannitol used were carried out. The solutions used were the saccharin-glucose mixture to which mannitol was added to make mannitol concentrations of 0, 0.1, 0.2, 0.3, 0.4, and 0.5 M.

The results of this experiment are summarized in Fig. 3. Since the model

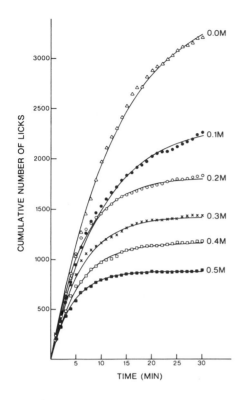

FIG. 3. The mean cumulative number of licks elicited by each of the test solutions during the 30-min drinking period. Numbers to the right of each curve, concentration of mannitol in the test solution. A printing counter printed the accumulated number of licks at each minute during the drinking period providing the data from which these curves were constructed.

predicts that the cumulative intake functions should be a negative exponential growth functions the data were fitted by the least squares method to functions of the form $y = a(1 - e^{-bt})$ where a corresponds to g/r and b to dr in the model. The solid lines in Fig. 2 are the functions generated by these least squares fits. As can be seen, predictions of the model conform well to the data.

A relationship exists between the two functions $I(t)$ and $C(t)$ which permits a test of the internal consistency of these data with respect to the model. If the initial rate of drinking, which is the value of $I(t)$ at $t = 0$, or gd, is multiplied by the reciprocal of the asymptote of C(t), which is r/g, the result is an estimate of dr $(gdr/g = dr)$. The value of this initial rate was estimated from our data by calculating the mean number of licks that occurred during the first minute after contact with each of the test solutions. It has a mean value of 216 (SD = 23.5). If the data are internally consistent with respect to the model this estimate of dr should agree with that obtained from the least squares fit. The values of dr obtained in this way are listed in the 3rd column of Table 1. Comparing column 2 with column 3 shows that the agreement is not very good. As agreement is approached with other pairs of dr and g/r the fit to the data is degraded. Figure 4 shows the best agreement we could find without allowing the fit to fall more than ±1 SE of the

TABLE 1

Mannitol concentration	Exponential Parameters			Mean amount consumed (ml)
	$a = g/r$ (licks)	$b = dr$	$dg(r/g) = dr$	
0	3607	0.077	0.060	28.4
0.1	2342	0.102	0.092	20.9
0.2	1821	0.161	0.119	14.5
0.3	1430	0.176	0.151	11.1
0.4	1171	0.179	0.191	8.9
0.5	885	0.231	0.244	6.6

data. The agreement is fair but not perfect as demanded by the model, that is, the xs and 0s are very nearly superimposed. Note, however, that the predictions of a direct proportionality between mannitol concentration and the exponent dr and the inverse proportionality between mannitol concentration and the asymptote are approximately supported by the data. (The open circles in Fig. 4 are a function of the reciprocal of the asymptotes and thus should increase with mannitol concentration as they do). The linear function that best describes these data has the form $y = 0.34(x + 0.17)$.

As a whole the model does a reasonably good job of predicting the outcome of this experiment. The internal consistency check was not as satisfactory as we would like and suggests that modifications of the model are needed. However, as a first approximation, which is what it is intended to be, it seems to be a pretty good start.

The explanation of our results rests on a number of reports in the literature that mannitol blocks absorption (7, 13). Since this is a crucial assump-

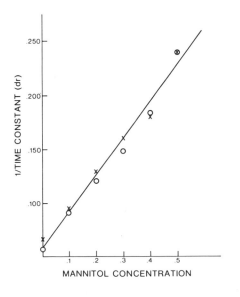

FIG. 4. Relationship between the reciprocal of the time constant (dr) and the concentration of mannitol in the test solution. 0s, values of dr derived from the relationship $dr = gdr/g$; Xs, closest values to these which generate exponential functions which fall within $\pm$ 1 SE of the cumulative intake functions; solid line, least squares linear fit to these data.

tion of our hypothesis and since we were assuming that a reduced absorption rate would lead to intestinal filling our next experiment was designed to determine if our assumptions were correct.

A new group of rats was first adapted to drinking the standard saccharin-glucose solution for 30 min/day after 8 hr of food deprivation. When the intakes of this solution had become asymptotic they were then assigned at random to one of five treatment groups. Four of these groups differed with respect to the amount of mannitol that was added to the saccharin-glucose test solution which was 0, 0.1, 0.2, or 0.3 M mannitol. The other group served as a control to be described below. The animals were offered the appropriate solution at the usual testing time. They were removed from the drinking cage 14 min after they began drinking. They were then anesthetized, the abdominal cavity was opened and hemostats were applied to the cardia of the stomach, to the pylorus, and to the junction of the ileum and the large intestine. The gastrointestinal tract was then removed, all adhering fatty tissue was removed and the stomach, the small intestine, and the large intestine were then weighed separately with their contents intact. After drying in an oven at 100°C for 24 hr they were weighed again. The difference between the wet weight and dry weight gave a measure of luminal contents and tissue water in the gut.

In order to determine accurately the distribution of ingested fluid, it was necessary to know the amount of fluid present in the gut prior to the initiation of drinking. To determine this the members of the fifth group were treated identically to the members of the other four, but were sacrificed at the time the members of the other four groups were given access to the test solutions. The difference between the wet and dry weight of the gut in these animals provided an estimate of the water content of the gut of the experimental animals just prior to the drinking test.

To determine the net acquired fluid caused by drinking, an estimate of the amount of fluid in the three compartments of the gut just prior to drinking was subtracted from the amount of fluid found in the corresponding compartments of the guts of the animals that drank the test solutions. Then to determine how much of the ingested fluid was actually retained by the gut, the net acquired fluid was expressed as a percentage of the mean amount of fluid ingested by the animals. The results of this analysis are displayed in Fig. 5. This figure shows a linear relationship between mannitol concentration and retention of the fluid by the gut over the range of mannitol concentrations used. A least squares linear fit to these data gives the function $y = 4.24 \, (x + 0.16)$.[1] The close linear fit to these data makes it possible to

---

[1] It is encouraging to note that the constant added to x (0.16) in this function is very close to the constant added to x (0.17) in the function which describes the relationship between dr and mannitol concentration illustrated in Fig. 4. They should agree since we interpret them to represent a contribution to the retention coefficient from the solutes other than mannitol in the drinking solution and the intestinal lumen.

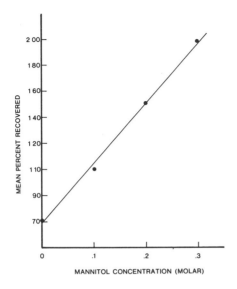

FIG. 5. Percentage of the ingested fluid recovered from the entire gut as a function of the mannitol concentration in the test solution. Solid line, least squares linear fit to these data.

estimate accurately the mannitol concentration that effectively blocks absorption. Solving this equation for $y = 100$ gives a value of 0.072 M mannitol in the test solution which is approximately the value found by Dillard et al. (7) and Launiala (13). Concentrations greater than this lead to a transfer of fluid from the body to the gut.

Since the smallest concentration of mannitol we used was one that led to a transfer of water from body stores to the intestinal lumen, it is conceivable that the inhibition of drinking with higher concentrations that we observed could have resulted from the activation of a thirst mechanism. McCleary (14) has argued that the graded reduction of intake with increasing concentrations of hypertonic carbohydrate solutions is due to the activation of an osmotically induced shift of water from systemic stores to the gut. This interpretation was based on the observation that hypertonic preloads of glucose introduced directly into the stomach increased the water intake of the animals.

To evaluate this interpretation of our results, we repeated our second experiment in which animals were permitted to drink saccharin-glucose solutions with the addition of different concentrations of mannitol for 30 min after 8 hr of food deprivation. The concentrations of mannitol added to the saccharin-glucose test solution were 0, 0.1, 0.2, or 0.3 M. The osmolar concentrations were 206 (saccharin-glucose alone), 306, 406, and 506 mOsm/kg bracketing a solution isotonic with body fluids. The same group of animals was offered each of these solutions on successive days in the order of increasing concentration. Immediately after drinking the test solutions they were returned to their home cages where they were offered tap water in a graduated cylinder for 30 min. At the end of this 30-min period, the amount of water consumed was recorded and the cylinders were replaced with standard water bottles.

The results of this experiment were that virtually no water was drunk in the 30-min period following drinking of the test solutions. There was not even a trend for water intake to increase with increasing concentration of mannitol in the test solution drunk previously. Thus, even though our previous experiment provided evidence for a net influx of water into the gastrointestinal tract when the animals drank the saccharin-glucose solution with 0.1 M mannitol or greater concentration, this experiment indicates that this transfer of water from systemic stores was not sufficient to activate either hypovolemic or osmotic thirst.

Why did McCleary (14) find such an effect and we did not? Jacobs (11) has suggested that the thirst-inducing effects of hypertonic gastric loads that McCleary reported were caused by the fact that his animals were run under a 16-hr water deprivation schedule. Under the conditions of systemic body water depletion a transfer of fluid into the intestinal lumen might be sufficient to induce subsequent water drinking, whereas such a transfer in animals in water balance might not. Our next experiment evaluated this possibility.

Rats were first adapted for 14 days to a water deprivation schedule that permitted them access to tap water for 30 min at the same time each day. Following this they were adapted to drinking mannitol solutions. After this adaptation period, they were offered, on each successive day, a solution of mannitol in water. Immediately after a 30-min access period to this solution they were returned to their home cage. A calibrated drinking tube containing tap water was attached to the home cage and the amount ingested 30 min later was recorded. Four concentrations of mannitol (0.4, 0.3, 0.2, and 0.1 M) were offered in order of decreasing concentration. The amount of water drunk in the 30 min following 30-min access to water was also recorded to provide a baseline measure.

The results of this experiment are summarized in Fig. 6. Two effects stand out clearly. One is that as mannitol concentration is increased the mean amount of fluid consumed increases to a mannitol concentration of 0.2 M and then decreases. The differences in intake among these five conditions is statistically significant ($F = 6.13$, $df = 4,20$, $p < 0.005$).

The second apparent effect is that as the concentration of mannitol in the solution ingested first is increased, the amount of tap water ingested in the following 30-min period increases proportionally. The differences in water intake across conditions is statistically significant ($F = 11.12$, $df = 4,20$, $p < 0.001$).

The ingestion of mannitol in water-deprived rats clearly appears to induce a state of thirst as measured by the amount of water ingested subsequently. Since there was no evidence for this in a previous experiment in which the animals were in water balance, it seems reasonable to conclude that the

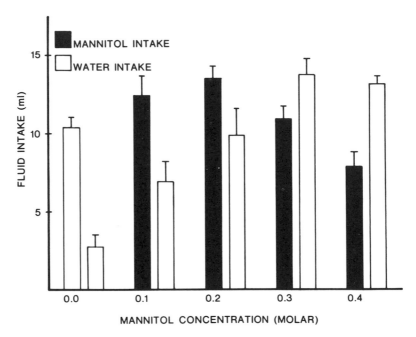

FIG. 6. Amount of mannitol solution drunk in 30 min and the amount of tap water drunk in the 30-min period immediately following by thirsty rats.

thirst-inducing effects of the ingestion of fluids that cause a shift of fluid into the gastrointestinal tract depends on the state of water balance of the animal. This, of course, is completely in line with Jacob's observations and conclusion that the thirst inducing effects of hypertonic glucose loads depends on the state of water balance of the animal.

An unexpected finding was that the addition of mannitol in concentrations up to 0.2 M significantly increased ($t = 2.66$, $df = 20$, $p < 0.02$) rather than decreased the amount consumed. This is in contrast to the results reported above showing that a 0.1 M mannitol concentration in the saccharin-glucose test solution significantly decreased intake. Here the increase could be due either to a palatability factor (mannitol in water tastes slightly sweet to humans) or, more likely, the effect of mannitol on absorption rate. Hall (1973) has reported that, when water absorption is prevented by clamping the pylorus, the intake of water during a 30-min access period in thirsty rats is significantly increased above the intake of these animals with the pylorus open. Since mannitol reduces the absorption rate, the increased intake of mannitol solutions that we have observed here in our thirsty animals may have occurred for the same reason that it increases when the absorption of water is prevented altogether.

Taken as a whole, these data are clearly consistent with the view that the intestinal absorption rate can play an important role in the control of the size of a meal. How is the effect mediated? Although we do not have direct evidence on this point, the evidence is consistent with the view that the negative feedback signal derives from activation of tension receptors in the wall of the intestine. These would be activated as the intestine distends to accommodate incoming fluid from the stomach and from systemic stores in response to a transient osmotic gradient.

We favor the intestine rather than the stomach as the source of the negative feedback signal for a number of reasons. The effect of mannitol on absorption acts in the intestine not the stomach. Initially, therefore, the effects of reduced absorption rate should be felt at the intestinal rather than gastric level. Another reason is that because of receptive relaxation (3) the tonus of the stomach is relaxed providing for the accumulation of considerable fluid before distention is likely to occur. A third and probably the most compelling reason is that Beck (1) has shown that while a rat drinks hypertonic sucrose solution the volume of fluid which can be removed from the stomach remains constant or decreases whereas the amount recoverable from the intestine increases. The intestine, not the stomach, becomes increasingly distended during the course of drinking hypertonic solutions.

In conclusion it should be pointed out that our results provide an alternative to Jacobs' (11) conclusion that caloric metering is responsible for the short-term control of carbohydrate solution intake. He based this conclusion on the fact that in nonthirsty rats hypertonic gastric loads did not induce thirst. In our experiments the ingestion of equicaloric and equipalatable solutions, differing only with respect to their absorption rates in the intestine, decreased in inverse proportion to their absorption rates and did not lead to thirst. We don't mean to imply by this that caloric metering cannot or does not play a role in the control of the ingestion of carbohydrate solutions. On the other hand, it is important to recognize that intestinal distention may play a more important role in the control of ingestion of carbohydrates than has been generally recognized.

APPENDIX. DERIVATION OF INTAKE FUNCTIONS FROM THE MODEL

The behavior of the model described in Fig. 3 in response to an input can be described by its transfer function. In Laplace notation this is

$$\frac{I}{G} = \frac{ds}{s + dr}, \tag{1}$$

where I is the ingestion rate, G represents some quantitative measure of gustatory input, d is the forward gain of the ingestion mechanism, r is the retention coefficient, and s is the Laplace Operator.

When an animal makes gustatory contact with a palatable solution it is equivalent to introducing a step input to the system. The step response of this system described by the transfer function (1) is

$$\left(\frac{g}{s}\right)\left(\frac{I}{G}\right) = \frac{gd}{s + dr},\tag{2}$$

where g is some specific value of gustatory stimulation and the other symbols are as defined above.

Converting to the time domain we have

$$\mathcal{L}^{-1}\left[\frac{g}{s}\frac{I}{G}\right] = I(t) = gde^{-drt}.\tag{3}$$

ACKNOWLEDGMENT

This research was supported by National Science Foundation Grant GB 25937 to John D. Davis.

REFERENCES

1. Beck, R. C. (1967): *J. Comp. Physiol. Psychol.*, 64:243–249.
2. Cagan, R. H., and Maller, O. (1974): *J. Comp. Physiol. Psychol.*, 87:47–55.
3. Cannon, W. B., and Lieb, C. M. (1910): *Am. J. Physiol.*, 27:xiii.
4. Cannon, W. B., and Washburn, A. L. (1912): *Am. J. Physiol.*, 29:444–454.
5. Davis, J. D. (1973): *Physiol. Behav.*, 11:39–45..
6. Davis, J. D., and Campbell, C. S. (1973): *J. Comp. Physiol. Psychol.*, 83:379–387.
7. Dillard, R. L., Eastman, H., and Fordtran, J. S. (1965): *Gastroenterology*, 49: 58–66.
8. Hindle, N., and Code, C. F. (1962): *Am. J. Physiol.* 203:215–220.
9. Fordtran, J. S., Rector, F. C., Ewton, M. F., Soter, N., and Kinney, J. (1965): *J. Clin. Invest.*, 44:1935–1944.
10. Gibbs, J., Young, R. C., and Smith, G. P. (1973): *J. Comp. Physiol. Psychol.*, 84:488–495.
11. Jacobs, H. L. (1961): In: *The Physiological and Behavioral Aspects of Taste* edited by M. R. Kare and B. P. Halpern. University of Chicago Press, Chicago.
12. Janowitz, H. D., and Grossman, M. I. (1949): *Am. J. Physiol.*, 159:143–148.
13. Launiala, K. (1968): *Scand. J. Gastroentemol.*, 3:665–671.
14. McCleary, R. A. (1953): *J. Comp. Physiol. Psychol.*, 46:411–421.
15. McFarland, D. J. (1971): *Feedback Mechanisms in Animal Behavior.* Academic Press, New York.
16. Millelstaedt, H. (1962): *Ann. Rev. Entomol.*, 7:177–198.
17. Mook, D. G. (1963): *J. Comp. Physiol. Psychol.*, 56:645–659.
18. Riggs, D. S. (1970): *Control Theory and Physiological Feedback Mechanisms.* Williams and Wilkins, Baltimore.
19. Russek, M. (1971): In: *Neurosciences Research, Vol. 4,* edited by S. Ehrenpries. Academic Press, New York.
20. Schally, A. V., Kedding, T. N., Lucien, H. W., and Meyer, J. (1967): *Science,* 157: 210–211.
21. Schwartzbaum, J. S., and Ward, H. A. (1958): *J. Comp. Physiol. Psychol.*, 51:555–560.
22. Sharma, R. N., and Nasset, E. S. (1962): *Am. J. Physiol.*, 202:725–730.
23. Shuford, E. H. (1959): *J. Comp. Physiol. Psychol.*, 52:150–153.
24. Ugolev, A. M. (1960): *Doklady Akedemii Nauk,* 133:1251–1254.
25. Valenstein, E. S., Cox, V. C., and Kakolewski, J. W. (1967): *Science,* 157:552–554.
26. Young, P. T., and Trafton, C. L. (1964): *J. Comp. Physiol. Psychol.*, 58:68–75.
27. Young, R. C., Gibbs, J., Antin, J., Holt, J., and Smith, G. P. (1974): *J. Comp. Physiol. Psychol.*, 87:795–800.

Hunger: Basic Mechanisms and Clinical Implications,
edited by D. Novin, W. Wyrwicka, and G. Bray.
Raven Press, New York © 1976.

The Relationship Between External Responsiveness and the Development and Maintenance of Obesity

Judith Rodin

Department of Psychology, Yale University, New Haven, Connecticut 06520

Experimental studies of hunger in animals investigate the central and peripheral biological mechanisms that influence feeding. These factors are presumably both necessary and usually sufficient to explain feeding behavior, and many of the chapters in this volume describe exciting work that brings us closer to understanding these processes. In human eating behavior, however, where habits and preference play so great a role, short- and long-term biological regulation may sometimes be overridden by environmental influences. All people are responsive to the sight of well prepared food, or fragrant aromas, or delicious tastes, and, although everyone overeats occasionally in the presence of abundant and tempting external food cues, for some this over-responsiveness may be far more frequent. If overeating continues, weight gain should follow.

RESPONSIVENESS TO EXTERNAL FOOD CUES

For the past few years, our studies have examined whether some overweight people eat more than is physiologically required because they are highly and sometimes uncontrollably responsive to external, food-relevant cues. Presumably this behavior could cause them to ignore internal regulatory signals to a greater extent than normal-weight people, although even normals show far from perfect internal regulation (1–3). Several experiments considering this question have demonstrated that the eating behavior of the human obese subject[1] is strongly determined by the cues that are associated with food and with the eating routine and ritual. In contrast to many normal weight subjects, the amounts eaten by the obese are markedly affected by such variables as the sight of food, its quality, and the time of day (5–7).

Further research has demonstrated that this heightened responsiveness appears confined to specific conditions. When the food cues are immediate and compelling, the obese are more likely to eat and overeat than normals; on the other hand, when the cues are remote, the obese may actually be less

---

[1] Unless otherwise specified, the criterion for obesity was 15% or more overweight on the basis of Metropolitan Life Insurance (4) norms. Normal-weight subjects always ranged between ± 10% overweight.

likely to eat than are normals. In a typical experiment that showed this inter-action, Ross (8) manipulated cue salience in two ways: first by manipulating the sheer physical prominence or inconspicuousness of the food cue; second, by manipulating the extent to which the subject's attention was focused on the food cue. When the subject's attention was focused on a prominent food cue, the obese ate roughly twice as much as normals. When the subject's attention was diverted from an inconspicuous food cue, obese subjects ate half as much as normals. Thus, obese subjects seem particularly sensitive in terms of the magnitude of their response to highly salient food; they are not particularly sensitive in terms of the level of stimulation required to initiate appreciable eating. This pattern of results helps us to understand why obese individuals eat larger but fewer meals than normal weight individuals (9) and are inverterate plate cleaners (10, 11). Similarly it explains why obese sub-jects in the Goldman et al. (5) study of religious fasting experienced very little discomfort when they remained in the synagogue shielded from all palpable or compelling food-related cues.

GENERALIZED EXTERNAL RESPONSIVENESS

On the basis of these studies, we next considered whether overweight people might simply be more reactive than normals to all prominent stimuli, and thus these various findings about eating behavior might be a special case of a much broader phenomenon. To test this hypothesis, a series of studies examined obese-normal differences in a variety of contexts unrelated to consummatory behavior. We reasoned that if the obese are generally more responsive to salient stimuli than are normals, they should react more quickly to external cues, take in more environmental stimuli, and possibly remember them better. To test these predictions, Rodin et al. (12) measured reaction time latency, immediate recall for items briefly presented on a slide and threshold for the recognition of tachistoscopically presented material.

Response latencies of obese and normal weight subjects were measured in a simple reaction-time task that required the release of a telegraph key with the forefinger of the dominant hand when a light appeared and also in a choice reaction time measure. In the more complex choice reaction time test, subjects were instructed to release the key controlled by the contralateral hand when a light appeared. While the obese appeared somewhat slower than normals on simple reaction time, their response latencies were shorter on the choice reaction time measure (393.38 msec for the obese; 423.95 msec for normals, $t_{18} = 2.07$, $p < 0.05$).

In the second part of the experiment, subjects viewed a series of slides, each showing 13 items (words or pictures). A slide was presented for 5 sec and the subject was immediately asked to recall what he saw. Obese subjects recalled, on the average, 6.52 items on a slide, whereas the nonobese recalled a mean of only 5.76 items ($t_{18} = 3.34$, $p < 0.002$).

In a third test, subjects were asked to identify a word that was flashed briefly in the visual field of a tachistoscope. Increasingly long flashes were presented until the subject correctly identified the word on two successive trials. For each subject a mean recognition threshold was obtained representing the average exposure duration at which he recognized the 21 experimental words. The data revealed a significant tendency for the obese to recognize words at shorter exposures than did normals (Mann Whitney $U = 126$, $p < 0.05$).

Despite the fact that these results were statistically reliable and replicable, we felt that their interpretation was questionable. The data may indicate differental stimulus sensitivity but they might also show differential motiva-

TABLE 1. Emotionality of obese and normal subjects

Subjects	Mean emotionality index		p
	neutral tapes	emotional tapes	
Normal	16.6	20.1	ns[a]
Obese	9.5	29.3	<0.002
p	<0.01	<0.05	

[a] ns, not significant.

tion. Certainly there is general consensus on what constitutes good performance on the sorts of measures employed in this study. In selecting subjects according to degree of obesity, we may have also inadvertently selected subjects who were differentially eager to please and to make a good impression. Because of this ambiguity, the next set of experiments was deliberately designed to test interaction predictions—to specify the conditions under which heavy subjects should do worse than normals as well as the conditions under which they should do better. These several experiments were designed to test implications of the interaction hypothesis suggested for eating that the relationship of cue prominence to responsiveness is considerably stronger for obese than normal subjects. First, Rodin et al. (13) considered emotionality. As Table 1 indicates, when subjects listened to either neutral or emotionally disturbing material, the obese behaved and reported themselves as more emotional than did normals when the tapes were upsetting and less emotional than normals when the tapes were neutral. As shown in Table 2, painful shock appeared to interfere more with the ability of obese subjects than normals to learn a complex task. Under conditions where no shock was given, the obese learned the task somewhat better than normals.

In a second experiment, Rodin (14) examined the effects of distraction on performance. We predicted that salient distracting stimuli should be more disruptive for obese than normal weight subjects when they are performing a task requiring concentration. Prominent irrelevant stimuli did distract the obese and led to less accurate proofreading, as shown in Fig. 1, and slower

TABLE 2. *Effects of electric shock on learning*

Subjects	Total number of errors made			No shock versus high-shock (p)
	no shock	low shock	high shock	
Normal	228.7	163.4	198.1	ns[a]
Obese	189.9	228.8	286.5	<0.05
p	ns[a]	ns[a]	<0.05	
		Interaction p < 0.03		

[a] ns, not significant.

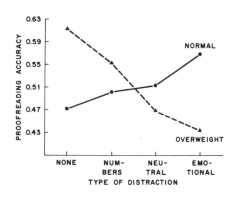

FIG. 1. Accuracy while proofreading under conditions of no distraction and increasingly interesting distractions.

reaction times than for normals. Under conditions of no distraction or when presented with minimal cues, the obese performed better than normals on both these measures. Rodin and Slochower (15) used an incidental verbal learning paradigm in which performance was evaluated in the absence of intent to remember, i.e., in the absence of explicit motivation to learn, and found that even in a task that minimizes conscious compliance the distraction effect was obtained.

These experiments all strongly support the hypothesis that the responsiveness of many obese subjects to external food cues is only one aspect of a more general responsiveness to external stimuli. One possible explanation is that the obese are more arousable and that these behaviors are indicative of differences in a nonspecific arousal system for motivation. Although work is still needed to clarify the underlying processes mediating such differences, the correlation between overweight and external responsiveness seems clear. We may then ask whether these two variables are causally related.

CONSIDERATIONS OF A CAUSAL RELATIONSHIP BETWEEN OBESITY AND EXTERNAL RESPONSIVENESS

At least three causal hypotheses seem tenable. First, it is possible that the obese condition makes an individual externally responsive; second, externality and obesity may be correlated but both caused by a third, more basic mechanism; and third, it is possible that externality produces overeating which is followed by weight gain.

A partial test of the first position was conducted by Decke (*unpublished data*) as part of a research program designed to examine metabolic and endocrine changes as a function of weight gain. Sims and his colleagues (16, 17) paid prison volunteers to overeat for an extended period of time. Decke tested these subjects after they had attained and stabilized at weights 20 to 30% higher than their normal weight. She found little evidence of external hyperresponsiveness in this sample suggesting that externality does not necessarily develop following weight gain.

A second hypothesis, which views the correlation between obesity and external responsiveness as the result of a third factor, has recently been considered by Nisbett (18) who suggested that external responsiveness is characteristic of all deprived organisms. He proposed that moderately overweight people are actually in a state of chronic deprivation because of dieting caused by social pressure and are consequently below their biologic set point. By this line of reasoning, extremely overweight people should be less external because they are less deprived, and therefore they should behave more like normals.

An alternative formulation is proposed by Schachter and Rodin (19) who suggest that externality might lead to overeating and weight gain in certain individuals whereas some forms of extreme obesity may simply be caused by other factors, for example, those that are metabolic or psychogenic in origin, and therefore would not be related to external responsiveness. This argument holds that externality is a general response style (acquired either biologically or through early experience), which tend among other things to affect weight in a world filled with potent food cues.

THE RELATIONSHIP BETWEEN DEGREE OF OBESITY AND EXTERNAL RESPONSIVENESS

Comparing different weight groups, Nisbett (18) and Rodin et al. (12) have reported some evidence that the extremely obese (50% or more overweight) are less external than the moderately overweight, whereas Grinker, Hirsch, and Smith (20) found the opposite. However, none of these studies had large enough super-obese samples to adequately test how the degree of overweight was related to external responsiveness. A second way to approach the question is to ask whether, within individuals, changes in body weight occasioned by extreme weight loss would be related to changes in external responsiveness.

To make both between- and within-subject comparisons, we tested females between the ages of 17 and 28 who were campers and counselors attending a weight reduction camp for overweight girls (21). At the time of the first test (week 1 of the camp season) the overweight girls ($n = 86$) ranged from $+14\%$ to $+122\%$ overweight and the normal weight girls ($n = 6$ counselors) ranged from -3.4% to $+7.5\%$ overweight. Weight loss was accomplished by a combined program of daily exercise and restriction of intake. The summer camp provided an ideal experimental setting because everyone was fed identical types and quantities of food at the same hours, engaged in comparable activity programs and lived in the same overall environment for 8 weeks. All participants were tested during the first and final weeks[2] on those measures of heightened external and lowered internal responsiveness that had most clearly discriminated between overweight and

TABLE 3. Mean externality scores divided by weight category

| | Composite externality score (standardized) | | Amount of milkshake drunk (cc) | | | |
| | | | before weight loss | | after weight loss | |
	before weight loss	after weight loss	before meal	after meal	before meal	after meal
Obese	−0.372	−0.098	432.3	363.4	625.0	596.9
Low overweight	+0.349	+0.172	450.4	374.1	644.4	630.2
Normal	−0.112	−0.035	287.4	179.7	369.0	294.2

normal weight people in previous experiments. These were: (a) amount eaten before and after a uniform preload (22, 23); (b) immediate recall of objects and words briefly presented on a slide (12), and a comparison of the number of food to nonfood items recalled when both were presented on a single slide; (c) extremity of affective responsiveness to positive and negative stimuli (13, 24); and (d) some exploratory measures including glucose tolerance thresholds.

The overweight sample was divided into thirds and the heaviest ($x = +79.2\%$ overweight) and lightest ($\bar{x} = +25.9\%$ overweight) groups compared to the data obtained from the six normal-weight ($\bar{x} = +2.1\%$ overweight) counselors. A composite externality score was devised based on the sum of the individual measures, each standardized on the entire sample. As indicated in Table 3, moderately overweight subjects were significantly more external than either the normals ($t_{33} = 2.12$, $p < 0.05$) or the extremely obese ($t_{56} = 2.45$, $p < 0.02$). Normals and the heaviest obese group were not significantly different from one another. However, considerable weight loss did not influence these response differences. When the means were compared within weight groups before and after weight loss, there were no significant changes although there appears to have been some re-

[2] The measures used at the end of the summer were the same (in the case of the slides) or conceptually equivalent to those at the beginning.

gression toward the mean in the retest data (see Table 3). Furthermore, the week 1 to week 8 correlation of standardized externality scores, summed across measures, was 0.76 ($p < 0.001$, $df = 27$) for the heaviest group and 0.74 ($p < 0.001$, $df = 28$) for the lightest overweight sample. The correlation for the small normal weight sample was 0.78. In addition, degree of weight loss was not significantly related to any changes in externality that did occur after weight loss.[3]

When each measure was examined separately, it was clear that the external nonfood-relevant measures remained the most stable. For the eating test, which measured internal regulation as well as responsiveness to sweet taste, some changes were evident. In this measure subjects had been given 800 cc of chocolate milkshake in a 1420 ml opaque container and instructed to drink as much as they needed in order to rate the milkshake on a three-page taste questionnaire (cf. 25). The containers were fastened to the table and thus subjects could not feel or see how much they were drinking. At the beginning of the summer, each subject was tested two times, once before and once after a calorically identical 500 cal meal. The measures were taken two to three days apart. They were then retested at the end of the summer using the same procedure. As Table 3 shows, before weight loss, both overweight groups drank far more than the normals [$F(1,62) = 7.56$, $p < 0.01$] and they showed somewhat poorer regulation than normals in response to consuming a 500 cal preload [Interaction $F(2,62) = 3.11$, $p < 0.05$]. At the end of the summer, they consumed even more than before weight loss and, although normals did not show increased consumption, they and both overweight groups were less responsive to the meal preload than they were before weight loss. Short-term regulation thus appears influenced by the deprivation occasioned by weight loss. These findings are consistent with Cabanac's (26, 27) suggestion that in a deprived organism, internal physiologic cues signalling short-term changes in nutritional state are ignored. According to Cabanac, one consequence of this condition is that the individual remains highly responsive to sweet taste. To determine whether increased consumption of the good tasting milkshake after weight loss was due to increased sensitivity to or preference for sweet taste, we examined the glucose sensitivity ratings given by these subjects before and after weight loss.

Subjects rated glucose dilutions of 0.125, 0.25, 0.5, 1, 2, and 3 M glucose in unsweetened cherry Kool-Aid for sweetness intensity and pleasantness. The order of presentation was randomly determined for each subject and for each trial. There were four trials, the first and third for judgments of sweetness intensity and the second and fourth for pleasantness. For each rating, the subject took a sip of the solution, rated it on a 9-point scale, and rinsed her mouth with clear water (cf. 28).

---

[3] The average weight loss for the camp was 30 lb and the average percent overweight for the three groups at the conclusion of the summer was: obese $\bar{x} = 51.3\%$, low overweight $\bar{x} = 10.9\%$, normals $\bar{x} = -4.0\%$.

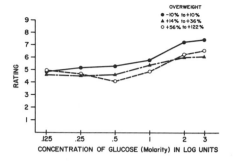

FIG. 2. Mean judgments of sweetness intensity of glucose solutions varying in concentration for normal weight, moderately overweight, and obese subjects.

First, let us consider the comparisons between weight groups before weight loss. As Fig. 2 shows, there were no significant differences in intensity judgments regardless of degree of overweight. This replicates findings by Grinker (20, 29) and Rodin (25) for different sweet substances. On perceived pleasantness, shown in Fig. 3, the average ratings for normals increased up to the 1 M solution and then decreased at 2 M and 3 M. For overweight subjects, progressively higher ratings of pleasantness were given at 2 M and 3 M. These results differ from the findings of Grinker and her associates (20, 29, and this volume) who reported that with sucrose solutions, extremely and moderately overweight subjects showed less preference than normals for the sweeter solutions. Another study (25) using increasingly sweet solutions of chocolate milkshake, found no differences between overweight and normal weight subjects in judgments of pleasantness. Perhaps perceived pleasantness varies more than judged intensity as a function of the type of taste substance being evaluated. For example overweight subjects prefer the taste of highly concentrated glucose to high concentrations of sucrose (30).

Whatever the basis for taste differences between weight groups, their ratings did not change with weight loss. For each glucose solution, the correlation between pre- and postweight-loss ratings were better than 0.51 for every weight group. Thus weight loss appears to have no effect on taste responsiveness, whereas, as indicated by the consumption data, it did affect regulation in response to a preload.

We conclude from this study that externality is not simply a consequence

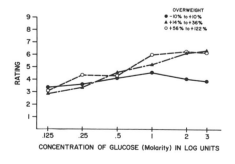

FIG. 3. Mean judgments of pleasantness of glucose solutions varying in concentration for normal weight, moderately overweight, and obese subjects.

of overweight since the most overweight subjects were not the most external. Nor is externality simply a consequence of deprivation which moves an individual further from his set point, as Nisbett (18) has suggested. External responsiveness remained relatively constant in these subjects although they lost considerable amounts of weight. Nisbett (18) based his hypotheses on Cabanac's notions (26, 27) about the effects of set point on short-term regulation and taste responsiveness. Our results supported the hypotheses about short-term regulation only. After weight loss when the overweight subjects were deprived and perhaps further from their biologic set point, regulation in response to a preload virtually disappeared when the test substance was sweet tasting. Thus, weight loss and/or deviation from set point may indeed influence internal regulatory processes but it does not affect externality as measured by the nonfood-related tasks and the taste tests.

In summary there are some obese people who are external and others who are not. Degree of obesity alone cannot predict who is external and weight loss apparently does not change this response. Does externality then predict and contribute to determining who will become fat?

THE RELATIONSHIP BETWEEN DEGREE OF EXTERNALITY AND WEIGHT GAIN

Again we selected an 8-week summer camp to test this question because of the constant environment (31). This was not a diet camp and the food was abundant, attractively prepared, and served family style. Candy and other treats sent by parents were plentiful in each cabin, and could also be purchased at any time at the camp canteen. It was predicted that the more external a child was, the more her eating behavior would be influenced by the shift to abundant food cues which coming to camp represented. This, in turn, would affect her weight. In contrast, nonexternal children were expected to be more responsive to internal physiologic signals and thus maintain a relatively constant body weight independent of alterations in the environment. The strong test of this hypothesis was provided by studying normal weight people with no history of overweight.

The same measures of external responsiveness used in the earlier study were given to all campers. Standardized externality scores for each subject ($N = 92$) were then correlated with her algebraic weight change from the first to final week divided by her starting weight. There was a significant positive correlation [$r = 0.387$, $p < 0.001$] between externality and this weight change measure suggesting that the most external children gained the most weight. Activity level and emotional adjustment were not related to weight change although age and initial weight and growth were. Externality appears to be an important correlate of weight change but it is certainly not the only one.

As indicated by their weight gain, many external children must have found camp an environment with more novel, abundant, or tasty food cues than home. It is also possible, however, that for others, camp actually offered fewer food cues. If this were true, then some external children may have lost weight at camp as a consequence of their externality. The mean standardized externality scores can be divided for children who lost weight ($\bar{x} = -1.94$), those whose weight remained relatively constant ($\bar{x} = -4.423$) and those who gained weight ($\bar{x} = 4.22$). As the means indicate, the weight gainers were clearly more external than the stables and the weight losers were a little more external than the stables. This nonmonotonic relationship is indicated in the stronger correlation between externality and absolute weight change ($r = 0.501, p < 0.001$).

The finding that there are normal weight externals who behave as do the moderately obese lends further support to the notion that externality is not purely a function of overweight, but instead reflects the underlying tendency toward hyperresponsiveness, and the data suggest that externality does influence amount of weight gain, at least in the short run. Since degree of overweight is unrelated to degree of externality, however (21), external responsiveness apparently does not play a major role in determining the level at which long-term weight regulation occurs. Full prospective studies that address these issues are currently in progress.

In summary the data suggest that, on the basis of pretested differences in external responsiveness, one can predict with some degree of accuracy the relative magnitude of weight change within a population placed in a novel external environment, and to a lesser degree the direction of the change. In fact it might be expected that any time externally responsive individuals are exposed to a new or different food setting for a sufficient period of time, their weight should be affected. Because the present data were obtained from a sample of subjects with no present or past history of overweight, we can conclude that externality is not simply a correlate of corpulence. The theoretic and practical implications of the notion of external responsiveness are clearly enhanced by this finding.

ACKNOWLEDGMENTS

The research reported in this chapter was supported by National Science Foundation Grant GS-37953 and a grant from the Weight Watchers Foundation.

REFERENCES

1. Jordan, H., Stellar, E., and Duggan, S. (1968): *Commun. Behav. Biol.,* 1:65–67.
2. Spiegel, T., (1973): *J. Comp. Physiol. Psychol.,* 84:24–37.
3. Wooley, O., Wooley, S., and Dunham, K., (1972), *J. Comp. Physiol. Psychol.,* 80: 250–258.
4. Metropolitan Life Insurance Company (1959): *Stat. Bull.,* 40:1–4.
5. Goldman, R., Jaffa, M., and Schachter, S., (1968): *J. Pers. Soc. Psychol.,* 10:117–123.

6. Nisbett, R. E. (1968): *J. Pers. Soc. Psychol.*, 10:107–110.
7. Schachter, S., and Gross, L., (1968): *J. Pers. Soc. Psychol.*, 10:98–106.
8. Ross, Lee, (1974): In: *Obese Humans and Rats*, Chapter 7. Erlbaum/Halsted, Washington, D.C.
9. Ross, L. D., Pliner, P., Nesbitt, P., and Schachter, S., (1971): In: *Emotion, Obesity and Crime*, Academic Press, New York.
10. Nisbett, R. E. (1968): *Science*, 159:1254–1255.
11. Beaudoin, R., and Mayer, J., (1953): *J. Am. Diet. Assoc.*, 29:29–33.
12. Rodin, J., Herman, C. P., and Schachter, S. (1974): In: *Obese Humans and Rats*, Chapter 12. Erlbaum/Halsted, Washington, D.C.
13. Rodin, J., Elman, D., and Schachter, S. (1974): In: *Obese Humans and Rats*, Chapter 3. Erlbaum/Halsted, Washington, D.C.
14. Rodin, J., (1973): *J. Comp. Physiol. Psychol.*, 83:68–78.
15. Rodin, J., and Slochower, J., (1974): *J. Pers. Soc. Psychol.*, 29:557–565.
16. Sims, E. A. H., Goldman, R. F., Gluck, C. M., Horton, E. S., Kelleher, P. C., and Rowe, P. W. (1968): *Trans. Assoc. Am. Physicians*, 81:153–170.
17. Sims, E. A. H., Danforth, E., Horton, E. S., Bray, G. A., Glennon, J. A., and Salans, L. B. (1973): *Rec. Prog. Horm. Res.*, 29:457–496.
18. Nisbett, R. E. (1972): *Psychol. Rev.*, 79:433–453.
19. Schachter, S., and Rodin, J., (1974): *Obese Humans and Rats*, Erlbaum/Halsted, Washington, D.C.
20. Grinker, J., Hirsch, J., and Smith, D. (1972): *J. Pers. Soc. Psychol.*, 22:320–325.
21. Rodin, J., Slochower, J., and Fleming, B. (1975): Unpublished manuscript, Yale University.
22. Schachter, S., Goldman, R., and Gordon, A., (1968): *J. Pers. Soc. Psychol.*, 10:91–97.
23. Pliner, P. (1974): In: *Obese Humans and Rats*, Chapter 5. Erlbaum/Halsted, Washington, D.C.
24. Pliner, P. (1974): In: *Obese Humans and Rats*, Chapter 14. Erlbaum/Halsted, Washington, D.C.
25. Rodin, J. (1975): *J. Comp. Physiol. Psychol.*
26. Cabanac, M., and Duclaux, R. (1970): *Science*, 168:496–497.
27. Cabanac, M., Minaire, Y., and Adair, E., (1968), *Commun. Behav. Biol.*, 1:77–82.
28. Moskowitz, H., (1971): *Am. J. Psychol.*, 84:387–405.
29. Grinker, J. (1973): *Proceedings of Meetings on Nutrition and Psychology*, edited by Bovet, Croffi, and Ricci. Sasso Foundation. Rome, Italy.
30. Rodin, J., and Moskowitz, H. (1975), Unpublished manuscript, U.S. Army, Natick Laboratories, Natick, Mass.
31. Rodin, J. and Slochower, J.: Externality in the nonobese: Effects of environmental responsiveness on weight. *J. Pers. Soc. Psychol.*, (In press).

Hunger: Basic Mechanisms and Clinical Implications,
edited by D. Novin, W. Wyrwicka, and G. Bray.
Raven Press, New York © 1976.

Salivation as a Measure of Appetite: Studies of the Anorectic Effects of Calories and Amphetamine

Orland W. Wooley, Susan C. Wooley, and Barbara S. Williams

Department of Psychiatry, University of Cincinnati, College of Medicine, Cincinnati, Ohio 45267

Investigations of hunger and satiety in humans have focused on changes in food intake, in hunger ratings, and, to a lesser extent, on hedonic ratings of sweet stimuli as indices of internal hunger state.

FOOD INTAKE AS A MEASURE OF INTERNAL STATE

When the food intake of human subjects has been measured or manipulated in an experimental situation, the food consumed is usually crackers (1, 2) or liquid food (3–8). In order to conclude that changes in cracker or liquid food consumption reflect internal states, all external cues that would lead or allow subjects to hypothesize about internal state must be systematically controlled. Studies in which external cues, such as time since the last feeding or the flavor, appearance, and volume of preloads of varying caloric content, were controlled reported no effect on food consumption at a given meal of internal state, or prior caloric intake (3, 4, 8). Some studies reported no effect of prior caloric intake even when external cues were present (9, 10).

HUNGER RATINGS

When hunger ratings have been used as an index of internal state, subjects' beliefs about internal state have often been a more powerful determinant of hunger ratings than actual prior caloric intake (5, 8). An apparent exception to this general finding is the report by Silverstone and Stunkard (11) that amphetamine significantly reduced hunger ratings within 105 to 120 min after administration. These investigators did not report whether or not subjects could, on the basis of side effects or subjective effects, tell on which days they had ingested amphetamine and which days they had been given a placebo, although they do report that upon postexperimental questioning no subject had ascertained the aim of the investigation or the nature of the drug under examination. The effect on hunger ratings was greater with 10 mg of amphetamine than with 15 or 20 mg.

HEDONIC RATINGS

When hedonic ratings have been used as an index of internal state, the results have been mixed. Cabanac and his associates (12–15) and Guy-Grand and Sitt (16) have reported that in persons who are not below their penderostat weight, ingestion of 200 cal of glucose will reduce, within 1 hr, hedonic ratings of the taste and smell of various sweet stimuli. Wooley, Wooley, and Dunham (17) found as great a decrease after ingestion of an equal amount of noncaloric, but equally sweet cyclamate solution as after ingestion of a glucose solution identical to that used by Cabanac and his associates. Grinker (18) found an instability of the Cabanac effect—Cabanac's term is negative allesthesia—in that subjects' hedonic ratings of sweet stimuli were not consistently related to caloric intake in repeated trials.

CONDITIONED SALIVATION AS A MEASURE OF INTERNAL STATE

In an effort to discover a measure of appetite that would reflect internal state and would be free of cognitive influences, we began a series of studies of salivation elicited by palatable foods. Our result, when viewed within the context of prior animal work on salivation, allowed us to formulate the working hypothesis that variables that affect lateral hypothalamic activity in animals affect conditioned salivation in humans.

In the first experiments, we measured salivation elicited by food stimuli at different levels of deprivation (19). In one condition, subjects delayed lunch for 2 hr, and salivation was measured before and after presentation of lunch—lunch consisted of sandwiches selected by subjects on the basis of preference. In another condition salivation was measured before and after presentation of lunch at subjects' regular lunch time. In a third condition, salivation was measured before and after presentation of a dessert 20 min after lunch. The amount of salivation elicited by the food stimuli over and above baseline was a direct function of length of deprivation; baseline salivation was unaffected by deprivation.[1]

Obviously, subjects knew in this study at what level of deprivation they were when the food stimuli were presented. So, the next experiments (21) were designed to control for this kind of cognitive information. We gave subjects—obese and normal—liquid meals of either 900 or 450 cal. One hour later we measured the amount of salivation elicited by a palatable food stimulus. The high- and low-calorie meals were identical in volume (900 cc)

---

[1] The SHP method of measuring salivation was used [20]; this method consists of putting three preweighed 1.5 inch cotton dental rolls in the mouth, leaving them in place for 2 min, removing and reweighing them. The mean weight of saliva collected in grams in three 2-min periods separated by 2-min rest intervals constitutes a single measure for a single subject. When salivation is measured with no food present, the measure is called baseline salivation. When food is present it is called salivary response. See ref. 19 and 21 for a more detailed description of the SHP method.

and could not be distinguished by taste. On postexperimental questioning only 11 of 20 subjects guessed correctly on which day they had consumed 900 cal and on which day they had consumed 450 cal.

As Table 1 shows, among the nonobese subjects the palatable food stimulus elicited less of a salivary response following the high-calorie meal ($\bar{x} = 1.41$ g) than following the low ($\bar{x} = 2.19$ g).

An analysis of variance of the salivary responses (ignoring the baseline salivation data) revealed that caloric content of the liquid meals had a significant overall effect ($p < 0.01$) and the interaction between body weight and caloric content was very nearly significant ($p < 0.053$). One-tailed t tests showed that for the normal, but not for the obese, subjects salivary response was greater following the low-calorie meal than following the high ($p < 0.005$). Salivary response in the normals was greater than baseline

TABLE 1. *Salivary response and baseline salivation (in grams/2 min.) by obese and nonobese subjects after high- and low-calorie meals*

		High-calorie meal (900 cal)		Low-calorie meal (450 cal)	
		Baseline salivation	Salivary response	Baseline salivation	Salivary response
Obese (n = 10)	Mean	1.19	1.83	1.16	1.95
	S.D.	0.49	0.85	0.56	0.65
Nonobese (n = 10)	Mean	1.20	1.41	1.34	2.19
	S.D.	0.47	0.41	0.57	0.65

following the low-calorie meal ($p < 0.001$), but not significantly different from baseline following the high calorie meal. For the obese, salivary response was greater than baseline following both the high-calorie meal ($p < 0.01$) and the low ($p < 0.001$).

An analysis of variance of the baseline salivation data alone yielded no significant main effects or interactions. The salivary response of the nine subjects who guessed incorrectly about the caloric content of their meals showed the same pattern as those who guessed correctly. In both cases, salivary response to the palatable food stimulus following the low-calorie meal was greater than following the high-calorie meal. Hunger ratings, made just before the presentation of the palatable food stimulus, were unrelated to the caloric content of the liquid meal for the obese and the normals.

This experiment was replicated and the results, shown in Fig. 1, were essentially the same. However, in this experiment, there was a significant ($p < 0.025$), but small difference between the salivary response in the obese following the high- and low-calorie meals (2.25 g after high-calorie meal versus 2.61 g after low-calorie meal). Again salivary response in the obese was greater than baseline following both the high-calorie and the low-calorie

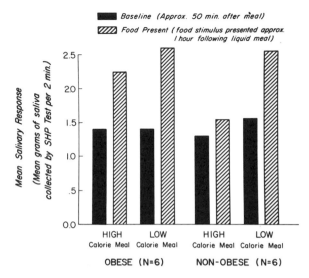

FIG. 1. Baseline salivation and salivary response (g/2 min) by obese and nonobese to a palatable food stimulus (PFS) at 1 hr after high- (900 cal) and low- (450 cal) calorie meals.

meals. And again salivary response in the normals was greater than baseline following the low-calorie meal only.

A second replication shows the same pattern of results; the results are presented in Fig. 2. There was a significant difference between salivary response to the palatable food stimulus following the high- and low-calorie

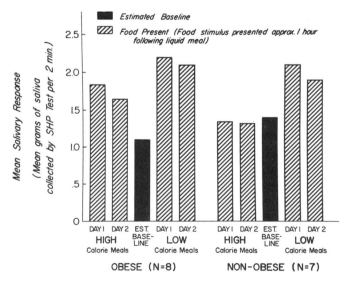

FIG. 2. Salivary response (g/2 min) and estimated baseline salivation (i.e., mean of individual subjects' baseline salivation data from prior experiments with identical procedure) by obese and nonobese at 1 hr after two high- (900 cal) and two low- (450 cal) calorie meals.

meals for both the obese and nonobese. But salivary response for the obese was greater than baseline following both kinds of meals; for the normals following the low-calorie meal only.

In summary a liquid meal of 900 cal suppresses appetite for a palatable food stimulus presented 1 hour later more in normal subjects than in obese subjects.

THE PHYSIOLOGIC MECHANISM OF CONDITIONED SALIVATION

Pavlov's (22) was probably the first systematic investigation of the physiology of digestive secretions. He discovered that salivation and gastric secretion elicited by food-related stimuli reflected learned appetite.

The Pavlovian concept of appetite was based on the experimental conditions that were necessary for demonstrating the secretions. These conditions include the following: (a) the animal must be sufficiently hungry;[2] (b) the food must be one the animal recognizes and wants; (c) the animal must think he will be allowed to eat the food.[3] In agreement with this last point, we (23) have demonstrated that when human subjects know they will not be allowed to eat a food stimulus, it elicits less salivation than when they know they will be allowed to eat it.

Teitelbaum (24) has identified salivation with lateral hypothalamic activity: "By measuring saliva flow in response to presentation of stimuli paired with food, Pavlov was probably studying lateral hypothalamic activity almost as directly as if he had a microelectrode there to record action potentials." This statement is based on the results of a series of experiments in which Teitelbaum and his associates demonstrated that the development of regulatory eating was a process of encephalization, and that recovery from lateral hypothalamic lesions was a process of reencephalization. Both processes involve: "Incorporation and transformation of . . . simple reflex patterns into more complex feeding behavior . . . as development [or recovery] proceeds; therefore, the development of higher parts of the nervous system, i.e., the diencephalen and telencephalen, must be necessary for the transformation of simple reflexive oral ingestion patterns into motivated regulatory behavior" (25).

Conditioning of salivary responses also involves these higher parts of the nervous system as Pavlov's later work showed (26). Rozkowska and Fonberg (27) found that lateral hypothalamic lesions diminished both condi-

---

[2] "A psychic response is only obtained when the animal is hungry. To explain this, it may be supposed that the salivary secretory center is influenced by the state of the blood in hunger" (Pavlov, 1910).

[3] Of this last condition Pavlov wrote: "Often the animal perceives at once that it is not intended to receive the food, becomes annoyed thereat, and turns away offended at the farce enacted before it. We must, therefore, so arrange matters that the dog does not get the impression that it is going to be disappointed, but on the contrary, that it is to be fed in reality."

tioned and unconditioned salivation. Although the lesions impaired conditioned salivation more than unconditioned salivation, the authors were unable to rule out the possibility that the reduction in salivation was "caused by a general decrease of function of the salivary mechanisms."

AMPHETAMINE ANOREXIA AND SALIVATION

Blundell and Lesham (28) have shown in rats that lateral hypothalamic lesions eliminate the anoretic effects of amphetamine, but not of fenfluramine. In accordance with our working hypothesis, i.e., any factor that affects lateral hypothalamus activity in animals will affect conditioned salivation in humans, we gave subjects either 10 mg of amphetamine or a placebo 1 hr before presentation, at lunch time, of a palatable food stimulus. The next day subjects who had received amphetamine were given placebo, and those who had received placebo were given amphetamine.

As Fig. 3 shows, amphetamine suppressed salivary response to the palatable food stimulus, but did not affect baseline salivation, which, as usual, was measured just before the food stimulus was presented.

However, for the subjects who received amphetamine on the 1st day, salivary response to the palatable food stimulus was still suppressed 24 hr later. Analysis of variance yielded a significant order effect; Table 2 presents baseline salivation and salivary response of subjects who received amphetamine and placebo in different order.

Fortunately we had included several placebo trials prior to the first experimental day. The two bars on the right of Fig. 3, labeled predrug placebo, represent the means of the baseline salivation and salivary responses for these days. These data give a better picture of the anorectic influence of amphetamine as measured by its effects on the conditioned salivary response to a

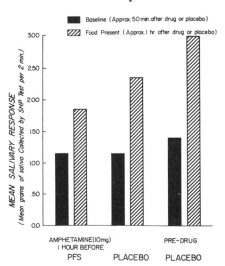

FIG. 3. Salivary response elicited by a palatable food stimulus (PFS) and baseline salivation (g/2 min) approximately 1 hour after ingestion of 10 mg of amphetamine, placebo, or predrug placebo (see text).

TABLE 2. Baseline salivation and salivary response as a function of the order in which amphetamine and placebo were administered

| | Subjects who received amphetamine on first day, placebo on second | | | | | | Subjects who received placebo on first day, amphetamine on second | | | | | |
| | Amphetamine | | Placebo | | Pre-Drug Placebo | | Placebo | | Amphetamine | | Pre-Drug Placebo | |
	Baseline	Salivary Response	Baseline	Salivary Response	Baseline	Salivary Response	Baseline	Salivary Response	Baseline	Salivary Response	Baseline	Salivary Response
Mean	1.18	1.96	0.94	2.02	1.39	3.34	1.35	2.66	1.15	1.77	1.51	2.58
SD	0.30	0.36	0.29	0.78	0.49	0.93	0.48	1.26	0.47	0.92	0.41	1.22

palatable food stimulus. Table 2 presents the predrug placebo values (baseline and salivary response) of subjects in the two orders of drug-placebo administration. For the amphetamine-placebo subjects, salivary response on both days (1.96 g on the day amphetamine was administered; 2.02 g on the placebo day) was highly significantly less—$t(5) = 3.8$ and 3.7, $p < .01$ in both cases—than on the predrug placebo day (3.34 g). But for the placebo-amphetamine subjects, salivary response on the two placebo days (2.66 g and 2.58 g) were not different from each other, but were both significantly greater than salivary response on the day amphetamine was administered (1.77 g)—$t(5) = 4.2$ and 2.8, $p < 0.005$ and 0.025, respectively.

Baseline salivation on the drug day was not significantly less than baseline salivation on the placebo day for either group, although the difference approached significance among the amphetamine-placebo subjects—$t(5) = 1.89$, $p < 0.10$.

Hunger ratings made just prior to the presentation of the food stimuli were not affected by the drug. Only five of the 12 subjects correctly guessed which day they got the drug and which the placebo.

In summary amphetamine, a drug the anorectic effects of which are mediated by the lateral hypothalamus in rats (28), reduces the amount of salivation elicited in human subjects by a palatable food stimulus, presented one hour after drug ingestion. This effect on salivation was observed before any effects on hunger ratings were seen, suggesting that conditioned salivation is more sensitive than hunger ratings to amphetamine's anorectic action, just as it is more sensitive than hunger ratings to calories (21).

REFERENCES

1. Schachter, S. (1967): In: *Neurophysiology and Emotion,* edited by D. C. Glass, pp. 117–144. The Rockefeller University Press and Russell Sage Foundation, New York.
2. Schachter, S. (1968): *Science,* 161:751–756.
3. Spiegel, T. (1973): *J. Comp. Physiol. Psychol.,* 84:24–37.
4. Jordan, H. (1969): *J. Comp. Physiol. Psychol.,* 68:498–506.
5. Wooley, O., Wooley, S., and Dunham, R. (1972): *J. Comp. Physiol. Psychol.,* 80: 250–258.
6. Wooley, O., and Wooley, S. (1975): In: *Obesity: Pathogenesis and Management,* edited by T. Silverstone and J. Fincham. Medical and Technical Publishing Co., Lancaster, England.
7. Wooley, O. (1971): *Psychosom. Med.,* 33:436–444.
8. Wooley, S. (1972): *Psychosom. Med.,* 34:62–68.
9. Singh, D. (1973): *J. Personality Soc. Psychol.,* 27:220–238.
10. Price, J., and Grinker, J. (1973): *J. Comp. Physiol. Psychol.,* 85:265–271.
11. Silverstone, J., and Stunkard, A. (1968): *Br. J. Pharmacol. Chemother.,* 33:513–522.
12. Cabanac, M. (1971): *Science,* 173:1103–1107.
13. Cabanac, M. (1974): Presented at the Fifth International Conference on the Physiology of Food and Fluid Intake, Jerusalem.
14. Cabanac, M., and Duclaux, R. (1970): *Science,* 168:496–497.
15. Cabanac, M., Duclaux, R., and Spector, N. (1971): *Nature,* 229:125–127.

16. Guy-Grand, B., and Sitt, Y. (1974): Presented at the First International Congress on Obesity, London.
17. Wooley, O., Wooley, S., and Dunham, R. (1972): *Physiol. Behav.,* 9:765–768.
18. Grinker, J. (1975): *This Volume.*
19. Wooley, S., and Wooley, O. (1973): *Psychosom. Med.,* 35:136–142.
20. Peck, R. (1959): *Arch. Gen. Psychiat.,* 1:35–40.
21. Wooley, O., Wooley, S., and Woods, W. (1975): *J. Comp. Physiol. Psychol.,* 89: 619–625.
22. Pavlov, I. (1910): *The Work of the Digestive Glands.* G. Griffin, London.
23. Wooley, S., Wooley, O., and Dunham, R. (1975): *Physiol. Behav. (In Press.)*
24. Teitelbaum, P. (1971): *Progress in Physiological Psychology,* IV, edited by E. Stellar and J. M. Sprague, pp. 319–350. Academic Press, New York.
25. Cheng, M., Rozin, P., and Teitelbaum, P. (1971): *J. Comp. Physiol. Psychol.,* 76: 206–218.
26. Pavlov, I. (1927): *Conditioned Reflexes: An Investigation of the Physiological Activity of the Cerebral Cortex.* Dover Publications, New York.
27. Rozkowska, E., and Fonberg, E. (1972): *Acta Neurobiol. Exp.,* 32:711–720.
28. Blundell, J., and Lesham, M. (1974): *Eur. J. Pharmacol.,* 28:81–88.

Hunger: Basic Mechanisms and Clinical Implications,
edited by D. Novin, W. Wyrwicka, and G. Bray.
Raven Press, New York © 1976.

Food Intake and Taste Preferences for Glucose and Sucrose Decrease After Intestinal Bypass Surgery

G. A. Bray, R. E. Barry, J. Benfield, P. Castelnuovo-Tedesco, and J. Rodin

Departments of Medicine, Surgery, and Psychiatry, University of California at Los Angeles, Harbor General Hospital, Torrance, California 90509

The jejunoileal bypass is the one surgical approach to obesity that has met with measured success. This technique was introduced in several institutions in the early 1950s. In 1963, Payne et al. reported a series of 11 patients in whom they had anastomosed 15 inches of jejunum to the transverse colon (1). Diarrhea with loss of electrolytes in the diarrheal fluid were the unsatisfactory sequelae of this operation. To reduce these complications, surgeons increased the length of the jejunum to 20 or 25 inches. However, the high mortality rate and severe side effects even with these longer jejunal segments terminated the use of this type of operation. In its place, two kinds of jejunoileal anastomosis have been introduced (2–5). Weight loss with this operation depends primarily on the length of the functional intestinal segment left in continuity (2, 6). Weight loss varies with a number of factors including the length of functional intestine, the duration of time after the operation, and the initial weight of the patient. The rationale for introducing this operation was to produce malabsorption of food stuffs by the intestine and thus facilitate the loss of calories from the body. In all of the published and unpublished reports available to us, however, there has been no critical assessment of the possibility that decreased food intake rather than malabsorption might account for the weight loss. To test this, we have examined the relationship between caloric intake on the one hand and losses of calories in the stools on the other.

METHODS OF APPROACH

Patients

Twenty-two patients, all under 30 years of age, are included in these studies. The first group of eight patients were operated on between June 1972 and November 1973. Their initial weights were 150 ± 4 kg. Weight loss after surgery is plotted in Fig. 1. Caloric intake was measured before and after surgery. Measurements of fat loss in the feces were made before and on two or three occasions after surgery during periods when the subject was in-

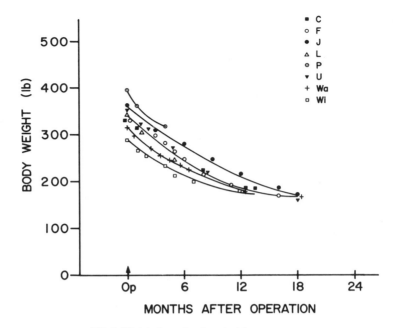

FIG. 1. Weight loss after intestinal bypass surgery.

gesting 100 g of fat in the diet. Intestinal absorption of D-xylose following 25 g oral load and of vitamin B_{12} (Schilling Test) were also performed pre- and postoperatively.

Operations on the second group of 14 patients who weighed on average 161 ± 5 kg, were initiated in June 1974. For this group of patients, several additional studies were performed. (a) Sucrose test: The preference rating for solutions of sucrose was tested using the procedures of Cabanac (6). This involves tasting solutions containing 2.5, 5, 10, 20, and 40% sucrose. The subjects are presented in a randomized double-blind order with each of the five solutions and asked to take a spoonful of the solutions into their mouth for 15 sec, to provide a rating of sweetness between +2 for very pleasant and −2 for very unpleasant. After rinsing out their mouth with water, a second so- lution is tasted until all have been rated. Following this, the subject is given a solution containing 50 g of glucose to drink and the rating procedure for sucrose solutions is repeated 30 min later. (b) Pleasantness: Rating of pleasantness for glucose, salt, citric acid, and quinine solutions was tested in the afternoon after a standard breakfast and lunch. Each subject received six concentrations of each flavor in a random order for each taste. Rating of pleasantness was done using a scale from 0 for very pleasant to −9 for very unpleasant. These tests were performed before, and again after surgery. (c) Caloric preload: This procedure involved measuring the effect of two preloads on food intake. The subjects were led to believe that they were participating in studies on the absorption of two different vitamin capsules which were given to them with their second meal on two different days. Thirty minutes before giving them the vitamin and their second meal, each subject received a good tasting chocolate milkshake in which the quantity of calories differed but in which the volume and taste did not. Thirty minutes later, they were presented with their regular lunch and one of two vitamin pills. A blood sample was drawn 1 hr later and the quantity of calories consumed during this lunch period was measured. (d) Caloric ingestion of self-selected diet: The calories ingested each day were averaged over a 4-day period in which subjects could select the kind of food they wished to eat and during which they were given these foods in excess of what they actually consumed. The quantity of food eaten on each of the 4 days was assessed pre- and postoperatively. (e) Liquid formula diet: Each subject was fed a liquid lunch of chilled chocolate-flavored formula through a straw and the quantity of fluid consumed each 2 min for 20 min was measured by weighing the diet remaining in the thermos bottle from which the subjects were ingesting the meal. These tests were repeated daily for 4 days both before and after surgery.

RESULTS

Group 1

The first study was designed to measure caloric intake before and for various intervals of time following surgery. These data are plotted in Fig. 2. Preoperatively, the caloric intake averaged 6,750 cal for the eight subjects. During the first 6 months postoperatively, there was a marked drop in caloric intake which averaged only 1,320 calories per day. Between 6 and 9 months, caloric intake rose slightly but there was a substantial jump between 9 and 12 and a smaller additional increase between 12 and 18 months. By a year after operation, the subjects were eating an average 3,700 calories per day, or just over half of the preoperative level. This decrease in dietary intake was associated with repeated comments by the patients that preferences for sweet-tasting substances had diminished. Both the psychiatrist and the endocrinologist who saw these patients commented about the altered taste preferences. One patient, for example, who had eaten a pound of chocolate almost daily prior to surgery, had eaten no candy for over 6 months after operation. Fatty foods and liquids, which were the foods most frequently associated with increased diarrhea, continued to be eaten. This finding suggests that the altered preference for sweet-tasting substances was not solely attributable to conditioned aversion to these substances due to the appearance of diarrhea. The rate of weight loss during the first 6 months was most rapid and by the end of 1 year, the average weight loss was 150 lb (Fig. 1). The extent of malabsorption is summarized in Table 1. The losses of fat in the stools postoperatively ranged anywhere from 30 to 60% of a 100-g fat

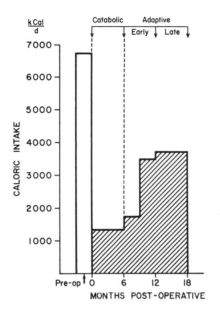

FIG. 2. Caloric intake before and after intestinal bypass surgery.

TABLE 1. *Three indices of malabsorption*

	Fecal fat (%)	D-xylose (g)	Schilling (%)
Preoperative	7.8 ± 1.3	6.7 ± .8	18.7 ± 9.3
Postoperative			
4–6 weeks	44.4 ± 6.6	2.9 ± .4	2.9 ± .73
5–8 weeks	32.9 ± 7.0	3.2 ± .5	7.9 ± 1.5
15–18 weeks	33.7 ± 6.4	2.7 ± .4	

n = 8.

diet. These patients claimed, however, that they rarely ingested this quantity of fat. The malabsorption of D-xylose and vitamin B_{12} is also apparent in Table 1. With time after surgery, these tests gradually became less abnormal.

Group 2

Figure 3 shows the effects of a glucose load and of intestinal bypass on the rating of sucrose solutions. Whether the taste tests were compared before ingesting glucose or after ingesting glucose, there was a significant reduction in preference for the 40% sucrose solutions after surgery. This dislike for sucrose solutions was manifested only at the higher concentrations. With the 2.5, 5, or 10% solutions, there was no detectable difference. The ratings of concentrated solutions of sucrose showed a significant reduction after surgery whether the test was made before or after giving glucose by mouth. This

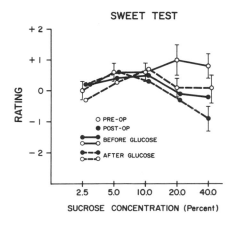

FIG. 3. Ratings of sucrose. The rating of pleasantness for five concentrations of sucrose was tested preoperatively before and after ingesting 50 g of glucose orally and again postoperatively

differs from the data of Cabanac et al. (7). They found no change in the preference for sucrose solutions after giving glucose to their obese subjects. In our obese patients, there was a clear suppression both before and after surgery and similar data have been reported by Grinker (8). An altered preference for glucose was also observed. Preoperatively, the ratings for glucose solutions were variable with no consistent pattern (Fig. 4). Postopera-

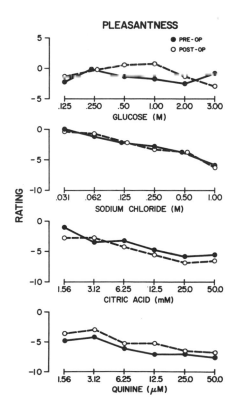

FIG. 4. Ratings for pleasantness of several substances. Solutions with various concentrations of glucose, sodium chloride, citric acid, and quinine were tested before and after surgery.

TABLE 2. *Caloric intake at lunch time and over 24 hr before and after surgery*

Procedure	Preoperative	Postoperative	p
Lunch of liquid milk shake	378 ± 10	198 ± 11	< 0.01
Self-selected diet	4811 ± 67	3011 ± 45	< 0.01

$n = 14$.

tively the preference for glucose rose with a maximum rating at a concentration of 1 M, and then declined. This is similar to the curves obtained by Rodin, Moskowitz, and Fleming (9) on normal subjects. The preference for the 1 M solution after surgery was significantly greater than before surgery ($p < 0.05$). With the 3 M concentration, however, there was a significant reduction in pleasantness after surgery when compared to the preoperative rating. The ratings of pleasantness for sodium chloride, citric acid, and quinine showed no significant changes after jejunoileostomy for obesity.

The number of calories eaten with a self-selected diet is presented in Table 2. Postoperatively there was a significant reduction in caloric intake. The ingestion of a liquid lunch is shown for one subject in Fig. 5 and the data for all subjects are summarized in Table 2. Food ingestion in most of the obese patients showed two phases. There was an initial rapid ingestion of liquid formula which then leveled off to be followed by a second burst occurring in most patients between 8 and 15 min. The timing of this second burst of food intake was variable but was present in over ⅔ of the patients. Postoperatively, at 1 and 6 months, there was a reduction in the quantity of liquid formula ingested. This significant effect is shown for 11 patients in Table 2.

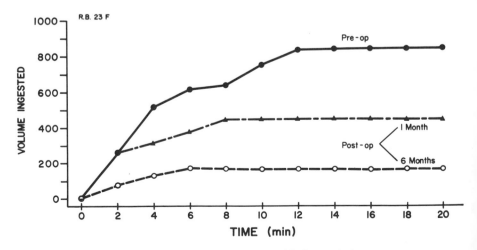

FIG. 5. Volume of a liquid formula diet ingested before and after surgery.

The effect of a caloric preload was examined before, and again after, surgery and the results presented in Table 3. The caloric preload contained either 200 or 440 calories. Preoperatively, the obese patients ingested approximately 1,300 cal whether the preload contained 200 or 440 cal. After surgery patients ingested fewer calories with both preloads. Of more importance is the significant reduction in caloric intake after surgery when fed the higher caloric preload. These data suggested that after surgery, the obese

TABLE 3. *Effect of preload on caloric intake*

Calories in preload	Caloric intake		
	preop	postop	p
200	1375 ± 99	757 ± 84	< 0.005
440	1284 ± 99	651 ± 103	< 0.001
p	> 0.2	< .025	

Each subject received either 200 or 440 cal in a milk shake which was indistinguishable by taste. Each subject received a standard meal 0.5 hr later and the amount eaten was recorded. (Statistical comparisons were paired differences.)

subjects have become responsive to a caloric preload which could not be demonstrated preoperatively.

DISCUSSION

In the present study, the major reason for weight loss after jejunoileostomy is the decrease in food intake. If an average of 3,500 cal/day are required for weight maintenance (10) during the 1st year after surgery, these patients would require 1.27 million cal during that time. Estimated caloric intake from dietary history would be 741,600 cal and the subject would be in deficit by 528,400 cal. Since each pound of fat contains approximately 3,500 cal, a loss of 150 lb would provide 525,000 cal or essentially all of the caloric deficit. This indicates that decreased food intake was primarily responsible for the negative caloric balance and for the rapid and sustained weight loss that these subjects experienced. Although malabsorption was demonstrated in our patients and by others in the medical literature (3, 11, 12), this does not appear to be the major reason for weight loss.

A decrease in food intake could occur for one of several reasons. It might occur to reduce the frequency of diarrhea in the early postoperative period. The diarrhea associated with jejunoileostomy is worsened by drinking liquids and by eating foods containing significant amounts of fat. A conscious effort to reduce diarrhea may well be one component in the decreased food ingestion. However, food intake remains below preoperative levels even after diarrhea and rectal irritation have essentially disappeared suggesting that other factors are involved. In addition it is difficult to conceive that the altered taste preferences result from the diarrhea alone since the things that cause the diarrhea were not the sweet-tasting foods that the patients disliked.

Decreased intestinal absorption of carbohydrate may be a second factor which reduces food intake. Soulairac (13) showed that experimental manipulations which decrease carbohydrate absorption may, in turn, reduce food intake directly or through altered taste preferences. This concept is supported by the significant changes in response to a caloric preload which was demonstrated after surgery. After the jejunoileostomy, the 440 cal preload depressed food intake more than a 200 cal preload, whereas there had been no detectable difference between the two preloads before surgery.

Intestinal distention may be a third mechanism for reducing food intake. Before surgery, these patients rarely experienced fullness or other sensations emanating from the intestinal tract. In contrast, after surgery all of the patients commented on the increased awareness of intestinal activity. Following jejunoileostomy, they became full when eating and frequently felt they had eaten enough. The shortened intestine may respond to a smaller volume of food more readily and may thus serve as a satiety signal.

Patients who lose weight in an out-patient clinic by restricting caloric intake show a high incidence of depression. Indeed this syndrome of dieting depression (14, 15) is a frequent reason why patients stop dieting. The nervousness, anxiety, and irritability associated with dieting are similar to changes found when normal men are deprived of food. During semistarvation of healthy volunteers, Keys et al. (16) noted depression, nervousness, and an increasing preoccupation with food as weight declined. This deprivation syndrome or dieting depression thus occurs in both normal and overweight subjects when they lose weight. In contrast patients who lose weight after jejunoileostomy do not become depressed (17, 18). Indeed Solow et al. (17) and Castelnuovo-Tedesco and Schiebel (18) have found less depression than before surgery. This finding suggests that shortening the intestine by jejunoileostomy prevents the deprivation syndrome. The changes in taste which we are reporting are also consistent with a reduction or absence of sensations of caloric-deprivation. In experimental animals deprivation of food increases the preference for good-tasting food and reduces the preference for bad-tasting food even though the bad-tasting food contains needed calories (19). If our subjects were having a deprivation syndrome, we might expect them to like the concentrated solutions of sugar or glucose more after surgery than before surgery; but the contrary was true. The dislike for sweet tastes after surgery would be consistent with the conclusion that after jejunoileostomy, obese patients are not experiencing metabolic or caloric deprivation.

SUMMARY

The food intake and degree of malabsorption were measured in 22 obese patients before and after jejunoileostomy for obesity. Fecal fat excretion rose from 7.8% before surgery to 44% postoperatively. Absorption of D-xylose and vitamin B_{12} (Schilling test) were also impaired. Essentially all of the weight loss, however, could be accounted for by the reduction in food intake. A disliking for sweets was noted by most patients. Preferences for concentrated solutions of sucrose and glucose were reduced after surgery but the ratings for citric acid and salt solutions and solutions with quinine were not altered. Postoperatively patients showed a depression of food intake by a 400 cal preload, which had not been detected before surgery.

ACKNOWLEDGMENTS

The authors thank the nurses and dietitian of the Clinical Study Center, without whose help these studies could not be done. We are grateful for the superb secretarial help of Ms. J. Martinez. This grant is supported in part by U.S. Public Health Service grant AM 15165 and RR 425.

REFERENCES

1. Payne, J. H., DeWind, L. T., and Commons, R. R. (1963): *Am. J. Surg.,* 106:273–289.
2. Payne, J. H., DeWind, L. T., Schwab, C. E., and Kern, W. H. (1973): *Arch. Surg.,* 106:432-437.
3. Scott, H. W., Jr., Dean, R., Shull, H. J., Abram, H. S., Webb, W., Young, R. K., and Brill, A. B. (1973): *Ann. Surg.,* 177:723–735.
4. Salmon, P. A. (1971): *Surg. Gynecol. Obstet.,* 132:965–979.
5. Weismann, R. E. (1973): *Am. J. Surg.,* 125:437–446.
6. Cabanac, M., Duclaux, R., and Spector, N. H. (1971): *Nature,* 229:125–127.
7. Cabanac, M., and Duclaux, R. (1970): *Science,* 168:497–497.
8. Grinker, J. A. (1975). In: *Obesity in Perspective,* Fogarty International Center Series on Preventive Medicine, Vol. II, Part 1 and Part 2, edited by G. A. Bray. U.S. Government Printing Office, Washington, D.C.
9. Rodin, J., Moskowitz, H. R., and Fleming, R. (1975): *Unpublished manuscript*
10. Bray, G. A., Schwartz, M., Rozin, R. R., and Lister, J. (1970): *Metabolism,* 19:418–429.
11. O'Leary, J. P., Thomas, W. C., Jr., and Woodward, E. R. (1974): *Am. J. Surg.,* 127:142–147.
12. Sandstead, H. H. (1975): In: *Obesity in Perspective,* Fogarty International Center on Preventive Medicine, Vol II, Part 1 and Part 2, edited by G. A. Bray. U.S. Government Printing Office, Washington, D.C.
13. Soulairac, A. (1967). Alimentary canal. In: *Handbook of Physiology.* Vol. 1, Control of Food and Water Intake, Chap. 28, edited by C. F. Code, pp. 387–398. American Physiological Society, Waverly Press, Inc., Baltimore, Md.
14. Stunkard, A. J. (1957): *Am. J. Med.,* 23:77–86.
15. Stunkard, A. J., and Rush, J. (1974): *Ann. Intern. Med.,* 81:526–533.
16. Keys, A., Anderson, J. T., and Brozek, J. (1950): *The Biology of Human Starvation,* pp. 1385. University of Minnesota Press, Minneapolis, Minn.
17. Solow, C., Silberfarb, P. M., Swift, K. (1974): *N. Engl. J. Med.,* 290:300–305.
18. Castelnuovo-Tedesco, P., and Schiebel, D. (1975): *This volume.*
19. Jacobs, H. L., and Sharma, K. N. (1969): *Ann. N.Y. Acad. Sci.* 157:1084–1125.

Hunger: Basic Mechanisms and Clinical Implications, edited by D. Novin, W. Wyrwicka, and G. Bray. Raven Press, New York © 1976.

Studies of Taste in Childhood Obesity

Joel A. Grinker, Judy M. Price,* and M. R. C. Greenwood**

The Rockefeller University, New York, New York 10021, * San Diego State University, San Diego, California 92115, and ** Institute of Human Nutrition, Columbia University, New York, New York 10032

Considerable evidence suggests that the obesities seen both in humans and in animal models can be classified on the basis of adipose tissue morphology, metabolic anamolies, and behavioral and genetic differences. Nonetheless, the interrelationship of these factors is yet to be elucidated. Although the inheritance of obesity is clearly documented in rodents (4, 10, 75), evidence for a genetic component in human obesity is based on epidemiological studies. Whereas obesity occurs in only 7% of the children born of normal weight parents, 40% of the children born in families with one obese parent, and 80% of the children from two obese parents are overweight (45). A higher correlation also exists between the weights of parents and natural offspring than between the weights of parents and adopted children (72). The high correlation in parent-child obesity reflects both genetic and environmental components. Studies have indicated that individual environments can alter the risk for obesity. For example, there is a strong inverse relationship between obesity and social class, which has been demonstrated in both adults and children (16, 68).

In the genetic animal obesities, the early development of obesity is associated with hypercellularity of the adipose tissue (31, 33), whereas obesity that develops later in life is characterized by hypertrophic enlargement of the fat depots only. In experimentally produced obesity (electrolytic or chemical lesions of the ventromedial hypothalamus, VMH), the obesity is accomplished solely by enlargement of the adipose tissue cells. In normal rats, the timing of fat cell proliferation has been carefully documented by both nutritional studies (41) and recently by ^{3}H-thymidine incorporation into fat cell DNA (19). These studies have shown that the hyperplastic growth period of adipose tissue in normal rats is complete at, or shortly after, the end of the suckling period. In contrast, the genetically obese rat has been shown, both in early nutritional manipulation studies (32) and by proliferation enzyme studies (18) to differ in its pattern of adipose depot development.

In humans, there appears to be a good, although not invariable, correlation between early onset of obesity and later hypercellularity of the adipose depots (2). Furthermore, recent data collected by Knittle (40) on obese children suggest that they differ in the developmental pattern of cell proliferation compared to normal nonobese controls. Absolute amount of fat was unchanged in the nonobese population between the ages of 2 and 10, whereas obese children developed significant increments throughout this age range. Cell size did not change in obese subjects during this age period, although it was significantly greater than in nonobese children. Cell number, however, continued to increase. In contrast, nonobese subjects showed increases in adipose cell size and number after age 10 when adult levels are reached in normal children. Thus qualitative and quantitative differences in adipose cell development are evident by age 2 in obese and nonobese children.

In most populations of obese, the severity of obesity is correlated with early onset of the obesity (27, 58). Therefore, the most obese individuals are usually those with early onset and hypercellularity. Although morphological findings and nutritional studies strongly suggest that early developmental patterns may be crucial in the genesis or maintenance of the obese state, it is not clear how hyperphagia and hypercellularity are related or causative.

In experimentally obese rats, the accompanying hyperphagia is associated with characteristic differences in taste parameters. Lesioned rats demonstrate a hyperresponsiveness to good-tasting (e.g., high-fat or high-carbohydrate) diets and an underresponsiveness to less palatable diets (e.g., adulterated with quinine). Lesioned animals may even fail to exhibit hyperphagia and weight gain on diets low in palatability, and may lose weight as the palatability of the diet is further decreased (7, 38, 63). This is in contrast to the behavior exhibited by normal rodents who will maintain normal weight in the face of considerable dietary manipulations (1, 69, 70). The constellation of behavioral patterns considered to be an invariant consequence of these lesions, such as hyperphagia, hyperreactivity to taste, and impaired food motivation, may well be a function of the conditions of training, size and placement of lesions, and the degree of obesity. Graff and Stellar (17) concluded that obesity and finickiness could be disassociated. Others questioning the importance of taste or sensory factors in this syndrome noted that VMH-lesioned animals, feeding themselves intragastrically, continued to overeat in spite of the absence of oral-pharyngeal sensations (47). Still others failed to obtain differential taste responses between VMH obese and lean rats to nondietary solutions (44, 49). More recently, several investigators reported that preoperative training considerably modifies the expression of the behavioral deficits found in dynamic VMH-lesioned animals (42, 64, 71). Other experiments have shown that taste responsiveness to good- or bad-tasting substances depends on methods of presentation and amount of preoperative training and not on obesity per se (3, 43, 57, 65). Perhaps of even more importance is the finding that genetically obese rodents with no gross hypothalamic pathology do not display at least some of the behavioral deficits associated with the experimentally produced obesities (5, 8, 20).

In studies of human obesity, it is particularly difficult to separate primary from secondary effects or to separate causation from correlation, since the behavioral and metabolic pathology found in the obese is a combination of genetic predisposition, cultural variables, cognitive and social consequences of obesity, and other early environmental factors. And yet it has been suggested that an integral part of the human obese hyperphagic syndrome is the result of an overresponsiveness to sensory cues or to cues in the external environment and an inattention to or nonresponsiveness to internal physiological cues. Schachter (59, 61), in particular, has focused attention on the importance of sensory and cognitive factors in both the genesis and the maintenance of the obese state.

Theories of hyperresponsiveness to external stimuli, particularly taste, have been advanced to explain both animal and human obesity. Indeed, overindulgence in "sweets" has been singled out as a cause of human obesity (50). Numerous studies on the consummatory behavior of humans have attempted to document this hypothesis (61). Studies of food intake in the obese are to some degree confounded by the prejudice that obese individuals experience in social situations (46) and their concern and possible covert behavior in feeding situations. Thus it remains unclear to what degree any excessive reliance on external or sensory cues by the obese is truly an etiological factor in the obesity or merely a secondary consequence of the obesity.

The deception experiments (62) attempt to avoid the problem of the obese individuals' sensitivity to observation by deliberately misleading subjects and using hidden measures of food intake. Although obese individuals usually eat more than normal weight individuals, in one typical experiment (60) the obese actually ate fewer crackers than did the normal weight subjects in the low-fear and food-deprivation condition. This decreased intake merits some attention. Is the reported externality of the moderately obese an inability to sense internal cues or a denial of their importance and a deliberate shift to reliance on external cues? We have attempted to replicate the finding of a high degree of correspondence between manipulated hunger in normal weight subjects and the amount of food ingested but, in our experiment, both obese and normal-weight subjects were unresponsive to satiety signals and consumed equivalent amounts in the deprivation and nondeprivation conditions (54). Other investigators (73, 74) have reported that the eating behavior of normal weight as well as obese can be controlled by external or cognitive cues. Even when subjects were instructed to use the metabolic cues associated with satiety, their hunger ratings were better correlated with their beliefs about the caloric value of ingested food than with actual caloric intake. Studies of normal weight subjects on feeding machines document the slow adjustments that are made to changes in the caloric concentration of liquid diets or to variations in the rate of delivery (34, 66, 67). Although one investigator reports no differences in the responses of obese and normal weight subjects (H. A. Jordan, *personal communication*), other investigators report differences in feeding behavior between obese and normal weight subjects when caloric concentration of the diet is changed (6).

DEVELOPMENTAL STUDIES OF TASTE

In our efforts to avoid the social and cognitive expectations that the obese bring to an eating situation, we employed two experimental paradigms. The first series of experiments examined taste parameters independent of food intake in obese and normal weight adults. The second series consisted of a developmental study of taste parameters in obese and normal weight children.

STUDIES IN ADULTS

In a series of experiments using appropriate psychophysical procedures, a variety of taste parameters were examined (21, 22, 24, 25). Using a criterion-free signal detection procedure, we found no differences between obese and normal weight subjects in their ability to detect low concentrations of sucrose. We attempted to manipulate the perception of sweetness by the addition of a cherry color. With a magnitude estimation procedure, all subjects rated suprathreshold solutions of sucrose colored red more sweet than colorless solutions of the same concentration. Marked differences in taste preference, however, were found. Normal weight subjects preferred the concentration of medium strength (a pattern similar to that reported by Pfaffmann, ref. 52), whereas the preferences of obese subjects were an inverse function of concentration: the more concentrated the solution, the less it was preferred. These findings were independent of experimental procedures or psychophysical methodology, since comparable results were obtained with both hedonic ratings and the method of paired comparisons. Differences in taste preferences were found to be specific for a sweet taste. Most obese subjects showed the typical aversion patterns for sodium chloride solutions described by Pfaffman (52). Furthermore, in a thirst experiment, intake was highly correlated with taste preferences (hedonic ratings) in normal weight, moderately overweight, and severely obese subjects.

Thus the obese subjects tested with these psychophysical procedures have an aversion to sucrose solutions. This finding is in contrast to popular *a priori* reasoning that the obese have a "sweet tooth." This phenomenon is consistently found and correlates with the degree of obesity. Since this is the only taste parameter predictably different in the obese and appears related to the degree of obesity, one might ask if the ontogeny of sweet aversion and the ontogeny of obesity are related. Accordingly, we examined the sweet preferences of obese and normal weight children and adolescents.

STUDIES IN CHILDREN

It was necessary to utilize several populations and to employ a variety of techniques for measuring taste parameters in children and adolescents. In particular, in the camp setting we found it easiest to enlist the overweight

TABLE 1. *Summary of subject characteristics and experimental procedures*

Location	Age (years)	Sex		x̄ % Fat	x̄ Height	x̄ Weight (lb)	x̄ lb lost
Mt. Sinai Pediatric Clinic[a]	8–10 obese	Female	n = 5	32.13	4'5"	108.53	
		Male	n = 3	35.08	4'6"	123.49	
San Diego civics class[a]	8–10 normal	Female	n = 5	17.92	4'4"	57.5	
		Male	n = 5	18.27	4'2.75"	56.1	
San Diego civics class[a]	8–10 moderate	Female	n = 2	31.45	4'7"	108.25	
		Male	n = 6	25.07	4'7"	83.0	
Weight Watchers camp in N.C.[b]	10–21 x̄ 14.5	Female	n = 90	38.20	5'3.5"	174.61	17.37
		Lightest	n = 30	28.47			
		Middle	n = 30	37.88			
		Heaviest	n = 30	51.37			
		Male	n = 7	38.12	5'3"	174.46	25.93
San Diego summer camp[c]	14–16	Female	n = 14	38.92	5'4.75"	175.96	22.3

[a] Paired comparisons of sucrose (1.95, 3.42, 6.16, 10.95, 19.5% wt./vol.)
[b] Hedonic ratings and magnitude estimation of cherry Kool-Aid sweetened with sucaryl (0, 0.5, 1, 2× manufacturer's recommended sweetness).
[c] Hedonic ratings, paired comparisons, and magnitude estimations of Kool-Aid sweetened with sucaryl, (0. 0.5, 1, 1.5, and 2× recommended sweetness).

camper's cooperation by using flavored but unsweetened Kool-Aid as the taste stimulus and by using a nonnutritive sweetener. When possible, in the clinic, both flavored and unflavored solutions were used for comparison.

Engen (12) demonstrated the feasibility of using a paired comparison procedure with young children. Older children and adolescents are able to use a hedonic rating procedure. Table 1 outlines the subjects' characteristics, location, age, degree of overweight, experimental procedures, and solution concentrations.

SUCROSE PREFERENCE IN CHILDREN AGED 8 TO 10

Taste preferences for sucrose solutions (1.95 to 19.5%) in normal weight and obese children aged 8 to 10 were measured by the method of paired comparisons. Eighteen children were students in a civics class in San Diego. Ten of them were normal weight and eight were moderately overweight (18.09% fat and 26.66% fat, respectively). Eight obese children were selected on the basis of age from those referred to the Mount Sinai Pediatric Clinic for treatment of simple exogenous obesity and were tested on their initial visit to the clinic (23). Percent body fat was calculated from height and weight using the Friis-Hansen nomograms (14). Normal weight girls averaged 17.92% fat and boys averaged 18.27% fat, whereas severely obese girls averaged 32.13% fat and boys averaged 35.08% fat. Normal weight children were middle class Caucasians of normal I.Q. and were tested in the classroom. Obese children were predominantly lower class, Spanish speaking, normal I.Q., and were tested individually in the clinic. Both normal weight and obese children sipped two solutions on each trial and indicated their choice by writing the number of the solution they preferred or indicating their choice orally to the experimenter. All subjects rinsed between trials with distilled water. Each of the five solutions was paired once with every other solution for a total of 10 trials. Every concentration was presented four times.

Preference was inversely correlated with percent fat. The heavier the child, the less the preference for the sweetest solution ($r = -0.5858$, $p < 0.005$). The overall responses of the severely obese children were similar to those of obese adults; the more concentrated the solution, the lower the frequency of choice (see Fig. 1). Only 50% of the moderately overweight children showed a strong preference for the 10.95% solution, whereas 80% of the normal weight children showed a strong preference. A strong preference was defined as greater than 50% selection. Less than 40% of the moderately overweight children chose the most concentrated solution on each presentation compared to 70% of the normal weight children ($z = 1.395$, $p < 0.08$). The preferences of the normal weight children were a direct function of solution concentration (see Fig. 1). There were no sex differences (analysis of variance: groups $\times$ solutions, $F = 6.2493$, $p < 0.005$).

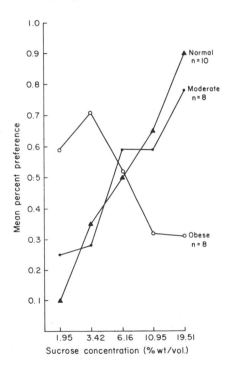

FIG. 1. Sucrose preferences of extremely obese, moderately obese, and normal weight children (ages 8–10) using the paired comparison procedure. Percent preference is a function of the number of times a solution was chosen over all other solutions.

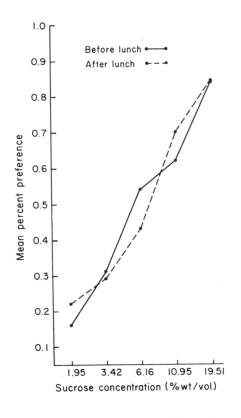

FIG. 2. Sucrose preferences of 18 normal weight children (ages 8–10) tested before and after a meal using the paired comparisons procedure.

Additional data on the effects of short-term food deprivation were obtained from the 18 normal and moderately overweight children in San Diego. Preferences for sucrose solutions were measured immediately before and after lunch. There were no significant changes in the choice responses as a function of these short-term changes in satiety (see Fig. 2).

HEDONIC RATINGS OF KOOL-AID SOLUTIONS IN OBESE CHILDREN AGED 8 TO 11

Ratings of the pleasantness of four cherry Kool-Aid solutions of varying sweetness concentration were obtained from 15 obese children from the Mt. Sinai Pediatric Clinic population. Kool-Aid solutions, sweetened with sucaryl, ranged from 1 to 2.5 times the manufacturer's recommended sweetness. Ratings were made on a nine point category scale that ranged from +4 ("great") to −4 ("lousy"). As a group, children liked the 2× recommended sweetness solution best. Children were divided into three groups on the basis of percent fat ($n = 5$ per group). The percent fat averaged 31.77% in the lightest group, 34.48% in the middle group, and 40.73% in the heaviest group. The hedonic ratings were inversely related to percent fat. The heaviest children showed the least liking for the 2× solution, whereas the lightest children showed the greatest liking ($t = 2.188$, $p < 0.05$, $8df$).

HEDONIC RATINGS AND MAGNITUDE ESTIMATES OF KOOL-AID SOLUTIONS IN OBESE ADOLESCENTS AT SUMMER CAMP IN NORTH CAROLINA

Ninety adolescent girls and seven boys attending a Weight Watchers summer camp for weight reduction in North Carolina made hedonic ratings and magnitude estimates of cherry Kool-Aid solutions sweetened with sucaryl (0, 0.5, 1, and 2 times the manufacturer's recommended sweetness), in the first and last weeks of camp. The 0.5 sucaryl solution corresponded to a 5.6% sucrose solution and the 2× solution was equivalent in sweetness to a 22.38% sucrose solution. Subjects were instructed to sip each solution, spit it out, and rinse with water between trials. Subjects rated the pleasantness of each solution on a nine-point scale, which ranged from "tastes great (+4) to "tastes lousy" (−4) and estimated the sweetness intensity on a scale from 0 to 100. Subjects received one presentation of each solution in random order.

The total sample of girls was divided into thirds on the basis of percent fat. The lightest girls averaged 28.47% fat, the middle third, 37.88% fat, and the heaviest girls averaged 51.37%. Circumference measures (midarm, abdomen, and forearm, for boys and midarm, abdomen, and wrist in girls) were used to calculate percent fat from equations developed by Katch and McArdle (35). Initial magnitude and hedonic ratings were calculated from all campers. However, 25 campers left camp before the second taste test. Data from these campers are not included in the calculations on the effect of weight reduction.

Comparisons of magnitude estimates (log transformation) of sweetness intensity showed no differences between heavier and lighter campers. Hedonic ratings, however, were related to the degree of overweight: the heaviest girls liked the most preferred solutions significantly less than did the least over-

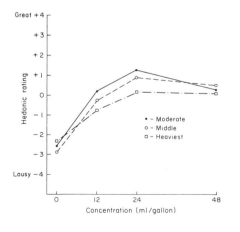

FIG. 3. Hedonic ratings of Kool-Aid solutions (0, 0.5, 1, 2 times the manufacturer's recommended sweetness) by obese adolescents, divided into groups on the basis of percent fat. Sweetness was varied through the addition of 0, 12, 24, 48 ml of sucaryl per gallon of Great Bear Water, respectively.

TABLE 2. Changes in mean hedonic ratings for Kool-Aid solutions as a function of weight loss and degree of overweight in obese adolescents

Weight group	Normal concentration (solution 3)		Twice normal (solution 4)	
	Before	After	Before	After
Girls lightest ⅓ (n = 19)	0.94	0.94	0.16	1.26
Girls middle ⅓ (n = 25)	0.60	0.92	0.48	0.92
Girls heaviest ⅓ (n = 21)	0.19	0.38	0.09	0.95
Boys (n = 7)	0.51	0.90	0.30	1.06

weight girls ($t = 2.16$, $df = 58$, $p < 0.05$) (see Fig. 3). Age was also significantly related to rated pleasantness; oldest campers, 16 and older, liked the solutions less ($F = 4.9189$, $p < 0.01$). Following weight reduction, the obese adolescents showed significant changes in the rated pleasantness for the sweeter Kool-Aid solutions. Solution 4 ($2\times$ the manufacturer's recommended sweetness), increased in pleasantness, whereas solution 3 ($1\times$ the recommended sweetness) decreased in pleasantness ($t = 2.02$, $p < 0.05$). These changes were most marked in the heaviest group (see Table 2). Magnitude estimates of sweetness intensity remained unchanged.

KOOL-AID PREFERENCES, MAGNITUDE ESTIMATES, AND HEDONIC RATINGS IN OBESE ADOLESCENTS AT CAMP IN CALIFORNIA

Fourteen obese adolescent girls (aged 14 to 16) at a summer camp for weight reduction in California made hedonic ratings, paired comparisons, and magnitude estimates of cherry Kool-Aid sweetened with sucaryl (0, 0.5, 1, 1.5, $2\times$ the manufacturer's recommended sweetness). Ratings were made four times during camp: before and after dinner, prior to weight loss, and again after weight loss. Order of testing was counterbalanced. Subjects estimated sweetness intensity on a scale of 0 to 100 and rated their liking for each solution on a nine point category scale as described above. Each solution was presented once. When the method of paired comparisons was employed, subjects received six pairs of solutions. Four solutions were presented (0 to $1.5\times$ recommended sweetness). Each solution was presented three times. Percent fat was estimated from the sum of skinfold measures at four sites (suprailiac, triceps, biceps, and subscapular).

Hedonic ratings, paired comparisons, and magnitude estimates were direct functions of sweetness concentration; the sweeter the solution, the greater the liking and rated intensity. Magnitude estimates of sweetness intensity did not change significantly before and after a meal either before or after weight reduction. Hedonic ratings changed minimally following a meal. Only after weight reduction was the sweetest solution rated more pleasant after a meal than before (Anova: before and after dinner, not significant; after weight reduction for solution $2\times$, $t = 2.488$, $p < 0.03$). Weight reduction, however, produced increases in the rated attractiveness of all Kool-Aid solutions (Anova: pre- and postweight loss, $F = 13.6246$, $p < 0.01$) and an increase in the magnitude estimates of sweetness intensity (Anova: pre and post $F = 8.0387$, $p < 0.01$) (see Fig. 4). Preferences were correlated with sub-

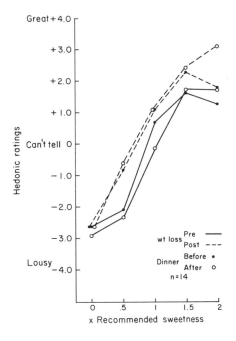

FIG. 4. Hedonic ratings of Kool-Aid solutions (0, 0.5, 1, 1.5, 2 times recommended sweetness) by obese adolescents before and after a meal prior to and after weight reduction. Sweetness was varied through the addition of 0, 12, 24, 36, 48 ml of sucaryl per gallon of spring water, respectively.

jects' self-reported age at onset of obesity. Age at onset ranged from early infancy to early adolescence. The younger the age of onset, the less the sweetest solution was preferred ($r = 0.4969$, $p < 0.05$). There were no changes in the results of the paired comparisons procedure following weight reduction. Small but significant differences in preference did occur when subjects were asked to choose between solutions before and after dinner (Anova: solutions $\times$ before and after dinner, $F = 3.7199$, $p < 0.01$). Following dinner, preference for the $0.5\times$ sweet solution was decreased and preference for the $1\times$ solution was increased.

   These data strongly suggest that the sucrose aversion of adult obese subjects obtained in our laboratory is meaningfully related to the degree and nature of the obesity. Aversion to sucrose appears in obese children as early as 8 years of age. In addition, the degree of overweight reliably discriminates the extent of this aversion. Preferences for Kool-Aid were also a function of the degree of overweight. The more overweight children liked the sweetened Kool-Aid least. Data obtained from different populations by different experimenters in different locations were consistent. In the California camp, it was possible to request that children report their age at onset of obesity. Children with the earliest ages of onset showed the least liking for the sweetest Kool-Aid solutions. In general, weight reduction produced an increased liking in obese campers for the sweeter solutions. Obese children tended to prefer the sweeter solutions after a meal rather than before a meal and this effect was accentuated with weight reduction.

DEVELOPMENTAL STUDIES OF OTHER COGNITIVE AND SENSORY FACTORS

It has been suggested that the externality in the obese described by Schachter and Rodin (62) can be extended to include a hypersensitivity in non-feeding situations. Responses such as simple and disjunctive reaction times and recall and recognition thresholds are significantly different in the moderately obese compared to individuals of normal weight. It has even been suggested that differences in externality may precede subsequent weight changes (56). However, the direction of the weight changes could not be predicted.

We undertook to obtain a meaningful measure of external responsiveness that could discriminate between obese and normal weight adults. Results from many of these experiments are outlined in Table 3. Moderately overweight subjects ranged from 30 to 50% overweight, whereas severely obese subjects were greater than 60% overweight (48). Severely and moderately overweight subjects showed no differences from normal weight subjects in simple and complex reaction times. Simple measures of reaction time were obtained by asking subjects to depress a key when a light appeared. Complex reaction times involved a choice; subjects were requested to press the right key when a red light appeared and the left key when a green light appeared. Other measures of externality such as persuasibility also failed to discriminate among severely obese, moderately obese, and normal weight individuals. A modified version of the persuasibility procedure developed by Janis and Field (30) and used by Glass (15) was administered. Questionnaire measures were also unsuccessful in distinguishing these populations. Personality inventories included measures of self-esteem (30) and externality-internality (Bach). Although significant differences were obtained between normal weight subjects and severely obese subjects, normal weight subjects appeared more external. Subjects' willingness to undergo further conditioning experiments and their resistance and anxiety were assessed following a classic eyelid conditioning experiment (39). Obese subjects were not more reactive in this experiment.

Nonetheless, the development of a device for the prediction of weight

TABLE 3. *Measures of external responsiveness in obese and normal weight adults*

Group		Visual reaction time	
		Simple	Complex
Severe obese	$\bar{x}$	330.53	694.94
	S.D.	46.60	134.07
	n	37	37
Normal wt.		307.45	726.71
		37.55	157.31
		10	10
		$t = 1.447$ N.S.	$t = -0.635$ N.S.

	Persuasibility scores topic		
	Cancer	Cold Remedy	Ice Cream
Severe obese (n = 23)	1.09	1.41	1.22
Moderate obese (n = 16)	1.33	1.40	1.47
Normal wt. (n = 39)	1.90	1.62	1.94

Questionnaire measures of externality

		External-Internal (Bach)			Personal Reaction Inventory		
		General	Obesity			Self-Esteem	Social Inhibition
Sev. Obese	$\bar{x}$	5.89	2.92			71.82	34.76
n = 69	S.D.	2.85	1.65	n = 63		14.79	7.13
Moa. Obese	$\bar{x}$	6.00	2.29			76.64	27.28
n = 14	S.D.	2.15	1.07	n = 14		7.86	4.27
Normal Wt.	$\bar{x}$	8.00	2.52			76.36	38.42
n = 27	S.D.	2.73	1.78	n = 25		12.00	5.185
	$t = -3.301$	$p < 0.01$			N.S.		

	Eyelid Conditioning			
	Willingness to return	Value of experiment	Resistance and suspicion	Anxiety and annoyance
Severely obese (n = 21)	75.92	52.30	41.19	26.98
Moderate obese (n = 16)	73.75	58.02	50.62	37.81
Normal weight (n = 20)	68.5	49.0	49.5	33.5

change would be extremely useful. Therefore, we continued our attempts to measure "externality" using procedures similar to those that have been reported to distinguish between the performance of moderately obese and normal weight individuals (55). Adolescent girls at camp in San Diego were asked to recall food-related and nonfood-related items after a brief exposure (15 sec). Twenty items were presented on a tray. Subjects were tested before and after dinner, prior to weight loss, and again after weight loss. Weight reduction resulted in greater recall in the total number of items, but not in the number of food items recalled. Use of homonyms (e.g., wait and weight or flower and flour) was measured. Subjects listened to 15 words read aloud by the experimenter and were asked to write each word and their first association with this word. No differences occurred before and after weight reduction in the number of food related homonyms or associates.

DISCUSSION

Our finding that obese children show less liking for sweetened solutions has strengthened our conviction that the taste aversion seen in obese adults is a real phenomenon. In the area of obesity research, much popular mythology persists. One of the most prevalent myths is that obese people become obese by overindulgence in sweets or carbohydrates. There are few direct observations or questionnaire studies that compare the intake of obese and normal weight subjects. In one study of a large number of subjects at a County Fair, no differences were found between obese and normal weight subjects in their preferences for desserts of varying sucrose concentrations (51). Obese teenagers reported a lower consumption of bread, sweets, and sugar than normal weight children (36), and similar findings of lower carbohydrate intake have been reported in studies of obese adults (37). The lack of significant differences in fatty acids of adipose tissue in obese and normal weight subjects suggests that, in general, obese individuals eat the same proportion of fats, carbohydrates, and protein as do normal weight subjects (26).

The ontogeny of feeding behavior follows distinct patterns in man and animals. At birth, the organism is virtually parasitic with little active control of patterns of ingestion, but this becomes rapidly transformed into a complex phenomenon with multifactorial control (28, 67). It has been shown that preweaning rats are more responsive to the state of gastrointestinal fill than to glucose metabolism in the control of food intake (29). In man, there have been similar studies (11, 13) indicating that early in life the human infant is responsive primarily to gastric filling but, after 4 to 6 weeks, many more complex factors begin to govern food intake.

Reports in both man and animals document neonatal taste preferences for sweet solutions. All studies suggest that there is a universal preference for sweet-tasting solutions (9, 53). We find it puzzling then, that obese children show a decreased liking for sweetened Kool-Aid and an aversion for sucrose solutions as early as 8 years of age. Furthermore, preliminary data suggest that the sucrose aversion can be elicited as early as 3 years of age in obese children. Since children who are obese at these early ages invariably show hypercellularity as well as hypertrophy of their adipose depots, it is particularly intriguing that the taste differences occur simultaneously. It may be that early dietary intake plays a determining role in both the ultimate adipose tissue cellularity and in the ontogeny of the aversion to sucrose and decreased liking seen in obese children, adolescents, and adults. Studies in animals emphasize the importance of early nutritional effects on fat cellularity in both obese and normal animals, but the effects of early nutritional treatments on the development of subsequent taste preferences are far from definitive. It may be that the feeding of diets of varying caloric density to infants or animals prior to the activation of hypothalamic regulation of food intake may determine fat cellularity, body size, and taste preferences.

The sucrose taste aversion in the adult is correlated with adipose cell number. The greater the number of cells, the greater the aversion to sucrose. After weight loss, this aversion persists in the adult (25). Although we are not able to draw conclusions about the relationship of the hypercellular state and the development of this aversion, we find it an increasingly valuable tool for distinguishing among obese individuals. However, we are not at all certain whether the aversion is endogenous and related to metabolic variables or a learned response correlated with social factors and denial.

It is possible that at least two feedback mechanisms are involved in the control of food intake. Certainly one can speculate that the energy demands of an organism are reflected in, and monitored by, sensing systems for lipid and carbohydrate stores. Among the candidates for a peripheral monitor of carbohydrate and lipid intake, taste is the obvious sensory cue. In children, the increased liking for sweet tasting solutions that we find after weight reduction may in some way reflect metabolic demands for increased consumption.

ACKNOWLEDGMENTS

This research was supported in part by Nutrition Foundation grant to Joel Grinker, National Institute of Health Grants TI AM-5168 and HD-02761-08, and San Diego State University Research Funds.

The authors thank Barbara Kibler, John Sheposh, Beth Swartzel, and Janet Tenney for collecting data at the camps and school. We also gratefully acknowledge the assistance of Florence Oetjen for writing our computer program and Anna Maria Resnikoff for technical assistance.

REFERENCES

1. Adolph, E. F. (1947): Urges to eat and drink in rats. *Am. J. Physiol.*, 151:110–125.

2. Batchelor, B., Hirsch, J., Grinker, J., Stern, J., and Cohn, C. (1975): Adipose cellularity and human obesity: A review in 106 individuals. (*In preparation.*)
3. Beatty, William W. (1972): Influence of type of reinforcement on operant responding by rats with ventromedial lesions. *Physiol. Behav.,* 10:841–846.
4. Bray, G., and York, D. A. (1971): Genetically transmitted obesity in rodents. *Physiol. Rev.,* 51:598–646.
5. Bray, G. A., and York, D. A. (1972): Studies on food intake in genetically obese rats. *Am. J. Physiol.,* 223:176–179.
6. Campbell, R. G., Hashim, S. A., and Van Itallie, T. B. (1971): Studies of food intake regulation in man. Responses to variations in nutritive density in lean and obese subjects. *N. Engl. J. Med.,* 285:1402–1407.
7. Corbit, J. D., and Stellar, E. (1964): Palatability, food intake and obesity in normal and hyperphagic rats. *J. Comp. Physiol. Psychol.,* 58:63–67.
8. Cruce, J. A. F., Greenwood, M. R. C., Johnson, P. R., and Quartermain, D. (1974): Genetic versus hypothalamic obesity: Studies of intake and dietary manipulation in rats. *J. Comp. Physiol. Psychol.,* 87(2):295–301.
9. Desor, J. A. (1973): Taste in acceptance of sugars by human infants. *J. Comp. Physiol. Psychol.,* 84(3):496–501.
10. Dickie, M. M. (1969): Mutations of the Agouti locus in the mouse. *J. Hered.,* 60:20–25.
11. Dubignon, J., Campbell, D., Curtis, M., and Partington, M. W. (1969): The relation between laboratory measures of sucking, food intake and perinatal factors during the newborn period. *Child. Devel.,* 40:1107–1120.
12. Engen, T. A., Gasparian, F. E. (1973): A study of taste preferences in young child. Dept. of Health, Education, and Welfare, U.S. Public Health Service, Research Report.
13. Fomon, S. J., and Filer, L. J. (1971): A pediatrician looks at early nutrition. *Bull. N.Y. Acad. Med.,* 47:569–578.
14. Friis-Hansen, B. (1961): Body water compartments in children: Changes during growth and related changes in body composition. *Pediatrics,* 28(2):169–181.
15. Glass, D., and Lavin, D. (1969): Obesity and persuasibility. *J. Pers.,* 37(3):407–414.
16. Goldblatt, P. B., Moore, M. E., and Stunkard, A. J. (1964): Social factors in obesity. *JAMA,* 192:1039–1044.
17. Graff, H., and Stellar, E. (1962): Hyperphagia obesity and finickiness. *J. Comp. Physiol. Psychol.,* 55:418–424.
18. Greenwood, M. R. C., Cleary, M., Brasel, J. A., Stern, J. S., and Johnson, P. R. (1974): The regulation of fat cell number in normal and obese rats. *Proceedings of the XXVI International Congress of Physiological Sciences,* Jerusalem, October, 1974, Abstract.
19. Greenwood, M. R. C., and Hirsch, J. (1974): Postnatal development of adipocyte cellularity in the normal rat. *J. Lipid Res.,* 15:474.
20. Greenwood, M. R. C., Quartermain, D., Johnson, P. R., Cruce, J. A. F., and Hirsch, J. (1974): Food motivated behavior in genetically obese and hypothalamic-hyperphagic rats and mice. *Physiol. Behav.* 13:687–692.
21. Grinker, J. Taste parameters in obese and normal weight individuals. In: *Nutrition and Psyche.* Eighth International Meeting, sponsored by Fondazione Sassi (*in press*).
22. Grinker, J., and Hirsch, J. (1972): Metabolic and behavioral correlates of obesity. From *Physiology, Emotion, and Psychosomatic Illness,* edited by J. Knight, pp. 349–374. A CIBA Foundation Symposium 8, ASP, Amsterdam.
23. Grinker, J., and Knittle, J. (1975): Metabolic and behavioral parameters of obese children. *Proceedings of the International Symposium on the Adipose Child,* Spring. (*In preparation.*)
24. Grinker, J., Smith, D. V., and Hirsch, J. (1971): Taste preferences in obese and normal weight subjects. *Proceedings of the Fourth International Conference on the Regulation of Food and Water Intake,* Cambridge, England, Abstract.
25. Grinker, J. (1975): Obesity and taste: Human and animal studies. U.S. Government Printing Office. Presented at Fogarty International Conference on Obesity, 1973.

26. Goldrick, B., and Hirsch, J. (1963): A technique for quantitative recovery of lipid from chromatoplates. *J. Lipid Res.,* 4:482–483.
27. Hirsch, J., and Knittle, J. L. (1970): Cellularity of obese and non-obese adipose tissue. *Fed. Proc.,* 29:1516–1521.
28. Hirsch, J. (1972): Regulation of food intake: Discussion. In: *Advances in Psychosomatic Medicine, Vol. 7, Hunger and Satiety in Health and Disease,* edited by F. Reichsman. Karger, Basel: 229–242.
29. Houpt, K. A., and Epstein, A. N. (1973): Ontogeny of control of food intake in the rat: G. I. fill and glucoprivation. *Am. J. Physiol.,* 225:58–66.
30. Janis, I. L., and Field, P. B. (1959): A behavioral assessment of persuasibility: Consistency of individual differences. In: *Personality and Persuasibility,* edited by C. I. Hovland and I. L. Janis, Yale University Press, New Haven: 29–54.
31. Johnson, P. R., and Hirsch, J. (1972): Cellularity of adipose depots in six strains of genetically obese mice. *J. Lipid Res.,* 13:2–11.
32. Johnson, P. R., Stern, J. S., Greenwood, M. R. C., Zucker, L. M., and Hirsch, J. (1973): Effects of early nutrition on adipose cellularity and pancreatic insulin release in the Zucker rat. *J. Nutr.,* 103:738–743.
33. Johnson, P. R., Zucker, L. M., Cruce, J. A. F., and Hirsch, J. (1971): Cellularity of adipose depots in the genetically obese Zucker rat. *J. Lipid Res.,* 12:706–714.
34. Jordan, H. A. (1975): Physiological control of food intake in man. U.S. Government Printing Office. Presented at Fogarty Conference on Obesity.
35. Katch, F., and McArdle, W. (1973): Prediction of body density from simple anthropometric measurements on college-age men and women. *Hum. Biol.,* 45:445–454.
36. Kaufman, N. A., Poznanski, R., and Guggenheim, K. (1974): Eating habits of teenagers and self perception of body weight. *Proceedings of the XXVI-International Congress of Physiological Sciences,* Jerusalem, Abstract.
37. Keen, H. (1974): Incomplete story of obesity and diabetes. *Proceedings of the First International Congress on Obesity,* London, 1974.
38. Kennedy, G. C. (1953): The role of depot fat in the hypothalamic control of food intake in the rat. *Proc. R. Soc. [Biol.],* 140:578–592.
39. Kimble, G. A. (1967): Attitudinal factors in eyelid conditioning. In: *Foundations of Conditioning and Learning,* edited by G. A. Kimble. Appleton-Century-Crofts, New York: 642–659.
40. Knittle, J., Ginsburg-Fellner, F., and Brown, R. (1975): Adipose cell development as an indicator of obesity. *Society for Pediatric Research,* April, 1975.
41. Knittle, J. L., and Hirsch, J. (1968): Effect of early nutrition on the development of rat epididymal fat pads: Cellularity and metabolism. *J. Clin. Invest.,* 47:2091.
42. Larkin, R. (1971): How hard will hyperphagic rats work for food? *Eastern Psychol. Ass. Ann. Mtg. Abstract.*
43. Levison, M. J., Frommer, G. P., and Vance, W. B. (1973): Palatability and caloric density as determinants of food intake in hyperphagic and normal rats. *Physiol. Behav.,* 10:455–462.
44. Maller, O. (1964): The effect of hypothalamic and dietary obesity on taste preference in rats. *Life Sci.,* 3:1281–1291.
45. Mayer, J. (1965): Genetic factors in human obesity. *Ann. N.Y. Acad. Sci.,* 131:412–421.
46. Mayer, J. (1968): *Overweight: Causes, Cost, and Control.* Prentice Hall, Englewood Cliffs, N.J.
47. McGinty, D., Epstein, A. N., and Teitelbaum, P. (1965): The contribution of oral-pharyngeal sensations to hypothalamic hyperphagia. *Anim. Behav.,* 13(4):413–418.
48. Metropolitan Life Insurance Company, Statistical Bulletin, 40, 1959.
49. Nachman, M. (1967): Hypothalamic hyperphagia, finickiness and taste preferences in rats. *Proceedings of the 75th Annual Convention of the American Psychological Association,* 2:127–128.
50. Nordsiek, F. W. (1972): The sweet tooth. *Am. Sci.,* 60:41–45.
51. Pangborn, R. M., and Simone, M. (1958): Body size and sweetness preference. *J. Am. Diet. Assoc.,* 34:924–928.
52. Pfaffmann, C. (1961): The sensory and motivating properties of the sense of task.

In: *Nebraska Symposium on Motivation, Vol. IX,* edited by M. R. Jones, pp. 71–110. University of Nebraska Press.

53. Pratt, K., Nelson, A., and Sun, K. (1930): The behavior of the newborn infant. Ohio State University Studies (contributions in Psychol. No. 10, Ohio State University Press), 105–125.

54. Price, J. M., and Grinker, J. (1973): Effects of degree of obesity, food deprivation and palatability on eating behavior of humans. *J. Comp. Physiol. Psychol.,* 85:265–271.

55. Rodin, J. (1973): Effects of distraction on performance of obese and normal subjects. *J. Comp. Physiol. Psychol.,* 83(1):68–75.

56. Rodin, J. (1974): Obesity and external responsiveness. *First International Congress on Obesity,* London, October, 1974.

57. Roswell, V. A., and Grinker, J. A. (1974): Palatability and intake in two obese animal models: Genetically obese rats and ventromedial hypothalamic lesioned rats. *Proceedings of the Eastern Psychological Association,* Philadelphia, Pennsylvania, 1974.

58. Salans, L. B., Cushman, S. W., and Weismann, R. E. (1973): Studies of human adipose tissue: Adipose cell size and number in nonobese and obese patients. *J. Clin. Invest.,* 52:929–941.

59. Schachter, S. (1968): Obesity and eating. *Science,* 161:751–756.

60. Schachter, S., Goldman, R., and Gordon, A. (1968): Effects of fear, food deprivation, and obesity on eating. *J. Pers. Soc. Psychol.,* 10:91–97.

61. Schachter, S. (1971): Some extraordinary facts about obese humans and rats. *Am. Psychol.,* 26:129–144.

62. Schachter, S., and Rodin, J. (1974): *Obese Humans and Rats.* Wiley, New York.

63. Sclafani, A., Springer, D., and Kluge, L. (1975): Effect of diet palatability on the body weight of hypothalamic hyperphagic rats: Further evidence for a dual lipostat model. *Physiology and Behavior,* (in press).

64. Singh, D. (1973): Effects of pre-operative training on food-motivated behavior of hypothalamic hyperphagic rats. *J. Comp. Physiol. Psychol.* 84:47–52.

65. Singh, D. (1974): Role of pre-operative experience on reaction to quinine taste in hypothalamic hyperphagic rats. *J. Comp. Physiol. Psychol.,* 186(4):674–678.

66. Spiegel, T. A. (1973): Caloric regulation of food intake in man. *J. Comp. Physiol. Psychol.,* 84:24–37.

67. Stellar, E. (1967): Hunger in man: Comparative and physiological studies. *Am. Psychol.,* 22:105–117.

68. Stunkard, A. J., d'Aquille, E., and Filion, R. D. L. (1972): Influence of social class on obesity and thinness in children. *JAMA,* 221:579–584.

69. Teitelbaum, P. (1955): Sensory control of hypothalamic hyperphagia. *J. Comp. Physiol. Psychol.,* 48:156–163.

70. Teitelbaum, P., and Epstein, A. N. (1963): The role of taste and smell in the regulation of food and water intake. In: *Olfaction and Taste, Vol. 1,* edited by Y. Zotterman, pp. 347–360. Pergamon Press, Oxford.

71. Wampler, R. S. (1973): Increased motivation in rats with ventromedial hypothalamic lesions. *J. Comp. Physiol. Psychol.,* 84:275–285.

72. Withers, R. F. J. (1964): Problem in the genetics of obesity. *Eugen. Rev.,* 58:81.

73. Wooley, S. C. (1972): Physiological versus cognitive factors in short-term food regulation in the obese and nonobese. *Psychosom. Med.,* 34:62–68.

74. Wooley, O. W., Wooley, S. C., and Dunham, R. B. (1972): Can calories be perceived and do they affect hunger in obese and nonobese humans? *J. Comp. Physiol. Psychol.,* 80:250–285.

75. Zucker, L. M., and Zucker, T. F. (1961): Fatty, a new mutation in the rat. *J. Hered.,* 52:275–278.

Hunger: Basic Mechanisms and Clinical Implications,
edited by D. Novin, W. Wyrwicka, and G. Bray.
Raven Press, New York © 1976.

Studies of Superobesity
II. Psychiatric Appraisal of Surgery for Superobesity

Pietro Castelnuovo-Tedesco and Douglas Schiebel

Harbor General Hospital, Torrance, California 90509 and UCLA School of Medicine, Los Angeles, California 90024

Over the past 15 years, increasing attention has been devoted to patients with extreme forms of obesity (variously called superobesity, morbid, or intractable obesity) in an effort to evaluate both their principal personality characteristics (1–5) and their response to treatment (6–13). There has been a long-standing awareness that approaches that are based on diet, anorectic agents, and/or on psychotherapy have been of limited effectiveness and, ultimately, are disappointing (14–16). Hopes rose during the 1960s when programs based on starvation (6–8) were introduced. In time, however, this approach too proved disappointing when it became apparent that it is an expensive one requiring prolonged hospitalization and, more importantly, the weight loss thus obtained is short-lived. After discharge from the hospital, patients generally tend to return to their original weight levels. The most recent effort to deal with the problem of superobesity has involved surgery on the gastrointestinal tract aimed at reducing the amount of bowel available for absorption of foods. Several intestinal bypass operations (17–19) have been tried. The first attempt involved an ileocolic anastomosis but later a jejuno-ileal (end-to-side or end-to-end) anastomosis came to be preferred because of fewer side effects. The characteristics of these operations have been dealt with in the surgical literature. Here we simply point out that these are major procedures inevitably carrying some risk of mortality and morbidity. The more serious postoperative complications include fatty infiltration of the liver and, occasionally, liver failure, various electrolyte disturbances, and the formation of urinary tract stones. In addition to the possible physical complications, attention must be given to the emotional aspects of this radical form of treatment, which causes a loss of almost half the body weight in approximately 1 year. There is need to evaluate both its benefits and any psychiatric risks attendant upon such a marked alteration of bodily configuration.

Of the psychiatric reports that have appeared to date both in this country

---

This article is reprinted with modifications with the permission of the *American Journal of Psychiatry*.

and in Europe, most have given a generally positive view of the bypass procedure emphasizing its beneficial psychological effects (3, 10–13). In particular, Solow et al. (10) noted postoperatively "an improvement in mood, self-esteem, interpersonal and vocational effectiveness, body image and activity levels, as well as notable decrease in the use of denial." They observed that the most important psychologic change was "the loss of a pervasive sense of entrapment, helplessness and failure associated with massive obesity" and added that "symptom substitution did not occur." On the other hand, Espmark (11) from Sweden has drawn much more tentative conclusions. In a preliminary report, he notes that 40 of his 65 patients postoperatively needed psychotherapy "due to anxiety and depression." Three had "serious psychogenic vomiting," four "made serious suicidal attempts," and seventeen "reported thoughts of suicide or weariness of life." Still others experienced what Espmark calls "crises of self-assertion" and "body image crises." He concludes by saying that "bypass surgery is an important tool in the treatment of extreme obesity, but . . . the psychological problems involved should be emphasized and cooperation with a psychiatrist, familiar with obesity problems, is necessary."

This chapter derives from a larger study of superobese patients. An earlier article (5) has dealt with the psychological characteristics of these patients, whereas the present one examines their response to bypass surgery and its effects on their psychological adjustment. Consideration of the psychosocial consequences is needed to help assess the value of this form of treatment and the extent to which it may be broadly applicable to patients who are superobese.

MATERIALS AND METHODS

Twelve white superobese women, aged 18 to 30 years, were studied psychiatrically for up to 3 years in conjunction with their treatment by means of jejuno-ileal bypass surgery. All were selected serially from a larger group of patients who had been seen in the Obesity Clinic of Harbor General Hospital and chosen for bypass surgery by members of the departments of Medicine and Surgery. All were of lower class or lower middle class extraction. All weighed between 300 and 350 lb and were in good general health. Most had come to the clinic specifically requesting bypass surgery, whereas a minority had been advised to have this procedure at the conclusion of their work-up. Preoperatively three patients dropped out from the study of their own volition because of increasing anxiety and ambivalence about the forthcoming surgical procedure. Of these, two decided to temporarily give up further attempts at treatment, whereas the third chose to seek care at another medical center offering a nonsurgically oriented program based on strict diet and rehabilitation. Postoperatively, one patient had to be dropped from the study because she declined to return for medical or psychiatric follow-up appointments; approximately 2 years later, her bypass was taken down at another hospital but the circumstances that prompted this decision are not known to us. The four above-mentioned patients were replaced in the study with four other patients. No patients were excluded from surgery because they were considered poor risks on psychiatric grounds.

One month prior to surgery, all were seen for several semistructured psychiatric interviews to review their personal histories. They also received a battery of psychological tests, which included the Minnesota Multiphasic Personality Inventory (MMPI), a variant of the thematic apperception test, a sentence completion test, human figure drawings, and the multiple affect adjective check list. A specific attempt was made to involve each patient in a psychotherapeutic relationship and an opportunity was offered to discuss issues of personal concern. Followup interviews occurred two to three times per week during the period of hospitalization and approximately once a month after discharge from the hospital. In addition, all were invited to take part in a monthly group consisting of pre- and postbypass patients. Psychological tests were repeated shortly after surgery and then at 6-month intervals. Detailed process notes were made immediately after each interview.

The psychological characteristics of these patients have already been described at length in an earlier paper (5). It will suffice here to say that none in our group had serious psychiatric illness. Ten showed mild to moderate personality disturbances with predominant passive aggressive traits, whereas two seemed reasonably normal and did not warrant a personality diagnosis. Depressive features, although common, were not severe and most patients presented an appearance of equanimity and lack of obvious distress. They also showed a limited awareness of emotional problems and generally tended to concern themselves with here-and-now external and "realistic" issues. None chose to avail herself of the offer of psychotherapy, except very briefly when in a crisis. A noteworthy finding was that none in the group sought the bypass operation primarily or exclusively to improve appearance. Rather they wished to forestall the medical complications of extreme obesity. Although patients commonly said that they wanted the operation because they could no longer accept some of the consequences of their obesity (such as being unable to get a job or becoming fatigued and short of breath on very slight exertion), none asked for surgery simply for cosmetic reasons.

RESULTS

Effects of Surgery on Body Weight and Attitudes toward Weight Loss

During the first postoperative year, 10 of the 12 patients lost between 8 and 15 lb/month. Two patients, however, lost a total of only about 30 lb and this was a source of considerable unhappiness and dissatisfaction, which finally led them to obtain a revision of the bypass elsewhere. Following the second operation, they lost weight at a similar rate as the other members of the group. These two patients were the first in our series and probably had received a somewhat more conservative operation than the ones who followed them. In view of their clearly atypical status it was decided to exclude from the analysis all psychometric data obtained from these two cases.

The critical weight loss occurs during the first postoperative year. It then gradually slows down and the patient's weight generally stabilizes in 2 to 3 years at the 150- to 180-lb level. Typically, patients are very pleased by their weight loss, which at first they report with clear signs of accomplishment and pride. Most say that they "can't wait" to get down to a normal weight and although a few, transiently, express the hope of weighing in the 125- to 130-lb range, they are generally quite satisfied when their weight eventually stabilizes at a level that is 25 to 50 lb above their "ideal."

Effects of Surgery on Appetite and Food Intake

A striking finding, which, to our knowledge, has not been mentioned in the literature, is a distinct postoperative change in food intake. All our patients reported that they were not only losing weight but also eating significantly less, as well as less often, than before surgery. They said they ate only one or two meals per day and a few claimed that occasionally they went a whole day without eating. There was general consensus that snacking between meals had markedly decreased. Probably a variety of physiologic factors are involved, of which at least the following may be identified with assurance. Patients repeatedly referred to the occurrence of diarrhea, borborigmi, abdominal cramps, and flatus, which, especially in the first 2 to 3 months after surgery, are promptly activated by food intake. Some also became aware of the food's transit through the intestine "like it's falling down a shute." Thus there is both physical discomfort associated with eating, spontaneously creating an aversive conditioning, as well as simply greater awareness of a variety of sensations arising from the gastrointestinal tract. As these problems tend to subside after 6 months to 1 year postoperatively, there is a tendency for food intake gradually to increase again. After 2 years or so, approximately 1/3 of the patients say that they eat again as much as they did preoperatively, but it is difficult to gain more than general impressions.

Following surgery, patients also report some changes in the type of diet preferred. Whereas preoperatively these patients eat freely of everything, postoperatively they tend to restrict fried and spicy foods, sweets (including soft drinks), and roughage, which tend to produce symptoms. On the other hand, they also report cravings for other foods, especially fruits and vegetables which generally had not been an important part of their preoperative diet.

Somatic Complications of Surgery and Their Psychological Significance

Various somatic complications of bypass surgery were noted, some rather serious.[1] As already mentioned, two patients had to have a second bypass procedure because the first had produced insufficient results; much disappointment and resentment were engendered by the first but largely subsided after the second operation. Four patients developed megacolon with recurrent abdominal distension, one requiring surgery for intestinal obstruction. Another patient required removal of a renal stone (another stone was passed spontaneously). Four patients needed a panniculectomy for removal of an abdominal fat apron. Six patients had difficulties with vomiting, associated with electrolyte disturbance and liver involvement; in two cases, they were severe enough that consideration was given to undoing the bypass, although ultimately this proved unnecessary. In five of these six cases, anxiety also appeared to have a prominent role in the patient's vomiting. During the first 6 to 10 months, nine patients experienced some thinning of the hair (associated with hypoproteinemia); whereas in all cases this condition eventually reversed itself, it became temporarily a source of embarrassment and of concern that it might progress to a frank alopecia. Overall, five patients had an essentially uncomplicated postoperative course with only minor, if any, difficulties. There were no deaths among our 12 patients, although two deaths occurred in another group of bypass patients treated at our hospital. This caused considerable anxiety among the survivors and may have had some influence on the three who preoperatively withdrew from our program. Despite direct evidence that fatalities can occur, most patients did not seriously waver in their resolve to proceed with surgery.

Adaptive Reactions and Psychiatric Status of Patients during the Postoperative Period

Typical Postoperative Course

Postoperatively, our patients' reaction to the bypass operation generally was a positive one; with only minor qualifications, they were pleased with its effects and its overall results. All obtained a great deal of gratification and sense of achievement from their weight loss.[2] They felt, especially at first, as if it could not proceed fast enough and they would report with pride their latest weight. They clearly conveyed the feeling that their life at last had

---

[1] In addition, other complications secondary to any major abdominal procedure but not specifically related to bypass surgery also occurred. These included gastrointestinal stress ulceration with bleeding, homologous serum jaundice, thrombophlebitis, intra-abdominal abscess with intestinal obstruction, repair of an incisional hernia, etc.

[2] See ref. 20 for a patient's enthusiastic account of her reaction to surgery.

taken a new turn and that they were about to enjoy a new sense of freedom from the burdens and limitations imposed upon them by their obesity. All spoke with anticipation of the pleasures of becoming more active. They emphasized variously the satisfactions of being able to walk comfortably and take part in physical activities, of obtaining employment and becoming self-supporting, and of having a fuller social and sexual life. Particularly in the immediate postoperative period, the typical reaction was mildly euphoric as the patient looked ahead to these new opportunities. Thus, at first, one noted an upsurge of enthusiasm and a new sense of confidence. This was reflected in patients' appraisal of their body size. Immediately after the operation they "felt slimmer" and tended to regard themselves already as definitely less obese, even before enough time had elapsed for significant weight loss to occur. We have regarded this as a "placebo" effect of the surgery (see Fig. 1).[3]

The index of patients' appraisal of their body size used in Fig. 1 was obtained from their human figure drawings. In this test, patients were asked to draw both a self-sketch and a sketch of an average person. The ratio of the abdominal widths of these two sketches became the index of self-perceived obesity. Figure 1 contrasts this phenomenological index of obesity to the patients' actual overweight as obtained from statistical tables, adjusted for age and body height.[4] It will be seen in Fig. 1 that there is a tendency for the superobese to exaggerate their overweight prior to surgery, and conversely to underestimate their residual obesity 1 year following surgery. The placebo effect noted 1 week postsurgery has already been mentioned.

As weight loss continued,[5] patients were especially encouraged by the realization that they now were less prone to shortness of breath and had greater capacity for activity. After approximately 6 months, other physical milestones became important. They felt a great sense of accomplishment when they became able to cross their legs, fit comfortably in ordinary-sized arm chairs (which permitted them for the first time in years to attend the movies or the theatre), and pass through turnstiles at the supermarket. Somewhat later, during the second 6 months and afterward, they noticed that it became easier to obtain clothes. These generally were more shapely and colorful than the ones they had worn before surgery. They began also to pay more attention to grooming and to use lipstick and other beauty aids; their appearance became more feminine and attractive. Gradually, they began to break through their earlier restrictions on social activity, to be more active socially, and also to date. They enjoyed their new opportunities for sexual

---

[3] In Figs. 1 and 2, $n = 8$ because at the time of writing the last two patients in this series had not yet completed 1 year's follow-up.

[4] From National Center for Health Statistics, PHS Publication No 1000, Series 11, No 14.

[5] Most patients weighing between 300 and 350 lb must lose between 25 and 45 lb or approximately 10% of their weight to become subjectively aware that weight loss has occurred.

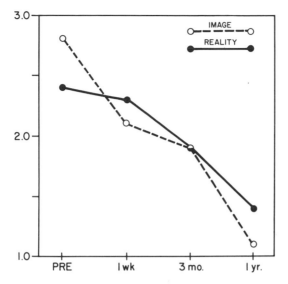

FIG. 1. Average ratio of body image inflation compared to average ratio of normative overweight (n = 8).

affairs, but also felt that they had lost the protection they used to receive from their fatness. Moreover, as noted in our first paper (5), they appeared wary and disinclined toward marriage, although one married postoperatively. Three patients became pregnant; one, who already had three children, chose a therapeutic abortion. Patients often sought additional education to help improve their prospects for employment. Of nine unmarried patients, preoperatively six had been unemployed, whereas 1 to 3 years postoperatively seven were either employed or going to school or both. Of the three who were working preoperatively, two had risen postoperatively to more remunerative employment.

Further Characteristics of Postoperative Personal Adjustment

In conjunction with their new sense of confidence, patients typically remark that they are less concerned about pleasing others, more outspoken about their views, and less likely to "turn the other cheek." These changes in behavior, objectively observed as well as subjectively reported, clearly convey that the overall effect of the surgery on the patient's life has been a positive one. We never heard any of our patients say, even during some of the more difficult periods, that they would like to have the bypass taken down. In fact, when such a step was considered in the case of two of our patients because of electrolyte and liver complications, both became upset and said they would rather risk death from complications of the bypass than allow the bypass to be undone and "go back to the way I was before." Both were immensely

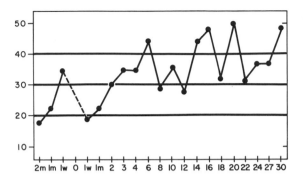

FIG. 2. Relative degree of dysphoria (anxiety, depression, hostility) expressed by 13 patients over 2.5-year period. Composite picture.

relieved when eventually they managed to overcome their difficulties with the bypass still intact.

On the other hand, despite their accomplishments and their obvious satisfaction with these, most patients found their postoperative course far from simple or devoid of stress. Grumblings about the program were common. We have mentioned the extent of somatic complications to emphasize that there were periods when patients felt distinctly unwell and worried about their condition. Even the five whose surgical postoperative course was essentially uncomplicated experienced emotional stresses of some significance. Most patients showed greater emotionality and the "ups and downs" of anxiety, depression, or hostility became more noticeable (see Fig. 2). In particular, patients seemed more prone to, and expressive of, anger. This was well demonstrated by their responses to the multiple affect adjective check list (Fig. 3 shows response patterns of patients M.J. and D.M.).

At the same time, we wish to note that postoperatively we have not seen major psychiatric complications and that, despite awareness that they were going through a stressful period, none of the patients decompensated. Several had mild-to-moderate emotional crises in connection with various interpersonal issues, which will be described in more detail below, but all were effectively handled through brief outpatient intervention. It is interesting to note here that patients' performance on the MMPI was essentially the same 1 year after as before surgery (see Fig. 4). This suggests that despite fluctuations in mood, episodic crises, and increased assertiveness, these patients' personality characteristics have not fundamentally changed.

Patients' greater assertiveness brought not only greater social effectiveness but, in some areas, more interpersonal strain. One patient separated from her husband just prior to surgery; divorce followed shortly thereafter. A significant factor seemed to be the husband's inability to accept that his wife would no longer be fat; he promptly found himself another fat woman. Two other patients divorced during the follow-up period. One of these, who was

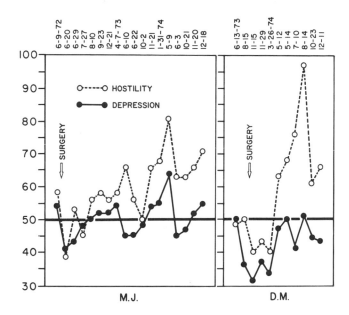

FIG. 3. Fluctuation in level of self-reported depression and hostility.

married to a superobese man, became increasingly intolerant of her husband's fatness. She complained that even though she had gone through the rigors of surgery, he "had done nothing about himself." A separation resulted and finally he agreed to also undergo bypass surgery; this, however, did not result in a reconciliation. Unmarried patients became sexually much more active than had been preoperatively. They enjoyed both sexual intercourse and the fact that men now found them more desirable. However, problems often arose when they received marriage proposals because of wariness about a lasting commitment. They also tended to become more independent of their

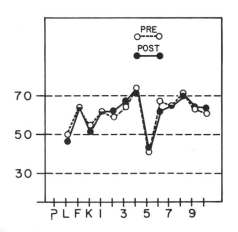

FIG. 4. Comparison of average MMPI profile 1 month presurgery to 1 year postsurgery ($n = 8$).

parents and to move into apartments of their own; this was accompanied by some of the commonly expectable frictions. Several felt that their mothers now were envious of their newly found slimness; one patient's mother felt spurred to have a bypass herself.

A recurrent theme among postbypass patients was that they increasingly did not like to mingle with those who are fat. This attitude became prominent about 6 months after surgery and was forcibly expressed by a growing reluctance to attend group therapy sessions. They explained that by associating with fat people they were not helping themselves to develop a normal identity. It only served to remind them of when they were fat, a part of their life they would just as soon forget.

DISCUSSION AND CONCLUSIONS

Our findings suggest that the psychological effects of bypass surgery are mainly positive and that most patients derive substantial benefit from the procedure. In particular, social and vocational effectiveness are enhanced. The more serious emotional difficulties we observed were associated with the somatic complications of the operation. Weight loss *per se,* although undoubtedly stressful, was not the cause of severe reactions or outright decompensations. Major depressions did not occur. Patients who had a smooth surgical postoperative course typically did well psychiatrically as well. At the same time, one must realize that major life adjustments are required of the patient during the postoperative period and that these commonly have emotional repercussions. Thus patients typically showed increased emotionality with fluctuations in anxiety, depression, and irritability. For this reason, it is not possible to state absolutely, as Solow et al. (10) do, that substitute symptoms do not occur. There was evidence particularly of increased assertiveness. This generally had positive social consequences and was usually associated with greater self-confidence and self-esteem; however, it also became a new source of friction, especially with spouses and parents. As patients lose weight, they achieve a more accurate and realistic view of their size. This suggests that the distortion of body image may be more reversible than Stunkard (21) has indicated.

A consistent feature of the postoperative course is that, on one hand, patients are quite pleased with the results of surgery and with their new social accomplishments and, on the other, that they complain of feeling more anxious and easily upset. This seeming paradox can be resolved, at least in part, by noting that the dysphoria is a byproduct of the new adjustments that patients are attempting and also that it is an expression of a decrease in the use of denial. Why the latter occurs is not quite clear but we have observed repeatedly that postoperatively patients seemed more in touch with their feelings and their conflicts. Thus clinically they looked better even though subjectively they were more conscious of inner distress.

Like Solow et al. (10), we were impressed by the profound consequences of the obese state and we concur with them that surgery "broke the vicious circle of unrelieved ineffectiveness, guilt and resignation" and facilitated new hopes and new constructive adjustments.

Some comments are in order about the need for preoperative psychiatric screening and for postoperative psychiatric follow-up. Our impression is that psychiatric diagnosis rarely is a contraindication to bypass surgery. However, we believe that the motivation for surgery should be carefully assessed (17, 19), and that it may be wise to withhold the procedure from those who are noticeably ambivalent; at any rate, the staff should not exert pressure, however subtly, to overcome the misgivings that beset some patients. A positive feature of our approach was that at least 1 month elapsed between entrance into the program and surgery. During that time, the patient spoke repeatedly with the psychiatrist as well as with the internist and the surgeon and had ample opportunity to drop out of the program if she so chose. In our experience, also, psychiatric participation helps to provide these patients needed emotional support and offers them an outlet for dissatisfaction which, in turn, enhances their collaboration with follow-up.

In conclusion, we believe that bypass surgery has much to offer to well-motivated superobese patients and that this procedure represents a decisive step forward in the treatment of a condition which has shown itself largely refractory to conservative approaches. At the same time, however, we also must remind ourselves that follow-up has thus far been relatively short and that we do not know how these patients will fare psychologically and/or somatically in the years to come. At present, it would appear that the drawbacks to the bypass procedure are more somatic than psychological. For reasons not yet identified and seemingly quite unpredictable, more than 50% of the patients experience troublesome organic complications, whereas the others make very satisfactory progress. If the procedure can be further refined to achieve greater control over the occurrence of metabolic complications, the overall value and applicability of this approach will be distinctly enhanced, and it will be possible to endorse it, without some of the reservations that of necessity still remain, as a truly effective treatment for otherwise intractable extreme obesity.

SUMMARY

Twelve superobese women were studied psychiatrically for up to 3 years in conjunction with treatment of their obesity by jejuno-ileal bypass surgery. All responded with significant weight loss to near-normal levels. They were pleased with the results of surgery and by their new ability to be physically, socially, and sexually more active. Self-esteem, initiative, and assertiveness were enhanced. Whereas no serious psychiatric complications occurred, postoperatively patients experienced more lability of mood and greater awareness of anxiety, depression, and irritability. New adjustments tended to strain relationships with spouses and parents. Principal drawback to the surgery was the occurrence in seven patients of major somatic complications with concomitant discouragement and apprehension.

ACKNOWLEDGMENTS

This research was partially supported by U.S. Public Health Service grant RR-425. The authors are indebted to Drs. George Bray and John Benfield, respectively, professors of Medicine and Surgery, UCLA School of Medicine, for the active support of the psychiatric portion of the study.

REFERENCES

1. Fink, G., Gottesfeld, H., and Glickman, L. (1962): The "superobese" patient. *J. Hillside Hosp.*, 11:97–119.
2. Reivich, R. S., Ruiz, R. A., and Lapi, R. M. (1966): Extreme obesity—Psychiatric, psychometric, psychotherapeutic aspects. *J. Kans. Med. Soc.*, 67:134–140.
3. Atkinson, R. M., and Ringuette, E. L. (1967): A survey of biographical and psychological features in extraordinary fatness. *Psychosom. Med.*, 29:121–133.
4. Swanson, D. W., and Dinello, F. A. (1970): Severe obesity as a habituation syndrome. *Arch. Gen. Psychiatry*, 22:120–127.
5. Castelnuovo-Tedesco, P., and Schiebel, D. (1976): Studies of superobesity. I. Psychological characteristics of superobese patients. *Psychiatry Med. (In press.)*
6. Kollar, E. J., and Atkinson, R. M. (1966): Responses of extremely obese patients to starvation. *Psychosom. Med.*, 28:227–246.
7. Kollar, E. J., Atkinson, R. M., and Albin, D. L. (1969): The effectiveness of fasting in the treatment of superobesity. *Psychosomatics*, 10:125–135.
8. Swanson, D. W., and Dinello, F. A. (1970): Follow–up of patients starved for obesity. *Psychosom. Med.*, 32(2):209–214.
9. Harris, J., and Frame, B. (1968): A Psychiatric study of patients undergoing intestinal bypass for treatment of intractable obesity. *Proceedings of the 124th Annual Meeting of the American Psychiatric Association*, Boston, May 13–17, 1968.
10. Solow, C., Silberfarb, P. M., and Swift, K. (1974): Psychosocial effects of intestinal bypass surgery for severe obesity. *N. Engl. J. Med.*, 290(6):300–304.
11. Espmark, S. (1974): Psychological adjustment before and after bypass surgery for extreme obesity—A preliminary report. *Proceedings of the First International Congress on Obesity*, London, Oct 9–11, 1974.
12. Ishida, Y. (1974): Sexuality after small bowel bypass. *Curr. Med. Dial.*, 41(12): 659–662.
13. Crisp, A. H., and Kalucy, R. S. (1974): Some psychological accompaniments of major fat loss in a series of women who had undergone ileo-jejunal bypass operation. *Proceedings of the First International Congress on Obesity*, London.
14. Conrad, S. W. (1954): Resistance of the obese to reducing. *J. Am. Diet. Assoc.*, 30:581–588.
15. Stunkard, A., and McLaren-Hume, M. (1959): The results of treatment for obesity. *Arch. Int. Med.*, 103:79–85.
16. Mendelson, M., Weinberg, N. and Stunkard, A. J. (1969): Obesity in men: A clinical study of twenty-five cases. *Ann. Intern. Med.*, 54:660–671.
17. Payne, J. H., and Dewind, L. T. (1969): Surgical treatment of obesity. *Am. J. Surg.*, 118(8):141–147.

18. Salmon, P. A. (1971): The results of small intestine bypass operations for the treatment of obesity. *Surg. Gynecol. Obstet.,* 132(6):965–979.
19. Buchwald, H., Schwartz, M. Z., and Varco, R. L. (1973): Surgical treatment of obesity. *Adv. Surg.,* 7:235–255.
20. Briscoe, J. P. (1973): I chose surgery to lose weight. *Good Housekeeping,* 176(5):50–58.
21. Stunkard, A., and Mendelson, M. (1967): Obesity and the body image: Characteristics of disturbances in the body image of some obese persons. *Am. J. Psychiatry,* 123:1296–1300.

Hunger: Basic Mechanisms and Clinical Implications,
edited by D. Novin, W. Wyrwicka, and G. Bray.
Raven Press, New York © 1976.

Neural Mechanisms of Hunger: Current Status and Future Prospects

G. J. Mogenson

Department of Physiology, University of Western Ontario, London N6A 3K7, Ontario, Canada

The foundations for the study of the neurology of hunger were established in the 1940s and 1950s. The stereotaxic technique used by investigators during this period enabled them to make fundamental discoveries of the effects of lesions and stimulation of the hypothalamus on food intake. In interpreting the experimental findings and trying to develop explanatory theoretical models, they were strongly influenced by two great traditions in physiology, the traditions of Cannon and Sherrington. According to Cannon, energy balance was an important condition of homeostasis resulting from both behavioral regulations (feeding) and physiological regulations (energy utilization). Feeding was initiated and terminated by signals integrated by the central nervous system. From studies in which the hypothalamus was lesioned or stimulated, it was concluded, in accordance with Sherrington's concepts of central excitatory state and central inhibitory state, that the lateral hypothalamus (14) was an "appetite center" and the ventromedial hypothalamus (VMH) a "satiety center."

Following the dramatic effects of lesions and stimulation of the hypothalamus on food intake reported in the 1940s and 1950s and the influence of the Sherrington-Cannon heritage on the interpretation of these effects, it was only natural to ask, what is "the nature of the changes within the body which are capable of providing signals to the hypothalamus"? (6) Related questions were also raised: What are the receptors for these signals? What are the integrative actions of the hypothalamus? How do these integrative actions influence the motor system and thereby initiate feeding behavior?

Figure 1 depicts the general approach to the neural mechanisms of hunger that has been followed during the last two or three decades. The stars in Fig. 1 identify the aspects that have received the most attention, the larger the star the greater the degree of interest by investigators. The major efforts have been studies of the integrative systems, particularly the hypothalamus and limbic structures, and studies of feeding behavior *per se* by behavioral scientists. Although there has been a continuing interest in signals and receptors, the number of studies is considerably fewer. The question marks designate aspects for which there is little or no definitive evidence, the larger the question mark the greater the degree of uncertainty. In some cases, such

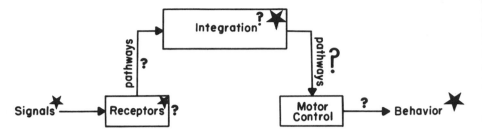

FIG. 1. The dramatic effects of lesions and electrical stimulation of the VMH and LH focused attention on the integrative role of the hypothalamus. The hypothalamus was, in the Cannon tradition, "the organ of homeostasis" and according to the Sherrington tradition was said to contain a central excitatory system (LH, "appetite center") and a central inhibitory system (VMH, "satiety center"). A good deal of effort has been devoted to the study of the integrative mechanisms in the hypothalamus and to the signals and receptors that project to them. However, there is still a good deal of uncertainty about the signals and receptors that influence feeding and about the pathways that transmit feeding and satiety signals. It is assumed that when hunger signals have been integrated command signals initiate feeding reflexes. There has been little effort, however, to investigate the interface between hypothalamic integrative mechanisms and the neural systems for motor control. Recent interest in the role of catecholamine pathways in ingestive behaviors has shifted attention to this important interface.

as the neural pathways from neural structures that integrate hunger and satiety signals to neural structures involved in the motor control of feeding behavior, and the neural pathways from receptors to integrative structures, the large question marks reflect a limited amount of investigation. However, for signals and receptors, there are question marks in spite of a good deal of research.

SIGNALS AND RECEPTORS FOR FEEDING

For a number of years, three major signals have been recognized associated with three classic theories (Fig. 2). From the chapters in this volume, it is clear that there is still considerable interest in the contribution of thermostatic, glucostatic, and lipostatic signals to hunger and satiety. Blass (*This Volume*) presented evidence supporting the hypothesis that temperature may serve as a primary feeding signal. Several papers dealt with glucostatic sig-

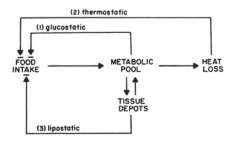

FIG. 2. The glucostatic (22), thermostatic (5), and lipostatic (15) theories of food intake were formulated more than 20 years ago. (After Brobeck, ref. 7.)

nals, receptors, and pathways and the current status of this research is considered herein. It was recognized that fat stores, rather than body weight *per se,* are monitored and regulated (e.g., Borer, *This Volume*), although the signal and the neural integrative mechanisms are not known. A number of other signals that influence feeding were also considered (amino acids, Harper; duodenal hormones, Smith and Gibbs; energy flow, Booth; gastric and duodenal distention, Davis, Epstein, Sharma; hepatic energy reserves, Russek; insulin (via CSF), Woods; all in *This Volume*).

Two or three chapters in this volume raise the possibility of one crucial signal that might be necessary and sufficient for the control of food intake (e.g., detection of energy flow or hepatic energy reserves). Although such parsimony has considerable appeal, most authors favor the view that feeding is under multifactorial control and that a number of signals contribute to the control of food intake. But which ones are physiologically relevant? With a few exceptions (e.g., gastric distention), the physiological significance of the numerous putative hunger and satiety signals in normal feeding is uncertain. Since the ultimate goal of research in this field is to account for normal, spontaneous feeding the criterion of physiological relevance is a critical one in considering hunger and satiety signals.

Recent studies of the ontogeny of feeding have provided an interesting approach to feeding signals. Epstein (*This Volume*) presented results from his laboratory showing that infant rats are able to utilize various hunger and satiety signals at different ages. Although the consummatory response capabilities are present in the rat soon after birth the appetitive reactions to hunger signals are not available until later.

Another interesting chapter discusses the view that signals do not merely impinge on a passive central nervous system. Sharma (*This Volume*) showed that gastric distention and gustatory signals depend on the nutritional and metabolic state of the animal. The principle that peripheral signals that influence feeding may be modulated by the brain was also supported by evidence presented by Vanderweele et al. (46) and by Booth (4).

CURRENT STATUS OF STUDIES OF THE GLUCOSTATIC SYSTEM

Several chapters deal with glucostatic signals and receptors and with the neural systems that transmit and process glucostatic signals. Since this is a major theme of this volume, it deserves special treatment in this summary chapter.

Central Glucoreceptors

Although it is two decades since Mayer postulated that glucoreceptors in the VMH are responsible for satiety, the status of central glucoreceptors is still uncertain. The evidence from goldthioglucose experiments (23) is not critical, as assumed initially, since it has been pointed out that goldthioglucose, a "vascular poison," which shuts down circulation to several regions of the brain, destroys neurons indiscriminately (10). Glucosensitive neurons have been identified in the LH as well as in the VMH using electrophysiological recording techniques (1, 31, Marrazzi and Oomura, *This Volume*) but their role in feeding behavior remains to be established. Epstein and co-workers (10), after failing to reduce food intake by infusing glucose into the VMH[1] and after failing to alter food intake by infusing 2-deoxy-D-glucose (2-DG) into either the VMH or the LH,[2] concluded that "the glucosensitive units in at least the lateral hypothalamus are not concerned with feeding but with autonomic-endocrine mechanisms for gastric secretion and maintenance of blood sugar levels" (10).

Since the administration of glucose to the ventricles reduces food intake (14) and 2-DG to the same site initiates feeding (25), it appears that the brain does contain glucoreceptors for feeding; their locus, however, remains uncertain and their contribution to feeding may be limited to emergency conditions (38).

Peripheral Glucoreceptors

Several years ago, Russek (36) postulated glucoreceptors in the liver and in this volume he presents a mathematical model that attempts to account for various aspects of feeding behavior and energy balance in terms of hepatic glucoreceptors. Three recent studies in which infusions of glucose into the portal-hepatic system did not reduce food intake (43, 46, 48) cast doubt on this hypothesis. However, VanderWeele and co-workers (46; *This Volume*) reported that such infusions of glucose did reduce food intake if the animals were food deprived. Novin and co-workers (29) provided further evidence for hepatic glucoreceptors by showing that the infusion of 2-DG into the portal system initiated feeding in rabbits. Russell and Mogenson (*unpublished observations*) have obtained similar results in rats (see Fig. 3).

There is also evidence suggesting glucoreceptors in the gastrointestinal tract. Several investigators have reported that infusing glucose into the stomach (2, 4, 32, 48) or the duodenum (28, 46, 48) reduces food intake, although for the duodenum the reduced food intake apparently occurs only in free-feeding, not food-deprived animals (28, 46). Novin and co-workers (28, and *This Volume*) presented additional evidence in support of duodenal glucoreceptors.

---

[1] Wagner and De Groot (47) and Panksepp and Nance (33), as well as Epstein (9), reported that infusing glucose into the VMH did not reduce food intake.

[2] The 2-DG experiments are equivocal. Balagura and Kanner (3) reported feeding when 2-DG was administered to the LH, Epstein and co-workers (10) failed to replicate this finding, and Gonzalez and Novin (13) obtained inconsistent results.

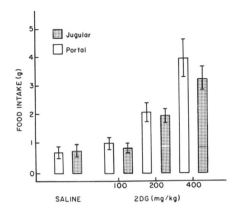

FIG. 3. Food intake of rats during a 3-hr period following the infusion of 2-DG via jugular catheter or portal catheter. Food intake was increased significantly by the 200 mg/kg and 400 mg/kg doses. There was no significant difference for the two routes of administration.

A Neural System for Peripheral Glucostatic Signals

If there are hepatic and possibly duodenal glucoreceptors, it is appropriate to ask how glucostatic signals from these receptors reach the brain and what role they have in the control of feeding and satiety. Table 1 summarizes relevant experimental evidence.

The studies reviewed previously that suggest hepatic-portal and duodenal glucoreceptors, are listed in Table 1. The vagus nerve was first implicated by Niijima (27) as a pathway for glucostatic signals from the liver. Novin and co-workers (29, also *This Volume*) provided further support for the role of the vagus by showing that food intake initiated by portal infusions of 2-DG was reduced by sectioning the vagus. There was a further reduction of feeding when the splanchnic nerves were cut suggesting that sympathetic afferents might be involved. Vagotomy also eliminates the reduction of food intake produced by infusing glucose into the duodenum or hepatic-portal system (28). This is consistent with the view that duodenal glucoreceptors transmit signals to the brain via the vagus. Alternatively, the duodenal glucose might be reaching hepatic glucoreceptors.

Schmitt (40) recorded from single neurons in the hypothalamus while infusing glucose into the portal vein. The activity of some hypothalamic neurons was altered by the infusions providing further support for the hypothesis that there are glucoreceptors in the region of the hepatic portal veins or liver. Both increases and decreases in discharge rates were observed for neurons in the LH, but no changes were found in the paraventricular and supraoptic nuclei, or, it should be noted, in the ventromedial nucleus. The responses of LH neurons to the glucose infusions were eliminated by sectioning the splanchnic nerves bilaterally or the spinal cord at level T5.

The conclusion from Schmitt's study that glucostatic signals are transmitted to the LH is also supported by lesioning experiments. Booth and Novin have both reported that the attenuation of food intake to infusions of

TABLE 1. *Evidence for peripheral glucoreceptors*

With glucose	With 2-deoxy-D-glucose
Lateral hypothalamus + (40)	
Vagus Nerve + (27)	
Hepatic-portal + (37) − (48) − (43) − (46) + (28)	hepatic-portal + (29) + (50)
Gastric + (2) + (32) + (4) + (48)	
Duodenum + (48) + (46) + (28)	
Intraperitoneal + (39)	intraperitoneal + (41)

Evidence was (+) or was not (−) found for peripheral glucoreceptors.

glucose into the portal system or duodenum is eliminated by lesioning the LH.

A good deal of attention will be devoted in the near future to the study of the receptors, pathways, and central integrative mechanisms for peripheral glucostatic signals. It is important to determine the role of this system in spontaneous feeding and the results of the relative contribution of peripheral and central glucostatic signals in the control of food intake.

CATECHOLAMINE PATHWAYS AND FEEDING

Beginning with the classic paper of Ungerstedt (44), there have been a number of studies implicating catecholamine pathways in feeding behavior (11, 21, 34, 42, 49). Ungerstedt suggested that the syndrome of aphagia and adipsia following lesions of the LH was caused by damage of catecholamine pathways that project rostrally through this region and in particular to damage to the dopamine nigrostriatal pathway. Stricker (*This Volume*) presented a good deal of experimental evidence in support of this hypothesis. He proposed that the basis of the deficit in ingestive behaviors is a disruption in the arousal component of behavior. In support of this suggestion Stricker as well as Wolgin, Cytawa, and Teitelbaum (*This Volume*) reported that in animals with damage to the catecholamine pathways feeding could be elicited by amphetamine or arousal stimuli.

From careful investigation of the deficits following lesions of catecholamine pathways using 6-OH-dopamine or following classic electrolytic lesions of the LH, it appears that the major deficit is in consummatory behavior. Stricker showed that rats with such brain damage could respond to regulatory challenges if the challenges were relatively mild. It appears that such animals have difficulty in coping with stress.

Formerly, it was thought that the LH was an integrative site for hunger signals and that the LH syndrome of aphagia was the result of damaging this integrative mechanism. Investigations of the role of catecholamine pathways in feeding have led to a reassessment of this view; it appears that the LH syndrome is the result of a disruption in the consummatory stage rather than in the appetitive stage.

Other catecholamine pathways have also been implicated in feeding behavior. Hoebel (*This Volume*) presents evidence from his laboratory that hyperphagia results from damage to the ventral noradrenergic pathway; this has been confirmed by Mogenson and co-workers (Fig. 4). Following damage to this pathway the anorexogenic effect of amphetamine is reduced, suggesting that it subserves amphetamine anorexia. Leibowitz (*This Volume*) presents evidence that the paraventricular nucleus is a very sensitive site for elicited feeding by the central administration of norepinephrine and suggests that the exogenous norepinephrine might act at synapses of the periventricular pathway recently mapped by Lindvall and co-workers (19). It has been claimed that lesions of the periventricular pathway cause hyperphagia, which

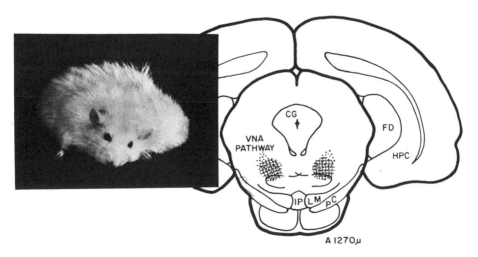

FIG. 4. Rats with bilateral, electrolytic lesions of the ventral noradrenergic pathway are hyperphagic when fed a high-fat diet and become moderately obese. The hyperphagia was not observed when the rats were fed Purina chow pellets (*unpublished observations*).

is difficult to reconcile with Leibowitz's chemical stimulation data. Studies of feeding elicited by electrical stimulation have implicated the dorsal norepinephrine bundle (8, 24).

Research on the relationship of feeding to catecholamine and other transmitter-specific pathways is only beginning. However, it has already had a major impact on our thinking about the neurology of hunger and has been a major factor in the current reassessment of the role of the hypothalamus in ingestive behaviors (26).

THE NEUROLOGY OF HUNGER: CURRENT STATUS AND FUTURE PROSPECTS

"Nervous systems are built for action. . . . Actions are directed towards goals." (20).

Reassessment of the Role of the Hypothalamus in Feeding and Satiety

Early studies of aphagia from lesions of the LH were considered evidence that this was the locus of the central excitatory system for feeding. Subsequent reports that animals with LH lesions failed to respond to glucoprivic and other deficit signals were considered evidence that the LH was the integrative site for appetitive behavior. However, recent studies discussed previously showed that the decrements in consummatory behavior are related to a disruption of behavioral arousal and difficulty in coping with stress. Since animals with LH lesions can respond to glucoprivic and other challenges if they are not too intense, the view that the LH is an integrative site for appetitive behavior should be reassessed.

The Neurology of Action

An important outcome of the recent studies of the role of catecholamine pathways in ingestive behaviors is that we know less about the role of the hypothalamus and about the integration of hunger signals than was believed a few years ago. However, an unanticipated benefit of these studies is a shift of attention to the neural events that trigger feeding reflexes.

Earlier it was indicated that there has been little effort to understand how hypothalamic integrative systems influence the motor systems and feeding reflexes (see Fig. 1). The important neural interface between the intention to respond (e.g., hunger) and the motor control of feeding behavior has been largely neglected. The catecholamine pathways that are implicated in feeding behavior, the dopamine nigrostriatal and dorsal norepinephrine pathways, project to the striatum, the cerebral cortex, and the cerebellum, structures that make important contributions to the motor control of behavior. These pathways may be an important link between the intention to respond and the motor control of feeding. A new direction of research has been initiated, which eventually may provide a neurology of action.

A speculative hypothesis concerning the contribution of the catecholamine pathways to motor control has recently been proposed by Roberts (35). The axon terminals of the dopamine and norepinephrine pathways exert inhibitory effects on neurons in the striatum and cerebral cortex (see Fig. 5). In order to account for the influence of these inhibitory pathways on behavior Roberts assumes that the dopamine and norepinephrine neurons synapse on γ-aminobutyric acid (GABA) inhibitory interneurons and that the GABA interneurons exert inhibitory effects on preprogrammed neural circuits ("motor tapes") represented in the cerebral cortex and striatum. Thus nerve impulses transmitted along the dopamine and norepinephrine pathways disinhibit preprogrammed neural circuits, so that, depending on the environmental context, biting, chewing, swallowing, or other sequences of reflexes occur. Disinhibition, according to Roberts, may be an important organizing principle of the nervous system.

From this model it is easy to understand the behavioral deficits in animals with damage to the catecholamine pathways. The lack of exploration and apparent difficulty in the initiation of movements is explained by the unchecked inhibitory effect of the GABA interneurons on preprogrammed neural circuits. The model is also consistent with the observations of Stricker (*This Volume*) and of Wolgin, Cytawa, and Teitelbaum (*This Volume*) that amphetamine or arousing stimuli could initiate feeding in animals with dam-

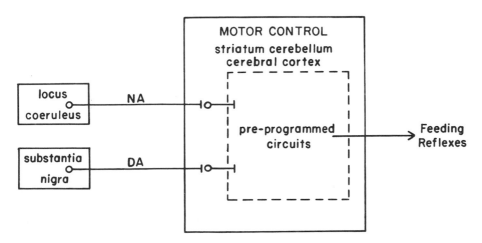

FIG. 5. Neurons of the dorsal noradrenergic pathway (NA) and of the nigrostriatal dopaminergic pathway (DA) inhibit neurons in the cerebral cortex and striatum. According to Roberts (35), these NA and DA neurons synapse on GABA inhibitory inerneurons, which inhibit preprogrammed neural circuits ("motor tapes") represented in the cerebral cortex and striatum. The NA and DA thus disinhibit the preprogrammed circuits and feeding reflexes occur.

age to the catecholamine pathways. Presumably, these conditions result in a larger release of transmitter from the remaining undamaged fibers. Ungerstedt and Ljungberg (45) have also observed that animals can overcome akinesia under conditions of high stress or motivation and compare this to the paradoxic kinesia seen in Parkinson patients under similar circumstances.

The Neurology of Anticipation

Because of the strong impact of the Sherrington and Cannon traditions and because of the widely held view that the hypothalamus is the organ of homeostasis, it is not surprising that the major emphasis for many years has been on deficit signals for hunger and on hypothalamic integrative mechanisms for such signals. One of the consequences of the current reassessment of the role of the hypothalamus in control of ingestive behaviors is an increasing recognition of the importance of nonregulatory signals and of non-homeostatic feeding.

Feeding is associated with habit, with circadian rhythms, and with complex environmental and social stimuli (17, 18). Such factors influence ingestive behaviors so that food and water intakes may occur prior to and in anticipation of energy and water deficits (12, 26). For example, LeMagnen (16) fed rats three meals a day spaced 7 hr apart. One of the meals was withheld and food intake increased for the meal that followed the 15-hr fast. After a few days, however, food intake increased for the meal that preceded the 15-hr fast; apparently feeding responses were anticipating energy needs.[3] Oatley (30) has suggested that for such anticipatory or nonregulatory feeding the animal utilizes representational processes of the external environment "deployed not in the feedback mode so that deficits are corrected, but in a feed-forward mode so that they can be anticipated" (p. 221). These representational processes presumably involve the highest levels of neural integration (cerebral cortex, limbic system), but the nature of these integrations is poorly understood; we lack a neurology of anticipation.

There is a need for theoretical models and rigorous experimentation to elucidate the neural mechanisms for representational and other cognitive processes. If this need is recognized, it may become possible within a decade to provide a more satisfactory account of the factors and mechanisms responsible for normal spontaneous feeding in rats and other experimental

---

[3] Russek (38) has pointed out that food intake and body weight are loosely regulated and suggests that ". . . the supposed body weight regulation . . ." is readily broken as ". . . evidenced by the increasing number of obese people in wealthy countries." He goes on to say: "Why do we need to 'watch our diet' in order to avoid overeating . . .?" (p. 129). People, as well as rats, frequently eat in excess of needs and a good deal of food intake is apparently not in response to deficit signals.

animals. We will then also have a better understanding of the controls of food intake in normal and obese people.[4]

SUMMARY

A neurology of hunger developed two or three decades ago to account for the effects on feeding behavior of lesions and stimulation of the LH and VMH. It was strongly influenced by the traditions of Sherrington and of Cannon and assumed a central excitatory system in the LH and a central inhibitory system in the VMH. Much effort has been devoted to identifying signals and receptors that initiate hunger and satiety and to investigating hypothalamic integrative mechanisms for these signals.

There is still considerable interest, as reflected by the contents of this volume, in the numerous signals that influence hunger and satiety, but the physiological significance of most of these remain unclear. Controversies still exist concerning the signals that initiate and terminate spontaneous feeding and those that regulate energy balance and body weight regulation.

Studies of the neural mechanisms of the glucostatic system are a major theme in this volume. Much work remains to be done to elucidate the neural systems for peripheral and central glucoreceptors and their contributions to feeding and satiety.

Studies of the contribution of central catecholamine pathways to feeding behavior have made it clear that we know less about the role of the hypothalamus in ingestive behaviors than previously assumed. These studies have shifted attention from the integrative site for hunger signals to the neural mechanisms that trigger feeding reflexes. Another consequence of the recent reassessment of the role of the hypothalamus in ingestive behavior is an emphasis on nonregulatory or anticipatory feeding and drinking. It is becoming clear that in order to account for spontaneous feeding behavior it will be necessary to formulate a neurology of action and a neurology of anticipation.

ACKNOWLEDGMENTS

The manuscript was read by Blanche Box, Mark Evered, Alan Faiers, and John Kucharczyk who made helpful suggestions. I also acknowledge the assistance of Marianne Jeffery who typed the manuscript and of Rebecca Woodside who prepared the illustrations.

The author's research was supported by grants from the Medical Research Council of Canada and the National Research Council of Canada.

---

[4] Reports of intestinal bypass surgery to treat human obesity (Bray and Benfield, *This Volume;* Castelnuovo-Tedesco, *This Volume*) are a clear indication of the limitations of our research and of our theoretical models to provide an understanding of the neurology of hunger.

REFERENCES

1. Anand, B. K., Chhina, G. S., and Singh, B. (1962): *Science,* 138:597–598.
2. Baile, C. A., Zinn, W., and Mayer, J. (1971): *Physiol. Behav.,* 6:537–541.
3. Balagura, S., and Kanner, M. (1971): *Physiol. Behav.,* 7:251–255.
4. Booth, D. A. (1972): *Physiol. Behav.,* 9:199–202.
5. Brobeck, J. R. (1948): *Yale J. Biol. Med.,* 20:545–552.
6. Brobeck, J. R. (1957): *Gastroenterology,* 32:169–174.
7. Brobeck, J. R. (1974): Invited lecture, XXVI International Congress of Physiological Sciences, New Delhi, India, 24th October 1974.
8. Cioe, J., and Mogenson, G. J. (1974): *Fed. Proc.,* 33:342.
9. Epstein, A. N. (1960): *Am. J. Physiol.,* 199:969–974.
10. Epstein, A. N., Nicolaidis, S., and Miselis, R. (1975): In: *Neural Integration of Physiological Mechanisms and Behaviour,* edited by G. J. Mogenson and F. R. Calaresu, pp. 248–265. University of Toronto Press, Toronto.
11. Fibiger, H. C., Zis, A. P., and McGeer, E. G. (1973): *Brain Res.,* 55:135–148.
12. Fitzsimons, J. T. (1972): *Physiol. Rev.,* 52:468–561.
13. Gonzalez, M. F., and Novin, D. (1974): *Physiol. Psychol.,* 2:326–330.
14. Herberg, L. J. (1960): *Nature,* 187:245–246.
15. Kennedy, G. C. (1953): *Proc. R. Soc.,* 140:578–592.
16. LeMagnen, J. (1959): *C. R. Acad. Sci. (Paris),* 249:2400–2402.
17. LeMagnen, J. (1967): In: *Handbook of Physiology, Section 6, Alimentary Canal, Vol. 1: Control of Food and Water Intake,* edited by C. F. Code, pp. 11–30. American Physiological Society, Washington, D.C.
18. LeMagnen, J. (1971): In: *Progress in Physiological Psychology, Vol. 4,* edited by E. Stellar and J. M. Sprague, pp. 203–261. Academic Press, New York.
19. Lindvall, O., Bjorklund, A., Novin, A., and Stenevi, V. (1974): *J. Comp. Neurol.,* 154:317–348.
20. Livingston, R. B. (1967): In: *The Neurosciences, A Study Program,* edited by G. C. Quarton, T. Melnechuk, and R. O. Schmitt, pp. 499–515. Rockefeller University Press, New York.
21. Marshall, J. F., and Teitelbaum, P. (1973): *Brain Res.,* 55:229–233.
22. Mayer, J. (1955): *Ann. NY Acad. Sci.,* 63:15–43.
23. Mayer, J., and Marshall, N. B. (1956): *Nature,* 178:1399–1400.
24. Micco, D. J. (1974): *Brain Res.,* 75:172–176.
25. Miselis, R. R. (1973): *The Glucostatic Control of Feeding Behavior in Rats.* Ph.D. Dissertation. University of Pennsylvania, Philadelphia.
26. Mogenson, G. J., and Phillips, A. G. (1975): In: *Progress in Psychobiology and Physiological Psychology, Vol. 6,* edited by A. N. Epstein and J. M. Sprague. Academic Press, New York.
27. Niijima, A. (1969): *Ann. NY Acad. Sci.,* 157:690–700.
28. Novin, D., Sanderson, J. D., and VanderWeele, D. A. (1974): *Physiol. Behav.,* 13:3–7.
29. Novin, D., VanderWeele, D. A., and Rezek, M. (1973): *Science,* 181:858–860.
30. Oatley, K. (1972): *Brain Mechanisms and Mind.* Dutton, New York.
31. Oomura, Y., Ono, T., Ooyama, H., and Wayner, M. J. (1969): *Nature,* 222:282–284.
32. Panksepp, J. (1971): *Psychon. Monogr. Suppl.,* 4:85–95.
33. Panksepp, J., and Nance, D. M. (1972): *Physiol. Behav.,* 9:447–451.
34. Phillips, A. G., and Fibiger, H. C. (1973): *Behav. Biol.,* 9:749–754.
35. Roberts, E. (1974): *Adv. Neurol.,* 5:127–143.
36. Russek, M. (1963): *Nature,* 197:78–80.
37. Russek, M. (1970): *Physiol. Behav.,* 5:1207–1209.
38. Russek, M. (1975): In: *Neural Integration of Physiological Mechanisms and Behaviour,* edited by G. J. Mogenson and F. R. Calaresu, pp. 128–147. University of Toronto Press, Toronto.
39. Russek, M., and Stevenson, J. A. F. (1972): *Physiol. Behav.,* 1972:245–249.
40. Schmitt, M. (1973): *Am. J. Physiol.,* 225:1089–1095.

41. Smith, G. P., and Epstein, A. N. (1969): *Am. J. Physiol.*, 217:1083–1087.
42. Smith, G. P., Strohmayer, A. J., and Reis, D. J. (1972): *Nature [New Biol.]*, 235: 27–29.
43. Stephens, D. B., and Baldwin, B. A. (1974): *Physiol. Behav.*, 12:923–929.
44. Ungerstedt, U. (1971): *Acta Physiol. Scand.* (Suppl.), 367:95–122.
45. Ungerstedt, U., and Ljungberg, T. (1973): In: *Frontiers in Catecholamine Research*, edited by E. Usdin and S. H. Solomon, pp. 689–693. Pergamon Press, Oxford.
46. VanderWeele, D. A., Novin, D., Rezek, M., and Sanderson, J. D. (1974): *Physiol. Behav.*, 12:467–473.
47. Wagner, J. W., and De Groot, J. (1963): *Am. J. Physiol.*, 204:483–487.
48. Yin, T. H., and Tsai, C. T. (1973): *J. Comp. Physiol. Psychol.*, 85:258–264.
49. Zigmond, M., and Stricker, M. (1972): *Science*, 177:1211–1214.
50. Russell, P. J. D., and Mogenson, G. J. (1975): *Am. J. Physiol.* (*In Press.*)

Subject Index

Subject Index

A

Absorption 131-134

Acetyl CoA, relationship to appetite 115-124

Activation
aggressive behavior and, 182-183
hypothalamic lesions and, 186-188
loss of, 180-181, 186-188
regulation of food intake, 179-189
sensory stimuli, 185-186

Adipsia, 50-58, 62, 251-254

Aggression, mechanisms of, 71-72

Aggressive behavior and activation, 182-183

Alimentary regulation and emotion, 61-74

Alpha-adrenergic receptors
feeding initiation and, 1-4
feeding potentiation and, 2-3
mechanism of action, 2
mediation pathways for, 3-4

Amino acids
imbalance of, 103-104
regulation of feeding, 103-112

Amitriptyline, 69-71

Amphetamine (AMPH), 6, 9-15, 25, 184
anorectic effects of, 421-428
satiety and, 38-41

Amygdaloid complex
alimentary regulation by, 61-74

Amygdaloid complex (contd.)
depression and, 68-69
hypothalamus and, 64-66
lesions of, 67-68

Androgens and sex differences in feeding, 257-270

Anorectic drugs, 421-428
neurochemistry of, 41-48
satiety and, 33-48

Anorexia nervosa, 73

Anticipatory feeding, 98

Antidepressive drugs and amygdaloid complex, 69-73

Aphagia, 50-58, 62-64, 66-67, 215-128

Apomorphine, 27

Appetite
determinants of, 78-81, 103-112, 127-141
enhancement at cold temperature, 77-87
obesity syndrome and, 281-293
relationship to metabolite flux, 115-124.
salivation as measure of, 421-428
surgical effects on, 462

Arousal and catecholamine-containing neurons, 22-25

B

Beta-adrenergic receptors
mechanism of action, 11-13

DATE DUE

NO 15'78		
SEP 1 '78		
DE 18'01		
OC 25 '82		
DE 17'86		
ILL		
7-13-9		
JA 11 '95		
FE 13'96		

DEMCO 38-297